War and Nationalism in China

In 1937, the Nationalists under Chiang Kaishek were leading the Chinese war effort against Japan and were lauded in the West for their efforts to transform China into an independent and modern nation; yet this image was quickly tarnished. The Nationalists were soon denounced as militarily incompetent, corrupt, and anti-democratic and Chiang Kaishek, the same.

In this book, Hans J. van de Ven investigates the myths and truths of Nationalist resistance including issues such as:

- The role of the USA in East Asia during the Second World War.
- The achievements of Chiang Kaishek as Nationalist leader.
- The respective contributions of the Nationalists and the Communists in the defeat of Japan.
- The consequences of the Europe First strategy for Asia.

War and Nationalism in China offers a major new interpretation of the Chinese Nationalists, placing their War of Resistance against Japan in the context of their prolonged efforts to establish control over their own country and providing a critical reassessment of Allied Warfare in the region. This groundbreaking volume will interest students and researchers of Chinese history and warfare.

Hans J. van de Ven, educated at Leiden and Harvard universities, is a Reader in Chinese Studies at the University of Cambridge. He is also the author of the award-winning book *From Friend to Comrade*.

RoutledgeCurzon studies in the modern history of Asia

War and Nationalism in China

1925–1945

Hans J. van de Ven

RoutledgeCurzon
Taylor & Francis Group

LONDON AND NEW YORK

First published 2003
by RoutledgeCurzon
11 New Fetter Lane, London EC4P 4EE

Simultaneously published in the USA and Canada
by RoutledgeCurzon
29 West 35th Street, New York, NY 10001

RoutledgeCurzon is an imprint of the Taylor & Francis Group

© 2003 Hans J. van de Ven

Typeset in Baskerville by
Newgen Imaging Systems (P) Ltd, Chennai, India
Printed and bound in Great Britain by
MPG Books Ltd, Bodmin

British Library Cataloguing in Publication Data
A catalogue record for this book is available from the British Library

Library of Congress Cataloging in Publication Data
van de Ven, Hans J.
    War and nationalism in China 1925–1945; / by Hans J. van de Ven.
        p. cm.
    Includes bibliographical references.
    1. China – History – Northern Expedition, 1926–1928.
    2. China – History – 1928–1937. 3. China – History – 1937–1945.
    4. Nationalism – China – History – 20th century. I. Title.
    DS777.46.V36 2003
    951.04–dc21   2002155141

ISBN 0–415–14571–6

For Johan, Derek, and Willem

Contents

Illustrations

Acknowledgements

This book is the product of archival research in Nanjing and Taipei. Friends and colleagues in both places contributed in many ways to its gestation. In Nanjing, Chen Qianping, Guan Yumin, and Chen Rangzhi were hosts of rare generosity who made sure that my family was made at home and my research time productive. Zhang Xianwen, Cai Shaoqing, Chen Hongmin, and Shen Xiaoyun of the History Department at Nanjing University all helped me in countless ways. At the Second Historical Archives of China, Ma Zhendu ensured a steady supply of documents and enlightened me about many aspects of KMT history. In Taipei, the Institute of Modern History provided accommodation and an office, and a profoundly stimulating academic environment, which has saved me from many errors of fact and interpretation. I am profoundly grateful to its directors during my stay, Ch'en San-ching and Lü Fang-shan. Chang Jui-te was a superior guide to Republican military history and Ch'en Yung-fa a delightful source of insight into many obscure aspects of Republican history, including personal backgrounds and relations. Shen Huai-yu, Lin Man-houng, Chen Tsu-yu, Chu Hung-yuan, Yu Miin-lin, and Chang Ning all were generous in sharing their expertise. Much of my time in Taipei was spent in archives. The staff of the KMT archives, then still at Yangmingshan, and the Academia Historica went beyond the call of duty to assist me in deciphering difficult handwritten documents.

At Cambridge, it has been my good fortune to be surrounded at St Catharine's College by a group of outstanding historians. I am especially thankful to Chris Bayly for his support for this project and his insightful comments on successive drafts of the manuscript. John Thompson shared his knowledge of US foreign policy and the Second World War, asked pertinent questions, ensured that I kept on a manageable track, and supplied a stream of Churchill anecdotes. In the wider Cambridge community, David Reynolds provided important corrections to my chapter on Joseph Stilwell, while at the Faculty of Oriental Studies Mark Lewis, Boping Yuan, Susan Daruvala, and Stephen Large not only were tolerant of a distracted colleague but also provided important help with various major and minor aspects of my research. Further afield, Stephen MacKinnon, Diana Lary, and Arthur Waldron invited me to participate in always stimulating and friendly meetings of an informal group of China historians interested in warfare. I have benefited greatly from comments on the manuscript by Bruce Reynolds, Joseph Yick, Timothy Cheek, Diana Lary, Susan van de Ven, and Denis Showalter, as well as from opportunities to present parts of the research at conferences and seminars at Nanjing University, the Institute of Modern History of the Academia Sinica,

Colorado College, the University of British Columbia, Heidelberg and Tübingen Universities, and here at Cambridge.

The British Academy's Research Readership scheme, providing two years of leave, made it possible for me to develop this new direction in my research and spent a year in China. The Pacific Cultural Foundation, the Universities' China Committee in London, and the Chiang Ching-kuo Foundation too have provided generous financial assistance.

Military history is not an easy subject, but nonetheless one that young and old can share. My sons Johan and Derek accompanied me on trips to military museums and sites in Beijing, Nanjing, Taipei, Duxford, and London. They illustrated the power of propaganda by accumulating People's Liberation Army paraphernalia in China and wearing them in Taipei before switching to an interest in Taiwan's military and finally settling on Buddhist warrior gods. Johan proved an invaluable source of knowledge about Second World War aircraft, while Derek's examination of the Doolittle Raid for his school newspaper is a model of historical argument. Both also, of course, helped me keep a balance in my life and reminded me that if I did not conclude this study soon, they would have completed their primary school years before I had finished this book. To them, and their younger brother Willem, this book is dedicated.

The author and publishers would like to thank:

The Random House Group Limited for granting us permission to reprint 'Where are the War Poets' by C. Day Lewis from *The Complete Poems* by C. Day Lewis, published by Sinclair-Stevenson (1992), copyright (c) 1992 in this edition, and the Estate of C. Day Lewis.

The Second Historical Archives of China for allowing us to use their images of Liao Zhongkai, Chiang Kaishek, Sun Yatsen, and Song Qingling at the Opening Ceremony of the Whampoa Military Academy; Firefighters during a Japanese bombing attack on Chongqing; Chiang Kaishek, Roosevelt and Churchill at Cairo; Building the Burma Road and Chiang Kaishek's victory parade in Chongqing.

Conventions

This book uses the Pinyin transliteration system, with a few arbitrary exceptions. In the case of some well-known Chinese and geographical names, I have used established English spellings. Thus, I use Chiang Kaishek rather than Jiang Jieshi and the Yellow River rather than the Huanghe. I also refer to the Nationalists' political party as the KMT (Kuo-min-tang) rather than the GMD (Guomindang), as some now do. In the Notes, I follow the conventional format except that in referencing documents from published collections of primary sources I provide only a translated title. These titles are long and were added by the compilers of these collections. To omit a long Pinyin transliteration seemed justifiable to keep the Notes accessible to a non-specialist audience and saved considerable space. Translations of titles of Chinese books and articles in the Notes can be found in the bibliography.

Introduction

When China's War of Resistance against Japan broke out in 1937, many foreign correspondents rushed to China. Peter Fleming covered the war for *The Times*. Joris Ivens, the Dutch Left-wing film-maker, led the History Today film crew. He as well as Robert Capa, the war photographer, had moved on straight from Spain, where Franco had just prevailed in the Spanish Civil War. Christopher Isherwood and W.H. Auden felt like 'characters in one of Jules Verne's stories about lunatic English explorers' when they travelled to the battlefields of China. Isherwood wrote with sympathy about Chinese soldiers and Auden in his poems expressed the sad absurdity of war.[1] Franco's victory in Spain, the spread of militarism and fascism in Europe, the callousness of appeasing West European democracies, the alternative of Communism, and the dread of another world war were the themes featuring in their reporting on the events unfolding in China.

When the books came out in the following year, all were opposed to the Japanese and many wrote favourably about the Nationalists, the ruling party, which led the Chinese war effort. In 1939, Robin Hyde in *Dragon Rampant* described the first great battles of the war praising the Chinese. In the same year, Charles Shepherd in *The Case Against Japan* detailed Japanese violations of international law and disregard for the League of Nations. Harold Timperley of the *Manchester Guardian* gave publicity to the Nanjing Massacre in *What War Means: the Japanese Terror in China*. Johan Gunnar Andersson's *China Fights for the World* stated that 'among the democratic powers, China alone has for twenty-five months fought singled-handed and against tremendous odds to uphold the right of a nation to live its free and independent life'.[2] Andersson had lived for many years in China and praised the Nationalists for what had been achieved in state-building and economic reconstruction, but also wrote that rural poverty remained a serious problem, commenting, however, that 'Chiang Kaishek knows where the shoe pinches'.[3]

In 1940, Hallett Abend, writing to awaken the US public to the USA's destiny in China, criticised Nationalist corruption, profiteering, and nepotism, but also praised the Nationalists for responding well to the challenges of the war and argued that China was experiencing a revival. In *China's Struggles with the Dictators*, which had a foreword by Guo Taiji, the Chinese Ambassador in London, O.M. Green, closely following Nationalists propaganda, described the Nationalists as having bedded down a new unity in China and as capably leading its transformation into a modern nation.

Even Theodore White, whose *Thunder out of China* of 1946, written together with Annalee Jacoby, became a best-selling indictment of the Nationalists, reported on

China with considerable sympathy and even admiration for the Nationalists during the first two years of his stay, which began in 1939. White was the China reporter of Henry Luce's *Time* magazine. He wrote of Chiang Kaishek as an 'Olympian' whose tranquillity reassured 'all who come into contact with him' and praised Madame Chiang as brave, anxious to promote American efficiency, a philanthropist, and a social worker who believed in 'the democratic process'.[4] As late as 1941, he praised Chiang Kaishek's refusal to make peace with the Japanese and believed that their time in East Asia was running out.[5] But, as Robert E. Herzstein put it in his biography of Luce, 'White wanted to equate antifascism with democracy',[6] and was first 'confused, and then angered' about signs, such as the harsh use of force by the police, financial mismanagement, and Japanese military successes, which suggested that China was neither liberal nor efficient in an American way.

Early foreign views of the Nationalists, then, were generally sympathetic although not uncritical and stand in sharp contrast with those that have since come to dominate. Before the war, there had been a group of Leftist critics of the Nationalists, including R.H. Tawney, whose *Land and Labor in China* grew out of a conference held by the Institute of Pacific Relations in Shanghai in 1931. They did not fall silent once the fighting began. Edgar Snow, Israel Epstein, and James Bertram were firmly with the Communists, with whom the Nationalists had been fighting a civil war in the 1930s until just before the beginning of the War. Snow had lived and worked in China for seven years when as the war clouds gathered he published *Red Star over China*, based on his visit to Yan'an, the Communist capital, and his interviews with Mao Zedong the year before. Snow, who revised the second edition of his book in order to fall in with policies of the Communist International in Moscow after pressure of the Communist Party of the USA,[7] held that Communist revolution would 'defeat the external tumour of imperialism and the internal cancer of class oppression'.[8] Writing before the fighting had begun, he looked forward with eager anticipation to a 'great imperialist war', which he believed would become a world war, because it would 'release the forces that can bring to the Asiatic masses the arms, training, the political experience, and the moral weakening of internal policing powers which are necessary accessories for any conceivable successful revolutionary ascent'.[9] Epstein's *The People's War* cast the history of Republican China as a struggle by the people to free themselves from state oppression.[10] Bertram, who dedicated his *North China Front* of 1939 to 'Griff McLaurin, killed in Spain, November 1936',[11] too argued that a popular front under Communist leadership would solve China's problems.

But, the negative appraisal of the Nationalists would not come to prevail until after the US entry into the Second World War. Initially, as Barbara Tuchman has written, following Pearl Harbor China was 'the favourite ally', naturally so since China was fighting the country that had just attacked the USA.[12] When on 6 January 1942 President Franklin Roosevelt discussed in Congress the new allies that the US had acquired, he praised the Chinese as 'those millions who for four and a half years have withstood bombs and starvation and have whipped the invaders time and again in spite of superior Japanese equipment and arms'.[13] Set against the crumbling of the British, Dutch, and US military presence in East and South-east Asia (the French had already become powerless in 1940), Nationalist resistance gained a new aura of pluckiness against all odds.

However, as US service men and journalists moved to China in 1942, they did not find a gallant country bravely resisting the Japanese, but rather factionalism, poverty, filth, stench, greed, ignorance, corruption, disunity, and trading with the enemy. As the likelihood of a Chinese counter-offensive against Japan declined, the image of the Nationalists in the US public mind began a rapid decline, although Roosevelt continued to support China partly for strategic reasons and partly to further his vision of a post-war world order in which China would be one of the policemen of the world. In the last years of the Pacific War, many China correspondents, including Brooks Atkinson, Jack Belden, and Theodore White, wrote with growing disillusionment about the Nationalists in leading US newspapers and periodicals.

The story of 'Vinegar Joe' Stilwell became a foil around which a story of Nationalist military incompetence and of a militarist and authoritarian regime mired in corruption was constructed. Lieutenant General Joseph Stilwell was the ranking US military officer on the Asian mainland. He was commander of US forces in China and Chief-of-Staff to Chiang Kaishek of the Allied Armies in the China Theatre, besides controlling the distribution of Lend–Lease supplies to China. Stilwell led Chinese forces during the 1942 defeat of the Allies in Burma. He became the advocate of a strategy of recovering north Burma in order to build a supply line to China. Properly equipped and trained Chinese forces would then drive Japan from China and cut off its connections with oil- and rubber-rich South-east Asia, thus bringing Japan to its knees.

US journalists focused on Stilwell as the US public was hungry for stories illustrating that the US was taking on the Japanese. Stilwell was portrayed as a man heroically battling to force a reluctant Chiang Kaishek to reform his armies, co-operate with the Communists, and finally launch offensives against the Japanese as well as a sound opponent of British imperialism. In October 1944, after Japan's Ichigo Offensive had cut through Nationalist defences and in the US the conviction took hold that the Nationalists might yet be knocked out of the war, Stilwell was dramatically recalled after Chiang Kaishek refused a US demand to put Stilwell in charge of all Chinese forces not just in Burma but also in China itself. A Brooks Atkinson article in *The New York Times* described Stilwell's recall as the 'political triumph of a moribund anti-democratic regime' with Chiang Kai-shek 'bewildered and alarmed by the rapidity with which China is falling apart'.[14] The continued support of the Nationalists, this article went on, 'has the effect of making us acquiesce in an unenlightened cold-hearted autocratic regime'.

The dismissal of the Nationalists as a militarily incompetent, corrupt, and authoritarian clique became entrenched after the end of the war, when the issue of whether or to what extent the USA should support the Nationalists in their Civil War with the Communists became politically divisive in the USA. White's *Thunder out of China*, advertised as giving 'the background for an understanding of China today and of America's role in the Chinese revolution',[15] confirmed a wholly unsavoury image of the Nationalists. According to White, Chiang Kaishek's regime was a nasty and corrupt dictatorship. It had not been interested in fighting the Japanese and had no concern for the Chinese population, having done nothing, for instance, to ameliorate the great Henan famine of 1943. He described the communists positively: they ruled the areas under their control effectively and fairly; they had been determined to fight the Japanese; and they were popular.

Subsequent publications strengthened this perspective. In 1948, Theodore White helped edit and publish *The Stilwell Papers*, after Stilwell had died in 1946. It became a bestseller in which Stilwell associated the KMT (Kuo-min-tang) with 'corruption, neglect, chaos, ... black market, trading with the enemy',[16] and the Communist with 'reduce taxes, raise production and standard of living ... practice what they preach'.[17] Chiang Kaishek, memorably called 'the Peanut', was a 'stubborn, ignorant, prejudiced, conceited despot'[18] who 'failed to keep his agreements',[19] who never said 'a single thing that indicated gratitude to the President or our Country',[20] and who 'wants to be a moral potentate, a religious leader, a philosopher. But he has no education. How ridiculous this is. If he had four year's of college education, he might understand conditions in the modern world'.[21] Senior Nationalist commanders were dismissed likewise. He Yingqin, the head of the Board of Military Administration, was the 'Blocking Back' who lacked 'military education and ability', and was 'a joke'. The senior strategist Liu Fei made 'inaction a virtue by proving conclusively the impossibility of action. ... Everything full of false assumptions, and mistakes of fact, and twisted viewpoints'.[22]

Stilwell was positive about few people. His bad relations with Claire Chennault, the head of the US 14th Air force, were legendary. When a rumour that Albert Wedemeyer might replace him reached Stilwell, he noted 'Good God-to be ousted in favour of Wedemeyer-that would be a disgrace'.[23] The British came in for similar treatment. Harold Alexander, who commanded British Empire forces during the first Burma campaign, was, Stilwell moped, 'astonished to find ME – mere me, a goddam American – in command of Chinese troops. "Extrawdinery!" Looked me over as if I had just crawled from under a rock'.[24] Although at first he had liked Mountbatten, the Supreme Allied Commander of the South-east Asia Command, by 1944 Stilwell 'went to the zoo first to look at the monkeys just to get in the mood' before meeting 'his Lordship'.[25]

The US government adopted Stilwell's belief that the US had done its best but the Nationalists had caused their own defeat to defend its China policy. In August 1949 – weeks before Mao Zedong announced the founding of the People's Republic of China – the State Department published *The China White Paper*. Following the failure of George Marshall's mediation efforts to end the Civil War, the *White Paper* justified US withdrawal of support for the Nationalists in terms of the latter's incompetence and corruption. The publication of the *White Paper* took place just after the unexpected Democratic victory in the 1948 elections, when the Democrats gained control of both houses of Congress. In his letter of transmittal, Dean Acheson, the Secretary of State, argued that Chiang Kaishek's government had 'lost the confidence of its own forces and its own people'.[26] Intervention would require 'the expenditure of even greater sums than have been fruitlessly spent thus far' as well as US command of Chinese forces and the participation of huge US armies. Because the China Lobby in Congress, which supported the Nationalists, had made US policy towards China a major political issue, the *White Paper* was an attempt to close the debate on China, or at least to take the political sting out of it, by letting, as Lyman Vanslyke put it in his introduction to the Stanford University Press edition of 1968, 'the record speak for itself'.[27]

It did not do so. The American media again threw themselves upon the China issue, and questions about omissions, distortions, and falsifications were raised in the House of Representatives. Senator Joseph McCarthy exploited the White Paper to press his pursuit of Communists in the Department of State. As Ambassador to China, Patrick Hurley had come to blows with China specialists in the Department of State such as John Service and John Carter Vincent who in their despatches had described the Nationalists negatively and the Communists favourably. Hurley charged in a letter to President Harry Truman in November 1946 that 'our professional diplomats continuously advised the Communists that my efforts in preventing the collapse of the National Government did not represent the policy of the United States. These same professionals openly advised the Communist armed party to decline unification of the Chinese Communist Army with the National Army'.[28] Following the publication of the *White Paper*, in 1950 McCarthy began to make speeches about Communist subversion of the US Government.

McCarthy's charge that the Roosevelt and Truman administrations were virtually the product of a Communist conspiracy was an act of gross demagoguery, wild speculation, and paranoia. He and his supporters exploited a scare about the enemy within to attack Roosevelt's New Deal liberalism in a very nasty way. Nonetheless, as Allen Weinstein, Alexander Vassiliev, John Earl Haynes, and Harvey Klehr have shown on the basis of research conducted in Soviet archives in the 1990s and as a result of the release, finally, of 3,000 war-time telegrams between Soviet spies in the USA and Moscow deciphered by the Venona project, the consensus of the 1970s and 1980s that there were no Soviet spies in the US government was also wrong.[29] Although some of their specific conclusions have been challenged,[30] it is clear that high-ranking US officials in the Treasury, in the Department of State, in the Office of Strategic Services (OSS) (the forerunner of the CIA), in other US government agencies, and in the Manhatten Project were indeed Soviet agents. They included, among many others, Lauchlin Currie, Roosevelt's Special Advisor, and Harry Dexter White, Henri Morgenthau's aide, who had a hand in delaying gold shipments to China for the purpose of stabilising the Nationalist currency.[31]

In the feverish atmosphere that followed McCarthy's allegations and his subsequent hearings in Congress, the nature of the Nationalist government became a political issue with deeply serious consequences. Service, Vincent, and John Paton Davies suffered greatly in their careers and in their lives. The argument became that the Americans had tried their honest best, but that the Nationalists had been beyond salvation, as men like Service, Davies, and Vincent had charged all along, and as Dean Acheson had asserted in the Letter of Transmittal of *The China White Paper*.[32] Stilwell was an excellent vehicle to make this case. No one could accuse him of being a Communist or even a Democrat, his views about the Nationalists seemed all too prescient, and he had worked with great energy. Service and White had developed a genuine admiration for him, and an equally honest loathing for the Nationalists. Like White, Service had been close to Stilwell. The State Department had loaned him to Stilwell as his political advisor.

In 1971, when the ground of McCarthyism and the China issue 'was still hot',[33] Barbara Tuchman distilled what had been implicit in much of the reporting about the Stilwell–Chiang clash into a grand tragedy of American values running into the blinkered authoritarianism of Chiang Kaishek. In her *Stilwell and the American Experience in China*, which won the Pullitzer Prize and which concluded the public debate about the Nationalists, she described Stilwell as 'quintessentially American'.[34] Stilwell, to her, was an American hero precisely because despite the fact that the National Government was beyond salvation, 'he made the maximum effort because his temperament permitted no less'.[35] He was given to 'plain talk' and could not stand the 'phoney propaganda,' as he himself called it, about Chinese victories.[36] Perhaps too honest and outspoken for his own good and unsuited to the Byzantine politics of Nationalist China, Stilwell was a good guy: honest, dedicated, incapable of scheming and self-aggrandisement, and essentially on the right track. In Tuchman's version of Stilwell, he failed because 'the KMT military structure could not be reformed without reform of the system'.[37]

Tuchman built on the work of White and others who had reported on China or produced memoirs, as well as on Stilwell's papers. She also relied on the research of the official US Army historians, Charles Romanus and Riley Sunderland. In their three-volume account of the war published between 1953 and 1959, they praised Stilwell's attempts to reform the Chinese army, argued that his strategic views had been correct, and lauded his command capabilities. Tuchman agreed with their views, but put the political at centre stage. According to her, the Nationalists were doomed to waste America's 'supreme try in China' because the 'regenerative idea', for which America stood, could not 'be imposed from outside' on a politically debilitated 'husk'.[38]

Most other academic historians agreed with the negative appraisal of the National Government. None have challenged Stilwell's depiction of their military capabilities, the appropriateness of his own strategic preferences, or his command capabilities. Our understanding of the Nationalist prosecution of China's war against Japan has been shaped heavily by Stilwell and by people who had close connections with him. Romanus and Sunderland defended the US Army's point of view and Stilwell against charges of gross incompetence and criticism made by detractors such as Captain Joseph Alsop,[39] who had good relations with Harry Hopkins, Roosevelt's special advisor, and Claire Chennault who commanded the 14th US Air Force in China.[40] Romanus and Sunderland were heavily influenced by Stilwell's papers, commenting that 'for an understanding of events in China in the years 1942–44 their importance can hardly be overestimated'.[41]

Frank Dorn published *The History of the Sino-Japanese War, 1937–1941: From Marco Polo Bridge to Pearl Harbor* in 1974 which was highly critical of Nationalist strategy and military forces. Dorn was assistant military attaché under Stilwell when Stilwell himself served as military attaché in China when the War of Resistance broke out. Dorn later was Stilwell's Aide-de-Camp in Burma and Chief-of-Staff of Y-Force, the army trained in Yunnan in south China as part of Stilwell's programme to train a Chinese force to recover north Burma. As Dorn stated in *Walk-out*, his 1971 memoirs of the retreat from Burma, 'my friendship and regard for General Stilwell were highly subjective, and still are'.[42] Lloyd Eastman described the account of Romanus and Sunderland about the US role as 'near definitive'.[43] Edward Dryer in *China at War, 1901–1949* based his chapters on the War of Resistance almost entirely on their work.[44] They, as well as Dorn, Tuchman, and *The Stilwell Papers*, shaped Eastman's account of Nationalist military and its operations in *The Cambridge History of China*.[45] Bruce Elleman in *Modern Chinese Warfare, 1795–1989* relied heavily on Eastman and Dryer.[46]

In writing about the Nationalist state during the War of Resistance, most commentators and historians have taken as their starting point the validity of the criticism of the Nationalist military by Stilwell, Romanus, Sunderland, and Dorn, and then sought to explain it in terms of a pathology endogenous to the Nationalist state predating the War of Resistance. Ch'i Hsi-sheng's *Nationalist China at War* saw the Nationalists' inability to produce offensive warfare during the War of Resistance as laying bare a malady that predated the war and that rendered Nationalist rule stillborn. Discussing several

Nationalist attempts at offensive warfare, Ch'i concluded that 'the root causes of the KMT's failure were in existence long before the outbreak of the war. ... The militari-sation of politics, the pursuit of etatist objectives, the exceedingly narrow definition of revolution as the elimination of domestic and foreign political–military rivals had all been firmly established as features of the KMT's programs of the Nanking decade'.[47] According to Ch'i, these features made it impossible for the Nationalists to mobilise Chinese society effectively during the War of Resistance.

The purpose of Eastman's *Seeds of Destruction* was to counter the China Lobby's argu-ment that the Communists won in 1949 because the 'US government betrayed the Nationalists by withholding support and material aid at critical junctures of the Civil War'.[48] He concluded that responsible for the victory of the Communists was 'the inherent structural infirmities of a military-authoritarian regime lacking a base in society'.[49] The failure to institute social, military, economic, and political reform along liberal lines before 1937, according to Eastman, made it impossible for the Nationalists to gain the loyalty of warlord troops, to tax rural society efficiently, reform the military, and establish a fair conscription system so that the National Army became 'incapable, at least after 1942 and probably earlier, of sustained effective military operations'.[50]

Subsequent monographs worked on different aspects of this general interpretative framework. Parks Coble in *The Shanghai Capitalists and the National Government* argued that the Nationalists were not even friendly to capitalist business.[51] In *Facing Japan*, he described the Nationalists during the 1930s as failing to stand up to Japan, thus holding them indirectly responsible for Japanese militarism. He agreed with Eastman that the Nationalists were an authoritarian and conservative regime without a mass base and obsessed with the Communists.[52] William Wei described the Nationalists' campaigns against Communist bases in the early 1930s and argued that its military approach then led to the dominance of the military.[53]

Recent studies have begun to bring the Nationalists back into the historiography of twentieth-century China. Thomas Rawski, David Faure, and Loren Brandt have argued for impressive economic progress both in industrial and agricultural productivity during the 1930s.[54] William Kirby discussed Sino-German relations in the 1930s. He argued that after 1931 the Nationalists pursued a vigorous industrialisation programme and suggested that dismissals of the regime as fascist were not fully appropriate.[55] Christian Henriot has written about the Nationalists' efforts to bring order to chaotic Shanghai with its powerful Green Gang, arguing that their policies were sensible and effective.[56] Julia Strauss undermined the depiction of Nationalist officialdom as invari-ably corrupt and incompetent by showing that before 1940, the Ministries of Finance and Foreign Affairs, as well as the Sino-Foreign Salt Inspectorate made themselves into relatively effective and honest bureaucracies in a very difficult environment.[57] Studies of Shanghai,[58] a new interest in Republican culture, mentalities, and discources,[59]and a special issue of *The China Quarterly* on the history of the Republican China too have revitalised interest in the period.[60]

Yet, in our understanding of the Nationalist military and the War of Resistance, the influence of what perhaps might be called the Stilwell–White paradigm remains over-whelming. Its basic tenets, of military incompetence, corruption, a debilitating obses-sion with the Communists, authoritarianism, and a blind refusal to fight Japan remain in place. Even if the Communists have lost their shine, we continue to think in terms of a stark dichotomy between the Nationalists and the Communists. Because it is assumed that the Nationalists suffered from an endogenous pathology predating the war, we continue to neglect extraneous factors, including the geo-political situation and the complicated domestic situation, and to regard the War of Resistance as historically irrelevant. A depressing consequence is that we still lack a good operational history of the War of Resistance in the English language, or of most of the wars in which the Nationalists were engaged previously, let alone treatments of their effects on collective memory, economic developments, politics, culture, and society.[61]

To develop a new approach, it is necessary first to discuss some of the ideological foundations that have shaped evaluations of the Nationalist military and their prosecution of the War of Resistance. Important in shaping the views of Dorn, Stilwell, Romanus, and Sunderland was the pronounced influence on them of what Jack Snyder with reference to the First World War called the 'ideology of the offensive'.[62] In that war, according to Snyder, the ideological commitment to the offensive by military establishments led all sides to mobilise for massive offensive operations not in accord with military realities, with horrendous consequences.

Military strategy during the Second World War was of course shaped by the experience of the preceding world war. The avoidance of trench warfare and man-wasting offensives such as those of the Somme or Paschendaele were aims for all belligerents. If Japan and Germany remained highly offensive-minded, this was not the case for Britain, the Soviet Union, and of course China. Churchill followed a 'peripheral' strategy, aimed at surrounding Europe, stimulating resistance movements, and using strategic bombing offensives to wear out Germany before counter-attacking. The Soviet response to the German invasion was withdrawal. Mark Stoler has shown that until 1939, the USA followed a strategy of extreme defensiveness. If shaped by isolationism, in the US army this attitude was also the result of resentments nursed at leisure about perfidious British attempts to use the US Expeditionary Force during the First World War to safeguard the interests of the British Empire. Lieutenant General Stanley Embick, head of the Army's War Planning Division, who had been at Versailles, developed a strategy of hemispheric defence, which was based on the assumptions that the USA was economically self-sufficient, that neither Europe nor Asia was of vital interest to US security, and that the USA should not again be drawn into imperialist projects. Until 1939, some US war plans continued to speak about Britain as 'our most probable antagonist' because it would go to war to protect its imperial trade network.[63] It was only in November 1940, following German military successes, that Plan Dog, formulated by Admiral Harold Stark, the Chief of the Naval Office, substituted this strategy for one that saw the prevention of a German conquest of all of Europe as a vital US interest. Plan Dog called for 'an eventual strong offensive in the Atlantic as an ally of the British and defensive of the Pacific'.[64]

But, this cautious geo-strategic orientation was accompanied by a highly offensive operational doctrine in the US army itself. This was promoted by General George Marshall, who became the US Chief-of-Staff in 1939. During the First World War, Marshall served as a staff officer in charge of planning under John Pershing, the commander of the American Expeditionary Force. Loath to become stuck in the trenches like his European counterparts, Pershing masterminded US offensives at Saint-Mihiel near Verdun and the Meuse-Argonne area. Marshall planned the critical transfer of

600,000 men rapidly from one combat area to the next.[65] The First World War was not decided by these battles: Ludendorff's offensives had exhausted and demoralised the German army while British and French offensives had driven the Germans from the Channel Coast and broken the Siegfried Line.[66] But the experience did shape Marshall's views about warfare.

When in charge between 1927 and 1932 of Fort Benning, the leading US Infantry School, Marshall implemented what has become known as his 'Benning Revolution'. Marshall believed that the US army's experience in the First World War had been misleading in that the Americans had arrived at the end of a static campaign when trenches, arms dumps, railroads, and intelligence services had all been neatly in place. To fight an enemy mobile offensive or to conduct one without the availability of such support would be an entirely different proposition. He stressed independent initiative by local commanding officers and simplicity in operations because 'a citizen army was not going to have more than a few highly trained officers'.[67] He inveighed against the complex orders that staff officers tended to draw up and sought to eradicate as much complexity and formalised thinking in the army as possible. As Chief-of-Staff, Marshall set about weeding out older officers and rapidly testing and promoting younger ones. Promotions in the US army had depended strictly on seniority.[68] A culture of 'can do' improvisation and camaraderie fitted his tactical preferences.

Once war began, as we shall see, Marshall's aim was to end the war as quickly as possible through a large-scale infantry offensive directly aimed at Germany. Marshall was convinced that infantry offensives remained decisive in warfare. He had reacted furiously in 1941 when Roosevelt had slowed the US army build-up in favour of aiding Britain and the Soviet Union.[69] In 1942, Marshall opposed Churchill's peripheral strategy and regarded the invasion of north Africa as militarily of no significance. With many in the US army suspecting the British of again trying to use US military resources for the good of the British Empire, Marshall advocated preparations for a forty-eight division cross channel attack in 1943 and emergency operations straight away across the channel, partly to aid the Soviet Union.[70]

That the ideology of the offensive shaped the views of US analyses of the Sino-Japanese War is easily demonstrated. One of the quotes on the frontispiece of Dorn's *The Sino-Japanese War* is General George Patten's famous phrase: 'In war, the only sure defence is the offence; and the efficiency of the offence depends on the warlike souls of those conducting it'. Dorn praised the Japanese army for its offensive strength and for being 'deeply imbued with a sense of patriotism for their Emperor and their cause',[71] while he repeatedly chastised the Nationalists for lacking the 'will to offensive action',[72] and for 'refusing to believe the axiom that no war has ever been won from previously prepared positions'.[73] Commenting on the plans for the defence of Wuhan in the fall of 1938, he wrote that 'the whole tone of the directive was one of delay, step-by-step withdrawal, and defence in depth that presaged defeat. Like most antiquated Chinese military thinking, the operational guidelines for the defence of Hankou were a product of a sort of dream world of correct words and resounding phrases'.[74]

Marshall selected Stilwell as commander of US forces in China, Burma, and India partly because of his commitment to the offensive. At Fort Benning, Stilwell had been head of the Tactical Section.[75] Many of Stilwell's views reflected those of Marshall and the US Army generally. It is unsurprising that Stilwell frequently fulminated against the lack of the 'offensive spirit' in Nationalist armies.[76] Marshall himself too judged China by its capacity to mount offensive warfare and when he concluded that it would not be able to deliver that he refused to commit significant resources, let alone US troops, to China. Stilwell may have been commander of US forces in the China theatre, but that meant that for much of the time he commanded only a very few people. Stilwell too was not convinced of the utility of air power, although Marshall would change his views about this; he was deeply suspicious of British motives; and he looked for a single large infantry offensive to bring an end to the war in East Asia. His denunciations of senior generals and his programmes to train a new Chinese army seems to have aimed at repli-cating Marshall's Benning Revolution. Stilwell wanted to be to China's military what Marshall was to the US Army, and to the war against Japan what General MacArthur also promised to be.

As Stoler has shown, US army planners, including Embick, after the US entrance into the war talked about Britain as a decadent power that was in decline and saw the USA and the Soviet Union as young and virile powers.[77] Albert Wedemeyer, who did succeed Stilwell following his recall in 1944, articulated similar views.[78] Wedemeyer was Embick's son-in-law. After graduation from Fort Leavenworth, he studied at the German Kriegsakademie. As a member of the War Planning Division of the Army General Staff from 1941 to 1943, he used his knowledge to help draft the Victory Programme of September 1941.[79] Aimed at defeating Germany in Europe, including by a large infantry offensive, the Victory Programme detailed the army build-up to prepare the US Army for this task.[80]

The preference for the offensive, suspicion of Britain, and an organicist view of history in the US Army meshed in Stilwell and Dorn with an Orientalist discourse about Chinese civilisation and warfare whose origins and development I have sketched elsewhere.[81] In that discourse, modern offensive warfare was associated with modernity, industrialisation, honesty, manly vigour, science, initiative, mastery of nature, and progress,[82] while defensive strategies stood for emasculation, backwardness, degenera-tion, passivity, traditionalism, lack of discipline, and deceit. Such views depended on an essentialised understandings of Chinese culture and a juxtaposition between martial, modern, and aggressive countries like the USA (and latterly Japan) and an a-martial, passive, and backward China. They also universalised and idealised nineteenth-century European ways of organising military force and conducting offensive warfare. Such warfare was conducted by a military led by a professional officers corps with specialist skills and was subordinate to the will of the state and served its purposes and interests. Armies were clearly separated from society, by their distinct uniforms, an elaborate set of rituals that socialised recruits into the army, and by housing armies in closed barracks. Warfare too was bureaucratised, in that it was guided and disciplined by large bureaucracies, and industrialised, in that it was armed by the products of modern industry and adopted many of its managerial practices. Armies fought, or were supposed to do so, on clearly demarcated battlefields in well-defined time frames, when the military was in charge and peace time civil rule made way for military law on the battlefield.[83]

Chapter 1 will provide ample evidence for the influence of Orientalist views on Stilwell and Dorn. But to suggest its significance here briefly, Dorn dismissively talked about 'Confucian attitudes towards the settlement of difficulties by discussion and compromise',[84] and wrote that 'feudal in their thinking and strongly influenced by politics of one kind of another, the Chinese looked upon the scene of a campaign as a gigantic military chessboard about which pieces were shifted in various formations to check the enemy'.[85] Just after Pearl Harbor, as the US and Britain were being defeated everywhere, Stilwell wrote that 'most of the despised people (Chinese Russians, Greeks, and Filipinos) are doing the best work for civilisation'.[86] When he was nearly removed in 1943, he blamed 'the suspicious, jealous Oriental mind, listening to lies'.[87] To the *Stilwell Papers* was appended a transcription, meant to illustrate the difficulties of getting anything done in backward China, of a conversation in which Stilwell addresses with growing frustration and fury a Chinese worker who constantly wants more money and whose explanations of problems in carrying out a certain task Stilwell interprets as excuses for laziness, duplicity, inscrutability, and stupidity.[88] He referred to Chinese politics as Byzantine, Chinese strategy as amateurish and based on fear, and himself as a regenerative force with the mission to reform China so that it then would be capable of taking offensive action against the Japanese.[89]

A lack of reliable information also made it difficult for Stilwell and Dorn to develop new understandings of the Nationalists' military. As Harry Hinsley showed in his magisterial study of British intelligence during Second World War, before signals intelligence became available in 1939 and the institutions were created in the course of the next year to assess the information delivered by it and to put it in the hands of field commanders, the British Joint Chiefs-of-Staff could not establish Germany's order of battle, let alone its strategic and tactical plans. He found that 'intelligence bulletins' compiled by the Foreign Office from reports by embassies with their military attachés 'were regurgitating embassy rumours and foreign misinformation' and that, because foreign states were neither inclined nor forced to provide accurate information on their militaries or their war plans, 'diplomatic missions, like the press, the radio, and other overt sources, were alive with conflicting rumours and warnings'.[90]

Yet, it was on this type of source material that Stilwell and Dorn based their assessments as military attachés. When the War of Resistance broke out, Stilwell and Dorn found that 'reliable information was scarce' and that they were in the dark about the position of Chinese and Japanese divisions.[91] On orders of Stilwell, Dorn attempted to gather information, first by driving around Beijing, an effort that failed because of roadblocks; then by squeezing into trains crowded with refugees to make his way to battle fields in north China;[92] by reading the English-language *Ts'ing-tao Times* in Ji'nan;[93] by attending press conferences during the Battle of Shanghai in the Cathay Hotel held by Japanese authorities where 'all drinks … were at the expense of His Imperial Majesty'; and finally, in the fall of 1938 during the Battle of Wuhan, by attending the parties of the foreign community frequented by young embassy secretaries such as John Paton Davies, John Service, and the 'eccentric Agnes Smedley' who was friendly with Chinese Communist Party (CCP) leaders.[94] If Dorn hammed up his exploits in the interest of readability and no doubt also did do some serious hard work, the 'Situation Reports' filed by Joseph Stilwell nonetheless confirm that he and Dorn relied on 'press reports', 'rumours', 'well-informed sources', and information from journalists, including Edgar Snow, who, when the fighting broke out in July 1937 was in Beiping and wrote for the *London Daily Herald*.[95] In his reports, it should be mentioned, Stilwell spent much time agonising about the reliability of the information available to him and evaluating his own hunches about what actually might be happening.

In short, war-time judgements on the Nationalist prosecution of the war were based on certain ideological preferences about the organisation of armed force and the prosecution of warfare, Orientalist views of Chinese civilisation, and a plain lack of information. In all this, men like Stilwell were, of course, simply products of their time and their environment. In seeking to develop a new understanding of the Nationalists and the wars in which they were involved, my intention is not to argue that their opponents had it right after all. Coming several decades after the issue lost its political relevance, that would be a pointless exercise.

Nor is it my purpose to argue that the situation in China was not awful or that the Nationalists were persistently wise and able leaders of their country during one of its gravest crises. Instead, I hope to suggest that the standard by which the Nationalists military has been judged, namely that of modern Western warfare, is inappropriate and has led to a serious misreading of Nationalist war-making. Neither am I convinced that the concepts of authoritarianism, derived from Western political discourses based on classical theories revived in the nineteenth century and often rather idealist about Western practices, or that of corruption are adequate tools to analyse the Nationalists politically.

White, *The China White Paper*, and Tuchman turned China's war against Japan into an affirmative myth in which the US and especially Stilwell stood central and whose purpose it was to validate US wartime actions in East and South-east Asia. This myth crowded out other actors, including the British as well as many Americans, but also the Indians who officered and manned the India Army and did much of the fighting for their own purposes, including post-war independence, and others who did so elsewhere. It sidelined other developments than the US entry into the area, especially local nationalist mobilisations against both imperialism and Japanese aggression in many countries of East and South-east Asia, and including China.

These nationalisms had long histories predating the war, but found new opportunities in it. This was true in India, the Dutch East Indies, Burma, Malaya, French Indo China, and Korea. The war proved in all these areas the forcing house of history, as populations mobilised themselves to resist Japanese aggression, were armed by the Allies to fight the Japanese, made deals with them to gain post-war independence, and accumulated the symbolic and material resources to make themselves masters of their countries. I will put at the centre of my account what the Nationalists themselves did to mobilise their country against Japan and against imperialism. It is not an uncomplicated story and certainly not one of continuous triumphs all along the way. Nor is it one of a great leader and his followers uniting their society with uncommon skill, without internal rivalries, and without greed, or one in which the livelihoods of local populations were always put first. As elsewhere in East and South-east Asia, the result was not a unified and secure nation ready to take up its place in a new world order. VJ-Day did not often mean an end to warfare in East and South-east Asia, as conflicts then broke out to gain control over the new states born by the war. But to look beyond Stilwell and see how China, warts and all, mobilised against Japan is nonetheless important.

I stress four themes in my analysis. First, I place the role of warfare and the military central in the history of the Nationalists from their emergence as a revolutionary organisation with a substantial military force in the middle of the 1920s until the end of the War of Resistance following Japan's surrender in August 1945, by which time, I believe, their defeat was predictable if not inevitable. In emphasising the military, I am following the growing trend in Chinese studies that takes war seriously.[96] That trend is the result of the new military history that has changed our views of warfare and the military in European history and that regards warfare not as a surface phenomenon but as an important historical factor, both in opening or foreclosing certain developments on the battlefield but also in shaping long-term political, economic, social, and cultural developments.[97] In analysing Nationalist approaches to warfare, I seek to move away from stark dichotomies between the traditional and the modern, and the West and the East that dominated an earlier generation of scholarship but which now have long been recognised as of little use.

Second, one element of the Nationalists' nationalism was the refutation of depictions of China as an emasculated a-military culture. In the late nineteenth and early twentieth centuries, the Western view of China as an a-martial, passive, and backward country was domesticated. Kang Youwei, the Confucian leader of the reform movement in the latter part of the 1890s, bemoaned Chinese military weakness, and suggested that China should recover its military strength including by following the German example and 'making all people into soldiers'.[98] Liang Qichao, Kang's disciple who became a leading constitutionalist and essayist, wrote in a text designed as a school history textbook about the fading of martial values following the unification of the empire after the Warring States.[99] In 'On Respecting Martial Qualities', he wrote that 'respect for the martial is the fundamental animus of a people. States depend on it to establish themselves and civilisations rely on it to maintain themselves'.[100] Following the Boxer Rebellion, China's military weakness became thought of as a cause for deep shame. The idea of 'shangwu' – respecting the martial – became in vogue; a popular phrase exhorted the Chinese to 'strengthen the race to protect the country'.[101] Even sons of elites enrolled in military academies to join the modern army that the Qing sought to built after the Sino-Japanese War of 1894–5 and the Boxer Rebellion.[102] Martial arts clubs were established that downplayed magical elements but promoted martial arts as a way to strengthen the body and cure the 'sick man of Asia'.

Such ideas faded after the 1911 Revolution, but re-emerged in the 1920s. One characteristic of Chiang Kaishek's speeches about the military was to denounce the Chinese military for all the ways in which it was inferior to modern Japanese and Western armies. Building a modern standing army, introducing national military service, constructing efficient bureaucracies, and creating a disciplined and patriotic population oriented towards the state were efforts, which had both instrumental and cultural aims. They were to give the Nationalists the means to carry out revolution, consolidate their power, eliminate Western imperialism, and resist Japanese aggression. They also were to demonstrate that the Chinese were not a degenerate race and China not a decadent civilisation.

Third, although they were influenced by Western military models and cultural critiques, the Nationalists did not forget China's own history and their policies adapted past traditions. Precisely at the time that Chiang Kaishek with Soviet help built up a modern army in the mid-1920s, he also edited a collection of sayings of Zeng Guofan and Hu Linyi, the determined and tough-minded Confucian suppressors of the Taiping

Rebellion in the middle of the nineteenth century.[103] He ordered its distribution to his armies during the Northern Expedition of 1926–1928.[104] During the War of Resistance, he frequently referred to China's military classics, including Sunzi's *The Art of War*, as well as the Ming general Qi Jiguang, and again Zeng Guofan. Jiang Baili, a military thinker of the 1920s and 1930s, who influenced both Mao Zedong an Chiang Kaishek, talked at length about Chinese military traditions and prevailing conditions, insisting that approaches to the military and to strategy should be based on them. In the 1930s, he insisted that a defensive strategy aimed at the attrition of Japan met those conditions best.[105]

Even if much had changed as a result of the fall of the Qing dynasty in 1912 and the rise of secular nationalism, some of the practices and strategies of the Nationalists, nonetheless, echoed earlier times. This was, for instance, true in their attempts to demobilise the interior after the Northern Expedition of 1926–8, their attempt to resurrect a disciplined bureaucracy, and their efforts to implement the traditional system of local mutual surveillance, the *baojia* system, to re-establish order over local society and gain control over the means of violence, although they also sought to make the *baojia* the basis for a system of national military service and used it as a device to spread their redemptive nationalism. The Nationalist response to warlordism and the Communists, too, also was informed by a long tradition of dealing with regional armed forces and border problems. During the War of Resistance, the strategy of attrition, the creation of multiple centres of resistance across China, reliance on areas with grain and men surpluses, the collection of the land tax in kind, and a revival of mercenary recruitment too echoed earlier periods.

It is noticeable, too, that the Nationalists, like the Communists, were reluctant to give free reign to their generals or allow personality cults to grow up around them. Neither did they think in terms of a sharp demarcation between civil and military spheres, with politicians in charge of the first, and once war began, the military having complete authority over the other. Yuan Shikai, the first President of the Republic, Chiang Kaishek, and Mao Zedong would all claim both civil and military skill and ultimate authority. Perhaps one reason for the difficult relationship between Chiang Kaishek and Stilwell was that Stilwell did claim unique military expertise, did indulge in heroic gestures, and did not want to be Chiang Kaishek's subordinate but have full authority in his own sphere of action.

Fourth, I pay close attention to geo-politics. On the one hand, this requires attention to the Nationalists' own geo-strategic calculations. In these, from 1935 until 1939, the Nationalists sought to make use of conflicts between Japan and the Soviet Union, which shared a long border in Manchuria. If the Nationalists hoped to draw the Soviet Union into the war, the Soviet's own aim was to diminish the threat of a war on two fronts by providing enough aid to China to bolster its resistance to Japan and so prevent a Japanese attack on themselves. Afterwards, the USA and Britain, never irrelevant, replaced the Soviet Union as the most important geo-strategic partners of the Nationalists. Each had their own geo-political strategies. Allies were also adversaries who sought to make use of their partners to secure their own strategic objectives. Before Pearl Harbor, avoidance of war with Japan was the dominant aim for both Britain and the USA, a goal best served by keeping the war in China going. Afterwards help to China became important but had to compete with activities elsewhere which, because of the 'Europe First' strategy, were usually accorded a greater priority. Concentrating maximum resources for the invasion of Europe, support for operations in the Pacific, aiding the Soviet Union, and keeping the US public on board were important in shaping the US policies towards China, while for Britain preserving the Empire was an additional aim.

Let me finally outline the chapters. I begin, against chronological dictates, with a re-appraisal of the fighting in Burma between 1942 and 1945 and the role of Joseph Stilwell. The chapter will demonstrate that his preference for the offensive made no sense in this theatre. It led him into two operations, the attacks on Tounggoo in 1942 and on Myitkyina in Burma in 1944, which went disastrously awry. Burma became an obsession which reached such proportions that in 1944 he insisted that Chiang Kaishek release a large army from south China to Burma to assist two Chinese divisions led by himself when these had run into problems at a time when the Japanese were destroying Chinese armies in China itself during the Ichigo Offensive, of which Stilwell was badly informed, and occupied recruitment grounds and agricultural areas critical to the Nationalists' survival.

We then move backwards to the 1920s. I begin by examining a military turn in Chinese nationalism in the 1920s, the construction with Soviet help of the National Revolutionary Army (NRA) in Guangdong that would enable the Nationalists to seize power during the Northern Expedition of 1926–8, and the financial measures that made this possible. Chapter 3 discusses the Northern Expedition, long considered a turning point in Chinese history. Many have seen it as the fall from revolutionary grace of a revolutionary party, the KMT, after it was usurped by a military dictator, that is, Chiang Kaishek. Using a variety of new archival resources, including the telegrams that Chiang Kaishek sent during the Northern Expedition, I argue that the Northern Expedition led to the gestation of cultures of violence to which all parties contributed. During the Northern Expedition, the Communists, the Nationalists, and warlord forces all scrambled to develop new sources of power over which they exercised only a limited control. The Communists, I argue, lost out and suffered greatly as a consequence, but they too contributed to bringing about a culture of violence, which would prove difficult to eradicate. Chiang Kaishek emerged as a victor, although this was by no means inevitable, because of his ability to construct personal networks, because he followed shrewd political and military strategies, and because he had the greater ability to raise large sums of money.

Chapters 4 and 5 cover the period between the Northern Expedition and the beginning of the War of Resistance. The Northern Expedition did not end with a Chinese nation embracing a new future, but with a country that remained divided by several large military groupings. Attempts to demobilise them failed, political unity proved illusive, civil war intensified, and government organisations were incapable of discharging their normal functions, let alone deal with the natural disasters of these years. The Japanese seizure of Manchuria in 1931 and its attack on Shanghai in 1932, however, concentrated minds and marked a new beginning. If internal KMT rivalries persisted and the problems of a divided military continued, nonetheless, the need to prepare for war and actual war drove the Nationalists to devote their energies to state-building, with the military at its core. Around this core, the Nationalists attempted to construct a new disciplined nation, using a variety of economic, fiscal, cultural, and political means.

They first worked to wring the means of violence and the sources of warlordism out of Chinese society, rebuild a centralised and disciplined bureaucracy connected to a variety of constituencies, and construct a modern elite army. Through local systems of militarisation controlled by their government, they sought to link this army to Chinese society and through campaigns such as the New Life Movement they attempted to orient the population to their state and its armed forces.

The final two chapters focus on the War of Resistance itself. Chapter 6 provides an operational history, in which I stress, following current scholarship in China itself, that the Nationalists were serious about fighting the Japanese and did so in ways suited to domestic conditions and the international situation. In analysing the fighting, I pay attention not only to underlying Nationalists strategy, but also geo-strategic issues and domestic political developments. When full-out war came in 1937, the first problem the Nationalists encountered was to make China fight as a unity. They failed in this objective in north China and even their lines of retreat to Sichuan Province in the west were not secure. If sound military reasons were behind the decision to open a second front in Shanghai, the Nationalists did so also because they were unable to make militaries in the north stand and fight and to bed down the full co-operation of the Guangxi Clique and the Communists. Another objective was to ensure that the war was put firmly in the mind of Western powers so that when a new world war would come, as was expected, China would not again be forgotten and its interests slighted during any post-war settlement. Internationally the most important objective of the Nationalists was to draw the Soviet Union into the fighting. Operations were designed to shepherd the war in the direction of the Soviets as much as possible and exploit Soviet–Japanese tensions. The Nationalists did gain significant Soviet aid, but not full Soviet military involvement.

After the fall of Wuhan in October 1938 and the Japanese defeat at Nomonhan a year later, the War of Resistance changed in character. The Japanese, with their supply lines fully stretched, abandoned the idea of eliminating the Nationalists on the battlefield. Instead they worked to secure their gains and build up a Chinese alternative to Chiang Kaishek's Nationalists in the hope of reducing Chiang to an irrelevant warlord in a border region. The withdrawal of the Soviet Union from the war in East Asia following the Battle of Nomonhan and a Soviet–Japanese truce agreement in September 1939 meant that the Japanese northern flank became safe and that they could concentrate on China before, as they expected would happen, they would have to confront European imperial powers and the USA. They thrusted further west along the Yangtze River and moved the war south, including into Guangxi in south China once European powers became involved in war in Europe. They supported a new National Government under Wang Jingwei, launched offensives to cut Nationalist lines of communications, engaged in punishing strategic bombing campaigns, captured grain areas, and hardened their economic embargo. The Nationalists developed a set of tactics that delivered them some battlefield victories, but they were not able to prevent the loss of grain and recruitment grounds nor of the city of Yichang on the Yangtze River which connected the Nationalists' Sichuan supply base with fronts elsewhere in China. Although the fighting changed in character, I do not believe it right to speak of these years before Japan's Southern Offensive, of which the attack on Pearl Harbor was part, as a period of stalemate. For China, these were the hardest years. It faced Japan alone, the fighting was dispersed but frequently intense, and the stakes were nothing less than the future shape of East Asia.

The final phase of the war saw the Nationalists become the allies of the USA and Britain. That development ensured the eventual defeat of Japan. Yet, the price the Nationalists paid for their involvement in the alliance would be substantial. Neither the USA nor Britain wished to make China itself a major theatre of operations. The Europe First strategy, the British focus on Empire, the USA's belief that the participation of the Soviet Union would be needed to defeat Japan, and Stilwell's obsession with Burma would all prove detrimental to Nationalist interests. During Japan's 1944 Operation Ichigo, China's best forces were in Burma and the majority stayed there in 1945, when Britain used them for the recovery of Burma. In the spring and summer, Albert Wedemeyer, who did succeed Stilwell, opposed the Nationalists' desire to go on the offensive and recover grain and recruitment areas along the Yangtze River but deployed China's forces in the south to prevent Japanese troops in South-east Asia from retreating through China and so make the USA's Pacific offensive more difficult.

The last chapter examines the political economy of Nationalist mobilisation during the war. It argues that until 1941 the Nationalists were relatively successful. They drew nearly 2 million men per year into the army while maintaining social stability. They did so by protecting rural productivity, concentrating mobilisation in areas well known for producing soldiers and capable of sustaining recruitment, and protecting bureaucratic control over the recruitment process. They also kept army service reasonably attractive and permitted flexible local accommodations to dampen the disruptive effects of recruitment and taxation.

Afterwards, the Japanese embargo, complete isolation from outside military supplies and grain markets, the collapse of transport networks, and the Japanese capture of Yichang caused financial and monetary chaos. The Nationalists made most of their forces live off the land and kept up only a small number of divisions capable of sustained operations. Large parts of their army became militarily useless, engaged in smuggling, and traded with the Japanese. The Nationalists did work to overcome the crisis. They switched to taxation of the land tax in kind, instituted ration systems for officials and educators, and worked to establish control over an increasingly compartmentalised bureaucracy in which most organs saw securing resources for their own constituencies as their priority.

They, nonetheless, did not succeed. The loss of many grain and recruitment areas and the destruction of transport networks meant that the Nationalists' resource base became too small and that what was available was difficult to transport to the front. After 1941 the pool of men that could be recruited without serious consequences for local productivity had dried up. The result was that to sustain the war the Nationalists could no longer use a set of minimal but, nonetheless, acceptable inducements and various sorts of local accommodations to draw men into their armies, but had to beat them out of the countryside. Taxation too now hit the agricultural population directly. The Nationalists' local agents and their armies used brute force to collect taxes, obtain food, and collect equipment.

The result of the crisis was that in 1945 the Nationalists were in a bad position. Many of their armies were worth little on the battlefield and were politically an unreliable instrument. Their forces, the central bureaucracy, and their local agents were resented. The economy, the fiscal and monetary systems, and marketing and transport networks were in disarray. Rivals to Chiang Kaishek internally had grown strong, war zone commanders had developed a considerable degree of independence, so-called puppet forces had grown up around the Wang Jingwei Government and the Japanese in central and north China, and the Communists had built a series of interlocking base areas in China north of the Yangtze River. By the end of the War of Resistance, the demise of the Nationalists would take a further four years and was perhaps not inevitable, but peace was unlikely and the future of the Nationalists unpredictable.

1 Stilwell revisited

Out of the crooked timber of humanity
Nothing entirely straight was ever made.
(Isaiah Berlin)

When I prepared for this study, I had been determined to avoid writing old forms of military history focusing on operations, generals, and statesmen, inspired as I was by European military historians writing about the importance of warfare in the creation of identity, its impact on state making, and the formation of national memories. I had least expected to want to write extensively about Stilwell and the Nationalist military during the War of Resistance. To a graduate student at a time when the USA repeatedly backed nasty governments, when the Nationalists imposed a harsh martial law in Taiwan, and when Communist rule still retained the vestiges of promise, Tuchman's *Sand against the Wind*, *The Stilwell Papers*, and Theodore White and Annalee Jacoby's *Thunder out of China* were convincing and confirmed that the Nationalists had deserved their fate.

As I read around what I then still thought of as the Pacific War, initially with the restricted aim of providing a short synopsis, it became clear that the Stilwell story could not stand up. I concluded that a new presentation of Stilwell's activities, placed in the context of Allied strategy, was unavoidable. Only when a more complex understanding of the war, US and British strategies, the Nationalists' approach to it, and Stilwell's actions was established would the ground exist for the proper exploration of the topics that first drove me to undertake this study. This chapter, and much of the rest of the book, is the result.

To challenge Stilwell's views about Nationalist military incompetence, their refusal to gather up China's resources to fight Japan, and their blinkered failure to make use of the opportunities provided by the USA, it will be necessary to analyse the Burma War and the position of China in Allied strategy in detail. What I shall suggest is, first, that to understand Stilwell's role in China his actions have to be placed in the context of US strategy in the Second World War, generally, and in the Pacific War, specifically. Neither Roosevelt nor the USA's Chief-of-Staff, George Marshall, shared Stilwell's conviction that Japan had to be defeated in China and that therefore it was necessary to build a supply line through north Burma to equip National Army divisions with advanced munitions and to retrain them. The key aims of Roosevelt and Marshall were to avoid fighting in China and make use of Chinese forces to prevent the fall of India and later on to support the US Pacific Offensive. The British too sought to make use of China's forces, but in their case in support of their Empire.

Most US military planners, including George Marshall, were convinced that an offensive against Germany launched from Britain should have priority. While they did come to back a programme to build heavy bomber bases in China to support the operations of the US Pacific Fleet, for Roosevelt and Marshall the problem after Pearl Harbor was that US public opinion demanded action against Japan. Stilwell was useful because of his status as a war hero to suggest that the USA was doing all it could against Japan on the Asian mainland, first after Pearl Harbor when the USA simply did not have the strength to do anything at all in East Asia and later to avoid the dispersal of US resources over too many theatres.

My second suggestion will be that neither descriptions of Stilwell as a great war hero representing the USA at its best nor depictions of him responsible for much that went wrong can stand. In Stilwell there was something of Kurtz in Joseph Conrad's *Heart of darkness* or the film *Apocalypse Now*. He was deeply dismissive of the Chinese and especially Chiang Kaishek. He believed that they could not save themselves, and was convinced that only he, knowing modern warfare, could do so. Stilwell certainly made serious tactical mistakes and his failures in organisation, administration, and intelligence have been acknowledged even by his staunchest supporters. Few, and certainly not Marshall, agreed with his strategic proposals for the defeat of Japan. At the same time, the actions for which he has been most criticised, including the withholding of supplies to the Nationalists and the US 14th Airforce in China that sought to support them in the spring of 1944 when Japan's Operation Ichigo penetrated deep into south China, were carried out on the orders of Marshall. It is furthermore difficult to see that any of the operations in which Stilwell was involved profoundly affected the course of the war.

Stilwell became an important figure in the Pacific War less because of his military exploits, his strategic views, or his attempts to build up the Nationalist army than for political reasons. In the same way that he was useful to Marshall, who did not always support him wholeheartedly, he was similarly useful at times to Chiang Kaishek, who assigned command over Chinese divisions in Burma to Stilwell in order to keep him out of British hands, to attract US aid, and draw the USA into the fighting on the Asian mainland. Like Chiang, the British also found Stilwell difficult to deal with, but they used him, during the first Burma campaign in the hope of establishing some influence over Chinese forces in Burma and later because they feared that insisting on Stilwell's recall would lead to a backlash in the US press.

Third, Stilwell's dramatic recall in October 1944 came at a critical time in the war. Allied offensives in Europe were suffering setbacks. Following the breakout from the Normandy beachheads, General Montgomery's attempts to seize the bridges over the Rhine in preparation for a 'pencil-like' thrust to Berlin failed in mid-September. While German resistance was stiffening and supply problems intensified, in the Pacific events had not gone well. The Japanese had put up very fierce resistance in the Marianas until the middle of July. The Ugo offensive in Burma had been stopped, but the recovery of Burma would still take much time and hard fighting. In China, the Ichigo Offensive had broken Chinese resistance and it seemed possible that the Nationalists might yet be defeated. The beginning of Kamikaze attacks during the Battle of Leyte

Gulf in October frightened all, and made clear that an attack on Japan even after the destruction of its fleet would demand huge sacrifices.

These developments came in the run-up to the US elections of that year, in which the conduct of the war was a major issue. Opinion polls suggested that Roosevelt's lead was uncomfortably small and declining. In that context, it became useful for Roosevelt to distance himself from the Nationalists to avoid being tainted by their collapse in a critical moment in the Second World War and in US politics.

Stilwell's recall served these purposes. Roosevelt approved the publication of articles by sympathisers of Stilwell, which suggested that the USA had done its best in China and that it had sought to reform the National Army, but that the Nationalists had never been interested in fighting the Japanese and instead had become a nasty dictatorship that was corrupt, oppressed the Chinese people, and with which the USA should no longer be associated. This view became entrenched subsequently, as the introduction has made clear, when China figured largely in political rivalries in the USA, in which the fate of New Deal liberalism was as much an issue as US foreign policy.

Many of the conflicts between Chiang Kaishek, Stilwell, and the USA had their origin in the complexities inherent in Allied warfare. For example, when in 1944 Chiang refused to let a US equipped force in south China join the fighting in Burma, he did so not because he did not want to fight the Japanese. With the USA and Britain having decided to put all possible resources into the invasion of Europe and to retract the promise of the participation of sizeable amphibious forces in the reconquest of Burma to focus all effort on the invasion of Normandy, Chiang's refusal is better seen as an attempt to avoid committing his best forces to a campaign in Burma to which his Allies appeared to attach little significance while his greater need was to confront Japan in China itself.

The correctness of Allied strategy has been debated at length, and will no doubt continue to be so. It may well be the case that Churchill's peripheral strategy was appropriate before 1943 and that afterwards the USA was correct to insist on the early invasion of Europe as the speediest way to bring an end to the war. But that is not to say that Allied strategy especially in East and South-east Asia was well designed, that people always did their honest best, that all was done altruistically to help China, or that promises were not abandoned when that seemed expedient. We need not accept as truth a presentation of events to the public that flowed from political expediency, especially the suggestion that the Nationalists were not willing to fight the Japanese. No one has a monopoly on virtue; and no one on incompetence.

A surprise battlefield and a surprise appointment

Japan's official history of the war has made clear that Japan did not intend to take its Southern Advance as far as north Burma. Throughout 1941, Japanese operational plans called for the navy and the 25th Army to seize Hong Kong and Singapore and occupy the Philippines, Malaya, and the Dutch East Indies. The aim of the Southern Advance, according to these plans, was to create a defensive perimeter in anticipation of Allied attacks, secure access to primary resources such as oil and rubber in South-east Asia, and cut international supply lines to China so as to gradually strangle the Nationalists into submission. Japan's access to oil had been severely curtailed by Roosevelt's haphazard imposition of an oil embargo in July 1941. Until then the USA had provided Japan with 80 per cent of its oil supplies.[1] The embargo followed Japan's occupation of the southern provinces of French Indo-China.[2] Yet, both Roosevelt and Churchill remained determined to avoid war with Japan while also seeking to keep the Soviet Union in the war. They hoped to prevent the Japanese from joining the Germans in their assault on the Soviet Union.[3]

In October 1941, the Japanese took the decision to add the 15th Army to the Southern Advance and to include in its plans the occupation of Thailand to protect the flank of the units of the 25th Army that were to take Singapore. Although subsequently Burma was mentioned in operational plans, what was meant, according to Japan's official history, was not the whole of Burma, but Moulmein to the south of Rangoon, where the British had an important air base from which they might attack Japanese forces in Thailand. Shipping allocation lists confirm that no plan existed to attack Burma before Pearl Harbor.[4] It was simply not believed that the Japanese navy had sufficient capacity to be able to support a large-scale attack on Burma in addition to its other assignments. Besides the attack on Pearl Harbor, these called for a two-pronged attack on South-east Asia, one from Taiwan to the Philippines and one from Hainan and French Indo-China to Malaya. After securing these areas, the two forces then were to converge on the Dutch East Indies. The operation, which was to succeed in 150 days and involved Japan's entire navy and eleven infantry divisions, reflected perfectly Japan's strategic ideology of a combined arms offensive aimed at a quick victory.

The Nationalists too had made few serious preparations for a move into Burma. Since Japan's occupation of north French Indo-China in August 1940, the Nationalists worried about a Japanese attack from there into Yunnan, the Chinese salient into South-east Asia bordering French Indo-China and Burma but also a backdoor into Sichuan where China's wartime capital, Chongqing, was located. Long the preserve of the shrewd Long Yun, the province was poor, lacked good supply lines, and depended on imports from French Indo-China, as Long suggested to Chiang and as he acknowledged, and therefore would find it difficult to support more forces.[5] However, in August 1941, Chiang and Long Yun reached an agreement that two central divisions would enter the province. In October 1941, the 60th Army, consisting, in fact, of two divisions and three independent brigades, was ordered to take up positions near Kunming, the provincial capital, as well as Kaiyuan and Jianshui to protect Yunnan's border. Fortifications along the Yunnan section of the Burma Road were also to be built to protect the road from attack by paratroopers.[6] Long Yun was promised that the centre would not interfere in internal Yunnan affairs.[7] After protests by Long Yun, Chiang informed him that initially only a few thousand soldiers would be sent. These would be increased when the necessary infra-structural facilities had been built up.[8]

Even though the British were concerned about a Japanese offensive in South-east Asia, their preparations did not focus on Burma either. The British had decided that Hong Kong could not be defended, but had strengthened Singapore with two capital ships, five cruisers, nine destroyers, six submarines, and 120,000 troops. Although Singapore was the cornerstone of the British Empire in South-east Asia and critical to the protection of the dominions of Australia and New Zealand, Churchill had prevailed in a debate with Sir John Dill, then the Chief of the Imperial General Staff, about strategy to defend the Empire. Dill had advised to concentrate not on the Middle East but on India and Singapore and argued that the Middle East had become something of an obsession for Churchill. Churchill, however, was convinced that the Middle East, with its critical oil reserves, was central to the survival of Britain, that it was unlikely that Japan would attack South-east Asia, and that if it did so, the USA, with its interests in the Philippines, would not be able to stay out of the war. He refused airforce and naval requests to reinforce Singapore.[9] The security of Singapore depended on Britain's ability to despatch the Mediterranean Fleet and the Royal Air Force (RAF) and that, by 1942, was impossible.

As to Burma, British and Chinese officials began discussions in late 1940 about co-ordinating their military actions in case of a Japanese attack somewhere in South-east Asia and they did consider the defence of the Burma Road. These discussions took place between Air Chief Marshall Robert Brooke-Popham, the Commander-in-Chief Far East, headquartered in Singapore and a Chinese Military Delegation under General Shang Zhen. According to a Chinese report, Brooke-Popham suggested that the Nationalists would focus on the defence of the Burma Road in Yunnan while the British would do so in Burma itself. Brooke-Popham also promised the delivery of 100 aeroplanes and mentioned that Rangoon, then the terminus of the Burma Road, had been reinforced with anti-aircraft guns and that an RAF squadron had been stationed in Burma. In case the Japanese attacked Burma through Thailand, which under the ardently nationalistic Phibun Songkhram was pro-Japanese and strongly anti-Chinese, Brooke-Popham suggested that the Nationalists should attack French Indo-China from Yunnan so as to cut off Japanese lines of retreat.[10] However, a Japanese attack on Burma was thought unlikely. The British stationed only 2,600 British and 8,000 Empire troops in Burma and left southern Burma virtually undefended.[11]

Burma, from Rangoon to the north, became a serious Japanese objective only when 'victory fever' took hold of the Japanese. After Pearl Harbor, the Southern Advance went far more swiftly than the Japanese had anticipated. The British battleship *Prince of Wales* and the battle cruiser *Repulse* were sunk on 10 December as they tried without air cover to prevent Japanese landings on the eastern coast of Malaya. The remaining naval forces of the Allies, including those of the Dutch, were destroyed in the Battle of the Java Sea in February 1942 in the same month that Singapore fell. The USA did no better. Guam and Wake were in Japanese hands before Christmas, while the US airforce in the Philippines was caught on the ground and General MacArthur made what was referred to euphemistically as a 'fighting withdrawal' to Bataan.[12]

Burma did not become a Japanese target until well into February 1942. The war plan of the 15th Army of 11 December called only for the capture of Moulmein and the nearby mouth of the Salween river in order to protect the flank of Japan's army in Thailand. On the 21st, the possibility of moving on to Rangoon was for the first time included in Japanese war plans as a serious objective; but until 9 February, the 15th Army in Moulmein remained deployed in a defensive formation. Its staff opposed offensive operations in Burma, preferring to foster a Burmese independence movement.[13] On 9 February, however, the Japanese Southern Army, following instructions from the Japanese Supreme Headquarters, ordered the 15th Army to occupy 'important cities in central Burma' in co-operation with the navy, first by taking Rangoon and then swinging north toward Tounggoo, Mandalay, and the nearby oil fields at Yenangyaung.[14]

The USA was of course even less prepared to fight in Burma. It had organised a volunteer airforce of 100 planes under Claire Chennault, which did arrive in time and fought in Burma, but after Pearl Harbor and the loss of the Philippines, Guam, and

Wake, the USA could not have constructed the supply lines to sustain significant numbers of troops in Burma. It is easy to forget how small the US Army was. In 1939, it ranked nineteenth in the world in terms of size, most of its divisions were under-strength by half, and it carried out joint manoeuvres only every fourth year. It was supported by an airforce of 160 fighters and 52 bombers.[15] The adoption of the Victory Programme in July 1941, envisioning a rapid build-up to over 8 million men, would deliver the USA the forces it needed for meaningful operations, but it was not anti-cipated that they would be ready before 1943. At the time of Pearl Harbor, the US had some 200,000 infantry troops. Of these, eight divisions were to be sent to Europe, including some weaker ones to take over garrison duties in northern Ireland to release the better British divisions there. Two were sent to Brazil to defend South America. None went to China or Burma.[16]

If limited military strength, the Mediterranean crisis, and the lack of air and naval power made it impossible for the USA and Britain to do much about Japan's Southern Advance, so did the USA's Europe First strategy. Immediately after Pearl Harbor and Hitler's subsequent declaration of war on the USA, US and British war planners met in late December 1941 and early January 1942 in Washington for the Arcadia Conference to discuss allied strategy. Prime Minister Winston Churchill advocated taking a defensive attitude in East Asia while in Europe building a 'ring of steel' around Germany, first by securing north Africa and then launching simultaneous offensives from various fronts combined with uprisings by resistance forces.

Marshall opposed Churchill's indirect approach. He objected to operations in north Africa as of no utility and also because it seemed that Britain was again intent to use US forces not to defeat the enemy but to protect its empire. Marshall wanted the concentration of US forces in Britain for an offensive with maximum resources against Germany at the earliest possible date as 'a democracy could not indulge in a Seven Year's War'.[17] In a memorandum to operational planners of 27 March he wrote that western Europe was 'the only place in which a powerful offensive can be prepared by the United Powers in the near future'.[18] General Eisenhower and the Army's Operations Planning Division urged a forty-eight division invasion in 1943 and an emergency assault on Europe in the summer of 1942, although the USA could not send ground forces before 1 July and only 66,000 troops by 1 October.[19] Although it was recognised that a 1942 operation could only end in disaster, US strategy-makers nonetheless pressed for this in the belief that the operation was important to keep the Soviet Union in the war.[20]

The traditional view of what happened next is that Marshall, after running into the British refusal to forego an offensive in north Africa and attack the Germans in Europe, threatened to switch US resources to the Pacific but that this was a bluff, a version of events to which Marshall, Admiral Ernest King, and Henry Stimson, the Secretary of War, all adhered after the war.[21] Mark Stoler, on the other hand, has made a convinc-ing case arguing that the USA's Joint Chiefs of Staff had been serious when they suggested that the USA should opt for a Pacific First strategy.[22] On 10 July, Marshall proposed to the Joint Chiefs of Staff that if Britain continued to insist on an invasion of north Africa, the USA should turn to the Pacific.[23] The always quotable Churchill, who wanted to hold the Mediterranean to safeguard oil supplies, characterised the Joint Chiefs of Staff's position with 'just because the Americans can't have a massacre in

France this year, they want to go sulk and bathe in the Pacific'.[24] On 12 July, Stoler has made clear, Roosevelt put a stop to the Joint Chiefs of Staff's demarche after they had to reveal that they did not have any worked-out plans for Pacific operations. Roosevelt commented that a turn to the Pacific was 'precisely what Germany hoped we would do after Pearl Harbor' and observed that it would achieve little else than the occupation of countless useless islands.[25]

Even if Marshall wobbled in the spring and summer of 1942, nonetheless, his aim throughout the war was to concentrate maximum force for an invasion from Britain of Europe aimed at the annihilation of the Germans. On 8 February, before the fall of Singapore, the US defeat in the Philippines, or the fall of Java, Marshall objected to the US Navy's proposals for a Pacific First strategy, arguing that 'we realise that flanking attacks would be useful, but the Japanese are protecting that flank at Wake and Guam'.[26] On 6 May, in response to a memorandum by Admiral King, a proponent of a Pacific First strategy, Marshall stated:

> While I agree that we must hold in the Pacific, I do not concur that this is our basic strategy. My view, and I understood it to be your decision prior to my visit to England, was that our major effort would be to concentrate immediately for offensive action against Germany from the British Islands.[27]

Marshall may have prevaricated during his conflict with Churchill over the invasion of North Africa, but from then on he would be steadfast in maintaining that the invasion of Europe was the best way to bring the Second World War to an early close. He pursued this aim single-mindedly, although that of course did not mean that significant resources were not shifted to the Pacific.

Burma, then, was a surprise battlefield for all and one to which Marshall was not willing to commit significant resources, something that even in the context of a Pacific First policy would not have made sense. However, US public opinion was gripped with hatred of Japan. The attack on Pearl Harbor was fresh in the mind. Some actual and some supposed sightings of Japanese submarines off the coast of California led to scares of an imminent Japanese invasion. Many Americans, like the strategic decision makers in the US Army, remained dubious about involvement in European affairs, with its empires that had colonised so much of the world and with its Machiavellian statesmen. Marshall then could not be seen to abandon the campaign in Burma and had to suggest seriousness of purpose in supporting it. For the assignment, Marshall first approached General Drum, one of the only three remaining generals in the US Army with experience of large-scale operations in the First World War. Drum believed that Marshall was not serious about the mission and demanded as his condition for accepting the appointment that ground forces would be made available to serve in China and that US supplies be increased significantly. Marshall refused and then appointed Stilwell.[28]

Stilwell was a surprise appointment. He had never been in command of any troops, he had not attended command courses at Leavenworth, and had no experience in combined operations. His career had been in the not particularly glamorous areas of intelligence and training. But Marshall had met Stilwell first in China when Stilwell was military attaché and had come to know him well at Fort Benning.[29] Although Marshall recognised that Stilwell treated his subordinates harshly and sometimes unfairly, he also believed that Stilwell was 'ahead of his period in tactics'.[30] For the paternalistic but also coolly calculating Marshall, Stilwell was useful because he knew him well, could count on him to seek offensives that would convince the US public that the USA was doing its best, and could rely on his loyalty and support. The latter may have been important to offset the imperious and unpredictable General MacArthur, then in charge of the US army in the Far East. A dyed-in-the-wool Republican opponent of the New Deal, he had been Chief-of-Staff before Marshall.[31] The British spied on him while Roosevelt feared that MacArthur would challenge him for the presidency.[32]

Stilwell also did not insist on a substantial commitment of US military resources. In a memorandum to Marshall before his departure, he had suggested that MacArthur's South-west Pacific theatre should be a defensive one and that at least one US Army Corps should be assigned to the China theatre to develop 'maximum offensive capacity' there.[33] In his formal instructions to Stilwell, Marshall declined that proposal, stating that Stilwell would 'command such Chinese forces as may be assigned to him'.[34] Stilwell furthermore was presentable as someone with a long familiarity with China and opposed to any imperialist designs of the British. Before his departure, Stilwell was promoted to Lieutenant General to keep up appearances.[35]

In August 1942, after the Japanese had conquered Burma, Marshall concisely set out his views about China's strategic significance in a memorandum for the Combined Chiefs of Staff of the British and the Americans. He saw China as the weak reed among the Allies. According to Marshall, it was 'impossible to release US ground forces for duty in China or Burma', but 'because the Pacific is a secondary theatre, we must depend on the Chinese to contain increasingly more Japanese divisions than at present'. Marshall advocated 'the re-opening of the Burma Road' as the best way to 'keep China in the war'.[36] China was an ally in which Marshall had no faith but from which he hoped to extract the maximum effort at the lowest possible price, so that he could concentrate on the invasion of Europe. Stilwell had the unenviable task of implementing this policy.

The loss of Burma

Burma may have been a surprise battlefield, but it was an important one (Map 1.1). Burma was so to the Nationalists partly because it might open up access to Allied and especially US productive capacity, which China lacked. Rangoon and the Irrawaddy River formed the only major open supply line to China. Burma's plains were highly productive. Burma was the largest rice exporter before the Second World War. Yenangyaung had large oil-fields which China itself lacked, other than in a remote part of Gansu. Burma provided a dangerous backdoor for Japan into south-west China, which the Nationalists had built up into their major base of resistance. Traditionally, China had been influential in north Burma.

If these reasons would suffice in their own right for the Nationalists to involve themselves in Burma, a huge economic and financial crisis, explored in Chapter 7, made it imperative for Chiang to get stronger armies than his own stuck into his war against Japan and to direct that war out of China as much as possible. In making his allies fight his enemies, Chiang was doing the same as the USA, the Soviet Union, and Britain

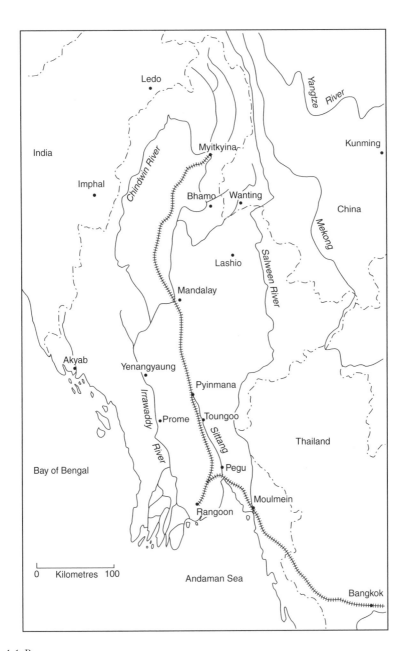

Map 1.1 Burma.

were trying to do to him. As suggested in the Introduction, before the acceptance of Plan Dog, the USA had first tried to stay out of the Second World War altogether. Lend–Lease was an effort at arming proxies so that the USA itself did not have to go to war. Before Pearl Harbor, the USA and Britain had sought to avoid war with Japan and they had done so in part by seeking to trap Japan in China. The Soviet Union successfully followed the same policy. Allied warfare is a complex business in which each of the partners will seek to get the most out of the other in pursuit of its own objectives.

Burma was important for the Nationalists also to make the war against Japan one in which the USA and Britain were fully involved and in which China participated on equal terms with them. The Nationalists probably believed that only in this way they could prevent a disadvantageous peace between the USA, Britain, and Japan after the defeat of Germany. It was only at the Casablanca conference of January 1943 that the unconditional surrender of Germany and Japan became established as Allied war aims. Even so, in the US army, as US forces encountered strong resistance on their march towards Japan, there were those who argued that a negotiated settlement should be considered.[37] The Yalta agreements would be unfavourable to China. It should be mentioned as well that to draw the USA into the war in East Asia was important to Chiang Kaishek to develop a counter-weight to Britain.

Given the previous lack of thought about defending Burma, it is not surprising that none of the Allies fought well there in the spring of 1942. Serious fighting began in late February. The Japanese first took Moulmein, where the British lacked the artillery and the airforce for effective defence. The Japanese then crossed the Salween River and advanced towards Pegu, in preparation for an attack on Rangoon at the mouth of the Irrawaddy River and the only major port left through which Allied forces could have been supplied. General Harold Alexander, the Hero of Dunkirk who like Stilwell was sent to Burma in lieu of serious military reinforcement, ordered counter-attacks on the advancing Japanese, but when these failed, the decision was made to evacuate the city after destroying its harbour installations. The Japanese took possession of Rangoon on 8 March. With the monsoon looming, the Japanese then decided immediately to advance towards Tounggoo where an important British airbase was located. After capturing this city, they rushed towards Lashio in upper Burma, which they took on 29 April, completing a Blitzkrieg that turned Allied flanks and cut off Chinese lines of retreat. Besides seeking to acquire Burmese oil resources, one Japanese aim was to stir up opposition to the British in India.

The rapidity of the collapse of the Allied defence in north Burma is easy to explain. The lack of an adequate airforce was critical. During the deciding phase of the battle, the Japanese operated 400 aircraft, including a good number of the mighty Zeros, while the Allies had withdrawn their air power to India and retained only 35 aeroplanes in Burma, including those of Chennault's, most of which were in fact outmoded.[38] Had more air power been available, Allied naval forces could have been better protected; had there been more of both, Japanese landings could have been made more difficult. Allied resources simply did not stretch to offering significant resistance to the Japanese in Burma.

Many Burmese living in the country's lowland areas, in contrast to the Karens and Kachins there and in the northern hills, were either indifferent or hostile to the British. Some Burmese personnel critical to defence, such as those working on the railroads, left once the Japanese invaded. Promised independence by the Japanese, Aung San was able to draw others into a Burmese Independence Army of 30,000 troops.[39] Deficient or virtually non-existent supply lines meant that heavy artillery and tanks could not be brought into play. Important too, however, were serious logistical problems on the Nationalists side, the British decision to withdraw first to north Burma and then to

India, mutual suspicion especially between Britain and China, and finally an attempt by Stilwell to begin an offensive, which broke up the Allied position.

An internal Nationalist report illuminates the failings of the Nationalist divisions sent to Burma. Its author, Lin Wei, had been a member of Chiang Kaishek's Personal Staff Office and in the spring of 1942 served as the head of the Chinese staff delegation, co-ordinating operations at Lashio with the British and later Stilwell as well.[40] The report discussed in detail the various battles in which the Chinese participated, the problems of co-operation with the British, and logistics.

The report was highly critical of the British. Lin described them as arrogant and gripped by defeatism. He lamented that the British had failed to inform Chinese liaison officers of the British logistical arrangements and their order of battle. He also denounced British unwillingness to share telegraph and radio communications facilities and their distrust of the Chinese reports on troop strength and hence ration require-ments. Lin did write that British logistics had performed well until the fall of Lashio. They had supplied China's divisions with all their food, fuel, ammunition, and transport needs until then.

As to the Nationalists, Lin criticised logistical and staff weaknesses. China's supply lines simply did not reach as far as Burma. After the order for retreat had been given, Chinese troops had to depend on their own supply lines. Food shortages immediately became severe, so that, as a British report stated, 'the Kachins suffered some rather rough treatment from some Chinese formations'.[41] Lin was frank about the short-comings of China's own staff work. The National Army essentially fought blind, as no Chinese maps for Burma were available. Just before the campaign, the British Embassy in Chongqing and the Consulate in Kunming had supplied a few English maps. These were of the wrong scale for strategic and tactical planning. Staff officers had not worked out a standard transcription system to translate Burmese place names into Chinese. A shortage of signals technicians capable of laying telephone and telegraph lines hampered communications. Radio equipment was insufficient and of poor quality, so that most sets suffered fatal breakdown. Staff officers furthermore had failed to draw up regulations for the transmission of messages, so that they were not graded in importance and private communications to family members vied with urgent military ones. Long delays occurred between the receipt of a message and its delivery to the appropriate officer. The avoidance of taboo words such as 'withdrawal', usually replaced with 'transfer' or 'advance', meant that staff officers in the rear had to scurry around the available maps before they figured out actual movements on the ground. Intelligence in the field was dismal, with the result that often no one knew where Japanese units were located. The available artillery essentially fired at random and therefore made little impact.

Mutual suspicion between the British and Chinese provoked severe tensions, with serious repercussions for the co-ordination of action. On 2 March, just before the fall of Rangoon, Chiang Kaishek had suggested to Archibald Wavell, the Commander-in-Chief in India and Supreme Commander Far East for the British, that he defend Pegu and Rangoon and wait for the Chinese 5th Army to arrive at Tounggoo in preparation for a counter-offensive.[42] Wavell did not believe this plan to be feasible and refused entrance to the Nationalist 5th and 6th Armies on the grounds that the logistical infrastructure could not support them. Not to have the Chinese in Burma was also an important motive behind the refusal. In a communication to Churchill, Wavell wrote that it was 'obviously better to defend Burma with Imperial troops than with Chinese, and the Governor particularly asked me not to accept more Chinese for Burma than absolutely necessary'.[43]

Defeatism too was a factor. When Churchill sent Harold Alexander to take command of British forces in Burma, he commented 'never have I taken the responsibility of sending a general on a more forlorn hope'.[44] Alexander's association with Dunkirk cannot have reassured Chiang Kaishek. Following the fall of Rangoon, the cause was lost and British priorities switched to the defence of India. During conversations on 25 and 27 March, Alexander set out a deeply pessimistic view of the fighting. According to Alexander, the lack of air power was a serious problem. He mentioned that although two RAF squadrons were on their way, they had to come from Britain and therefore could not be expected to arrive for several weeks. He went on to explain that the Empire forces had no experience of jungle warfare while the Japanese, mobile and lightly armed, excelled in it. Because the British with their heavy armoury were tied to the two main roads in Burma, the Japanese had turned their flanks constantly. Alexander mentioned that he had instituted training programmes for jungle warfare and had ordered his forces to abandon vehicles for mules and horses. A further problem, Alexander reported, was that the Burmese component of the Empire forces had deserted and that the morale of Indian units had slumped.[45]

Chiang Kaishek explained in conversations with Stilwell that he believed, as was the case, that the British aim was to use Chinese divisions to protect their retreat to India.[46] During a conversation with Alexander of 6 April, Chiang took Alexander to task for wanting to withdraw British forces from Prome to Allanmyo and demanded a 'no retreat' agreement.[47] He furthermore challenged Alexander about the lack of defence preparations for Mandalay, something which he probably saw not only as evidence of British intentions to abandon Burma but also of keeping the Chinese out. He accused Alexander of not trusting the Chinese to defend Mandalay and seeking to prevent its stores of equipment and ammunition from falling into Chinese hands.[48]

A rattled Alexander replied that the Chinese were welcome to the supplies at Mandalay, that his three divisions had been fighting for three months and had been reduced to a third of their full strength, and that they were defending a front of 80 kilometres while the Chinese were only fighting on a front of 40 kilometres. Doubting whether Chiang really wanted to assist the British, he stated that if Chiang was worried about the British, 'I am equally concerned about the assistance of China's armies' and then went on to say that 'if you do not dispatch your forces, my army also will not be able to operate in Burma'.[49] Chiang Kaishek instructed Stilwell that the Chinese divisions in Burma, command over which he had assigned to Stilwell, should not take up positions 'too far forward' until the British, who were then some way to the south of Mandalay, had shown that they were willing to stand and fight. He also threatened to withdraw them altogether if the British did not do so.[50] Such mistrust, as well as the lack of staff structures able to co-ordinate the activities of the various forces in Burma, meant that Allied forces were spread out over large distances, providing the Japanese with easy opportunities to advance through the empty spaces between them.

Stilwell's preference for the offensive and his disdain for Chinese strategy also contributed to the loss of Burma. Stilwell arrived in India on 23 February, and then flew on to Chongqing to confer with Chiang Kaishek on 9 and 10 March after Rangoon had fallen. Chiang began his first meeting with Stilwell by mentioning the counter-offensive plan that on 2 March he had suggested to Wavell. He stated that because of a British failure to deliver promised petrol, some Chinese tanks and heavy artillery had not yet moved to the front, but that some units of the 5th Army, including China's only mobile division, the 200th, had been moved to Tounggoo while the rest was on its way, while the 6th Army had been deployed from Jiangmai in north Thailand to the west in north Burma. Chiang went on to say that following the fall of Rangoon, the counter-offensive had to be scrapped. He feared an immediate Japanese offensive towards Tounggoo and stated that the defence of Mandalay should now be the main concern. He advocated a strategy of defence in depth, with a series of strong points between Tounggoo and Mandalay. With the local population sympathetic to the Japanese, Chiang argued, only in this way could troops fight without having to worry about security in the rear. Fearing that the available British Empire forces were too weak to shoulder the responsibility for the defence of Mandalay, he told Stilwell to liase with them in order to obtain their consent to hand over Mandalay.[51]

Even if mutual suspicion kept the Chinese and British apart, they did agree that after the fall of Rangoon, the best option was to retreat to the north. Wavell instructed Alexander on 3 March that if Rangoon could not be held, he should withdraw to northern Burma to protect the oil fields at Yenangyaung and the Ledo Road from Assam to China.[52] The British suggested that their forces take up positions in the Irrawaddy Valley, the Chinese 5th Army in the Sittang Valley, while the 6th Army was to guard the frontier with Thailand.[53]

Stilwell's decision to push south to assault Tounggoo and Rangoon was based on his faith in the offensive. During their 9 March meeting, Stilwell had responded to Chiang's proposal to concentrate on the defence of Mandalay by stating that 'our best option is to begin an offensive at Tounggoo … if we begin a counter-offensive immediately then we shall score a huge victory'.[54] Chiang disagreed on the grounds that the Chinese had only one division nearby and that a counter-offensive required tanks, which due to the lack of gasoline remained at the rear.[55] The next day, Chiang Kaishek explained that the 5th and 6th Armies were China's best, the loss of which would mean that there would be no reserves to fight in the Yangtze or defend Yunnan against possible Japanese attacks. He stated that the Allies lacked an airforce, naval support, and artillery. Chiang further pointed out that for a counter-offensive China's forces would have to be concentrated, which would take several weeks. Everything, according to Chiang, was in Japan's favour: they had the airforce, the artillery, the naval support, and the supply lines that would enable them to build up a massive force well before Chinese forces could do so.[56]

Stilwell characterised these discussions in his diary as a 'session of amateur tactics by Chiang Kaishek, backed up by a stooge staff general [Shang Zhen]. Chiang Kaishek gave me a long lecture on the situation and picked on Mandalay as the danger point. I showed him the solution, but the stooge jumped in and made a long harangue about how right Chiang Kaishek was. I let them rant'.[57] According to Stilwell, Chiang did agree during their discussions on the 19 March that one division could be moved south of Mandalay to Taungdwinggy and that an offensive could be contemplated in time. Stilwell believed this was a major victory and that 'continued butting is wearing down resistance'.[58] The Chinese record of the conversation shows that Chiang approved the transfers in order to set up defensive positions to the south of Mandalay in preparation of the arrival of three or four more divisions from China to strengthen the defences of

Mandalay. He also stated to Stilwell that 'I will inform you when the time has matured for an offensive'. By the end of April, Chiang mentioned, the monsoon season would begin, five or six Chinese divisions would be near Mandalay, and thirty aeroplanes would have arrived. He stressed that 'for now we must assume the defensive'.[59]

When Stilwell returned to Burma on 21 March, the Japanese had already arrived on the outskirts of Tounggoo and Japanese reinforcements had left Singapore on 19 March.[60] Without heeding the advice of Chiang or consulting the British, Stilwell ordered the Nationalist 55th and 22nd Division south to Pyawnbwe and Pyinmana to begin a counter-offensive.[61] Four days later Stilwell had suffered the indignity of seeing the Japanese encircle Tounggoo and with it the 200th Division. Chiang had mentioned to Stilwell that the 200th Division would not retreat unless Stilwell ordered it to do so. Stilwell did not issue the order and the 200th Division was forced back into the city so that its mobility could not be brought into play. Even when food and ammunition had run out and the Japanese had brought up reinforcements, Stilwell refused to order a retreat from Tounggoo. With Chiang Kaishek's approval, the commander of the division ordered a break-out.[62]

Realising, in part because of information provided by documents captured at Tounggoo, that China's forces were now too far south of Mandalay, on 3 April, the Japanese decided on an immediate thrust towards Lashio, between the Nationalist forces near Tounggoo and those on the Thai–Burma Border. Lashio was to the north-east of Mandalay and the seizure of this city would turn Allied flanks, destroy the Allies' logistical and command centre, and prevent China's 5th and 6th Armies from retreating to China.[63] The Japanese took Lashio on 29 April. Confusion then descended, the order of command collapsed, and logistical and supply networks broke down. Chiang ordered an attempt to rally at Myitkyina, but by this time, the concern of most commanders, including of Stilwell, was the removal of their forces from Burma.[64] When Chiang learned of Stilwell's order that the Chinese 5th Army retreat to India, he responded 'This is contrary to my order to concentrate the entire army at Myitkina; isn't Stilwell losing his nerve?'[65]

The organisation of an orderly and timely retreat back to a safe area is an important military skill. Napoleon during his invasion of Russia, Hitler in Operation Barbarossa, and the Japanese would all pay with defeat for their inability to realise when the time for retreat had come. They instead persisted with doomed offensives. Stilwell's attack on Tounggoo did not have the same consequences and was in the scale of things only a minor event. But it revealed the same deficiency.

The inexperienced Stilwell could not see the defeat as the result of overwhelming Japanese advantages and the consequences of a very risky move that had gone horribly wrong. He blamed Chinese stupidity and a backward preference for the defence. He commented in his diary that 'through stupidity, fear, and the defensive attitude we have lost a grand chance to slap the Japs back at Toungoo'.[66] During his first conversation with Chiang Kaishek after the debacle on 4 June, Stilwell responded to Chiang Kaishek's statement that 'we have learned a valuable lesson' with 'Yes: the price for taking the offensive is always far lower than for taking the defensive'.[67] It was also at this point that he came to the conclusion that 'The Chinese government is a structure based on fear and favour, in the hands of an ignorant, arbitrary, stubborn man. Only outside influence can do anything for China – either enemy action will smash her or some regenerative idea must be formed and put into effect at once'.[68]

Chiang Kaishek did not see it this way. He wrote

> The cause of failure in Burma rests in our loss of autonomy in decision making …
> I am compelled to yield to the US. However, the sacrifice has been enormous.
> If my original plan had been followed and the main body had been concentrated
> in the highlands Northeast of Old Mandalay, today's defeat would not have
> happened.[69]

The same strategy that Chiang had proposed for the defence of north Burma and
which Stilwell had so derided had just brought success in the Second Battle of
Changsha.

The British were not as negative as Stilwell about China's effort in Burma.
A Chongqing embassy report noted that 'the Chinese troops appear to have fought
well'.[70] The Commander of the Burma Corps, William Slim, although not unsym-
pathetic to Stilwell and in tune with his offensive instincts, described the Chinese
contribution as largely positive. Their armies, according to Slim, suffered from a lack
of organisation and were handicapped by a lack of munitions and communications, but
'the Chinese soldier was tough, brave, and experienced – after all, he had already
been fighting on his own without help for years. He was the veteran among the Allies,
and could claim up to this time that he had held back the Japanese more successfully
than any of the others. Indeed, he registered his arrival in the forward areas by several
minor but marked successes against enemy detachments'.[71] Slim appreciated the tactics
that the Chinese had used during the first Battle of Changsha. These involved drawing
the Japanese beyond their staging points so that their food and ammunition would
run out. When a Chinese general informed him of them, Slim noted that 'later, I acted
on it'.[72]

Burma in Allied strategy

On 25 May 1942, just after he had arrived in India following his retreat from Burma,
Stilwell wrote in a message to the War Department of his 'belief in the decisive
strategic importance of China' and averred that 'a serious mistake is being made in not
sending American units into this theatre'.[73] In June 1942, Stilwell outlined a strategic
rationale for the recovery of Burma, stressing the importance of building a land-based
line of communication from Assam to Yunnan. Once established, according to Stilwell,
the USA could supply and train Nationalists divisions. These were then to drive to south
China, open harbours there, and swing north to dislodge the Japanese from the rest of
China and bring Japan to its knees by cutting it off from primary resources in China
and South-east Asia. Stilwell proposed that three Chinese divisions be trained at
Ramgarh in India and that another Chinese force be trained in Yunnan.[74]

Tuchman, Romanus, Sunderland, and more recently Dreyer argued that Stilwell was
right, and that Chiang Kaishek's failure to support Stilwell's army reform programme
and reluctance to commit his Yunnan force to the campaign for the recovery of north
Burma was symptomatic of his military incompetence, his lack of anti-Japanese patriotism, and his ploy to let the USA do all the fighting against Japan. The following
sections will suggest that the USA and Britain were never serious about fighting Japan
in China and certainly not with ground forces. They will also argue that the USA and

Britain failed to anticipate the Japanese offensives of 1944 or heed Chiang Kaishek's warnings about them.

In the aftermath of defeat

The USA's Joint Intelligence Committee produced a report in June 1942, called the 'Situation in China', just after Stilwell had made his views known. In contrast to Stilwell, the report was dismissive of China's strategic importance and did not agree that Japan had to be defeated in China. 'The Chinese army', it wrote, 'despite great improvements of late, has so many inherent weaknesses that it will not be able to stage a major offensive'. It noted that the Chinese were 'bitterly disappointed that the Pacific War has brought them no relief' and observed that the Chinese feared that 'the Allies may not continue the war with Japan when Germany is beaten'. However, according to the report, 'local resources are sufficient to produce as many small arms as their limited forms of resistance require, provided Japan stages no major offensive against them'.[75]

The USA at the same time could not simply abandon China. The US public was perhaps even more passionate about Japan than Germany. The Doolittle Raid of 18 April 1942 was one demonstration of the concern for public relations. Sixteen B-25s were launched from the US carrier Hornet to drop some bombs on Japan. It was impossible for the heavy B-25s to return to the Hornet. They had hardly been able to take-off. One wing extended out over the water and a special line drawn over the flight deck guided the pilots to prevent them from veering into the ocean. The plan was for the B-25s to fly from Japan to China, but because they had to take off earlier than anticipated after the Hornet had been sighted by the Japanese, most ran out of fuel or were prevented by bad weather from landing on airfields in China. Most ditched somewhere along the China coast.[76] Some crew members were executed or held for ransom by the Japanese. Chiang Kaishek had objected to the raid for fear of Japanese retaliation, but Roosevelt and Marshall had insisted on it going ahead.[77] The damage inflicted on Japan was limited, but the US press celebrated the raid. It gave a huge immediate boost to US public morale and Roosevelt awarded James Doolittle the Medal of Honour in White House ceremony, although questions were raised later.[78] The Japanese, however, laid Zhejiang to waste and destroyed a large Nationalist airbase.[79] However understandable, the raid had been a public relations stunt for which China paid a heavy price and which harmed its military position.

Stilwell's fighting in Burma in the spring of 1942 served Marshall in much the same way. It had been depicted in glowingly heroic terms. The US press published stories with headlines such as 'Invading Jap force crushed by Stilwell' and 'Stilwell's China troops trap Japs'.[80] Stilwell's portrait appeared on the front cover of *Life* magazine.[81] His retreat from Burma was reported as an act of extreme courage and endurance. After reaching India, Stilwell declared on 26 May that he had suffered a 'hell of a beating' and that Burma 'could be – and must be – retaken from the Japanese'.[82] The recovery of Burma became an obsession for Stilwell.

Marshall did not agree with Stilwell's strategic views. The extent of his commitment to the Burma campaign in the spring of 1942 is well illustrated by the fact that he kept the US 10th Airforce in India out of the fighting and ordered it into action only after Japanese planes threatened Ceylon and the Japanese Fleet seemed about to explode into the western part of the Indian Ocean.[83] Reports of bravado and a determination to take on Japan, however, were very welcome. It was similarly useful for Marshall to suggest support for Stilwell in his endeavours to build up the National Army. The US public would be re-assured and it would cost the USA little. No troops needed to be made available, as luck had it that Stilwell had brought the 22nd and 38th Nationalist divisions out to India. 45,000 tons of Lend–Lease supply had piled up in India which could not be transported to China and which therefore could be used to equip the National Army divisions in India.[84] Far larger amounts – 149,000 tons – originally assigned to China were kept in the USA or allocated to the British.[85] The Ramgarh programme fitted Marshall's aim of keeping China in the war at little cost to the USA.

Chiang Kaishek had been suspicious of Stilwell's decision to retreat with two of his best divisions to India rather than China, and the British too were not happy to see a large Chinese force in India. But Chiang also realised that after the fall of Burma, little US aid could be delivered to China. On 16 June Chiang stated to Stilwell that he agreed with his plans for a campaign to recover north Burma and then went on with stating that 'we must make preparations for our own contribution to this campaign and therefore would like the 5th Army to remain in India, but under US responsibility'.[86] Chiang clearly did not want the British to have control over this force and stated to Stilwell that an American should be in charge. After Chiang Kaishek assured Stilwell that this US officer 'would have complete responsibility and full authority', Stilwell stated that 'in accordance with our original proposal of training a Chinese army of 100,000 troops, the USA genuinely desires to assume responsibility for training them, provide them with weaponry such as heavy artillery available in India, and supply barracks and medicines'.[87] If for Chiang the retention of Stilwell was useful to keep control over forces now in India and for gathering up US supplies, for Stilwell here was an opportunity yet to obtain command over an army and be involved in a campaign against Japan and avenge his defeat.

The USA's best effort in China and Burma would always have to take place within the strict limits imposed by locally available resources. It also had to conform to its grand strategic design and the commitment to a massive offensive at the earliest possible moment against Germany. China was militarily important only to the extent that it tied down half a million Japanese troops. It was however important in US public opinion.

China in the planning for victory

The strategic situation for the Allies changed for the better quite quickly. India did not fall or disintegrate. The USA was able to recover its naval strength in the Pacific remarkably quickly after Pearl Harbor. The Battles of the Coral Sea of May 1942 and of Midway in June, the latter triggerd in part by the Doolittle Raid, were a shock to the Japanese. The Battle of Guadalcanal between August 1942 and February 1943 was a clear US victory and signalled that the tide in the Pacific had turned. From then, the USA pursued a 'Twin Axis' strategy in the Pacific. General MacArthur wanted to concentrate resources in his South-west Pacific Command for a drive through New Guinea towards the Philippines. The US navy, under Admirals Chester Nimitz, William Leahy, and Ernest King, favoured a strategy of cutting Japan's lines of communication to

South-east Asia by establishing control over the central Pacific to be followed by sea borne assaults on Taiwan or the Philippines. In order to keep both MacArthur and the navy satisfied, Roosevelt approved both strategies, although command relations were organised in such a way as to favour the navy.[88] Roosevelt, like Churchill, was a navy man.

As a result of these developments, Marshall articulated a new strategy towards Burma and China. In a memorandum for the Joint Chiefs of Staff of 7 December 1942, on the anniversary of the attack of Pearl Harbor, Marshall still called for the recovery of north Burma, not to strengthen the Nationalists' army, but because 'the opening of the supply route will permit the rapid build-up of air operations out of China. Already the bombing attacks, with very light US casualties, have done damage out of all proportion to the number of planes involved'.[89] For Marshall, the point of the Ledo Road became that it allowed the build-up of the US Airforce and especially its strategic bombing capacity in China. By bombing Japanese supply lines and Japan itself, important assistance, it was hoped, would be provided to the US navy and the Marines in the Pacific in preparation for a direct attack on Japan itself. This would make it possible to bypass Japanese forces in China itself and elsewhere. This was the time when the USA and Britain had come to place great emphasis on strategic bombing campaigns, partly because it was a way to avoid large-scale land offensives with all the risks attached to them, partly because it was a way of doing something without committing infantry resources, and partly because destroying the industrial capacity of the enemy and interdicting his lines of communication were sensible aims.

Roosevelt and Marshall now had reason to support Claire Chennault. Since October 1942, Chennault had pressed for a strategy that privileged his 14th Airforce. Chennault's American Volunteer Corps of 100 pilots and P-40s that had been sent to China in November 1941 had been re-absorbed in the US military as the 14th Airforce stationed in China after Pearl Harbor.[90] In a letter to Roosevelt, who had asked Chennault to correspond with him outside military channels, Chennault argued that he could 'accomplish the downfall of Japan'.[91] He argued that even with quite a small amount of air power he would be able to destroy the Japanese airforce in China and develop the bombing capacity to interdict Japan's transport lines, attack Japan itself, and support the US Pacific Fleet.[92] Neither Marshall nor Roosevelt are likely to have accepted such extravagant claims, but they did object to Stilwell's plan for the build-up of China's armies because it would take too much time.[93] Supporting Chennault and building up an airforce in China to strike at Japan and co-operate with the US Pacific Fleet provided a more economical way to deliver demonstrable results more quickly. Even if Chennault's air strategy has been derided by pro-Stilwell historians, he was no doubt right that a strong US airforce could make a large difference there. The Southern Advance had meant that Japan had to disperse its air power over a large area. The Japanese reduced the number of aeroplanes in China from over 800 to over 300, with no elite units remaining.[94]

Stilwell objected to the new strategy as it could not but come at the cost of his programme to equip and train National Army divisions and then lead them to recapture north Burma. Marshall urged Stilwell to accept the change, criticising him in a memorandum of January 1943 for failing to understand the significance of air power in modern warfare, 'particularly in your theatre', and admonishing him to reconcile himself to Chennault, stating: 'would it not be wise in the light of your successes to give Chennault his chance'.[95] Marshall wrote to Roosevelt on 16 March 1943 that 'as to air operations, Stilwell is cognisant of our planned air effort out of China which will take place immediately upon the establishment of bases' and 'I will further impress upon him to assist Chennault'.[96] The differences between Chennault and Stilwell became so serious and their refusal to co-operate so detrimental to the war effort that both were called to Washington in May 1943, at the time of the Trident Conference. At this time, Marshall was frustrated with Stilwell. He had sent a message to Stilwell in March, quoting Roosevelt's response to a negative report by Stilwell on Chiang Kaishek. Roosevelt had stated that 'he is going about it precisely the wrong way. You can't treat him [Chiang Kaishek] like the Sultan of Morocco'.[97] And in a memorandum of 9 April Marshall quoted a letter from a soldier under Stilwell, which had stated that 'the opinion of most of us is that if the different commands would stop fighting amongst themselves, we might get somewhere'.[98]

In Washington, during a discussion at which both Churchill and Roosevelt were present, Stilwell was extremely critical of Chiang Kaishek, continued to insist that the Japanese army had to be defeated in China, and emphatically argued that the opening of a road through north Burma should have priority.[99] Marshall later wrote to Stilwell that Roosevelt had drawn the 'conclusion from his interview with you that the air activities were in effect largely to be suspended while the more tedious ground build-up was being carried out'.[100] Roosevelt decided in favour of the air campaign also because Chiang had warned that the situation in China was critical and Song Ziwen (T.V. Soong), then Foreign Minister, had suggested that China might have to surrender.

Roosevelt promised an increase in supplies to China flown in over the Hump (the air route that skirted the Himalayas) to 10,000 tons per months at a time when the Hump route was not delivering even half that.[101] He also ordered that Chennault should receive the first 4,700 tons of supplies earmarked to China.[102] The Trident Conference itself confirmed the downgrading of the Stilwell's strategy.[103] The build-up of especially the Yunnan force was not stopped. However, the strategic rationale for the programme was changed. It was no longer to be used for the recovery of north Burma, as Stilwell had intended, but to protect the bases for heavy bombers in China itself. Marshall stated in a memorandum to Stilwell of 3 May 1943 that the task of the Yunnan Force would be to 'prevent a successful Japanese operation against Kunming'.[104]

Roosevelt was in the habit of dealing with differences of opinion among his commanders by allowing each to pursue their own strategy, and it therefore was not surprising that the Trident Conference still approved a campaign to recover north Burma. Outright cancellation too would have been difficult to explain publicly and would have damaged relations with China. The conference scheduled the campaign to begin after the monsoon season in the autumn of 1943. A plan agreed in July by the Combined Chiefs of Staff provided that it would be accompanied by substantial naval operations to establish control over the Bay of Bengal and by amphibious landings along the Burmese coast.[105] Chiang Kaishek put his stamp of approval to this plan, including the possible use of the Yunnan force in Burma, but also stipulated three conditions. These were the participation of an airforce of 500 planes, to be increased to 1,000 if necessary, a naval task force of 3 battle ships and 8 carriers, and a substantial US infantry force.[106]

Chiang made these demands in part to ensure that Japanese supplies through Rangoon to their troops in Burma would be cut off. They also suggest that Chiang was not willing to fight in Burma alone. This was not only because he confronted Japanese forces in China itself. As Marshall had noted, Chiang feared that the USA and Britain would after the defeat of Germany settle for a negotiated peace with Japan. The failure of both the USA and Britain to commit substantial infantry, naval, and air forces to the Asian mainland no doubt strengthened that suspicion. What a negotiated peace might have looked like was unpredictable, but might perhaps have left Japan in control of Korea and Manchuria. Historical precedent suggested that such a deal would sacrifice China's interests. The Versailles Treaty concluded after the First World War had accepted the Japanese take-over of German possessions in China and the League of Nations failed to take firm action against Japan after its seizure of Manchuria in 1931. The failure of the 'international community' to back up China during the First World War against Japan had helped trigger a rebellion against Yuan Shikai when Japan presented its Twenty-One Demands and the Versailles Treaty itself had precipitated the May Fourth Movement. The Manchurian Incident had led to widespread demonstrations against Nanjing and compelled Chiang to go into an artificial retirement for some time. With Chiang having staked all on the War of Resistance and defeating Japanese imperialism, an unfavourable negotiated settlement would have seriously affected the chances of survival of his government. Rather than suggesting that China was seeking to get the most out of the USA while being unwilling itself to fight Japan, Chiang's conditions were a product of his anxieties about the extent of the US and British commitments to the Burma campaign and China itself.

Postponement and intrigue before Cairo

The schedule for the Burma operation agreed in Washington in the spring proved unrealistic. The Allies became involved in heavy fighting in north Africa and began the invasion of Italy. The troop build-up in Yunnan also proceeded slower than anticipated, due to the fighting in May–June 1943 in western Hubei.[107] Churchill and Roosevelt met for the Quadrant Conference in mid-August 1943. At that meeting, they confirmed that 'establishing land communications with China and improving and securing the air route' would constitute 'the main effort' in respect to China. However, they also stated that 'no decision was reached on actual operations'.[108] They resolved instead that Overlord – the code name for the Normandy landings – 'will be the primary US and British ground and air effort'.[109]

The Quadrant conferees decided to set up a new Allied Command for South-east Asia under the Combined Chiefs of Staff, separate from the British India Command as well as from China. The creation of South-east Asia Command (SEAC) followed the failure of a British invasion of the Akyab mountains along the Arakan coast in late 1942 designed to control coastal shipping. The debacle had convinced Churchill that a shake-up was needed. Churchill, moreover, wanted Britain fully involved in the defeat of Japan, not just because, as he would claim, he was afraid that US public opinion might conclude that Britain abandoned the USA as soon as Germany was defeated,[110] but also to be in a good position to recover Britain's colonies. SEAC's American nickname was Save England's Asian Colonies. Louis Mountbatten, a navy man and Britain's specialist in combined operations, was appointed Supreme Allied Commander.

The Quadrant decisions as well as the creation of SEAC must have given Chiang cause for concern. They had confirmed the low priority given by the USA and Britain to East and South-east Asia. They had furthermore made Burma and Thailand part of SEAC. Thailand had, after Pearl Harbor, been designated part of China's war theatre and China too had claims in northern Burma. The allocation of these areas to SEAC was therefore difficult to accept for Chiang Kaishek and the subsequent tensions were untidily resolved by an unwritten Gentlemen's Agreement between Mountbatten and Chiang, which allowed each to operate in Thailand and French Indo-China on a first come first serve basis.[111] The creation of SEAC again raised the possibility that Nationalists forces would be used not to support China in resisting Japan but in aiding Britain in the recovery of Burma.

Mountbatten explained to Chiang during a meeting in October that in August Roosevelt and Churchill had considered abandoning the campaign for the recovery of Burma altogether. They had agreed not to do so, Mountbatten continued, but also had come to the conclusion that an early campaign in north Burma would mean reducing military supplies for China. Mountbatten informed Chiang that no plans existed for the participation of US ground forces in the Burma campaign and asked Chiang to agree that he be given command over all Chinese forces once they entered Burma.[112] When Chiang Kaishek raised the issue of Allied naval and airforce support, Mountbatten reported that 'he had not yet been assured by telegram on this point' but that he was 'hopeful'.[113] What Chiang was asked to do, then, was to agree to the deployment of his Ramgarh and Yunnan forces in Burma under British command, in an operation to which, he had been told, the Allies attached little priority, for which neither the USA nor the British were willing to promise air or naval support, for which the USA would not make ground forces available, and which would see Britain's position in South-east Asia strengthened.

The hope of making use of Stilwell in a similar way as he had done in the spring of 1942 to maintain control over his Burma forces may be one reason why Chiang dramatically retracted a request for the recall of Stilwell on 15 October. At this time, Marshall, still frustrated by Stilwell's spring performance in Washington, according to Stimson, 'regretted he didn't make the decision to relieve Stilwell months ago'.[114] Able to justify the act as part of the general re-organisation that accompanied the creation of SEAC, Roosevelt too had indicated that he would approve the recall of Stilwell.[115] On 15 October, Chiang formally requested Roosevelt to do so, but he then immediately reversed himself, to the consternation of all concerned.[116] Retaining Stilwell, who did want a more substantial US commitment in China and did ultimately want to fight there, may have appeared to Chiang the best way yet to secure a greater effort from the USA as well as to maintain leverage in SEAC. If this was a consideration, another one probably was that retaining Stilwell would undercut Song Ziwen, Chiang's brother-in-law but also one of the main contenders for power in China. In June 1940, Chiang Kaishek sent Song to Washington. Song would remain in Washington until October 1943, part of this time as Minister of Foreign Affairs. He negotiated a series of large loans, took a lead in the discussions that would lead to agreements with the USA and Britain for the abolition of extraterritoriality and leased territories, and worked hard to enhance China's representation at US and British war councils. If all that could be seen as helping Chiang and China, Song also had made use of his time to increase his own power base.

It was Song rather than Chiang who had been pressing since August for Stilwell's recall. Just before his return to China, on 15 September Song had proposed to Harry Hopkins, Roosevelt's close advisor who lived in the White House, a re-organisation of the China theatre. Besides the removal of Stilwell, Song had suggested that a US vice Commander-in-Chief be appointed, that under a Chinese Chief-of-Staff there would be a US vice Chief-of-Staff, and that this system of mixing US and Chinese officers would be replicated throughout the army.[117] With Song widely regarded as a pro-American progressive liberal as well as with carefully nurtured contacts in the USA, Song would have been able to have men favourably disposed to him appointed to these posts. With the Yunnan Army also set to slip out of his control once it entered Burma, it is possible that Song was engineering a situation in which Chiang's power would decline while his own influence would be greatly strengthened.

One reason Song failed was because his power grab ran into the opposition of his sisters, Song Meiling and Song Ailing, who were married to Chiang Kaishek and Kong Xiangxi (H. H. Kung), the latter the then Minister of Finance. Fearing implications for their husbands and hence their own positions, they mollified Stilwell and induced him to express to Chiang Kaishek regret for past misdeeds and make promises for future good behaviour.[118]

Mountbatten too may have had a hand in the affair. In early October, Song had involved Mountbatten in his efforts to recall Stilwell when they met in New Delhi en route to Chongqing.[119] In July and August, Song had visited London, where he had clashed with Foreign Secretary Anthony Eden about Tibet, insisting that Tibet was a part of China. Just before his departure, a Foreign Office official had expressed concern about the increase of Nationalist forces near Tibet's border.[120] On 10 October, Song informed Mountbatten that he and Chiang Kaishek wanted Stilwell to be recalled and that Roosevelt and Marshall had agreed. Song may have hoped that Mountbatten, as the Supreme Allied Commander of SEAC, would lodge the formal request.[121] Mountbatten refused, because, SEAC reported to London, 'political opponents have made capital in the USA over rumours that Mountbatten's appointment would diminish MacArthur. If Stilwell now goes as well, the US press will jump on Mountbatten and Anglo–US relations will suffer'.[122]

The Cairo house-of-cards and miscalculations in the run-up to Overlord

The Cairo Conference of 22–27 November 1943 was the only Allied conference attended by Chiang Kaishek. Militarily it was his opportunity to secure greater British and especially US effort in South-east Asia and perhaps even China. As important was the opportunity to demonstrate in a highly visible fashion China's new status of independence and equality with its Allies. The Unequal Treaties had been abolished the year before and in October China had been one of the signatories in Moscow of the Four Power Declaration between the USA, Britain, the Soviet Union, and China. It committed all to fight for the unconditional surrender of Germany, its tripartite occupation, and post-war co-operation in international security.[123] During the Moscow negotiations, Cordell Hull had worked hard to secure Soviet agreement to the inclusion of China in the Four Power Pact, something that was difficult for the Soviets because of its non-aggression treaty with the Japanese.

The Cairo Conference took place when the Soviet Union had become increasingly central in US strategic thinking. US army strategists feared that a Soviet collapse, withdrawal, or separate peace would mean the defeat of Britain and they did not believe that even a fully mobilised US army would be able to put enough divisions into the field to overcome Germany alone.[124] Embick and the US Joint Chiefs of Staff in 1943 had analysed conflicts between Britain and the USA over strategy. They concluded that Britain's 'politically inspired strategy was a hindrance to victory' and that a 'strong relationship with the Soviets was necessary' for that victory.[125]

Cairo was difficult for Churchill because it signalled the beginning of US ascendancy in his 'special relationship' with the USA to which he had devoted so much energy and rhetorical effort and on which the future of Britain depended. A particular difficulty was the issue of Overlord. While Churchill was committed to its eventual implementation, he remained 'haunted by the possibility of a bloodbath on the assault beaches of France, or a subsequent stalemate and prolonged wasting carnage'.[126] He had hoped to meet with Roosevelt alone to discuss once more the timing of Overlord, for which a date of May 1944 had been set at Quebec, but the USA did not want the issue of the timing of Overlord discussed further, for fear that delay might once more lead to the postponement of the operation that Marshall regarded as the key that would unlock the door to victory.[127]

A second difficulty was that the USA opposed operations in the Eastern Mediterranean, which Churchill favoured because it would tie down twenty-five German divisions there and in the Balkans so that they could not be redeployed in France and because with the Eastern Mediterranean in Allied hands, the Soviet Union would not have to be supplied through Iran so that the British naval assets in the Indian ocean could be deployed elsewhere, including the Pacific.[128] A further problem was that the US military was determined not to be 'outgunned' by their British colleagues, as they believed they had been at earlier joint deliberations.[129] Finally, and perhaps most fundamentally, if Churchill hoped for a post-war world in which an Anglo–American alliance would dominate, Roosevelt wanted a new world order anchored by the USA, Britain, the Soviet Union, and China together with an end to European empires.[130]

In contrast to Churchill, Roosevelt 'was determined not to expose himself to Churchill's blandishments if he could possibly help it'.[131] Somewhat deviously, continuing a personal and improvisational mode of operation that he had regularly found useful in US politics, he on the one hand signalled to Churchill that there would be opportunities for discussions before meetings with the Soviets and the Chinese, while on the other inviting them to arrive in Cairo at the same time.[132] When the Soviets learned that the Chinese would be present, they declined to come, as they did not want to provoke the Japanese, with whom they were still bound by a Non-Aggression Treaty. The near simultaneous arrival of Chiang Kaishek and Churchill meant that Churchill did not succeed in coming to an agreement with Roosevelt about European issues in prior meetings Roosevelt's desire to build up China meant that, as Churchill wrote, 'all hope of persuading Chiang and his wife to go and see the Pyramids and enjoy themselves till we returned from Tehran [to meet with Stalin] fell to the ground'.[133]

Churchill did not share Roosevelt's 'excessive estimates of Chiang Kaishek's power or the future helpfulness of China',[134] thinking it 'an absolute farce' that the Chinese should be treated as a Great Power and given a say in the affairs of Europe.[135] Churchill wrote to Anthony Eden, the Foreign Secretary, that China would simply be a 'faggot vote' for the USA in any Four Power organisation.[136] Sir Alan Brooke, the Chief of the Imperial General Staff, thought similarly that China 'had nothing to contribute to the defeat of Germany, and for the matter of that uncommonly little towards the defeat of the Japanese'.[137] He believed that the Americans possessed little strategic sense. He noted in his diary that the USA 'was a drag on Mediterranean strategy' and 'I despair of getting the Americans to have strategic vision'. He believed that he should have resigned rather than accept a fixed date for Overlord, kept to inflexibly regardless of subsequent developments on the battlefield.[138]

Discussions about operations in South-east Asia took place against the background of these tensions between the USA and Britain. Despite the abolition of the Unequal Treaties relations between Britain and China remained shaped by Britain's long history of imperialism and China's desire to end it. Churchill's Imperial mindset made it impossible for him to understand that Asian nationalism could be mobilised for an Allied victory and perhaps for the good of Britain's future.[139] 'Early Kipling' is how the Secretary of State for India, Lord Amery, described Churchill's views towards Asians.[140] The rapid collapse of Britain's military position in East Asia and Wavell's inept refusal to agree to the deployment of Chinese armies in Burma in 1942 had both astonished and infuriated the Nationalists, and led to an anti-British propaganda drive. Chiang Kaishek, in 1942, angered the British when during a visit to India he had asserted himself as a supporter of Asian nationalism, while Chiang himself had been put off by the patronising attitude of Indian colonial leaders who he saw probably as local officials who should treat him with the respect he deserved as a central government leader. He had insisted over British objections on meeting Gandhi and Nehru and supported their calls for immediate independence, arguing that such an act would greatly motivate Asian nations to fight against the Japanese.[141]

At Cairo, three possible operations for SEAC were discussed: 'Tarzan', the re-invasion of Burma by British Empire and Chinese Forces; 'Culverin', the occupation of the tip of Sumatra, an operation favoured by Churchill and something of an obsession for him; and 'Buccaneer', an amphibious operation in the Sea of Bengal with the aim of taking Andaman Islands 300 miles south of Rangoon from which Burma, Thailand, and Malaya could be threatened and which would cut Japanese supply lines. As Commander-in-Chief of SEAC, Mountbatten suggested the following plan for Tarzan. Four Indian divisions of the 15th Corps of Slim's 14th Army Group would concentrate at Chittagong and in mid-January cross the Maungdaw–Butthidaung line. Its objectives were the protection of Chittagong itself and the occupation of Akyab on the Burma coast. At the same time, at Imphal, three divisions of the 4th Corps of the 14th Army Group were to concentrate and advance eastward, with the aim of destroying Japanese communications. In March, Orde Wingate's Chindits, a long-range penetration force, were to be dropped behind Japanese lines and seize Mogaung and Myitkyina. They were to assist Chinese forces, which would start off from Ledo and move through the Hukawng Valley, proceed towards Myitkyina, and in April take Bhamo. The Yunnan Force was to begin operations on 15 March, advance towards Lashio in April, and then link up with

British forces there and at Bhamo. Large-scale amphibious operations were to take place in the Bay of Bengal and 3,000 US and British Long Range Penetration Forces were also to participate.[142]

The problem was shortage of available resources, especially of 'landing and tank-landing craft, which had now become the bottle-neck'.[143] Chiang Kaishek declared himself in support of Tarzan, which would involve both the Ramgarh and Yunnan Forces, but insisted that it could only succeed if accompanied by large-scale naval operations in the Bay of Bengal to establish sea and air supremacy. Chiang had made clear to Mountbatten in October that he believed that the re-invasion of Burma was doomed otherwise.[144] While the British supported Tarzan, they were less keen on simultaneous large-scale naval operations in the Bay of Bengal. Churchill argued in response to Chiang Kaishek that naval forces could be released from the Mediterranean and assembled in the Indian Ocean only following the defeat of Italy, while Sir Alan Brooke suggested that Buccaneer could only go ahead if Overlord was postponed.[145] His assessment of Chiang Kaishek was that he was 'shrewd and foxy … no grasp of the larger aspects of the war, but determined to get the best of all bargains'.[146]

During initial discussions by the US and British Combined Chiefs of the Staff, the British were surprised to find that the Americans were not, in fact, willing to push very hard for large-scale operations in SEAC. Admirals King and Leahy supported Brooke's view that these operations should be seen in relation to overall plans for the defeat of Japan, which had not yet been agreed. They believed that Pacific operations should be the main element in these and that large-scale operations of infantry forces on the Asian mainland might well not be necessary. Their meeting ended with an agreement that Buccaneer would go ahead as 'soon as possible', but that no date should be fixed and that it should always be considered in relation to other operations. All other options in SEAC would be submitted to 'further study'.[147] At a meeting of the US military chiefs the next day, Marshall made clear that he did not want to make US aircraft available to maintain the airlift to China at 10,000 tons per month as Chiang insisted against both British and US objections and that he opposed making ground forces available for any operations.[148]

Roosevelt, however, overrode the military experts. In an evening meeting with Chiang Kaishek, he promised that Tarzan would be accompanied by large-scale amphibious operations in the Bay of Bengal. He pressured Chiang to begin negotiations with the Communists. With Roosevelt probably already thinking ahead to his meetings with Stalin, they also discussed Soviet aims in East Asia, especially their desire for access to ports in Manchuria. Roosevelt promised support to Chiang in his efforts to combat imperialism and the two agreed that French Indo-China would not be restored to France. In return for negotiations with the Chinese Communists and the Soviets, Chiang requested Roosevelt to gain assurances from Stalin that he would not interfere in his relations with the Chinese Communists and that he would respect Chinese sovereignty in Manchuria.[149]

Chiang Kaishek could look back with some satisfaction at the Cairo meetings. Politically, they were carefully stage-managed to signal the acceptance of China as a full member of the Allies and equality of status between Roosevelt, Churchill, and Chiang. This was caught neatly on the famous and much reproduced photograph that shows Churchill, Roosevelt, and Chiang sitting together on a bench with an array of high commanders standing behind them. Chiang too gained the Cairo Declaration, which re-affirmed China's position as one of the Big Four and promised that 'all Chinese territory obtained by Japan shall be returned to China', that Korea 'will attain freedom and independence', and that 'all Japanese public and private property in China wholly will be given over to the Chinese government'.[150] He had gained Roosevelt's support for ending imperialism in East Asia. Militarily, too, Roosevelt had promised that Tarzan would be combined with large-scale amphibious operations while the plans for the re-invasion of Burma demanded that Chinese forces from Yunnan would only set off in the spring of 1944, by which time other Allied forces, including the Ramgarh forces, already would have been in the field for several months.

Yet, he had not been given firm paper assurances about naval operations in the Bay of Bengal and had been alerted to the reality that the USA wanted the Soviet Union involved in the war against Japan. Chiang Kaishek's domestic position was also precarious. In China he had to contend with the Young Generals Coup, which aimed at disposing not only Chiang Kaishek but all senior Nationalist government and military leaders. The plot was discovered by Dai Li while Chiang was at Cairo. Little is known about the event.[151] Stilwell too appears to have been playing with the idea of a coup. He recorded in his diary a personal conversation with Roosevelt in which he had again set out his negative opinion of Chiang Kaishek and stated that 'an attack might overturn him'. Roosevelt, according to Stilwell, replied 'Well, then, we should look for some other man'.[152] While no conclusions should be drawn about Roosevelt's true beliefs from Stilwell's account, Stilwell interpreted Roosevelt's response as consent. According to Frank Dorn, when Stilwell returned to China he stated that he had been given a 'hush-hush' order to engineer the elimination of Chiang Kaishek and asked Dorn to plan an assassination attempt, which he did.[153]

Churchill and Roosevelt flew from Cairo to Tehran to discuss strategy with Stalin at the Eureka Conference, held from 28 November–1 December. At this meeting, Stalin declared himself to be unimpressed with the Italy campaign, stated that Overlord should be the key operation of 1944 while all other operations were mere diversions, and that it should be accompanied by landings in southern France – code-named Anvil – to ensure that the Germans would not be able to transfer reserves to the north. Stalin promised that he would step up operations on the Eastern front once Overlord was underway. He also agreed to join the fight against Japan after the capitulation of Germany.[154] What Stalin offered at Tehran was first of all a strategy for the rapid defeat of Germany. Once Overlord began, the Germans would face war on two fronts. The Soviets also promised significant assistance with the defeat of Japan. If the Soviet's armies would be unleashed on Manchuria, with its substantial industrial base, its mining resources, and its large Japanese army presence, the task of the US navy and marines would be much simpler. At a time when the USA and Britain were gearing up for Overlord, when they were desperately short of means to take the war to Japan, when there was no agreed US and British plan for that war, and when the atomic bomb was not yet operational, Stalin offered a way to end the Second World War quickly. The Soviets further agreed to co-operation in international institutions after the war, something to which Roosevelt attached great importance but of which the British were sceptical.[155]

Tehran was for Churchill even more difficult than Cairo. Roosevelt elaborately charmed Stalin and suggested that the Pacific was at least as important as western

Europe to the USA. Churchill, then, saw his 'special relationship' further downgraded by Roosevelt, while he also had to witness the USA and the Soviet Union claiming the kind of role in Asia to which the British Empire was accustomed. Churchill felt compelled to remind his interlocutors that 'nothing would be taken away from the Empire without war'.[156] He also was forced to abandon his peripheral strategy.

For China, the consequence of Tehran was that its strategic significance became even less than it had already been. Roosevelt and Churchill returned to Cairo for further discussions between 2 and 7 December. After the first set of Cairo meetings, Mountbatten had returned to India, and, as ordered, had drawn up new operational plans for SEAC. Mountbatten telegraphed these from India. For Buccaneer, he envisioned the deployment of 50,000 men. The inclusion of Anvil in the 1944 plans of the Allies meant that the pressure on the supply of landing craft had only become more intense. Roosevelt and Churchill agreed that Mountbatten could not have more than the 14,000 men originally promised. While Roosevelt and Marshall argued that an operation with that number of men should go ahead, Churchill argued that it would be better to scrap it altogether and instead use the resources so released for an operation in the Aegean.[157] On 5 December, Roosevelt agreed to the cancellation of Buccaneer, on which he could hardly insist given that most US military leaders were lukewarm about it, because the US was not willing to commit further resources to SEAC itself, and because the issue threatened to undermine the US–British relations. He sent a telegram to Chiang Kaishek informing him that 'because of European offensives, especially the requirement of landing craft, the Bay of Bengal amphibious operations are impracticable'.[158]

Chiang Kaishek tried to force a reversal of the decision. General Carton de Wiart, Churchill's representative at Chongqing and SEAC's liaison officer, informed Churchill that Chiang would continue to build up the Yunnan Force but would not agree to its deployment in Burma unless the promised amphibious operation would go ahead.[159] In response to this message, on 21 December, Churchill told Mountbatten that he could use 20,000 troops for an amphibious operation.[160] According to General William Slim, instead of attacking the Andaman Islands, the idea now became to invade the Arakan coast behind Japanese forces.[161] This news was relayed to Chiang Kaishek on 24 December by Major General T. S. Hearn, Stilwell's Chief-of-Staff in Chongqing, who informed Chiang Kaishek, inflating Churchill's promise, that 'naval and air strength available to support strong amphibious force of thirty thousand troops is said to be overwhelming'.[162] However, on 23 December, a telegram from the Chiefs-of-Staff to Churchill stated that 'it was agreed that Overlord and Anvil were to be the supreme operations for 1944 and that nothing must be undertaken anywhere else in the world which hazards the success of these operations'.[163] Chiang refused to accept a small attack on the Arakan coast as a substitute for Buccaneer. It was cancelled and all SEAC's landing craft were sent back to Europe.[164] The Nationalists assented, nonetheless, to the continuation of Tarzan because it was thought necessary to achieve 'joint warfare by Chinese, British, and American forces and realise the hope for direct US participation in China in the War of Resistance'.[165]

After Cairo and the cancellation of Buccaneer, Marshall found new reasons to support the north Burma campaign and Stilwell, both because he feared that Chiang Kaishek would retaliate by withdrawing his approval to deploy the Yunnan Force in Burma,[166] and because Japan might threaten US air bases in China. To press ahead with the north Burma campaign might provide sufficient diversion to forestall such an outcome. The campaign, and especially the recovery of Myitkyina, was also important to eliminate the Japanese airbase there, which forced the Allies to take the difficult route along the Himalayas to fly supplies from India to China. On 25 February 1944, Roosevelt wrote to Churchill that 'our occupation of Myitkina will enable us immediately to increase the air-lift to China', and so keep China in the war.[167] On 1 January, Marshall sent a telegram to Stilwell, stating that 'your acceptance of the strategy of concentrating all necessary means to defeat Germany first unites us all completely'. He went on to say that 'the major contribution we can make is to drive a road across north Burma'. He noted that Mountbatten would have to 'undertake operations within the means available to him' and that 'supply difficulties' would make it difficult for the airforce to fight 'at their full potential'.[168] With that he meant not the strategic bombing operation but the fighters of the 14th Air Force of Chennault that supported National Army divisions.

Chiang Kaishek was alert to the danger that concentrating Allied efforts in Europe while sitting still in South-east Asia would be an invitation to Japan to take action before the might of the Allies would be turned against it. On 1 January he wrote in a telegram to Roosevelt:

> From the declaration of the Tehran Conference, Japan will rightly deduce that practically the entire weight of the UN forces will be applied to the European Front, thus abandoning the China theatre to the mercy of Japan's mechanised land and air forces. It would be strategic on Japan's part to liquidate the China affair in the coming year. It may therefore be expected that before long Japan will launch an all-out offensive against China so as to remove the threat to their rear.[169]

This was not an instance of crying wolf for a foreign audience. In February 1944, Chiang Kaishek warned at the Fourth Nanyue Military Conference that he feared that Japan would mount a large offensive in China.[170]

The USA and Britain failed to heed the warning, not just because Chiang had rung the alarm bells previously. Faulty intelligence and mistaken assessments led the USA and Britain to ignore the possibility of new Japanese offensives. A Joint Intelligence Committee paper on Japanese intentions of 12 January 1944 argued that in 1944 Japan would assume a defensive strategy and would begin to withdraw from south and central China in order to strengthen its defences in the Philippines. It argued too that 'with Allied air bases no nearer than Chengtu it is most unlikely that Japan will be in a position to undertake any land operations against them'.[171]

This assessment of Japanese intentions could not have been further from the truth. In August 1943, the Japanese Staff Department considered responses to the eventuality that the Japanese navy would lose control over the Pacific. In November, an operational plan was adopted for the establishment of overland links through China to South-east Asia. In early January 1944, the Japanese Supreme Headquarters approved Operation Ichigo. A war plan approved by the Supreme Headquarters on 24 January called for Japanese divisions in north China to begin operations to secure the Ping–Han Railroad in April. In June, Japanese forces in Wuhan would begin actions to conquer Hunan and Guangxi, to be joined one or two months later by Japanese armies concentrated in

Guangdong. Nanning in Guangxi was to be taken by early 1945 in order to secure the railroad from Guilin to Hanoi.[172] The Supreme Headquarters furthermore decided to begin offensives at the China–French Indo-China border and in Burma in order to tie down Chinese troops there.[173] To achieve their aims in China, the Japanese mobilised 500,000 men, 200 bombers, and 67,000 horses. In the China theatre, they had stocked aviation fuel for eight months and ammunition for two years. Meticulous logistical preparations preceded the offensive.[174] If Allied intelligence, especially Ultra, played an important role in the defeat of Germany, its failure *vis-à-vis* Japan's plans in 1944 led to huge miscalculations in East Asia.

The decision to concentrate on Overlord was understandable. Overlord was an enormously difficult operation. Although enjoying air superiority, the USA and Britain did not have overwhelming superiority in numbers or even fire power. The price of failure would have been so devastating that even now one shudders at its possible consequences. Allied strategy would have been in ruins and armies would have had to be rebuilt. Governments would have tumbled, the German genocide would have continued, and the pain inflicted on German-occupied territories would have become even worse. The strategy evolved at Tehran made sense: to attack Germany from two flanks and then turn Allied might against Japan surely offered the quickest road to ending the war. Given the shortages of resources, especially landing craft, it inevitably meant curtailing operations elsewhere. Even if Marshall worried about implications, Buccaneer seemed the one operation that was least dangerous to curtail. The military issue the Allies faced was to devise a quick end to the war and to allocate available resources to maximum effect with that goal in mind.

Yet, the decision had significant implications. The failure to heed Chiang Kaishek's warnings about Japanese actions in 1944 and to support the Chinese war effort adequately would prove damaging. To signal so clearly that little would be done on the Asian mainland was surely a grave mistake. Had more been done, for instance by strengthening tactical airpower in China, the Japanese would have found it far more difficult to launch the Ichigo and Ugo offensives in China and Burma. These two operations would cost the Allies and the local populations in the areas where the fighting took place very dearly indeed. The geo-strategic situation too was profoundly affected. The centrality of the Soviet Union in US strategic thinking would have devastating consequences for eastern Europe during and after the war. In East Asia, the determination not to deploy US forces on the Asian mainland, to rely on the Soviets to deal with Japan's Kwantung Army in Manchuria, and to keep the British out of the Pacific would similarly have grave consequences.[175]

The recovery of Burma

The stated justification for Japan's offensives in China and Burma was to construct overland lines-of-communication through China to south-east Asia and eliminate the National Army in order to strengthen Japan's Defence Perimeter. If these were the military goals, a recent study of discussions at the highest level of the Japanese military and government, involving the Emperor, suggests that the offensives also had political goals. According to Edward Drea, soon after Pearl Harbor, Emperor Hirohito wanted an end to the fighting and a settlement which would safeguard the future of Japan as well as his own position. As we have seen, Japan went to war in the belief that it would ultimately not be able to prevail over the USA and Britain, especially not after they had begun to re-arm. According to Drea, after the setbacks of the summer of 1942

> Hirohito spent the next three years hoping in vain for a military or naval victory that would lead to a negotiated settlement. Underestimating the American determination to fight Japan to the finish, Hirohito clung to the illusion that one great military victory would extract Japan from its war with the West. The chimera of the decisive battle, be it on land or sea, became not only the Emperor's mantra, but also that of the court, the bureaucracy, and ultimately the die-hard military itself.[176]

If military objectives were also important, the Ugo and Ichigo Offensives were surely fought with diplomatic aims in mind. Perhaps they can be best understood as desperate acts, aimed at the British at Imphal and in China in part at the US airbases to get the USA and Britain, facing a difficult campaign in Europe, to the negotiation table.

Further trouble in US–British relations

In Burma, both Allied and Japanese armies had already begun to move when the cancellation of Buccaneer led to discord and confusion. In accordance with the plans laid at Cairo, Field Marshall William Slim's XVth Corps had set off in November. At the same time, two Chinese divisions had been moved from Ramgarh to Ledo in Assam and in the last week of December had begun to make contact with the Japanese.[177] The Japanese, for their part, had been building up their forces in Burma and had begun their own offensive towards Chittagong. They were able to surround two divisions of Slim's forces trying to break into the Arakan mountains.[178]

Following the cancellation of Buccaneer, SEAC's planners decided that a campaign in north Burma to re-open the Ledo Road would not work. Myitkyina might be reached, so they argued, but there would not be enough time before the monsoon to construct a supply line to it and therefore 'it would be logistically impossible to hold it'.[179] Even if Myitkyina might be taken and held, they concluded, it would be impossible to secure a connection to the Chinese border, a task that without the participation of Chiang's Yunnan force would have to be undertaken by either British Empire forces or Stilwell's Chinese Ramgarh divisions. Even so, the Ledo Road could not be completed before 1946, so that it could not play a role in the defeat of Japan, which was to be accomplished within one year after the defeat of Germany. SEAC drew up a new plan, involving an amphibious operation to take Rangoon to cut Japanese supply lines and link up with British forces in India, all in preparation for an invasion of Sumatra and the opening up of a harbour in south China after the monsoon season of 1944, that is, in the autumn when landing craft could be released from Europe.[180]

In January 1944, Mountbatten sent a delegation to London and Washington to discuss this plan.[181] General Albert Wedemeyer, who had been appointed Chief-of-Staff at SEAC, was one of its members. Emboldened by Marshall's message of January that he was to press on with the north Burma campaign, at a meeting convened in Delhi on 31 January, Stilwell objected to SEAC's change of plan. According to Mountbatten's political advisor, Stilwell 'had been extremely rude in defence of his own strategy of an overland march to Canton'.[182] He was invited to put his ideas in writing so that they could be discussed, but had instead refused an invitation for dinner.[183] Without inform-ing Mountbatten, Stilwell sent his own representatives, including John Paton Davies and Hayden L. Boatner, the Chief-of-Staff of the Ramgarh Force, to Washington to plead for the retention of his Ledo operation.[184] They arrived before Wedemeyer. From a meeting with Roosevelt, Davies and Boatner gained the impression that Roosevelt supported them.[185]

Wedemeyer, on the other hand, also came away from his own meeting with Roosevelt in the belief that Roosevelt had agreed to SEAC's point of view. He wrote to Churchill on 21 March 1944 that he 'recommended strongly against the construction of the Ledo Road through Upper Burma and explained very carefully our reasons'. To his surprise, he wrote, Roosevelt had not voiced any objections.[186] No decision about SEAC's proposals was, in reality, taken.[187]

A mighty row then broke out between Mountbatten and Stilwell. Two articles appeared in *Time* magazine in early February. One reported that 'Admiral Mountbatten differs with Stilwell. The US commander admitted that a southern port must be opened. But Vinegar Joe who knows China better than any brasshat in Delhi stoutly held that the Ledo Road and the hump can fill the immediate gap'.[188] These articles were followed up, as Marshall noted in a message to Stilwell, by numerous write-ups by columnists, all calculated to 'stir up anti-British feelings'.[189]

Mountbatten as well as the British War Cabinet responded by pressuring Marshall to recall Stilwell. This was partly because Mountbatten believed it 'disloyal and improper', as a memorandum to Churchill by the War Cabinet Office put it, for Stilwell to have sent a delegation to Washington without informing him.[190] Important too for Mountbatten, for whom security always was a high concern, was that 'the Battle of Asia article confirms that somebody is blabbing. This is a security issue; it gives our strategy away'.[191] From London, the War Cabinet Office too informed Marshall that the article had been 'dangerous in its references to Mountbatten's intentions, accuracy of which shows that there has undoubtedly been a leak'.[192]

Who had been 'blabbing' is not clear. There is no shortage of candidates: Stilwell, Davies, Boatner, or Brooks Atkinson all could have been behind the leak. Marshall himself suggested to Stilwell that the US navy was behind it, with the motivation being to bring pressure on the British navy to participate in Pacific operations.[193] In the summer of 1943, a series of negative reports appeared about the National Army in such papers as the *Reader's Digest* and the *New York Herald Tribune*. Cordell Hull wrote to Stimson that such articles 'originate from military people in Washington' and that they 'should be shut up'.[194]

British pressure did not lead to Stilwell's recall. Marshall informed John Dill, Churchill's representative in Washington, that 'Stilwell, as built up by the American press, is something of a hero whose burning desire to beat Japan is being thwarted by the British'.[195] His recall would lead to a storm of protest in the USA at the eve of the Normandy invasion and, somewhat further out, the presidential elections in the fall. The next day, Churchill ruled that he was 'not prepared to press for Stilwell's removal, on broad political grounds. Marshall is a good friend of ours'.[196] Stilwell escaped recall once more, not because anyone was convinced of his sense of strategy or his command abilities, but because Marshall was worried about the US press and Churchill about good relations between Britain and the USA.

Trouble on the ground

While much time and energy in the upper echelons was spent on debating strategy, dealing with personal conflicts, and warding off negative reports about SEAC in the US press, developments on the ground took their own course. The offensive of the Japanese 55th Division on Chittagong was prevented from destroying two of Slim's divisions only because air superiority allowed Slim to airdrop ammunition and food and put in a relief force. At the same time, Wingate's Chindits had been launched to the south of Myitkyina, but they too ran into trouble, as did a Chinese division under Stilwell trying to advance through the Hukawng Valley. Japan's major offensive, towards Imphal and Kohima, began on 8 March with 80,000 troops. Its aim was to break into the Assam Valley and threaten the British in India itself, something that fitted the political aims of trying to bring the Allies to the negotiating table. But the operation also would have cut off Stilwell's forces and destroyed their supply base in Assam. Sixty thousand British and Indian forces became trapped at Imphal and Kohima. Their rescue was a close-run thing. The Battle of Imphal remains etched in British public memory of the war. It was only on 22 June that a British force was able to break through and force the Japanese to retreat. Long lines-of-communication and the onset of the monsoon season meant that the Japanese had run out ammunition. Sixty-five thousand Japanese died in this battle.

At the same time that the British became stuck at Imphal, Stilwell became encircled at Myitkyina. After his Chinese forces had 'disappointed' in their advance through the Hukawng Valley,[197] Stilwell decided to risk a dash to Myitkyina just before the monsoon. Japanese strategy had been to withdraw gradually through the Mogaung Valley east of Myitkyina so that Stilwell's forces would be lured to an ever greater distance from their supply base in Assam. Stilwell failed to inform Mountbatten of his plans, with the result that his relationship with Mountbatten deteriorated further.[198]

Stilwell's dash for Myitkyina quickly went awry in the same way as his earlier assault on Tounggoo. He forced an exhausted and diseased American brigade, New Galahad, which had been trained by Wingate and whose strength had already been halved, to undertake a difficult march over high mountains, which its members themselves compared to the charge of the Light Brigade.[199] While the Myitkyina airstrip was taken on 17 May, the Japanese were able to reinforce the city rapidly, using the railroad to the south. Miytkiyna became a hell hole, with Stilwell's forces, restricted to supply by air, besieged by the Japanese. Mountbatten wrote to Churchill following the capture of Myitkina that defending it would be difficult because of 'problems of supply lines from Ledo to Myitkina.[200] The siege of Myitkyina lasted nearly three months and sacrificed enormous numbers of troops.[201]

Again, public opinion played a role. Stilwell wanted this to be an American victory. On 17 May, after taking the airstrip, Stilwell allowed radio broadcasts that announced his victory over the Japanese to the whole world and Stilwell became an even more celebrated figure.[202] To take Myitkyina itself, Louis Allen has argued, Stilwell could have flown in a fresh British division from India. One reason he delayed was because lack of intelligence left him unaware that the town was lightly defended and might well have fallen to an immediate thrust before the Japanese could reinforce it.[203] But his Anglophobia as well as the presence of US press officers at the Myitkyina airstrip made Stilwell insist on US forces. Stilwell went as far as to scour rear hospitals. He also kept the New Galahad troops at Myitkyina, although he had promised them immediate relief after the taking of the airfield. Their commander was shipped home after the siege by ship 'to silence him'.[204]

The situation at Myitkyina became truly desperate. Stilwell's treatment of his troops was abominable. He berated his commanding officers, and kept both the Chindits and New Gallahad, the USA's Long Range Penetration Force, well after, in the words of General William Slim, 'they had shot their bolt'.[205] Mountbatten at one point flew in medics who declared up to 90 per cent of the forces unfit for service to force Stilwell to agree to their relief. Mountbatten was so disgusted that in June he again pressed Marshall for Stilwell's recall.[206] The Japanese abandoned Myitkyina on 3 August, as the end of the Monsoon season approached. By then the British had broken up the Japanese Ugo Offensive and had advanced through the Mogaung Valley. This made the Japanese position at Myitkyina untenable. In some of the most moving pages of his book, Louis Allen compares Stilwell's huge sacrifice of men during the Mitkyina siege with the decision of Mizukami, the Japanese commander, to commit suicide, thus satisfying the demands of honour and allowing the remaining Japanese forces to withdraw.[207]

The re-conquest of Burma was less the result of Stilwell's march to Myitkyina than of the Indian Army's success first in defeating the Japanese offensive at Imphal and then taking the offensive. Most US historians of China have treated the recovery of Burma as essentially a US operation that illustrated Stilwell's heroic leadership. With less than a few thousand troops on the ground, and many of them diseased, that is untenable. Stilwell's Myitkyina operation was a gamble that did not work out and that did little to contribute to the defeat of Japanese forces in Burma, let alone to that of Japan itself.

Trouble in China

In China, Operation Ichigo proceeded according to plan. Within a month after its start in early April, the Japanese had taken Henan and cleared the Ping–Han Railroad. In May, the attack on Hunan followed, which was completed by the middle of June. Having resisted Japanese offensives three times in the past, Changsha finally fell to the Japanese. Japanese operations then concentrated on clearing the Canton–Hankou Railroad from Canton to Wuhan and the Xiang–Gui Railroad from Hunan to Guizhou in south-west China. Hengyang in southern Hunan fell on 8 August, days after Stilwell had taken Myitkyina. The Japanese then moved into Guangxi and Guizhou (Map 1.2).

In the spring, reports began to reach Roosevelt that the National Government was about to collapse. On 19 April, Chennault wrote to Roosevelt that Japan's aim was to secure the Ping–Han and Yue–Han Railroad and to take Henan in preparation for an offensive against Chongqing. He continued: 'I wish I could tell you I had no fear of the outcome. But owing to the present concentration of our resources on the fighting in Burma, little has been done to strengthen the Chinese armies in the interior'.[208] He furthermore reported that the Soviet Union had begun bombing Chinese troops in Xinjiang and Outer Mongolia, and believed that this was 'the first step in asserting Soviet influence in East Asia' which 'eventually will take the form of a Russian attack on the Japanese in Manchuria, junction between the Russians and Chinese communist in north China, and ultimately the establishment of a Chinese communist state or states

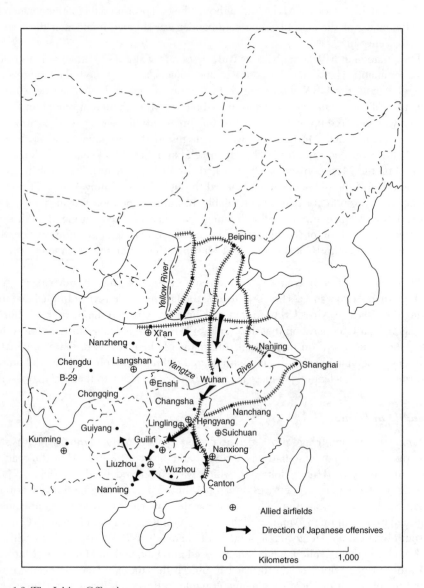

Map 1.2 The Ichigo Offensive.

in north China'. Chennault was not the only one in the US military and diplomatic
world to have become concerned about Soviet intentions, but others, including Embick,
believed that Soviet desires were historically determined by its conflict with Britain, and
hence limited, and that in any case nothing could be done because Soviet forces would
be needed against Japan.[209]

The US Ambassador Clarence Gauss reported on 20 May that the Japanese had
shattered Nationalist forces in the 1st War Zone. The armies of Jiang Dingwen and
Tang Enbo, two of the better ones in the National Army, had been destroyed and the
'best crop in years' in Henan had fallen into Japanese hands. Gauss furthermore stated

that 'Hu Zongnan's position is critical'. Hu was the head of the war zone headquartered in Xi'an in north-west China close to Yan'an. With Henan in their hands, the Japanese could easily attack it. Moreover, he had lost his 9th Army that had been sent to Henan and two of his Group Armies that had been sent to Xinjiang. According to Gauss, the 'Japanese may wish to seize Xi'an, the cotton crop, and the airfield'.[210]

Panic began to spread. On 12 May, upon the advice of the US military, the US Consulate in Guilin sent out a warning to US citizens in south-west China to leave because 'the Japanese are believed to have strongest concentration of troops ever gathered in China' and were planning to attack the south-west.[211] Chennault's desire for increased supplies for himself, his lack of enthusiasm for the north Burma campaign, as well as his acrimonious relation with Stilwell in part explain the contents of his letter to Roosevelt. But his letter, Gauss's report, and the advice to US citizens to leave suggested that imminent collapse was now being anticipated. It was only natural to assume that US army personnel and citizens would be prime targets for the Japanese.

It has been argued that, aware of the danger that the bomber bases would attract Japanese offensives, Stilwell had opposed them and that Chennault and the Nationalists had supported them. The purpose of this argument was to suggest that Chennault and the Nationalists had brought Ichigo on themselves and that Stilwell's Burma campaign had been correct. Although the US bases were a target, this is nonetheless a misrepresentation, in several ways. Roosevelt and Marshall had pushed the heavy bomber base programme. The Nationalists were anxious about it. Gauss reported in January 1944 that the Nationalists opposed 'airfields which might draw Japanese retaliation'.[212] He similarly reported in May that the Chinese military 'show signs dislike expansion United States air activity in their theatre as likely to result in Jap land invasion to destroy or seize air bases'.[213]

The build-up of the heavy bomber bases as well as the Burma campaign reduced the number of airplanes of Chennault's 14th Airforce that could be used to support the National Army in its efforts against Ichigo. The 14th Airforce had 500 aircraft. In support of the USA's strategic air strategy, 200 were assigned to protect the B-29 bombers and airfields at Chengdu. Another 150 were allocated to the fighting in Burma. Only 150 remained therefore to assist the Nationalists in resisting Operation Ichigo.[214] On 2 May, Marshall instructed Stilwell, who controlled the allocation of Lend–Lease supplies, that his 'main task was to provide air support from Chinese bases for Allied offensives to Japan and Formosa. It is recognised that major curtailment of 'Hump' support to Ground Forces in China and to such other activities as do not directly support our air effort will be required'.[215] These other activities referred to Chennault's units supporting the Nationalists. Chennault objected, stating in a memorandum that 'the combined air forces in China may not be able to withstand the expected Japanese air offensive and will certainly be unable to offer air support to Chinese ground forces over the areas and on the scale required. Drastic measures to provide them with adequate supplies and adequate strength must be taken'.[216]

Trouble in US–China relations

On 27 March, Chiang sent a message to Roosevelt that made clear that he would continue to refuse the deployment of the Yunnan Force into Burma. Chiang explained that he faced a Japanese offensive in China and that the Soviets had begun to move into

Xinjiang. With China not able to hold its current positions against the Japanese, he argued, the removal of the Yunnan Force and the US air force to India would further undermine Nationalist fronts in China itself, allowing the Japanese to advance into south China and perhaps threaten Chongqing itself. Although he was willing to send one or two divisions to re-enforce the Ramgarh Force, he went on, he would not order the Yunnan Force to move until Allied amphibious operations had begun to support the Burma campaign.[217]

Roosevelt responded to Chiang Kaishek in a tough message on 3 April. He stated that US aid would be 'unjustified' if the Yunnan force did not cross the Salween River into Burma.[218] Stilwell had suggested in a message to Marshall that the USA should stop Lend–Lease aid to China if the Yunnan Force did not immediately begin operations. On 13 April Marshall transmitted a message to Stilwell ordering him to stop supplies to the Y-Force in Yunnan and allocate them to the US airforce in China.[219] Chiang Kaishek caved in and ordered the Yunnan Force to move.[220]

It is important to remember that when Roosevelt and Marshall coerced Chiang to send the Yunnan Force into Burma, the extent of the Ichigo Offensive had yet to become fully clear in Washington. Chiang had spoken unambiguously, and anxiety was expressed by US diplomatic personnel in China, although their reports were vague. The reports show that Ichigo came as a surprise and that even by late May there was no real certainty about Japanese intentions.[221] John Carter Vincent, then the head of the Division of Chinese Affairs at the Department of State, played down Ichigo's significance in a memorandum of 15 May, stating that 'we do not view the present fighting in Honan [Henan] Province as being as critical as reports of the Chinese Central News Agency at Chungking would indicate. … Reports from our military people in China support our view. … Our American air and other forces in south-west China would not be directly affected, and it is not clear that the over-all Chinese strategic position would be drastically affected'.[222] As we have seen, in US strategy, building a supply line through Burma so as to make possible US air support of operations in the Pacific were regarded as of greater strategic significance.

Stilwell himself was completely misinformed about Operation Ichigo. John Paton Davies, a Stilwell supporter who had pleaded his case in Washington, wrote a memorandum to Stilwell on 17 July 1944. He stated that 'the inadequacy of our intelligence is being painfully revealed in the Central China campaign. We weren't sure that the blow was coming, when it came we didn't know how far it was going, and now we don't know whether it's over'. Stilwell commented in the margin that this was 'True', capitalising and underscoring the word.[223] Davies noted as well that the quality of Stilwell's staff ranged from 'pleasant mediocrity to senile incompetence', urging him to undertake a general clearing out.[224]

Stilwell left Chongqing when the deployment of the Yunnan Force became an issue between Chiang and Roosevelt. Gauss reported to the Department of State that 'Stilwell moved HQ from Chongqing to Delhi without informing Embassy, the National Government, and perhaps the US President. This will have an effect on local politics, money market, and Japanese intentions'.[225] Stilwell's sudden departure, which was damaging to the Nationalists at a moment of great crisis and which also had the result of leaving him out of the information loop, cannot have re-assured Chiang about what would happen once the Yunnan Force entered Burma.

Marshall's message, which had stated that all resources should be focused on the north Burma campaign and the heavy bomber bases and the fact that Stilwell was badly informed about events in China explain why he refused to allocate supplies to China during Operation Ichigo. In June, with the situation at both Imphal and Myitkyina still highly critical, Chiang asked Stilwell, who was in charge of US aid to China, to approve the diversion of 1,500 tons to Chennault's airforce, which had run out of spare parts and fuel. Stilwell refused with Marshall's support.[226] In July, Stilwell similarly prevented assistance to Nationalist forces at Hengyang in south Hunan. The Nationalists had succeeded in driving off a Japanese first assault. On 14 July, Chennault wrote to Roosevelt, 'the Japanese have lost momentum at Hengyang and the Generalissimo has ordered a counter-attack. However, just when our air support of the Chinese should be intensified, our own supply line eastward has broken down'.[227] Stilwell responded to a plea for 1,000 tons of aid to the Hengyang commander, Xue Yue, with: 'Let them stew'.[228]

By June 1944, Allied strategy in East Asia lay in ruins as a result of Japanese offensives in China and Burma. Personal relations between top commanders had broken down. Various operations now worked at cross purposes. On 4 July, Marshall set out the situation as he saw it to Roosevelt. He warned that 'if the Japanese offensive continues, the 14th Air Force will be rendered ineffective, the long-range bomber airfields in Chengtu will be lost, and the collapse of China must result'. He counselled against any further assistance to Chennault's 14th Airforce because the Nationalist armies were patently 'impotent' and because 'air alone cannot stop ground forces'. He concluded by saying that 'the time has come when all the military power and resources remaining in China must be entrusted to one individual capable of directing that effort in a fruitful way against the Japanese' and noting that 'the Chinese can't' and therefore recommended Stilwell for the post.[229] For Marshall, the priority was to rescue the heavy bomber bases, regardless of its consequences for National Army operations against the Japanese.

Stilwell's dismissal

Following Marshall's advice, Roosevelt sent a message to Chiang Kaishek suggesting Stilwell's appointment as commander of all Chinese forces on 6 July.[230] Chiang agreed because he could not afford a rift with the USA. He demanded however the stationing of a personal emissary of Roosevelt in Chongqing and guarantees that Communist forces would not be incorporated in the Chinese chain-of-command until they had accepted Nationalist authority. He also made agreement dependent on transfer of authority over Lend–Lease Supplies to the Nationalists and a precise definition of Stilwell's command authority.[231]

Even now Stilwell continued to refuse aid to the Nationalists in their hour of need. On 8 September, after the fall of Hengyang but with the situation in Burma turning for the better, Chiang suggested to Stilwell that he stage a diversionary attack on Bhamo, in order to relieve the Yunnan Force, which had run into determined opposition at Longling. Chiang feared that if the Japanese broke through, they might attack Kunming. In the dark about Ichigo and having been ordered by Marshall that 'the early bombing of Japan will have a far more beneficial effect on the situation in China than the long delay in such an operation which would be caused by the transfer of these stocks to Chennault', Stilwell refused Chiang's request and also continued to withhold fuel for the 14th Airforce.[232]

Chiang Kaishek responded by threatening to withdraw the Yunnan Force from Burma. Stilwell, fearing that his campaign to complete the recovery of the Ledo Road through north Burma might yet fail, was furious.[233] Marshall reported Chiang's threat to Churchill and Roosevelt, who were again meeting in Quebec. The British and the Americans continued to differ about strategy in Burma. 'In spite of recent successes', Churchill was of the opinion that 'it was most undesirable that the fighting in the jungles should go on indefinitely'.[234] He again floated the idea of an amphibious operation, focusing on Rangoon and supported by an advance of Slim's troops from Central Burma, suggesting that the US make one or two divisions available from Europe in return for British naval and air support in the Pacific. Marshall refused.[235] Churchill too did not press hard: 'landing craft would have to be taken from either the Mediterranean or Overlord. Was it yet safe to start weakening our effort in Europe?'[236]

Marshall's remedy for the crisis in China was to continue to push for the appointment of Stilwell as commander of all Chinese forces. He drafted a memorandum on 16 September to be despatched by Roosevelt to Chiang Kaishek, which Roosevelt sent and which stated

> I have urged time and again in recent months that you take drastic action to resist the disaster which has been moving closer to China and to you. Now, when you have not yet placed General Stilwell in command of all forces in China, we are faced with the loss of a critical area in east China .... The advance of our forces across the Pacific is swift. But this advance will be too late for China unless you act now and vigorously. ... I am certain that the only thing you can now do to prevent the Jap from achieving his objectives in China is to reinforce your Salween armies immediately and press their offensive, while at once placing General Stilwell in unrestricted command of all your forces .... It appears plainly evident to all of us here that all your and our efforts to save China are to be lost by further delays.[237]

Five days later Chennault sent a message to Roosevelt that began by saying that the 'policy of concentrating all our major military investments in Burma has now led to the loss of east China'. Preventable if enough supplies had been given him to support China's ground forces, according to Chennault, the consequence was that the USA would not be able to conduct air strikes from China. Of China's armies, only those in north China headquartered at Xi'an, the depleted armies of the 6th War Zone, and the reduced units of the Yunnan Force remained, so that even when supplies would begin to flow over the Ledo road it would simply be too late for China.[238]

Roosevelt's message had threatened to withdraw US aid and had demanded that Chiang hand over all Chinese military forces to a US commander in whom Chiang had no faith. What Chiang, and China, needed was Chinese victories in China.[239] Important furthermore were not just the tone of the message – which did treat Chiang like the Sultan of Morocco – but also the fact that Roosevelt was clearly allocating responsibility to Chiang for the turn of events in China. With his claim to legitimacy staked on the successful prosecution of the war, Chiang could not afford to let that charge go unchallenged.

In an Aide Memoire to Roosevelt on 9 October, Chiang rejected Roosevelt's accusation. It recounted that he had disagreed with Stilwell on the significance of the Burma campaign and that at Cairo all had agreed with the need to accompany it with amphibious landings. The Burma campaign, he went on, 'had drained off most of the properly trained and equipped reserves in China'. Japan's Ichigo Forces in China, he noted, had been six times as large as those that the USA and Britain faced in Burma, but 'Stilwell had been completely indifferent and refused to release Lend–Lease already in Yunnan'. He had opposed the north Burma campaign, but agreed to the deployment of the Yunnan force after Stilwell had stated that the failure to do so would lead the US public to believe that China was not willing to fight the Japanese. Only after June had Stilwell relented, but 'in all we have received 60 mountain guns, 320 anti-aircraft guns, and 506 Bazookas'. Chiang concluded by saying that 'we have taken Myitkyina but lost all of East China'.[240] Chiang put the blame on Stilwell and implicitly the USA.

To both Chiang and Roosevelt, it was no longer Stilwell's retention but his dismissal that became useful. Neither could afford to be seen to be responsible for China's recent defeats. On 2 October, after Hopkins had passed a message to Chiang that Roosevelt was willing to recall Stilwell,[241] Chiang addressed a meeting of the KMT Central Executive Committee and heatedly insisted that Stilwell had to go, denouncing US attempts to impose Stilwell as 'imperialism'.[242] Stilwell was deeply unpopular with Chinese divisional commanders. General Sun Liren, usually seen as pro-American and praised for his effectiveness, wrote to Chiang that Stilwell sought to break up Chinese command organs, demanded that they behave like slaves, and even then blamed them for everything that went wrong.[243] Sun and others also resented the rapid promotion of Americans and Stilwell's reduction of their own authority.[244] Mountbatten had come to dislike him intensely, and even Marshall and Roosevelt were willing to abandon him. Chiang had reason to believe that scapegoating Stilwell might be achievable.

A factor that has been overlooked is that Chiang by this time may no longer have been so worried as Roosevelt and Marshall about Operation Ichigo. In Tokyo, a faction favouring immediate peace negotiations and strict control over the army had forced the Tojo cabinet from power. On 30 August, the new cabinet adopted 'A plan for political work to be carried out with regard to the Chongqing Government'. It declared that the current priority was to bring a halt to the war with the Nationalist Government and outlined eight conditions for a settlement. These included the return of Chiang Kaishek to Nanjing, with relations between Chiang and the Wang Jingwei Government settled by direct negotiations between the two. Japan had recognised that government as China's National Government to isolate Chongqing. Japan, according to the document, would accept a single unified government for all of China under Chiang Kaishek and would withdraw Japanese forces if the US and Britain did the same. The document further declared that the status of Manchuria should not be changed, but that Japan would recognise Chinese control over Mongolia and Xinjiang. Chiang was to accept neutrality *vis-à-vis* Britain and the USA and adopt a treaty of friendship with Japan.[245]

The Japanese cabinet wanted the Wang Jingwei Government, some of whose leaders, having seen the writing on the wall, were in direct contact with Chongqing and provided important assistance to it,[246] to be its intermediary in opening negotiations. On 13 September, the Commander-in-Chief of Japan's China Expeditionary Force met Zhou Fohai and Chen Gongbo, its most powerful members after Wang Jingwei himself, who by then was on his deathbed in a Tokyo hospital. He stated that Japan now offered a complete Japanese retreat from China in return for US withdrawal of its heavy bomber bases. Japan would accept whatever relation Chongqing wished to have with the US and Britain. Negotiations would take place on the basis of complete equality.[247]

No information is available on the actual contacts with Chongqing or its response. In early October Zhou Fohai did send several emissaries.[248] Given the secret channels that existed between Nanjing and Chongqing as well as the fact that Dai Li's secret service had many contacts in the Wang Jingwei government, it is likely that Chongqing was well informed. The significance of the fall of the Tojo Government would not have escaped Chiang Kaishek. Nor would he have failed to realise that if the Japanese wanted a peace settlement to avoid complete defeat, they would have to achieve it before Germany was defeated. He also would have been aware that his National Government would be the only feasible Chinese negotiation partner.

These developments strengthened Chiang's negotiation position. He wanted Stilwell dismissed not only because he had no faith in him and did not want to lose control over his armies, but also because Stilwell had been loudly supportive of US army contacts with the Chinese Communists. Stilwell believed that the Communists unlike the Nationalists would fight the Japanese and had pressed for their inclusion in the war since 1943.[249] John Paton Davies, his advisor, advocated the dispatch of a military mission to Yan'an in order to explore military co-operation with the Communists in late 1943 and the spring of 1944 when it appeared that no significant operations would take place in SEAC or mainland East Asia. His efforts were important to the realisation of the Dixie Mission, which finally went ahead in June 1944, at a time when the Ichigo Offensive destroyed the Nationalist military position and when therefore it became reasonable to look for alternatives especially in north China if US landings there were still to take place.[250] As Maochun Yu has shown, OSS officers part of the Dixie Mission in December 1944 offered massive aid to the Chinese Communists, including for the arming of 25,000 guerrillas.[251] Chiang demanded in the negotiations with the USA that the Communists would only be included if they agreed to their incorporation in the Nationalist battle order.

It should be mentioned that US expectations of effective Communist assistance against the Japanese were misguided. Bruce Elleman has written that 'top secret documents from the Japanese Foreign Ministry archives in Tokyo reveal that on 3 October 1940, Soviet and Japanese diplomats agreed that: "The USSR will abandon its active support for Jiang [Chiang Kaishek] and will repress the Chinese Communist Party's activities; in exchange, Japan recognizes and accepts that the Chinese Communist Party will retain as a base the three north-west provinces of [Shaanxi, Gansu, and Ningxia]" '.[252] Joseph Yick has argued that in 1945 the Communists negotiated with representatives of the Japanese army who offered the Communists eight bases in the lower Yangtze region if they agreed not to fight the Japanese.[253] An intelligence source considered reliable by the British stated, with reference to the Communists, that 'Their military strength is considerable and they are offering some resistance to the Japanese, but their resistance is controlled to such an extent that I am led to the personal observation that there must be some collusion between Yennan and the Japanese High Command'.[254]

According to Nationalist intelligence, probably gathered by the *Juntong*, the Communist leader and future mayor of Shanghai, Chen Yi, secretly visited Shanghai in April 1945 to meet with Japanese officials. The deal he suggested was that if the Japanese surrendered to the Communists at the end of the war, they would allow the Japanese to retreat to Japan through Communist areas. He also suggested that Shanghai should be offered to a neutral country like the Soviet Union. During a meeting in June between Chen Yi, Pan Hannian, and Liu Shaoqi, on the one hand, and Japanese officials, on the other, according to this intelligence, a deal was signed which stipulated that the Japanese would inform the Communists one week in advance of their withdrawal. The Communists would not attack while the Soviet Union would formally take over control of the city and hand over Shanghai later to the Communists.[255]

Remarks made by John Paton Davies, who cannot be accused of a pro-Nationalist bias, to Fu Bingchang, the Nationalist ambassador to the Soviets, in Moscow on 7 April 1945, also suggest that the Communists followed a careful policy aimed at preserving their own forces. According to Fu, Davies told him that the Communists

> purely use guerrilla warfare to fight the Japanese. As soon as the Japanese army arrives, they disperse. Once the Japanese retreat, they regroup and occupy the towns and villages. They do not have the strength to fight the Japanese army because their armaments are very poor and they will not waste the arms they already have. They try to preserve them for future use to gain power. The Japanese do not want to attack them either because their areas are of little military value. The CCP tries to avoid attacking the Japanese army for fear of reprisals. It probably goes too far to say that they have an agreement, but neither side really wants to fight.[256]

This is not to say that the Communists were not nationalistic or did not seek to oppose the Japanese, not that they did not suffer from Japanese mopping-up campaigns. But given their weakness, the Communists too had to be concerned simply with survival.

Stilwell's recall became useful not only to Chiang, but also to Roosevelt. He could not accept Chiang's charge that Allied strategic decisions and Stilwell's actions were responsible for the crisis in China, especially not when the outcome of the 1944 election came in doubt, when the invasion of Europe was undergoing setbacks and when US Pacific operations encountered very stiff resistance. Roosevelt's opponent, Thomas Dewey, was doing well in public opinion polls, with some suggesting a 'photo-finish'. Gallup in 'his headlines as well as the figures publicised indicated a very close race and played up factors favourable to Dewey'.[257] The polls in October suggested that support for Roosevelt was slipping, especially in the New England, the Pacific Coast, and the Mountain states.[258] For the USA to be held accountable for the crisis in China and perhaps the defeat of the Nationalists would have been a boon for Dewey's campaign.

If Chiang used the Stilwell issue for political ends, so did Roosevelt. In the run-up to the elections, military developments around the globe suggested not a glorious allied advance on all fronts but a string of difficulties and miscalculations, especially in China, the country about whose future the influential publisher of *Time* magazine, Henry Luce, cared so much. Roosevelt decided that the best course of action was to distance himself from Chiang Kaishek. On 28 September, Marshall had prepared 'a sharp rejoinder' to Chiang's request for Stilwell's relief. But Roosevelt opposed and sided against Stilwell.[259] In a draft message for Roosevelt to send to Chiang to cover Stilwell's recall, Marshall included the sentence that 'I now am inclined to feel that the US Government should not assume the responsibility involved in placing an American officer in command of your ground forces'.[260] Roosevelt retained that sentence in his actual message of 5 October, but suggested to Chiang that Stilwell be given control only over the Ramgarh and Yunnan forces and that he would be relieved as Chiang's Chief-of-Staff.[261]

In his reply, Chiang stood by 'my original request that you will relieve Stilwell'.[262] Marshall drafted a response for Roosevelt, which denied that 'Stilwell lacks the essential qualification for the command which I had hoped you would give him' and defended US strategy as 'inescapable', but stated that Roosevelt acquiesced in Stilwell's recall because of Chiang's insistence. It went on to say that Stilwell would not be replaced by any other US commander. If China was going to collapse, this would not happen with a US officer in charge. The message made clear that the Nationalists would have to pay an enormous price in public relations, stating that 'a full and open explanation of the reasons for General Stilwell's recall will have to be made. The American people will be shocked and confused by this action and I regret the harm that it will inevitably do to the sympathetic attitude of the American people toward China'.[263]

Although Roosevelt did not include Marshall's defence of Stilwell in his formal reply to Chiang Kaishek's insistence that Stilwell be relieved,[264] he made sure that the event was explained to the US public. At first a terse press release was issued, which asserted that Stilwell 'stated that the had no public statement to make'.[265] Stimson recorded that 'we are trying to keep him out of reach of all newspaper men and not give them an opportunity to catch a distorted or unwary word just before the Election'.[266] However, US journalists friendly to Stilwell prepared articles describing Stilwell as a hero who had done his best to save China, but had been thwarted by Chiang Kaishek. Before his departure, Stilwell had called in Brooks Atkinson of *The New York Times* and Theodore White, giving them his version of events and urging them to make them known. He also ordered John Service back to Washington to make his case.[267] In their articles, Atkinson and White described Chiang as a nasty military dictator whose sole aim had been to hoard US military aid to fight the communists who were described as truly patriotic. Brooks Atkinson got his story out by travelling with Stilwell, while Theodore White send his copy with Atkinson.[268] In Cairo, censors demanded to see all of Atkinson's papers, but he carried his article about Chiang in his pocket. In Tunis, he gave it to Service, who had a high travel priority, with the instruction to hand it straight to *The New York Times*. Censors prevented publication for three days, but when the decision to publish was submitted to Roosevelt, he approved and it appeared on 31 October, days before the election.[269] The 1944 election campaign was, in Roosevelt's words, 'the dirtiest in history'.[270] Roosevelt was re-elected.

Conclusion

What I have suggested is, first of all, that Stilwell was neither the great war hero as made out in the US press at the time and as subsequently argued by historians, nor the villain as suggested by Chennault and Chinese opponents. He was a man of limited military skill, both as a commander and a strategist. Launching an offensive at Tounggoo was misguided, as was his dash for Myitkyina during the re-conquest of Burma. His belief that the recovery of north Burma was critical to the defeat of Japan was accepted by few at the time and disproved by subsequent events. Even his supporters agreed that his logistical and intelligence operations were a shambles. He remained wedded to pre-First World War infantry warfare and sought victory through offensive efforts without the necessary means available and without making any plans for retreat. He failed to appreciate the importance of air power.

Stilwell, however, was not that important as a military leader nor were the operations he led decisive. Both the praise and the criticism of Stilwell have overestimated his significance for the war. It should be remembered too that behind the most controversial decisions that would affect the Nationalists were US and British strategic decisions on which Stilwell had little influence. These included the cancellation of Allied amphibious operations to support the re-conquest of Burma, the building of heavy bomber bases in China, and the withholding of supplies to Chennault's airforce during the Ichigo Offensive.

Stilwell's position depended on the uses that others could make of him. In 1942, Chiang Kaishek gave him command over Chinese divisions fighting in Burma in order to keep them out of the hands of the British. He also hoped through Stilwell to secure greater amounts of US aid. Later he found him again useful when SEAC was established and apparently also to counter T. V. Soong, even if the details of that particular incident remain shrouded in mystery. For General Alexander, Stilwell was useful because he knew that the Nationalists would not allow the British to command Chinese forces and so Stilwell offered a way to co-ordinate Chinese and British operations at a remove. Mountbatten and Churchill supported him in the autumn of 1943, when Marshall and Roosevelt had agreed to his recall, because they did not want to endanger US–British relations. For Roosevelt, Stilwell's press coverage was useful in keeping US public opinion on board and in suggesting that the US was doing its best against Japan while in reality focusing on the invasion of Europe.

In the same way that Stilwell's position depended on his political utility, so did his demise. In October 1944, Chiang Kaishek could blame Nationalist reverses on him and Stilwell seized to be useful, and even had developed into a threat, to Chiang's control over Chinese armies in Burma and access to US supplies. For Roosevelt, Stilwell's recall was useful to distance the USA from Chiang Kaishek and China in the run-up to the elections. Stilwell was not an innocent man himself. What he tried to get out of the situation was military glory as a great commander. His close contact with the US press served this purpose.

I have furthermore suggested that neither the British nor the Americans believed in the strategic value of China. While many in the US, including Roosevelt, were deeply sympathetic to China and were convinced that they were destined to play an improving role in China, this did not translate into actual military assistance. Despite the fact that the issue of Lend–Lease supplies led to enormous bickering, the amounts actually allocated to China, let alone delivered, were infinitesimal compared to what the USA sent to Britain and the Soviet Union, and a good part of what was delivered was hoovered up by Stilwell. China was an ally from which maximum effort was demanded at a minimum price. Before Pearl Harbor, US policy consisted of articulating high principles, at which Cordell Hull was good, while appeasing Japan. Afterwards, the aim was to limit US commitments to China and avoid the deployment of US army resources while keeping China in the war, first to tie down the Japanese army and then as a base for a strategic bombing offensive against Japan in support of the US Pacific Fleet. From 1943, US strategy aimed at relying on the Soviet Union first in the war against Germany and then Japan. British strategic policies remained driven by imperial aims.

In the same way that the US did not have a monopoly on virtue, the Nationalists did not have a monopoly on military incompetence. Neither Britain nor the USA performed well in the aftermath of the attack on Pearl Harbor. Stilwell's belief in the offensive led him twice to undertake seriously misguided operations. Marshall's pursuit of a strategic bombing offensive was dangerous to China. If one failure was to make clear at Tehran that nothing would be done in East Asia, the lack of accurate military intelligence as well as better political intelligence about Japan were others. Chiang Kaishek's views were not taken seriously, although he often was right, including about Stilwell's Tounggoo offensive, the risks in beginning the reconquest of Burma without cutting Japan's naval supply lines, and the danger of running down military resources in China itself.

The charge that Chiang Kaishek did not want to take the offensive in China against the Japanese is partly disingenuous. The strategies of the USA and Britain were predicated on not having such an offensive. Before Pearl Harbor, Britain, the USA, and the Soviet Union each sought to avoid war with Japan, and afterwards none did much to assist China. The USA and Britain sought to make use of Chinese forces each for their own purposes, Britain to defend and then recover the Empire, and the USA to suggest to the US public that it was fighting the Japanese. The accusation is also mistaken. If after Pearl Harbor, in a situation of great domestic difficulties, the Nationalists sought to shepherd their war against the Japanese out of China as much as possible, as we shall see, in 1944 and 1945 they did want offensives in China but were held back. The view that the Nationalists refused to fight the Japanese but let the USA do so to accumulate resources for waging war on the Communists must be seen for what it was: an expedient argument first advanced by Stilwell to explain his own failures and further his own obsessions. It was then given weight by Roosevelt when he needed to explain a possible collapse of China, and was sustained finally during US political battles in the late 1940s and 1950s.

I have also stressed that during the Second World War allies were also competitors. This has of course long been recognised as true for Britain and the USA.[271] Their differences were expressed perhaps most strongly in South-east Asia. That Stilwell rebelled against Britain's elaborate military ceremonies, the attitudinising of its officers, the high-living of senior officers, including Mountbatten, and claims to imperial greatness is readily understandable. So is Mountbatten's frustration with Stilwell's crude anti-Britishness, his penchant for fleeing the Allied chain of command, his self-righteousness, and his talking to the press. These tensions were so severe that to Louis Allen, who served in Burma, it seemed that Stilwell was 'fighting the War of Independence all over again'.[272] It was also true for China. If Chiang Kaishek pursued his own agenda, that of the USA and Britain was to make use of China for their own objectives. The deployment of substantial ground forces or tactical air power in China did not fit in with these, while its interests were sacrificed by the British for the sake of the recovery of Burma and by the USA in order to gain the co-operation of the Soviets in the war against Japan.

The British Left-wing poet, C. Day-Lewis, who had broken from Communism in 1939, wrote the following poem in 1941 to express his reluctance and discomfiture when pressed to defend Allied warfare in the heroic language and mythologies propagated by US and British propaganda machines and so loved by Churchill.

> They who from panic or mere greed
> Enslaved religion, market, laws,
> Borrow our language now and bid
> Us to speak up in freedom's cause.
>
> It is the logic of our times
> No subject for immortal verse
> That we who lived by honest dreams
> Defend the bad against the worse.[273]

No one doubts that the cause of the Allies was just and that the fight against genocidal fascist dictatorships had to be waged. But Lewis's scepticism about the myths spun around the war, his disinclination to believe in the imminence of a perfect world, and his refusal to subordinate his writings to the ends of ruling politicians continue to have much to recommend themselves, especially in a time when memories of warfare are again used for political ends and sustain often rosy images of the collective past. The cause was just but mistakes were made and took place as war was waged with limited resources, with imperfect and sometimes seriously mistaken understandings of the plans and capabilities of opponents and allies, with national objectives firmly in mind, and with personal reputations and political power at stake. Such is human.

2 Raising the National Revolutionary Army

This chapter returns to the beginning: the raising of the NRA in Guangdong. Arthur Waldron argued in *China's Turning Point* that in the middle of the 1920s, a situation developed in which national regeneration on the back of armed revolution could latch on to new opportunities. In 1924, two factions of the Northern Government that ruled China went to war. The fighting affected nine provinces, involved half a million troops, undermined the economies of large cities such as Shanghai, and weakened the political cohesion of the Northern Government. The result was a 'political and emotional vacuum' filled by the radical ideologies of the CCP and the KMT.[1] It would be the Nationalists who prevailed in the warfare that followed. In 1926, they set out from their base in Guangdong on the Northern Expedition. Two years later the NRA made it to Beijing and unified China, even if more nominally than in fact.

To explain the Nationalist victory, scholars have focused on the history of the First United Front between the Chinese Communists and Nationalists, peasant and labour movements, and Soviet involvement.[2] What still needs to be done is to explain why the Nationalists again turned towards armed revolution during the 'second rise of revolution', as the Taiwanese historian Lü Fangshan called the revitalisation of the KMT in the early 1920s.[3] The renewed positive evaluation of military action was surprising because Nationalist military efforts during the 1911 Revolution, the Second Revolution of 1913, and the Movement to Protect the Constitution of 1917 ended in a disaster and because the May Fourth Movement espoused strong anti-militarist convictions. The movement began in 1919 in protest to the Versailles Peace Treaty that assigned German privileges in Shandong Province to Japan at a time when the slaughter of the First World War abhorred all.

Further, the Nationalists still need to be placed firmly in the contemporary domestic context, especially that of warlordism, rather than seen as something quite apart from it. Warlordism provided opportunities to accumulate military force and build alliances, but also posed challenges, including the disciplining of co-opted forces that possessed local bases and gathered taxes themselves. The Nationalists, too, had to develop their military strategy in response to warlord conflicts. As well, while the Soviet intervention in the 1920s has been analysed in detail, the initial precariousness of the Soviet's commitment to the Nationalists has not been brought to the fore. It was the Nationalists' good luck that domestic developments made them the most promising partner in the middle of the 1920s in Soviet efforts to prevent a Japan-dominated China and foster revolution.

This chapter will begin by examining the new belief in the possibility of organised military action for the sake of national revolution. I then examine how the Nationalists used the opportunities of warlordism and the Soviet interest in developing a strong pro-Soviet force in China to build up a base in Guangdong Province and amass military force. With respect to the latter, I will stress the operation of a military–fiscal cycle in which military campaigns were conducted to enhance the Nationalists' resource base and the resources so gained, in turn, used to strengthen the military.

Ideas about the military in the 1920s

The May Fourth Movement developed out of the New Culture Movement. That movement began in 1915 when Yuan Shikai, the man who had built the Beiyang or Northern Army and became first President of the Republic, had shut down democratic institutions, re-introduced Confucian classics in the school curriculum, restored Confucian rituals, and instigated a campaign to construct a constitutional monarchy with himself as emperor.[4] New Culture Movement activists held that a modern republican polity could only emerge as a willing union of modern and enlightened citizens who had thrown off the shackles of the past. They derided Yuan's re-introduction of Confucian ritual as a retrograde step and saw his use of the military as a sign of backwardness, which had to be overcome before real progress towards a modern republican order could be made.[5]

It is important to note that if the New Culture Movement would be consistently anti-warlord, those involved did not initially oppose the military *per se*. In 1916, an article by Liu Shuya in *The New Youth*, the standard-bearer of the New Culture Movement, still argued that China had better adopt German-style militarism, not because it was admirable, but because it offered a way out of national disunion and all the problems that came with that. According to Liu, militarism had caused all to work for Germany's strength whereas 'the Republic of China is the state that venerates the martial least of all the states of the world'.[6] Liu argued that peace was an illusion and war a natural state of affairs. He feared racial conflict between white and yellow races, making the adoption of virile attitudes all the more necessary.[7]

In 1918, after the end of the First World War when 'never again' became the hope of the day around the world, such a view became unpopular. *The New Youth* published an article that called for the demobilisation of all military forces. It argued that in future peace and order would depend not on force, but on education, the law, and effective government, while a nation's strength derived not from the size of its army but its educational system and its economic prosperity.[8] Hu Shi, one of the leading figures of the movement who had studied under John Dewey, argued under the influence of Wilsonian idealism that the First World War had shown that national armies solved nothing and that peace in the future should be preserved by a global military force.[9] Edward McCord has rightly argued that the anti-military Zeitgeist was important in convincing military and political leaders in 1919 to convene a peace conference, even if international pressure to stop civil wars in China at the time of the Versailles negotiations were also important.[10]

Contextualising the anti-militarism of the New Culture Movement

If New Culture Movement adherents believed that cultural backwardness was behind civil war and that once modernity was embraced the military would wither away, that view was vulnerable to charges of idealism and of playing into the hands of imperialists. Jiang Baili was a military expert and theoretician who had headed the Baoding Military Academy, China's most famous military academy in the late Qing and early Republic. Interested in the European Renaissance, he was well connected with leading intellectual and political figures of the time, including Liang Qichao and Wu Peifu, who dominated the Northern warlords in the 1920s. In a letter to Liang, he wrote that he wanted to write about military problems, but feared that the May Fourth Movement made this difficult because it generated 'a lot of empty talk' about the military.[11] In his writings of the 1920s, he analysed why China's first attempt under Yuan Shikai to build a modern army had gone awry, described the nature of warlord forces, suggested that despite everything China did need a strong military, and drew up a highly detailed programme for demobilising warlord forces, instituting national military service, and creating a new army suited to Chinese conditions and able to support a modern republic and defend China.[12] A peace conference in 1925, held after the end of the civil war discussed by Waldron, discussed these issues and similarly adopted concrete programmes for the demobilisation of warlord armies, the reduction of military expenditures, national political unification, and the rehabilitation of civil administration.[13]

Others wrote from a more passionate nationalist perspective. In his essays of the time, Zhou Zuoren, the brother of the still revered May Fourth author Lu Hsun, expressed respect for military citizenship education (junguozhuyi jiaoyu). In a July 1923 article called 'Militarism May Not Be So Bad' he argued that he approved of using military means to defend China and that fostering a more military spirit might therefore be right. Militarism, Zhou stated, was 'relatively OK'.[14] Zhou reported on a revival of interest in martial arts among urban youths, reflected in the popularity of the Jingwu Sports Club, the China Martial Arts Society, the Shanghai Society for Martial Arts and the Advancement of Virtue, and various provincial martial arts societies.[15]

In a 1925 overview of the development of his thinking, Zhou Zuoren described his ambivalence about the radical cosmopolitanism of the New Culture Movement:

> My thinking has returned to nationalism. At first … I believed in venerating the monarch and resisting foreigners. At the time of the Boxer Uprising, I was delighted when I heard that in the countryside 'a foreigner' had his legs broken and his felt hat smashed and recorded it in my diary. Later, when I read *The New Citizen, The Citizen, The Revolutionary Army* and *New Guangdong* I changed completely. … During the May Fourth Period, I dreamed about cosmopolitanism and expressed some rather unrealistic views. Last spring I narrowed its scope to Asianism. However I have become aware of my own pedantry. We must seek truth from facts. Our starting point must be nationalism.[16]

Just after the May Thirtieth Massacre of 1925, when British police in Shanghai had gunned down demonstrators, Zhou bitterly wrote that 'Civilised people have guns, barbarians do not. Westerners have guns and therefore they are civilised. Chinese do not and are therefore barbarians'.[17]

That such views emerged after incidents such as the May Thirtieth Massacre is understandable. But, the interest in the military did not begin then. The well-known military historian of the Republican period, Wen Gongzhi, described how he had secretly been interested in Chinese military history from his boyhood days in his foreword to his still seminal *The Military History of China of the Last Thirty Years* of 1930. When at school, Wen claimed, he had a real interest in history, but not of the moralising variety. He therefore kept the approved books on top of his desk and mouthed along as sentences were droned out in recitation, but kept his preferred reading about battles and knight-errands in his desk drawer together with his crickets, and read them until inevitably a furious teacher punished him. In retelling this, Wen's aim was to call for greater attention to military affairs even if high culture regarded them as uncouth.[18]

Many before and after the May Fourth Movement also connected the recovery of military qualities with promoting modernity and nationalism. In 1917, Mao Zedong wrote about the need for physical education, stating that 'it is extremely worrying that our nation is weak, martial customs are not encouraged, and the physical quality of our people deteriorates daily' and then declaring that 'the main aim of physical education is martial bravery'.[19] He organised healthy walks through the countryside for himself and his friends, once covering 450 kilometres in one month,[20] and read traditional novels about military heroes and battles. Mao claimed that he knew many celebrated passages by heart and that, like Wen, at school he secretly read such novels.[21] In 1920, he expressed admiration for the great leaders of the Qing struggle against the Taiping such as Zeng Guofan, whose writings he knew well, as well as Huang Xing, who had led the revolutionary armies during the 1911 Revolution.[22] Chiang Kaishek himself stated that as a youth 'I carefully listened to the stories told by local elders about the Taiping Heavenly Kingdom' and that after the 1911 Revolution, like Mao, he developed a strong interest in their opponents and read their works.[23] In the early 1920s, when in charge of the Whampoa Military Academy, he compiled a collection of excerpts of the writings of Zeng Guofan and his colleague Hu Linyi for the instruction and inspiration of his students. Mao's personal name, Runzhi, was the same as that of Hu Linyi.

As argued in the introduction, Chinese nationalists reacted to Orientalist ideas about Chinese civilisation as degenerate, effeminate, and a-military. In a 1925 article, Wang Jingwei, who succeeded Sun after his death in that year, wrote that following the Boxer War Chinese perceptions of foreigners had switched from dismissal to an abject acceptance of their superiority in all areas. He urged his readers to abandon this inferiority complex and work both to unite China and oust imperialism by creating a modern and disciplined national army.[24] In January 1927, Chiang Kaishek convened a military re-organisation conference during the Northern Expedition. In addressing his fellow generals, he criticised shortcomings in the NRA, mentioning the lack of discipline, integrated planning, reliable statistical information, low morale, and disorganisation. He termed these 'the problems of us Chinese' and the reasons 'why we can't do anything right'.[25] For him, achieving a disciplined army had everything to do with the recovery of national self-worth.

The 1924 visit of Rabindranath Tagore, the first Asian author to receive the Nobel Prize for literature, ran into trouble because of this urge to prove militarily equal to the West. Tagore talked at length about aggressive Western cultures and harmonious and pacificistic Eastern ones and urged that the latter should be valued for those qualities. His lectures in China provoked a storm of hostility. He was seen as having imbibed reprehensible Western dismissive attitudes about Eastern civilisations.[26]

Sun Yatsen too was attracted to the modern army built along European lines as a cultural project. In a July 1917 letter to Liao Zhongkai, one of the KMT's Left-leaning Elders who would play a leading role in the formation of the NRA, Sun wrote that he was preparing a book entitled 'Plans for National Defence'.[27] Sun would never write the book, but did list the titles of its sixty-two chapters. They indicated that Sun envisioned a National Defence Army as the exemplar of the modern nation. He wanted to 'turn the whole nation into expert soldiers' and spoke of 'training thirty million basic national defence personnel' and 'ten million experts in the material construction of national defence'. The purpose of the army was to safeguard domestic peace, guarantee constitutional government, and resist foreign aggression. It would be supported by efficient and disciplined national bureaucracies, which enforced central control over all military forces, drew up national war plans, and studied the most advanced military technologies of the West. Sun's admittedly vague chapter titles suggest that he saw a modern army with its sparkling armour and healthy bodies vigorously marching in neat rows as a necessary accoutrement of the modern nation. It expressed the vigorous, upright, and disciplined nationalism that he sought to bring about. Sun's text became important after the Northern Expedition, as in 1929 the KMT's National Defence Committee turned Sun's letter to Liao Zhongkai into a canonical scripture sanctioning the idea of an elite army of national self-defence recruited on the basis of a national military service obligation.[28]

In explaining the renewed interest in the military, some scope need to be given to a plain yearning for action. In Chiang Kaishek's summer residence on Yangming Mountain north of Taipei one immediately notices a huge copy of a piece of calligraphy in Sun Yatsen's hand stating 'to know is difficult, to do is easy'. Copies could be found in many places during the years of Nationalist rule. The background is a chapter in Sun Yatsen's *Basic Strategy of National Reconstruction* of 1918 that carried the phrase as its title. In *Basic Strategy*, Sun set out a vision about a new Nationalist China, elaborating grand schemes for industry and transport, discussing at length how a Republican system was put together, and describing how civilised people should behave in public assemblies.[29] Sun's projected 'Plans for National Self-Defence' may well have been intended as a companion volume.

Basic Strategy was a visionary statement, often poopoo-ed for its grand dreaming, but Sun's purpose was to call for a re-dedication to action. The chapter on action and knowledge criticised a famous phrase from the Classics which held that 'knowledge is easy, to act difficult' as well as the famous dictum of the Ming philosopher Wang Yangming, who believed in intuitive knowledge, stating that 'knowledge and action must be combined into one'.[30] Sun argued that past revolutionary attempts and efforts to save the Republic had failed because people believed that action was difficult, leading to passivity as well as a lack of boldness and determination. He called for a new commitment to action and argued that even without certain knowledge action was possible.[31]

One wonders what Chiang Kaishek really thought of the problem of knowledge and action in his tranquil summerhouse of understated but refined comfort, not only because he had been defeated or because he had renamed Grass Mountain into Yangming Mountain and displayed Sun's calligraphy there, after having been forced out of mainland China. In addition, Chiang Kaishek in the 1920s argued that Sun's vision was great but that in action he had disappointed and that the responsibility to do better in that regard fell on his successors, including, of course, himself. In 1923, he wrote that 'Dr Sun has scored his success. But if it means success in deeds related to the present period, the responsibility falls on us'.[32]

It should be mentioned that the debates about the military, the nation, and revolution echoed late Qing discourses, already referred to in the Introduction, about these topics. In the 1920s, the attitude towards the military and martial values was different in two ways. First, instead of individual heroism, Nationalists stressed the importance of disciplined collective action and the effacement of individuality. Second, in the later Qing, revolutionaries assumed that once Qing rule had been overthrown through a violent uprising, the Chinese people would instinctively and spontaneously embrace their inherent nationalism. In the nineteenth century, that was a common view of the emergence of nationalism. In the 1920s, after Yuan Shikai's destruction of the national assemblies and the rise of warlordism, that view became seen as too naive and optimistic. The old order would not simply crumble. The conviction took hold that what was needed, as Sun Yatsen suggested in his writings, was a period of military rule to prevent the forces of the old from making a come-back when the new was still fragile and a period of political tutelage to instruct the people in how to be modern citizens of a new nation.[33]

The army as revolutionary instrument

Prominent followers of Sun Yatsen considered the military in connection to strategies for revolution. Zhu Zhixin was a close collaborator of Sun Yatsen until his accidental death in 1920. Born in 1885 in Canton, as a student Zhu read the popular anti-Manchu tracts of the time and translations of Adam Smith's *On the Wealth of Nations* and Darwin's *On Evolution*. After the Boxer Rebellion, he studied in Japan where he joined the Revolutionary Alliance and in 1906 published the first partial translations of *The Communist Manifesto* and *Das Kapital*. During the 1911 Revolution, Zhu helped organise military uprisings and mobilised New Army units as well as local militia and bandit forces during the 1911 Revolution.

Important in contextualising the changes in Zhu's attitude towards the military is the Movement to Protect the Constitution of 1917, which called for the restoration of the 1912 Constitution and the assemblies formed after the elections of that year and which were dominated by the KMT. Sun Yatsen led this movement from Guangdong and sought to co-opt Lu Rongting, the Guangxi warlord who then was influential in Guangdong as well. Lu proved a fickle ally. While he opposed the Northern Government and had welcomed Sun, he favoured a loose association of southern provinces and opposed Sun's plans to use southern forces to unify the country. He declared that 'with the President still in [Beijing], there is no need to set up another government. The rather confusing title of Grand Marshall [which Sun had adopted] is particularly subject to question'.[34] Sun was forced to leave Guangdong and began a period of two years of virtual exile from Chinese politics in 1918.

In June 1919, Zhu wrote a letter to Chiang Kaishek in which he declared that he had foresworn any further involvement in military affairs.[35] He published articles about the lack of discipline, the bribe-taking, and the extortion that had taken place even in his own forces.[36] The First World War illustrated, Zhu believed, that neither 'money', as in the case of Britain, or 'military power', as Germany had tried, provided the real instruments of power, as he had believed previously.[37] Zhu argued that China's armies had carved out areas to secure a resource base and that civil wars were inevitable as each tried to strengthen his position.[38] He also described contemporary military leaders with the derogatory term 'warlords' (junfa), discussed the lack of discipline in China's armies, depicted soldiers as lacking in a sense of responsibility for the nation, and rejected that current strongmen could unify the country.[39]

A year later, in June 1920, Zhu argued that Trotsky's Red Army provided a model for a military that could play a positive role in revolution. The New Culture Movement, Zhu now stated, had not come to terms with the issue of the military. He argued that a new army built along Soviet lines had to be raised. He stated that Sun Yatsen's practice of co-opting existing military units to carry out revolution should not be tried again. He claimed that 10,000 Chinese had served in the Red Army and inspired by ideology had fought with bravery. A new army, Zhu stated, should be recruited from workers in industrial areas.[40]

Dai Jitao, a leading KMT ideologue most famous for arguing that 'Sun Yatsen-ism' was a moral philosophy rooted in traditional Confucian concepts, also called for a return to military action. Like Zhu, he too believed that existing military forces should never again be used. Interested in Marxist economic theory, in 1919 Dai argued that economic imperialism had created numerous 'drop outs'.[41] Many had become bandits, but then had been recruited into armies. As military people they had linked up with old officials and politicians, and this unholy alliance had destroyed the political realm after the 1911 Revolution. In January 1920, however, Dai wrote a letter to Chen Jiongming, who had first emerged as a result of Yuan Shikai's support during the 1911 Revolution but who also had close connections with progressives and had joined Sun's Revolutionary Alliance. After conquering Canton in 1920, he invited Sun Yatsen to return to Guangdong. In his 1920 letter, Dai urged Chen Jiongming to turn his Guangdong Army into 'an intensely enthusiastic and bright red model army'. Dai contrasted the revolutionary army with armies of the past, which had been led by brutish generals who, lacking education, had regarded themselves as the 'household slaves' of their masters and had supported their regimes. Dai argued that the strength of the revolutionary army depended not so much on its arms or discipline, but on individual commitment to the ideals of revolution. 'This kind of revolutionary army', Dai wrote, 'is indispensable for destroying the forces of the old, and creating a new world'.[42]

Chiang Kaishek himself too believed that revolution could not be carried out in China without building an army. An important episode in his personal development and in his rise among Sun Yatsen supporters was Chen Jiongming's attack on Sun Yatsen in June 1922. When Sun, on 6 May 1922, began a military offensive to unite China, Chen refused to participate, favouring a federal approach to reconstituting China politically. In June, Sun dismissed Chen as Governor of Guangdong and military commander. Chen retaliated by shelling Sun's residence. Sun took refuge on a gunboat with a few followers, where Chiang Kaishek joined him.[43] The protection of a British gunboat was necessary to secure Sun's safe return to Shanghai.

Following these events, Sun, in September 1922 in Shanghai, met with Adolf Joffe, a Soviet envoy.[44] In August 1923, he sent Chiang Kaishek as his representative to Moscow to discuss collaboration. In Moscow, Chiang produced a paper for the Soviets in which he argued that the disintegration of China's political system, the weakening of China's national strength, and the rise of warlordism were the result of the fact that during the 1911 Revolution Sun Yatsen had focused only on political and international affairs, leaving military matters to subordinates who had not been loyal to the KMT and had used the revolution to set up their own bases and build up their own forces. In contrast to the October Revolution, the result, according to Chiang, was that the Chinese revolution had failed and that power had fallen into the hands of Yuan Shikai. He concluded that 'the only strategy for today is to use the military' to eliminate the warlords.[45]

Sun Yatsen himself, as a revolutionary, always had endorsed the use of military force. He may well have drawn inspiration from the Taiping rebellion in the middle of the nineteenth century. According to Chiang Kaishek, Sun 'often spoke to me about the strategy and tactics of the Taiping as well as their great commanders such as Li Xiucheng, Chen Yucheng, and Shi Dakai'.[46] When Sun founded the Revolutionary Alliance in 1905, he envisioned revolution as taking place in three stages, the first of which was the military seizure of power. A period would then follow in which a provisional constitution would readjust relations between military and civil government, after which the transition to a constitutional republic could be made.[47] Sun believed that revolution could make use of existing sources of violence, including the military, local militia, secret societies, and mercenaries. In 1914, after he had lost his battle for power with Yuan Shikai, Sun did not conclude that the lack of an army controlled by his own party had undone him, but that his followers had not been loyal enough to him and his cause. He therefore insisted that those who would join his new party, the Chinese Revolutionary Party, swore an oath of personal allegiance to him, something that many were unwilling to do.[48] He also became convinced that a period of military rule would need to follow revolution, to make sure that carpetbeggars would not run away with the spoils of victory. He disbarred anyone who had not joined before or during the revolution from holding office and participating in elections until the transition to constitutional government had been made.[49]

It should be noted here that despite the counsels of Zhu, Dai, and Chiang, Sun would continue to co-opt existing military forces, as we shall see. He agreed to Soviet proposals to raise a new army probably because it was one way to acquire a force and one that would be loyal to him. In April 1924, in *Fundamentals of National Reconstruction*, he wrote:

> without a period of military rule, the counter-revolutionary forces could not be eliminated and our revolutionary ideology could not be made known to the masses so that it could not obtain their sympathy and commitment. And without a period of political tutelage, the shackles of the people may have suddenly been released, but they did not know what to do, and if they did not simply continue in their old habit of not assuming any responsibilities, they were exploited by others and unknowingly went over to the counter-revolution.[50]

An army tied to himself would prevent that outcome. But before his death in 1925, Soviet assistance and the Guangdong base were not secure enough for Sun to foreswear co-opting local militarists. If some of his followers called for that in the early 1920s, after his death they too were not, in fact, able to do so.

In short, the early 1920s was marked by a return to a new belief in military action. The hope that following the 1911 Revolution a new republican political order would flourish almost spontaneously could by this time only be seen as naive. But, the strengthening of nationalism, imperialist outrages in China, the desire to take action, and the example of the Soviet Red Army led to a new appreciation for collective military action both as an instrument of revolution and as a way to demonstrate that Chinese civilisation too could be martial, aggressive, and modern.

The context of warlordism

Good reasons exist not to use the term warlordism at all. It was first employed not as a tool of social or historical analysis but as a political smear. Nationalists and Communists made resort to it to denounce their enemies.[51] As used by the Nationalists and the Communists, the term is underpinned by a teleological view of history. They portrayed warlordism as a pathology stemming from backwardness and a lack of patriotism, which was to be overcome by the forces of modernity, nationalism, and revolution.

Attempts to define warlords by less politically implicated standards have proved not entirely successful. The warlords were a highly diverse group. If some maintained a fairly stable base, others did not, while yet others usually regarded as warlords did not even primarily rely on military power.[52] Their backgrounds varied greatly in terms of social origins, education, and institutional position. The sharp distinction drawn between the Nationalists (or the Communists) and those commonly called warlords is often difficult to maintain once one looks at their actual practices. Despite all the claims that they were different, the Nationalists incorporated warlords. To regard warlords simply as regional strongmen is also problematic. Many played an active role in national affairs. There is, finally, a problem with dates. The period between 1916 and 1928 is often termed the warlord decade. Historians have made clear that warlordism did not emerge suddenly in 1916, and James Sheridan rightly remarked that 'residual warlordism' continued after the Nationalist assumption of power in 1928.[53] He left it to others to explore its significance. One of the tasks of this book is to do precisely this. I will suggest that the problems of a divided military remained a key issue, including during the War of Resistance.[54]

Despite the shortcomings of the term, I shall, nonetheless, use 'warlords' and common synonyms such as 'militarists'. In part, this is a convenient way of referring to all those who struggled with Chiang Kaishek and his most loyal followers for supremacy. But, warlordism as a term referring to military fragmentation draws attention to an important reality with which anyone who claimed to be the legitimate government of China had to struggle, which the Nationalists did with a broad array of symbolic, ritual, military, and institutional tools. In addition, not to use the term is to eradicate an imagery that had considerable meaning to the Nationalists themselves, as it did to others. It was an idea around which they constructed understandings of the nature of Chinese society, of the Chinese nation, and of the stage in history in which they believed they found themselves.

Origins

The fragmentation of China's military forces into competing units was a key characteristic of warlordism. No unified and centralised military bureaucracy supplied all forces with their needs, controlled military recruitment, appointed and rotated officers, and imposed a common strategy. US military intelligence reports of 25 January 1927 described the reality of military fragmentation in detail. It noted that after the end of Yuan Shikai's regime, the Ministry of War had ceased to function, that many divisions had become localised, and that each controlled its own appointments and revenue collection systems.[55]

If after the death of Yuan Shikai the situation became worse, in reality, military fragmentation had begun well before the 1911 Revolution.[56] If an earlier generation of scholars traced warlordism to the Qing's mobilisation of regional armies outside the regular military system during the Taiping Rebellion,[57] more recent historians have made clear that no direct link existed between these and warlord armies. McCord argued that warlordism originated in 'the continuing crisis of political authority that followed the fall of the imperial system' following the 1911 Revolution as a result of which 'military men were indeed called into the political arena to resolve the seemingly irreconcilable conflicts of civilian politics'.[58] While this is so, this analysis depends on drawing a stark distinction between civil and military realms and is, therefore, shaped by nineteenth-century European concepts.[59]

Studies of the recent resurgence of warlordism in various areas of the globe, adopting a broad comparative perspective, are useful in suggesting that warlordism was connected to contemporary global developments. Paul Rich suggested that one factor that tends to be conducive to the emergence of warlordism is the lack of a single superpower or a cohesive international order able to sanction a single authority as the legitimate power in a given area.[60] This was clearly true for China. European powers exported their conflicts to East Asia during the late Qing, where they were joined by Japan and the USA. Competition between them undermined the Qing. During the Boxer War, regional officials sought local accommodations with foreign powers. Arthur Waldron has described the destabilising effects of the failure after the First World War by the Great Powers to come to an international agreement on China.[61] Sun Yatsen was able to regain a significant role and build up a base in Guangdong, as we shall see, because of Soviet support.

Other factors in the contemporary situation conducive to warlordism were the narcotics and arms trades. Although opium consumption had a long history in China, its popularisation in the middle of the nineteenth century, the spread of domestic cultivation across China at the same time, and the development of refined opiates made it difficult for central authorities to control this highly lucrative trade. Although domestic cultivation was to an extent suppressed in the late Qing and early Republic, Edward Slack has suggested that after the death of Yuan Shikai, opium cultivation in China spread rapidly once more.[62] As he has shown, all warlords were to a greater or larger extent dependent on the opium trade, as were the Nationalists, and as is now clear, the Communists.[63]

The revenues from the opium trade were used in part to sustain armed forces and to purchase arms. After the First World War, when the world suddenly had a glut of arms and when arms industries searched for new customers, the value of the international arms trade with China, according to a League of Nations report, rose steeply, peaking at times of war when Chinese imports of arms could reach to 15 per cent of the global total. In 1920, Chinese imports of arms and ammunition amounted to US$ 300,380.

In 1922, its value reached US$ 777,942. The amounts for 1924 and 1925 were respectively US$ 1.2 and 5.4 million.[64] They then dropped to US$ 1.4 million, but in 1927 again rose to 4.2 million US dollars.[65] No central government, as reports from the Chinese Maritime Customs Service show, was able to control arms imports as provincial authorities issued import licences.[66]

Warlordism too was the result of problems inherent in raising any large force in a country as large and diverse as China that remained agricultural. As Mark Lewis has suggested, Chinese dynasties had consistently relied on hereditary households and sought to de-militarise the interior. They did so because mobilising the population would not produce the skilled warriors needed at the frontier, because staffing armies from the regular population on a rotation basis decreased rural productivity, because it was prohibitively expensive and administratively too complex, and because it spread military skills through society. As, for instance, during the Taiping Rebellion, dynasties turned to mobilising the population only in times of great crisis, and then they consistently sought to do so by recruiting the settled population under strict bureaucratic control. Chinese history is littered with examples of frontier generals turning their armies around to march on the capital and regional strongmen building up large followings more loyal to themselves than to the centre.

In the late nineteenth century the Qing was reluctant to raise a large force even when it faced strong external challengers. When confronted in the autumn of 1894 after the Japanese had destroyed the Qing's modern navy with the possibility that Japan would march on Beijing from Manchuria, the Qing first decided to raise a 100,000-man infantry force with German help, but then scaled down the plan because of Soviet pressure but also because the loyalty of this force could not be guaranteed.[67] It was only after the crisis of the Boxer Rebellion that the Qing sanctioned the construction of a large European-style army.[68] As the Qing had feared, this army, which developed into Yuan Shikai's Beiyang Army and which would spawn a number of warlords, would prove of doubtful loyalty. Factions at court and in the bureaucracy were replicated in it, while, as Edmund Fung showed, it was also infiltrated by revolutionaries.[69]

During the crisis of the 1911 Revolution, Yuan Shikai was able to use his hold over parts of it to seize power, but his victory was achieved by narrow margins. He had to make deals with regionally powerful men such as Yan Xishan in Shanxi, Li Yuanhong in Wuhan, and Zhang Zuolin in the Northeast. He also had to accept KMT dominance in Guangdong, Jiangxi, and Anhui provinces. Yuan succeeded not just because of his access to military force, but also because of British support, which enabled him to seize important sources of revenue, including from the Maritime Customs Service, against which he could raise large loans from foreign banks and so pay his forces and keep the administration going. He also offered high appointments to co-opt potential enemies, made large sums available to some, and resorted to murder. Where he could not install a loyal follower, he chose between two local competitors, helping one to consolidate his power, including by using his control over legitimate appointments and, more brutally, executing their opponents' representatives and fundraisers in Beijing.[70]

After the 1911 Revolution, Yuan attempted to retrieve central control over the military, over appointments, and over fiscal power, and sought to draw many constituencies, including constitutionalists such as Liang Qichao and followers of Sun Yatsen into his administration. He further attempted to reduce the role of the military in civil administration. He did not succeed. Following the KMT's victory in post-revolution elections, they challenged his authority to appoint provincial officials in areas they controlled and objected to foreign loans he had negotiated. Yuan then used secret society thugs to murder Song Jiaoren, the KMT leader who had emerged victoriously in the elections.[71] Although Yuan crushed the Second Revolution which then followed, these events damaged greatly the prestige of his regime, a problem that all late Qing and Republican governments failed to avoid. In 1916, he fell to what was only a minor rebellion in the south after the Beiyang Army had become divided, sources of foreign funding during the First World War had dried up, and popular opinion had swung against him not only because of the brutal measures he had taken but also because he had been shown impotent in the face of Japanese aggression.

Fundamental reasons of China's inability to raise and maintain a large modern army had much to do with its fiscal system and, of course, the size of the country. European-style armies and navies were above all expensive. As John Brewer has argued, the British state was able to accumulate financial resources, which for a long period allowed it to prevail in the European competition for power because it was able to create a centralised and nation-wide excise and customs system between 1688 and 1783. This enabled the British state to tax capitalist agriculture and expanding domestic trade efficiently, and raise large funds by instituting the National Debt in 1694. Most European states were able to borrow heavily in financial markets. The need to issue debt affected Britain's political system as well, as it forced the authorities to accept a greater degree of scrutiny by parliament, thus making its tax collection and revenue disbursement more efficient. Debt, which can only be based on trust, furthermore tied government and, at least, the elites together while in the nineteenth century National Savings schemes also connected financially the poorer segments of society to the state. The increased resources allowed the British government to expand its navy and use it to protect what was presented as its 'national interest' and made war a national affair. Trade with overseas territories, in turn, increased revenue and fostered a sense of common purpose among the different communities of the British isles.[72]

Fiscal problems formed one set of reasons why the Qing was not able to make the transition to the high tax regime of the modern state that enabled the maintenance of well-armed standing armies loyal to the centre. The Qing held county magistrates responsible for land tax collection. However, officialdom had not been able to keep land registers and land ownership registers up-to-date and thus tax collection became an exercise in levying fixed conventional sums on a given area, with the result that a divorce emerged between assessment and ability to pay, with the burden shifted on those who were most powerless. A further problem was that revenues did not cover government expenditures, leading to the levying of surcharges often in excess of formal tax obligations. County magistrates, who served for limited periods and in areas not their own, relied on staff who usually served far longer than themselves. One of the ways this staff made a living was by lending money at usurious rates to tax payers who could not meet their obligations. In addition, local elites engaged in the illegal but, nonetheless, common practice of paying taxes for local residents, also, of course, for a profit.[73] This system was inefficient, a cause of many disturbances, difficult to reform, and left much revenue at the local level.[74]

The Qing, unlike European states, did not borrow but financed its military campaigns from accumulated reserves and if these were not sufficient it relied on 'donations' of rich merchants while armies lived off the land and raised *tanpai*, or levies on local communities.[75] The Qing endured after the Taiping Rebellion and was able to construct a modern navy and engage in self-strengthening efforts because the lucrative Maritime Customs revenues, handled outside the local bureaucracy and managed largely by the British, formed a substantial new source of revenue. The heavy indemnities imposed after the Sino-Japanese War and the Boxer Rebellion, however, knocked this pillar from under the Qing. From then and throughout much of the Republican period, debt payment consumed around one-third of central revenue. This fiscal crisis took place just when the Qing needed new funds for the New Army. For the military, the consequence was a serious shortage of funds so that the centre could not provide for the needs of the military. If this meant that the overall quality of the military declined, and that the Qing was unable to raise the armies it believed it needed, other consequences included involvement by local military units in tax collection, demands for payments from local businesses, recruitment on the cheap, and negligence in training. Relations with society inevitably suffered, the prestige of the army declined, and the quality of the army was reduced. In addition, in response to the fiscal crisis, the Qing ordered local governments to make funds available to support army units stationed in their areas. The result was that the centre had a limited grip on the military.[76]

Besides fiscal reasons, it was also important that the Qing ruled a very large empire. In Europe, from the eighteenth century, the institutions and practices that oriented populations to the centre multiplied, giving rise to what has been called a new sociability. Such institutions included local councils, churches, sports clubs, pubs, schools, charitable organisations, and gentlemen's clubs, as well as annual or multi-annual cycles of events, such as the opening of parliament, elections, and the London Season. Shared patterns of consumption, dress, and approved behaviour, even if also expressing differences in class and status, proliferated. The spread of literacy, cheap books, and the burgeoning press helped to cement national communities. In the nineteenth century, wars became national endeavours in Europe. With the growth of industry and the strengthening and deepening of state structures in the nineteenth century, the mobilisation of the population into national armies became therefore more easy to contemplate for rulers, although it was never without risk, as the Romanovs found out during the First World War. The *levee en masse* during the French Revolution had shown that a population in arms could rally to the national cause and play an important role on the battlefield. The mid nineteenth-century rebellions cannot have convinced Qing authorities that it was safe for them to raise large armies.

Warlordism, then, arose in part from the fall-out of the 1911 Revolution and the failure of the international community to develop a co-ordinated policy towards China. Its deeper causes, however, must be found in the different security requirements of a country as large and complex as China's, its blighted fiscal system, and its size. It was perhaps never difficult to raise troops in China. There would always be many poor people willing to join an army. To create a large standing army, staff it with well-educated troops and officers, equip it with modern arms, keep it separate from society and the economy, orient it towards the state, and, if war came, to keep armies stuck in at the front for many years was an entirely different matter.

Repercussions

If Edward McCord has detailed how the military and the civil interpenetrated each other, the military leached also into other areas. The military penetrated fiscal, economic, social, and administrative organs and they, in turn, the military.[77] Reports from Soviet advisors after they arrived in 1923 described the consequences for Guangdong. Armies from neighbouring provinces had decamped to Guangdong. After having been forced out of the areas in which they were raised, they sought to establish a new base in Guangdong with its rich resources. They included the Yunnanese forces of Yang Ximin; the Guangxi forces of Liu Zhenhuan; and two separate Hunanese of armies, one of Tan Yankai and one of Cheng Qian. Local Guangdong forces existed as well, including those of Chen Jiongming from north Guangdong, the gendarmery of Wu Tiecheng, and the Cantonese army of Xu Chongzhi. Guangdong was further inundated with petty armies from Hubei, Jiangxi, Fujian, and elsewhere. These were personal armies with their own bases out of which, a Soviet report stated, 'each army strives to get out as much as possible.'[78] Helen Siu has described the resulting brutalisation of society in Guangdong.[79]

For their commanders, these forces were the assets on which they relied for their influence and on which they and their subordinates depended for their livelihoods. As Jiang Baili made clear in an exhaustive social analysis of the make-up of warlord armies, personal relations and local bonds were more important than formal bureaucratic relations and procedures.[80] Officers in higher ranks were usually engaged because of close personal connections with the commander. Routine administration, training, tax collection, and recruitment fell to junior officers, usually promoted from the ranks. Rank-and-file soldiers, according to the Soviets, were physically in bad shape and were often ex-bandits. Maltreatment was common. Training was done by junior officers on the basis of the manuals that had been introduced in the early part of the century. Lack of knowledge and ammunition meant that 'most did not know how to shoot'.[81] There was of course no such thing as a central staff, a logistical department, or the rotation of officers. The estimate was that there were about 150,000 soldiers in Guangdong.[82]

Before it set out on the Northern Expedition, in June 1926, the staff department of the NRA drafted a report on the forces of its enemies.[83] It provides a concise description of warlord forces outside Guangdong. It estimated that the number of troops arrayed against the NRA was about 1.5 million. Usually large concentrations of troops (one or two divisions) were stationed at provincial capitals, major centres of communications or marketing, and along railroads. The report showed that Sichuan, the most populous province in China with a rich agriculture and flourishing opium trade but little industry and few railroads, was carved up in Defence Areas with 30,000–50,000 troops in each. Prosperous Manchuria possessed a much better system of communications and a degree of industrialisation. It was separated from the rest of China by easy to defend passes. Zhang Zuolin controlled the entire region and had welded New Army divisions and local military forces into a force that used railroads and to an extent modern technologies. His forces numbered 195,000 men.

In north China were the armies of Yan Xishan and Feng Yuxiang. Yan ruled the province of Shanxi, surrounded by high mountains. Feng's army was the product of his rebellion against Wu Peifu in October 1924, when Wu was at war with Zhang Zuolin.

He had seized Beijing, but to strengthen his position, he sought to develop a base in Chahar and Suiyuan and accepted Soviet aid. His forces numbered about 200,000 troops. Zhang Zongchang in Shandong, an ally of Zhang Zuolin, had a force of 170,000. Sun Chuangfang had used the wars of 1924 and the subsequent tensions to form an unstable alliance of forces spread through the five provinces of Jiangsu, Zhejiang, Anhui, Jiangxi, and Fujian. Sun himself had captured Shanghai. According to the report, smaller units of militias, protecting towns and villages, and bandit gangs, trying to break into them, were ubiquitous in the countryside.[84] The NRA Staff Department's report gave information on these for Fujian, the province to the north of Guangdong. It listed forty units, with normally 100–500 troops, but several as large as 3,000. The total came to over 20,000.

War was one consequence of military fragmentation. Even if Arthur Waldron's comparison of the 1924 Zhili-Fengtian War with the First World War is useful to force us to consider the effect of war in creating the conditions in which the second rise of revolution could find a broad resonance, it, nonetheless, risks overstating similarities between warlord warfare and the total warfare of the First World War. When European armies took to the battlefield in 1914, the expectation was that the result would be a conflict of short duration on a clearly demarcated battlefield by bureaucratically controlled armies. Once the armies became stuck in the trenches, the war itself became a long hard slog lasting four years. European states then improvised the institutions that geared their economies to war production, secured a constant stream of trained recruits for the armies that devoured them at a horrid pace, and mobilised domestic society to support the war.

The Zhili-Fengtian War was not this kind of war. It was short, did not involve as large a part of the population as in Europe, and did not have the same type of consequences. Warlord armies imitated pre-First World War warfare, whose models had been domesticated in China largely as part of Yuan Shikai's efforts to build up the Beiyang Army, but they did not, in reality, fight such wars. No centralised bureaucracy controlled the armies that fought in them and officers and soldiers had not gone through the elaborate training and rituals that characterised European armies. Nor were peace and war, war zones and civil areas, military and civil leaderships, and combatants and non-combatants demarcated by law. Warlord wars were not fought to defend or alter fixed territorial boundaries, but to capture significant resources, weaken domestic opponents, and alter alliances with a view to prevailing in the struggle for national power. Bureaucracies were not capable of delivering the same number of recruits and material resources to the front as those of the combatants of the First World War.

This discursion into the phenomenon of warlordism, I hope, has suggested the enormous difficulties that the Nationalists faced when in the early 1920s they set out to mobilise an army, unify China, and begin the construction of a modern nation. Due to international developments, especially the involvement of the Soviet Union in China, the civil war between Northern Government factions, and the strengthening of nationalist sentiments, there were opportunities. But, the task was militarily difficult. The Northern Government came close to recovering its position in 1926, as we shall see. In addition, it would not prove easy to keep control over co-opted armies and destroy the local sources of militarism.

The NRA

Sun Yatsen, following his ouster by Chen Jiongming in 1922, returned to Canton in February 1923 by co-opting the Yunnan Army of Yang Ximin. Few could have been certain that this time his actions would make it possible for the Nationalists to bring the province under Nationalist control, build a substantial army, and use the area for a military campaign to re-unify China. Guangdong was militarily fragmented and Sun had many enemies. Large armies blocked the roads out of the province to central China and the north with its all-important capital. The KMT was itself a divided party, some of whose constituencies, including overseas Chinese in South-east Asia and entrepreneurs in Canton and Hong Kong, were likely to be concerned about collaboration with the Soviets. Sun's financial resources were limited and the extent to which he would be able to mobilise the wealth of Guangdong for an expensive project not necessarily in the interest of Guangdong's elites was unpredictable.

The backing of the Soviets would be critical to the Nationalists as they strengthened their Guangdong base after 1925, but when Sun returned to Guangdong, Soviet policy in China was in flux. In 1921 and 1922, the Soviets had hoped to bring about an alliance between Wu Peifu, the most important military and political leader in north China at the time, Sun Yatsen, and the Chinese Communists.[85] The aim of the Soviets was to prevent the emergence of a Zhang Zuolin-dominated China, as they believed that Zhang was beholden to the Japanese. This strategy proved unworkable because of Wu Peifu's suppression of a Communist strike at the large Kailuan coalmines in 1922 and along the Beijing–Hankou Railroad in January 1923; because of Wu's links with Sun's enemy in Guangdong, Chen Jiongming; because of Wu's insistence in the fall of 1922 that the Soviets return the China Eastern Railroad and withdraw Soviet troops from Mongolia; and because internal factional rivalries undermined Wu's general political and military position.[86]

Adolf Joffe, instructed to strengthen relations with Sun, travelled to Shanghai in January 1923. He and Sun signed the famous Joint Declaration, Joffe as Ambassador and Sun as Dr Sun Yatsen, in which the Soviet Union declared its readiness to help China achieve 'national unification' and 'full national independence', and in which Sun Yatsen accepted Soviet special interests in the Chinese Eastern Railroad as well as the continued presence of Soviet troops in Outer Mongolia. Probably to assuage elites in the Treaty Ports, gripped by the fear of Communism, the Joint Declaration also stated that Sun did not believe that Communism could be implemented in China.[87]

This document bolstered Sun Yatsen's public prestige as, although a private citizen, he was now seen as negotiating with an important country about national matters. However, it did not lead to immediate agreement on financial support or the delivery of military aid. Even though such topics had been discussed, and even if reports to Moscow about Sun by Soviet emissaries were generally positive at this time,[88] without some territorial base, Sun Yatsen would be a risky investment for the Soviets. Sun realised this. In a letter to Chiang Kaishek of 21 November 1922, referring to the Soviets, he wrote 'we have to have a base before we can deal with them'.[89]

Sun was able to secure that base with the help of Yang Ximin's Yunnan forces, which drove Chen Jiongming from Canton. Sun co-opted Yang by providing him with

400,000 *yuan*, raised among Hong Kong and Cantonese elites as well as overseas Chinese. To keep these groups on board, Sun promoted the 'Prince's Clique', who included Sun Fo, his son who would become mayor of Canton; as well as Wu Chaoshu and Fu Bingchang who had married daughters of Ho Kai, a wealthy Hong Kong citizen with whom Sun had close connections since the days of the Revolutionary Alliance.[90] When Sun made his way back to Canton in February, he went out of his way to cultivate these constituencies, meeting the Chinese business elite in Hong Kong, having lunch with the governor of the colony, drinking tea with the head of the Hong Kong and Shanghai Bank, and at an address at the University of Hong Kong praising British rule.[91] Still without any firm promises of Soviet support, Sun could not afford to alienate them.

In March 1923, after negotiations between Liao Zhongkai, the Nationalists' financial expert, and Joffe in Japan,[92] the Soviet Politburo decided to dispatch a political and military advisors group to Sun in Canton and make 2 million Mexican dollars available to him.[93] However, much divided the Soviets and the Nationalists. Sun favoured a strategy that was anathema to the Soviets. He proposed a north-western strategy, of which opposition to Wu Peifu, co-operation with Zhang Zuolin, and the raising of an army in the north-west on the Mongolian–Chinese border were the main features.[94] When Chiang Kaishek visited Moscow, this was the strategy he advocated,[95] which the Soviets rejected.[96] Concerned about reports that Sun's claims of popular support were excessive and that his behaviour in Guangdong left much to be desired, they advised Chiang Kaishek that building up political institutions and conducting propaganda were at present more important tasks than immediate military action.[97] They insisted that the Nationalists train a cohesive army in Guangdong and consolidate their base by building up popular support.[98] Chiang Kaishek objected that the large cities, where propaganda would have to be delivered, were controlled by foreigners. He also argued that while in Russia it had been possible to conduct propaganda campaigns and seize power by a revolution in the capital, this strategy was not possible in China. He continued to insist that military action had to come first.[99]

However, the Soviets did send Michael Borodin to Canton. He arrived in October 1923 as the head of the Soviet mission and political advisor to Sun. Borodin was a Russian who had joined the Bolsheviks in 1903 and from then had been active in England and America as a revolutionary. When Borodin arrived, Sun was encountering great difficulties. The Guangxi military faction, which had supported his return and with whose support he sought to consolidate his control of the Canton delta, had turned against him and even tried to take Canton. Chen Jiongming too had launched an offensive, the Yunnan forces refused to carry out his orders unless he paid with cash in advance, and Wu Peifu had begun to aid hostile armies on Guangdong's borders with Hunan and Guangxi.[100] According to the first report filed by Borodin, workers had initially welcomed Sun but they had turned against him. The continuous warfare had alienated the petty bourgeoisie, coolies were being sent to the front and thus transport systems had collapsed, and Sun's need for money had led him to institute various local taxes, which had angered peasants.[101] Those in Hong Kong who hoped that Sun might be good for business by bringing some peace to the area were of course disappointed, making further support from that direction unlikely. Sun Yatsen's future became dependent on Soviet support.

Reforming the party

Upon his arrival, Borodin made it his priority to reshape the KMT. As a Leninist, he was, of course, dedicated to creating a disciplined and hierarchical party to serve as an efficient tool of its leadership and with cells at the local level to mobilise the masses. Borodin reported to Moscow that Sun Yatsen claimed that the KMT had 30,000 members in Guangdong, but that only 6,000 paid dues, while revised registers suggested that the KMT had no more than 3,000 members. According to Borodin, there was no party constitution or programme, there were no meetings, and no party publications existed to inform the membership and tie it together.[102] Borodin proposed to end military campaigning as it usurped all of Sun Yatsen's energies and was costing him dearly both financially and politically. Instead, he proposed to re-organise the KMT, establish a military academy, publish a party journal, and begin a radical land reform programme.[103]

Sun agreed. He had few alternatives, as the chaos in Guangdong had alienated his supporters in Hong Kong and he could not risk loosing the support of the Soviets as well. In October 1923, Sun sanctioned the creation of a Provisional Central Executive Committee to draft new statutes and prepare a national congress for January 1924. The tasks of the provisional Committee, in which Communists participated, included the creation of active party branches in Guangdong. A branch of the Provisional Committee was established in Shanghai, which began to function by December. Its activities included the organisation of KMT branches, printing propaganda pamphlets, and convening public meetings. The Shanghai Branch was not just active in Shanghai, but was responsible for the development of the KMT throughout China with the exception of Guangdong and Guangxi. Especially in view of all that happened later, its minutes make pleasant reading. Hu Hanmin, Wang Jingwei, Mao Zedong, and briefly Liao Zhongkai all worked together in Shanghai.[104] All would later turn against each other. By the time of the First KMT Congress, the new KMT had 1,023 registered members in Shanghai, 475 in Hunan, 8,218 in Canton, and 5,377 in the rest of Guangdong. Total membership may have been slightly over 20,000, with a substantial number living abroad.[105]

The congress opened on 20 January in Canton, and proved a discordant affair. Many KMT members disapproved of dual party membership for Communists. They also objected to the Manifesto, which stated that China's problems were caused by imperialism and militarism, called for the struggle against both, and demanded the mobilisation of peasants and workers. At one point, Sun suggested the retraction of the Manifesto, proposing that instead the congress should declare the establishment of a national government, which would be guided by Sun's *Outline for National Construction* and of which he would be the president. Borodin furiously refused and in the end a modified Manifesto was adopted. It omitted mention of land confiscations, an idea which Borodin believed crucial for peasant mobilisation. Leninist party statutes requiring members to be active in a strictly centralised and hierarchical party organisation were adopted, but with the difference that Sun was named president of the KMT for life and given veto powers over the decisions of the Central Executive Committee. He too had the right to appoint Central Executive Committee members, which he used to create a body that mixed Left-wing members, of which Liao Zhongkai was the most influential, with a large number of Right-wing KMT members and three Communists, who were appointed to the directorships or vice-directorships of the three critical labour, workers, and organisation departments.[106]

It is one thing to re-organise a party on paper, and quite another to make it cohesive and disciplined in practice. The tensions between the various constituents that made up the United Front – between the CCP and the KMT, between various local military figures, between younger and older generations of KMT supporters, and between those like Liao Zhongkai who supported close co-operation with the Soviets and Hu Hanmin and Deng Zeru who opposed this – remained unresolved.[107] After the KMT Congress, opponents of collaboration with the Soviets and the Communists, with close links to Overseas Chinese, Hong Kong, and Cantonese elites, brought about a new crisis in July 1924, when they succeeded in convening a Central Executive Committee meeting to discuss a proposal to expel the Communists. Until then Sun had prevaricated, but possibly as a result of a threat by Borodin to withdraw Soviet support altogether, or perhaps because the campaign challenged his leadership, Sun moved against the opposition and expelled one of its leaders.[108]

The uncertain military situation in Guangdong, as well as a quickly deepening financial crisis, helps explain why Sun decided to travel to Beijing to participate in a convention to settle national affairs. That convention was called after Feng Yuxiang had rebelled against Wu Peifu in October and seized Beijing. Sun hoped, perhaps, that the outcome would be his installation as the new President of the Republic. In a letter to Chiang Kaishek, Sun expressed his misgivings about the viability of the Guangdong base when he stated that 'British pressure', 'Chen Jiongming', and 'the greed and arrogance of expatriate armies' threatened its existence.[109] Strong reservations to Sun's journey to Beijing existed in the KMT. Some feared that Sun would end up losing all in the same way as had happened after the 1911 Revolution when he had entered into negotiations with Yuan Shikai. Others believed that given all that the KMT had said about imperialism and warlordism, the party's reputation in the arena of public opinion would suffer irredeemably.[110] The Soviets, however, enthusiastically supported Sun's step. Co-operation between Sun, the Communists, and Feng Yuxiang, they stated, provided favourable prospects for a national revolution in China, and also was a way to prevent Duan Qirui, friendly to the Japanese, to emerge as President and to keep Zhang Zuolin from capturing north China. That outcome to the uncertain situation in the north would have rendered Soviet efforts to expand their influence, foster revolution, and secure their eastern borders stillborn.[111]

Sun set off in November, but his efforts came to a naught and he died from cancer on 12 March 1925. His death became an important ritual moment when KMT representatives were able to put their stamp on funeral arrangements for Sun and turn Sun's passing into a national affair that challenged the authorities in Beijing, including Duan Qirui, and pointed towards a new future under the KMT.[112] The KMT's new popularity, Zhang Zuolin's rapid expansion of influence in north China, and uncertainty about Feng Yuxiang's ability to hold north China prompted the Soviets to step up very substantially their aid programme to the Nationalists. This new aid enabled the Nationalists to expand their military power and strengthen their base in Guangdong.

Military reform

Following Chiang Kaishek's return from his mission to the Soviet Union in the fall of 1923, Sun appointed him head of the Preparation Committee for the Whampoa Academy, the military academy that was to train the officers for the new military force that was to give the Nationalists the muscle to seize power. Even before the Committee began its work, however, Chiang Kaishek departed for his home in Zhejiang Province following a dispute over funding for the academy.[113] Military reform went off to an uncertain start.

It is possible, as has been suggested, that Chiang Kaishek objected to Soviet origins of the funds.[114] Chiang's diary, on the other hand, suggests that he departed from Canton because he objected to Sun's continued reliance on local militarists and financial interests.[115] Sun had ordered the Provincial Finance Office to remit 30,000 *yuan* monthly to the Whampoa Academy. It managed only 6,000 *yuan*, while the Soviets were slow in delivering the funds that they had promised.[116] According to memoirs, the finances of the Whampoa Academy were so tight that the feasibility of the whole project was in serious doubt.[117] Liao Zhongkai had to scurry around to raise funds, which indeed he did by appealing to local militarists.[118] Liao Zhongkai wrote several besieging letters to Chiang to return 'for the sake of the nation and the KMT'.[119] On 21 March, Liao stated in one of these letters that 'the finances of the Academy have now been arranged and you can announce them upon your return. As to other reforms, these we should plan together upon your return. If we fail, it will not be too late to resign together then'.[120] Chiang gave in, but also urged Sun in a telegram 'to carry out financial reform and put Liao Zhongkai in charge'.[121]

Liao Zhongkai himself acted as the head of the Preparatory Committee during Chiang's absence. Under his guidance statutes were drawn up, staff selected, a site prepared at the old Canton military and naval school, and through KMT branches, cadets recruited. By October 1924, the Whampoa Academy was training 1,000 students.[122] By the end of 1929, 7,399 cadets had passed the final examination – a sufficient number of officers for several divisions.[123]

The aim was to nurture a new type of officer: literate, honest, disciplined, militarily competent, drawn from across the country, and dedicated to revolution. The course was set at six months, and later extended to a year.[124] Of the above mentioned 7,399 cadets, half came from Hunan and Guangdong. The rest was made up in about equal number by other provinces.[125] The academy recruited youths between the ages of 18 and 25 with at least a middle school education in a clear sign that the army was to be radically different from warlord forces. Cadets had to be KMT members, or willing to become such, and had to be recommended by a KMT branch.[126] They did not pay tuition fees, but had to agree to serve in the KMT's army one year for every two months of instruction received. Cadets lived at the school and had to accept its discipline.[127] Military training included tactics, rifle practice, logistics, engineering, communications, hygiene, and geography. Field exercises trained the cadets in the command of units, battlefield logistics, and the implementation of tactics. From the second year of Whampoa's existence, cadets specialised in infantry, artillery, engineering, transport, or military police courses. From the fourth year, further options became available in political work, aviation, cavalry, and radio communications.[128] Advanced courses in strategy, history of warfare, staff work, and war planning were also given.

Speeches by various KMT and CCP leaders at the academy indicate the new kind of force they had in mind. Sun Yatsen in June 1924 stated that the reason for the revolutionary success of Russia had been party discipline. Discipline, organisation, and party were key, according to him, rather than individuality. Zhou Enlai stressed discipline, not to be enforced, but as a consequence of revolutionary conviction. This commitment would make the army the 'vanguard of the revolution'.[129] Li Jishen, a Guangdong general, stressed closeness to the population, 'united purpose' and 'spirit of solidarity'.[130]

Political training was meant to instil such outlooks and attitudes. Political instruction focused on KMT history, Sun Yatsen's Three People's Principles, the history of imperialism, world revolution, social and political sciences, and economics.[131] Emphasised were concepts such as the army as the vanguard of revolution, unity, discipline, obedience to the will of the party, anti-imperialism, anti-feudalism, and awakening, that is the process of becoming aware of the inequities, the oppression, and the backwardness of the old society and the embracing of modernity, rationalism, nationalism, and revolution. For Yun Daiying, a Communist political instructor at the school, political training was to cleanse one's 'old anti-revolutionary habits of mind'.[132] Awakening also meant valuing discipline, cleanliness, hygiene, honesty, and integrity. Political commissars enforced such attitudes and practices.[133]

In August 1924, with the first class of cadets in training at the Whampoa Academy, the KMT Political Council approved Chiang Kaishek's plan for the gradual training of a division in a period of one year, at a cost of 2.7 million *yuan*. In October, a model regiment was set up under the command of He Yingqin. He would be the commander of the 1st Army Corps during the Northern Expedition and would from then on play a leading role in Chiang Kaishek's National Army. Its soldiers were recruited from Jiangsu, Anhui, and Zhejiang. Junior officers were graduates from Whampoa, while the academy's staff filled the higher command functions.[134] The regiment had political commissars down to the company level.[135]

The regiment and the Whampoa cadets were involved in several campaigns that extended the authority of the KMT in Guangdong and would greatly enhance the prestige of Whampoa and its army. In October 1924, the regiment played a role in the suppression of the Merchant Corps Uprising. Opposed to the heavy taxation that the Canton government imposed and worried about its attempts to bring Canton workers into unions under its control, the Canton merchants had revived their militia and purchased 10,000 Mauser rifles in Belgium. Chiang Kaishek intercepted these rifles. In the inevitable clash, the regiment led the successful attack on the Headquarters of the Merchant Corps.[136] The arms seized during this operation strengthened the new force greatly.

A second success was the defeat of an offensive by Chen Jiongming, who hoped to exploit Sun Yatsen's absence in Beijing. Chen mobilised perhaps 50,000 troops. The defence of the Guangdong base was conducted by Yunnanese forces under Fan Shizheng in the north of the province, a part of the Guangxi Army of Liu Zhenhuan, and the Whampoa force that had grown to 3,000 troops. The latter's success in clearing the Canton–Kowloon Railroad and then taking the offence along the coast towards the East River Area and Shantou impressed all. Chen Jiongming was not decisively defeated, but was forced to the north of the province. The fierce battle of Mianhu, when the Whampoa forces destroyed a strong position defended by Chen Jiongming, has become legendary.[137] The troops were disciplined, morale was high, and popular support was mobilised efficiently and without corruption. War booty was substantial, including 12,000 rifles, 110 machine guns, 8 million cartridges, and 30 artillery pieces. Following this operation, in April 1925, the Training Regiment became the Party Army under the command of Chiang Kaishek.[138]

In June 1925, the Yunnanese Army of Yang Ximin and the Guangxi Army of Liu Zhenhuan occupied Canton. The Party Army, which had been campaigning against Chen Jiongming, turned back, and with the cadets then being trained at Whampoa recovered Canton. The defeat of Yunnan and Guangxi armies further increased the prestige of the Whampoa forces. Booty was again substantial: 16,600 rifles, 120 machine guns, and 6 gunboats.[139]

These victories, the increase in Soviet assistance, and the new public opinion climate created by the May Thirtieth Movement generated the conditions in which the Nationalists could begin the rapid expansion of their military forces. They had a substantial base, even if their actual control remained limited. They had become more important to the Soviets. Feng's rebellion had weakened Wu Peifu, but to prevent a resurgence of the Northern Government or of a north China dominated by Zhang Zuolin, their best hopes lay in supporting Feng in the north and the Nationalists in the south. Public opinion following the May Thirtieth Massacre in Shanghai had turned against Western imperialism and the Northern Government. The prospects for a Nationalist military campaign to re-unify the country, which the Soviets had disparaged and about which Sun Yatsen himself had been pessimistic, had gained in feasibility. But before any idea along those lines could be entertained, the Nationalists' military forces had to be expanded and unified. The Military Affairs Council was the institution that led this effort.

The Military Affairs Council

The KMT's Military Affairs Council (MAC), established in June 1925, was 'to take charge of all military affairs in the Nation'.[140] After Sun's death, the KMT had resolved to form a National Government, thus formally declaring that it claimed to be the legitimate government of China. Its forces from then on would no longer be known as the Party Army but as the NRA.

The Council met under the chairmanship of Wang Jingwei, who had won the first round in the struggle for succession that followed Sun's death.[141] Wang Jingwei also held the chairmanships of the Central Executive Committee of the KMT and the Government Counsel. It was made up of four civilian party members (Wang Jingwei, Liao Zhongkai, Hu Hanmin, and Wu Chaoshu) and the four main military leaders of the armies that the Nationalists hoped to co-opt. They were Tan Yankai of the Hunan Army, Xu Chongzhi of the Guangdong Army, Chiang Kaishek of the KMT's Party Army, and Zhu Peide of the Yunnan Army.[142] The MAC sought to impose a standard military organisation on all units, centralise command, develop a general staff, unify tactics and strategy, remove the military from involvement in the local economy, create unified systems of supply and command, and establish a single personnel system.

The minutes of the MAC's meetings prior to the Northern Expedition are now available.[143] They allow us to follow the MAC as it pursued these goals until the beginning of the Northern Expedition. They also make it clear that army reform became a vehicle for a vary rapid extension of Soviet influence, something that added greatly to the tensions that would explode on the eve of and during the Northern Expedition and which would greatly affect its development.

Financial concerns were never far removed from the deliberations of the MAC. A June 1925 Chiang Kaishek proposal for army re-organisation, surely drafted with Soviet assistance, argued that Guangdong could produce 35–45 million *yuan* per year in revenue. If 20 million were allocated to the military, according to Chiang, a force of 65,000 would be feasible. He argued that the core of this army should be the Party Army with 10,000 troops, divided into two divisions, which could be expanded quickly in time of war and as money and officers became available.[144]

The MAC attempted to remove the militarists from their forces and bring these together into one single armed force. On 2 July 1925, the MAC began by abolishing the posts of Commander-in-Chief of the various armies. Yet, the move had more symbolic than actual significance, as the regional commanders were re-appointed as commanders of what were called Army Corps (juntuan) of the NRA. The MAC created a central Staff Department to achieve a more actually effective integration of Guangdong's military forces. The MAC's Staff Department was headed by a Soviet, and had offices for Military Affairs (investigation, intelligence, secret communications), General Administration, Artillery, Military Industry, Transport, Aviation, Naval Affairs, and Supply. To each a Soviet advisor was attached. One of the first activities of the General Staff was to issue forms to all military units to collect information on personnel, equipment, and geographical location. Investigation Teams were to be sent to each division for verification.

On 4 August, the MAC re-organised the armed forces into numerically identified Army Corps. Each corps was to consist of two or three divisions. Armies and divisions were from then on no longer officially identified with a specific region or commander. Appointments of officers were formally confirmed by the MAC. On 3 September, it was suggested that Soviet advisors be assigned to divisions.

Proper budgeting and accounting were important MAC concerns. On 10 September, the MAC held a joint meeting with the Finance Committee. The latter reported a daily deficit of 11,837 *yuan* in the MAC's budget and a deficit of 255,313 *yuan* for the Military Supply Office in the three months of its existence. Whether or not these calculations reflected increases in Soviet aid is not clear. The Finance Committee estimated military expenditures at 2.7 million per month. To improve the financial situation, proposals were formulated for a government monopoly on opium trade and sales, a central bank to issue debt, the introduction of strict budgets for each Corps, an end to the retention by local army units of county revenues, and the abolition of Military Fundraising Offices (Chouxiangju) controlled by Army Corps. Before the meeting, the MAC had drawn up a preliminary budget of 3 million *yuan* per month. Most Army Corps would receive 250,000–300,000 *yuan*.

In the fall of 1925, the MAC concentrated its military activities on bringing Guangdong under control and suppressing banditry. In this time, the KMT's own 1st Army Corps conquered the East River Area with its abundant economic resources and finally eliminated Chen Jiongming as a serious military force. It seems likely that Soviet aid and advice were important in tipping the balance of power in Guangdong in favour of the Nationalists. Other Corps operated in the south of the province and in the west extended the Nationalist power towards Guangxi. The MAC minutes make clear that it was not able to have great influence over these units. With the exception of the 1st Corps, the other Corps acted on their own, and merely reported victories or problems after they had occurred. They also submitted requests for ammunition, rifles, and funds. The ability of the Nationalists to make these available was important in securing the co-operation, even if only of a limited nature, of these Corps. The MAC also conducted negotiations with military leaders in neighbouring provinces. In return for joining the NRA they were given an area to station their troops and draw revenues.

After Guangdong Province had been more or less unified, the MAC initiated a second wave of expansion and reform. Chiang Kaishek proposed a scheme for army expansion at the 15 December 1925 MAC meeting. His reasoning was that following the unification of Guangdong, revenues could be expected to rise to 40–50 million *yuan*. According to Chiang, if 70 per cent was used for the military, the Nationalists could afford a force of around 15–18 divisions, given that the maintenance of one division required 130,000 *yuan* per month.[145]

In the spring of 1926, the decision was taken to establish a military tribunal to strengthen military discipline and end the maltreatment of troops by officers. The General Staff was strengthened, and more detailed information was collected on the armies themselves. One of its tasks was to produce standard military training manuals for all military academies and all field exercises and to oversee military training through all armies and divisions. It also was to publish a journal for the army to build up a common *esprit de corps*. In January, a plan was adopted to re-allocate various divisions to different Army Corps and to re-arrange the army as five Corps and two independent divisions. Some commands too were reshuffled.[146]

On 19 March 1926, the MAC published regulations for political commissars. Commissars had been introduced in the 1st Army Corps, but political commissars were now to take up position in the other armies as well. The regulations stated that political commissars represented the KMT in the army, guided party cells, and directed the activities of soldiers and officers clubs. Political commissars were to countersign the orders made by commanding officers at the same level. If they disagreed, according to the regulations, they still had to sign but report their objections to a higher level. Political commissars also were to liaise with local government officials and mass organisations. While responsible for military discipline, they also were charged with ensuring proper living standards for soldiers and their good treatment by officers. Commissars themselves had to be exemplars of valour, discipline, and revolutionary commitment. Party cells in the army were at all times to support the commissar in any public situation. They could only challenge them in closed party meetings.[147]

In the year after the death of Sun Yatsen, in short, the Nationalists rapidly expanded their power in Guangdong and the MAC developed into an increasingly assertive institution that worked hard to transform Guangdong's varied military forces into a cohesive army. While it made progress, there were limits to what could be achieved in so short a time. Soviet reports of March 1926 stated that 20,000 unfit soldiers had been weeded out from the Yunnan and Guangxi armies and that the MAC had some control over these two forces. The reports took great satisfaction of this development, but also realistically noted that much remained to be done. It stated that co-operation between Army Corps and even between divisions within any Corps continued to be weak. The supply system was not yet centralised, which suggests that most armies and divisions continued to live off the land in various ways. Political commissars and political departments had been established in the 1st Army Corps, according to these Soviet reports, but they did not exist in the other Corps.[148] The reports further make clear that the General Staff was not popular and that recruitment remained the prerogative of division commanders. The quality of officers and the standard of equipment were low.[149]

The following poem precedes the formal minutes of the MAC's meetings. It is not signed but may have been written by Tan Yankai.[150] Tan had a long history of involvement in national and Hunanese politics, and is usually seen as a pragmatic and skilful politician. The poem is interesting because it is written from a different perspective than that of the Soviets, the Communists, or the Nationalists. It is expressive of a sceptical and ironic voice too rarely heard.

> Mr Chiang [Kaishek's] proposals are marvellous
> . . .
> However the foreign money is just not enough
>
> Coffee, milk, sweets, tea
> Only the bananas are not touched
> Surely because foreigners are afraid of diarrhoea
> They also never touch watermelons
> They have meetings everyday as Deputies
> But worry that they have no money to send home
> They just eat and don't say anything.[151]

Financial reform

The issue of finance is not usually put central in accounts of warfare in China. Yet, without financial resources, armies could not be supported and without armies, financial resources could not be secured. As in the case of the modern military, the Nationalists sought to build-up a modern fiscal system not only to accumulate military resources. Creating a centralised fiscal system was also a way of demonstrating that China could be modern, with budgets separating private and public resources and the state enforcing distinctions between the military, the party, and the government. Financial reform was also seen as central to rehabilitating the military, as only in this way could an end be brought to the military units sponging off local society and transforming them into a unified force with no other objective than supporting the project of bringing a modern nation about.

Liao Zhongkai was in charge of financial reform. Liao was well qualified for this position because of his familiarity with financial affairs, his strong local contacts in Guangdong and Hong Kong as well as among overseas Chinese, and his long dedication to the Nationalist cause. He was born in 1877 or 1878 in San Francisco, where his father worked in the local branch of the Hong Kong and Shanghai Bank. He returned with his ailing mother in 1894, who would die a few months later. Three years later he married He Xiangning. Her family had grown rich in Hong Kong from the tea trade. Because members of the Liao family had worked for the Qing government, this was a marriage between 'rich merchants of Hong Kong and officials from Canton'.[152] In 1902, the couple moved to Japan where Liao studied economics at Waseda University and in 1905 joined the Revolutionary Alliance. Liao developed a close relationship with Zhu Zhixin, and his home became a meeting place for Revolutionary Alliance members. Liao busied himself with fund-raising, a task for which his close connections with Overseas Chinese in South-east Asia and the USA were useful. Following the 1911 Revolution, he took charge of provincial finance in Guangdong. Although Yuan Shikai's suppression of the 1913 Revolution forced him back into exile to Japan, he returned to China in 1916 and again assisted Sun by raising funds and by participating in the negotiations with the Soviets. Liao became one of the most outspoken supporters of close collaboration with the Soviets, for military and financial reform, and for a strong labour movement.[153]

In 1924, Liao headed the KMT's Financial Committee, served as the KMT representative at the Whampoa Military Academy, head of the Military Supply Office, provincial governor of Guangdong, and head of the Provincial Finance Office. The minutes of the Financial Affairs Committee, established under the chairmanship of Sun Yatsen, make clear that in the spring and summer the Nationalists in Guangdong faced grave difficulties.[154] The business of the committee consisted of dealing with requests of various military units for funds and ammunition, which it frequently had to deny. In July, the committee reported to Sun Yatsen that it required 24,183 *yuan* per day for military expenditures, but that its income was 15,700 *yuan*. It proposed that 'except for military forces who have a local base and can provide for themselves, all other forces receive funds as our revenue allows'.[155] Sun informed the various militarists accordingly.[156]

To deal with the situation, Liao sought to centralise control over revenue collection. In a telegram to Yang Ximin, the Yunnan Army general, and other militarists, Liao wrote

> Although Guangdong is famed for its riches, since armies were mobilised, the financial system fragmented, the *lijin* and land taxes were all retained by these armies, and they also controlled gambling and opium taxes. They have sliced up the opium taxes like a melon. In the last two years, financial orders had no impact beyond the gates of the Finance Office.[157]

In this telegram, Liao estimated that revenue in Guangdong amounted to 30 million *yuan* and that the cost of the military was in reality only half this amount, so that there was no real need for the severe shortages. He called on the militarists 'to hand over financial authority' and to agree to 'the centralisation under our financial institutions of the land tax, the *lijin*, local defence revenues, and opium taxes'. He called on them to intervene no longer in the activities of his personnel and also to report their troop strength honestly and not to demand rations for soldiers who existed only on paper.[158]

Liao's plans could not be implemented as long as their realisation depended on the goodwill of the militarists. But the suppression of the Merchant Corps uprising, the defeat of Chen Jiongming's attack, the invasion of the East River area, and the defeat of the attack by Liu Zhenhuan and Yang Ximin on Canton in June 1925 bolstered Liao's position, as did the increase in Soviet aid. On 15 June 1925, Liao Zhongkai as Minister of Finance of the newly established National Government issued the 'Order to Unify Revenue Collection Agencies', which insisted that 'all revenue must be collected and managed by legal organs. No civil or military officials may intervene under whatever pretext in tax collection or without authorisation retain funds. Those who disobey shall be regarded as criminals and dealt with under military law'.[159] This kind of tough language would not have been possible only a few months earlier.

Liao would pay with his life for his efforts to remove armies from tax gathering operations.[160] On 20 August, three assassins killed him. Although the details of the plot remain unclear, implicated were Hu Hanmin, the Minister of Foreign Affairs who had strong local connections and was associated with the Right-wing of the KMT, as well as Xu Chongzhi, who was the Minister of Military Affairs.[161] Xu's Guangdong forces had controlled about half of the province's revenues and Liao had impeached him. Wu Tiecheng, the head of the Department of Public Safety in Canton, too may have been involved.[162] Following the assassination, the KMT Political Council appointed Wang Jingwei and Chiang Kaishek to a Special Committee and declared martial law, which Chiang Kaishek enforced with his 1st Army Corps. Hu Hanmin and Xu Chongzhi were sent into exile, Hu as Ambassador to the Soviet Union. Xu's forces were broken up into two divisions.[163]

Song Ziwen succeeded Liao Zhongkai. His father, Charlie Song, had roamed through South-east Asia before gaining the patronage of a rich American, Julian Carr. He trained to become a missionary, but upon his return to Shanghai decided that this vocation was not for him. He became an entrepreneur, selling cheap Chinese bibles for the American Bible Society, founding the Commercial Press, and building up an industrial and financial empire. He was a close friend of Sun Yatsen, with his house and printing press in the International Concessions serving as a meeting place for revolutionaries. Charlie Song himself raised substantial funds for Song's Revolutionary Alliance, including from his American patron. His daughter Qingling married Sun in 1914. Song Ziwen, born in Shanghai in 1894, was a graduate of St John's, Shanghai, and Harvard Universities. Following his graduation, he worked for the Hanyeping Coal and Iron Works before joining Sun Yatsen in Canton. Another of Charlie Song's daughters, Meiling, would marry Chiang Kaishek in December 1927.

In reforming Guangdong's finances, Song Ziwen built on the basis laid by Liao Zhongkai.[164] The destruction of enemy forces, the extension of KMT territorial control, and the gradual take-over of county governments made rapid progress possible, but the KMT's military was insatiable. In November 1926, Song reported on financial reforms over the last twelve months. According to Song, when he took over, the destruction of land tax records made the collection of land taxes impossible, a huge variety of taxes were imposed without authorisation, no budget or accounting systems existed, the military ran its own revenue collection agencies, and many taxes were farmed out to merchants. Song then set out how he had been able to increase National Government revenue in one year to 80.2 million *yuan*, a large increase compared with the 7.9 million that had been raised in Guangdong in the whole of 1924. He had achieved this, he wrote, by issuing debt, rationalising collection agencies and dismissing superfluous staff,

Table 2.1 Income of KMT Guangdong Government,
November 1925 to October 1926 (in millions)

Public debt	24.3
Lijin	11.8
Military tax collection (chouxiang)	11.5
Salt Gabelle	8.9
Opium monopoly	3.4
Miscellaneous taxes	4.1
Stamp tax	3.0
Land tax	3.0
Tobacco and alcohol	2.4
Other	2.7
Fuel taxes	1.7
Native customs	0.2
Extra revenue collections	1.6
Registration of reclaimed land (shatian)	0.6
Total	79.2

Source: ZHMGDAZL, IV: 2, 1400.

creating an opium monopoly, registering land, holding county magistrates responsible for revenue quotas allocated to them, forcing the military to remit revenues, and enforcing a comprehensive budget system. The extension of Nationalist territorial control was no doubt important as well, and few of Song's reforms would have been possible without the increased military might of the Nationalists.

According to Sun, the revenue collected by him came from the sources as shown in Table 2.1. This table illustrates that the issue of public debt had been the most important revenue source. It was made possible by the central bank that Liao Zhongkai had introduced. Song argued that public debt, a device which imitated Western practices, had been important in creating stability in the financial system and gaining the financial resources for large economic projects, such as setting up a mint, but also for harbour development. The debt was underwritten by Guangdong's taxes and according to Sun, the new National Government's credit was sound.[165]

It should be noted that the people of Guangdong were coerced into purchasing National Government debt. After a first attempt at issuing 5 million *yuan* worth of debt had failed, a second attempt, for 10 million *yuan*, was successful, but only because households and shops had been forced to purchase debt to the value of one month rent's or 1 per cent of the value of their real estate. Also, one-third of military pay was issued in the form of promissory notes, redeemable in areas to be conquered by the Northern Expedition and hence a charge on the resources of these areas.[166]

Song stated that he regretted the opium monopoly and hoped that it would be phased out in future. Yet, he reported that the abolition of a farmed-out opium tax and a full government monopoly over its transport and sale had proved lucrative in the extreme. He expected that revenues from opium would rise to 10 million *yuan*. The monopoly had also deprived local militarists from one of their main sources of revenue.

Although Song had abolished a variety of taxes, he had also introduced new ones, for instance on petrol and luxury items. Hotels paid policing fees and prostitutes paid each twenty-five *yuan*. Song had also registered re-claimed land. Military protection had been needed for this task, but once accomplished, the land so bought on the books of the National Government provided a lucrative and increasing source of revenue.[167] Tax farming too, Song argued, could not yet be abolished. But the reduction of the number of tax agencies, greater competition in tax farming, and inspections of tax farming operations had led to a trebling of revenues from this source.

Song's report expressed pride in the achievements of the past year. But he also wrote that 'in the previous year, we needed enormous amounts of money to pay for the deployment in the East River area, the pacification of the southern circuit, and the incorporation of forces from Sichuan; this year the same is true for our preparations for the Northern Expedition to pacify the Central Plains, for the defence of the rear, for the fight against local bandits, for payments to the military for accounts fallen in arrears as well as for new outlays on arms, ammunition, uniforms, and equipment'.[168] Song estimated that military expenditures had come to 61 million *yuan*, leaving little for domestic affairs, justice, education, or the promotion of trade and industry. He noted that the National Government's resources had suffered greatly from the Canton–Hong Kong Strike, which meant that it had to provide for all the striking workers. Despite the great increase in revenue, the issue of public debt, and drastic savings exercises, the National Government still ran a deficit of more than 20 million *yuan*. He warned that 'Before we have reached the time when our military campaigns are concluded, military expenditures are reduced, and the state can begin peaceful reconstruction, it will not be possible to dedicate the uses of our revenue fully to increasing the prosperity of the nation'. Locals in Guangdong expressed themselves more pithily. During the rallies that were then regularly conducted in Guangdong they shouted: 'Guomindang Wanshui! (The ten thousand taxes of the KMT) – a pun on 'Guomindang Wansui!' (Long Live The KMT).[169]

Conclusion

This chapter has stressed the re-thinking of the military in the 1920s, the interplay between domestic and international military and political developments, and the pressures imposed by the military–fiscal crisis in analysing the rise of the NRA. This is not to deny the relevance of nationalism. Beyond the rapid and often unexpected changes that generated new opportunities as well as dangers, the clash of personalities and ambitions, and the spectacle of men trying to impose their will on a fractious and intractable environment, the nationalist aspirations of those who transformed Guangdong into a new political and military base always shone through. It was moulded by the experience of past failures. If the stress in the late Qing was on individual acts of heroism and intellectual innovation, in the 1920s, bureaucratisation, organising military force, and building institutions to make possible disciplined collective action came to the fore. The aim was to make manifest a new China as a prosperous and cohesive nation, which had shed its reputation as the Sick Man of Asia and in which all could live as citizens.

Without the opportunities provided by the international and domestic context, the NRA would never have come into being. They made it possible for the Nationalists to accumulate financial and military resources in Guangdong. Especially important was the

October Revolution and the decision of the Soviet Union to foster nationalist revolutionary movements in European and Japanese colonies. The Soviets provided financial and military support without which it is unlikely that the Nationalists would have been able to establish a beachhead in Guangdong and then prevail against the forces that attempted to destroy it. Perhaps just as important, their association increased the symbolic prestige of Sun Yatsen and the Nationalists, while Soviet advisors transferred knowledge about army organisation, party construction, and social and political mobilisation.

Rapid changes in China domestically meant that the Nationalists would benefit from the Soviet search for allies in China. With the petering out of the German revolution and the stabilisation of European governments, the danger for the Soviets was that the same would happen on their eastern front. They first hoped to use Wu Peifu as the main pillar in an alliance involving the Nationalists as well as the Communists. Because of Wu's opposition to Soviet expansionism, his bad relations with Sun, and Feng Yuxiang's coup against him, that strategy had to be abandoned. The Soviet's then stepped up aid to both Feng Yuxiang and the Nationalists. But the importance of the Soviet Union can be overplayed. It was the Nationalists themselves who sought to mobilise their society against imperialism and warlordism.

I have suggested that the lack of a cohesive international order, a rapidly growing opium trade, and the arms trade were factors conducive to the rise of warlordism. More fundamental were China's fiscal system, the huge indemnities imposed on China, and the large size of the country, which made it both difficult and risky to raise large armies against imperialist challengers who competed for influence in China in the late nineteenth century. Even if the warlords, as a group, have been excessively demonised in history, any rehabilitation of the warlords should not go so far as to ignore the damage that the fragmented, ill-disciplined, and resource-hungry warlords inflicted on Chinese society. They disrupted economic, financial, and social institutions and their involvement in the opium trade fostered the spread of gangs and secret societies. They often brought a modicum of stability to their regions, built up new bureaucratic structures, and promoted economic enterprise. But their rule was harsh and their competition for national power brought misery.

In analysing the growth of the NRA itself, I have stressed the operation of a military–fiscal cycle. Fiscal shortages drove the need to strengthen the military while military weakness necessitated the extension of the Nationalists resource base. Virtually continuous warfare increased the necessity to accumulate financial resources. The aims were to gain the means with which to carry out a national revolution and to demonstrate that Chinese could be just as disciplined, efficient, vigorous, competent, rational, and martial as Westerners.

It is clear that despite the very rapid expansion of the NRA and the increased Nationalists' ability to tax Guangdong, their base was never secure. It was repeatedly buffeted by attacks from armies, which the Nationalists first had co-opted but then turned against them. Financial resources were strained while the NRA was never a unified army but one in which a host of conflicting interests could at any moment break out into hostilities. The contradictions between the various constituencies of the Nationalists – Overseas Chinese, commercial elites, workers, peasants, some militarists, and even some landlords – too proved difficult to reconcile and bring together into a cohesive political order.

3 Cultures of violence during the Northern Expedition (1926–8)

The Northern Expedition has spawned a sizeable literature, including some of the best writing on modern China, combining meticulous research with elegant prose and strong convictions about important issues. English accounts have written about the Northern Expedition as a revolutionary movement, which began with the May Thirtieth Movement of 1925, entered into a decisive phase when the NRA set off from Guangdong in July 1926, and reached a disastrous end in the spring of 1927 when two centres of power in the KMT competed for supremacy and when the Nationalists unleashed a White Terror in which many thousands of Communists and tens of thousands of others died. Who was to blame for this end to what many believed could have been a successful revolution became an important concern.[1]

Martin Wilbur, who with Julie How compiled important collections of sources on the National Government, the Soviets, and the Northern Expedition from materials obtained in the famous raid on the Soviet Embassy by the Manchurian warlord Zhang Zuolin on 6 April 1927,[2] described the events as a 'national revolution', which 'succeeded because of a remarkable mobilization of human energy and material resources in the service of patriotic and revolutionary goals'. According to Wilbur, the Northern Expedition 'combined military prowess, effective propaganda, and subversive activity in the enemy's rear', but ended in 'tragedy' when 'the leadership split over the issue of violent social revolution'.[3] Wilbur's work remains the most thorough study to date.[4]

This chapter suggests that the Northern Expedition certainly was the product of a remarkable effort at mobilising Chinese nationalism but also that it is limiting to see the Northern Expedition as a second fall from revolutionary grace. There is no doubt that the hopes of revolution, its romantic *élan*, its templates for action, and its analytical terminologies were influential, and not just among the Communists. The Northern Expedition cannot be understood if one ignores the call of revolutionary imaginings of a new future. Yet, the Northern Expedition was also shaped by military developments elsewhere, financial and military stresses in Guangdong, and criss-crossing internal rivalries. The forces associated with the Northern Expedition were deeply divided amongst themselves and each tried to establish their dominion over events by accumulating military force, establishing new military and financial bases, and developing new sources of symbolic and social power. Many reached for increasingly unorthodox and brutally violent measures.

When the Northern Expedition finally took Beijing in 1928, the result would not be, as Arthur Waldron argued, 'the assumption of control by the Guomindang with its new and stable political and military institutions'.[5] Instead, new military groupings had established new bases, the already demoralised bureaucracy lay in ruins, and the barriers that had contained violence had crumbled. Paranoia, intrigue, murder, and brutality had become common. The harvest of the Northern Expedition was the entrenchment of nasty cultures of violence.

The 20 March Incident

The Northern Expedition began formally on 9 July 1926. That day NRA forces were participating in an oath swearing ceremony in Canton.[6] Chiang Kaishek announced that same day that he had accepted appointment as Commander-in-Chief of the NRA.[7] However, we must begin our investigations with the 20 March Incident of that year. On that day, Chiang Kaishek arrested the acting head of the NRA's Naval Bureau, Li Zhilong; placed Canton under martial law; and disarmed guards at residences of the Soviet advisors and the offices of the Canton–Hong Kong Strike Committee, which had led a blockade against Hong Kong since June 1925. A part of the nation-wide protests and actions that broke out following the May Thirtieth Massacre in Shanghai, it made life in Hong Kong difficult but also placed great financial strain on the National Government because it had to support the strikers.[8]

The Incident is of great importance. It is likely that the Northern Expedition would never have taken place had Chiang not acted and demanded as his price for continued co-operation the go-ahead of the Expedition. Beforehand, many of the top leaders in Canton, including the Soviets, had argued for postponement. The Incident solidified divisions within the KMT, including between Chiang Kaishek and Wang Jingwei. It also split the Communists about the issue of how to respond to it. It became an iconic moment; subsequent events, including during the Northern Expedition, were interpreted through lenses coloured by the fears, paranoias, anxieties, and hatreds it generated.

Sun Yatsen's death and the crisis of leadership

While a variety of factors went into the gestation of an atmosphere of intense distrust, Sun's death was an important factor as it left the Communist–Nationalist United Front without any figure around whom to unite. Given that Sun too had faced a series of mutinies during his lifetime, it is by no means clear that had he lived, his persona would have been able to keep the various constituencies of the Nationalist–Communist United Front together. But, most revolutions in their violent phase have thrown up a charismatic figure, needed precisely because revolution destroys regular institutions. No other obvious candidate for this role was present.

Wang Jingwei made a powerful bid to take over Sun's mantle of leadership. On 1 July 1925, at the time of the formal establishment of the National Government, he was elected chair of the National Government Council and its Standing Committee. He also was the chair of the KMT's Central Political Council and the MAC. In June, just before the establishment of the National Government and Wang's inauguration, a KMT statement had been remarkably frank about the impact of Sun's death on its own cohesion:

> Following the death of our leader, the KMT with a sincere and firm resolution accepted his Last Testament to complete the national revolution. We carefully considered government re-organisation, and decided to adopt a system of joint deliberation. But elements plotting our overthrow were hidden everywhere and day and night they looked for opportunities. If we had given them power, it would have been no different than giving arms to our enemies and help them rebel. ... Now, internal rebels in the government have been completely eliminated and we can shoulder our tasks united in mind and heart.[9]

The author of this statement was Hu Hanmin – the man implicated in the assassination of Liao Zhongkai in August 1925.[10] Liao's death and Hu's departure removed two important challengers in Canton to Wang's position. Wang had emerged as Sun's successor when as a member of Sun's entourage in Beijing he had prevailed on Sun to sign a testament he had written and even more so when he had taken charge of an audacious ritual move by turning Sun's burial into a huge mass event in support of the KMT and opposed to Duan Qirui, Zhang Zuolin, and other warlords in north China.[11] He could do so because Feng Yuxiang's troops held the capital in their grip and, one suspects, because the Soviets supported an alliance between Feng Yuxiang and the Nationalists in opposition to Zhang Zuolin. However, Wang's ritual coup provoked resistance among the Nationalists. On 23 November 1925, Right-wing KMT leaders, including eleven Central Executive Committee and three Central Supervisory Committee members, gathered around Sun's body, which had been given a temporary resting place in the Western Hills near Beijing. Following this attempt to partake of Sun's aura and display their loyalty to him, the Western Hills faction convened as a Central Executive Committee Plenum.[12] While not entirely quorate, the numbers were, nonetheless, large enough for this gathering to amount to a serious challenge to Wang Jingwei who by then was back in Canton. The meeting demanded the dismissal of Borodin, the impeachment of Wang Jingwei, the transfer of the Central Executive Committee to Shanghai, an end to dual-party membership for CCP members, and the convocation of a new KMT Congress.

Such a Congress would be an opportunity to re-adjust the leadership. The Canton KMT therefore decided to convene a Second Congress first in Canton. At the conference, Wang Jingwei reported how he had been at Sun's bedside in Beijing, took care of him, acted on his behalf, and had discussed with Sun's entourage the need for Sun to indicate his will to the party. He had drafted various papers together with an Emergency Political Council in which Michael Borodin was involved, he had discussed them with Sun, and finally, as Sun's death approached, convinced him to sanction them.[13] Thus were born Sun's *Political Testament*, a *Letter of Farewell*, and a private testament, which bequeathed all of Sun's earthly belongings to his wife Song Qingling.[14] Sun's testament included the phrase 'we must rouse the popular masses and unite with the peoples of the world that treat us on an equal footing' and expressed the hope that 'the day may soon dawn when the USSR will greet, as a friend and ally, a strong and independent

China'.[15] During another conference speech, Wang argued that Sun's 'testament was his last words to us and form the spirit which he wanted us to continue'.[16]

The suggestion was that Wang, rather than the Western Hill's faction, was Sun's most trusted disciple who had been anointed by Sun as his successor and who faithfully carried out the path indicated by him. The Soviets could not but be pleased by these developments, and probably were involved in all these events behind the scenes. The Congress duly confirmed Wang Jingwei in his positions and approved his policies.[17] Song Qingling added lustre to Wang's claims by announcing that 'I am much consoled by the fact that political and militarily progress has been impressive. These are now implemented even better than when my husband was alive'.[18]

Despite this important symbolic victory, Wang's position remained fragile in Canton as much as in the broader KMT, especially because he lacked a military base. He moved quickly to address this problem. On 7 January 1926, according to the MAC minutes, Wang Jingwei re-arranged the order of battle of the NRA, removing Chiang Kaishek from command over the 1st Army that had conquered the East River Area. The MAC under Wang's chairmanship took direct control over the 2nd and 20th divisions, one of which garrisoned Canton.[19] Within the NRA, the Soviet Military Advisor General N. V. Kuibishev, who used the pseudonym Kisanka – Pussycat – and was head of the military group of Soviet advisors, became increasingly influential. He arrived in October 1925 and was the driving force behind the creation of centralised institutions to control the NRA and for increasing the influence of political commissars in its armies.[20] A report likely drafted by him or on his orders noted that General Rogachev, a member of the Soviet group in Canton, 'acts, in reality, as the Chief of the General Staff' of the MAC while 'our instructors were, in fact, at the head of' all General Staff departments.[21]

Kuibishev described Chiang Kaishek as a 'communist, but looking deeply at his convictions, one sees that he belongs to typical "intelligentsia" of the radical kind, after the pattern of the French Jacobins. Theoretically he is strong enough in military science, but on account of his irresoluteness, could not have obtained much success as leader of troops without the aid of our instructors. He is so connected with us that the possibility of a rupture on his part can hardly be admitted'.[22] He could hardly have been more wrong.

For Wang Jingwei, through whom the Soviets clearly had decided to work, the deployment of the Soviets and Communists was a useful device to increase his influence over the military forces that made up the NRA. Zhou Enlai, who would become the most powerful man in the CCP after Mao Zedong, became the political commissar of the 1st Army in the East River Area.[23] In the 1st Army, 69 political commissars and 37 officers were Communists, and the total in the NRA was 227.[24]

Wang Jingwei also brought in new domestic allies. On 26 January, Wang met Li Zongren and Bai Chongxi, the leaders of the Guangxi Clique who had established control over Guangxi. Subsequent negotiations led to the incorporation of their forces into the NRA.[25] Wang also formed an alliance with Tang Shengzhi, a Hunan militarist, on 24 February 1926.[26]

Wang Jingwei, in short, had moved rapidly to expand his control of the National Government. He had removed his most important political opponents, brought in new allies with strong military and financial resources, and increased his control of the KMT and the NRA by strengthening Soviet and Communist influence. Such steps could not but generate opposition among military forces already gathered in Guangdong, local business and commercial elites, KMT members in Canton and across the country, and of course those who themselves had aspirations to succeed Sun.

The problem of the Northern Expedition

Chiang Kaishek was one of those whose position declined as a result of Wang's steps. Because he had built up the NRA, defended the Canton base against Chen Jiongming, and then led the NRA in unifying Guangdong, this was difficult for him to accept. Chiang turned the issue of whether to begin a Northern Expedition – something that manifestly had always been close to Sun's heart – into a major issue. On 30 January, an internal publication of the Guangdong Maritime Customs House, *Canton Events and Current Rumours*, reported that a 'private source' had stated that on 30 January, Chiang Kaishek had decided to begin the Northern Expedition after the Spring Festival.[27] In February, Chiang Kaishek formally proposed 'a plan for an early Northern Expedition in order to aid [Feng Yuxiang's] North-west National Army'.[28]

Soviet advisors, including General Kuibishev, did not agree with Chiang Kaishek's call for an early Northern Expedition, and on 13 March, the two had a row about the issue.[29] One reason was the deterioration of Feng Yuxiang's position in north China. The Soviets had built up Feng and provided him with a large amount of materiel and a significant number of advisors. Dan Jacobs suggests that after Sun Yatsen's death, the Soviets had entertained the idea of promoting Feng as Sun Yatsen's successor, something which, if true, must have been a worry for Wang Jingwei.[30] Throughout 1925, Feng had worked hard to build up a base in Beijing, Suiyuan, and Chahar, while also absorbing defeated units of Wu Peifu's armies in Henan and Anhui.[31] However, in December, Feng suffered heavy casualties during a campaign to capture Tianjin. On 23 December, furthermore, a revolt involving 50,000 men against Zhang Zuolin by Guo Songling, a member of a younger generation of commanders in Zhang's army, was defeated decisively near Shenyang.[32] Had Guo Songling been successful, Feng Yuxiang would have been in a strong position to take all of north China and emerge as China's supreme leader. However, following the collapse of Guo Songling's attempt to take the north-east, Wu Peifu and Zhang Zuolin joined forces in a campaign to drive Feng, who had closely co-operated with Guo, from Zhili, the province in which Beijing is located and which subsequently became known as Hebei. Knowing when a battle could not be won, on 1 January 1926, Feng announced his 'retirement' and took up residence in Kalgan, the capital of Suiyuan Province north-west of Beijing. In March, his allies in Henan were routed by Wu Peifu while Zhang Zuolin pressed into Zhili Province and defeated forces of Feng's still at Tianjin. Feng first withdrew these to Beijing but on 16 April abandoned the capital as well. His most forward troops were then at Nankou, the pass in the Great Wall to Suiyuan Province.[33] Rather than a military situation ripe for a *coup-de-grâce* by the combined militaries of Feng and Canton, in the spring of 1926, a powerful new alliance between Zhang Zuolin and Wu Peifu threatened to establish its dominance.

In February 1926, Moscow sent a secret investigative delegation to China to determine the future of its course in China. Borodin joined its deliberations in Beijing.[34] There the Soviet delegation and Borodin witnessed the suppression on 18 March of a student protest in Tian'anmen Square against a Western ultimatum that insisted that all fortifications and troops be withdrawn from the Dagu forts in accordance with the Boxer Protocol. Communist and Nationalist organisers of the protest went into hiding, while Borodin and other Soviets had to make an ignominious withdrawal through Suiyuan. On 6 April, Zhang Zuolin, who by then had taken control of the city, raided the Soviet embassy.[35]

Russian reports from the spring of 1926 furthermore were not optimistic about the NRA's military strength. A March 1926 report was dismissive of the NRA and its fighting capacity, noting that the logistical system was virtually non-existent and that arms and ammunition were in short supply.[36] Kuibishev argued that despite very significant improvements, staff officers were not yet accepted, no central logistical system existed, and that the quality of officers was low.[37] NRA tactics, he wrote, remained those that German and Japanese armies used in the late nineteenth century. According to Kuibishev, only 30 per cent of the NRA's machine guns were usable and no ammunition was available for 50 per cent of the available rifles, which he believed were short of requirements by 20,000 in any case. One Soviet report of March 1926 stated that 'training must be considerably improved' before the NRA could take on 'the better prepared armies of central and north China'.[38]

Chiang Kaishek became increasingly concerned with Wang Jingwei's apparent subservience to the Soviets and with the *lèse majesté* of the abandonment of the Northern Expedition, which he saw as his historical mission to deliver. In a letter to Wang Jingwei after the 20 March Incident, Chiang stated that after he had returned to Canton from his victory over Chen Jiongming in the East River Area, Wang first had agreed to his proposal for a Northern Expedition. According to Chiang, Wang 'approved wholeheartedly and to show your resolution, you allocated funds. However, when Kuibishev opposed, you changed your attitude, and the proposal for the Northern Expedition was cancelled, so that we lost our opportunity'.[39] If not all Chinese Communists, those associated with Chen Duxiu, the CCP leader, also were opposed to the Soviet decision to abandon the Northern Expedition. According to Chen, if Feng Yuxiang was abandoned and he lost his position in north China, 'the Canton government could hardly continue to exist'.[40]

Chiang Kaishek's entries for this period in his diary, no doubt perfected in the editing, suggest a man who had become deeply hurt by the haughty attitude of Soviet advisors and who had convinced himself that the fate of China now rested on his shoulders. On 19 January, he wrote with reference to Kuibishev and Rogachev that 'I treat them with sincerity, but they reward me with duplicity. These are not comrades with whom I can work'.[41] He noted also that many Soviets 'have doubts about me and insult me. I can only deal with them on the basis of sincerity, in the hope that they will change their minds'.[42] On 7 February, he lamented that 'when Kuibishev talks about the political situation and military organisation with me, his words are often scathing and it seems that he has not faith in me. China's society and atmosphere can be compared to Turkey's, and China's military is corrupt. I am afraid that I will grow into a warlord and am thinking of resigning all my posts'.[43] Four days later he wrote 'The situation is extremely dangerous. No revolution will happen if we do not take drastic action to break through this difficult impasse. If not, I have to muddle on and lighten my responsibilities as a way of resigning. Yet, to protect the party and safeguard the nation, I must bear insults and shoulder heavy burdens. To advance and retreat, to move forward and backward, isn't that what a revolutionary does?'[44]

After attending a banquet on 22 February, held by the Soviets who at the occasion argued for the postponement of the Northern Expedition,[45] Chiang went to Wang Jingwei to argue that 'Kuibishev's tyrannical behaviour means that if he is not dismissed, it will not only harm our Party but also influence Sino-Soviet relations. He acts on his own; it is not the idea of Soviet authorities'.[46] Expressing a sense of isolation, he wrote on 5 March that 'My situation now is that of somebody who faces tigers and wolves on all sides single-handedly. I am completely without support. Please let the souls of Sun and the late revolutionary martyrs in Heaven take pity on me, support me, and not let me end up in a hopeless situation'.[47] His doubts reached such a pitch that on 15 March he wrote 'I have enemies everywhere. All I can do is fight a decisive battle and seek life in death'.[48]

With the Guangdong base under financial strain and the commitment of several NRA armies to the Canton Government in question, Chiang may have thought, like Chen Duxiu, that the survival of the Canton Government was in doubt if nothing was done to support Feng Yuxiang. Wu Peifu was already building up his influence in south China. In February 1926, the death of one warlord in Hubei, who had been allied with Wu, allowed Wu to acquire the plentiful resources of Hubei province. These he used to support the efforts of Zhao Hengti to re-enter Hunan Province. Wu also allied himself with Sun Chuanfang in the Lower Yangtze region. Together they secured the removal of the military governor of Jiangxi who had maintained an accommodation with the National Government.[49]

Chiang's apprehensions could have only been worsened by the efforts of Wang Jingwei and the Soviets to reduce his role in the NRA. Wang Jingwei not only removed Chiang as commander of the 1st Army. Perhaps to test Wang Jingwei's commitment to him, on 9 February, Chiang offered his resignation as member of the MAC and Garrison Commander of Canton and only asked to keep his position as head of the Whampoa Academy and member of the KMT Central Political Counsel, to which he had been elected in January at the Second Congress.[50] On 3 March, the National Government accepted his resignation as Canton Garrison Commander.[51] Chiang publicly explained the change as the logical conclusion of the unification of Canton and the consolidation of order.[52] Chiang's letter to Wang Jingwei following the 20 March Incident suggests that Chiang in reality interpreted these actions, and Wang's reduction of financial assistance to the 1st Army and the Whampoa Academy, as efforts to undermine him.[53]

It should be stressed that these were times of great insecurity. *Canton Events and Current Rumours* recorded all kinds of stories about Chiang Kaishek, the Northern Expedition, Wang Jingwei, and the Soviets. On 10 February, for instance, it reported that Hu Hanmin had left Moscow and would soon return.[54] On 5 March, it said, 'rumours' circulated of 'differences of opinion between Chiang Kaishek and other government leaders, and that Chiang was preparing to leave Canton'.[55] On 11 March, there were rumours that Chiang Kaishek and the Cantonese General Li Jishen, appointed head of the NRA Staff Department on 25 February,[56] had fallen out and that 'the government had ordered an investigation as well as punishment of who had fabricated these rumours'.[57] In the week before the March 20 Incident, the Guangdong Customs Office reported on further rumours of the Guangdong Army preparing to 'oppose the

Revolutionary Army under Chiang Kaishek'. Anti-Chiang fliers had been sent around by the post office and there were indications of Right-wing KMT members preparing for a coup.[58] Chiang mentioned in his diary the distribution of leaflets against him, as well as the fact that he had been frightened when he learned that the British were spying on him.[59]

The possibility of a Right-wing plot seems to have been taken seriously. On 18 March, the National Government proscribed meetings of the Western Hills faction and on 6 April arrest orders were issued for its most prominent members.[60] Fears for a KMT Right-wing coup were increased by the growing activity in Guangdong, including at the Whampoa Military Academy, of the Sun Yatsen-ism Study Society, which had links to the Western Hills faction, and which in the NRA vied for influence with the Young Soldiers Association.[61] In February, it was preparing for an armed march through the city.[62]

Many other incidents fuelled suspicions and tensions. Gao Yuhan, a Chinese Communist at the Whampoa Academy, had called for the ouster of the 'southern Duan Qirui' before attacking the one in the north.[63] This probably was a reference to Chiang Kaishek who had links in Japan where he had attended Japan's most prestigious military academy. Chiang stated in his letter to Wang that he had also been infuriated by Wang's address to the Sun Yatsen-ism Study Society. Wang had stated that before the Turkish Revolution had been completed, Turkish communists had been killed. Wang had asked whether the same was going to happen in the Chinese case. According to Chiang Kaishek, this sowed discord between officers in the NRA and the Communists.[64] The officers in the NRA had been 'astonished', according to Chiang, as this was 'no different than inciting the members of the NRA and the Whampoa Academy to kill each other'.[65]

Chiang first took action when on 26 February he dismissed Wang Maogong, the commander of the 2nd Division of the 1st Army and acting Garrison Commander, which, according to Chiang, 'had shocked Kuibishev, as now his plan to use Wang had been derailed and he will not succeed in overthrowing the revolutionary force of our Party'.[66] Behind this was the decision to incorporate the Guangxi Clique forces as the 8th and 9th NRA Armies. Given that this left a 7th Army, which did not yet exist, Chiang suspected that Kuibishev and Wang Jingwei were about to appoint Wang as head of a new 7th Army, thus reducing his own power and position further. Chiang replaced Wang with a loyal follower.[67] Wang Maogong himself argued that he had prohibited a march by the Sun Yatsen-ism Study Society out of concern for local order and that one of its members then spread the rumour that he was a Communist.[68] The next day, Chiang Kaishek asked Wang Jingwei for Kuibishev's dismissal. These steps seem to have quieted some of Chiang's tensions. He noted in his diary that 'my will has become settled and for the first time I slept peacefully'.[69]

The 20 March Incident

The 20 March Incident was triggered by the sudden appearance of the SS Zhongshan, the most powerful gunboat in the NRA Navy, at Whampoa on the night of 18 March. According to Communist orthodoxy, the incident was manufactured by Chiang Kaishek, who by falsely accusing Communists of being behind the unauthorised journey of the Zhongshan from Canton to Whampoa gained the pretext to declare martial law. Nationalist orthodoxy, on the other hand, has maintained that Li Zhilong, a Communist and the acting head of the NRA Naval Office as well as acting captain of the Zhongshan, ordered the Zhongshan to Whampoa to take in the coal prior to kidnapping Chiang and removing him to Vladivostok.[70]

An incisive article by Yang Tianshi of the Chinese Academy of Social Sciences in Beijing has put forward a new interpretation.[71] According to Yang, there was no plot by either Chiang Kaishek or the CCP: the Incident was triggered by a series of miscommunications and misunderstandings, not helped by faulty telephone connections; officers and officials being away from their offices for one reason or the other; and by ambitious juniors scheming to undo rivals and issuing orders in the name of their superiors. According to Yang, if the Incident itself was unplanned, it nonetheless was made virtually inevitable by Chiang Kaishek's increasing suspicions, fed by Right-wing KMT members, about Wang Jingwei's close co-operation with the Soviets.

The journal *Minguo Dang'an* (Republican Archives) recently published telephone log-books, telegrams, letters, and testimonies made by those involved in the days after the Incident during investigations.[72] These materials are contained in Chiang Kaishek's Personal Files held at the Second Historical Archives in Nanjing and which Mao Sicheng used in compiling Chiang Kaishek's Chronological History. Let me summarise here what the evidence suggests. Ouyang Zhong was the head of the Transport Office of the Whampoa Academy as well as of the Whampoa Academy's Canton Office. According to Ouyang Zhong's report shortly after the Incident, in Canton his subordinate had received a telephone call from Whampoa stating that Deng Yenda, the Head of Education at the Whampoa Academy, had requested two vessels for the Whampoa Academy. Ouyang Zhong went to the Naval Office, but found Li Zhilong absent. The head of the War Office of the Naval Office then approved an order for two vessels to be sent, without making clear which ones they should be.[73] Testimony from Li Shiyong, who made the call from the Whampoa Academy to Canton, stated that a request for vessels from Canton had been made because a ship at Whampoa had been dispatched to protect a steamer that had been attacked by pirates.[74] In Canton, Ouyang Zhong's subordinate, Wang Xuechen, had received this call. He declared in his testimony that because the telephone line had been faulty, he had not understood who had given the order, but that he assumed it had come from Deng Yenda. He then reported to Ouyang Zhong.[75]

Li Zhilong himself stated in his testimony that he had decided to send the Zhongshan, because Ouyang Zhong had told him that a telephone call had been received from Deng Yenda, which stated that Chiang Kaishek had requested the immediate dispatch of two vessels. Only two were available, of which the Zhongshan was one. He had originally hesitated to dispatch the vessels without a formal written order, but had done so because, as a graduate of the first class of the Whampoa Academy and a loyal servant of Chiang Kaishek and Deng Yenda, he feared that if something untoward had happened at Whampoa, he could not risk not sending a vessel. When he then had learned that no order had been given, he had instructed the Zhongshan to return to Canton.[76] He furthermore stated that

> Although Ouyang Ge [the Vice-Director of the Naval Academy] and I were not on bad terms, I did know that he had hoped to become head of the Naval Bureau and Captain of the Zhongshan. Chairman Wang Jingwei stated that several persons nourished ambitions for these posts, and so the Government decided not

to appoint them and for the time being appointed me as acting head of the Naval Bureau, the Naval Staff Office, and Captain of the Zhongshan. Last Sunday, the Vice-Captain of the Zhongshan, Zhang Chentong, reported that he feared that Ouyang Ge would seize the Zhongshan. I reported this to Chairman Wang, who appointed Zhang acting captain and ordered two platoons of the Second Division to guard it. After Ouyang's plot was defeated, he sought to set a trap for me.[77]

This evidence, then, suggests that an effort by Ouyang Ge to fulfil his ambitions and prevent Wang Jingwei and Li Zhilong from capturing control over the Zhongshan were behind the strange movements of the Zhongshan that triggered Chiang Kaishek's imposition of martial law.

In a report of 23 March to the MAC, Chiang Kaishek stated that his suspicion had been aroused when he learned that the Zhongshan had sailed to Whampoa and that its commander had told Deng Yenda that he had acted on an order of Chiang Kaishek himself. Because he had not given this order and because the vessel then had sailed back to Canton, Chiang went on, 'I became aware of preparations for a rebellion and for bringing harm to myself' and therefore 'I acted immediately. I ordered Ouyang Ge … to take charge temporarily of the Navy, arrested Li Zhilong for questioning, and ordered troops to place Canton under martial law to prevent disturbances'.[78]

Chiang had hesitated before acting. On the 19th, after his suspicions were increased by telephone calls from Wang Jingwei and his wife asking about his whereabouts, he had first decided to return to the East River Area, where his most reliable forces were located. He had already purchased a ticket for a Japanese steamer that night to Shantou. He may have considered that this was the one area where he could be safe, although Communists too had begun to be active there. In Canton, Wang Jingwei and the Communists had built up influence in the Whampoa Academy itself; Zhu De, the future leader of the Red Army, had a force there; and Zhu Peide, of the Guangxi Clique, too would naturally be more sympathetic to them. In addition, if the Communists and Wang would establish control over the navy, Chiang would have few allies left in Canton. Rather than fleeing, however, Chiang decided to act.[79]

No 'smoking gun' document, then, exists to prove that the Incident was a plot by the Soviets or the Chinese Communists or that Chiang Kaishek engineered the whole Incident. Whether anyone told the truth in their testimonies is not certain. All naturally denied personal responsibility for the Incident. The testimonies may have been part of an attempt to prevent the situation from spiralling out of control. After the Incident, which took place while Borodin was in Beijing, Chiang Kaishek and A. S. Bubnov, the head of a Soviet delegation visiting Canton, decided to find a basis for continued co-operation. Both sides needed each other, the Soviets because they could not afford to lose another ally now that Feng Yuxiang's position had become fragile and Chiang Kaishek because he needed Soviet military aid, advice, and their support in the north if the Northern Expedition was to have any chance of success. The Soviets agreed to Chiang Kaishek's terms for a settlement, which included the departure of Kuibishev, an end to Communists holding top ministerial positions, and the submission of a list of all CCP members in the KMT.[80] On 3 April, Chiang Kaishek stated in a public telegram that the Incident was an 'individual and limited matter' involving 'a small number of members of our Party who had carried out an anti-revolutionary plot'.[81]

If some questions remain, it does seem clear, first, that the relation between Chiang and Wang was critical and that this worsened because Chiang objected to the growth of Soviet influence that Wang accepted. Chiang was also unhappy with Wang because he did not treat him as a trusted supporter whose advice was heeded. Whereas Sun had made Chiang feel valued, Wang had done the opposite. On 9 April, Chiang wrote a lengthy and emotional letter to Wang Jingwei.[82] He began by writing that he had respected Wang Jingwei greatly as a revolutionary elder. He stated that he had always been sincere with him and had remained loyal to him as Sun's successor, even when he believed that Wang was being misled by Soviet advisors. According to Chiang, after he and Kuibishev had clashed about the idea of the Northern Expedition, Kuibishev had suggested that Chiang go to the Soviet Union for recuperation. According to Chiang, Kuibishev's aim was to reduce 'the strength of our party', but, according to Chiang, Wang 'did not see through this, and even agreed with and supported his suggestion'.[83] Chiang Kaishek then, he wrote, had offered to resign from all his posts, but Wang had refused, placing him in the impossible situation where he could not do anything but still would be held responsible. Chiang too stated that he had been deeply angry at Wang because of his failure to support the NRA financially. He maintained that he had acted because he believed that the Soviets had decided to abandon the Northern Expedition and hence had turned against the call in Sun Yatsen's testament to continue the revolution. He stated that he had explained all this to Wang, but that Wang had failed to listen.[84]

Furthermore, although Chiang maintained that he acted in response to a sudden crisis, and although he decided to impose martial law rather than leave Canton at the last moment, his diary suggests to the extent that it is reliable that he had prepared himself mentally for something drastic. It is also clear that once he acted, he did so with deliberation, purpose, and caution. Throughout the Incident, he was careful not to accuse the CCP as a whole, he did not call the United Front into question, and did not demand the withdrawal of all Soviets but only of Kuibishev. He quickly released Communist prisoners, lifted martial law, moved against Right-wing KMT members, and forbade Right-wing demonstrations.

Finally, a tense situation existed in which the movements of the Zhongshan could be taken as evidence of a plot and trigger extreme reactions. A whole series of events and incidents gave rise to deep suspicions: mutinies and assassinations had happened in Canton; Hu Hanmin had been taken to the Soviet Union; rancour and ill-feeling had built up between Kuibishev and Chiang; the latter may have demanded that Chiang leave Canton; and Wang had clipped Chiang's wings. With rumours swirling around, with the national military situation poised on a knife-edge, and with the Northern Expedition in doubt, on which so much would depend and in which Chiang had invested much personal prestige, it is not strange that unexpected movements aroused dark thoughts and grave suspicions, and were seized upon to force through radical changes.

The 20 March Incident would have many long-term consequences, but of immediate significance was Wang Jingwei's decision, made public on 7 April, to resign his posts and go abroad. After polite attempts to persuade him otherwise, a week later Tan Yankai was appointed head of the Political Council of the KMT and Chiang of the MAC.[85] These steps did not have the endorsement of a KMT Congress and hence enjoyed weak legitimacy. When the Northern Expedition began, the groups that supported it were already deeply divided among themselves. This was not an auspicious beginning.

The first phase of the Northern Expedition (July 1926–March 1927)

On the eve of the Northern Expedition, the NRA consisted of the following seven armies with a total of perhaps 100,000 troops.[86] The 1st Army, with five divisions made up of the former Party Army, was commanded by He Yingqin and with 20,000 reasonably trained and armed troops was regarded as the strongest. The 2nd Army of Tan Yankai consisted of Hunanese forces. The 3rd Army of Zhu Peide had three divisions with troops from Jiangxi and Guangxi. Li Jishen commanded the 4th Army of four Guangdong-ese divisions. Li Fulin's 5th Army was made up of local Guangdong militia, while Cheng Qian's 6th Army consisted of Wu Tiecheng's Gendarmery and troops from Jiangxi. Li Zongren's four Guangxi regiments made up the 7th Army, while Tang Shengzhi's Hunan forces, which formally joined only after the beginning of the Northern Expedition, constituted the 8th Army.[87]

The NRA was not a unified army subject to the will of a single state or a single party. It was a loose alliance of military interest groups that were often not well integrated internally. As they set out on the Northern Expedition, their actions aimed not simply at the defeat of a common enemy, but also at seeking new territories for recruitment and fundraising and for successes on the battlefield with which to increase their own political power and diminish those of their competitors. As an instrument to get a revolutionary job done, the NRA was imperfect at best.

To make matters more complicated, the Nationalists, the Communists, and the Soviets were all divided among themselves and sought to use developments on the battlefields and political events to weaken their internal rivals and capture control over the Northern Expedition. Such rivalries were played out in a heightened atmosphere when revolutionary triumph seemed within reach at the same time that imaginations were gripped by fears of the loss of a great opportunity to put China on the right course and by deep suspicions about the ultimate aims and motivations of comrades in arms.

Some aspects of these conflicts, including the Wuhan–Nanchang split and the military events of the first few months of the Northern Expedition have been discussed at length before. The next section will survey these briefly. Less well known are the efforts of Chen Duxiu, the leader of the Chinese Communists, to bring about radical peasant and labour movements and build up the KMT Left-wing. This was his strategy to prevent a Chiang Kaishek victory and bring about revolution. It brought him into conflict with Borodin and his supporters among the Chinese Communists. Further sections will detail how the Northern Expedition gave way to the spread of devastating violence and ultimately the victory of Chiang Kaishek.

The NRA's capture of Wuhan and Nanchang

The first phase of the Northern Expedition lasted from July 1926 to April 1927 when the NRA took Nanjing and Shanghai. The strategy for the Northern Expedition had been drawn up by Chiang Kaishek, who became Commander-in-Chief, Li Jishen,

Chiang's Chief-of-Staff, and General Bliukher, who had returned to Canton in May 1926 after an absence of a year following disagreements with Borodin. On 23 June, they had agreed that the Northern Expedition would first attack Hunan and occupy Wuhan and then seek to link up with Feng Yuxiang.[88]

At this time, Tang Shengzhi's Hunan forces were already engaged in a battle with Wu Peifu's Hunan ally, Zhao Hengti. Tang, who professed Buddhist leanings, had been a subordinate of Zhao, but in March 1926, had rebelled and taken Changsha, the capital of Hunan Province. With the help of Wu Peifu, Zhao had then driven Tang back to the south of the province, after which Tang had appealed for help from Canton. When Wu Peifu then turned his armies north to confront Feng Yuxiang and the forces of Li Jishen and Li Zongren moved into southern Hunan in early July, Tang himself advanced towards Changsha, which he retook on 11 July.[89] On 30 July, Tang organised a Hunan provincial government and assumed the post of provincial chairman and military commissioner.[90] In some ways, the NRA always played catch-up to military developments elsewhere in China.

Following his appointment as Commander-in-Chief, on 27 July, Chiang Kaishek left Canton to establish a Headquarters at the front. Following an arduous journey to Changsha, he arrived on 11 August and called a military conference there. This conference affirmed the correctness of the strategy of an immediate advance on Wuhan. Tang Shengzhi was placed in command of the Central Army made up of the 4th Army of Li Jishen, the 7th of Li Zongren, and the 8th of Tang himself. The 3rd Army under Zhu Peide protected the right flank from a possible attack by the forces of Sun Chuanfang through Jiangxi. The left flank was protected by the 9th and 10th Armies made up of Sichuan and Guizhou forces, who too found it opportune to join the NRA. Two divisions of the 1st Army, which had moved into Hunan were designated as a general reserve and watched the border with Jiangxi.[91]

Li Jishen's forces did most of the arduous fighting that opened the road to Wuhan, including at the famous battles of Dingsi Bridge, Hesheng Bridge, and Pingjiang River. Following these battles, Wu Peifu withdrew his forces in Hubei into Henan, leaving 10,000 men to defend Hankou, one part of the Wuhan tri-city well protected by the Yangtze to the south and the Han River to the west. Two NRA assaults on Wuchang, the part of Wuhan to the south of the Yangtze, in early September by the 2nd Division of the 1st Army and units of the 4th and 7th Armies failed, with especially the 4th Army suffering heavy casualties. The decision was then taken to lay siege to the city and starve it into submission.[92]

In the meantime, Tang Shengzhi crossed the Yangtze River at Yueyang to the south-west of Wuhan on 22 August. On 6 September, he took Hanyang, a second part of the Wuhan tri-city to the north of the Yangtze. Wu Peifu's forces in Hankou surrendered to Tang the next day. In a greatly strengthened position, Tang Shengzhi began to woe the Soviets, requesting that they send advisors and military aid to him. He criticised Chiang Kaishek's military and political capabilities. To Soviet advisors he expressed his hostility to Li Jishen, stating that he did not want the 4th Army to take the remaining unconquered part of Wuhan.

When Tang Shengzhi's forces entered Wuhan, Chiang Kaishek himself, on 4 September, suddenly ordered an attack on Jiangxi province, using three routes of advance from Hunan into north and central Jiangxi as well as one from Guangdong.

Besides re-deploying his own divisions, Chiang was able to convince Li Zongren's 7th Army to join him. This move was partly a response to Wu Peifu's decision to invite Sun Chuanfang to reduce NRA pressure on Wuhan by investing Jiangxi. Part of Chiang's aim, however, was also to establish his own territorial base in Jiangxi and Fujian after Tan Shengzhi threatened to take control of much of Hunan and Hubei and to prevent others from doing so themselves elsewhere. Tan Yankai of the Second Army and Cheng Qian of the Sixth had made an agreement to co-operate in a plan in which Tan would occupy Jiangxi while Chiang Kaishek's forces would be used in Hunan to resist Tang Shengzhi's expansion of power.[93] Had they succeeded, Chiang would have been left without a reliable base. The offensive into Jiangxi was accompanied by an attack by divisions of the 1st Army under He Yingqin from the East River Area into Fujian and towards Zhejiang in late September.[94]

These moves, which would radically change the course of the Northern Expedition and would prove critical to Chiang's rise to power, nearly failed. The invasion of Jiangxi initially went smoothly. On 19 September, the NRA took the provincial capital Nanchang. But, Sun Chuanfang struck back on 21 September, retaking Nanchang, occupying Jiujiang, and driving the NRA from the Jiangxi lowlands. In the next week, the 7th Army was pushed back towards Hunan, and the 1st Division of the 1st Army – Chiang's 'own' – had been badly mauled. Forces of Sun Chuanfang even sailed up the Yangtze and landed close to Wuhan to threaten the NRA there.[95] Tang Shengzhi sought to make use of these troubles to move Li Jishen's forces out of Hubei by sending them east in support of Li Zongren's 7th Army. Chiang, who needed to approve such moves as Commander-in-Chief, had initially agreed, but then reversed himself. Li Jishen's forces finally captured Wuchang on 10 October, not coincidentally on the fifteenth anniversary of the 1911 Revolution, which had begun in Wuhan.[96]

In Jiangxi, Chiang Kaishek was able to reinforce his army with the Whampoa Cadets and also now gained Tan Yankai's support. Tan had ample reason to be concerned about Tang's ascendancy in his home province. Chiang's forces were further strengthened by a new 14th Army made up of defected units of Sun Chuanfang's armies.[97] On 9 November, the NRA took Nanchang again, and this time held it.[98] In mid-November, Tang Shengzhi in contrast had suffered his first setback when his forces campaigning in eastern Hubei were defeated and suffered significant casualties.[99]

The break-out of the NRA from Guangdong had succeeded militarily far better than most people had anticipated in the spring. But during the campaign, the forces that made up the NRA had been pulled apart. The capture of Wuhan and Nanchang raised difficult questions, militarily about what to do next and politically about the division of power and authority.

Wuhan versus Nanchang

Two centres of military and political power began to take shape after the decision was made in December to move a first group of KMT and National Government officials to Wuhan. The Temporary Joint Council in Wuhan, to which Borodin was attached as Political Advisor, claimed to be the supreme political authority prior to the convocation of a new CEC meeting. Left-wing KMT figures such as Song Qingling, He Xiangning (Liao Zhongkai's widow), Eugene Chen, and Song Ziwen joined it.[100] The Temporary

Joint Council sought to strengthen its military base by seeking the support of Tang Shengzhi, Feng Yuxiang, and Li Zongren. According to Li Zongren's memoirs, in Wuhan Borodin wanted him 'to succeed Chiang as Commander-in-chief'.[101] Seeking to exploit the relative decline of Chiang Kaishek's military status, the Temporary Joint Council was an attempt by those whose position had declined as a consequence of the 20 March Incident to regain the political initiative and rebuild their military base.

These moves sidelined Chiang Kaishek. On their way to Wuhan, National Government and KMT figures did meet Chiang Kaishek, who remained the Commander-in-Chief of the Northern Expedition. Chiang was conciliatory: he welcomed them with great ceremony and argued that the Northern Expedition was part of a world revolution. He also stated that representatives from Yan Xishan in Shanxi and Zhang Zuolin in Manchuria had informed him that they were ready to join the NRA, thus suggesting his continuing importance to the Northern Expedition, although perhaps not everybody was happy to hear about these potential allies. With Feng Yuxiang at the Tongguan Pass able to make a comeback in north China if the strategic situation changed, according to Chiang, the future for the Northern Expedition was highly favourable. The meeting decided to appeal to Wang Jingwei to return to China. Chiang Kaishek proposed the elimination of the post of Chairman of the KMT. If some of Chiang's opponents welcomed that, according to Chen Duxiu, this was in fact a trap as it would mean that Wang Jingwei 'would have no post to which to return'.[102] The conferees in Nanchang further agreed not to strike north immediately, but instead attack Sun Chuanfang in the Lower Yangtze.[103] Although a sensible response to the threat of Sun Chuanfang's military, the offensive would prove to the advantage of Chiang Kaishek.

It was not unreasonable for the supporters of the Wuhan Temporary Joint Council to believe that they were in a strong position. They had the support of Song Ziwen, the Minister of Finance in charge of the National Government's treasury who at this time declined funds to Chiang Kaishek.[104] With Feng Yuxiang likely to support them, given that the Soviets had supplied him with 6 million rubbles worth of guns, cannon, aeroplanes, and ammunition, they also could believe that they had the military power to make their claim to political leadership stick.[105] The Soviets furthermore had learned from one of their spies that various units campaigning with Chiang Kaishek in the Lower Yangtze, in Fujian, and in Zhejiang were ready to join Wuhan.[106] If they could defeat Sun Chuanfang and then with Feng Yuxiang occupy the north and take Beijing, the future would be theirs.

Events would not work out in this way. In late December, Chiang asked Tan Yankai, then still in Canton, that the remaining National Government and Party Headquarters staff meet him in Nanchang on their way to Wuhan. This they did, and on 31 December, Tan Yankai as the head of the National Government and Zhang Jingjiang as the acting leader of the KMT made it known that the Party Headquarters and the National Government would remain in Nanchang and that they would convene a Central Executive Committee plenum on 1 March. Both Tan and Zhang threatened to be sidelined by the Temporary Joint Council in Wuhan. Zhang Jingjiang was a wealthy entrepreneur from Zhejiang, thus sharing common province relations with Chiang Kaishek. He had gone to Canton after the 20 March Incident to help negotiate a settlement and had become the acting head of the KMT when Chiang accepted appointment as Commander-in-Chief of the NRA.

The split between Wuhan and Nanchang quickly deepened. In Wuhan, the Temporary Joint Council decided to maintain its position and Borodin concluded that a break with Chiang Kaishek was inevitable. In January, Borodin refused an invitation to travel to Nanchang to discuss with Chiang the location of the new capital.[107] Chiang Kaishek responded by travelling to Wuhan himself where he stayed for a week from 11 to 18 January. At a welcoming banquet, Borodin insulted Chiang Kaishek publicly by telling him not to suppress mass movements.[108] He refused Chiang's suggestion that the KMT Political Council meet in Nanchang.[109] By the end of February, both sides were calling the legality of the other side publicly into question,[110] mass meetings in Wuhan denounced Chiang Kaishek, while Chiang himself sent a telegram to Wuhan demanding the recall of Borodin.[111]

Military campaigns gained a tremendous political significance. The plan to take the Lower Yangtze area went ahead, which would prove greatly to Chiang's benefit. Soviet advisors, including Bliukher, drew up the 'Memorandum on the Liquidation of the Enemy in the Area of the Lower Yangtze'.[112] The plan called for a drive towards Hangzhou, the Zhejiang provincial capital, as well as Shanghai and Nanjing in Jiangsu Province. The participating NRA forces were regrouped as three Route Armies. He Yingqin's divisions of the 1st Army made up the Eastern Route Army, which also included Guangxi forces under Bai Chongxi. These would strike from the south through Zhejiang to Hangzhou and Shanghai. Chiang Kaishek, the Commander-in-Chief, commanded the Central Route Army. Made up of two columns, it would advance along the north and south sides of the Yangtze River. Li Zongren's 7th Army divisions on the north side would aim at the Tianjin–Pukou Railroad, which would make a counter-attack by Sun Chuanfang's forces there difficult, while Cheng Qian, the Hunan militarist, would aim at Nanjing.[113] Helped by defections from Sun Chuanfang's armies, these campaigns went smoothly. On 22 March, Bai Chongxi was at Shanghai and He Yingqin had cut the Nanjing–Shanghai Railroad, a move which precipitated the defection of Sun's navy. Nanjing was taken on 23 March.[114]

With NRA forces poised to take Shanghai and so make itself master of China south of the Yangtze River, the Northern Expedition had reached a climactic and chaotic phase. The NRA had achieved great victories, but it also had become divided and problems of supply, always most difficult in the spring when stocks had run out but new harvest had not yet come in, had become acute. Politically, two competing centres of authority had emerged. Which side Feng Yuxiang would support became a critical factor. In north China, the remaining leading warlords, especially Yan Xishan and Zhang Zuolin, had to decide how to respond to the Northern Expedition.

Communist responses to weakness

In the spring of 1927, the Communists faced a difficult situation. A moment of great historical significance had emerged, yet the political situation was delicately balanced and opportunities existed to turn events in their favour. How this was to be done, however, was less obvious, and deeply divided the Chinese Communists. The 20 March Incident loomed large in considerations among the Chinese Communists about what to do next.

Borodin's strategy of seeking to establish a Communist hegemony by controlling KMT institutions and working through them has been described.[115] Borodin had the support of many CCP members who had worked with him in Canton. Chen Duxiu's strategy was very different. Fearing that the Northern Expedition could lead to a victory for 'new militarists' such as Tang Shengzhi, Chiang Kaishek, and Li Zongren, Chen supported radical labour and peasant movements, sought to arms these, and wanted to build up an independent CCP organisation. His aim was to support the KMT Left-wing of Wang Jingwei and build up a social base for it so that the fight for control over the Northern Expedition would not be seen as primarily one between the Communists and the Nationalists, but between the KMT Right-wing and the rest of the KMT. He opposed Borodin's approach, believing that it would unify the KMT against the Communists.

Chen's fear would become reality, but his own policies not only divided the CCP at a moment when it could not afford to be such, but also contributed to a KMT backlash. In late March and April, it may briefly have seemed that his policies would carry the day. Wang Jingwei returned to China and mass movements in the cities and the rural hinterland of the Wuhan Temporary Joint Council came out in support of citizens assemblies supportive of the KMT Left-wing and the CCP. However, urban and rural chaos and violence provoked powerful reactions.

Fears of 'another 20 March Incident'

The 20 March Incident had come as a great shock to the Communists. It had alerted them to their vulnerability as they did not have their own armed force at a time when decisions were reached by arms. When the Northern Expedition began, CCP members argued that the situation was 'very dangerous' and required a very careful response to avoid 'another 20 March Incident'.[116] Similarly, in April 1927, Chen Duxiu stated that the 20 March Incident had been a 'pivotal incident'.[117] Quite different lessons could and were drawn from it.

Within the CCP, the 20 March Incident led to serious divisions. It raised first of all the issue of the CCP's relation with the KMT, a point of contention from 1922 when Moscow's emissary, Maring, had suggested that all Communists should join the KMT *en bloc* in 1922. Many Chinese Communists had objected, and considerable Comintern pressure had been necessary before the Third Congress in June 1923 formally approved the policy.[118] That the issue would again become contentious after the 20 March Incident was understandable.

Whether the Communists and the Soviets should have struck back too became an issue of serious disagreements. In 1929, Chen wrote that although at the time of the Incident he had accepted that the CCP could not break with the KMT and actively oppose Chiang Kaishek, he had proposed that the CCP 'should build up an independent military force to oppose Chiang Kaishek'.[119] Chen certainly rejected an immediate counter-coup in Canton. As he stated at the CCP's Fifth Congress, 'we did not have the forces to crush Chiang Kaishek', while Chiang had behind him not only military force, but also the support of a sizeable proportion of the KMT and even 'public opinion'.[120] However, that does not mean that Chen bowed to Chiang Kaishek's predominance. In 1929, he stated that he had asked the Soviets to divert to the CCP some military equipment that they now liberally provided to Chiang Kaishek so that they could 'arm the peasantry'. In a 1926 report to Moscow, Chen argued that the form of the alliance should be changed to that between two separate parties, as he had proposed in the past.[121] The request for arms was denied by Soviet representatives in Guangdong on the grounds, according to Chen, that 'it will provoke KMT suspicions and lead the peasants to oppose the KMT'.[122]

In rejecting the idea of a counter-coup, Chen was in agreement with the Soviet delegation under Bubnov visiting Canton but not Borodin, then in Beijing, and his acolytes in Guangdong. As Chen stated at the Fifth Congress of the CCP of April 1927, 'the view of our party comrades working in Guangdong and Comrade Borodin was that we should not tolerate the 20 March coup, but launch our own 20 March coup'.[123] Borodin, according to Chen, believed that this would secure good relations with Wang Jingwei, which no doubt would have been true, but Chen did not believe that the CCP had the means to carry out a coup.[124]

Chen Duxiu's policies

The 20 March Incident not only raised the issue of the CCP's relation with the KMT, but also its future policies with respect to the peasant movement and in urban areas. In the aftermath of the Incident, Comintern policy was to avoid actions that could alienate Chiang Kaishek. Chen Duxiu's alternative strategy was set out in a political report he made to a CCP Central Executive Committee meeting of July 1926. The CCP should, Chen argued, develop its own organisation, 'unite with the masses of workers and peasants, and ally with the petty bourgeoisie to pressure the big bourgeoisie'.[125] If this failed, he warned, 'the revolutionary movement will expire in mid-life'.[126]

A resolution on CCP–KMT relations, adopted at a Central Committee meeting of July 1926, attributed the 20 March Incident and the spread of 'the anti-CP movement … throughout the country' to several factors, including the resurgence of northern warlord Wu Peifu, but also to 'the mistake in our previous formula for leading the KMT'.[127] As a result of trying to monopolise the KMT, according to this resolution, the CCP had 'forced the Left not to participate in party affairs or struggle against the Right'.[128] The result had been that the conflict between the KMT Right and the KMT Left had become seen as a conflict between the CCP and the KMT. The resolution instructed CCP members, while increasing their own organisation, to 'expand the KMT Left' and to 'actively develop the Left's mass organisation outside of the party'.[129]

Chen Duxiu also called for the recall of Wang Jingwei. He explained in a letter of 22 September 1926 to the Guangdong Committee of the CCP that he favoured this because Wang Jingwei would be able to dampen the conflicts between Chiang Kaishek and the 'new warlords' such as Li Zongren and Tang Shengzhi, who Wang had brought into the NRA. He also wrote that Chiang Kaishek should be re-assured that they supported him as the military leader of the NRA. Chen argued that the return of Wang Jingwei would serve to separate military authority (junquan) from party authority (dangquan).[130] Chen suggested that this policy might be made palatable to Chiang Kaishek by asking him to build an even greater army at Wuhan, with '10 divisions at the minimum', as a way of 'meeting his desire for great glory'.[131]

Chen also denigrated the Northern Expedition as 'a military action to punish northern warlords' rather than 'the Chinese national revolution'.[132] This position, made public in the CCP's *Guide Weekly*, could not but be interpreted as a slap in the face of Chiang Kaishek and damaging to the United Front. Qu Qiubai, a follower of Borodin, who would succeed Chen Duxiu as CCP leader in August 1927, reported following a visit to Canton that it had led to KMT Right-wing attacks on him, especially at the Whampoa Military Academy.[133]

Chen strongly supported the peasant movement. In a Central Executive Bureau report of 5 December, covering October and November, he described his support for it as arising from his anger at the suppression of the interest of the revolutionary peasant masses for the sake of the NRA. He argued that after the March 20 Incident, 'the KMT Right-wing and the reactionary Hong Kong Government...attacked the peasants. Later, because of the issue of the Northern Expedition, the early collection of the land tax and the issue of public debt gave the reactionaries further opportunities to make trouble and the peasants were suppressed, just like in areas controlled by the warlords'.[134] In 'On the Northern Expedition of the National Government', Chen stated that the Northern Expedition had led to 'collection of land taxes in advance' and had only benefited 'compradors, local bullies, corrupt officials, and traitorous businessmen'.[135]

In October 1926, the CCP adopted a Draft Peasant Policy which stressed that 'KMT political power cannot last long without a peasant policy that satisfies the demands of the peasant masses'.[136] It called for a 'united front' of the KMT and the CCP in the countryside which would 'overthrow the political power in the villages of the evil gentry'. The arming of the peasants and the confiscations of land were part of this.[137] In a letter to all party offices of 17 October, Chen Duxiu expressed his faith in the peasant movement:

> Modern industrial workers truly are few [in China]. Most of China's territory is a peasant world. In provinces such as Guangdong, Guangxi, Hunan, Hubei, Henan, Sichuan, Shaanxi, and Jiangxi peasant movements now exist. In these provinces our party should shout the slogan 'The party must go amongst the peasants'.[138]

A radical peasant movement was part of Chen's strategy to build a base in society for the KMT Left-wing. His December 1926 Political Report stated:

> Not only must we in the peasant movement cooperate with the KMT Left-wing elements, and lead them actively to attack the reactionary forces. It is most important that we create a Left Wing among the peasantry and a broad Left-wing peasant base within the KMT. If it is not possible to have the whole peasant association join, then they must join as individuals. We must establish district and sub-district KMT offices to represent the interests of the peasants.[139]

The strategy on which Chen Duxiu pinned his hopes was to use peasant associations to undercut warlord power in the countryside and provide a social basis for the Left-wing KMT.

To further this strategy, Chen Duxiu set up the Peasant Movement Committee of the CCP Central Committee and appointed Mao Zedong as its secretary in early November 1926. Until the 20 March Incident, Mao had worked in various capacities in the National Government in Canton. Wang Jingwei had appointed him acting head of the KMT Propaganda Department and editor of the *Political Weekly*.[140] After the Incident,

Mao, like Zhou Enlai, had been among those who believed that a counter-coup was possible.[141] In October, Chen Duxiu called Mao to Shanghai to head the Peasant Movement Committee, perhaps to remove a significant CCP figure from Borodin's orbit. After sending his wife and children to Hunan, Mao travelled to Shanghai, where Mao drafted the 'Plan for the Peasant Movement at the Present Time', which was approved by the Central Bureau under Chen Duxiu.[142] The Plan called for the development of the peasant movement in the four provinces of Hunan, Hubei, Jiangxi, and Henan, the critical areas in the Northern Expedition at this time, and demanded that 'the peasant movements in these areas must genuinely co-operate with the KMT Left-wing'.[143]

In his December 1926 Central Bureau Report, Chen expressed satisfaction with the revival of the peasant movement in the previous few months. He stated that after the 20 March Incident, gentry militia and military figures such as Li Jishen had stopped supporting peasant associations and that Chinese Communists had halted their earlier peasant movement activities, but that the peasant movement had strengthened again in Guangdong and elsewhere.[144] He pointed out that in Hunan in 'the last two months, peasant movement work has spread to 65 counties'. CCP-controlled peasant association, according to Chen, existed in 45 counties, with a membership of 416,000.[145] Chen noted that 'during the Northern Expedition, Hunanese peasants obtained quite a few arms and battle experience'.[146]

In the English secondary literature, Chen Duxiu is usually described as having been unable to pursue his policies because of Comintern policies that insisted that the CCP stay in the United Front. In Chinese scholarship, Chen is said to have opposed the peasant movement and have taken a 'defeatist' attitude towards the KMT. Both views have downplayed the idea that Chen played an active role during the Northern Expedition. If Chen did not believe that the CCP could end up as the victorious party, he nonetheless supported radical peasant and labour movements and hoped to turn events in favour of the CCP.

After Wuhan

The divisions between Chen Duxiu and Borodin became acrimonious in the spring of 1927 when the outcome of the Northern Expedition hung in the balance. The situation was made more complicated by the growing involvement of the Comintern and the struggle for power between Trotsky and Stalin. The Comintern held its Seventh Plenum in Moscow in November 1926. What policies to follow in China was naturally a contentious topic, made none the easier because Trotsky had, in September, begun to exploit the Comintern's insistence that the CCP stay in the KMT as a vehicle to attack Stalin.[147] On 30 November, Stalin, concerned to exert his authority, made comments that did little to help reconcile factions in China.

Stalin criticised Chen Duxiu for having belittled the Northern Expedition as a military rather than a revolutionary affair.[148] He insisted that the CCP had to stay in the KMT. However, Stalin objected to the downplaying of the peasant movement, as Borodin did at this time, criticising those 'in the KMT and even the CCP who believed that we must not arouse revolution in the countryside'.[149] In fact, in the 'transitional stage in the development of the revolution, the land issue became sharp and is now the key issue. The class which will maintain a firm attitude toward this issue and provide a thorough resolution, will become the leader of the revolution'.[150] Stalin also argued that the CCP should 'pay special attention to the military', which Chen Duxiu had called for but which Soviets advisors had believed too provocative.[151] Stalin's pronouncements could only fuel the divisions in China. Both Chen and Borodin were criticised, but also saw some of their policies re-affirmed. Conflicts in the Soviet Union between Stalin and Trotsky and in China between Chen and Borodin reinforced each other.

According to a report by Qu Qiubai, Borodin believed that where the CCP had gone wrong in the past was not to make use of its position in the KMT, thus rejecting Chen's claim that it was the attempt to dominate the KMT that had led to the 20 March Incident.[152] In a Political Report of 13 December 1926, Chen described the different views as follows.

> This idea of entirely negating the Left-wing is especially pronounced among the comrades from Guangdong. In their report to the Central Bureau, they said, 'As to the Left-wing, there is no such thing. This is curious logic. The result of negating the Left-wing is that there are only the following two options. One is to collaborate with the Right-wing, the other is to break with the KMT and lead the masses to fight the KMT. Neither are possible. The only option we now have is to stay in the KMT and unite with the Left-wing to oppose the Right-wing. Borodin ... ignores the issues of the struggle in China today. The present struggle is to continue the anti-imperialist national movement and the democratic movement to oppose the warlords, landlords, evil gentry and local bullies. Whoever in the KMT supports this is Left-wing, the others are the Right-wing.[153]

The peasant movement too continued to be a source of friction. In Wuhan, Borodin was faced with a deteriorating economy and a military staffed by officers with important interests in the countryside. Borodin moved to slow down the peasant movement. Qu Qiubai wrote in 1928 that Borodin argued that the Wuhan Government should yield to landlords so as not to undermine the Northern Expedition.[154] Cai Hesen, an early CCP member from Hunan, stated also in 1928 that during the Wuhan period, Borodin had denied that the CCP was leading any peasant movement and that he had called peasants 'riff-raff' at a Politburo meeting.[155] In his memoirs, Li Weihan argued that at the Special Meetings of the CCP Central Executive Committee convened in December, Borodin argued that it was too early for land confiscations in Hunan.[156]

Borodin himself discussed the land issue at an April meeting of the Wuhan Land Committee. Even if demands were minimal, he argued, it would still be difficult to obtain their realisation because village power was not in the hands of the peasants. He wrote that 'we must establish a special organisation, the Peasant Policy Department, which must use a scientific method to research the land question, and then in the name of the party submit it to provincial congresses, and use local regulations to implement it'.[157] Borodin suggested a complex bureaucratic machinery to dampen rash local action.

Borodin was not only opposed by Chen. Provincial and local level peasant movement organisers in especially Hunan, over which Wuhan had in reality little control, struck out on a more radical path than Borodin and others in Wuhan wanted. In March, the Hunan Peasant Union had directed county organisers to set up Peasant Association Self-defence forces and establish rural self-government throughout the province. In mid-April, directives called for the arming of the peasants, support for peasant demands for land, and struggle against feudal forces. At the end of the month, a propaganda week was organised, centred on the argument that to mobilise the peasants for the Northern Expedition and to make rural society flourish, the land problem had to be solved immediately. It was argued that this would also solve the Temporary Joint Council's financial problems as peasants no longer would have to pay taxes and hence could make more available to the Wuhan government.[158]

It was in this context that Mao produced his famous 'Report on an Investigation of the Hunan Peasant Movement' and his report to the Central Bureau in Shanghai. These texts were not, as Benjamin Schwartz argued, a 'side current' or 'simply a blunt and passionate plea that the peasant associations be given complete freedom of action'.[159] They also did not constitute, as CCP orthodoxy maintained, an appeal to a wayward Chen Duxiu, who had turned against the peasant movement. Even if heart-felt, they constituted a deliberate intervention in the debates about the peasant movement aimed at countering Borodin's conservative policies. Mao chose to do so by arguing that Chen Duxiu's strategy was correct.

In the report to the Central Bureau, Mao stated that during his trip he had helped correct the unanimous view on the part of the Government, the Guomindang, and all sectors of society that the 'peasant movement is terrible' and stated that 'the fact that "the poor peasants are the vanguard of the revolution" has been used to correct the opinion universally held in all circles about "a movement of riff-raff"'.[160] In conformity with Chen's strategy, he maintained that the peasant movement had to be conducted 'under the banner of the Guomindang; we must absolutely not raise immediately the banner of the Communist Party'.[161] He remarked too that 'we must develop the organisation of the Guomindang in a big way among the peasantry'.[162] At the traumatic 7 August Emergence Conference, which deposed Chen Duxiu, Mao stated that following his Hunan trip he did come to the conclusion that the CCP leadership was wrong, but also that 'I gave up my view because I always thought the ideas of the leading comrades correct'.[163] It is quite possible that Mao had come to a personal conviction about the need for radical rural revolution and the need of the CCP to take charge of it but did not believe that he could make that case and that the best way forward was to work within Chen Duxiu's policies and limit Borodin's conservatism.

Mao Zedong's Hunan Report itself, as Stuart Schram emphasised, was directed to the KMT in Wuhan. It was a beautifully crafted piece of propaganda by a man known for his writing abilities. It was meant to shift opinion, in Wuhan, in favour of the policies that Mao had outlined in his report. As he stated, 'Many of the arguments of the peasant movement were the exact opposite of what I had heard from the gentry class in Wuhan and Changsha ... all criticism directed against the peasant movement must be speedily set right and the various erroneous measures adopted by the revolutionary authorities concerning the peasant movement must be speedily changed'.[164]

If Mao's reports on the Hunan peasant movement provide ample evidence that in January 1927 the peasant movement in Hunan already experienced a 'high tide', following his departure the Hunan peasant movement intensified further. At the turn of the year, local elites had established militia to fight the growing assertiveness of peasant associations. Once in March the Hunan Provincial Peasant Association supported the arming of peasants and land seizures, the peasant movement spread quickly. Soon it claimed a presence throughout the province and a membership of more than 5 million people.[165]

The violence so unleashed proved difficult to contain. Mao noted many instances of this and famously declared that 'revolution is not a dinner party, or literary composition, or painting, or embroidery'.[166] In one instance, the father of Li Lisan, the pioneer of the CCP labour movement, who later became CCP chairman, was killed despite Li's letter stating that his father would not oppose the peasants and would share out his land. There are many reports of score-settling, revenge-taking, and summary trials, pitting angry peasants against local elites who mobilised militia to defend their property.[167] Mao predicted that if 'assassinations of local bullies and evil gentry continue to occur without end, a violent end would ensue should there be a military setback'.[168] This statement would prove prophetic.

At the same time that Chen Duxiu and Borodin clashed about policy towards the KMT and the peasant movement, Chen Duxiu also pushed for uprisings in Shanghai. Chen did so when, as Stephen Smith has shown, in Shanghai, police brutality and political terrorism already had become well established.[169] In 1926, as a long hot summer dragged on, rice prices soared, and the value of copper in terms of silver plummeted, 'the CCP raised terror to official policy' in a vain attempt to rekindle the May Thirtieth Movement.[170] They used ill-disciplined 'dog beating squads' to attack 'running dogs' and a wave of murders of foremen followed.[171]

In October, the CCP attempted a first uprising, but this was badly prepared and came after Sun Chuanfang had regained Nanchang and repulsed an advance by a Zhejiang militarist, who had switched sides from Sun to the NRA.[172] Following the failure of this uprising, the Communists in Shanghai put their energies in improving the quality of their pickets, which numbered about 1,000, and in organising a separate militia so that pickets would be solely responsible for keeping order during strikes while the militia would be able to carry out properly organised military actions. Although some pickets behaved better then others, CCP documents confirm that many had gang backgrounds and that workers were often reluctant to join them. In December, Chen called Zhou Enlai back from Guangdong to help with the organisation of a new uprising.[173]

Li Baozhang, the Garrison commander, in January used draconian means to maintain order. A judge went about the streets, accompanied by someone carrying a shield with the martial law text on it. Anyone suspected of revolutionary activity, even something like leaf-letting, was executed on the spot by two broad-sword executioners, after which their heads were displayed on bamboo pikes.[174] Smith recounts the story that one street hawker, shouting 'Buy My Cakes' (Mai Dabing) was stabbed by a soldier who thought he was crying 'Defeat the Army' (Dabai Bing). Several hundred people were killed.[175]

On 18 February, Shanghai workers went on a massive strike, less to fulfil the CCP's political demands than to welcome the NRA forces, which now closed in on the city. The CCP itself was overtaken by events. Some of its leading members learned of the strike only when they woke up to find trams halted. Two CCP attempts to translate the strike into an armed uprising petered out quickly due to a lack of military strength,[176] but did lead to nasty incidents of mob violence and revenge-taking. On 22 February 1927, Zhang Weizhen, CCP branch secretary at a Japanese cotton mill, executed a police spy after a crowd of 1,000 workers had been asked for their verdict.[177]

On 23 February, at a Joint Meeting of the CCP Central Executive Committee and the Shanghai Regional Committee, the CCP called a halt to the Second Uprising, but also decided to prepare for the next one. A Special Committee was set up, which included Chen Duxiu and Zhou Enlai, with the latter in charge of military affairs. As in the case of Mao, Chen may have brought Zhou to Shanghai to dilute the Canton faction close to Borodin and which had favoured a counter-coup following the 20 March Incident. According to its minutes, the Committee would prepare for a Red Terror. Assassinations of 'running dogs' were carried out of suspect union members, especially foremen.[178] The Special Committee further resolved to call for a 'citizens government' in Shanghai that would exclude the KMT Right-wing. An uprising to oust the Sun Chuanfang warlord government was to precede this.[179] It also oversaw a programme to restructure pickets into eight battalions with more than 2,000 troops.[180] On 5 March, Zhou Enlai reported to the Special Committee about military preparations. According to Zhou's report, the CCP could mobilise 700 pickets, 180 shock troops, and a Peasant Self-Defence Corps from the Shanghai countryside. Zhou stated that the CCP had 13,000 arms at its disposal.[181]

Just before the Third Uprising, timed to take place as Sun Chuanfang's forces left the city and before the NRA entered it, the Special Committee conducted negotiations with local militarists as well as representatives of the KMT. Agreement was reached for the creation of a Shanghai citizen's assembly that would include KMT and CCP members as well as army representatives. The KMT and the local military figures, however, questioned the need for an uprising, arguing that hoodlum (liumang) were bound to create disorder. Du Yuesheng, the leader of the Green Gang, also had made known that he opposed a violent uprising.[182]

Nonetheless, the Third Shanghai Uprising went ahead on 21 March. Some 3,000 armed pickets attacked police on the streets and seized police stations, while thousands of workers of the General Labour Union went on strike. Thousands of Nationalist flags adorned the city.[183] The first units of the NRA were welcomed by half-a-million people in the Chinese city. Bai Chongxi, the Guangxi Clique commander of these units, took over Longhua Garrison. On 24 March, he made clear that he would use his troops to maintain order and disarm the pickets. Bai also made known that his forces would not try to take the International Settlement of the Foreign Concession.[184]

Chaos quickly spread. As had happened during the Second Uprising, mob rule and mass trials of despised plainclothes policemen and hated foremen became features of an already explosive situation. Following one such incident, the *Guide Weekly* wrote about 'exceedingly revolutionary behaviour' and stated that 'the enemy have killed dozens of us; now we shall try each of them'.[185] The Shanghai Communists further discussed plans for a general uprising to take the International Settlement and the French Concession. Upon advice, so it seems, of Soviets, these plans were abandoned, although mass rallies and strikes focused against the British continued to take place.[186] Foreigners in the International Settlement were understandably concerned.[187]

Chen Duxiu's policies aimed at bringing about a KMT Left-wing government supported by the CCP as well as by workers and peasants. As tensions in Shanghai escalated, he continued to work for this outcome. The arrival on 1 April of Wang Jingwei, who had travelled from France via Moscow, provided a last hope. After meeting Wang, on 3 April, Chiang Kaishek issued a telegram stating that from then on he would only concern himself with military affairs and that Wang Jingwei would again take over as chairman of the KMT.[188] Wang and Chen Duxiu issued a Joint Statement made public on the morning of 5 April, which called on the CCP and the KMT to work closely together to prevent the enemies of the revolution from exploiting the conflicts between them.

Addressed to the Comrades of the KMT and the CCP, it declared that 'the CCP is wholly convinced that the KMT and its Three People's Principles are absolutely necessary for the Chinese revolution. Only those who do not want the Chinese revolution to advance seek to overthrow them'. It warned against rumours by the enemies of the revolution that 'the CCP will organise a worker's government, enter the Concession areas, attack the NRA, and overthrow the KMT' or that 'KMT leaders will drive out the CCP and suppress labour unions and their pickets'.[189] Wang Jingwei left for Wuhan the next day to take up leadership of the Wuhan Government there.[190] Within a week, it would become clear that constructing a reconciliation around Wang Jingwei was clutching at straws in the wind.

The conflagration

No evidence exists for the idea that the violence that would grip China in April and which would take the rest of the year to work itself through, was the product of revolutionary or counter-revolutionary master plan conceived in advance. Much of what happened was the product of tensions that had built up over time, *ad hoc* attempts to yank history back to a course favoured by this or that party, struggles for power in which policy issues were mixed in with personal rivalries, and memories of past traumatic events such as the 20 March Incident. Violence too was not just the product of those usually regarded to have been the makers of history. Local vendettas, shortages, abysmal living conditions in the cities and in the countryside, and both rural and urban lower cultures long habituated to rough violence also played their role.

Most scholarship has focused on the 12 April Shanghai Massacre when Guangxi forces of Li Zongren, with the support of Chiang Kaishek and the Shanghai Green Gang, ruthlessly massacred Communist pickets and began the White Terror. It is important to remember, however, not only that violence had become endemic in the countryside especially in Hunan, but had also affected other cities than Shanghai. On 30 March in Hangzhou, where bloody conflicts had been going on for a month, NRA troops fired on demonstrators. Led by pickets and supported by the General Labour Union, they had surrounded NRA headquarters. On the same day, in Chongqing, the attempt by the Garrison Commander to prevent a demonstration against imperialism and Chiang Kaishek led to a bloodbath when the pickets tried to resist the army. In Nanchang, on 2 April, a CCP–KMT Left-wing alliance staged a coup. Some twenty people died, and people's courts condemned several KMT leaders to death. In Fuzhou, a struggle between forces for and against Chiang Kaishek led to the latter's victory on 7 April. In Nanjing, the struggle for power turned bloody on 10 and 11 April, after Chiang Kaishek had sent his own forces into the city. Armed thugs, police, and the military suppressed Leftist mass organisations during those two days. In Ningpo the same happened on 9 and 10 April.[191]

In Shanghai itself, the crackdown came on 12 April. Bai Chongxi, who had reiterated his determination to disarm pickets and keep order at a welcoming rally for Chiang Kaishek on 26 March,[192] proved ruthless. The hows and whys of the White Terror, formalised and bureaucratised from 5 May as a party purification drive (qingdang),[193] remain obscure. However, leaders of Shanghai's business community had pressured Chiang Kaishek to re-establish order and offered financial support. The *North China Daily News*, the leading English-language paper, urged Chiang to act 'swiftly and ruthlessly'.[194] The KMT Central Supervisory Committee, dominated by the KMT Rightwing, urged expulsion of leading CCP members from high KMT offices. Du Yuesheng, the leader of the Green Gang, too supported the crackdown and his toughs were given arms by the NRA.[195]

On 11 April, Du invited Wang Shouhua, the head of the General Labour Union, for dinner and had him murdered. The next day, Green Gang thugs and Bai Chongxi's troops, with at least the connivance of the Settlement and the French Concession authorities, began rounding up pickets. On 13 April, they fired on a rally organised in protest by the General Labour Union that had been proscribed by Bai.[196] The White Terror had begun in earnest. In the next few months alone, it led to the death of 3,000–4,000 CCP members and 30,000 others. A further 40,000 were injured and 25,000 were imprisoned.[197] Following the 12 April massacres in Shanghai, the hope that the result of urban action would be citizen's assemblies made up of Communists and Left-wing KMT figures with broad urban support lay in utter ruins. Brutal suppression took place not just in Shanghai, but also in Canton, Shantou, Amoy, Ningbo, and various places in Guangxi.[198]

After 12 April, the Wuhan Government, supported by the KMT Left-wing of Wang Jingwei, the Communists, the Soviets, and Tang Shengzhi did not accept defeat. They refused to sanction Chiang Kaishek's move to transfer the National Government and the Party Headquarters to Nanjing on 18 April. In May, both the Wuhan and Nanjing camps sent forces into north China. From Wuhan, Tang Shengzhi and Zhang Fakui moved into Henan in the hope of linking up with Feng Yuxiang and together with him to take Beijing. The fate of the Wuhan Government now depended on the success of this offensive.

The Wuhan campaign met with fierce resistance by first Wu Peifu, who was decisively defeated on 14 May, and then Zhang Zuolin's Fengtian Army. Wu Peifu's defeat would bring an end to his role in Chinese political or military affairs. On 1 June, the Wuhan forces reached Zhengzhou, which Feng had also reached by this time by moving down the east–west running Long–Hai Railroad. From Nanjing, Chiang Kaishek sent the 4th Army of the Guangxi Clique into Anhui and Jiangsu. The 4th Army took Xuzhou on 3 June.

For Wuhan, the problem was that the campaign to the north left their rear to the south as well as their western flank virtually undefended. From Sichuan, Yang Sen, who had joined the NRA as commander of the 20th Army, struck eastwards and took Yichang on the border with Hubei. Yichang's garrison commander, who had also joined the NRA, withdrew and turned his army against Wuhan. When they approached the city from the south, communications between Wuhan and Hunan were cut. On 21 May,

Xu Kexiang, a regimental commander in Tang Shengzhi's forces, began a crackdown, possibly with Tang's support who had less to gain from supporting Wuhan now that the Temporary Joint Council was wooing Feng Yuxiang, after military units and militia had clashed with peasant organisations throughout the province and in Changsha garrison forces and armed pickets of the Changsha General Labour union had engaged in running battles. A communist attempt at a counter-coup failed miserably a week later. Illustrating the lack of control and the increasing desperation in Wuhan, its grain purchasing mission to Changsha had been turned back and some of its members killed.[199] In the weeks afterwards, Tang Shenghzi blamed peasant movement organisers for the disorder in Hunan and demanded the expulsion of all the Communists.[200]

The last hope of the Wuhan Government depended on which side Feng Yuxiang would support. Wuhan's leaders, including Wang Jingwei, met Feng at Zhengzhou in Henan Province between 10 and 12 June. The Zhengzhou meetings gave Henan Province, important as a recruitment and supply ground, to Feng and ordered the remaining forces of Tang Shengzhi back south. A week later, Feng met Chiang Kaishek in Xuzhou on 20 and 21 June. Prior to this meeting, Chiang's forces had conquered the Long–Hai Railroad east of Xuzhou. In return for substantial grants from Nanjing and recognition of his control over the territories that he had entered, Feng issued a public telegram demanding the dismissal of Borodin, the disciplining of radical elements in the peasant movement, and the submission of Wuhan KMT figures to the authority of Nanjing, suggesting that those who refused should go abroad for a vacation.[201] The Wuhan Government's strategic position had collapsed. It no longer had the support of any significant military force.

The Communists in disarray

In late April and early May, a Wuhan commission attempted to reconcile the conflicting imperatives of the peasant movement and keeping the loyalty of its armies. Involving several Communists, including Mao Zedong, as well as Soviet advisors, all agreed that all land should be nationalised, but also that at this time this could not yet be accomplished because it would affect the soldiers and officers who just then had begun the campaign to link up with Feng Yuxiang. The resulting document called for the protection of small landlords and Nationalist military men, while it approved the confiscation of land of 'enemies of the revolution', such as usurers, militarists, local bullies, bureaucrats, and so on. However, it carefully specified which government institutions could carry out land confiscation and determined that the recipients of new land would pay rent and that all proceeds would go to the government.[202] The Wuhan Government was not in the position to enforce this law. It could not have reined in peasants who were acting on their own initiative, nor could it have done much to stop army commanders and militia from suppressing peasant movements. When the document was submitted to the KMT Political Council, the majority view was that its contents were too explosive for publication.

These developments left the Communists in an impossible situation. Following the beginning of the White Terror in the cities, their fate depended on the survival of the Wuhan Government. At the same time, they were ideologically and emotionally committed to the peasant movement. Increasingly marginalized, it was also their last remaining source of actual influence. Their situation was complicated further by the arrival on 1 June of a telegram by Stalin, who had clashed hard with Trotsky about policy in China at the Eighth Plenum of the Comintern. Stalin ordered seizures of land from below, something that would inevitably be chaotic and generate much violence; the raising of an independent army of 70,000 troops made up of Communists, workers, and peasants; and the replacement of KMT Central Committee members opposed to the Communists by peasant and working class leaders. While ordering the CCP to stay in the United Front, it also demanded that any officer in contact with Chiang Kaishek be punished.[203] Chen Duxiu characterised the telegram as 'taking a bath in a toilet'.[204]

Although Stalin's order has been rightly criticised,[205] it should not be forgotten that substantial appetite existed within the CCP for some parts of Stalin's advice, especially armed uprising in the cities and the countryside. A further telegram from the Comintern, ordering a withdrawal from the Wuhan Government, although not yet an end to the United Front, and a 'land revolution under its own leadership' gave the green light. Even before Chen Duxiu was replaced by Qu Qiubai as CCP leader on 7 August, a plan was drawn up for an uprising in Nanchang in Jiangxi Province 'to give rise to a broad struggle for land revolution' centred on the provinces of Hunan, Hubei, Jiangxi, and Guangdong.[206]

The Nanchang Uprising, in which such great future Communist generals as Ye Ting, He Long, Liu Bocheng, Zhu De, Nie Rongzhen, Luo Ruiqing, and Lin Biao participated, was a military success, in the sense that Nanchang was taken and the Communists gained important amounts of ammunition and money. But politically the uprising had been badly organised. None of the high level KMT Left-wing figures invited to head a new government came out in support, and after four days the new Communist army withdrew. No agreement existed about what to do next. Some forces withdrew altogether, while the main force moved to the East River Area in Guangdong in the hope of finding a base there. Peasants in Jiangxi did not rise up in support of an army that would not be able to protect them. Battle casualties, desertion, and rebellion weakened these forces. Reprisals followed in both Wuhan and Jiujiang.[207]

Peasants in other provinces also did not come out in support of the Communists during the Autumn Harvest Uprising. In Hubei, a bandit leader on whom the Communist had hoped to rely betrayed them. In Hunan, Mao was able to cobble together a ragtag force of deserters of some NRA armies, bandits, unemployed miners, local militia, and peasants. An attempt to give rise to peasant uprisings around Changsha and then pounce with this force had failed by mid-September. In north-east Guangdong, Haifeng and Lufeng counties were briefly seized, but Communist forces there too had to withdraw within days following a period of mayhem in the city. In all these instances, the reaction was bloody.[208]

The last act in this series of increasingly desperate revolts was the Canton Uprising of December. The Chinese Communists hoped to make use of a struggle for power in the province between Li Jishen, who hoped to capture the city, and Zhang Fakui. With most military forces away, the Communists were able to capture most of the city's police stations, military headquarters, the railroad station, the telegraph office, government offices, and the treasury. But the population did not support the uprising and refused to attend mass rallies to give popular legitimacy to the Canton Soviet. After three days of street fighting, looting, revengism, and arson, 1,000 buildings had been destroyed and thousands of bodies lay dead in the street. This was a Communist own-goal. The uprising put paid to Wang Jingwei's last throw of the dice when he had allied himself with Zhang Fakui to make a comeback in Guangdong Province and seize Canton. The Canton Soviet destroyed whatever chances of success this move had. Zhang Fakui's forces, sent to the East River Area, were defeated there, while in January, Li Jishen took Canton.[209]

The decline and rise of Chiang Kaishek

It is often assumed that the 12 April Massacre led inexorably to the victory of Chiang Kaishek. This is not the case. The collapse of military unity in the NRA and the spread of violence in cities and the countryside made possible a counter-offensive by northern warlords. The National Pacification Army, headed by Zhang Zuolin and supported by Sun Chuanfang, who had re-grouped in north China, as well as Zhang Zongchang's substantial Shandong forces, nearly succeeded in capturing Nanjing. In early July, the National Pacification Army used an attempt by the Wuhan government to begin an offensive down the Yangtze River on Nanjing to strike back against the NRA forces in north China and to recover the Lower Yangtze provinces. The National Pacification Army forced the NRA out of north China and by August only the Yangtze River stood between it and Nanjing.[210]

In consequence of these defeats, on 12 August Chiang Kaishek announced his 'retirement' and left Nanjing for Shanghai, something that would facilitate a reconciliation between Wuhan and Nanjing. The Minutes of the Joint Conference illustrate that intense negotiations between Wuhan and Nanjing did take place. However, the Joint Conference refused to break completely with Chiang and the Left-Wing KMT in Wuhan with Wang Jingwei as its leader refused to come to a settlement with Nanjing or come to its aid when attacked by the National Pacification Army.[211]

Following a bombardment, on 25 August, National Pacification Army forces crossed the Yangtze and the fate of Nanjing hung in the balance. At the battle of Longtan on the south shore of the Yangtze, the NRA, led by Li Zongren, Bai Chongxi, and He Yingqin, prevented the National Pacification Army from breaking out of its beachhead. The battle, however, raged until 31 August and saw troops under Sun Chuangfang numbering between 40,000 and 70,000 nearly succeeding in taking Nanjing.[212] The fall of Nanjing would have led to the removal of the NRA from the entire lower Yangtze Area and likely to the end of the Northern Expedition.

The struggle for power was now between Wang Jingwei and Li Zongren. Li Zongren's victory at Longtan against the National Pacification Army had increased his prestige greatly. He did not include Wang Jingwei or Tang Shengzhi in new leadership organs formed in September. In response, Tang Shengzhi, Wang Jingwei, and Li Jishen formed an alliance in opposition to Nanjing and refused to recognise its legitimacy. Li Zongren's forces then undertook an offensive which on 15 November succeeded in taking Wuhan.[213] Tang Shengzhi had announced his retirement four days earlier and left for Japan. [214]

Wang Jingwei, however, agreed to negotiations with Chiang Kaishek. He also joined the uprising by Zhang Fakui in mid-November in Canton against Li Jishen. Wang's position, however, was made impossible, as mentioned, by the Canton Uprising.[215] A month after Tang Shengzhi had gone to Japan to study Buddhism, Wang Jingwei left Shanghai, on 17 December, for a rest cure in France.[216]

Conditions had now matured for Chiang Kaishek's return to active duty. That had always been anticipated; retirements were often simply one political device to get through a difficult impasse. The minutes of the Joint Conference in Nanjing show that many had anticipated that Chiang would return to take charge of the army once unification had come about. Many high level KMT members had gone with Chiang to Shanghai. In addition, Chiang had emptied the treasury and the new joint government could not make ends meet.[217] The collapse of Wang Jingwei's position had removed one obstacle preventing Chiang's return; the inability of the Guangxi Clique to prevent Li Jishen, whom Chiang Kaishek had supported in Guangdong throughout the Northern Expedition, from taking Guangdong illustrated the limits of their power. Rather than controlling both the Lower Yangtze Region as well as Guangxi and Guangdong, they now faced a serious threat on their own base while they were losing their grip on the situation in the Lower Yangtze region.

In Shanghai, Chiang Kaishek suggested the following deal to the remaining centres of power. In return for an acceptance of his overall military leadership and the legitimacy of the Nanjing Government, he proposed that four Branch Political Councils be established in Wuhan, Canton, Kaifeng, and Taiyuan and that there would be four Group Armies. Li Zongren was offered the headship of the Wuhan Branch, Li Jishen that in Canton, Feng Yuxiang that in Kaifeng, and Yan Xishan that in Taiyuan. Each would also have under their command one Group Army and serve as its Commander-in-Chief.[218] This proved acceptable. Chiang was formally invited back, on 1 January 1928, by the Nanjing Government.

On 16 February, at a meeting in Kaifeng in Henan Province these arrangements were formalised and an agreement was reached about the second phase of the Northern Expedition. Chiang's own forces became the 1st Group Army with 290,000 troops, Feng's formed the 2nd Group Army with 310,000 troops, and Yan's became the 3rd with 150,000. The Guangxi forces of Li Zongren's became the 4th Group Army with 240,000 troops.

Fierce battles still had to be won, but they were. By 1 May, the tide of battle had swung in favour of the NRA forces. As Zhang Zuolin withdrew his forces from north China, the NRA's component armies began to race to Beijing. Yan Xishan arrived first on 8 June 1928, bringing the tumultuous Northern Expedition to a close with the nominal unification of China.

Reasons for Chiang's victory

In Chiang's rise, good fortune and co-incidence played their roles. Tang Shengzhi, Li Zongren, Li Jishen, and Wang Jingwei could all have won the struggle for power, while Chiang himself came close to being sidelined during the first few months of the campaign and again after the 12 April Incident. Nonetheless, some good reasons do exist for Chiang's ultimate victory.

It was important that Chiang Kaishek did command a substantial military force. The presidency of the Whampoa Academy provided Chiang the opportunity to build student–teacher relations with Whampoa cadets and to train up the officers corps of the 1st Army. The first group of Whampoa cadets included future favourites such as Chen Cheng.[219] The Whampoa Clique would always remain an important pillar to Chiang's power base.

The importance of the *esprit de corps* that Chiang purposefully fostered around the Whampoa Academy is illustrated by an incident at the Wuhan branch of the Whampoa Academy, established quickly after the NRA took the city. Fights had broken out between workers, shouting slogans for the ouster of Chiang, and the cadets. Chiang ordered the cadets, in a letter to their commander, to ignore attacks on 'the Academy' and on Chiang personally. Cadets, he wrote, had to maintain strict discipline and dedicate themselves to revolution. Such interventions, in which Chiang could show himself as a selfless leader and played on ideas of revolution and teacher–student relations, fostered this *esprit de corps* as well as Chiang's leadership position.[220]

The strict application of the Mutual Responsibility Law (Lianzuofa), which made troops and officers responsible for each other on pain of execution, was one device that Chiang used to instil discipline in the army.[221] Although later its application was relaxed, during the unification of Guangdong and the Northern Expedition Chiang was remorseless.

Chiang was able to rise rapidly in the Nationalist hierarchy before the Northern Expedition not just because of his command of these forces, but also because he repeatedly demonstrated his capacity for resolute and decisive military action. Yet, Chiang's 1st Army simply was not large enough to conquer all of China. Chiang had to cultivate personal relationships with other military leaders, rich businessmen, and financiers, China's leading families, as well as the Shanghai underground. Chiang was shrewd in managing these relationships and turning them to his benefit.

Chiang was careful to establish connections with top generals of the various NRA armies not considered his 'own', such as Chen Mingshu in Li Jishen's 4th Army. Chen played a leading role in the occupation of Wuhan. Tang Shengzhi perhaps believed that Chen might support him, as they had collaborated in a reform movement at the Baoding Military Academy.[222] When Tang Shengzhi and Borodin tried to oust Chiang Kaishek, however, they found that Chen, whom Chiang had ordered to re-organise his divisions as the 11th Army and appointed Garrison Commander, decided to support Chiang Kaishek. Chen Mingshu was in telegraphic contact with Chiang throughout the great crisis of March 1927. Chen resisted much pressure to join the Wuhan Government or to go abroad.[223]

Chen also supplied detailed information to Chiang on the attitudes of the various generals and politicians in Wuhan.[224] A letter from Chen, for instance, informed Chiang that Song Qingling, Song Ziwen, and Sun Fo would agree with his demand that Borodin be recalled in return for his agreement to come to Wuhan. Only Tang Shengzhi and one of his allies opposed, according to Chen.[225]

Chiang supported Chen Mingshu and built up his status at the same time that he also fostered that of his superior, Li Jishen. Chiang used Li as a counter-weight to the Guangxi Clique. CCP members in Canton reported that Chiang Kaishek was 'allowing' Li Jishen, whose own base was in the West River, to take control over Guangdong and Guangxi. Chiang sowed dissension between Li Jishen and Li Zongren by suggesting to Li Jishen that Li Zongren was less interested in expanding into Hunan than into Guangdong.[226]

Part of Chiang's strategy during the Northern Expedition was to keep the garrison forces of important cities – Canton, Wuhan, Shanghai, and Nanjing – under as close a control as possible. Chen Mingshu was garrison commander in Wuhan. Even if Chiang helped Li Jishen in Guangdong, he was sure to keep Canton under his own control by having Qian Dajun, the Canton Garrison Commander and head of the 20th Division, take over the concurrent headship of the Public Security Bureau. Qian was not from Guangdong but from Jiangsu. He had come to Canton in 1921 and served in the Guangdong Army, but had then joined the Whampoa Academy, becoming its acting head in 1925 when Chiang was on campaign.[227] Qian was closer to Chiang than to Li Jishen.

Chiang Kaishek's control over appointments as the Commander-in-Chief of the NRA was one device he used to foster military networks tied to him and to manage them. Chiang made sure that the appointments were seen to be made by him. On 18 February 1927, for instance, he ordered He Yingqing to append his own name to any appointment that he made or any order that he issued.[228] He similarly insisted that local troop recruitment and the incorporation of local militia be approved by his Headquarters at all times.[229] For commanders to be the legitimate heads of their forces, they needed Chiang's sanction. He could withhold promotion of people he distrusted. He did so in the case of Zhang Fakui who had, Chiang acknowledged, performed with great merit but whom he, nonetheless, did not want to advance quickly.[230] It seems likely that Li Jishen was pleased with Chiang's efforts to undermine a threat to him.

Chiang used his control over military supplies in a similar way. While Chiang was encountering great difficulties in Jiangxi and Tang Shengzhi seemed about to take Wuhan, he refused permission to provide Tang with new guns.[231] Similarly, on 14 November 1926, he ordered that arms seized by the 7th Army of Li Zongren be given partly to the 6th Army.[232] Following the capture of Shanghai, he demanded monthly reports on production at the Jiangnan Arsenal.[233] He caused an arms shipment to Yichang in Sichuan to be intercepted in September 1926.[234]

Technology, especially the telegraph, was important as well. The telegraph allowed Chiang to shape affairs over very large distances, important because action was spread out over wide areas. It also allowed Chiang to be in touch, often on a daily basis, with the people whose goodwill or co-operation he required. During the crisis of the Wuhan–Nanjing split, for instance, he was in touch regularly with Song Ziwen.[235] He tried to exclude others from access to the telegraph, something that he could do as Commander-in-Chief. He, for instance, forbade any party member to communicate by telegraph from Shanghai to Wuhan.[236]

Chiang would not have been able to manage these military networks had he not had access to substantial financial resources. Even before the Northern Expedition began, Chiang had cultivated relations with important financial figures, including Song Ziwen, Kong Xiangxi, Zhang Kia-ngao, Xu Fu, Chen Qicai, and Zhang Jingjiang. These men were part of the community of rich bankers and businessmen of Shanghai, Jiangsu, and Zhejiang. As Parks Coble has shown, it is wrong to see the KMT under Chiang Kaishek as the party of the Shanghai Capitalists. Especially during the financial crises during and after the Northern Expedition, Chiang Kaishek resorted to extortionist methods to secure from them the vast amounts of money he needed to finance his troops and purchase loyalties all around.[237] However, if the relationship between the KMT and the Shanghai rich was one of conflicting interests, the two were also mutually dependent. The KMT needed to pay its armies, while Shanghai businessmen needed the military to secure stability, not just to be able to trade, but also to re-establish fiscal order and tax collection on which the loan business of their banks depended.

The relationship between Song Ziwen and Chiang Kaishek illustrates the ambiguous relationship between Shanghai finance and Chiang Kaishek. Song Ziwen never had an easy relationship with Chiang Kaishek and competed with him for power. As Minister of Finance, Song was the paymaster for the Northern Expedition. Chiang Kaishek needed his help to provide funds to the various armies of the NRA and to tie these to himself. In August 1926, Chiang enquired whether 400,000 *yuan* of campaign funds for the 7th Army of Li Zongren had indeed been sent to Li and ordered that Li be issued with a further 200,000 *yuan* each month.[238] He supported the 6th Army of Cheng Qian in a similar way.[239] Already by August 1926, Chiang's war chest was nearly empty. Telegrams from Chiang Kaishek to Zhang Jingjiang and Song Ziwen in Canton stated that he was running out of funds and he asked both for assistance, including by sending experts to help him.[240] A telegram from Chiang to Song of 20 September 1926 scolded Song for not sending sufficient money and accused him of still lacking faith in him.[241] Chiang at this time also instructed Xu Fu to secure funds raised in Shanghai and transfer them to Changsha.[242]

Both their personal rivalry and the fact that Chiang Kaishek's battlefield setbacks made him a dubious business proposition probably led Song to withdraw his support of Chiang Kaishek. In December, Song stopped remitting funds to Chiang. In a series of telegrams, Chiang pressed Song to pay the 9th and 10th Armies, which were then in western Hubei; informed Song that the 7th Army units in Hubei had mutinied because they had not been paid; and asked Song if it was true that the 1st Army from now on had to depend on raising funds locally. Chiang went so far as to urge Song to set personal disagreements aside and to re-institute payments to NRA armies campaigning with him so as not to endanger the whole Northern Expedition.[243] On 19 January 1927, Chiang was forced to halt all campaign payments to all armies.[244] On 12 February 1927, Chiang sent a telegram to Tan Yankai, who was then in Wuhan, to tell Song that if he did not receive 1.5 million *yuan* immediately he would 'regard this as the final rupture in our relations'.[245] On 1 March 1927, Chiang ordered Song to prepare 3 million for campaign expenditures for the armies that would be sent into the Yangtze delta.[246]

Song did not comply at first, but on 5 March, Chiang offered Song control over the finances of Jiangsu and Zhejiang. In the same telegram he suggested to Song that he could appoint his own people and follow his own policies. Song thereupon did throw his support behind Chiang. Besides Chiang's attractive offer, Wuhan's deteriorating financial position and attacks on him personally by Wuhan's labour pickets probably played a role in Song's decision to make common cause with Chiang.[247]

Chiang was able to weather the severe financial crisis of the first months of 1927 because he could turn to other financial connections. Zhang Kia-ngao, the younger brother of the great liberal Carsun Chang, was born in Zhejiang in 1888. In 1913, he joined the Bank of China, after having served in the Qing's Ministry for Post and Communications. In May 1916, as head of the Shanghai Branch of the Bank of China, located in the International Settlement, he defied Yuan Shikai's order to halt the redemption of the Bank's notes when Yuan's government faced a desperate financial crisis. In 1924, when Wu Peifu tried to force Zhang Kia-ngao to release funds from the Bank of China's Shanghai Branch, Zhang refused again. He later similarly thwarted Zhang Zuolin. As his memoirs indicate, he despaired of the Northern Warlord Government, and through Huang Fu, a sworn brother of Chiang Kaishek, established a channel to the National Government in Guangdong. He secretly sent an envoy to Song Ziwen and approved a secret 500,000 *yuan* loan. The NRA was under strict orders not to attack Bank of China offices during the Northern Expedition.[248]

Chen Qicai was a Zhejiang man who had attended a military academy in Japan and had taught at various Chinese military academies in China, including Baoding. He had been a consultant to Sun Yatsen during the 1911 Revolution. Afterwards he became the head of the Zhejiang branch office of the Bank of China. Chiang Kaishek invited him to Canton in July 1926 and appointed him chair of the Jiangsu Zhejiang Finance Committee.[249] After Zhejiang had been secured, in May 1927, Chen was appointed head of the Zhejiang Finance Office.[250] In the same month, Chiang warned Chen Qicai in Shanghai that if he had not produced 4 million *yuan* by the end of the month he would deem him as having turned his back on the revolution.[251]

Zhang Kia-ngao secretly remitted 300,000 *yuan* to Chiang in Jiangxi. After Chiang took Nanchang, the local branch of the Bank of China loaned Chiang a further 200,000 *yuan*.[252] Such support allowed Chiang to re-instate payments to Tan Yankai's 2nd Army and Cheng Qian's 6th Army in late January.[253] On 23 February, Chiang sent Li Zongren and Chen Mingshu 200,000 *yuan* from Jiujiang.[254] On 30 April 1927, Chiang ordered that 100,000 *yuan* be sent to Bo Wenwei, the Anhui military figure who had played an important role in the 1911 Revolution. Anhui Province was strategically important.[255] Bo Wenwei's agreement was useful to the northern offensive of the 4th Army that captured the Long–Hai Railroad, which prevented Feng Yuxiang from capturing the whole line and brought Feng's and Chiang's armies in close proximity. On 26 March, Chiang established a Jiangsu and Shanghai Finance Committee, to which he appointed leading local banking and business figures. The committee had full authority over local revenue collection and it took over tax administration. Shanghai bankers and financiers then loaned Chiang 10 million *yuan*.[256] On 1 May, the Nationalists issued 30 million *yuan* of debt certificates backed by Maritime Customs revenue. The issue was overseen by a committee on which sat government representatives as well as local bankers and financiers.[257]

The Wuhan Government failed partly because it could not compete financially. In April, when the Wuhan Government faced a deficit of 9 million, it ordered all transactions to be conducted in paper money issued by its banks. It prohibited trade and currency exchange with the Lower Yangtze and tried to issue 5 million *yuan* worth of public debt. By the end of the month, coal stocks were depleted and by June grain stocks had been reduced to 80,000 tons, sufficient only for ten days. Prices of fuel, grain, and cotton inflated, as factory closures caused the number of unemployed in the city to rise to 300,000. Armies, receiving no funds, then began to mutiny one after the other.[258]

Chiang's return to power, after his resignation in August 1927, was partly the result of his ability to raise funds. The minutes of the Joint Conference show that it immediately ran into financial problems. A drastic savings exercise was instituted, salaries were cut and even stopped, and armies that could not be financed were to be disbanded. The

Minister of Finance and provincial financial offices proved unable to remedy the situation. They found banks unwilling to provide funds and financial officials abandoned their posts.[259] Chiang Kaishek's recall in January 1928 was accompanied by an issue of a 40 million *yuan* in public debt. Almost 50 per cent of the Nanjing Government's budget of 140 million *yuan* until May 1928 was raised in this way.[260]

Chiang's personal networks in the military and in the Shanghai financial and business communities gave him the assets that he needed to secure the allegiance of the most significant military forces. Chiang's marriage to Song Meiling in 1927 illustrate the importance of such relationships. This was a marriage between a leading Shanghai family and a newly ascendant general with clear advantages to both. The liaison gave Chiang a new social prestige and made Chiang part of the leading families of his time. Chiang's relationships, however, also included leading figures in the underworld, including most famously Du Yuesheng in Shanghai.

The capture of the symbols of legitimacy were important too. Chiang Kaishek, on 18 April, declared that in conformity with Sun Yatsen's wishes, Nanjing would become the location of the capital of the National Government. Elaborate ceremonies were held in Nanjing. National Government and party flags adorned the city, a rally was conducted at the Jiangsu Provincial Sports Stadium, a three minute silence held for Sun Yatsen, and Sun's will read out in solemnity.[261] Capturing Beijing was perhaps more important symbolically than militarily. Because of the presence of Feng Yuxiang's, Yan Xishan's, and Zhang Xueliang's forces, Chiang's control in north China was limited, something that likely played a role in the decision to make Nanjing the capital. But Beijing's capture by forces formally part of the NRA and under Chiang's formal command fulfilled an ambition of Sun Yatsen, whose body remained in Beijing, removed competing symbols of authority and legitimacy, and gave the Nationalists a whole series of appointments to fill.

In conclusion, Chiang Kaishek's rise to power was partly the result of his control over substantial military forces. Important too were the networks he cultivated in various circles, including the military, Shanghai's financial communities, the underworld, and that of elite families. As Chiang's difficulties in the first months of 1927 illustrate, however, these relationships were tenuous and support could and was withdrawn when militarily Chiang Kaishek was not doing well. If Chiang would never have been able to succeed without the funds that were made available to him, his power too depended on his ability to prevail on the battlefield. Chiang had a knack for making sudden but decisive military moves, as in the 20 March Incident. Similarly, his decisions to abandon the Wuhan front and move into Jiangxi, and then not to strike north but march into the Lower Yangtze, also radically altered the military situation.

Conclusion

This chapter has made a number of more or less straightforward claims about the Northern Expedition. I have suggested that it should not simply be seen as a contest between different ideologies, the Communists and the Nationalists, or between revolutionaries, on the one hand, and warlords and imperialists, on the other. It is difficult to see the Northern Expedition as a promising revolutionary movement that began in 1925 but came unstuck in 1927 over the issue of social mobilisation. It was the result of a long-term effort to mobilise Chinese society and make manifest a new nation, but internal divisions ran deep and mobilisation was difficult, so that all reached for or made accommodations with irregular forms of violence. The Northern Expedition itself was the contingent product of the broader military situation in China, the Soviet Union's geo-political strategy, the military and financial weakness of the Canton National Government, the rivalry between Chiang Kaishek, on the one hand, and Wang Jingwei and the Soviets, on the other, and last but not least, the initiatives of warlords such as Tang Shengzhi, Li Zongren, and Li Jishen. The NRA was never a disciplined force and its armies lived from hand-to-mouth, searched for new bases, and absorbed and scattered bandit groups and militia.

The Northern Expedition itself was shaped by a myriad of issues: political and personal rivalries in the CCP and the KMT, the initiatives in the field of military commanders of those associated with the NRA and those who were not, finance, the supply needs of armies, the hopes for revolutionary success and the fear of failure, networks of personal connections, the ambitions of leading families such as the Songs, the spread of uncontrolled and undisciplined violence in the spring of 1927, and the Green Gang in Shanghai. Historical memories, mistrust, and iconic events such as the 20 March Incident were consistently at play.

In explaining the rise of Chiang Kaishek, I have brought to the fore some aspects that have hitherto been ignored. He thought of himself as a revolutionary, believed that his mission was to do better where Sun Yatsen had failed, and skilfully used the idea of Sun's legacy to move against his rivals. As to the Communists, I have stressed their internal divisions and rivalries and have suggested that their strategies not only could never have succeeded, but, in fact, worked at cross purposes and backfired, and are not without responsibility for the spread of brutality that characterised the Northern Expedition.

Militarily, the Northern Expedition solved little. The British were forced to give up the Wuhan Foreign Concession and adopt a more accommodating attitude towards Chinese nationalism. But Hong Kong and Shanghai remained theirs, and financially their influence remained. If Sun Chuanfang and Wu Peifu were eliminated, Zhang Zuolin and Yan Xishan remained, and new armies more loyal to their commanders than to the new government had emerged. Li Zongren, Feng Yuxiang, Li Jishen, Yan Xishan, Chen Mingshu, and Tan Yankai all had a good war. Most of these, and Zhang Zuolin and his son, would later turn against Chiang. It may have suited many, in 1928, to declare a victorious end to the Northern Expedition, but the struggle for national power would continue. During the fighting, all armies shed some of their units, some of which became bandits, others were co-opted as militia, and yet others were used by the Communists to build up bases in the countryside. Warlordism was not vanquished.

The Northern Expedition did not lead to a stable state, but bequeathed a difficult set of problems in terms of personal rivalries, a fragmented military, local brutality, and cultures of violence with which the Nationalists would have to deal and in which it was deeply implicated. The new National Government had little public prestige, was burdened by debt and a bloated military, faced powerful enemies, and it was tainted by its association with criminal gangs and the murderous suppression of opposition during the White Terror. Internally, the rivalry for power continued. It was in effective control of very little, lacked stable sources of revenue, and did not have a cohesive bureaucracy.

What, then, do we make of revolution in a broader sense? I have suggested that we must guard against teleological interpretations of history that underpin revolutionary narratives and which tend to partially allocate blame for undesired outcomes. Similarly, it is time to say farewell to romanticised views of revolution. At the same time, it will not do to dismiss the Northern Expedition as simply a nasty struggle for power. Although it is important to remember that many acted from different concerns which were not necessarily objectionable, revolutionary constructions of the present held a stronghold over the imagination, both among the Communists and the Nationalists. These were not unproblematic. Presentist and dichotomising tendencies fuelled irrational fears. Revolutionary obsessions foreclosed opportunities for compromise, creative re-adjustment, and syncretistic solutions. Revolution naturally demands violence and, in some ways, a deliberate bloodying of the nation or the class. Revolution too is a discursive practice, mobilised in the contest for power and later used to claim with more or less effectiveness an exclusive hold on power, an inequitable distribution of resources, and horrendous regimes of punishment.

Yet, it will not do to dismiss the urgings of revolution as ultimately a deeply destructive error born from a blind illusion about the human condition. If reality proved fractious and far less malleable than anticipated, it is also true that much in that reality was awful. Warlordism was a genuine problem, society was deeply unequal, justice unavailable to most, and economic opportunities open to only a few. Imperialism was offensive, destructive of the financial system, and politically debilitating. To seek to change that and build a new nation, and even to use violence to do so, was not unjustifiable.

No doubt some were swept up by a heightened revolutionary atmosphere, while others indulged baser instincts. But, although Chen Duxiu's policies may have backfired, he also feared the turn towards the military and his policies were designed to keep a broad coalition together. Borodin too attempted to stem the slide towards chaos. Chiang Kaishek fretted about becoming just another warlord, emphasised order and discipline in the exercise of military power, and sought to bureaucratise the White Terror. The times were not such that anyone had the means to impose their will.

4 Nationalism and military reform during the Nanjing Decade (1928–37)

The first three years of the Nanjing Decade were a time of terrible civil wars, debilitating KMT factionalism, and brutality. A study recently produced by the Seminar on Natural Disasters in Modern China makes clear the enormous scale of suffering. If adverse weather conditions may have played some role, the exactions of various military forces and the lack of government formed the main causes. Drought stuck north China in 1928. Four hundred and eighty-seven counties in the provinces of Shaanxi, Gansu, Suiyuan, Shanxi, Hebei, Chahar, Rehe, and Henan reported to have been affected, causing many millions of refugees. The situation worsened in 1929, when the Sino-Western Relief Association reported 20 million casualties, including 6 million deaths. The press reported instances of cannibalism. Storms, destruction by hail, plagues of insects, and epidemics were widespread. In 1930, in north China, 831 counties reported to have been affected by drought and the Yellow River burst its dikes in Shandong. The year 1931 proved a year of severe floods as well as earthquakes. The Yangtze, Yellow, Min, and Pearl Rivers, as well as the Grand Canal, all flooded. The east and central China provinces of Hubei, Hunan, Anhui, Jiangsu, Jiangxi, Zhejiang, Henan, and Shandong were all affected, with the worst hit areas being south Anhui, north Hunan, Henan, and north Jiangsu. In these areas alone, reports suggested, 420,000 people died and 5.5 million refugees took to the roads.[1]

Change came after 1931, largely as a result of Japanese aggression, including its seizure of Manchuria and its horrendous attack on Shanghai in 1932. If outside pressure was a stimulus for co-operation, change too was made possible by Chiang Kaishek's defeat during the War of the Great Plains of 1930 of his most important military rivals, Feng Yuxiang, Yan Xishan, and the Guangxi Clique. In addition, the Communists attempted to exploit the War of the Central Plains to launch attacks with sizeable armed forces on key cities along the Yangtze River, further making it clear that if things continued as they had, the Nationalists' hold on power would not last long. These developments led to a degree of military and political stability, which would last for the next several years and created the basis for a determined attempt to end warlordism, build up new state structures, and transform Chinese society.

From 1932, the Nationalists began to prepare for war with Japan. If in 1931 Chiang Kaishek concluded that war with Japan was impossible, from then on readying China for a major conflict with Japan became a central concern, although it was also hoped that an accommodation which would satisfy nationalist aspirations might be reached. The Nationalist approach was to construct a modern nation around the core of radically changed military. Militarily the goal was a small but modern elite force staffed by a professional officers corps and manned through a system of national military service. Politically, the ideal was an efficient state structure run by honest and expert officials committed to the state rather than for personal profit or power and able to guide the whole population to a common purpose. Socially, the aim was a disciplined, educated, and healthy population participant in the institutions of the new nation, enthusiastic about its armies, and free from what were seen as the vices of the past, such as opium consumption, superstition, disregard of the law, lack of attention to cleanliness and hygiene, rudeness, and slovenliness. Economically, China was to become a country with large modern industries capable of producing steel, radios, aeroplanes, tanks, and cars; a modern communications infrastructure with a national system of highways and railroads, radio broadcasting stations, and telephone and telegraph networks; and a financial system in which there was a single state currency, banks provided credit, deposit, and transfer facilities, and a fiscal system that created stability by dividing central and local taxes and balanced income and expenditure.

The aesthetic of a vigorous nationalist modernity shaped most policies. An advertisement in school textbooks promised that the Sun Yatsen suit, worn by officialdom, was 'healthy because they buttoned in the centre front, beautiful, and will inculcate a martial spirit'.[2] Hence, the promotion of supposedly healthy leisure activities such as sports, the stipulation of new rules for modern wedding ceremonies and funerals, the campaigns against waste and dissipation, and the creation of new rituals such as weekly memorial meetings for Sun Yatsen, required of all KMT, government, and educational organs. Hence too, the articulation of norms for polite intercourse, private behaviour, and public attitudes thought appropriate to modern, decent, and orderly societies. All meetings were to begin with three bows to the KMT and National Government flags as well as a portrait of Sun Yatsen, the reading of his Last Testament, and the observation of three minutes of solemn silence.[3] The first mooting of the Three Gorges Dam project, the construction of grand buildings with much modern concrete in the capital, the participation in the Berlin Olympics, and a fondness for mass rallies were all emblematic of this aesthetic.

Demobilisation

Chiang Kaishek once stated that 'it has been well said in our classics that soldiers are like water: they can carry the ship of state, or sink it'.[4] According to reports that Group Army Commanders filed with the Demobilisation and Re-organisation Conference of January 1929, at the end of the Northern Expedition the number of troops was:[5]

1st Group Army	224,000	(Chiang Kaishek)
2nd Group Army	269,000	(Feng Yuxiang)
3rd Group Army	206,000	(Yan Xishan)
4th Group Army	287,000	(Li Zongren)
Fengtian Clique	186,000	
Sichuan	200,000	(divided in separate military zones)
Yunnan	70,000	(Long Yun)
Guizhou	60,000	
Total	1,502,000	

These figures probably understated the true state of affairs. Chiang Kaishek later maintained that the 1st Group Army had at least 500,000 troops, the 2nd 600,000, and the 3rd 260,000.[6] The total number of armed forces, excluding militias and bandits, was then at least 2 million, and probably higher.

The political and military fudge that made the competing forces involved in the Northern Expedition co-operate in the march on Beiping – Beijing (Northern Capital) became known as Beiping (Northern Peace) once the Nationalists established their capital in Nanjing – laid the basis for the civil warfare that broke out almost immediately following the declaration of victory. While nominally subordinate to the Central Political Council in Nanjing, the Branch Political Councils were in reality autonomous administrations with their own military forces. Feng Yuxiang headed the Branch Council at Kaifeng and Yan Xishan was in charge of the one at Taiyuan. The Guangxi Clique headed two councils. Li Zongren was in charge in Wuhan and Bai Chongxi in Beiping, while Li Jishen, who maintained a complex relation with the Guangxi Clique, was in charge at Canton. A sixth council was established at Shenyang. It was headed by Zhang Xueliang, who had taken over from his father following the latter's assassination by the Japanese during his retreat from north China.[7]

The choice that Chiang Kaishek's regime in Nanjing faced was whether to leave the Branch Political Councils alone for the time being or abolish them and centralise power. The latter course of action was virtually inevitable. The Northern Expedition had been conducted in the name of ending warlordism and achieving national unity; not to confront regional military powers would make a mockery of that claim. Chinese history was full of examples of hostages to fortune resulting from a failure to confront regional military powers. The Taiping Rebellion had failed in part because the Taiping government had consisted of four separate administrative systems, each controlled by one of the four Taiping kings. The Qing victory had been facilitated by the civil wars between these four kings. A new dynasty that had allowed military leaders to hold on to separate bases after the conquest of power was likely to have to face them on the battlefield later. In the case of the Qing, in the 1670s, the Kangxi Emperor had faced three such feudatories in south China. They had co-operated with the Qing conquest, but had established independent fiefs, which they hoped to pass on intact to their sons. One of Chiang's advisors, Yang Yongtai, one of the main figures of the Political Science Clique, a group of tough-minded but pragmatic reformers, described the effort of abolishing the military forces of the new warlords as 'the elimination of feudatories' (xiao fan).[8]

Chiang Kaishek cast his attempt to defang his military rivals as an effort at demobilisation, necessary to free funds for national reconstruction and surely appropriate now that a new national government was in place. This allowed him to take the moral high ground and made it difficult for his opponents to resist his efforts. But they had not fought during the Northern Expedition, increased their military forces, and established new bases to be sidelined by someone still regarded as an upstart.

Ritual and political moves

On 18 June 1928, Chiang Kaishek began a tour by train that took him to the headquarters of his rivals to invite them to travel with him to Beiping to discuss demobilisation, military re-organisation, and political affairs. He first moved in the accompaniment of

Li Jishen, Cai Yuanpei, and Wu Zhihui to Wuhan to meet Li Zongren. For Chiang to travel to Wuhan, or to any other of the Headquarters, rather than order Li, Feng, or Yan to come to Nanjing was an ostentatious way to display his willingness to lose face for the sake of the nation. Li Zongren met Chiang at the train station, but at a banquet held in Chiang's honour, the three most prominent military leaders of the 4th Group Army in Wuhan failed to attend and left their seats empty. Although Li in his memoirs pleaded innocence and suggested that his chief commanders were not types who attended banquets, this was a snub calculated to embarrass Chiang.[9]

Nonetheless, on 2 July, Li Zongren left with Chiang on a train to meet Feng Yuxiang in Zhengzhou. Feng met the train with Chiang Kaishek and Li Zongren and their entourages at Zhengzhou. After a short stay, all travelled on to Beiping, where they were met by Yan Xishan and Bai Chongxi at the train station at Changxindian. On 6 July, Chiang Kaishek, flanked by Li Zongren, Yan Xishan, Feng Yuxiang, and several other military and political leaders, joined in a memorial ceremony for Sun Yatsen. In the presence of Sun Yatsen's imperfectly embalmed body in the Azure Cloud Temple in the Western Hills, Chiang, carefully positioned in the lead ritual role, made a report to Sun's spirit elaborating the great trials and ultimate success of the Northern Expedition. The double message was that Chiang Kaishek was the leader who had realised Sun's dream and hence was his legitimate successor and that no further military action could be condoned now that the task that Sun had set his followers had been completed. Chiang then broke down in tears. Li Zongren stated in his memoirs that Chiang's show of emotion had been excessive and that he regretted that he could not match Chiang in the skill of letting his tears flow at such an opportune moment.[10] Feng, forced into a subordinate role, took Chiang by the arm to lead him away to recover his composure.[11]

Chiang's sojourn was accompanied by a carefully staged series of events, that put heavy pressure on the Army Group Commanders. From 1 to 10 July, a financial conference was convened in Nanjing, attended by representative from various financially important institutions. They discussed the nation's financial problems and underscored the financial imperative of demobilisation while also by their presence signalling their support for the Nanjing Government of Chiang Kaishek.[12] On 2 July, in a lecture at the KMT Central Office that was part of a commemoration ceremony for Sun Yatsen, He Yingqin discussed the need for army demobilisation. On 7 July, he telegraphed Chiang Kaishek, Feng Yuxiang, Yan Xishan, and Li Zongren to re-iterate its importance.[13] On the same day, the Ministry of Foreign Affairs issued a declaration that called for negotiations with foreign powers about the Unequal Treaties.[14]

Chiang, Li, Feng, Yan, and several other leading military figures formally discussed demobilisation on 11 and 12 July and signed the 'Proposals for Military Re-organisation'. This document called for the organisation of a National Defence Council under the National Government to be made up of the most important military leaders and suggested the establishment of a National Army (Guojun) out of the four group armies. The National Army was to be formed by an Army Re-organisation and Demobilisation Council made up of the Army Group Commanders-in-Chief, their Chiefs-of-Staff, as well as three or five members of the KMT Central Executive Committee. The post of Commander-in-Chief, that of Chiang Kaishek, was to be abolished following the formal establishment of the Council. Demobilised soldiers, it was agreed, would be re-employed in a military police of 200,000 men strong, local police forces, land reclamation and colonisation projects, and industry.[15]

Chiang Kaishek issued a circular letter of 13 July 1928 to all ranking military figures.[16] He argued that demobilisation was necessary to free the funds required for national reconstruction and for constructing a small but strong military capable of protecting the nation and society. Chiang stated that annual revenue amounted to 500 million *yuan* a year. Payment of foreign debt required 20 per cent of this, according to Chiang. He noted that even if half of the budget was allocated to military expenditures, that still would mean that only 30 per cent would be available for national reconstruction. The upkeep of 500,000 troops required 15 million *yuan* per month, or 180 million per year. Seventy-eight million was required for the navy, the airforce, arsenals, and fortifications. If the military budget was to remain between 200 and 250 million a year, the government could afford no more than 500,000 troops. Chiang argued that this force should not be personal or local, but should be a National Defence Army (Guofangjun) as outlined in Sun's *National Defence Plan*. The centre should have control over all military affairs. The next day, at a press conference, Chiang made public 'A Proposal for Army Reform', 'Methods for Demobilisation of a Reformed Military', and 'Views on Demobilisation and Rehabilitation' and declared that he opposed 'the military occupying local bases' and that 'the key question for China's survival today is whether we are able to carry out demobilisation and reform the military'.[17]

On 14 August, these proposals were submitted to the 5th Plenum of the Second Central Executive Committee.[18] Its resolution about military re-organisation stated that the guiding principle of demobilisation was to 'eradicate the evil habit of military men controlling their own private forces and their own regional bases, to establish a new foundation for national construction, and make all armies in the country politicised forces, so that they become the army of the people'.[19] Feng Yuxiang was appointed Minister of War, Yan Xishan Minister for Domestic Affairs, and Li Zongren was appointed to the Military Advisory Council. All, then, were invited to leave there bases and come to Nanjing.

Besides endorsing the Proposals for Military Re-organisation, the plenum resolved that the period of military rule had ended and that now the period of political tutelage had begun. In accordance with Sun Yatsen's theory of five branches of government, a Legislative Yuan, Judicial Yuan, Executive Yuan, Examination Yuan, and Discipline Yuan were established. The plenum furthermore adopted resolutions about implementing a budget system, re-organising fiscal affairs, and economic policy. It elected a new Central Political Council, which included Chiang Kaishek, Wang Jingwei, and Hu Hanmin in an obvious bit to reconcile the interest of the main KMT factions. A Ministry for Army Administration, a Staff Ministry, and a Training Directorate took over the functions of the MAC. A National Defence Council was organised. Its members included the Chairman of the Government, the head of the Executive Yuan, the Chief-of-Staff, the Director of Training, the Ministers of Foreign Affairs and Finance, and the head of the Military Advisory Council to which the leading military figures were 'promoted'.[20] The Fifth Plenum also resolved to eliminate the Branch Political Councils.[21]

Despite the fact that the Army Group commanders in reality continued to increase their forces and took preparations for war, the Demobilisation Conference did begin on

1 January 1929, in Nanjing. The participants took the following oath during its opening ceremony:

> we solemnly swear before the grave of Sun Yatsen that we will respectfully obey his last will and commit ourselves to troop demobilisation and saving the country. I shall implement all the decisions of the meeting, without any consideration for selfish interest, resort to false pretexts, misrepresentations of the truth, or abandonment of our goal halfway. I shall accept the severest punishment in case of violation.[22]

The declaration issued at the opening of the conference by the Demobilisation Council stressed that the conference's decisions regarding a unified military system, the organisation and size of its armed forces, military expenditures, and the allocation of divisions to specific areas would affect China for a long time.[23] In a speech, Chiang drew a comparison with Japan. There, he argued, military power had been in the hands of the shoguns. Samurai had been subordinate generals, with their own lands and their own troops. Sometimes they had been loyal, sometimes rebellious. Before the Meiji restoration, Japan had been the same as China now, Chiang stated, but then the shoguns had been defeated. He continued

> Unlike the selfish Chinese militarists of today, the victorious generals immediately handed over all their powers and surrendered their lands and troops. Japan was unified and the troops formerly under different generals were re-organised into a state army. After that Western sciences were introduced and many improvements followed. These are the causes of Japanese greatness. Should you wish to remain militarists, and counter-revolutionaries, I have nothing further to say to you.[24]

Chiang then went on to say that the Northern Expedition had been completed and all leading military figures had been included in the government. The next steps to be secured by the meeting was to determine arrangements for the centre and the province to share financial and administrative power. While those arrangements were up for discussion, what was not, according to Chiang, was that the centre should have complete authority over all military affairs and foreign relations.

In a memorandum on the financial situation, Song Ziwen backed up Chiang's message by describing the desperate financial plight of the National Government. He expected a deficit for 1929 of 50 million *yuan*, on a total budget of 458 million. The central government depended largely on revenues from the Salt Gabelle (117 million), the Maritime Customs (192 million), and the *lijin* or transit tax (47 million). Song noted that foreign recognition and the recovery of tariff autonomy had been secured on the condition that Nanjing recognised all foreign debt. Revenue would suffer from the promised abolition of the *lijin* tax. Song proposed a limit on military expenditures of 192 million, which equalled 78 per cent of all revenue after collection costs (95 million) and debt service charges (155 million) had been subtracted.[25]

On 18 January, the meeting did adopt a formal agreement. Posts such as that of Group Army Commander and Army Corps Commander were abolished. Six demobilisation areas were to be set up, each with a Demobilisation Office appointed by the government and reporting to the national Demobilisation Council. A first project was to draw up registers of all army officers. In accordance with the needs of the new army, the best were to be re-trained at a central military academy to ensure uniformity and standardisation. Others would be re-assigned. Registers would also be made of all army equipment and stored under government supervision. The new army would not exceed sixty-five divisions, to be gradually reduced until military expenditures were limited to 41 per cent of the budget. The Ministry of Finance would arrange funding for demobilisation and would control its disbursement. Provinces would be allowed a force of no more than 3,000 troops, paid for from the provincial budget. Funds which in the past had been raised locally for the support of troops would be placed under the control of the Ministry of Finance.[26] Demobilisation was to be completed in six months.[27]

Li Zongren wrote in his memoirs that Chiang's purpose was 'to force his opponents into some move that would give him the necessary excuse for "punitive action"'.[28] If that was an extreme way of putting it, it is nonetheless true that Chiang had put the Army Group commanders in an untenable position. His ritual and political manoeuvres had sidelined them, his comparison of them to selfish militarists was insulting, demobilisation would reduce their military forces, while the elimination of the Branch Councils deprived them of their political roles.

The Civil Wars

The first war took place between the Guangxi Clique and Chiang Kaishek. Using the authority of the Branch Political Council at Wuhan, Li Zongren, on 21 February 1929, fired Lu Diping, the governor of Hunan who had decided that it was in his interest to ally himself with Chiang Kaishek. Hunan was strategically important to the Guangxi Clique as it connected Li in Wuhan and his base in Guangxi. Chiang had induced Lu to remit central taxes not to Wuhan but to Nanjing.[29] Chiang in return sent large supplies of arms and munitions to Lu. He also sent emissaries to Wuhan to induce generals of the 4th Group Army to come over to his own side.[30] Guangxi forces then attacked Changsha. Chiang secured his northern flank by promising Feng Yuxiang control over all of Shandong and by sending him substantial funds, perhaps as much as 2 million *yuan*.[31]

This war lasted two months, and left the Guangxi Clique thoroughly defeated and removed from Nanjing-controlled positions of power. Part of Chiang's strategy was to isolate the Clique's leading figures from each other and sow internal dissension. On 21 March, the National Demobilisation Conference at its 10th meeting decided to abolish the 4th Demobilisation Office, which had been headed by Bai Chongxi, and instead appoint second rank leaders such as Li Pinxian, He Jian, and Chen Jitang to handle responsibilities for demobilisation each in their own areas.[32] On 27 March, the Third Congress of the KMT expelled Li Zongren and Bai Chongxi. The Governor of Guangdong, Li Jishen, was also expelled and actually imprisoned. In May, the Guangxi Clique tried to attack Guangdong, but there they were resisted by the recently elevated Chen Jitang. They then attacked Hunan, but were defeated by Chiang Kaishek. By the end of June, Bai and Huang had to flee, momentarily, to French-Indo China. They soon regrouped in Guangxi.[33]

The second war, with Feng Yuxiang, began almost simultaneously.[34] After Chiang Kaishek and the Guangxi Clique went to battle, Feng had himself appointed 'Commander in Chief of the North-west Army to Protect the Party and Save the

Nation'. On 23 May, the KMT Central Executive Committee ex-communicated him. Chiang Kaishek bribed two of his allies, Han Fuju and Shi Yousan. With his alliance in disarray and after several nasty defeats, Feng announced his retirement. He secretly travelled to Shanxi. Yan, however, refused to join the war, but did allow Feng to stay in his area, probably as a signal to Chiang that he would let Feng lose and join him if Chiang Kaishek attacked him. By mid-July, Chiang had occupied Loyang.

After the conclusion of these wars, Chiang Kaishek again sought to push through demobilisation.[35] On 12 August, the Demobilisation Council, now shorn of the Guangxi Clique and Feng Yuxiang, adopted new regulations. Demobilised officers were to receive pay for three months from the government. Troops would receive back pay and a one-off payment of between 21 and 30 *yuan*, plus a set of clothes.[36] The Council decided to demobilise all forces in two stages before March 1930.[37]

Civil War broke out again in April 1930. The War of the Central Plains pitted the combined forces of Feng Yuxiang, Yan Xishan, and the Guangxi Clique against Chiang Kaishek. They gained the backing of Chiang's political opponents, including Wang Jingwei's Reform Faction. Yan Xishan took the lead in setting up the alliance. During the first two Civil Wars against the Guangxi Clique and Feng Yuxiang, Chiang Kaishek had kept Yan Xishan neutral with a grant of 6 million *yuan*. Soon after the conclusion of these campaigns, he stopped sending funds to Yan. Song Ziwen as Minister of Finance sent representatives to take charge of important revenue collection agencies in north China in Yan's control, including the Tianjin Maritime Customs Station and the Changlu Salt Commissioner's Office.[38]

In March 1930, Yan Xishan invited Chiang's opponents to a meeting at Taiyuan, the capital of Shanxi province, to discuss national affairs. All those who had lost out in past military and political struggles sent representatives. Political and symbolic manoeuvres aimed at casting Chiang's opponents as reasonable, accommodating, and acting in the interest of the nation. Yan Xishan in a telegram of 10 February offered his resignation and suggested that for the sake of the nation Chiang should do the same.[39] A series of telegrams were then issued to urge Yan Xishan not to resign. On 13 March, telegrams by Li Zongren, Zhang Fakui, and others supported the appointment of Yan, Feng, Li, and Zhang Xueliang as Commander-in-Chief and Vice Commanders of all military forces in China. A week later, Yan and Feng issued a telegram calling for a war of punishment against Chiang, again supported by a flurry of telegrams.[40]

Militarily, the strategy of the anti-Chiang alliance was to take the offensive in Henan in order to contain Chiang Kaishek along the Long–Hai and Beiping–Hankou Railroads. A simultaneous offensive in Shandong would establish control over that province. The forces would advance towards Xuzhou and Wuhan, by attacking eastward along the Long–Hai Railroad and southward along the Beiping–Hankou and Tianjin–Pukou Railroads. Zhang Xueliang would not join these attacks, but he promised munitions. In the south, the Guangxi Clique would attack Hunan and Wuhan to link up with the forces of Feng Yuxiang and Yan Xishan in the north. The order for attack was given on 23 April. Chiang Kaishek's forces numbered about 300,000; those of his opponents, although less well organised and less well armed, at 700,000 were vastly superior in numbers.[41]

The war took place in three different theatres across China. Battles were fought in Shandong, Henan, and Hunan and Hubei. The fighting lasted five months, involved more than 1 million troops, and exacted 300,000 casualties.[42] In the south, the forces of the Guangxi Clique never attained their objectives. They did advance through Hunan and without serious opposition reached the province's border with Hubei. However, their communications with their base in Guangxi were cut in early June when a Cantonese force occupied Hengyang in Hunan Province. Rather than trying to seize Wuhan, a strategy that had failed during the Northern Expedition, they decided to return to Hunan. Li Zongren concentrated his forces, but a drought meant that they could not live off the land. Li's forces had been defeated by the end of June and he was forced to retreat to Guangxi.[43]

In the north, however, the alliance came close to defeating Chiang Kaishek. In battles along the Long–Hai Railroad in May, forces led by Chen Cheng, one of Chiang's most trusted generals, were mauled and relief forces were defeated. Chiang had to retreat and was only able to stabilise this front by pouring in further relief forces. In June, he narrowly escaped capture. At the same time Feng Yuxiang defeated Chiang Kaishek in an important battle along the Beiping–Hankou Railroad, but Feng stopped the offensive towards Wuhan when he heard that Li Zongren had turned back south. Chiang also suffered defeats in Shandong. Yan's forces took the Shandong capital in mid-June and began an offensive down the Tianjin–Pukou Railroad.

Facing defeat, Chiang began a 'peace campaign' with Zhang Xueliang as intermediary. When, believing in the possibility of victory, Yan and Feng declined,[44] Chiang Kaishek launched an offensive towards Kaifeng to attack Feng Yuxiang. While the outcome of this offensive hung in the balance, the strategic situation changed when Chiang won the battle for the key railroad junction of Bangbu in Anhui. The large numbers of troops that had been tied down there became available for deployment elsewhere. A counter-offensive in August by Feng Yuxiang towards Xuzhou disintegrated when two of Feng's subordinates allied themselves with Zhang Xueliang.[45] By early September, Chiang Kaishek began offensives towards the Beiping–Hankou Railroad as well as towards Loyang to threaten Feng's flanks. Zhang Xueliang, induced by a bribe of perhaps 10 million *yuan* and the promise that he could rule over China north of the Yellow River, on 19 September issued a telegram announcing that he had accepted appointment as Vice-Commander of the National Army. This brought the war to a close.[46]

The Civil Wars dragged down everybody. Out of the wreckage of the old, no new nation gloriously embraced a new future. The National Government in Nanjing lacked any sort of mandate and huge disasters affected millions. Even such a disastrous and large-scale war as the Battle of the Central Plains did not bring an end to the violence. In October 1930, Chiang Kaishek called on the KMT to convene a National Assembly to draw up a constitution for the period of political tutelage and to dedicate itself to 'eliminating Communist bandits', 'reforming financial affairs', 'eradicating corruption', 'developing the economy', and 'implementing local self-government'.[47] Hu Hanmin, the President of the Legislative Yuan who feared that Chiang aimed at creating a US-style presidency, opposed on the rather technical ground that Sun Yatsen had not allowed for a constitution in the period of political tutelage. When Chiang imprisoned Hu, his military and political rivals called for Chiang Kaishek's immediate resignation and prepared for military action. In the fall, the Japanese attack on Manchuria prevented the outbreak of a full-scale civil war. In December, following complex negotiations and deals, Chiang Kaishek was retired and a new government under Sun Fo was installed. With Hu Hanmin, Wang Jingwei, and Chiang all biding their time, this government never had much chance. In December, it fell when Chiang Kaishek and Wang Jingwei struck a deal. Wang gained appointment as President of the Executive Yuan in January 1932, while Chiang Kaishek became head of a re-established MAC.

Ruling through the military

This deal held for the next several years. If Chiang's military victories, or perhaps military exhaustion on all sides, helped in creating a degree of stability, the Japanese occupation of Manchuria, the assault on Shanghai, and the intensification of the challenge of the Communists were probably the more important factors.[48] Chiang Kaishek increasingly ruled through Field Headquarters, in part to bypass Wang Jingwei in charge of the Executive Yuan but also to discipline local KMT and government organisations. He established the first Field Headquarters in Wuhan in August 1930. It was put in charge of combating banditry and Communism in Hunan, Hubei, and Jiangxi. Other Field Headquarters were subsequently created for the border regions of Yu E Wan (Henan, Hubei, and Anhui), Yu Shan Jin (Henan, Shaanxi, and Shanxi), and Jiangsu.[49] Following the Japanese occupation of Manchuria, a Beiping Headquarters was added for the provinces of Rehe, Hebei, Chahar, and Suiyuan.[50] Field Headquarters, from 1932 subordinate to the revived MAC, were far more than just military command posts. In the areas of their jurisdiction, they had supreme authority including over the KMT and the government. Especially the Nanchang Field Headquarters, established in 1933, was a powerful organisation as it functioned as the effective government for sizeable portions of Jiangxi, Hunan, Fujian, Hubei, and Guangdong.[51] It was through Field Headquarters that Chiang Kaishek pursued his reform programmes of the military and civil administrations and sought to consolidate his government.

Field Headquarters

Chiang Kaishek decided to act against Communist bases immediately after the end of the War of the Central Plains. Following defeat in the first three suppression campaigns, the last one of which had nearly succeeded but had to be called off because of the crisis caused by the Japanese attacks, the Nationalists adopted a new strategy, known as 'three parts military and seven parts civil'. Yang Yongtai, the man who had advised Chiang on 'the suppression of the feudatories', was one of the main proponents of this strategy, and became the chief official responsible for its implementation. Yang was a key official during the Nanjing Decade. Assassinated in 1936, in circumstances that remain unclear, in addition to the influences already outlined, Yang was one of the principal formulators of the policy of 'first pacify the country, then resist foreign enemies' that guided Chiang Kaishek's approach to the Japanese and Communists from 1931 to 1937.[52]

In the new strategy, broad economic, social, and administrative reforms accompanied military operations. These drew from dynastic ways of fighting rebellion. In one article, Yang traced the history of reform attempts since the Taiping Rebellion such as the Self-Strengthening Movement, the 1898 Reform Movement, the 1911 Revolution, and the May Fourth Movement, which, Yang argued, had focused, respectively, on technology, political change, constitutional change, and cultural change. He argued that his own reforms, combining aspects of statecraft, self-strengthening, and constitutional reforms were based on the premise that mindsets and habits needed to be changed in order for China to become a modern and disciplined society. Reform, according to Yang, had to begin at the lowest level.[53] Yang stated that the task of government was to institute 'guan, jiao, yang, wei,' or governance, education, sustenance, and security.[54] He believed that a strict and disciplined government by fair and clean officials provided the framework that would make modernisation possible. That government, initially to be resurrected with military assistance, should provide local security, foster nationalism, decency, and modernity, and promote economic productivity.

Yang Yongtai also built on recent experiences in bandit suppression. Bandit suppression in Hunan, as a report by its governor to Chiang Kaishek showed, had succeeded in pacifying Hunan following the Northern Expedition by restoring bureaucratic government, mobilising local elites to organise militias capable of maintaining local order, and strengthening sub-county bureaucratic authorities. In his writing Yang also discussed how the Guangxi Clique had brought Guangxi under centralised control by unifying local educational, governmental, and security institutions into one single structure, which also controlled local militia. Yang sought to realise this plan first while in charge of civil affairs at the Yu E Wan Suppression Command and then at the Nanchang Headquarters.[55]

The Nanchang Headquarters itself came under the MAC to 'unify organs of military command' on 24 May 1933.[56] The MAC was formally re-established, on 29 January 1932, by the KMT Political Council in the wake of Japan's attack on Manchuria and Shanghai. Feng Yuxiang, Yan Xishan, Zhang Xueliang, and Li Zongren were appointed to it, but now not as equals but as clear subordinates to Chiang, who was its chairman.[57] Beforehand, already on 6 July 1931, rules for the Staff and General Offices of the MAC had been adopted, which defined its task as organising 'resistance to foreign aggression and military reorganisation', and hence it may have begun operating before its formal establishment at a time when tensions with Japan were mounting.[58] Its remit included preparations for war with Japan and domestic pacification, illustrating that the two were not considered mutually exclusive. Regulations of 19 April 1932 stated that the head of the MAC – Chiang Kaishek – had to sign all orders and documents issued in the name of the MAC. Chiang also controlled appointment to MAC posts. The committee's tasks were simply said to assist him in carrying out these functions.[59] Through its Field Headquarters, the new MAC exercised control over local party organisations, civil administration, the economy, and of course military affairs.

Reform of government administration

Administrative reform aimed at centralising power in a few key officials at the provincial, regional, and county level. During the Republic, offices and personnel had proliferated at these levels, and authority had become dispersed in committees and special bureaus. A key official was to be the Special Intendent of Government (Xingzheng Ducha Zhuanyuan), a post first created in 1932.[60] The Special Intendent was the magistrate of one county and oversaw 4–15 other ones. Yang Yongtai stated that he had drawn on experiments with similar institutions earlier in several provinces.[61] He believed that they combined all the advantages of the prefectures, circuits, and independent *zhous* of the past, while avoiding the creation of a new tier of government, which would merely lead to the proliferation of offices, diffusion of authority, increases in expenditures, and further complications in the flow of documents.[62] By 1935, the intendencies existed not only in the area controlled by the Yu E Wan Bandit Suppression Command but also in Jiangxi, Fujian, Sichuan, Guizhou, Shaanxi, Gansu, Zhejiang, and other provinces.[63] Special Intendents supervised all civil and military affairs in their jurisdictions. Initially their most important task was to set up the *baojia* system and command the Peace Preservation Forces, to be explained in more detail in the next section. They were responsible directly to the Suppression Command and later the Nanchang Headquarters.

A second reform was the unification of executive authority at the provincial level. Before the reforms, a committee governed a province.[64] Although a chairman was formally in charge, members of the committee controlled their own bureaux (ting). They issued orders directly to subordinate agencies at the county level and reported to their ministries in the capital. In order to ensure financial discipline and unity of purpose, the Nanchang Headquarters issued 'Regulations for Administration from a Joint Office' (Sheng Zhengfu Heshu Bangong). It proscribed the proliferation of further government agencies and demanded that all documents were channelled through the Secretariat of the Provincial Chairman and signed by him. According to a 1935 report by the Nanchang Headquarters, financial accountability and bureaucratic downsizing produced savings of several hundred thousand *yuan* in most provinces. To make centralisation effective, Chiang Kaishek ordered that communications between Nanjing and the seven Yangtze Provinces was never to take longer than forty-eight hours.[65]

At the county level a similar reform – 'the substitution of bureaus for sections' (cai ju gai ke) – was implemented. In 1932, the Yu E Wan Bandit Suppression Command issued regulations to realise this reform.[66] Executive authority was to be unified in the magistracy, all tax collection should be undertaken by one agency under his supervision, all documents were to follow one channel, and all surcharges and customary fees should be eliminated. The magistrate was also to be in charge of local militia.[67]

The baojia system

A goal of the Nanjing Government from the beginning was the restoration of the *baojia*, a traditional system of local mutual responsibility and policing. On 23 May 1928, even before the Northern Expedition had been completed, Chiang Kaishek telegraphed Xue Dubi, the head of the Ministry of Domestic Affairs, ordering him to ensure that household registers were drawn up and verified, land measured, and militia trained in Zhejiang, Jiangsu, and Anhui, in order to secure the area around the capital. On the same day, he instructed the provincial secretaries of these provinces to complete the verification of household registers within three months and to order county magistrates to establish militia. The performance of magistrates would be judged by their completion of this task.[68]

Chiang could point to a basis for this policy in the KMT's Manifesto (Zhenggang), adopted by the 1st Congress in January 1924. He did so in 1932, when he again turned his attention to implementing the *baojia*.[69] Its revival was also accompanied by a series of publications outlining its origins in Chinese history. They stressed that the institution had deep roots in Chinese civilisation and hence was profoundly 'Chinese'.[70] They also emphasised that it fitted local conditions in the countryside, was familiar to local populations, and had often been important to making China strong and vigorous.

The *baojia* was to create the basis for compulsory military service. The KMT's Manifesto's had pledged the 'gradual transition from a mercenary system to compulsory national military service'.[71] In 1928, He Yingqin drafted a 'Proposal To Change To National Military Service' in which he proposed a system of national military service based on the *baojia*.[72] He argued that many of the problems China faced were the result of mercenary recruitment practices, which had given rise to private armies made up of the dross of society that constantly fought each other but were not able to defend China from external enemies. According to He, mercenaries were expansive, had no loyalty to the central state, were difficult to demobilise, and received little training.

He argued for universal military service also because it provided a way to recover Chinese national vigour. According to He Yingqin, China's weakness had been the result of a switch to mercenary armies in the Song Dynasty and the abandonment of traditional systems such as 'accommodating soldiers amongst the peasants' and 'recruit-ment on the basis of the number of males'. He pointed out as well that national mili-tary service would generate a large pool of people with military skills who could be mobilised in time of war without great cost to the state. The quality of the army would be much higher, as draftees would include people with good education.

Finally, according to He, national military service was a characteristic of both eco-nomically advanced countries in the West like Germany as well as of revolutionary countries like France. According to He, China's economic backwardness and low levels of education should not be considered an obstacle. He pointed to Guangxi, Yunnan, and Guizhou as examples of provinces that operated systems like the *baojia* with success and which based their armed strength on it. The *baojia* would lay the basis for national military service by registering the population and introducing military skills through regular training and exercises.[73]

He Yingqin was of course aware that not all eligible males could be drawn into the army, even for a short period. That would simply be too expensive. He held up the Japanese system as an appropriate model for China to follow. The Japanese, he explained, drafted a number of conscripts into a standing army for two years after which they became ready reserves (yubei bing) for five years and second reserves (houbei bing) for another ten years. Conscripts surplus to the requirement of the standing army served as First and Second Supplementary Soldiers (buchong bing) in territorial army units. He Yingqin proposed a standing army of fifty divisions based on this system.[74] Those surplus to requirement would be given some military training locally at convenient times.

The Nationalists, then, were deeply committed from 1928 to the *baojia* and compulsory military service as the basis to eradicate warlordism and banditry, and to revitalise China's strength. Civil War and provincial financial deficits prevented its implementa-tion before 1932. However, on 6 October 1932, Chiang ordered local officials from the province down to the Special Intendents and country magistrates to regard the imple-mentation of the *baojia* 'as a policy of the greatest priority. If higher level organs do not within the assigned time ensure its completion, then they will be held accountable for having failed in properly encouraging and implementing it and they will be punished together with lower level organs'.[75] A limit of two years was announced for the completion of organising the *baojia* and creating local militia.[76] The Provincial Chairman of Henan, a province with a notorious bandit problem where CCP influence had been spreading rapidly, was to recruit 3 million peasants into militia within three months.[77]

The Field Headquarters were primarily responsible for implementing the *baojia*, as they were highest local authority in their areas of jurisdiction. Again, the Yu E Wan Bandit Suppression Command under Yang Yongtai had taken the lead. In August 1932, it published regulations that stated that the *baojia*'s purpose was 'to organise the people (minzhong) closely, thoroughly survey households, advance self-protection capabilities, and complete the elimination of bandits and the cleansing of the countryside'.[78] The *baojia* system entailed the registration of all households. Groups of ten or so households were formed in a unit termed a *jia*. Ten or so *jia* became a unit known as *bao*. Several *bao* were grouped together in 'associated bao' (lianbao) at the district level. The *baojia* required households after registration to sign mutual responsibility covenants.

A report by the Yu E Wan Suppression Command attributed local disorder to abuses that had sprung up with the introduction of local self-government, as Yang Yongtai had done. At the county level, the report argued, self-government bodies possessed wide-ranging powers over finance, irrigation, agriculture, and local order.[79] Rather than providing the state with dependable allies in local society, it had spawned hostile agencies, who frequently abused their power. Militias raised by self-government agencies extorted money or other resources.[80] The *baojia* was to restore central government control over local society.

An important purpose of the *baojia* was to remove mercenaries from local militia and to localise them. All *zhuangding* ('healthy' males between the ages of 18 and 40) registered with the *baojia* were to be given military training and formed into local militia. While at first existing militias were simply incorporated, the aim was that over time the militia would be made up of locals only. However, the *baojia*'s military role was to be limited to assistance with local disaster relief, road building, protection against banditry, and the construction of blockhouses and stockades. The programme was less an effort to militarise local society than to discipline and control local sources of violence. Hence attempts to register all arms.

The *baojia* also provided intelligence on local conditions and assisted with scouting and sentry duties. The drawing up of local maps was an important task of *baojia* staff. The *baojia* also assisted with the implementation of the economic embargo against Communist-controlled areas. The *baojia* provided sentry posts and checkpoints to prevent smuggling in proscribed goods, which ranged from arms and ammunition to salt, medicine, petrol, and grains. *Bao* heads made lists of local requirements of proscribed goods using the *baojia* registers. The lists were sent to companies in nationalist areas. The military handled the delivery of the goods.[81]

Checks carried out on *baojia* implementation provide some insight in the effectiveness of the programme. Reports were drawn up that reviewed completion of *baojia* formation in terms of household registration, the appointment of family heads (not necessarily the most senior family member) and *bao* staff, arms registration and marking, the signing of mutual responsibility covenants, the compilation of *bao* maps, the posting of gate signs, as well as military training, militia formation, and the building of local fortifications. A spring 1933 report on Anhui showed that one year into the programme, many counties still were only in the early stages of household registration and *bao* formation, but in others, those steps had been accomplished, thousands and sometimes tens of thousands of arms had been registered, militia had been formed, maps drawn up, and hundreds of fortified positions constructed.[82] In February 1933, the Henan Civil Affairs Bureau reported to the Yu E Wan Bandit Suppression Command that sixty-two counties had advanced to the last stage in the implementation of *baojia* and that twenty-one would soon complete it.[83] This meant that registration, *bao* and *jia* formation, organisation of local militia, arms registration, and so on, were completed in about three-fourths of the counties in Henan.

No full report exists for the implementation of the *baojia* system in Hubei Province. However, an October 1932 report by the Special Intendent of the Third Region of Hubei stated that preparations proceeded according to schedule.[84] Households had been surveyed, household heads appointed and committees were established to draw up *baojia* registers. In early 1933, the Special Administrative Intendents of the Third, Fourth, and Sixth Regions reported completion of the tasks associated with the first stage.[85] The Seventh Region reported problems, partly due to large-scale population movements.[86] In 1935, the Headquarters published a report that included a full list of *baojia* statistics for Anhui, Henan, and Hubei. For each the number of *bao*, *jia*, and households was given. This suggests that in Hubei the programme was implemented to the same extent as in the other provinces. At least registers were drawn up and verified, *baojia* staff appointed, maps made, and covenants signed. A 1935 book on the *baojia* in Jiangxi Province by a local *baojia* inspector noted severe problems, with lax implementation a major issue. However, the *baojia* system had been set up in 72 out of 83 counties in Jiangxi.[87]

The Nationalists were able, by 1936, to link the *baojia* and army recruitment. In 1933, a Military Service Law was passed. In 1936, conscription began when under the Ministry of Military Administration the first twelve Divisional Conscription Headquarters (Shiguanqu Silingbu) set up Conscription Regions (Shiguanqu) in the lower Yangtze provinces. In co-operation with county governments, district offices, and *baojia* staff, the Divisional Conscription Commands compiled registers of *zhuangding*, called up conscripts, and trained them for army service. In December 1936, a first batch of 50,000 conscripts joined 12 National Army divisions, and in 1937 a further 8 Divisional Conscript Commands were activated. A February 1937 report by He Yingqin on military reform stated that by then 20 divisions had been staffed in this way, and that 60 Divisional Conscription Headquarters had been created to ensure that soon all main army divisions would be recruited in this way.[88]

In 1936, regulations were also promulgated for the training of citizen soldiers (guomin bing). All males after their 18th birthday were obliged to enrol in Citizen Soldier Units.[89] Administratively centred at the county level, Citizen Soldiers were trained by Social and Military Training Units at the district level. Instruction included basic military skills, including weapon handling, the construction of fortifications, reconnaissance, implementation of basic orders, and liaison, but also involved spiritual training, delivered in the form of lectures on Sun Yatsen's Three People's Principles, the New Life Movement, and National Economic Construction.[90] Citizen soldiers trained during short periods in the agricultural off-season. Although required 'to perform policing services in case of temporary emergencies', the purposes of the programme, as the MAC explained in February 1937, was to raise awareness of the nation, nurture heroic and martial attitudes, and prepare for conscription. The MAC criticised local government for having been too determined and enthusiastic in implementing the programme. Considerable local trouble had been the result, and that was precisely the opposite of what had been desired.[91]

Peace Preservation forces

Chiang Kaishek wrote in a report of November 1935 that in 1933, a programme had begun to bring local militia under control. They had, Chiang argued, been controlled by evil gentry and local bullies, which had brought much harm to their localities. The reforms attempted to create a Peace Preservation force built from the county upward, with uniform organisational formats, establishments, and training. Existing militia were to be drawn into the Peace Preservation troops, with county magistrates, aided by qualified military experts, appointing the officers of the Peace Preservation forces and directing their training. The Peace Preservation forces were to 'shoulder responsibility for cleansing their counties from banditry and maintaining local order'.[92] These forces were paid from county budgets. The collection of extra taxes locally (tanpai) for this purpose was proscribed.[93] Non-locals were to be eliminated from these forces, and weapons were to be guarded properly.[94]

In June 1934, the Nanchang Headquarters convened a local security conference.[95] Representatives from Jiangsu, Zhejiang, Henan, Hubei, Hunan, Anhui, Jiangxi, Fujian, and Shaanxi attended. Each reported on progress in creating Peace Preservation forces in their areas of jurisdiction. Yang Yongtai presided over the meeting. In his summary, he stated that there were four stages in achieving local security.[96] The first was to unify armed forces within a county, the next to do so within a region, then in a province, and finally within the nation. In Hunan, according to Yang, all Peace Preservation Detachments were under provincial control. Although Hunan was an exception, the first stage, of making sure that counties controlled the recruitment, transfers, training, and financing of Peace Preservation forces – that is of local armed units – had been essentially completed in all areas. 'Most provinces', he stated, 'were now proceeding from the first to the second stage'.[97] The cost of local security had been greatly reduced. In Hubei, the costs incurred by militias had amounted to 15 million *yuan*, which had been reduced by two-third due to the reforms. Savings had been at least half for Anhui, Henan, and Jiangxi as well.[98] Counties drew up budgets and supervised tax collection and disbursement for the local security forces.[99]

Table 4.1 was included with the minutes and papers of the Second Conference on the Peace Preservation forces, held at Nanchang in June 1934, just before the last suppression campaign against the Communists began.[100] The table was based on reports from provincial Peace Preservation offices and were obviously incomplete. The figures in Table 4.1 suggest reasonable success in creating Peace Preservation forces. Yang Yongtai summarised progresses at the meeting in establishing Peace Preservation as follows.

Table 4.1 The Peace Preservation forces (June 1934)

	Jiangsu	Zhejiang	Henan	Hubei	Hunan	Anhui	Jiangxi	Fujian	Shaanxi
Provincial establishment	7,810		9,217		33,824	3,531	9,391	21,727	16,542
County establishment			45,559	34,733		20,702	30,456	8,132	
Armaments – province									
Handguns	5,748	6,937	4,720		21,096	3,027	6,984	12,512	
Mortars	32	52	32				8	19	
Machine guns	70	375	73		30		103	42	
Armaments – county									
Handguns		15,300	17,877	28,682		17,795	27,399		16,243
Expenditures per month									
Provincial forces	150,000	210,000	103,428		460,000	39,709	176,413	362,462	
County forces	330,000	300,000	500,000	400,000		275,000	294,181	120,130	140,240

In Jiangsu, bandits now are active only in the two counties of Lianshui and Shuyang north of the Yangtze River. The interior of Zhejiang is quiet. Only pirates and Communist bandits disturb the coast and the border area between Fujian and Zhejiang. Henan used to be the province with most bandit bands. Large bandit bands have gradually been eliminated now. Large bandit bands also regularly hit Anhui. There bandits now create disturbances only in three counties in the Three Provinces Border Area. The Hunan Peace Preservation forces are strong enough so that they can maintain order within the province and moreover elements of it have accompanied the Western Route Army in bandit suppression outside of Hunan itself. Hubei's interior is quiet. Only scattered bandits still disturb counties in its northern, southern, and eastern borders. In Jiangxi, Peace Preservation forces have participated in bandit suppression more than 200 times in the last year. In this time the strength of provinces to suppress banditry has greatly increased.[101]

Economic assistance

Economic assistance focused on promoting co-operatives. Co-operatives provided peasants with loans and helped with the purchase of seeds, fertilisers, tools, and grains. They also organised repair shops, established rural enterprises such as weaving workshops or manufacturing workshops, and co-ordinated tree planting campaigns. Co-operatives further assisted in transportation and undertook improvements of irrigation works.[102] Rural Financial Assistance Bureaus (Nongcun Jinrong Jiuji Chu) assisted with the financial side. The scale of these programmes was small and their effects were limited, but I shall discuss them here for the sake of completeness as well as to indicate the ways in which the Nationalists sought to improve rural conditions.

In 1934, the Nanchang Headquarters established a Committee for Rural Co-operation in Jiangxi to lead the creation of co-operatives in Jiangxi itself.[103] The Headquarters attributed the decline in the agricultural economy to banditry and Communism, as well as to monopolies of rich traders, lack of access to capital and markets, and lack of equipment.[104] Banks were set up and a training institute educated staff for the co-operatives. In general, Jiangxi profited most. Its 5,194 co-operatives received 1.4 million *yuan* in emergency aid. Other provinces such as Hubei and Anhui received less than a tenth of that.[105]

Because of financial and personnel shortages, according to the Headquarters Report, the number of co-operatives was disappointing. Nonetheless, by June 1935 in Henan they had been established in 35 counties, in Hubei in 37 counties, in Anhui in 58 counties, and in Jiangxi in 77 counties, for a total of 6,223 co-operatives. Membership of co-operatives still in their preparatory stage numbered 452,000 and established co-operatives had 258,000 members.[106]

In the spring of 1934, during the most busy and crucial period in the agricultural season, the Headquarters dispatched teams of agricultural specialists with the army to assist in rural revitalisation as areas were recovered.[107] They provided money and assisted in the creation of co-operatives. According to the Headquarters report, 50 counties were aided in this way. The Nanchang Headquarters spent nearly 1 million *yuan* on agricultural aid, and loans from the Agricultural Bank and Jiangxi's People's Prosperity Bank provided another 1 million *yuan* in loans.[108] Nearly 2,500 ploughs, thousands of hoes and harrows, hundreds of oxen and water buffaloes, and nearly 3,000 *piculs* of rice seed had been provided.[109]

The Headquarters also sought to provide credit and issue rural means of exchange. This was important because many rural areas suffered from an agricultural crisis, not just due to the warfare itself, but also to the outflow of silver to the cities, caused by the USA's Silver Purchase Act. In March 1933, just before its transformation into the Nanchang Headquarters, the Yu E Wan Suppression Command established the Yu E Wan Gan Peasant Bank for the provinces of Henan, Hubei, Anhui, and Jiangxi. It had a capital of 10 million *yuan*, raised from the national treasury, the four provincial treasuries, as well as from the issue of stock to merchants. It issued rural exchange certificates, provided credit, set up granaries, and provided facilities for money deposits and transfers. It also conducted research into local economic conditions, and bought up currencies issued by local banks.[110]

Finally, it should be mentioned that the Headquarters also worked to restore dikes, implement irrigation projects, and re-establish a granary system. Twenty million was raised for irrigation works in Jiangsu to prevent flooding, and a large project in Hubei sought to prevent flooding there and to divert water for agricultural use. Irrigation works required a great deal of funds, and this limited progress. The Nanchang Headquarters had more success in restoring granaries, many of which had fallen into disuse since the late Qing. The goal was to ensure that each county granary would store a sufficient supply of grain for three months. By 1935, in the provinces of Hunan, Anhui, and Hubei, only 200,000 *piculs* had been accumulated, due to the problems of natural disasters and banditry. In Jiangsu, 280,000 *piculs* had been stored. In Jiangxi, 600,000 *piculs* had been accumulated. Most success had been achieved in Zhejiang and Hunan. In the first, 1.2 million *piculs* had been accumulated in granaries and in Hunan the amount had reached 2.5 million *piculs*.[111]

Militarily the new approach translated during the fourth and fifth suppression campaigns in the defeat of the Communists. During these campaigns, as William Wei has shown, many more troops, perhaps as much as a million, were mobilised to surround the Communist bases. They made use of heavy artillery and an airforce, built extensive networks of roads to enhance troop mobility, and constructed a system of linked fortifications both to interdict trade and thus starve out the bases, but also to give the Nationalist forces a secure point, safe from guerrilla raids, from which to advance. A strict mutual responsibility system in the army welded officers and troops together. Early retreat and disobedience of orders were punished by execution. Officers who abandoned their troops too were executed. First, Communist bases outside the main stronghold in Jiangxi were eliminated. During the final campaigns against the Jiangxi Soviet itself, the Nationalists suffered a defeat in the spring of 1933 and the Fujian Rebellion too caused a momentary halt to operations. But in the spring of 1934, after having re-grouped and secured Fujian, Nationalist forces pressed on inexorably. During a pitched battle at Guangchang, 'the northern main gate' of the Jiangxi Soviet, the Nationalist forces defeated nine Communist divisions, which had dug in there, after which the routes into the Jiangxi Soviet lay open.

By 1935, Chiang Kaishek and Yang Yongtai seemed confident that they had found the right strategy and they had begun to speak about the future with a new optimism. Not only had they defeated the Communists, local government bureaucracies in areas under the control of the Nanchang Headquarters, they believed, had been brought under control, their establishments had been curtailed, and their financial expenses limited. These bureaucracies had begun to take responsibility for what had been the routine activities of the Chinese state in imperial times, namely ensuring local order, overseeing a granary system, and supervising irrigation projects and water works. They had also begun to connect the *baojia* with the national army. The Nationalist Armies used the opportunity of pursuing the Communists as they went on the Long March to inject their forces into the provinces that had remained outside their control. Using the same approaches as they had done in the areas under the Nanchang Headquarters, they began to bring these areas under effective National Government control.

In conclusion, let me place the above in the context of the development of state–society relations in the Republican Period. Prasenjit Duara has argued that local networks able to mediate between state and society broke down as a result of state involution. According to Duara, the Nationalists, like their late Qing and early Republican predecessors, sought to increase their tax base through *tankuan* – an *ad hoc* tax levied on the local community and apportioned by local headman. According to Duara, *tankuan* generated entrepreneurial tax brokers. Their abusive taxation practices, their arbitrariness, and their pursuit of village office for profit drove away the local elites, who traditionally had mediated between the state and local society and handed the Communists the most important issues around which they could mobilise local society.[112]

While highly insightful, Duara argued that bureaucratic expansion was driven by a state 'dizzied by the brilliance of prospective modernity'.[113] He underestimated, I believe, the significance of the military and warfare. He wrote that wars were 'like natural disasters, utterly devastating but ultimately temporary' but that the effects of state involution 'like the slow erosion of the soil' were more profound.[114] This distinction, I would suggest, is not one that in reality obtained. If twentieth-century authorities were modernising, behind *tankuan* was also the unquenchable thirst for funds of warlord forces. Shortages of men, food, equipment, and money drove armies to exact what they needed, and often much more, sometimes directly but mostly through local bosses, from the areas through which they travelled or in which they were garrisoned, with urgency, hostile local attitudes, and the lack of reliable land and population registers precluding the observation of the local rules of decorum.[115] It was ever thus. As Chen Feng has shown, *tankuan* had accompanied war-making during the Qing dynasty, and had done so no doubt earlier as well.[116]

To what extent the Nationalists can be bracketed with the warlords is not clear. The levying of *tankuan* is what one would expect weak warlord regimes to do in the areas of north China, which formed the subject of Duara's study especially in a time when one military crisis followed the other. Shen Songqiao found support for Duara's ideas in the case of Henan, but ends his analysis in 1932, precisely when the reforms attempted by Chiang in the countryside began to be implemented with a degree of vigour. However, to consolidate their power and eliminate the local roots of warlordism, the Nationalists could not let continue a practice of which they, and their allies, had not been a stranger themselves. The reforms pursued under the auspices of the Field Headquarters aimed at eliminating the local roots of warlordism, demilitarising local society, and end the levying of *ad hoc* local taxes.[117]

The final chapter will suggest that during the War of Resistance the Nationalists instituted recruitment and taxation practices in which local bosses were left to meet state demands as best they could from their local communities. This occurred at a time when bureaucracies were destroyed and financial and fiscal systems had collapsed. Because the state could not provide for the huge armies that had been brought into being, they again turned to *tankuan* and recruited men for their armies by ordering local bosses to deliver the required numbers. The *baojia* then did become hated and abusive organisations that destroyed local relations. That this happened during the War of Resistance would illustrate again the significance of war.

Preparing for war with Japan

Parks Coble is right that the decision not to wage war on Japan after its occupation of Japan was unpopular. For any government to be shown to be weak cannot but damage its reputation and the refusal to stand up to an aggressor provides easy openings for its critics.[118] It is less clear that realistically Chiang had any other option. The northern militarists, including Zhang Xueliang, were not willing to risk their armies, while those in the south, poised to wage war against Chiang, would no doubt have pounced had Chiang begun an offensive. China's forces were also no match to the Japanese. In January 1932, Chiang Kaishek stated that 'China lacks real military power' and that if it declared war, 'within three days Japan would vanquish the coastal areas and the Yangtze River basin'.[119] He was probably right. In three weeks of fighting along the Great Wall between 6 and 21 March 1933, Nationalist units were badly mauled. In his diary, Chiang noted that 'it won't do to pretend that we are powerful. The urgent task is to stabilise the line of resistance against Japan and strengthen our defences in the north'.[120]

If Chiang refused to fight, it is simply not the case that he refused to prepare for war out of an obsession with the Communists. Chiang Kaishek established a secret National Defence Planning Council (NDPC), which formally began its work on 29 November 1932. Its tasks were (i) making practicable and timely proposals for dealing with all important issues that the government might confront in dealing with foreign aggression; (ii) reorganising the National Army and increasing China's productive capacity; and (iii) making proposals to strengthen national defence in the short term.[121]

A 1933 Defence Battle Plan, accepted by the Staff Department to which the NDPC was responsible, called for the implementation of eight 'priority measures'.[122] They included the provision that in case of war, the military should clear the Yangtze from enemy vessels and eradicate enemy forces from Treaty Ports; the construction of fortifications between Jiangyin and Nanjing and the area between Xuzhou and the coast; fortification of the Tianjin–Beiping–Kalgan region; preparations to defend the Wei River in Shandong; the strengthening of military forces in north Hebei and the training of local militia there; and the construction of anti-aircraft defences of key cities.[123] On 3 April 1932, Chiang Kaishek approved a 6-year, 80-million *yuan* allocation to fund these projects.[124] Measures were announced for the nationalisation of arsenals and the construction of new ones, including for chemical warfare and aircraft production.[125] In 1933, a comprehensive plan for the construction of the defences for Shanghai and surrounding areas was drawn up.[126]

With the help of German advisors, the NDPC at the same time turned to readying China for a military showdown with Japan. The aims were the creation of an elite army capable of advanced mobile warfare, a domestic arms industry, and a heavy industrial base to supply the army from domestic sources, and preparing the country for total mobilisation. Until 1935, the NDPC focused its efforts on collecting the necessary information to draw up a pragmatic plan. From then on, when the Communists had been defeated in central and south China, they were put into effect.

German advisors

Historians such as William Kirby and Ma Zhendu have provided thorough studies of Chinese–German collaboration in the 1930s. German advisors were important to the Nationalists in three ways. First, the advice they provided about military strategy, organisation, and tactics were crucial in reshaping the Nationalist military. Second, they made its implementation possible, not only because of the knowledge they provided, but also because Chinese–German barter trade provided the Chinese with the equipment and arms on which the feasibility of the strategy depended. Finally, because the German advisors included such highly respected men as Hans von Seeckt and Alexander von Falkenhausen, they provided a valuable symbolic endorsement to the strategy, useful to Chiang Kaishek to bring doubters into line.

Max Bauer was the first German advisor, appointed upon the recommendation of Erich von Lüdendorff after Zhu Jiahua, a KMT member who had studied mining at Berlin University, travelled to Germany to recruit new advisors in 1926. Bauer arrived in China in December 1927. During talks with Chiang Kaishek, who then was officially in retirement, Bauer already suggested the nationalisation of large enterprises, the construction of a heavy industrial base, the development of air transport, and the use of the media to promote Nationalist ideology.[127] In 1928, Bauer, appointed economic advisor, formed a group of foreign advisors consisting of ten military instructors, six experts in armaments and logistics, four in police affairs, and several specialists in general administration and fiscal affairs. Bauer died shortly afterwards in March 1929, in Shanghai, after having contracted a disease.[128]

His successor, Georg Wetzell, arrived in April 1930. Besides offering strategic advice during civil wars, Wetzell began the training of several elite divisions. In a memorandum to Chiang Kaishek of February 1933, Wetzell reviewed how, in 1930, he had proposed that first a few model divisions should be trained and that they gradually should be increased to five or six. By 1933, three such divisions had been created – the 87th, 88th, and 36th. He noted, however, that they continued to lack appropriate artillery guns and other arms. He also called for the development of an airforce, which he believed absolutely essential in modern war. Wetzell was not an all-out success because he failed to get along with his Chinese colleagues. He wrote that senior officers in the army resisted his reforms as they continued to be wedded to Japanese models of the early twentieth century. He noted that they did not understand the principles of indirect fire, essential to modern warfare, and did little in the way of field exercises. He criticised the Nationalist's underdeveloped staff system, 'the brains of the army', the inferior quality of military academies, and the often lackadaisical attitude of the officers of the Ministry of Military Administration.[129]

Perhaps it was to overcome this internal opposition that Chiang Kaishek invited Hans von Seeckt to come to China. He arrived on 22 May 1933. The 'Father of the National Defence Army', von Seeckt had been the chief architect of Germany's post-First World War army reforms. von Seeckt's vision of the army was as a symbol of national unity: it manifested the state and ensured its dominance, both domestically and internationally, but was not itself political. Neither he nor his successor, Alexander von Falkenhausen were Nazis; they had sought to combat Nazi influence in the army. Because of restrictions imposed by the Versailles Treaty on German troop strength, the new German army that von Seeckt constructed was small, but also highly mobile, superior in firepower, and able flexibly to combine artillery, infantry, and air operations. Building on earlier German military traditions, this army was commanded by a highly trained and disciplined professional officers corps. During war, its troop strength was increased by calling up reservists who had undergone training in peace time. Supplied through the bureaucracy, the army was not involved in fiscal affairs and it was kept separate from society in barracks. A domestic industrial base supplied the needs of this army to prevent dependence on foreign sources of supply.[130]

In June 1933, at the end of his visit to China, von Seeckt produced a memorandum for Chiang Kaishek. In conversations beforehand, von Seeckt had stated that China should aim at an army of sixty divisions,[131] but the memorandum emphasised that the Nationalists should begin on a small scale, gradually training up an officers corps in the most modern military techniques. The memorandum stressed that the army although small should be of superb quality, led by highly skilled officers, and capable of combined arms operations. The officers, according to the memorandum, were to be completely loyal to Chiang Kaishek as the Commander-in-Chief and no locality or general should ever again be allowed to pursue independent policies. A strict personnel system, rigidly enforced by a tough bureaucracy, was to ensure that loyalty. Seeckt furthermore suggested that China should develop its communications infrastructure and that the Lower Yangtze should be immediately fortified.[132]

Like Wetzell, von Seeckt stressed that China should develop its own arms industry. Scathing about the output of China's arsenals, von Seeckt proposed a trade agreement. In return for Chinese supply of such mineral resources as tungsten and certain foodstuffs, Germany would supply China with advanced military equipment as well as the industrial plants that were to make China industrially independent.[133]

Hans von Seeckt arrived back in Shanghai in March 1934, this time not as an eminent guest but as Chief Military Advisor. During a week-long series of talks, Chiang agreed that von Seeckt would not only be known as Chief Advisor but also as the 'Deputy of the Chairman of the Military Affairs Council' (*Junshi Weiyuanhui Weiyuanzhang Weituoren*), that is, of Chiang Kaishek himself. To stress further the close link between Chiang and von Seeckt, von Seeckt chaired twice-weekly meetings with Nationalist military authorities at Chiang Kaishek's official residence in Nanjing.[134]

Creating a knowledge base

The vision of the army set out by German advisors fitted Chiang Kaishek's desire to re-centralise military power, demonstrate that China too could be military capable, eliminate the social and economic consequences of warlordism, and bring about a modern nation. However, the small but elite modern army was by no means easy to realise. It was first of all necessary to gather information on China's financial and economic resources, transport networks, communication facilities, marketing structures, and revenue flows. To formulate a comprehensive strategy, furthermore, assessments had to be made of the intentions of the enemy, international relations, and domestic attitudes. Then concrete plans had to be drawn up and implemented, private armies had to be incorporated or overawed, and popular support secured.

The NDPC undertook the initial step of collecting the required data. German advisors provided information on requirements of an elite army, listing in long tables what an army of 6 and 18 divisions needed in terms of ammunition and equipment. These figures were broken down in terms of the required mining resources, iron and steel production quotas, and chemical inputs. To conduct its investigations and draw up plans, the NDPC was organised into a Secretariat, two Bureaus for Investigation and Statistics, and eight Teams for the investigation of military affairs; international affairs; population, land, and crops; primary resources and manufacturing; transport and communications; economics and finance; and culture. The NDPC reported to the Staff Department and Chiang Kaishek was its chairman.[135]

The scope of the NDPC's investigations was truly massive. Its work report for 1934 (which included the first half of 1935) listed some fifty completed research projects.[136] The Economic Team had investigated coal mining in Zhejiang, Anhui, Hunan, and Hubei; the Kailuan Coal Mines; and coal mines and railroads in Shanxi. It had compiled a report on the transport capacity, state of repair, management, and fuel needs of China's main railroads. Another report evaluated iron and steel plants in China. It had conducted investigations of China's light industry, price structures of water-based transport, and highways in central China.

The Financial Team had compiled detailed reports on the financial affairs of sixteen provinces.[137] Research also was conducted in central financial resources, the burden of the indemnities, and other loan obligations. A plan for monetary reform was drawn up that may have been the basis for the great currency reforms of 1935. In that year, with British help, China nationalised its currencies, placed monetary control in the hands of the state, and soon after, successfully switched to a paper currency and managed exchange rates.

The Team for Land, Crops, and Population had first of all investigated existing household registration systems. A fundamental problem, it reported, was the lack of reliable population statistics and much effort was expended on remedying this. The team also researched land holding patterns, crop cultivation patterns, and land rents. Other projects dealt with hydro-electric potential in Sichuan; water conservancy of the Upper Yangtze; copper mines of Hubei, Henan, Shanxi, and Hunan; and oil stocks in Shaanxi. The team produced plans to control copper mining and coal mining. It further compiled reports on how various countries controlled trade. Data were also collected on the grain markets of Yangtze harbours and coastal regions; grain storage facilities; and rice transport and distribution in Jiangxi.

The Military Affairs Team investigated all aspects of the military. Its main task was to draw up plans to assign divisions to specific localities in accordance with a national defence plan. It also compiled registers on the equipment of various armies, and investigated the use of short-wave radio, radio stations, and encoding machinery. Finally, it managed a project to produce maps on a scale of $1:200,000$ for all of China.

The Culture Team investigated education, as well as the Hitler Jugend, the organisation and activities of the Russian Youth Vanguards, and the British Child Protection agencies. It also busied itself with drawing up plans for promoting sports, youth training, and the compilation of text books in standard Chinese on Chinese history, geography, and citizenship. There were also plans for the physical examination of students, investigation of teaching methods, military training for the local population, and the compilation of songs to promote nationalism.

The International Affairs Team focused on the Great Powers and the League of Nations. Japan naturally received most attention. Another important NDPC project was the compilation of a database on experts in the natural sciences, industry, and management. In 1937, this research led to the 'Report on Experts in Mining and Metallurgy' and the 'Report on Specialists in Machine Industry' that covered 80,000 people.[138]

Good insight in the planning process and the way the German Advisors Group and the NDPC worked is provided by a meeting of the NDPC held in 1934 at the Guling resort on Mount Lushan, at which German advisors, including von Seeckt, were present. For the meeting, the NDPC produced a report entitled 'Information on Military Affairs, Finance, Economics, and Transport for the Guling Meeting of the National Defence Planning Committee'.[139] The meeting resolved predictably that China's national defence policy should aim at the recovery of lost territory, and that the army, navy, and airforce should be reformed on the basis of a national defence policy. A provisional plan for the distribution of sixty divisions on the basis of strategic needs, local resources, and population distribution was developed. Reflecting von Seeckt's concern with a high quality corps of officers, the capacity of China's military academies was reviewed and measures for improvement were suggested. A ten-year plan was suggested for the re-organisation of the army, to begin with six divisions.

In order to guide industrial development, the meeting discussed proposals to bring various sectors of the economy under state control. It decided that coal, abundant in China, should be China's main energy source. The meeting reviewed plans for the development of the machine tool and chemical industries as well as for the development of national communications, including railroads, highways, and telegraph lines.[140] A proposal for the development of heavy industry under state control was also reviewed. It suggested the relocation of key defence industries away from the coast to strategically safer areas in the hinterland.

The meeting also discussed state finance. A grim report argued that no immediate prospect for the improvement of the National Government's financial resources was in sight. State expenditures were high due to domestic and international debt obligations as well as military expenditures. Following the Japanese occupation of Manchuria, Maritime Customs revenue had declined substantially. Moreover, the adoption of the gold standard by most countries had led to panic in agriculture, reflected in price deflation. Therefore, according to the report, it was impossible to increase revenue. Furthermore, most provinces had begun to run large deficits. Administrative expenditures could not be reduced further. Although improvements in the management of railroads, alcohol and tobacco revenue collection bureaucracies, the Salt Gabelle, and the stamp tax system might yield some increase in revenue, the report stated, fundamental improvement would take a considerable period of time. It was against this background that the barter agreement with Germany became seen as the only way to finance China's military and industrial reforms.

Broad plans rapidly made way for more detailed ones, as a meeting of August 1934 suggests. That meeting established a special Committee for Economic Planning and formulated proposals for a national currency and regulations for moving bank reserves and accounts in time of war. It adopted a scheme for the promotion of commerce, as well as a 'profit guarantee' system for private military industries. It further discussed draft plans for iron and steel factories, chemical industries, and a plant for the manufacture of military vehicles. The meeting reviewed a plan for the military use of railroads in time of war. On the final day of the meeting, proposals were passed for the selection of students to pursue studies abroad, for strengthening education in border and coastal areas, for the establishments of departments of aeronautics and engineering in two universities, as well as for the education of women and of youth.[141] Finally, it discussed plans for the mobilisation of public opinion abroad and a network for information agencies in foreign countries.

The NDPC's aim was an economically feasible and strategically sensible national development plan, based on the reality that 'China remains a backward rural country using medieval technology. The level of its industrial development remains far removed from being able to meet the demands of a modern war of resistance'.[142] A report divided China into six regions in terms of primary resources, the material needs of the population, fuel supplies, edible salt provision, and mineral and mining resources. It assessed each region in terms of the surpluses and deficiencies in these categories, and then estimated their ability to meet the needs of the military, communications, access to coal, and expected enemy operations.[143] The end result, for instance, for economic planning was the Three Year Plan for Industrial Development of 1936. This plan defined Jiangxi, Hunan, and Hubei as the area where heavy industry and arms industry were to be located. Railroads were to connect it to supplies of key primary resources in neighbouring provinces. The plan also provided for the development of Iron and Steel Works at Xiangtan in Hunan, iron and copper mines in Sichuan, the development of coal mines in central and south-west China, and machine and electronic industries, also at Xiangtan.[144] By the outbreak of the war, many of these industries had been set up, although none had begun production.

Not just German advice, but Germany's willingness to supply industrial equipment and armaments was critical to the practicability of all these plans. After all, even if it was useful for the NDPC to know precisely how many tons of nitrate it might need to supply a division in time of war, it would not be able to do much with such information unless it could acquire the equipment to produce it. As William Kirby and others have pointed out, rich deposits of tungsten ore in southern Jiangxi provided China with an important asset.[145] Tungsten was used in the contemporary arms and electronics industries as a hardening agent. The tungsten of Jiangxi became available to the Nationalists once they had defeated the Communists there.

The activities of the NDPC and the German advisors illustrate that the Nationalists began to prepare actively for war with Japan from 1932. They also signalled the beginning of a new approach, which featured gradualism, detailed planning, and the nurturing of technical talent. Government bureaucracies formulated work plans and schedules of implementation on the basis of precise investigations. The new techno-nationalist approach set great store by the capacity of the state to direct society and the economy on the basis of accurate information assembled in registers, statistical tables, and surveys. A disciplined bureaucracy, free from parochial interests but serving the nation, was to co-ordinate its activities in all these areas on the basis of a common developmental strategy.

This new approach attracted some of the outstanding intellectuals of the time, as William Kirby has argued. These hailed mostly from northern universities, such as Beiping, Qinghua, and Nankai Universities, including Ding Wenjiang, who headed the Geographic Research Institute in Beijing, the bio-chemist Wu Xian, the sociologist Wu Jingchao, the political scientist Zhang Qiangzhao, who had studied under Harold Laski, and the economist Weng Wenhao. Such men may have been influenced by traditional ideas of government service, as well as by the idea that the state might yet be a beneficial force.

The formulation of a strategy

A 1935 secret memorandum 'Proposals to Meet the Current Situation' by Alexander von Falkenhausen and China's war plans of 1936 and 1937 show that by the mid-1930s, the Nationalists had arrived at a clear strategy to meet Japanese aggression. Von Falkenhausen had come with von Seeckt and succeeded the latter in March 1935 when von Seeckt left China. Von Falkenhausen had fought in China during the Boxer War, and then studied Japanese at Berlin University. In 1912, he was appointed military attaché in Japan. During the First World War he commanded Group Armies in Russia, Armenia, and Mesopotamia.

Von Falkenhausen's memorandum was submitted in the aftermath of Japan's intervention in May and July in north China, which had led to the He–Umezu agreement, whereby Nationalist as well as Manchurian forces were withdrawn from Hebei, KMT organs in the province were abolished, and the provincial government moved from Tianjin to Baoding. These developments, according to von Falkenhausen had made Japan's intentions clear. He counselled Chiang Kaishek that Japan would change its course only if it was confronted with a firm attitude in China. Although China's armies could not, he continued, 'fight a modern war', its forces could 'use a war of attrition'.[146]

Von Falkenhausen saw China's strategic situation as follows. In case of Japanese attack, north China would face severe threats. Because of the He–Umezu Agreement, the defences of Hebei could not be strengthened, and therefore, in case of a Japanese offensive, both the Long–Hai Railroad and the Yellow River would become front lines. The Yellow River, according to von Falkenhausen, was vulnerable to attack from Shandong. The Japanese navy would furthermore attack China's coastal provinces. With the Yangtze River navigable up to Wuhan, its defence would be difficult too.

Von Falkenhausen expressed doubts about the wisdom of plans that called for the withdrawal of China's line of resistance in the north to the Beiping–Hankou Railroad and in the Lower Yangtze area for abandoning Shanghai and concentrating on the defence of the Nanjing and Nanchang. He wrote that 'this strategy would rapidly result in the loss of the coastal provinces. Imports from abroad to the hinterland will be cut off, and the most important cities and factories will fall to the enemy'. Moreover, if Japan would take the Yangtze River basin from Shanghai to Wuhan, then 'China's powers of resistance will have lost a most important base ... and Japan would have thrust into China's hinterland and cut China into two parts'. Although von Falkenhausen's counsel contained much that was commonly agreed, and was reflected in the 1933 War Plan, it is probably true that in insisting on the defence of the north and of Shanghai he made an important impact on China's strategic stance in the first phase of the War of Resistance.

China's strategy, according to von Falkenhausen, should aim at preventing the Japanese from 'destroying our resistance in one go'. A second aim was to frustrate Japan's policy of 'divide and rule'. If resistance was a limited effort, then the danger was that Japan would separate north China and Shandong and perhaps establish a government in Beiping under Aysingyoro Puyi, the last Qing Emperor who had been re-installed in Manchuria. Japan would also, according to von Falkenhausen, establish a separate government in Nanjing. In case resistance was not a nation-wide effort, according to von Falkenhausen, the militarists in Guangdong and Guangxi would likely stay out of the war. Western countries would also find their way to an accommodation to the emergence of a Japan-dominated China, and while 'local populations would hate to be ruled by a different nation, if peace and livelihoods were ensured, they too would gradually accept it'. To bring about a national war and avoid partial accommodations would remain key Nationalist objectives from then on.

von Falkenhausen advised to concentrate most forces 'in the area between Xuzhou, Zhengzhou, Wuhan, Nanchang, and Nanjing'. Using interior lines of defence, they could be despatched to any danger area. This advice was important for the Battle of Xuzhou. Sichuan should be the 'last base of defence' in von Falkenhausen's view, because it was a rich province that could be defended easily. Its industrialisation, however, would take 'fifty years' and hence retreat to this province should be seen as a measure of last resort. von Falkenhausen counselled Chiang Kaishek that 'there was no point in continuing warfare with various provinces, because no one saw them as representing the Republic of China, but instead as destroying domestic peace'. As to international relations, he counselled that there should be no false hopes for foreign intervention because the Washington Treaties no longer had any practical value and because no foreign power was in the position to intervene. Only if China mounted full out resistance, 'perhaps then might it be given foreign assistance'.

von Falkenhausen's strategy, calling for meeting Japanese aggression first of all in north China, helps explain the adoption of a more aggressive forward policy towards north China followed by the Nationalists after 1934. Although the 1933 NDPC and MAC documents had called for concentrating on the north while counting on southern power holders to defend south China, following the War of the Central Plains and the occupation of Manchuria, Chiang Kaishek had focused on securing the Lower Yangtze provinces, and had settled for what can be described as co-habitation with Zhang Xueliang and his Manchurian forces, which were the dominant force in a divided north China and formed a buffer between Chiang Kaishek and the Japanese. As the next chapter will make clear, from 1935 the National Government pursued a forward policy in north China.

In early 1936, the National Government drew up the '1936 Draft Outline National Defence Plan', the 'Draft Plan for the Implementation of National Defence', and a 'War Plan'. They echoed the estimates of Japanese intentions set out by von Falkenhausen as well as his proposed counter-measures. In December 1936, the Staff Department drafted more detailed war plans in two versions.[147] Both plans shared the belief that the possibility of war with the Soviet Union or with the USA meant that Japan would seek a quick Blitzkrieg type war in north China. It would occupy the Beiping–Tianjin area, advance along the two north–south railroads to Zhengzhou, Ji'nan, and Xuzhou, and strike towards Shanxi. It would also land forces along the northern coast, and furthermore occupy the Lower Yangtze area. They estimated that Japan would be able to use 30–40 divisions, or about 600,000–800,000 troops, in China. Because Japan had absolute control of the seas, the war plans estimated that it would not increase its Third Fleet of twenty-three ships designed for coastal waters. Because of Soviet and Western airpower in East Asia, some of its airforce of 3,000 planes would have to be kept back, but the remainder, it was anticipated, would be used to bomb China's largest cities and destroy China's communications.

Like their 1936 predecessor, the 1937 war plans called for full-out resistance. This meant that in north China the Japanese attack should be resisted at the Great Wall, that landings along the north China coast especially in Shandong should be confronted immediately, and that all forces should be used to destroy the Japanese presence in Shanghai. Version 2, which posited offensive operations following a first phase of out-lasting Japan's initial punch, envisioned attacking the Japanese in Manchuria. Version 1 outlined lines of gradual retreat with the aim of wearing out the enemy. Both plans divided China into several war zones, detailed the order of battle for each of them, and made arrangements for supply lines and the mobilisation of reserves. Both envisioned the use of guerrilla warfare especially in the enemy's rear.

If von Falkenhausen's memorandum and the War Plans were secret, from 1934 the Nationalists began to signal publicly a tougher attitude towards Japan and to indicate that if it did come to war, it would wage a defensive war aimed at the attrition of Japan. Chiang Kaishek published 'Friend or Enemy', drafted by his advisor and secretary Chen Bulei, anonymously in the October 1934 issue of *Foreign Affairs*, a journal of the Ministry of Foreign Affairs. The article argued that Japan simply did not have the military power to occupy all of China. For the occupation of Manchuria, Chiang argued, Japan had used 100,000 troops, and even so it had not been able to suppress all resistance. According to Chiang, Japan's standing army had 300,000 troops so that it did not even have enough forces to create second and third Manchurias in north China and Mongolia, as it was then attempting to do. If Japan did begin an all-out war, according to Chiang, 'precisely because China's military is inferior to Japan's, the war will not be ended by a decisive battle on the battlefield'. Japan, Chiang believed, would at most 'be able to occupy some cities with good communicates and important harbours'. The Chinese government would retreat into the countryside and continue the fight from there.[148]

Jiang Baili expressed similar arguments in his 'The Japanese – An investigation by a Foreigner'. According to Jiang, the War of Resistance would be a long one – 8–10 years – and would see Japan take cities on the coast and along the major communication lines. However, if in advanced Western countries the loss of such cities would be serious, in China, 'because we are a rural county', the loss of Shanghai and Nanjing, 'with its few scattered modern buildings' – would have no impact on China's power of resistance'. Because of the superiority of Japan's army, Jiang Baili argued, China had no option but to engage in a war of attrition. 'If they place the centre of their force on the front line, we should place ours on the second, and moreover, preserve them deep in our hinterland, so that temporary predominance will not be of benefit to them'.[149]

The choice for a defensive strategy was not irrational. Offensive strategies required superiority in firepower, high mobility, logistical efficiency, as well as a highly trained officers corps, the ability to combine infantry, air, and naval power, the support of a strong industrial base, and an efficient bureaucracy. The Nationalists had none of these, or even the access to oil that was basic to the modern army. Even if they had, it is perhaps useful to remember that Japan and Germany, who did adopt offensive strategies, were defeated, while the Soviet Union, which also began the war with a massive retreat, emerged victoriously. China's defensive strategy aimed at surviving a Japanese Blitzkrieg, bringing about a national war of resistance, and outlasting the Japanese. It sought to make use of China's space, its supply of manpower, which was more easily mobilised to defend home areas than to die at far away fronts, and time.

Preparations

In March 1935, the Army Re-organisation Office, established under the Wuhan Headquarters of the MAC 'in order to minimise its visibility', began the re-organisation of China's armies. Chen Cheng was made the head of the Army Reorganisation Bureau. In a telegram of 19 December 1934 to Chiang Kaishek, Chen stated that he hoped to make the National Defence Army not just the best equipped and trained force in China, but also an organisation admired for its spiritual and ideological qualities. It was to embody the values of the modern nation such as discipline and patriotism, use the most advanced strategies and tactics, and be loyal to the centre. He argued that its officers should be drawn as much as possible from young and energetic Whampoa graduates.[150]

The establishment of this office followed the authorisation by Chiang Kaishek in December 1934 of a 'National Army Reorganisation Plan for Sixty Divisions', ordering its completion in 3–4 years. According to the plan, the sixty divisions were to be known as New Divisions (Xinbian Shi), while the remaining central forces, which also were to be reconstituted, were called 'Reformed Divisions' (Zhengli Shi). The New and Reformed Divisions were different first of all in that officers of the New Divisions were to be assigned randomly to 'eliminate factions'. To further strengthen central control and diminish the power of division commanders in the New Divisions, their staff system would be strengthened and staff officers would be appointed by the centre without consultation with the division commander. A centralised personnel system would regularly transfer New Division officers.

The 1935 reforms stipulated in case of the New Divisions that when units were called up for training, two Re-organisation and Training Centres, one of which was in Wuhan and one in Nanchang, would take over personnel, educational, financial, party, government, and health care affairs. Once a division completed its training and was equipped, central organs in Nanjing would take over these tasks.[151] According to a report by He Yingqin of February 1937, twenty New Divisions had been trained, equipped, issued their numerical designation, and assigned their station. He expected that a further twenty divisions would be completed by the end of the year.[152] China began war with Japan, then, with perhaps thirty New Divisions in place.

An important part of the reforms was to subordinate special armed units to the centre. Artillery units, which only had 567 artillery guns, cavalry formations, and an unknown number of engineer and signals forces were first to be brought together for centralised training at one of the two training centres. They were then assigned to specific divisions, but their pay was issued separately through the centre, which from then on also supplied them with their arms and equipment.[153]

If personal connections were to be discouraged among New Division officers, the reverse was true for the rank-and-file. Troops were drawn from existing units, but then grouped on the basis of their regional origin. After undergoing a period of training in a central training centre, they were assigned to divisions in their own region, 'so as to prepare for the implementation of national military service'.[154] As mentioned, in March 1936, the first twelve divisional conscription areas in Jiangsu, Shandong, Zhejiang, Anhui, and Hubei had delivered 50,000 new recruits.[155]

The Reformed Divisions were intended to perform garrison and bandit suppression duties in peace time, thus enabling the New Divisions to concentrate on training for frontline warfare. They also formed a ready pool of capable reserves that could replace casualties in the New Divisions in time of war. The changes demanded of the Reformed Divisions were much less. Even their officers corps was left in place. Their quality was to be improved mostly by weeding out personnel no longer fit for service and by bringing them up to strength through amalgamation.

This system, of a small elite force with a national officers corps but also with strong local links and a broader military made up of territorial army units, imitated the Japanese system. But it also reflected the Qing military set-up, in which the Banner Forces had been militarily dominant until the early nineteenth century. The Green Standard forces were a second rate force, kept purposefully dispersed, less well armed, and more closely involved in local society, but was also called upon to augment the Banners in case of emergencies.

As to the build-up of basic and arms industries, William Kirby and others have shown that considerable headway was made after the NDPC was transformed in 1935 into the National Resources Council (NRC) headed by Weng Wenhao.[156] In February 1937, He Yingqin reported that iron and steel works had been constructed at Xiangtan in Hunan and in the Lower Yangtze, coal mines at Chaling in Hunan and Lingxian in Hubei, copper mines and factories at Daye and Yangxin in Hubei and at Pengxian in Sichuan, and zinc and aluminium mines and factories in Guangxi and Hunan. Coal mines had also been dug in Jiangxi, Henan, and Hunan, and an oil field and refineries developed in northern Shaanxi and Sichuan. Plants for the production of nitrogen and ethanol were being developed. At Xiangtan, factories for the manufacture of aircraft engines, motors, and machine tool plants were being constructed, while textile and electronics factories were also being developed. A hydro-electric facility was being built in Sichuan to supply industries to be developed there. He Yingqin reported that besides the tungsten of Jiangxi, the National Government also had established state control over antimony and other minerals. Processing facilities had been established in Jiangxi and Hunan. According to He, 'within three years we shall have laid a firm basis for the metallurgical industry, fuel production, the chemical industry, the machine industry, and the electronics industry so that we can achieve self-sufficiency'.[157]

As to China's arms industry, He noted that all with the exception of one had dated from the late Qing. Following refurbishment, China's arsenals produced German-style rifles and Czech machine guns in adequate amounts. According to He, the Jinling Arsenal at Nanjing produced heavy machine guns of equal quality to those produced in Germany. China furthermore produced French-type mortars, artillery shells, aircraft bombs, and ignition devices. He reported 'progress' in the manufacture of armoured vehicles and two-way radios.[158]

According to He, detailed plans had been drawn up for economic mobilisation in time of war. Industries, mines, and oil fields had been registered and their productive capacity assessed. The NRC had conducted a project for a year-and-a-half to investigate the agricultural potential of uncultivated areas in the north-west and south-west. Detailed investigations had been made of railroads, highways, waterways, and the telegraph and the postal system, and plans drawn up for their military use. The NRC had investigated remittances of Overseas China as well as prices of various commodities to be able to impose state control in time of war.[159]

Another aspect of the reforms was the building of fortifications and the preparation of battlefields. China was divided into five 'war zones'. Main battle areas and key points were identified in each, which were fortified with machine gun emplacements, artillery bunkers, observation posts, and hide-outs, all made from reinforced concrete according to the 'most advanced' German and Soviet models and designed to withstand 100-pound aerial bombs.[160] By the spring of 1937, according to He's report, most projects to create three lines of fortifications between Shanghai and Nanjing as well as the fortification of Nanjing itself had been completed. In north China, pillboxes and trenches were built along the Beiping–Hankou and Long–Hai Railroads. Advance bases for their defence were established at Shijiazhuang, Baoding, and Xinxiang. Although Xuzhou's fortifications were completed, those of Bangbu had not. Forts along the entire Yangtze River as well as important coastal harbours had been strengthened. Important coastal harbours were also being fortified.[161] Chen Cheng was preparing the defences of Wuhan. Fortifications were connected by road, telephone, and radio networks.[162]

Railroads were constructed in order to facilitate the movement of troops and ensure supplies to main battle areas. In the Lower Yangtze, for instance, railroads were built to connect the three lines of defences there in such a way that trains did not have to travel through Shanghai. Four hundred kilometres of rail were laid from Lechang in Guangdong to Zhuzhou near Changsha in Hunan to connect Wuhan to Canton. In the first stage of the war, 2 million troops and 540,000 tons of material passed over this railroad. The Long–Hai Railroad was extended 170 kilometres westwards from Xi'an to Baoji, while the railroad in Zhejiang was connected from Baoshan to Nanchang in Jiangxi, and from there on to Pingxiang on the Jiangxi–Hunan border, from where there was a rail connection to the Xiang River. Another large project was repairing existing railroads in Shanxi and connecting them into a single north–south railroad from Datong in the north through Taiyuan and then on to the south of the province. A railroad was begun to connect Nanjing to Nanchang in Jiangxi, of which nearly 200 kilometres were completed. The 1,000 kilometres of highways that existed in 1927 was expanded to 109,000 kilometres to make up a national highway system. Even though their quality was uneven, roads stretched from Nanjing to Fujian and Guangxi; Guizhou and Yunnan; Shaanxi and Xinjiang; and Shandong, while roads were also built between Suiyuan, Sichuan, and Guangdong.[163]

Before the war, Nanjing's military academies trained about 15,000 officers. This number was not large, given that the total was 200,000.[164] German advisors shaped Nanjing's system of military education. A Central Military Academy was established in

Nanjing, with branch schools in the provinces. Cadets would first study for half a year at a provincial school, before being brought to Nanjing for a year of instruction, followed by half a year of practical training in the field. In 1930, the training period was lengthened to three years. Specialised academies existed for further training in staff work, infantry command, chemical warfare, anti-aircraft warfare, communications, and supply. Summer training programmes at Mount Lushan and military courses in high schools also helped to improve the quality of officers. 17,498 senior middle-school students completed courses for National Cadet Officer (NCO) status.[165] These training programmes strengthened the quality of lower- and middle-level officers. Higher levels, of Major General and above, continued to be dominated by officers trained in the late Qing and early Republic academies such as Baoding Military Academy.

Little headway was made in building up a modern airforce. In 1931, the National Government established its first Airforce Academy in Hangzhou, when China's disparate airforces numbered 100 aeroplanes. In 1936, a second academy was established in Nanchang and the Airforce Commission of the MAC began to oversee the development of a national air defence system. Little was accomplished. The Nationalists were not able to produce aeroplanes domestically. Together with sixty-eight aeroplanes purchased with funds 'donated' to celebrate Chiang Kaishek's fiftieth birthday, the Nationalist airforce consisted of 212 fighters and 257 bombers.[166] The Japanese airforce was not only far superior in numbers, the quality of its aeroplanes far exceeded that of the Nationalists. Given the great cost involved, the development of a navy was not even seriously contemplated.[167]

The achievements advertised by He in his report would, when they were put to the test, not prove as solid as he had asserted. Fortifications sometimes were ramshackle or badly sited, the fighting in Shanghai exposed the tactical and logistical limits of the officers corps, and communications frequently broke down. The Nationalists furthermore remained inferior in artillery. However, von Falkenhausen's secret 1936 year-end report to Chiang Kaishek stated that 'during 1936, impressive advances have been made in all areas. The authority of the central government has reached into many areas, and as a result, the people's sense of responsibility for the state and the unification of their patriotism have greatly accelerated'.[168]

The New Life Movement

The New Life Movement was an attempt to propagate a new Chinese identity around which to make the armed forces and society cohere. The movement began when in July 1933 Chiang convened the Lushan Officers Training Regiment at Mount Lushan near Nanchang following embarrassing defeats against the Communists as well as the conclusion of equally embarrassing treaties with Japan. During the first training session, nearly 8,000 officers and troops from Hunan, Hubei, Jiangxi, Zhejiang, Guangdong, and several northern provinces were brought together to receive tactical training in fighting the Communists. It was of course hoped that the exercise would weaken their links with their original armies and commit these officers to the new nation headed by the Nationalists. The Lushan training schedule paid attention to 'spiritual training' to foster a new common spirit. In speeches such as 'The Essential Meaning of Spiritual Education in the Military' and 'The Revolutionary Soldier First Respects Moral

Integrity', Chiang Kaishek presented himself as following in the footsteps of Zeng Guofan and Hu Linyi, the great leaders of the suppression of the Taiping Rebellion. Echoing their call to arms to defend Confucianism, Chiang talked about 'creating a new life for the nation' and 'creating a new life for the soldier.' According to Chiang, 'military spirit' meant 'knowledge, faith, humaneness, courage, and strictness'. 'National spirit' consisted of the 'four cardinal ethical principles' of 'propriety, righteousness, frugality, and modesty' (li, yi, lian, chi) and the eight virtues of 'loyalty, filiality, humaneness, love, faith, righteousness, peace, and equality'. Besides military men, government officials and party cadres too were brought to Lushan to undergo similar training.[169]

Chiang Kaishek inaugurated the New Life Movement as a civil campaign in Nanchang in February 1934, in the middle of the final campaign to oust the Communists from Jiangxi Province and just after the Fujian Rebellion of the dissatisfied 19th Army.[170] The New Life Movement, Chiang Kaishek stated, was to cause the citizens of the Chinese nation to conform in their 'eating, dress, private life, and public behaviour' (shi, yi, zhu, xing) to the ancient Confucian virtues of 'propriety, righteousness, frugality, and modesty'.[171] The *Basics of the New Life Movement* (Xin Shenghuo Yundong Xuzhi) attempted to specify these values. Propriety was to be disciplined, filial to one's parents, and respectful to people in authority. Righteousness meant impartiality, patriotism, honesty, dependability, and dedication. Frugality required not indulging in pleasure and luxury, and not mixing private and public funds. Being modest was living a life of integrity, working hard, and dedicating oneself to one's responsibilities. The New Life Movement was defined as seeking three transformations in Chinese life: cultural uplift, militarisation, and industrialisation.[172]

The *Basics of the New Life Movement* also supplied nearly one hundred simple prescriptions to guide behaviour. Their banality gave the New Life Movement a reputation, in the words of Lloyd Eastman, of being 'a futile and somewhat comic effort to regenerate the nation'.[173] Practising a new life, according to these prescriptions, meant purchasing only national products, eating at set mealtimes, being neat and clean, sitting upright, and not to slurp soup or spit bones unto the ground. China's new citizens were to wear sturdy rather than fashionable cloths, to wash and air them regularly, and to make sure that all buttons were fastened properly. They kept their living quarters clean, opened their windows regularly, and cleaned up all garbage inside and outside their houses. In public they moved around with purpose, kept to the left of the road, made little noise, got up early, were punctual, behaved orderly in meetings, looked straight ahead, and kept their chests out. They saluted the flag, stood up to sing the national anthem, gave up seats to women, queued orderly, and said Thank You and Excuse Me. They would not gossip, gamble, drink, take opium, visit brothels, be argumentative, wander into the road, use perfume, and urinate other than in a toilet.[174]

In terms of organisation, the 'New Life Promotion Association' steered the movement. It directed a hierarchical system that followed the bureaucracy down to local society. At each level, New Life Movement Promotion Associations were formed from the heads of the KMT as well as government organs for education and civil affairs, the Public Security Bureau, and various legal entities, such as factories, schools, and professional associations.[175] Propaganda weeks promoted desirable goals by holding mass rallies and parades, organising lectures, and conducting theatrical performances. Limits were imposed on spending at wedding banquets or entertaining. Youths were dispatched to teahouses, restaurants, and opera theatres to combat dissipation and extravagance. Groups of youths removed dirt and garbage from towns. Women were encouraged to wear short hair. Hygiene, physical education, and sports were vigorously promoted.

The issues that have so far stood central in analyses of the New Life Movement have been its association with fascism and with the existence of a Nazi-type Blue Shirt Society. In 1974, Lloyd Eastman argued that the movement was a disguised attempt by Chiang Kaishek to 'implant the fascist spirit among the Chinese people'.[176] Maria Hsia Chang attacked that argument, arguing that much of the evidence that Eastman marshalled was of dubious provenance.[177] Frederick Wakeman recently argued that the movement espoused a nativistic 'Confucian fascism', which was iconically ambiguous, but combined 'Confucian moralism' with the 'egalitarian righteousness of medieval knights-errant', and endorsed 'traditional social relationships', including 'imperial loyalism'.[178] Wakeman concluded that the movement was not analogous to European fascism, but was yet another example of the 'popular anti-foreignism and ethnic revivalism that characterised many movements in modern China, including the … Red Guards'.[179]

As to the existence of the Blue Shirts, Wakeman has created considerable clarity. Wakeman showed that in the crisis period of the autumn of 1931, Chiang loyalists among graduates of the Whampoa Military Academy formed the Society for Vigorous Practice (Lixingshe).[180] Chiang accepted the offer of becoming their patron and leader to gain an important source of support in times of great difficulty for him, in part in imitation of reformers and revolutionaries of the turn of the century, who had used similar associations to mobilise support against the Qing.[181] The Society for Vigorous Practice was founded in 1931 and continued to exist until 1938. It may have been a continuation of the Officers Moral Endeavour Society (Lizhishe), which Chiang Kaishek had founded in 1929 and was made up of 2,000 Whampoa Academy Graduates. Through various front organisations, the Society for Vigorous Practice may have encompassed 500,000 people.

According to Wakeman, the Blue Shirts 'never really existed as a formal Lixingshe instrument as such'.[182] One ambitious figure in the Society for Vigorous Practice, Liu Jianqun, who had not attended the Whampoa Academy and thus was regarded as an outsider, in a press conference of January 1933, made public a tract that he had written about the need for a Blue Shirts Society to strengthen discipline within the KMT. The result was widespread public association of the Renaissance Society, a public front of the Society for Vigorous Practice, with the Blue Shirts. Some foreign reporters, hostile to the Nationalists, and Japanese propaganda, eager to smear the Nationalists, built up the Blue Shirts and associated it with the Nazis. If perhaps a reality, as Wakeman does believe, the Blue Shirts also existed as a potent label used to blacken Chiang Kaishek and the KMT. That in the crisis of 1931 Chiang Kaishek decided to shore up his position with the Society for Vigorous Practice in which codes of personal loyalty and subordination were important and that this organisation operated secretly through various front organisations and engaged in nefarious activities is beyond doubt.

The New Life Movement is interesting not just for its association with the Society for Vigorous Practice but also for the message that it espoused and for what it hoped to achieve in doing so. It advanced, it seems to me, a secularised, essentialised, and militarised understanding of Confucianism to promote a new imagining of China, transcending regional, cultural, religious, and personal bonds. In the army, it aimed to make China's divided military forces cohere around a single *esprit de corps*, instil a new pride, and strengthen identification with the National Government. Socially, it was a movement of moral re-armament, deriving from fears about national and racial degeneration. Culturally, it aimed at dealing with what perhaps can be called a sense of disorientation, flowing emotionally from perceived irreconcilable conflicts between treasured traditions and the demands of modernity. Rapid economic change and the fracturing of hierarchies of status, for instance by the rise of professions in a more commercialised world, contributed to this disorientation. A sense of cultural inferiority to the West also played a role.

The New Life Movement was based on the premise that Chinese society was gripped by the lack of social trust and cultural malaise. 'The suspicions, jealousies, hatreds, and strife in our society today are diseases caused by the omission of promoting cultural uplift.'[183] Chiang described the consequences in the *Basic Outline for the New Life Movement* as follows:

> In our society today, the general attitude is one of moral laziness and apathy. It shows in that people do not distinguish between good and bad, do not separate the public and the private, and do not know what is basic and what is secondary. ... As a result, the bureaucracy is insincere and greedy, the people are disunited and listless, the youth is degenerate and indulgent, adults are corrupt and muddled, the rich live lives of elaborate but dissolute sophistication, and the poor are base and muddled. The result is that the bonds that tie the nation together have been weakened, that the social order has broken down, that national calamities cannot be resisted, that man-made disasters cannot be fought, that internal rebellion has spread widely, and that foreign aggression has come again and again.[184]

A lecture in 1935 at the Central Party Headquarters during commemoration ceremonies for Sun Yatsen explained the weakening of China's cultural spirit as follows:

> The last century has been a period in which the new and old thinking have struggled with each other. The basic spirit of establishing the nation has gradually disappeared in this struggle. On the one hand, it has been affected by remnants of the corrupt politics of the Manchu Qing and, on the other, it has been affected by the collision of currents from Eastern and Western nations. Because the will of the people has drowned, habits have been totally ruined ... few people have yet woken up to the danger for the nation.[185]

The New Life Movement's purpose was to make propaganda for the idea that its version of a secular and rational Confucianism constituted a uniquely Chinese 'spirit' compatible with modernity and shared by all Chinese, of whatever class, race, belief, background, and region, and which therefore could function as the principle around which to build the shared identities, institutions, social forms, and cultural life of a modern nation. The National Government pursued this goal not just through the New Life Movement, but also through a range of related cultural projects, for instance in education, in fixing social and cultural boundaries, in setting norms and standards for proper conduct in private as well as in public, in promoting certain forms of public address, in drawing up regulations for weddings and funerals, and in setting a calendar of state rituals.

This project required decisions about how to deal with China's many different religious practices and beliefs. Sometimes violent conflicts had resulted from attempts by KMT radicals to eradicate what they believed to be superstitious or backward practices. In 1930, the Central Executive Committee of the KMT issued a letter to party bureaus that tried to settle which gods, sects, religions, and temples should be preserved and which abandoned.[186] It did so, the text said, in response to local disturbances about this issue involving radical party offices. If sanctioned by eminent scriptures and long tradition, religious practices could be regarded as expressing China's unique and venerable culture and hence treasured. The committee declared that 'heterodox beliefs' that 'misled the people' had emerged mostly after the unification of the empire. These had always been combated by honourable officials and wise men with the welfare of the people in mind. The National Government should do so too, because they did not accord with China's cultural essence. Corruptions not sanctioned by ancient texts and distinctly backward practices such as idol worship, incense burning, and kowtowing before religious statues had to be combated, because if not, 'it makes us the laughing stock of the world and we will not obtain final victory in our struggle with the Great Powers'.

Daoism and Buddhism were accepted as ancient Chinese religions. However, the Committee declared that in corrupt forms they had influenced the White Lotus, the Boxers, the Big Knife Society, and the Red Spear Society. Such organisations were to be proscribed. Ancient Chinese Gods, such as the Gods of the Sun, the Moon, and the Earth, the City God, and the Kitchen God were, according to the text, respectable, but also had given rise to superstitious practices not confirmed in texts. It determined that there were twelve 'ancient philosophers' (xianzhe), including Confucius, Mencius, the Yellow Emperor, the God of Agriculture, Yue Fei, and Guanyu, who had represented and made China's culture. Temples and rituals involving them should be preserved. In worshipping them, such practices as incense burning and kneeling should be abolished while their personal qualities and their teachings should be brought to the foreground.

Chinese dynasties in the past had nurtured a dynastic cultural unity by issuing a calendar and maintaining cycles of rituals. Shortly after coming to power, in May 1928, the Ministry of the Interior called for the promulgation of a new national calendar and the proscription of old ones. The new calendar was to be based on the solar calendar. Several old festivals, such as Yuanxiao, Shangyi, Duanyang, Qixi, Zhongyuan Chongyang, and Laba, were to be included as they had throughout history provided rest days for the people. New ones to be included were to be the anniversaries of Sun Yatsen's death, National Day, the Oath-taking of the NRA as it set out on the Northern Expedition, and the birth of Sun Yatsen.[187] On the basis of historical evidence, various name changes were suggested and it was decided that a number of old rituals and practices would be listed in the new calendar, but that no holiday should be given to mark them. The main rituals that had traditionally marked the rural cycle too should be included, and KMT and National Government officials should participate in the rituals that marked them.[188] This way of casting the calendar was of course useful to the Nationalists to mark themselves out as modern leaders and enforce a hierarchy with themselves in a superior position.

The National Government also formulated new procedures for wedding and funerals. In 1930, it adopted detailed regulations that prescribed which kind of Western and Chinese music could be performed, what kind of banners in what colours could be displayed, and what kind and how many monks could be invited to participate.[189] During the New Life Movement, a new form of wedding was promoted. Couples were encouraged to wed in collective marriage ceremonies in town halls presided over by government officials.[190] The promotion of the *baojia* system too can be placed in this context. It required the National Government to define and legitimate what a family was, how its members should relate to each other, and how they should relate to neighbours and officials.

The New Life Movement was also an attempt at addressing the cultural deficit of which Chiang Kaishek personally and the KMT more broadly suffered. It suggested that the Nationalists were working for the whole of the Chinese nation and for its revival and that they were not a small clique out to monopolize power. It spoke out against corruption and sought to promote an image of National Government and KMT officers as honest and disciplined people. Such an interpretation is supported by the fact that in the summer of 1935, Chiang again attempted to convene a national assembly. In personal telegrams to his secretary and advisor Chen Bulei, he ordered Chen to draft laws for a two-chamber assembly. Half the upper chamber would be appointed by provincial, city, and local governments and the rest by the president. The higher chamber would focus on legislation. The lower chamber was to be elected from provincial and local assemblies, and focus on economic measures.[191] Chiang was not willing to weaken his grip on power, but he was interested in dressing up his rule in the more respectable clothes of democracy. Nothing would come of this initiative. Fears of further political trouble and civil war, first with the Guangxi Clique and then with Zhang Xueliang, caused its demise.

The New Life movement failed. It had a hectoring and petty quality. To accept its new presentation of the KMT and of Chiang Kaishek as grand nationalist visionary leaders was too much of a stretch with the civil wars still fresh in the mind, with so much suffering still around, with brutishness by no means eliminated, and with a KMT that continued to be deeply ridden by factionalism. It imposed straitjackets on social and cultural life that could not but be resented. Its failure is also interesting for what it reveals about Chinese nationalism. There is no doubt that nationalism was strong in many quarters. But, to make a country as large and diverse cohere around a common national identity, to give it political and institutional shape, to evolve the routines, the symbols, the festivals, the social networks, and the public practices to tie together the entire population and orient it towards a single state proved extraordinarily difficult. It did so as well for its successor.

Conclusion

This chapter has suggested that after the civil wars and political instability that followed the Northern Expedition, the Nationalists began actively to prepare for war with Japan. The policy of avoiding an immediate confrontation while pursuing military strengthening came at a price, but was given the state of China's military forces at the time, the tense domestic situation, and the unwillingness of the international community of the day to intervene probably unavoidable. The military build-up was first conducted in secret, with the German Military Advisors Group and the NDPC collecting the information necessary to produce workable plans for military reform and industrial development. After 1935, when the Nationalists signalled publicly that if Japan wanted to avoid war they would have to accommodate themselves to the Nationalists and their political claims, considerable progress was made in building up an industrial base, training and equipping an elite force, linking it to society through a system of universal military service, and building up fortifications. A clear and cohesive Nationalist strategy was developed that aimed to ensure that if war happened, China would fight as one entity and survive the initial Japanese onslaught.

The Nationalist approach was hybrid in nature. The influence of the past remained strong and showed itself destructively in the aftermath of the Northern Expedition when conflict was essentially about who would be China's leader with political, military, ideological, and ritual supremacy. More constructively, after 1930 Nationalist approaches to government, local security, and mobilisation aimed at demilitarising local society, tying the peasantry to the land, establishing bureaucratic control over the local sources of violence, reducing tax burdens, and eliminating nasty middlemen.

Even if hybrid, the Nationalists continued to link their efforts to a vision of national redemption in which the recovery of military and cultural vigour was a key part. In the countryside, the reconstruction of bureaucracy and the implementation of the *baojia* was intended to create new linkages between the population and Nationalist political and military structures. The elite force was to be a national army, embody the new nation, and support the development of Nationalist institutions throughout the country. The New Life Movement articulated an essentialised and secularised Confucianism and propagated it as a national ethos through various institutions, including at the local level in the training programmes for *baojia* staff, local administrators, and militia. The Nationalists, then, were neither blind modernisers nor simple revivalists, but evolved a symbiotic approach shaped by the Chinese past as well as the ideologies and the aesthetic of modernity.

This approach was not necessarily stillborn. At the eve of the War of Resistance, China was in better military and economic shape than a decade earlier. Nationalist political and military power had spread well beyond its initial base of the Lower Yangtze provinces. Conditions in the countryside had improved. Lloyd Eastman wrote that 'during 1936 and 1937, the agrarian crisis ended' and that bumper crops in those years, partly as the result of good weather conditions but surely also of stability, an end to military exactions, and a revival of markets, 'China's farmers generally enjoyed a prosperity they had not known for decades'.[192] Industry grew very rapidly during the Nanjing decade, in part because of government investment, although this should not be overstated, but also because of the unification of the currency, improvements in communications, the standardisation of weights and measures, a more predictable fiscal regime, and cheaper credit. In 1936, again as Eastman has pointed out, a new mood emerged, occasioned by better times for many, a new sense of unity, a peaceful end to the Guangxi revolt in the summer of 1936, and a sense that progress was being made, after all, on many fronts. According to Eastman, 'Chiang for the first time had become a popular and seemingly indispensable leader'.[193] The War of Resistance would change all that.

5 A forward policy in the north

After 1935 the Nationalists followed a forward strategy in north and north-west China. This was not an easy task as the Nationalists did not police clearly demarcated borders within which they controlled the means of violence. Rather, they faced a porous frontier zone populated by a number of larger and smaller military groups. These shaped their actions not only with an eye to Nanjing, but also to each other and to the actions of foreign powers, including Japan but also the Soviet Union, and even players further afield. To pursue their forward policy, the Nationalists needed to build mutually reinforcing domestic and foreign alliances, including with the Soviet Union, and develop more or less reliable local clients. They had to do so while not precipitating an early conflict with Japan and without alienating Germany, on whose military advisors and supplies of industrial and military resources they remained dependent. The task was further complicated by the reality that the militarists and the Communists in north and north-west China, no matter how patriotic and anti-Japanese they were, had much to lose not just from a war with Japan but also from the intrusion of the Nationalists themselves. This chapter examines how the Nationalists pursued this goal in the two years before the war and in the first months of the War of Resistance itself.

The He–Umezu Agreement of 1935 and the proximity of Japanese forces in Korea and Manchuria precluded too bold a policy in Hebei and Chahar, let alone the deployment of Nationalist forces. In Shandong, similarly, the Nationalists could not insert their armies. The best that could be done in these areas was to cultivate relations with regional power holders such as Song Zheyuan and Han Fuju, keep the National Government flag flying as best as possible, and prepare to insert forces quickly if war broke out.

In the north-west, by which I mean Shaanxi, Shanxi, and Suiyuan, the situation was different. Sufficiently far from Japanese armies, from 1935 the Nationalists sought to enhance their position there to make it possible to resist Japanese encroachment into Suiyuan and to weaken the local militarists and the Communists. In addition, firming up their position in the area would make it possible for the Nationalists from there to operate against the Japanese flank in case the Japanese moved south into Hebei, which is what Nationalist war plans expected and which would indeed happen after the Marco Polo Bridge Incident of 7 July 1937.[1] Zhang Xueliang's Fengtian forces (named after the province in Manchuria now known as Liaoning), Yan Xishan's Shanxi forces, Yang Hucheng's North-western Army, and the recently arrived Communist armies were the strongest in the north-west. The Nationalists' approach was to weaken them by pushing them together into an area with limited resources, by injecting their own forces, and by developing alliances through a mixture of offers of money and position and threats of dismissal.

This strategy nearly backfired. The Xi'an Incident was the result of an attempt by Zhang Xueliang, the Communists, and Yang Hucheng to form a North-western Alliance against Chiang Kaishek. They did so when Chiang pressed them to participate in a campaign against the Japanese, arousing fears, no doubt rightly, that Chiang's intention was to ensure their own demise or at least their weakening. The Xi'an Incident, however, ended with the release of Chiang Kaishek, the imprisonment of Zhang Xueliang, the break-up of his forces, and Communist and Nationalist promises to participate in a new United Front.

This outcome was due to a number of factors, including the unwillingness of Zhang Xueliang to oust Chiang Kaishek and the mobilisation of an expeditionary force by He Yingqin and others to attack Xi'an. Important too was the fear in Moscow that the Xi'an Incident might result in a pro-Japanese regime in China. Had that been the Incident's outcome, the Soviet Union would have been confronted not just with the possibility of a war on two fronts with undoubtedly the two best armies in the world, but also with a hostile China. To prevent this outcome, Moscow ordered the Communists to use their influence to safeguard Chiang Kaishek and help bring about a United Front against Japan under his leadership.

If geo-strategic reasons explain the Soviet attitude, it was also important that from 1934 the Nationalists courted the Soviet Union. For the Nationalists, to seek better relations with the Soviet Union as the likelihood of war with Japan increased was perhaps a counter-intuitive but nonetheless rational policy. The rivalry for influence in Manchuria between Japan on the one hand and Russia and the Soviet Union on the other had long been a feature of East Asian politics, and the Nationalists themselves had become thoroughly acquainted with its intricacies and potentialities in the 1920s. The Japanese occupation of Manchuria meant that the Japanese and the Soviets shared a long border and Japan's subsequent intrusion into Chahar and then Suiyuan enhanced Japan's threat to the Soviets further. Because isolationist policies dominated in the USA and appeasing ones in Britain, it was only the Soviet Union that was likely to aid China. In addition, the Soviets had leverage over the Chinese Communists and their attitude was watched too by the militarists of the north-west.

The Xi'an Incident, then, is useful in reconstructing the problems of defending a border area in a divided nation and analysing the considerations to which various players were subject. It also helps illustrate the interlocking nature of international and domestic alliance politics. The two are difficult to analyse separately. It should be stated that the Nationalists' forward policy in the north was only one part of their international strategy in the 1930s. A full examination of Nationalist foreign policy would include their activities in Japan itself, Manchuria, Korea, and, last but not least, South-east Asia with its thriving Chinese communities.

This chapter ends with an examination of alliance politics during the opening months of the War of Resistance. The Xi'an Incident did not lead to firm and formal agreements about a new United Front involving the Communists and supported by the Soviets. Nor did regional military forces commit themselves to fighting on the

Nationalist side. As military operations escalated after the Marco Polo Incident, the Nationalists were unable to make the militarists of the north and north-west stand firm. Some, in fact, sought to flee the battlefield and nearly succeeded in bringing about a new alliance designed to avoid Nationalist pressure to resist Japanese advances in north China. It was only after the Nationalists attacked Japanese positions in Shanghai, permitted under the 1932 truce agreement concluded following the Japanese bombing of the city, that the Soviets, the Communists, and a number of regional military forces committed themselves to a united War of Resistance. The Shanghai operation followed after the Japanese threatened to break through in north China and had concentrated massive naval forces at Shanghai itself. The most important force that then joined the War of Resistance was in fact the Guangxi Clique, which gained the opportunity to build a new base in north China. This development stabilised the situation on the north China front and allowed the Nationalists to pursue their strategy of confronting the Japanese in north China not too far from the Soviet Union.

The Nationalists' geo-political strategy

In studies of the international context of the War of Resistance, most attention has been paid to the USA. However, as John Garver has made clear in a study of wartime Soviet–Japanese relations, the Soviet Union's role was significant as well.[2] Threatened directly by Japanese advances in Manchuria, Mongolia, and north China, the Soviets could not but take an active interest in East Asian affairs and work to prevent China from joining the Japanese and the Germans, something that would be a possibility if pro-accommodation figures such as Wang Jingwei in the government or in the military held sway.

Much kept the two sides apart. Memories of antagonism during the Northern Expedition remained fresh in the mind. Chiang Kaishek's son, Chiang Ching-kuo, remained in the Soviet Union. The Soviets could not but be weary. Too close a co-operation with the Nationalists could drag them into war with Japan, at a time when the Soviet Red Army was going through Stalin's purges.[3] Soviet interventions in China in the 1920s had failed and had become part of destabilising power struggles in Moscow. The Soviet's most natural allies in China were the Communists. The Nationalists co-operated closely with Germany, potentially the most dangerous Soviet enemy. Only the fear of Japan was a common denominator between Chiang Kaishek and Stalin.

The Soviet Union

The National Government first proposed to the Soviet Union a non-aggression or mutual security pact in 1932 during discussions about the establishment of diplomatic relations. Given the weakness of the National Government at the time and its civil war with the Communists, it is unsurprising that nothing came of this approach. However, by 1934, the situation had changed in China domestically as the National Government had seemingly decisively defeated the Communists, and internationally because the Japanese had begun to expand into Suiyuan and Chahar while aggressive fascist regimes had emerged in Western Europe.

Chiang Kaishek initiated moves for a closer link with Stalin in the autumn of 1934, when he sent Jiang Tingfu in a personal capacity to Moscow, initially without informing the Chinese ambassador in Moscow or high officials in Nanjing. Born in 1895, Jiang had studied in the USA, including at Oberlin, and earned a PhD in history at Columbia University. In 1923, he returned to China to teach European history first at Nankai and then at Qinghua University and contributed articles to *The Independent Critic* and *The Impartial*. He thus belonged to that group of northern intellectuals who after 1932 began to make their expertise available to the National Government under Chiang Kaishek.[4]

Jiang Tingfu reported from Moscow that although the Soviets were not willing to sign a formal treaty, they were interested in improving relations. Jiang stated that like the Chinese, the Soviets believed that two opposing camps were emerging in the world, with China and the Soviet Union in one and the Japanese in the other. He concluded that it would be possible to 'open a new avenue in China's diplomacy' and asked that he be permitted to begin negotiations.[5] These took place partly in Moscow as well as in Nanjing between Chen Lifu and Dimitri Bogomolov, the Soviet ambassador to China.[6] In December 1935, Chen Lifu went secretly to Moscow to continue these negotiations.[7]

Jiang's visit to Moscow took place when Soviet foreign policy was undergoing radical change. In response to the rise of fascist governments in Europe as well as Japanese aggression in Manchuria, the Soviets toned down the rhetoric of class warfare and revolution and instead called for popular front governments. The Seventh Comintern Congress of July 1935 adopted resolutions stating that the threat of a new world war had increased and that in this war, German, Japanese, and Italian fascist forces would seek to suppress the Communist movement. If Communist parties remained isolated and continued to call for revolution, they would face this threat alone. Hence the call for governments representing a broad coalition of forces including Communists. In 'The Fascist Offensive and the Responsibility of the Communist International to Fight for the Unification of Proletarian Anti-Fascism', the Secretary General of the Comintern, Dimitrov, argued that the Chinese Communists 'should unite with all organised forces desiring to struggle genuinely for the salvation of the country and the people'.[8] Chinese representatives at the Comintern then drafted the famous '1 August' declaration, published only in October in Paris in the Chinese-language *National Salvation*, which called for a United Front in China of all forces opposed to Japan including the KMT.[9]

Within the CCP, it was Wang Ming, head of the CCP's mission to the Comintern and a leading Politburo member, rather than Mao Zedong who took the initiative in promoting the United Front. Wang had suggested a United Front already in 1933, although at that time he had in mind a coalition excluding Chiang Kaishek. Before 1935, CCP documents called for a 'broad Anti-Japanese United Front to win over all anti-Chiang forces'.[10] The 1 August Declaration was important because it did not mention Chiang Kaishek by name and so suggested that he might be included in such an alliance. In a 7 November 1935 article in *National Salvation*, Wang specifically stated that if Chiang Kaishek ceased attacks on the Red Army and fight Japan, the CCP 'will be prepared to unite with him and the Nanjing Army'.[11] For Wang, the promotion of the United Front was useful in strengthening his own status in the CCP. In late 1937, he returned to China as the promoter of the new United Front that then had come about and for a while vied with Mao for leadership of the CCP.[12]

Jiang Tingfu was appointed ambassador to the Soviet Union in August 1936, after which negotiations intensified. In a report of April 1937, he recalled that during his 1934 visit, anti-Nationalist propaganda had still been widespread and that many Soviet officials doubted that the Nationalists would be prepared to fight Japan. However, he went on, the atmosphere had changed: the Soviet media no longer criticised the National Government and carried no news about the Communists. At times of national crises, such as during the revolt of Guangdong and Guangxi in the summer of 1936 or the Xi'an Incident of December, newspapers had supported the National Government and called for a government of national unity under the Nationalists aimed at mobilising all forces to resist the Japanese.[13]

Soviet support for popular front governments intensified after Hitler's moves to build an alliance against 'Bolshevism, Socialism, and the Jews' led in November 1936 to an agreement with Japan to make common cause against Communism.[14] Jiang Tingfu stated that the Soviets' aim was not just to unite movements opposed to fascism, but also to open the door to improved relations, not just with China, but also with Britain and the USA, whose military strength the Soviets believed would be decisive in any new world war. According to Jiang Tingfu, the publication of Edgar Snow's *Red Star over China* should be placed in this context. In his conversations with Snow, Mao emphasised resistance to Japan and downplayed class warfare and land redistribution.[15] If Mao aligned himself with the rhetoric of the United Front, this did not mean that he was ready to accept a United Front under Chiang Kaishek's leadership. During negotiations with the KMT, which will be discussed later, he held out for an alliance based on equality between all partners, a suggestion that was anathema to the Nationalists, while also pursuing the North-western Alliance which would exclude the Nationalists altogether.

Although optimistic about co-operation between Moscow and Nanjing, Jiang Tingfu was a realist. He wrote to Chiang Kaishek that 'Soviet authorities on the one hand hope that we will resist Japan and in private conversations energetically encourage us to do so, but they have never discussed concrete steps. They want to avoid war with Japan'. He suggested that Soviet policy might in fact be aimed at war between China and Japan in the belief that China's rapid defeat would lead to US and British intervention in East Asia from which the Soviet Union then could profit.[16] If this was perhaps one Soviet goal, their interest would also be well served by a long and difficult war between China and Japan.

Chiang's suspicion of the Soviets was not shared by everybody. Yang Jie was the head of the Army Staff College who had received military training in Japan and had visited the Soviet Union when he headed a mission to investigate European militaries in 1933–4. Yang believed that the Soviet Union would enter the war. In December 1937, he went to the Soviet Union to plead for more military supplies and in May 1938 replaced Jiang Tingfu as ambassador.[17] If the Nationalists had reasons to be suspicious of Soviet intentions, the reverse was true as well. Significant elements in the KMT were weary of war with Japan and preferred an accommodation, including, of course, Wang Jingwei.

Negotiations between Jiang Tingfu and Maxim Litvinov, People's Commissar for Foreign Affairs, about a Chinese–Soviet Alliance began following Jiang's arrival as ambassador in Moscow. I shall discuss the role of the Xi'an Incident, which came only one month after the German–Japanese agreement to fight Communism together, in the evolving relationship later. In the discussions with Jiang Tingfu, Litvinov rejected a mutual security treaty, with its implied military commitment, not just because the Soviets wanted to avoid war with Japan, but also, Jiang reported, because the Soviets feared that such an alliance would provoke Western suspicions about Soviet intentions. As Garver has pointed out, Nationalist as well as Soviet foreign policy sought to bring about a 'non-aggressor front' involving Britain, the USA, and other Western powers. Given the deep suspicions of the Soviet Union in the West, this would not be easy.[18]

Both Chinese and Soviet diplomats sought to re-assure the West by informing them of the negotiations and by seeking their participation in security arrangements for East Asia. In March 1937, Jiang Tingfu told the US Ambassador in Moscow that an agreement on Soviet aid had already been agreed,[19] while Bogomolov, the Soviet Ambassador to the National Government, asked a journalist, perhaps Edgar Snow, to inform the US government about the Chinese–Soviet negotiations and attempts to bring about a settlement between the Communists and the Nationalists.[20] There were also suggestions that in East Asia security should be based on a revival of the Nine Power Treaty of 1922, the Paris Anti-War Covenant, and the League of Nations.[21] Jiang Tingfu suggested to Chiang Kaishek that China should attempt to bring about a multilateral alliance, including the USA, as a pillar of stability and security in East Asia.[22] The goal of such efforts was to make clear that closer Sino-Soviet relations were not a threat to Western interests in East Asia.

Even if by the time of the Marco Polo Bridge Incident, Sino-Soviet negotiations had progressed far, it was only after war began that they signed a Mutual Non-Agression Treaty and aid began to flow. A formal announcement earlier could only have antagonised Japan and alienated the Western powers. It is possible, too, that the two remained suspicious of each other and that the Soviets were not willing to begin the delivery of aid before the Nationalists had actually begun to fight Japan in deed.

Western powers

It has been suggested that Chiang Kaishek in 1937 decided to attack Japanese positions in Shanghai in a bid to gain Western support. Lloyd Eastman, who described the offensive as 'one of Chiang's greatest – and most debatable – gambles of his career',[23] believed that this was the case. Frank Dorn put the argument in an extreme form when he stated that the attack was a 'deliberate' but 'hopeless campaign' that 'sacrificed 240,000 Chinese troops in a ploy calculated to gain world support', by which he meant the Western powers.[24]

Ch'i Hsi-sheng rightly rejected these views.[25] Western military intervention on China's behalf was unlikely. The strategy of continental defence and isolationism prevailed in the USA. In the mid-1930s, Britain had become more actively involved in East Asian Affairs, but its attitude to the Spanish Civil War, Mussolini's annexation of Abyssinia in 1936, and the rise of Hitler suggested an unwillingness to intervene militarily even in Europe. On 26 May 1937, Neville Chamberlain became Prime Minister and implemented a policy of appeasement. If these realities counselled against any false hope of Western military support for China, so did history, as suggested by the Western failure to take measures against Japan earlier.

The Nationalists were aware of this reality. In his August 1935 memorandum, von Falkenhausen had stated that 'for now the Powers are disunited and they do not have the capacity to intervene separately' and therefore 'if China does not defend itself, no other country will use its forces to help it'.[26] In 1937, W. H. Donald, the Australian

Advisor to Chiang Kaishek, stated that Western help would come only after China had fought Japan alone for several years.[27] No false hopes existed about British or US military readiness to assist the Nationalists in 1937.

This did not mean that the Western powers were irrelevant in Nationalist geo-strategic calculations and that gaining their support was not a consistent aim of Nationalist policy. China's 1937 War Plan (Version 1) anticipated that 'if real war breaks out between the enemy and us, this will provoke war between Russia and Japan or the USA and Japan, or even a joint war by China, Russia, Britain, and the USA against Japan'.[28] If in 1937, the hope was realistic that the Soviets might become directly involved, as it would, for instance, during the Battle of Nomonhan, the involvement of Britain and the USA could only be a long-term prospect. A constant goal of Nationalist diplomacy was to keep the door open to this possibility.

One way in which Nationalist strategy was shaped in the immediate term with the Western powers in mind was in the assumption that Japan would not risk a war with them. This meant that it was believed that south China, abutting British and French colonies, would not become a theatre of operations.[29] It was for this reason that they built their industrial base there, concentrated their energies on a forward policy in the north, and made Sichuan into their last place of refuge.

Furthermore, it was in the interests of the Nationalists to obtain Western diplomatic support in case, if war broke out, it came to negotiations with the Japanese, or, if these would fail, to isolate Japan. In the months before the war, Chinese diplomats downplayed relations with the Soviets, and sought to involve them in a joint diplomatic intervention. In the spring and summer, China's diplomats directly and through generally respected Chinese public figures such as Hu Shi and Jiang Menglin as well as prominent Western journalists and academics in China, such as John Lossing Buck and Hallett Abend, repeatedly signalled to the USA on the one hand, that China would go to war with Japan if Japan did not withdraw from north China and, on the other, that it would welcome US diplomatic intervention.[30] Chinese diplomats too made sure to suggest to US diplomats that their relation with the Soviet Union was far from trouble-free, telling them, for instance, that trade negotiations had become stuck.[31] In December 1937, when Soviet military aid had begun to flow, Jiang Tingfu told the US Chargé in Moscow 'in confidence' that he had become bitter about the Soviets because of their refusal to put anything in writing.[32]

The following message of 23 August 1937 by Chiang Kaishek to Henry Morgenthau, the US Secretary of the Treasury, which was passed on by John Lossing Buck, was designed to push the USA to involve itself more actively in East Asian Affairs on behalf of China. Playing on the US self-image as an upholder of international justice and recalling the Mukden Incident when the British Foreign Secretary Simon had refused to join the USA in a policy to contain Japan, the message stated:

> I am truly disappointed that the USA did not co-operate with England in an attempt to avert the present crisis which could have been achieved by joint representation to Japan and China. China and the world will long remember Simon's failure to co-operate with the USA in 1931. The USA should not lose her prestige in the world as an upholder of international justice and if she will continue her Stimson policy the present conflict can be prevented from extending to other countries

including the USA. I do not want the USA to be dragged into the war, but I do look to her to maintain her position in the Pacific and to maintain peace there.[33]

Chiang's letter was crafted carefully to suggest that even within the limits of the doctrine of hemispheric defence, the USA could still take some measures beneficial to China. It followed a US refusal to participate in an internationally co-ordinated effort to forestall the war. Britain had brought concerted pressure on the USA to participate in this effort, and also called on the USA to join it in retaliatory measures against Japan and active diplomatic and financial support for China in case war did break out. The USA refused, even when the Japanese Ambassador in Washington assured Secretary of State Cordell Hull, when asked whether 'the making of any direct representations by the Powers, either individually or as a group, would contribute toward the maintenance of the peace', that 'it would tend to deter the Japanese from going to lengths which, if persisted in, would have to be resisted forcibly by China'.[34] Not just US public opinion, isolationist policies, the desire to avoid war and remain above international intrigue, but also the hope, expressed for instance by the US Ambassador to Japan, Joseph Grew, that anti-war forces in Japan might yet prevail led to this attitude.[35] As Dorothy Borg has made clear, the US desire to avoid war with Japan undermined its championing of China.[36]

In short, Nationalist strategy aimed at allying itself with those countries most threatened by Japanese expansionism. In the first instance, this was the Soviet Union which was threatened by the Japanese occupation of Manchuria and its growing interventions in Suiyuan and Chahar. The Soviet Union was useful to the Nationalists as a threat in the Japanese rear, a potential co-combatant, a supplier of war material, and as a power with influence in north China especially on the Chinese Communists. The Nationalists also pursued good relations with the USA and Britain, not because they believed that these countries would immediately intervene militarily, but because they had substantial interests in China and East and South-east Asia generally, they could be useful diplomatically, and in the long run, because they had the naval power and the productive capacity that would be decisive in a new world war.

Domestic strategy

During the Xi'an Incident, Zhang Xueliang imprisoned Chiang Kaishek and his entourage in Xi'an in the north China province of Shaanxi with the help of other local military leaders, including Yang Hucheng, the commander of the North-west Army, as well as the Communists. The Incident took place against two important backgrounds. The first was Chiang Kaishek's efforts to shepherd the Communists, Zhang Xueliang, and other regional military forces into the inhospitable terrain of north-west China. With winter having set in and with the usual period of spring shortages in the near future, for them the future looked bleak. At the same time, the Japanese were advancing into Chahar and Suiyuan. Chiang Kaishek needed the co-operation of local forces in his efforts to turn back the Japanese and Prince De's Mongolian force supported by them. These local forces, however, were negotiating about a Great North-western Alliance in opposition to Chiang Kaishek.

This situation illustrated the great difficulties of mounting warfare in a frontier zone. If Chiang Kaishek suggested that his actions were designed to resist the Japanese penetration of Suiyuan, regional leaders could not be certain of the extent of his commitment to this campaign and could reasonably believe it was designed to see their forces decimated. At the same time, if a serious war between China and Japan broke out, they would not want to fight alone and would want to secure the protection of a stronger force, such as the Nationalists. A radically different option for them was a broad anti-Nationalist alliance especially if it had the support of the Soviet Union. Such an alliance might make the Japanese think twice about offensives against them and would also reduce Nationalist pressures. During the Xi'an Incident, all had to consider which option would best secure their own future.

Moves towards a North-western Alliance

Zhang Xueliang headed the strongest military force in north China. A 1935 National Government document estimated that Zhang commanded 85,000 troops. According to the document, Yan Xishan controlled 43,000 Shanxi troops, while Han Fuju's forces in Shandong numbered 42,500, Song Zheyuan's forces in Hebei and Chahar came to 28,000, and Yang Hucheng's North-western forces in Shaanxi numbered 36,000.[37] US military intelligence of 1937 suggests that most of these forces had increased significantly in the following two years.[38] The 1935 document further mentioned that Shang Zhen, associated with Yan Xishan, controlled 17,000 troops and Liu Zhenhua, a former ally of Feng Yuxiang, 22,000. Communist forces had diminished greatly during the Long March, but became a factor in north China after the 1st Front Army under Mao Zedong established a base in north Shaanxi in October 1935 and the 2nd and 4th Front Armies arrived in Gansu in October 1936, having failed to establish a new base on the Sichuan–Tibet border.

The Fengtian Army had repeatedly been decisive in the history of the National Government. If Zhang Zuolin had nearly destroyed the Northern Expedition in 1927, his decision to withdraw from north China in 1928 had signalled its victorious conclusion and his son's stance in the last stages of the War of the Central Plains had been decisive in that conflict. If the loss of Manchuria was a severe blow to Nanjing's prestige, as it was to Zhang Xueliang's, the move of the Fengtian Army into north China was useful to Nanjing in its confrontation with Yan Xishan, Feng Yuxiang and other northern military leaders. Chiang appointed Zhang Xueliang head of the Beiping Pacification Office and Beiping Political Council.

From March 1933 until January 1934, Zhang Xueliang went abroad.[39] When he returned after the Fujian Rebellion and as the last campaign against the Jiangxi Soviet pressed ahead, he initially co-operated with Chiang Kaishek as vice-head of the E Yu Wan Bandit Suppression Office. Zhang later claimed to the Communists that he had done so wholeheartedly, but that he became disenchanted with Chiang Kaishek's policy of not resisting the Japanese but fighting the Communists in north China because it postponed any attempt at recovering Manchuria.[40] If that was no doubt a genuine concern, likely another one was that Chiang Kaishek had begun efforts to curtail Zhang Xueliang's power. The army reform programme called for the inclusion of Zhang Xueliang's best forces into the National Army. Chiang also reduced financial support to Zhang Xueliang.[41] Moreover, in October 1935, he appointed Zhang head of the North-west Bandit Suppression Office, making him responsible for fighting the Communists there and also forcing him and his forces into the poor north-west.

It was in this context that Zhang entered into discussions with the Communists. After the Long March, the CCP faced the problem of carving out their own base in north-west China. To achieve this end, the Communists mixed fighting and negotiation. In the fall of 1935, they attacked Fengtian Army units, inflicting considerable losses and killing three division commanders. In January 1936, Mao Zedong, Zhou Enlai and twenty-one CCP generals sent letters to Zhang and his most important generals, including Yu Xuezhong and Wang Yizhe, in which they wondered whether 'attacks on the Soviet area can offer a way out for the Fengtian Army' and stated that 'your enemies are the Japanese imperialist bandits and the traitor Chiang Kaishek'.[42]

In April 1936, Zhang Xueliang travelled to Yan'an and met with Zhou Enlai. According to Zhou Enlai's report on these meetings, Zhang Xueliang agreed to open up trading posts and promised to supply ammunition, radio equipment, as well as medicines to the Communists. He also informed them about some of his military plans for the next month. Both sides agreed to work together militarily to prevent Yang Hucheng, who would play a key role during the Xi'an Incident, from expanding his base in Shaanxi. Zhang furthermore guaranteed not to attack CCP forces making their way to their new base area.[43]

Although Zhang agreed with the CCP's demand for an end to Civil War and active resistance to Japan, he did not agree to the CCP's call to oppose Chiang Kaishek. According to Zhou, Zhang 'respected Chiang Kaishek and believed that he was highly patriotic and very capable' and therefore argued that 'helping Chiang Kaishek could further resistance against Japan'. Zhang Xueliang refused to oppose Chiang unless 'Chiang Kaishek submitted to the Japanese'. In that eventuality, which would entail a Nationalist recognition of the 'independence' of Manchuria, Zhang Xueliang would lose any prospect of being able to return to Manchuria and be left with an army that could no longer look forward to returning home. He furthermore stated, according to Zhou, that 'before the commencement of open resistance against Japan, he had to obey Chiang Kaishek's orders and occupy Soviet territory'. Zhang also told Zhou that he was negotiating with Sheng Shicai in Gansu and Yan Xishan in Shanxi, and urged the CCP to reduce its activities in Shanxi so as not to-pressure Yan. Surely in order to direct Red Army forces away from his own base, Zhang Xueliang argued that in case of war with Japan, he would not object to CCP forces entering Hebei, but that until then they should move to Suiyuan.[44] Following these meetings, both sides exchanged liaison officers and kept in radio contact, and on 22 September, Mao Zedong and Zhang Xueliang signed the 'Agreement to Resist Japan and Save the Nation'.[45]

One strand of Communist domestic diplomacy from the spring of 1936, pursued mostly by Yan'an, aimed at nurturing a Great North-western Alliance made up of themselves, Zhang Xueliang, and Yang Hucheng. They followed the same approach towards Yang as they had towards Zhang Xueliang. They first showed their teeth by attacking some of Yang's units and murdering his secret agents and personnel, including a brigade commander, but then began negotiations. In May 1936, the Communists and Yang Hucheng agreed on a mutual non-aggression pact and made arrangements to feign battles in case Chiang Kaishek pressed Yang to attack the Communists. They too exchanged liaison personnel and kept in radio contact.[46]

While Zhang and Yang had been on reasonably good terms, inevitably conflict arose and even turned violent as their armies were pressed together in north-west China. However, from the summer of 1936, the Communists urged co-operation between all three, telling Zhang 'to join together with Yang in allying yourself with the Communists' and Yang that 'the reason that Chiang Kaishek transferred the Fengtian Army into Shaanxi and ordered you and Xueliang to exterminate Communism is to cause us three to fight each other. For the interest of the nation, you should join together with friendly forces and ally with the Communists. Instead of fighting each other, we ought to join together'.[47]

Besides Zhang Xueliang and Yang Hucheng, the Communists also made diplomatic overtures to military and political leaders further afield. These included sympathetic figures in the KMT, military leaders in south China including the Guangxi Clique, as well as Liu Xiang, the Sichuanese warlord, and Yan Xishan. When Communist forces and cadres aggressively moved into Shanxi in September 1936, Yan initially turned to Chiang Kaishek, who sent several divisions to Shanxi to resist the Communist advance. However, clashes broke out between Shanxi troops and Nationalist units after the latter increased their presence and their secret service personnel began to operate in the province. In May 1936, Mao Zedong wrote Yan Xishan, suggesting that they co-operate in opposing Chiang Kaishek and resisting Japan. In September, a League for Sacrifice and Salvation was established and high CCP leaders, including Bo Yibo and Feng Xuefeng, took up posts in a joint CCP–Yan Xishan organisation in Shanxi. The two sides concluded an agreement not to attack each other.[48]

The North-western Alliance took shape in response to Nationalist efforts to extend their power into north China as well as Japanese penetration into Suiyuan and Chahar. The call for an end to civil war, political reform, and joint resistance to Japan created a platform around which they could rally together. However, significant differences existed between them. While the Communists under Mao's leadership were determined in their opposition to Chiang and called for his ouster, Zhang Xueliang, Yang Hucheng, and Yan Xishan did not want to go as far as that. Given recent Communist attacks on their own forces, they had reason to be suspicious of the Communists, who were also competitors for local resources.

CCP–KMT negotiations

While Zhang Xueliang and the Communists were working to give life to the Great North-western Alliance against Chiang Kaishek, in late 1935 Chiang Kaishek initiated efforts to begin negotiations with the Communists to establish a United Front against the Japanese. Chiang Kaishek opened three channels of communication with the CCP. Following the Seventh Comintern Congress and the publication of Wang Ming's articles calling for a United Front including the KMT, in December 1935 Chiang Kaishek ordered Deng Wenyi, the Chinese military attaché in Moscow, to interrupt his visit back to China and return to Moscow. Deng wrote a letter to Wang Ming suggesting discussions. Wang agreed, but cautiously first assigned Pan Hannian, a high ranking CCP secret service agent, as CCP representative.[49]

Deng Wenyi told Pan that Chiang Kaishek believed that war with Japan was imminent and that Chiang believed that he would need at least eighty divisions to fight the Japanese, but that many of these were now tied down by the Communists. Deng further told Pan that Chiang wanted to re-establish the United Front and would declare war once civil war between the Communists and the Nationalists had stopped. Deng also stated to Pan that Chiang's conditions for an agreement were the creation of a unified military command and Soviet support.[50] Informed by Pan, Wang Ming rejected these conditions, suggesting instead the formation of a National Defence Government based on equality between all anti-Japanese factions in China and military co-operation in a joint army called the Allied Resistance Army.[51]

Chen Lifu and Chen Guofu, leaders of the CC Clique and in charge of the KMT secret service, opened a second channel for negotiations when they contacted the CCP North China Bureau, also in December 1935. Through this channel Chiang Kaishek indicated that in return for CCP support for an alliance with the Soviet Union, incorporation of Communist forces into the National Army, and the restructuring of the Soviet government of the Chinese Communists, he would agree to allow the CCP to maintain an independent organisation and to control its own region as an experimental rural area.

Song Ziwen, Song Qingling, and Sun Ke opened the third channel in January and February 1936 when they made contact with Dong Jianwu and Zhang Zihua, CCP intelligence operatives, and asked each to travel to north Shaanxi via Xi'an to contact the CCP leadership directly. Song Qingling gave Dong Jianhua her secret telegraph identification code as well as a package of Yunnan medicines as a present for the Communists. Zhang Zihua carried a letter to Lin Boqu, a high-ranking CCP leader, from Tan Zhen, a Right-wing KMT member who then was a member of the Central Inspection Committee but in 1926 had joined the Western Hills Faction. The letter stated that

> The only thing to know is who is friend and who is enemy; the only method is to resist the former and join with the latter. I hope that you, Mao Zedong, and others, in deciding on this matter of the utmost importance, will seek to complete Mr Sun Yatsen's national revolution. I shall go through fire and water for this.[52]

Coming from someone so well known for his anti-Communism, this was a significant statement.

Dong and Zhang joined up in Xi'an, and there met Zhang Xueliang. After a telegram to Nanjing confirmed that the two were indeed allowed to proceed to Communist-held areas, Zhang could not be in any doubt that the Nationalists and Communists were in talks. This discovery may have influenced him in deciding to pursue his own discussions with the Communists.[53]

In meetings in February 1936 with the CCP leadership, the two stated that their mission had been arranged by Song Qingling, Sun Ke, and Song Ziwen, but that Chen Guofu and Chen Lifu were the key figures behind the démarche. They had come, so they stated, to learn the CCP's conditions for 'displaying sincerity' (shucheng), that is, to stop the fighting and recognise the legitimacy of the National Government. In return, they stated, Chiang would provide financial support, release political prisoners, arm the peasantry, stop attacks on the Communists, and resist Japan.[54]

The Communists believed that Chiang Kaishek's aim was to absorb the CCP and its armies. In a desperate situation, they nonetheless pursued the negotiations. In March 1936, they agreed to high level meetings and forwarded five conditions to Nanjing. The most important of these were a halt to Civil War, the formation of a National Defence Government, the organisation of an allied army, permission to move their forces to Hebei, and economic and political reform.[55] They aimed at a United Front in which the CCP and KMT, as well as other political factions and militarists, were equal members and in which the CCP would retain military and political independence.

The KMT response, which reached the CCP leadership in June, demanded that CCP armies in north China move to Suiyuan and Chahar rather than Hebei. It insisted that once war with Japan began, China's armies should be integrated. It also proposed that CCP leaders come to Nanjing to take up position in the government. Mao Zedong's response was that 'despite all the talk of resistance, in reality they have rejected our conditions and want us to move to Suiyuan, Chahar, and Outer Mongolia in order to ignite a war between Japan and the USSR'.[56]

The CCP, whose attempt to extend their base into Shanxi had in May been prevented by Nationalist divisions, had little option to continue the negotiations and scale down their demands. At the end of June, their representatives suggested that the CCP was willing to accept 'KMT leadership' of a National Defence Government and that once war began it would be willing to subordinate itself to 'national democratic unity'.[57]

In July and August, the revolt of Guangdong and Guangxi interrupted the negotiations. However, this incident was over by September. Moreover, in October Pan Hannian reached Yan'an and informed the CCP leadership that the Soviets wanted the CCP to come to terms with the KMT. The negotiations, taking place at various locations, including Hong Kong and Shanghai, intensified through September and early October. At the end of September, the CCP convened an expanded Politburo meeting to discuss the Comintern directive and on 11 October it accepted a 'Draft Agreement on Resistance to Japan and National Salvation'. Its main points were that once the document was signed the CCP and the KMT would stop attacks on each other's positions; the Nationalists would lift the economic embargo on Communist territory and supply food as well as military aid; and the Communists would agree to the creation of a unified command and a single military establishment, the disavowal of military means to overthrow the National Government, and participation in a National Assembly. They also would re-organise the political system of the Soviet area in accordance with the National Government's system of civil administration.[58]

This draft was sent to Pan Hannian in Shanghai and immediately passed on to KMT negotiators. To lay the groundwork in public opinion, in October the KMT began a propaganda drive calling for the revival of Sun Yatsen's Three Great Policies of alliance with the Soviet Union, co-operation with the Communists, and the mobilisation of workers and peasants. Song Qingling, Sun's wife, and He Xiangning, wife of the Liao Zhongkai, were brought out to make public announcements about the change in policy. Feng Yuxiang and other leading figures in Nanjing declared their support.[59]

Two comments are in order at this point. First, the fact that the CCP pursued both the United Front as well as the Great North-western Alliance was of course no more than sound politics on their part. Chiang Kaishek had engineered a situation in which the Communists faced the choice of moving into areas in which it was virtually guaranteed that they would be demolished by Japanese armies or weakened during the winter, or, if they accepted the lifeline of the United Front, be absorbed into the Nationalist armies and its government. Mao and his supporters in Yan'an, having been nearly wiped out by the Nationalist onslaught and pursued through the length and breadth of China, could not but be highly suspicious of Chiang's motives.

Second, it is useful to stand still for a moment to consider the cultural meaning behind what Chiang offered the Communists. What was anathema for him was not just to allow them a separate sovereignty, but also an independent identity outside the world of the National Government, with a claim to represent a different China. He did not demand that they give up their administrative and political organisations, although he sought to limit them. But he insisted that they 'display sincerity', by adopting the right titles, confirming the legitimacy of the National Government, and accepting that it stood for China. If Chiang sought to absorb the Red Army, he was willing even to let the Communists have their own force. But he did not accept, as the Communists surely knew he would not and as they themselves also never did, the idea of a new government made up of all parties and factions, precisely because it compromised his symbolic leadership and the claim of the National Government to represent China. As long as the Communists refused to acknowledge this, he fought them, but once they did, the fighting could end, all kinds of compromises were possible, and rather than facing trials for treason, long jail sentences, or lengthy investigations, the Communists could be incorporated into the world of the KMT, the National Government, and its armies.[60]

Crisis

Tensions mounted when the Japanese began to strengthen their position in Chahar and then moved into Suiyuan in May 1936. After having established an Inner Mongolian Government under Prince De in May, the Japanese issued supplies to his Mongolian Army, which in August 1936 took Taolin in eastern Suiyuan. Japanese forces at the same time occupied Zhangbei in Chahar.[61] Subsequently they established secret service stations in Guisui, the capital of Suiyuan, as well as in Ningxia and in Shanxi, and sent an emissary to Fu Zuoyi, the Suiyuan Provincial Chairman, suggesting that he 'improve Sino-Japanese relations'.[62] On 5 November, the Japanese convened a military conference that took the decision to occupy eastern Suiyuan and advance towards Guisui.[63] On 15 November, Mongolian forces supported by Japanese aeroplanes, tanks, and artillery units attacked Xinghe, Jining, Taolin, and Suiheng, cutting the Beiping–Suiyuan Railroad.[64] Now the roads into Shanxi and Shaanxi lay open to the Japanese.

The Xi'an Incident took place against the background of this Japanese advance. All the problems, and opportunities, of conflict with the Japanese in a border area where his forces needed the co-operation of local armies presented themselves to Chiang Kaishek in their full complexity. To resist, Chiang had to secure the co-operation of local forces and insert his own. Success would greatly increase his stature and, if he was able to make these local forces fight, he could count on them being seriously weakened. Caught between the vice of Japan's advance and the hammer of the Nationalist forward policy, local militarists and the Communists faced the difficult choice of falling in with Chiang's designs without knowing how serious he was about committing his own forces against the Japanese or following the equally risky option of the North-western Strategy.

Chiang made extensive preparations to meet the Japanese advance into Suiyuan. He despatched Chen Cheng to Taiyuan in Shanxi Province to direct the front from there and on 27 October suggested to Yan Xishan that he allow Tang Enbo's army, made up of main Nationalist units, to fight as part of his own forces in an offensive towards Zhangbei while Fu Zuoyi with his forces in Suiyuan would attack Shangdu. Chiang furthermore moved a number of divisions up into Henan and south Shaanxi and ordered the enlargement of airfields at Xi'an and Lanzhou.[65]

When the Japanese began their advance on 15 November, Chiang ordered resistance. Fu Zuoyi in Suiyuan began a counter-offensive on 17 November. On the evening of the same day, Chiang told Yan Xishan that to recover six counties occupied by the Japanese in Suiyuan he had ordered seventy aeroplanes to begin a bombing campaign against Japanese forces at Shangbei and Shangdu. Yan expressed his misgivings about this escalation of the conflict, fearing that the Japanese would respond in kind.[66]

Neither the Japanese threat nor Yan's reluctance were Chiang Kaishek's only problems. In October 1936, the 2nd and 4th Front Armies of the Red Army reached Huining in Gansu and linked up with the 1st Front Army. When these units then began to move east towards Shaanxi, the possibility emerged of a much stronger Communist presence, not only threatening the safety of Chiang's rear, but also increasing the viability of the North-western Alliance, which offered to military leaders like Yan Xishan a way out of Chiang's pressure to begin a risky offensive on the Japanese.

The Communists themselves faced one of the most critical situations in their entire history. The Soviet insistence on a United Front, the Japanese advance, the growth of Nationalist strength, the winter hardship, and the increased, even if reluctant, collaboration between regional military leaders such as Fu Zuoyi and Yan Xishan with Chiang Kaishek all were adverse developments for them. With the arrival of the 2nd and 4th Front Armies, which intensified Communist supply problems, came Zhang Guotao, who had begun the Long March with a larger army than Mao's and had rebelled against the Central Committee that had travelled with Mao. Although he had now lost most of his forces, the deep divisions in the CCP and the Red Army of the Long March had not been overcome.

After receiving an instruction from the Comintern, in September the CCP did finally jettison its slogan of 'Resist Japan and Oppose Chiang',[67] replacing it with 'compel Chiang Kaishek to resist Japan'.[68] At the same time, they kept their lines of communication with Zhang Xueliang open and the two continued to co-ordinate their actions. In October, Yan Xishan indicated to Zhang Xueliang that he would prefer Chiang Kaishek's leadership of a war of resistance against Japan, but that if Chiang chose not to fight, he would join with Zhang Xueliang and the CCP.[69]

As the Japanese threat increased, Nationalist conditions for a United Front became so onerous as to guarantee the CCP's demise. Just before the Suiyuan campaign began, on 11 November Chiang Kaishek through Chen Lifu informed Pan Hannian that the conditions for a United Front now included a sharp reduction in the establishment of the Red Army to 3,000 troops and assignment of all cadres and officers at division level and above to positions in the National Government and its armies after first a period of exile of half a year. In return, Chiang promised to release imprisoned CCP members and implement political and economic reforms.[70] Contact between the negotiators of the two sides in Shanghai did continue, but became acrimonious with Chen Lifu for instance remarking that if Chiang switched sides and joined the anti-Comintern alliance, the future for the CCP would be even bleaker.[71]

The hardening of Nationalist negotiation position was the result of Nationalist successes, both militarily and politically. The 'Situation Report' filed by US military intelligence for 29 November–10 December noted that 'Chinese resistance is stiffening and public opinion is rallying behind the resistance'.[72] Fu Zuoyi's counter-offensive was successful. His forces in combination with Shanxi troops retook Bailingmiao on 24 November.[73] This was a critical area, 'astride the road of advance for Japan', as US military intelligence observed.[74] Chiang Kaishek hailed the victory as the 'the beginning of China's rejuvenation'.[75]

In the last week of November, the Communist refused the Nationalist demands and declined Chiang's invitation for direct negotiations between him and Zhou Enlai. On 21 November, just when the fighting in Suiyuan reached a critical moment, they concentrated the 1st and 15th Army Corps of the 1st Front Army, the 28th Army, the 2nd and 6th Army Corps of the 2nd Front Army, the 32nd Army, and the 4th and 31st Army Groups of the 4th Front Army. The numbers involved were far smaller than these unit designations suggest. Nonetheless, they attacked Nationalist units under Hu Zongnan at Shanchengbao, placed between the 2nd and 4th Front Armies and the 1st Front Army and killed 600 troops.[76]

These developments provided new impetus for the North-western Alliance. Zhang Xueliang had continued to nurture the Alliance through the fall of 1936. He sent emissaries to the most important military figures in the north, including Yan Xishan, Han Fuju, and Song Zheyuan, as well as to Sheng Shicai in Xinjiang, Liu Xiang in Sichuan, and Li Zongren and Bai Chongxi in Guangxi. He worked to strengthen relations with Yang Hucheng. On 29 September, he organised a large mass meeting where both he and Yang spoke to commemorate the Japanese seizure of Manchuria and called for 'an allied army of the five provinces [of north China]' to make sure that 'no inch of land will be lost again'. On 28 November, Zhang organised a meeting in Xi'an to commemorate the tenth anniversary of Yang's defence of Xi'an during the Northern Expedition. Zhang and Yang Hucheng set up an Officers Training Regiment near Xi'an, inviting high Communist generals, including Ye Jianying, to join as instructors. Zhang maintained daily radio contact with the Communists, indicating areas to which the CCP could withdraw safely and promised that he would inform them in case he no longer could avoid to attack them.[77] On 30 November, Zhang stated that he would not undertake major attacks, and declared that 'in one or two month, there will be a major development. If the Red Army can continue to hold out, an alliance of armies in the north-west can be established'.[78]

The Communists too were careful to keep the option alive. In October, Mao and forty CCP generals promised Zhang Xueliang and Yang Hucheng in a letter 'to co-operate with you to the end'. The CCP also informed them about their negotiations with the Nationalists and revealed to them their draft agreement for a United Front government, which envisioned an alliance of all parties and factions and all armed units, thus suggesting that the Communists were negotiating for all and would not make a separate deal with the Nationalists.[79] On 2 December, the Communists also began negotiations with Fu Zuoyi and Yan Xishan, suggesting that they would be willing to subordinate their forces to Yan's command and would not interfere in his administrative apparatus.[80]

Climax

Chiang continued to press for an offensive against the Japanese in Suiyuan until 3 December, but then he suddenly cancelled the campaign. On 4 December, he flew to Xi'an for talks with Zhang Xueliang and his own commanders. After Fu Zuoyi's victory at Bailingmiao in Suiyuan, Zhang Xueliang had asked Chiang Kaishek's permission to move his army away. Chiang refused because he wanted Zhang Xueliang to check any Communist advances.[81] According to Zhou Enlai, he told Zhang that 'your responsibility now is Communist suppression and therefore I cannot permit you to transfer your army to Suiyuan. If you refuse, I'll remove you'.[82]

A meeting lasting three hours took place between Chiang Kaishek and Zhang Xueliang on 7 December. Zhang refused to implement Chiang Kaishek's order to suppress the Communists and urged Chiang to seek a political solution in his relations with the Communists. He also told Chiang that he doubted that his troops would follow orders to attack the Communists. Chiang Kaishek is reported to have told Zhang, 'even if you kill me now, the policy of Communist suppression will not change',[83] and he wrote in his diary that Zhang 'lacked the resolve of the last five minutes', when victory or defeat were decided.

That evening, Zhang and Yang agreed to carry out their mutiny. They decided that Zhang's forces would seize Chiang Kaishek, while Yang would apprehend senior Nationalist military figures in Xi'an.[84] Zhang sent a telegram to Ye Jianying, informing him that he had failed in convincing Chiang not to proceed with his campaign against the Communists and inviting him to come to Xi'an. On 9 December, they organised a mass demonstration in Xi'an which petitioned Chiang to stop Civil War and offer resistance to Japan. Zhang Xueliang declared his support for their goals and stated that 'in a couple of days, some facts will show this'.[85]

On 9 December, Chiang called his staff officers together and ordered preparations for an offensive against the Communists. He ordered Zhang Xueliang and Yang Hucheng to participate and told them that if they refused, he would move Zhang's forces to Fujian and Yang's to Anhui.[86] He moreover prepared to appoint Jiang Dingwen as Commander-in-Chief of Bandit Suppression in the North-west and Wei Lihuang Pacification Commissioner of the Shaanxi, Gansu, Suiyuan, and Ningxia Border region, thus threatening to demote Zhang Xueliang and Yang Hucheng.[87] A showdown became inevitable.

Even at this stage, KMT–CCP negotiations continued. In early December, the Nationalists moderated their conditions for a United Front with the Communists, suggesting an establishment of 30,000 for the Red Army and agreeing that they would not need to be re-organised.[88] On 10 December, just two days before the Xi'an Incident, the Communist too made concessions, stating that they were willing to change the designation of the Red Army to conform with the National Army, accept unified command, and defend a specific sector of the front, although they continued to decline any force reductions.[89]

On 12 December, Zhang and Yang took Chiang Kaishek prisoner in Xi'an. Zhang demanded that Chiang Kaishek re-organise the Nanjing Government by including all parties and factions willing to resist Japan and that he stop further civil war. The incident divided Nanjing. Some, like He Yingqin, called for a punitive expedition even at the risk of Chiang's life, or perhaps precisely because of this. Others, including Song Ziwen and Song Meiling, opposed the despatch of an expeditionary force to Xi'an and called for negotiations. Both travelled to Xi'an. In his telegraphic messages to them, Zhang guaranteed the safety of Chiang Kaishek, suggested that he continued to respect the legitimacy of the Nanjing Government, and that his aim was to make Chiang Kaishek resist Japan rather than fight a civil war.[90]

The CCP's initial response was to support the rebellion. On 13 December, the CCP convened a meeting of the Politburo Standing Committee, which concluded that 'the elimination of Chiang Kaishek can only have positive results' and called for a new national leadership around the Xi'an rebellion. They communicated this in a telegram to Moscow. They also sent a telegram to Zhang Xueliang stating that 'the whole world rejoices about the arrest of the mother of all criminals'.[91] On 15 December, CCP leaders sent a telegram to Nanjing demanding that the National Government 'fire Chiang Kaishek and hand him over to a people's tribunal'.[92]

This attitude changed on 17 December. That day, Zhou Enlai and Mao Zedong called for a peaceful settlement and the protection of the safety of Chiang Kaishek. On 18 December, they sent a telegram stating that their call for Chiang's dismissal and trial had been 'inappropriate', and that he should be released if a United Front against Japan would be formed.[93]

This u-turn was the result of a telegram on 16 December from the Comintern, which stated that 'regardless of Zhang Xueliang's intentions, objectively seen, his actions can only harm a united front to resist Japan and benefit Japanese aggression in China' and called on the CCP to 'firmly advocate a peaceful settlement'.[94] On the 14th, editorials in Pravda harshly condemned Zhang Xueliang, calling into question his motives and his past record in resisting Japan, while declaring Soviet support for Nanjing.[95]

The Soviet attitude was based on the calculation that a victory of the North-west Alliance would seriously endanger Soviet security. Records of meetings between Jiang Tingfu and Soviet officials of just before the Xi'an Incident show that the Soviets were deeply worried about the recently concluded agreement between Japan and Germany to fight Communism together, about which, despite its secret nature, they were well informed. These records also show that the Soviets feared that the growth of the Communist presence in north China might push the Nationalists to ally with the Japanese. The Soviets broached this issue in a meeting of 19 November. On 3 December, Jiang Tingfu was asked directly whether 'China might seek to make use of Japan's strength when the Red Army arrives in north China?'[96] Jiang Tingfu denied that this was so, stating that 'the Red Army in China is not the target of the Japanese'.[97] In response to expressions of doubt about Nationalist intentions to resist the Japanese, Jiang pointed to the fighting in Suiyuan as evidence of the Nationalist attitude and, referring to negotiations about fishing rights between the Japanese and the Soviets, hinted that the Soviet attitude was also not entirely unambiguous.[98]

The Soviets were not only worried that CCP expansion in north China might drive Chiang Kaishek into the arms of Japan. The Xi'an Incident raised the serious possibility that Chiang would be executed and that the Nationalists would have to find a new leader. One candidate for that position was Wang Jingwei. Chen Lifu's not always reliable memoirs suggest that the Soviets' decision to support Chiang Kaishek was the result of the arrival in Moscow of the news that Hitler had sent a plane to collect Wang Jingwei, who was again in Europe, to put him on a boat back to China.[99] Especially after the death of Hu Hanmin in 1936, Wang remained the most prominent opponent of Chiang Kaishek in the KMT and although Left-wing and a former supporter of close collaboration with the Soviets, he also had spent much of the 1930s seeking an accommodation with Japan in the belief that war could only be disastrous. Jiang Tingfu's report to Chiang Kaishek after the Xi'an Incident provides clear evidence that the Soviets were indeed concerned about an intervention by Wang Jingwei.[100]

Other factors, such as Zhang Xueliang's attitude, Song Ziwen and Song Meiling's journey to Xi'an, and the military expedition to Xi'an were important in determining the outcome of the Xi'an Incident. Zhang Xueliang ended the rebellion after receiving promises that Chiang would fight Japan. One story, no doubt spread by Chiang Kaishek's camp, has it that Zhang, after reading a portion of Chiang's diary captured during the Incident, came to Chiang Kaishek and stated that 'We have read your diary and other important documents, and from these we have learned the greatness of your personality, your loyalty to the revolutionary cause, and your determination to bear the responsibility of saving the country. If I had known one tenth of what is recorded in your diary, I would certainly not have done this rash act'.[101] He travelled back with Chiang Kaishek to Nanjing, was court-martialled, and sentenced to ten years hard labour, a punishment that was commuted into house arrest.[102] Precisely why Zhang gave up his rebellion and then preferred house-arrest in Nanjing to staying with his forces in the North-west remain something of a mystery which Zhang himself declined to clarify, although fear of mutinous subordinates who had wanted to kill Chiang Kaishek and were frustrated with their exile lives may have played a role.[103]

However, the Soviet attitude too was important to the outcome of the Xi'an Incident. They refused to back the North-western Alliance, which could have drawn them into a border war with Japan and which also might have led to a pro-Japanese government in China. They came to the conclusion that it was in their best interest to support a United Front led by Chiang Kaishek.

As Coble argued, it is possible to overestimate the importance of the Xi'an Incident.[104] It did not make either the Treaty of Non-Aggression or the United Front inevitable. However, the Incident ended with the survival of the Communists and Chiang Kaishek and the death of the North-western Alliance. This outcome would shape subsequent history very profoundly indeed.

The forward policy put to the test at the outbreak of war

The day after the Marco Polo Bridge Incident of 7 July 1937, when Japanese and Chinese forces clashed 15 miles south of Beiping, Chiang Kaishek made the following entry in his diary:

> The Japanese bandits have made provocative actions at the Marco Polo Bridge. Are they trying to subdue us before we can complete our preparations; or are they making trouble for Song Zheyuan. ... Is this the time to accept the challenge?[105]

This was a question difficult to answer because the alliances that Chiang had sought to construct with the regional militaries in the north and north-west proved of little military utility. As the crisis unfolded, they showed reluctance to face up to the Japanese. No formal agreement with the Communists or the Soviets had yet been signed.

Ambiguous signals emanated from Japan. One view, which had support in the Military Affairs Section of the Army Ministry, the Operations Section of the General Staff, the Japanese Kwantung Army in Manchuria, and some parts of the powerful South Manchurian Railway Company, hoped to use the Incident as a convenient pretext to launch a powerful strike into north China and settle a host of issues. Others, including other parts of the General Staff, feared that excursions into China would derail the army build-up against the Soviet Union.[106] On 30 June, Japanese and Soviet forces had clashed along the Amur. Prime Minister Konoe Fumimaro and Foreign Minister Hitoa Koki had come to power only a month earlier. At a meeting on 9 July, the Japanese Cabinet decided not to send reinforcements, a decision which was, however, reversed two days later.[107] The Cabinet issued statements saying that they hoped that the conflict could be contained and the Japanese domestic press, surely watched carefully in Nanjing, stressed the same message.[108] Yet, if the Japanese had decided on war, the Japanese were unlikely to signal this publicly. Herbert Bix has suggested that the Konoe Cabinet in reality had resolved within days after the Incident to expand the conflict. The belief that the war would be over 'within three months' was the deciding factor.[109]

Nationalist fears that Japan was about to go on the offensive in China must be placed in the context of developments over the preceding years. Despite their own military build-up, the Nationalists were in fact losing ground on Japan. After the Mukden Incident left it internationally isolated, Japan had begun to invest heavily in its armed forces. By 1933, its military strategy aimed at 'autonomous strength', so that it could defend itself against the Soviet Union, China, and the British and American navies.[110] Massive investment programmes in the heavy, chemical, and machinery industries followed to give Japan the industrial base to sustain itself in time of war, and also of course to deal with the problems of the Depression.[111] In 1936, Japan stepped up its military expenditures when a new cabinet accepted 'the build-up of national strength as Japan's highest priority'.[112] China's strategy aimed at wearing out Japan and was based on the assumption that the lack of a strong industrial base was Japan's critical weakness. The further Japan's industrial build-up advanced, the more dubious that assumption would become.

Despite the rapid build-up, the Japanese feared that their relative military strength *vis-à-vis* its major enemies would decline rather than improve. Japan therefore developed a strategic doctrine aimed at defending Japan by aggressive offensive operations of limited duration, to be concluded before its major enemies could concentrate their forces in East Asia. To defeat China before such a war was part of this strategy. Worried about war with the Soviet Union and the Western powers, the 'removal of China', as the belligerent General Tojo stated in a telegram from Manchuria to Tokyo in early 1937, would eliminate 'an important menace from our rear',[113] and release forces for service on more critical fronts.

If the military build-up and the political influence of the army in Japanese politics were causes for worry in China, so were the expansionist tendencies of the Kwantung Army in Manchuria and the North China Garrison Army at Tianjin. General Doihara Kenji was the driving force behind these tendencies. Reading Chinese expressions of interest in negotiations as a sign of weakness, Doihara argued that Japan should consolidate its hold over Manchuria and incorporate north China, including Hebei, Shanxi, Chahar, and Suiyuan. Following the February 1936 coup of the Imperial Way Faction, the Kwantung Army invaded six counties in Chahar and later that year, as we have seen, moved into Suiyuan and supported Prince De in forming his 'Mongolian Autonomous Military Government'.[114] Japan's military build-up, its strategic doctrine, and its aggressive penetration of north China all made it possible to fear that the Marco Polo Bridge Incident and subsequent Japanese military actions were the beginning of an attempt by Japan to knock China out of the war.

Uncertainty and prevarication

A situation of great uncertainty, then, came about after the Marco Polo Bridge Incident. The attitude of the north China militarists, especially Song Zheyuan, Han Fuju, and Yan Xishan, whose armies were located closest to the fighting, gained great significance. Under pressure of the Nationalists to stand firm and to allow the National Army to reinforce the north China front, they proved less then reliable allies for the Nationalists and once more illustrated the difficulties of concerted military action in a frontier populated by private armies.

Song Zheyuan was the commander of the 29th Army of about 60,000 troops in Hebei and Chahar.[115] Song had begun his career in Yuan Shikai's army, but in the 1920s became one of the 'five tigers' of Feng Yuxiang's North-west Army,[116] fighting for Feng in the War of the Central Plains. Afterwards he accepted nominal appointments in the National Government under Chiang Kaishek, for instance as a general and member of the KMT's Central Inspection Committee, but carefully maintained an ambivalent relationship with both Nanjing and the Japanese, joining the institutions of regional autonomy supported by the latter. It was Song's forces that confronted the Japanese at the Marco Polo Bridge. Song's attitude would be important. The Marco Polo Bridge was located near the junction of the Beiping–Hankou and Beiping–Suiyuan Railroads (Map 5.1). If the Japanese seized it, Beiping's defences could not be reinforced and the Japanese could then use these railroads to fan out across north China and advance towards the north-west.

Song Zheyuan adopted a careful wait-and-see attitude. On 8 July, three of his most important generals, Feng Zhi'an, Zhang Zizhong, and Qin Dechun, stated in a telegram to Nanjing that 'Although [the Japanese] want us to withdraw from Marco Polo Bridge City to prevent an escalation of the conflict, because of the consequences for national sovereignty, we cannot do so lightly. In view of legitimate defence, we cannot but do our utmost to contend with them if they continue to exert pressure'.[117] Song himself promised Chiang Kaishek that he would obey his order not to 'impair national sovereignty or abandon territory'.[118] If all that sounded tough, that same evening Qin Dechun reached a truce agreement with the Japanese that called for the withdrawal of both the 29th Army and the Japanese North China Garrison forces from Marco Polo Bridge City.[119] In subsequent days, telegrams to Nanjing by Song suggested that he was in fact searching for an accommodation with the Japanese.[120] An assessment by the Nationalist Staff Department expressed the concern that 'Song will split from the centre, mostly because central units assigned to Song's command are moving north and are gradually taking over his territory'.[121] On 11 July, Song met Japanese negotiators in Tianjin, stating that he hoped for a speedy 'legal and rational' settlement.[122]

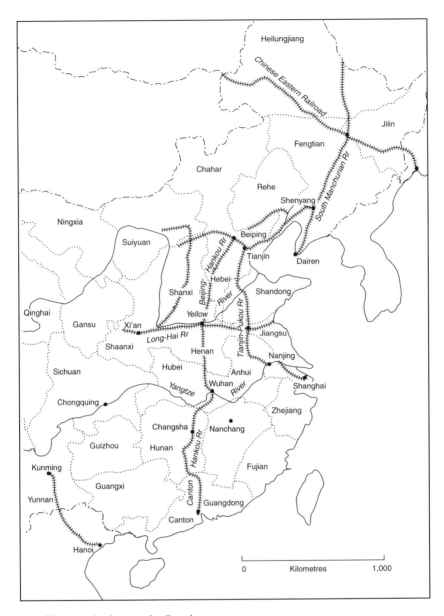

Map 5.1 China: main rivers and railroads.

Chiang Kaishek, too, did signal that he would not condone any further infringement of Chinese sovereignty, but also kept his options open. He did concentrate four divisions at Shijiazhuang and Baoding and set up headquarters in the first city. Immediately after hearing of the Incident, he also ordered 'a general state of alert to prepare for resistance'.[123] On 17 July, he issued a declaration stating that an agreement would be possible only if it did not infringe on Chinese sovereignty, would uphold the right of the

National Government to appoint local officials, and would not impose any restrictions on the 29th Army.[124] In the declaration he stated that 'if no hope remains and we have arrived at the final juncture, all we can do is to make sacrifices and carry out a War of Resistance. We don't want war, but we will resist armed aggression'.[125] That statement did allow a return to the *status quo ante* and Chiang did not forbid Song Zheyuan from continuing his negotiations and, as mentioned, asked Western powers to mediate.

In the first days after the Marco Polo Bridge Incident, the Nationalists' Supreme Command, which met daily under the chairmanship of He Yingqin, was uncertain about Japanese intentions as well as the advisability of war. At its 24 July meeting, a report stated that 'evaluation of intelligence over the last few days suggests two contradictory conclusions, namely (1) the enemy wishes to limit the incident and (2) the enemy is preparing for a broad attack'.[126]

The minutes of the meetings of the Supreme Command show disagreement about what course would be most in China's interest. At its 14 July meeting, Xu Yongchang, associated with Yan Xishan, a member of the Standing Committee of the MAC, and head of its General Office, counselled that policy should aim at minimising the incident so as to gain further time, because 'our preparations are insufficient and victory therefore cannot be guaranteed'. Tang Shengzhi at the same meeting maintained that the National Government should adopt a tough stance in public, but at the same time await the outcome of negotiations between Song Zheyuan and the Japanese before deciding what to do.[127] Two days later, during a discussion about the advantages of localising or expanding the war, several participants in the meeting argued in favour of preventing the spread of the war to the Yangtze River, but also stated that if Japan took action in Shandong or attacked Song Zheyuan's 29th Army, 'we should do something in Shanghai'.[128]

During the deliberations of the Supreme Command, the attitude of northern militarists was a major concern. Besides Song Zheyuan, Yan Xishan in Shanxi and Han Fuju in Shandong also were relevant. Following the War of the Central Plains, Yan had fled Shanxi and accepted the protection of the Japanese in Manchuria. Before the Mukden Incident, the Japanese had attempted to induce Yan Xishan, then in Dalian, to oust Zhang Xueliang. Yan had refused, but had aided the Japanese before the Mukden Incident by returning, on a Japanese plane, to Shanxi. This created a threat on Chiang's western flank in case he decided to move his armies north towards Manchuria.[129] If Yan, in 1935, invited Nationalist forces into Shanxi following the entrance of Communists into the province, he subsequently turned to the Communist to counterbalance them.

Following the Marco Polo Bridge Incident, Yan did send an emissary to Song Zheyuan, urging him to accept Nanjing's offer of military assistance, and in August travelled to Nanjing himself, after having submitted a request for 4.7 million *yuan* in assistance.[130] In discussions with He Yingqin on 6 August, after the Japanese conquest of Beiping and Tianjin meant that his own province was under threat, he declared himself committed to fighting the Japanese, stating that he agreed with the strategy of attrition and accepted the inclusion of Tang Enbo's forces in his command. But he also suggested that China's forces should be dispersed after a first major battle 'to correct world opinion',[131] referring presumably to widespread doubts about the Nationalists' determination to resist Japan. Given his track record and the fact that dispersal could easily be an excuse for not fighting, the Nationalists could not be confident that Yan would indeed throw his forces into the war with much energy and commitment.

As to Han Fuju, after attending a military academy, he joined Feng Yuxiang 's army and quickly rose through the ranks. During the second phase of the Northern Expedition, he played an important role during the battle for Xuzhou and the invasion of Hebei. As a reward, Feng Yuxiang recommended that Han be appointed to the post of chairman of Henan province, which had originally been assigned to Feng himself. While in 1929 Han refused to participate in a rebellion by Feng against Chiang Kaishek, during the War of the Central Plains Han Fuju told Chiang Kaishek that he would be willing to conduct operations against Yan Xishan but not against Feng's troops. Chiang then agreed that Han move his troops to Shandong to fight units of Yan Xishan's army there. Over the next seven years, Han built up a formidable position in Shandong and re-established order in the province following the misrule of Zhang Zongchang.

Like Song Zheyuan, he kept to an ambiguous attitude to both Nanjing and the Japanese. Just before the War of Resistance, Han refused to attend the Lushan Conferences convened by Chiang Kaishek in the aftermath of the Marco Polo Bridge Incident, but did send Liang Shuming, a highly respected Confucian reformer who ran a village experiment in Zouping County in Shandong and was an advisor to the Shandong Provincial Government, with a letter to Chiang, stating that he was making preparations to resist the Japanese. On 30 July, he travelled to Nanjing and met Chiang Kaishek. According to Liang Shuming, Han did not gain any clear idea about Chiang's intentions. Han had remarked that 'Chiang did not reveal an inch of what he had in mind. When I went to Nanjing I was confused; when I returned to Ji'nan, I was still confused'.[132] Yet, Han too had not made his attitude clear and remained in close contact with the Japanese.[133] Clarity, then, was at a premium.

Escalation and failure in the north

Chiang Kaishek surely would have preferred to wait. At the time of the Marco Polo Bridge Incident, the military reforms begun in 1935 required at least a further three years to complete. The basis had been laid for a domestic arms industry, but factories had not yet begun actual production. Arms shipments from Germany had begun to arrive, but Nationalist armies had not had much opportunity to train with them and most deliveries were yet to come. Alexander von Falkenhausen's 1936 report had reminded Chiang in unambiguous language that despite recent progress his armies possessed serious flaws, including in command organisation and staff work. Training up a strong officers corps would have taken many more years. Nor could Chiang be sure of the co-operation of regional militarists or the Soviet Union and the Communists. To broaden the war entailed great risks.

Containment, however, proved difficult, especially after Japan mobilised its army and navy. At the eve of the war, Japan had the following troops in China. Elements of the seven divisions and five independent brigades of the Kwantung Army with some 90,000 troops had occupied positions at the most important passes in the Great Wall, including Shanhaiguan, Gubeikou, Xifengkou, and Dushikou. Prince De's Mongolian forces numbered about 40,000, while those of the East Hebei Autonomous Government amounted to 17,000. If not simply a Japanese puppet force, they certainly were also not subject to Nationalist authority. The Japanese China Garrison Army headquartered at Tianjin by provision of the Boxer Protocol had 5,700 troops stationed along the railroads leading from Tianjin to Beiping and from Beiping to Shanhaiguan. In Hebei, from which Nationalist forces had been forced to withdraw in 1935, the Japanese only faced Song Zheyuan's 29th Army.[134]

Following the Marco Polo Bridge Incident, the Japanese government issued mobilisation orders. On 11 July, the Japanese Staff Department ordered two brigades from the Kwantung Army and one division of Japanese forces in Korea to be mobilised to settle what was now more ominously called the 'North China Incident'. Eighteen squadrons of the airforce were sent to Manchuria on 15 July. The Japanese Staff finalised their war plans on the 17th, which stated that 'the decisive moment for solving the situation speedily has arrived' and called for the elimination of the Song Zheyuan's 29th Army in two months and 'if full-out war breaks out, destruction of the central government in three to four months'.[135] On 18 July, the Operations Section of the Japanese Staff Department had adopted a resolution, which stated that 'although the fighting might spread across China', the aim of the Japanese army was to 'pacify' the Beiping–Tianjin area and restrict the fighting to north China 'as much as possible'. Operations, it had declared, should aim at 'destroying the Chinese armies [in north China] in one go and occupying the area north of Baoding'. It estimated that nineteen or twenty days would be needed to assemble the necessary three divisions.[136] After issuing several ultimatums, which were rejected by Nanjing, the Japanese began their offensive on 26 July. Beiping fell on the 28th, and Tianjin two days later.[137]

In response, the MAC ordered Tang Enbo and Gao Guizi's 13th and 17th Corps to move their forces into Chahar, to create a threat on the north-western flanks of Japanese forces in Beiping and Tianjin, protect the Beiping–Suiyuan Railroad, and defend Shanxi. These forces were made up of main National Army units augmented by local ones, including the 7th Army Group of Fu Zuoyi and Liu Ruming, made up of Suiyuan and Shanxi forces, and the 1st Calvarly Corps of Zhao Zhengzhou, belonging to Yan Xishan's forces.[138] These forces also threatened the units of the Kwantung Army as well as the forces of Prince De moving south. Furthermore, on 5 August, Tang Enbo led some of his forces to invest the strategic city of Nankou, 50 kilometres to the northwest of Beiping and on the Beiping–Suiyuan Railroad. Nankou would be crucial for the Japanese to take if they wanted to advance into the Hebei–Chahar border region or Shanxi itself. Besides the forces mentioned already, the forces assembled on the Chinese side included the 14th Army Group of Wei Lihuang, the 20th Army Group of Shang Zhen, and Liu Zhi's 2nd Army Group. These too were made up of main Nationalist army units augmented by local ones. Besides Nankou, they sought to safeguard Baoding and the Beiping–Hankou Railroad.

On the same day that Tang moved into Nankou and readied its defences, the Japanese Staff Department decided that Japanese forces in north China would begin an offensive along the Beiping–Hankou Railroad into Hebei and engage the Chinese in a decisive battle near Baoding by late September or early October.[139] A secondary offensive was to advance along the Beiping–Suiyuan Railroad to attack Chahar, Suiyuan, and Shanxi.[140] This would be supported by the Chahar Expeditionary Force of the Kwantung Army as well as the Mongolian forces of Prince De. Smaller Japanese forces were to occupy Shijiazhuang, strategically important because it would open up a route of southerly attack into Shanxi as well as points south, and Dexian. It still remained the hope of the Japanese to avoid fighting further to the south. Two Group Armies of three divisions with a total of 120,000 troops were assigned to participate in these offensives.[141]

These operations began on 7 August, when Tang Enbo's 13th Army Group clashed at Nankou with Japanese forces. During the following days, the fighting escalated as Japanese artillery, airforce, and tank units went into action, and as Chiang Kaishek ordered Wei Lihuang and Yan Xishan to act in support of the Tang Enbo at Nankou, including by attacking positions occupied by Japan in Chahar and Suiyuan in 1936. However, by 15 August, Nankou had become encircled and isolated, with little likelihood of a relief force being able to get through. The Japanese also besieged Shijiazhuang and took the city within a week. In defending Nankou, Tang Enbo suffered 26,000 casualties. Following these actions, the Japanese moved to consolidate their position, including by occupying Baoding, eliminating Song Zheyuan as a significant force, and occupying the northern parts of the Beiping–Hankou and Tianjin–Pukou Railroads.[142]

The Nationalist position had quickly disintegrated. The same problems that Chiang Kaishek had confronted in late 1936 in augmenting his forces with local militaries had re-asserted themselves. Fu Zuoyi and Liu Ruming beat a very hasty retreat as soon as Tang Enbo's defence of Nankou collapsed. Feng Yuxiang, who had been Liu's patron, wrote in an embarrassed letter to Chiang Kaishek that 'Liu's crimes are extremely serious', but pleaded that his erstwhile subordinate not be dismissed.[143]

A report by a German advisor sent to the north and covering the north China front from 22 September to 17 October illustrates the difficulties in making forces such as those of Yan stand and fight. The advisor noted that orders had called for 'firm defence of the line inside the Great Wall between Machang in Shanxi and Baoding followed by a counter-attack from two flanks on Datong'. However, the report went on, 'the speed of retreat of our armies appears to have exceeded the schedule of the Supreme Command. Even if orders called for a war of attrition, we surely should have used favourable terrain and strong prepared positions to achieve more attrition'. He wrote that he had considered suggesting that units at the central front be ordered to retreat 'to lure the enemy in deep', to be followed by attacks from the flanks, but decided against this, believing that these units would probably have continued their retreat. According to the report of this advisor, 'most forces simply have never offered resistance'. Another German advisor reporting on the fighting in Shanxi itself noted that Wei Lihuang's main Nationalist army units had offered strong resistance, but that Yan Xishan himself refused to have contact with him, had rejected liaison officers, and had only used inferior forces in the defence of Shanxi's passes.[144]

Han Fuju too refused to stand and fight. When the Japanese landed at Qingdao on 14 August, Han offered no resistance. He also did not do so when they advanced to the provincial capital of Ji'nan, which the Japanse occupied on 10 October. In late 1937, despite orders of Chiang Kaishek not to withdraw any further, Han again refused to give battle to Japanese forces then moving down the Tianjin–Pukou Railroad in south Shandong, greatly endangering Nationalist positions between south Shandong and north Jiangsu. Han was then arrested.[145]

This was not only because Han had withdrawn contrary to orders and exposed an important flank covering the approaches to Xuzhou, but also because it had been discovered that he and Sichuan's Liu Xiang were conspiring to withdraw their forces to Sichuan, the last place of refuge for the Nationalists. A Nationalist liaison officer with Han had first learned that Han planned to withdraw his forces to west Henan and south Shanxi. Song Zheyuan then revealed that Han had contacted Liu Xiang, suggesting that all 'co-operate in the protection of Sichuan and resistance against Japan'.[146] According to this plan, in return for Liu Xiang's financial and military aid, Han would take his forces to the Hubei–Sichuan border and subordinate them to the command of Liu Xiang. Song Zheyuan revealed these plans in part because he had moved his forces to south Henan himself and therefore Han's plans of withdrawal might come at his own expense.[147]

Even the re-appointment of Feng Yuxiang to lead his former subordinates in north China did little to stiffen their attitude. Feng had long spoken vigorously in favour of resistance, and following the Marco Polo Bridge Incident repeatedly wrote Chiang Kaishek, promising his support, making strategic suggestions, and arguing that morale in the north would be greatly strengthened if commanders and officials with strong local connections and dedicated to the war be re-appointed.[148] If for Chiang Kaishek it might be risky to put a former enemy back into the field, on 17 September he issued a secret order dividing the 1st War Zone into two, with the new 1st War Zone responsible for defending the Beiping–Hankou Railroad and a new 6th War Zone under Feng Yuxiang to protect the Tianjin–Pukou Railroad. This move failed, as Song Zheyuan refused to meet Feng and because Han Fuju also refused to follow Feng's orders. Their staff resented the return of Feng's personnel.[149] Feng's belief that armies would fight better if their former commanders were sent back into the field proved mistaken. By early October, the Japanese had occupied the Tianjin–Pukou Railroad from Tianjin to Ji'nan.

The decision to open a second front at Shanghai

There is little doubt that Chiang Kaishek's decision to open a second front at Shanghai was taken with public relations in mind. Although we do not know for certain, it is possible that he did hope that Western diplomatic intervention, combined with a determined show of strength at Shanghai, where this was possible unlike in the north, would cause the Japanese to pull back from the brink. But domestic opinion was at least as important. Undoubtedly Henri de Fremery, a Dutch observer on the scene who had been an advisor to Chiang Kaishek, was right in believing that the attack was meant less to impress Western than domestic public opinion.[150] Had Japan separated north China and Chiang given in, it is doubtful that his regime could have survived the backlash.

However, Chiang also had good military reasons. Chiang decided to take the initiative when the Japanese had encircled Tang Enbo at Nankou and had struck towards Zhangjiakou (Kalgan).[151] At the same time, Han Fuju, Song Zheyuan, and Yan Xishan had shown themselves unwilling to make a determined stance. Japan's navy in late July called for more aggressive action, suggesting the despatch of naval forces and five divisions to seize Shanghai and Nanjing 'to destroy the National Government and end the war as quickly as possible'.[152] Whether aware of this precise appeal or not, Zhang Zhizhong, the Shanghai–Nanjing Garrison Commander, reported that Japan's naval attaché had requested the Second Fleet to be diverted from Qingdao, where Han Fuju's accommodating attitude made its deployment unnecessary, to Shanghai. On 9 August, Zhang reported that 9 naval vessels had arrived in Shanghai from the Upper Yangtze, bringing the total to 12 vessels, with 3,000 marines on board. Because Japan already had 5,000 troops in Shanghai, this brought its combat personnel to 8,000, while it also had organised a volunteer force of 3,500. These vessels belonged to the Third Fleet. On 11 August, Zhang Zhizhong reported that a further 16 Japanese naval vessels were due to arrive in Shanghai, bringing the total then in Shanghai to 29. In addition, the Second Fleet, Zhang wrote, had set sail and mobilisation orders in Japan had been issued to reservists.[153] On 13 August, Zhang Zhizhong reported that 32 Japanese naval vessels had amassed at Shanghai. According to Zhang, the object of the 13 vessels of the Third Fleet was the Huangpu River, while the Second Fleet was to 'fight on the Yangtze'. Nineteen vessels that day had left the Huangpu River and begun to sail up the River.[154]

The Nationalists' Supreme Command initially had found it difficult to assess Japanese intentions and feared the consequences of full-out war. Bad news kept coming in, however. It was of course aware of Japan's military and naval mobilisation. On 23 July, Han Fuju revealed five secret plans of the Kwantung Army.[155] Anxiety mounted when it was learned on 26 July that trains were rushing Japanese men and material into the Beiping–Tianjin area,[156] and when the information was received that the Japanese had begun aerial attacks in various parts of north China and conducted aerial reconnaissance missions. On 27 July, the Shanghai municipal government reported that the Japanese were preparing to destroy the international telegraph station in the city. As such news accumulated, the conviction gained ground that war would be inevitable.

Prevarication then made way for preparation. Mobilisation orders were issued, troops transferred, and supply stations activated. Directives went out for the removal of lighthouses and beacons from the Yangtze. The Supreme Staff Department discussed plans to move civil populations out of large cities such as Nanjing and to disperse industry. Fortifications along the Yangtze River were strengthened and put on alert.

On 31 July, Chiang declared in 'An Admonition to All Officers and Soldiers in the War of Resistance' that 'since all hope for peace has been lost, all we can do now is to resist to the bitter end'.[157] A meeting of the Standing Committee of the KMT's Central Executive Committee established a Supreme Defence Council in Nanjing in early August, which included representatives from various regional military forces. On 7 August, a secret Joint National Defence Meeting, involving Chiang Kaishek, Wang Jingwei, Yan Xishan, Feng Yuxiang, Bai Chongxi, Liu Xiang, T.V. Song, Sun Fo, and thirty-three other high ranking civil and military figures met at the Endeavour Society in Nanjing. Chiang solicited opinions, spoke out forcefully in favour of war, and gained the support of Wang Jingwei, Yan Xishan, and Liu Xiang. At the end of the meeting, those who favoured war were asked to stand up as a sign that they pledged themselves to the war and to mutual co-operation.[158] The decision for war was thus made.

The next day, Chiang was appointed Commander-in-Chief of China's armed forces.[159] On 13 August, Chiang gave the order to his forces in Shanghai to 'drive the enemy in the sea, block off the coast, and resist landings'.[160] They only had a window of opportunity of about ten days before the Japanese would be able to land reinforcements in Shanghai. On 14 August, the 87th and 88th divisions of the National Army began an assault on Japanese positions running from the North Station along the Yangshupu district border to Hongkou Park. The next day, the National Government declared that it would 'carry out its sacred right of self-defence' in its 'Declaration of the War of Self Defence'.[161]

Seizing the initiative and beginning a war of attrition, as Chiang Kaishek explained on 18 August in a general address to the army, was an important objective.[162] Chiang argued that Japan 'wants a quick victory in a short war; we must therefore fight a protracted war of attrition'.[163] To achieve this, he went on, 'we must seize the initiative'.[164] According to Chiang, this was to be achieved by assuming a defensive stance in certain places while attacking Japan where it had not originally planned to fight. At the same time, such an attack was to end before the Japanese could gain a decisive victory.

Even after Chinese forces had begun their attack, debate continued about the wisdom of escalating the war. Chiang Kaishek sent Chen Cheng on an investigative tour to north China and Shanghai. Following his return to Nanjing on 20 August, one general, Xiong Shihui, argued that the Nationalist Army 'could not fight' in Shanghai. Chen opposed, arguing that given the Japanese attacks in north China, the escalation of the conflict was inevitable. The Japanese, according to Chen, would use their superior forces in north China to advance down the Beiping–Hankou Railroad and assault Wuhan. 'If we do not expand the war to tie down the enemy', he argued, 'the situation will be disadvantageous'.[165] Bai Chongxi, the strategic genius of the Guangxi Clique who at this point advised Chiang Kaishek in Nanjing, as well as Liu Fei, an important strategic councillor in Chiang's Personal Staff Office, were of the same opinion as Chen.[166] They argued that the Nationalists should not seek a decisive battle in the terrain south of Beijing and Tianjin, where the Japanese could easily supply their armies and bring their advantages in mobility and firepower into play.[167] On 19 August, Feng Yuxiang expressed the similar fear when he wrote to Chiang Kaishek: 'I admire greatly the willingness to die of our forces during the Nankou Campaign and their serious attacks on the enemy. However, the Japanese are rushing in reinforcements. They will be out to attack the Tianjin–Pukou and Beiping–Hankou Railroads.'[168]

On 20 August Chiang issued a 'General War Directive for the National Army'. Its assessment of Japanese intentions was that it would advance along the Beiping–Suiyuan Railroad and enter Shanxi in order to threaten the flanks of China's 1st War Zone (consisting of Hebei and north Shandong), attack Shanghai and Nanjing, advance into Shandong, and land forces to take Xuzhou. The directive stated that 'achieving a "war of attrition" is the basic principle guiding operations'.[169] Five war zones were designated,[170] setting out general operational plans for each.[171] In the 1st War Zone, limited offensives were to draw in Japanese forces. Operations in Shanxi, Suiyuan, and Rehe, the 2nd War Zone, should aim at preventing the broad encircling movement of Japanese forces, but avoid a decisive battle so that the Japanese would not be able to release troops from that front to Shandong and Shanghai. In the 3rd War Zone, made up of Jiangsu south of the Yangtze River and Zhejiang, the National Army was to destroy all Japanese positions and protect the Zhejiang coast so as to be ready for the arrival of new Japanese forces. The 4th War Zone, where little action was anticipated, consisted of Fujian and Guangdong provinces. The aim of operations in the 5th War

Zone, consisting of Jiangsu north of the Yangtze River and south Shandong, was to prevent Japanese landings or contain them.

The issue of the directive and the battle plans meant that the point of no return had, finally, been reached. These documents also make clear that the Battle of Shanghai was part of a much broader military operation, conducted in conformity with the strategic plans and the preparations that had been formulated after 1932. The aim was to prevent a quick military victory, compel Japan's armies to spread out, prevent it from penetrating the Yangtze River, and force it into a war of attrition.

Allies yet

It was only after the attack on the Japanese at Shanghai that the Soviets, the Communists, and some regional forces, especially the Guangxi Clique, agreed to formalise their participation in the War of Resistance. Many had beforehand announced their support. After Chiang Kaishek made public his conditions for a settlement, on 21 July Li Zongren and Bai Chongxi expressed their support. On 23 July, the Communists announced that Chiang's 'statements are the first correct declaration by the KMT about foreign relations for many years' and that 'all armies in the country, including the Red Army, support Mr Chiang Kaishek's declaration'.[172] Others, too, voiced their support, including Feng Yuxiang, Cai Tingkai, who had led the 19th Route Army during its heroic fight against the Japanese in 1932, but had then become hostile to Chiang and had participated in the Fujian Rebellion; and Liu Xiang.[173] However, only after the beginning of the Shanghai offensive did they commit their forces. Backroom negotiations no doubt had convinced the Nationalists that such a step was forthcoming, but the sequence of events does suggest that their condition was that Chiang would unambiguously commit his own forces in a meaningful operation. And even if Liu Xiang would commit his forces as well, as we now know, he simultaneously pursued other options.

On 1 August, Chiang Kaishek accepted Bogolomov's proposal for a Treaty of Non-aggression, which was publicly announced on 21 August, a day after Chiang issued the general mobilisation order. It stipulated that neither side would make a separate peace with Japan. In the first years of the war, according the Garver, the Soviets provided 348 bombers, 542 fighters, 82 T-tanks, 2,118 vehicles, 1,140 artillery guns, 9,720 machine guns and 50,000 rifles.[174] They were paid for by the Chinese supply of raw materials. Georgii Zhukov and Vasilii Chuikov, crucial to the Battle of Stalingrad and the whole Soviet war effort, were among the more than 3,000 Soviet military specialists that served in China. In rotation, as many as 2,000 Soviet pilots served in China and shot down hundreds of Japanese planes.[175]

As to the CCP, they did not formally agree to a United Front until September. Following the Xi'an Incident, negotiations between the CCP and the KMT experienced several ups and downs. In the first months after the Xi'an Incident, Yang Hucheng continued his resistance to Chiang Kaishek,[176] and the CCP, to avoid 'the defeat of the North-western Alliance by the Nationalists in detail', continued to 'consolidate the alliance of the armies of Zhang Xueliang and Yang Hucheng around the Red Army'. They refused top-level negotiations unless Nationalist armies were withdrawn and Zhang Xueliang permitted to return to the north-west.[177] In February, a new rebellion threatened, triggered by Nationalist demands that the Fengtain Army move to Gansu, but failed to materialise as a result of internal divisions in the Fengtian Army. Negotiations between the KMT and the CCP resumed only after Fengtian Army units were allowed to move to Henan and Anhui and after Yang Hucheng was dismissed.[178]

In the negotiations, the permitted size of the Red Army, its command structure, and the political form of the United Front continued to be the major points of contention. In June, Zhou Enlai and Chiang Kaishek met for the first time. Following the Marco Polo Bridge Incident, Chiang invited Zhou Enlai and several other high level CCP members to Lushan to discuss the war, but Chiang Kaishek's refusal to allow the Red Army their own Supreme Headquarters prevented agreement. After Chiang Kaishek conceded on this point and legalised the Red Army on 2 August, Zhu De, Zhou Enlai, and Ye Jianying flew to Nanjing and attended a meeting of the MAC.[179] In early September, the Communists committed two divisions to the war in north China, but the final hurdle was not overcome until Chiang assented to full political and military independence for the Communists and agreed that the Nationalists would not appoint staff officers or political personnel to the Red Army. On 23 September, public statements about the new United Front were finally issued and a third CCP division moved to the front.[180]

The most important force that joined the Nationalists was that of the Guangxi Clique. Li Zongren's Guangxi forces were following the disbanding of the Fengtian Army the best in China after the National Army itself. From the relative safety of Guangxi, Li had criticised Chiang repeatedly for failing to stand up to Japan and had rebelled against him only a year before the outbreak of war. After the Marco Polo Bridge Incident, Li declared publicly his support for Chiang, but also refused an invitation to come to Nanjing. Bai Chongxi, however, did travel to the capital, and although the details of the discussions that then took place remain unclear, we do know that on 28 August Li was formally appointed as Commander-in-Chief of the 5th War Zone headquartered in Xuzhou in north Jiangsu just south of its border with Shandong and that three Guangxi armies left Guangxi in late September and early October, destined for the 5th War Zone.[181]

We can only guess at the considerations of both sides. Li's bids for national power in the past had failed in part because he had been unable to secure a second base closer to the centre of power, as he had attempted to do during the Northern Expedition and the War of the Central Plains. Guangxi's limited wealth and population would always restrict Li's military strength. Guangxi was dependent on opium traffic, and access to opium markets could be cut off. A second base in the north would therefore increase his position greatly. As Commander-in-Chief of the 5th War Zone, Li had the opportunity to demonstrate that he was truly committed to fighting not just for Guangxi but for the whole of China. He would be able to do so with his own army re-inforced by northern military forces as well as the well-equipped divisions of Chiang Kaishek himself.

As for Chiang Kaishek, he needed desperately the extra forces that the Guangxi Clique could deliver to strengthen resistance in north China. Bringing about a large battle there, close to the Soviet Union, was part of his strategy in which he had so far failed. To leave the Guangxi Clique out of the war too was dangerous. Representatives of regional forces in Yunnan, Guizhou, Sichuan, Shaanxi, as well as the Communists were present in Guangxi, and Li and the Communists signed an agreement in June 1937 to co-operate.[182] During the National Defence Conference of July 1937, Zhu De and Long Yun too had exchanged secret codes. Ye Jianying and Zhu De were Long

Yun's schoolmates at the Yunnan Military Academy.[183] With the Guangxi Clique committed to the War of Resistance under Chaing Kaishek's command, any moves towards a southern alliance became difficult to sustain.

Chiang and Li Zongren co-operated in forcing northern regional militaries to stand firm. The events leading up to the execution of Han Fuju makes this clear. When Li Zongren called Chiang about Han's withdrawal from Shandong, which threw open a route of advance through southern Shandong to Li Zongren's 5th War Zone, Chiang responded with 'I am fully aware of this'. He arranged a meeting of high-ranking officers of the 1st and the 5th War Zones at Kaifeng on 11 January 1938. Chiang tele-phoned Han to tell him that he expected him and his senior officers to be present at the meeting.[184] At the meeting, Chiang spoke at length about the lack of concern for the nation of senior military leaders, their failure to co-operate with each other, their frequent disregard of orders, their inability to motivate their subordinates, the indiscipline of their forces who frequently looted, and their unwillingness to fight. He went on to say that in the face of the Japanese onslaught, no one would survive if all did not make common cause. He then criticised some 'senior commanders' for 'regarding the nation's armies as their own property' and 'for being unwilling to attack the Japanese to preserve their own forces'.[185] Chiang had referred to Shandong as an example, and pointed out that the unnecessary retreat there in the face of a few second-rate Japanese forces endangered the entire position in the north.[186] When the meeting ended, a guard informed Han that 'the Chairman of the Military Affairs Council [Chiang Kaishek] would like a brief word. Would you please stay?' The next day, Han was charged with 'disobeying orders and retreating without permission' and sent for trial to Wuhan. Han's indictment ended with 'let all forces take this as a warning and not defy the law'.[187] Han was executed on 25 January, condemned to death by a tribunal on which sat Li Zongren and Bai Chongxi, representing the Guangxi Clique; Chen Cheng and Hu Zongnan for the Nationalists; and Han's old patron, Feng Yuxiang, himself.[188]

Liu Xiang had been killed already. He had fallen ill before the fall of Nanjing, but had been moved to a hospital in Wuhan. He and Han Fuju had continued through secret telegrams and intermediaries discussions about their plan to retreat together to Sichuan and prevent the Nationalists from entering that province. Although Liu had sent troops from Sichuan to the front, these had been used in several different theatres in a piecemeal fashion which probably convinced Liu that Chiang was using the war essentially to disarm him. Causing Liu further alarm was Chen Cheng's replacement of him as commander of the 23rd Army Group on 1 January 1938. A plane sent from Sichuan on 18 January to collect him and take him back exploded in mid-air. On the same day, He Yingqin visited Liu in hospital. He informed him that Han Fuju had been court-martialled and then showed him copies of telegrams between himself and Han. Shortly after He Yingqin's departure, Liu became violently ill and died two days later.[189]

Conclusion

This chapter has attempted to elucidate the strategy that the Nationalists adopted in confronting Japanese advances in frontier areas populated by substantial regional armies. That strategy mixed international as well as domestic policies. From 1934, the Nationalists pursued closer relations with the Soviet Union. Because of the geo-strategic situation, the Soviet Union was a natural enemy of the Japanese and it therefore made sense for the Nationalists to pursue an alliance with them. Domestically, such an alliance was useful to undermine the North-western Alliance and to bring pressure on the Chinese Communists. European empires and the USA could not be as useful militarily, but nonetheless shaped Nationalist geo-strategic policies. With European Empires along China's southern borders, it was believed that these areas were relatively safe from Japanese attack. Hence, the Nationalists avoided conflict there, allowed greater autonomy to regional militarists such as the Guangxi Clique, and located their industrial base and their last place of refuge there.

In strengthening their influence in north and especially north-west China, the Nationalists used their increased military power to herd together various regional militarists in order to weaken them, while also keeping open the door to incorporation in the Nationalist order. Almost as soon as the Nationalists had defeated the Communists in central and south China, they began negotiations with them aimed at bringing them into the Nationalist order. The conditions for such co-operation were in some ways benign. A considerable degree of political, administrative, and even military autonomy could be considered. But, submission and incorporation in the Nationalist hierarchy and acceptance of the Nationalist order were principles to which the Nationalists held firm.

I have discussed the Xi'an Incident at length because it is a well-documented incident that allows us to examine closely the problems of frontier defence in a divided nation. We have seen how each party kept open various options, pursued different strategies simultaneously, and maintained a studied obscurity about their intentions. We have also seen how in the North-west international and domestic relations affected each other.

I have also discussed the beginning months of the War of Resistance when Nationalist alliance politics were put to the test. For the Nationalists, the problem was always that they needed the co-operation of regional military forces to increase their own limited military power, to blunt Japanese offensive power by forcing it to fight in different and widely separated theatres, to fight without having to worry about regional military forces conspiring against themselves, and to secure places of retreat. In north China, as the actions of Song Zheyuan and Han Fuju illustrated, the Nationalists were clearly not successful. They were able to secure Sichuan as a place of retreat only by drawing Liu Xiang's forces out of Sichuan, breaking up a conspiracy between Liu and Han Fuju, killing both, and fragmenting their armies.

The situation changed only after the Japanese concentrated a massive naval flotilla at Shanghai and threatened to break through in the North. Thus threatened, and probably with its survival at stake, the Nationalists then decided to open a second front at Shanghai. It was then that they were able to bring domestic and international partners into the War of Resistance, including the Soviet Union, the Communists, and the Guangxi Clique. With the Japanese having committed their forces in north China and at Shanghai, and with the proximity of European Empires to their base in Guangxi affording a degree of protection, the Guangxi Clique could deploy their forces outside their own province with relative safety. They did so not in Shanghai, but in the 5th War Zone, at a distance of the Japanese in north China and at Shanghai but also in the path of any Japanese advance from the north to the south. Their deployment stabilised the north China front for a while.

The Nationalist forward policy in north and north-west China, in short, had been successful only to a limited degree. It did lead to a useful alliance with the Soviet Union, the fragmentation of the Fengtian Army, and the inclusion of the Chinese Communists in a new United Front. Following the Shanghai offensive, a national War of Resistance did come about, but only to a degree. Armies were reluctant to stand firm, continued to keep their options open, and some sought to withdraw altogether.

Plate 1 Liao Zhongkai, Chiang Kaishek, Sun Yatsen, and Song Qingling at the opening ceremony of the Whampoa Military Academy. The Second Historical Archives of China.

Plate 2 Firefighters during a Japanese bombing attack on Chongqing. The Second Historical Archives of China.

Plate 3 Chiang Kaishek, Roosevelt, and Churchill at Cairo. The Second Historical Archives of China.

Plate 4 Building the Burma Road. The Second Historical Archives of China.

Plate 5 Chiang Kaishek victory parade in Chongqing. The Second Historical Archives of China.

6 The War of Resistance before Japan's Southern Advance

This chapter builds on research on the War of Resistance conducted in the 1980s in China itself. That scholarship resulted from deep dissatisfaction among contemporary People's Republic of China (PRC) historians with earlier accounts. According to a recent review by leading PRC historians, these held that 'the victory in the War of Resistance depended entirely on the CCP and the correct leadership of our Great Leader Mao Zedong, and was completely the result of the bitter protracted War of Resistance carried out by the people and the armies in the rear of the enemy'.[1] Earlier histories were wholly negative about the Nationalists:

> Because it was compelled to wage a war of resistance, in the beginning the KMT implemented a strategy that depended entirely on the government and the army [instead of the people], so that a great deal of national territory was lost. When the period of stalemate began [after the Battle of Wuhan in October 1938], the KMT pursued the War of Resistance only passively while actively opposing the CCP. At the eve of victory, the Chiang Kaishek Clique prepared to steal the fruits of victory to imprison China in the dark society of semi-colonialism and semi-feudalism.[2]

According to the review, pre-1980s scholarship, written in the aftermath of the Civil War when few were willing to say anything positive about an enemy against whom they had struggled bitterly, 'suffered from serious shortcomings' as it 'imprisoned research on the War of Resistance in the restrictive frameworks of CCP history and the history of the revolution'. It condemned past historiography as 'partial in arguments, simplistic in its conclusions, and abundant in falsehoods'.[3]

The new research of the 1980s highlighted the importance of Nationalist warfare especially 'on the battlefields at the front' before the fall of Wuhan. It did not portray the KMT as having been forced by the CCP to make war on Japan, but argued that they did so on their own accord for patriotic reasons. If the respective roles of the KMT and the CCP remained a subject of controversy, most scholars suggested that the Nationalists and the Communists each led the war in their own areas, with the Communists becoming dominant towards the end of the War.[4]

Some put forth the argument that the War of Resistance should be regarded as having begun in 1931 with Japan's invasion of Manchuria, a view that has become increasingly influential.[5] Others argued that the KMT began to turn decisively against Japan after

1934, after it had driven the Communists from central China and implemented its military reform programme. The new research denied that the Nationalists were simply the representatives of the large landlords and the big bourgeoisie, let alone, as some had argued, the stooges of the Four Great Households or British and US imperialism.[6]

My presentation of the War of Resistance has been profoundly influenced by the new PRC scholarship, but I do depart from it in several ways. A good case can be made to regard the Mukden Incident as the starting date of the War. Some Nationalists advanced the same view at the end of the War during discussions about Japanese compensation.[7] However, while previous chapters will have made clear that from 1931 the Nationalists prepared for war against Japan and that the Sino-Japanese conflict shaped their rule profoundly, I still believe that it is best to regard the War of Resistance as having begun with the Marco Polo Incident. Before then, the Nationalists kept anti-war figures such as Wang Jingwei in prominent positions, kept open the possibility of achieving their goals without large-scale warfare, and armed conflict remained limited.

If the new PRC scholarship focuses on the first phase of the War of Resistance, this chapter suggests that a re-valuation is also due for the period from the fall of Wuhan until the beginning of Japan's Southern Advance.[8] The usual depiction of a stalemate does not adequately describe the intensity of fighting in this period, its global and domestic significance, and the fact that both sides continued to be determined to prevail in a conflict in which the future of East Asia was at stake. These were the years in which the Nationalists fought without significant outside assistance, when Western powers and the Soviets sought to avoid war with Japan in part by keeping the Sino-Japanese conflict going, when Wang Jingwei's efforts to construct a rival National Government with Japanese help was at its strongest, and when the Japanese undertook large infantry offensives and punishing strategic bombing campaigns to support Wang Jingwei and render Chiang Kaishek's government irrelevant before war with Britain, the USA, and the Soviet Union became inevitable.

As in previous chapters, I relate Nationalist war-making closely to geo-strategic developments, both to illustrate their significance for the war in China but also to integrate the War of Resistance more fully into accounts of the Second World War. I also give greater play to Wang Jingwei's rival National Government. Finally, the distinction drawn in the recent scholarship in the PRC between a front dominated by the KMT and a rear in which the Communists were dominant is, I believe, too neat. The Nationalists initially conducted guerrilla warfare on a larger scale than the Communists, the Communists never launched major operations against the Japanese other than during the One Hundred Regiments Offensive, and at times, quite understandably, negotiated with the Japanese and the Wang Jingwei Government.[9] That is not to deny that the Communists too suffered hugely from Japanese aggression or to suggest that they were not nationalistic. But, they were also rivals of the Nationalists and worked to secure as favourable a position as possible for the post-war period, like the Nationalists.

This chapter ends in 1942. Nationalist campaigns in Burma have already been discussed in detail, while Chapter 7 will discuss developments in China after 1942. The re-assessment offered here can be no more than a preliminary offering. The scope of the topic is too large. According to the National Government's official history of the war, between 1937 and 1945 the Nationalists fought 23 campaigns, 1,117 major battles, and 38,931 smaller engagements with armies that just before the war consisted of 191 divisions and 52 independent brigades of infantry, a small airforce, and a navy unable to prevent smuggling let alone take on the Japanese navy.[10] The source base too remains inadequate. With a few exceptions, at least for now we lack access to communications between headquarters, commanders, staff officers, officers, and troops at the front – the stuff on which war histories should be based. Important archival sources, such as those of China's secret services, remain either closed or have been lost. The archives of Chiang Kaishek's Personal Staff Office, the MAC, most ministries and commissions of the Executive Yuan, the War Zone Commands, and military headquarters at all levels of the chain of command have yet to be opened and explored. Telegraphic communications between China's most important wartime leaders, including between Chiang Kaishek and Mao Zedong, but also for instance between either of these and regional military leaders such as Li Zongren, Feng Yuxiang, Yan Xishan, Zhang Fakui, Xue Yue, and Long Yun are not available except for a few scattered fragments. Nor are we well informed about the National Army's main field commanders, such as Chen Cheng, Tang Enbo, Wei Lihuang, Lo Zhoying, Hu Zongnan, Du Yuming, and Sun Liren. Much remains unclear.

Over the last two decades, nonetheless, many new sources have become available. I have used the operational plans, the battle reports, the orders, and the communications between battlefield commanders and the MAC collected in the 1,700-page collection of primary sources, published in China in 1987 and entitled *The Battlefields at the Front during the War of Resistance*.[11] Also important has been the four volumes of Chiang Kaishek papers relating to military operations during the War of Resistance edited on Taiwan by Ch'in Hsiao-i.[12] Archives in China, Taiwan, and Britain, a variety of other collections of primary sources, including foreign intelligence reports, and secondary works in Chinese and other languages were also useful.

From the Battle of Shanghai to the Battle of Wuhan

The Battles of Shanghai, Xuzhou, and Wuhan, which took place between August 1937 and October 1938, are usually described separately, as if they were events that followed each other without connection. They were in fact closely linked in strategy on the Nationalist side, although not for the Japanese, and can only be understood in relation to each other. If the Battle of Shanghai initiated full-out war, the Battle of Xuzhou was the critical encounter. Following the fall of Shanghai and Nanjing, Xuzhou provided the best opportunity for a counter-offensive. Here the Nationalists could make use of interior lines of communication to supply their forces and to move them about rapidly. Well beyond Japanese supply lines and the reach of its naval guns, the terrain, criss-crossed by rivers, canals, and lakes, neutralised the Japanese advantage in mobility. The loss of Xuzhou meant the inevitable loss of Wuhan. Wuhan, unlike Nanjing, was not made the subject of a fight to the death. Rather, the aim was to make the Japanese pay as high a price as possible for taking the city, frustrate their attempts at a decisive victory that would eliminate all Nationalist resistance, make use of the time that it would take the Japanese to reach Wuhan to move industries, government offices, and educational establishments to the rear, and to prepare defensive bases in key strategic areas from which to continue resistance.

In this phase of the war, an important element of Nationalist strategy was to exploit the Soviet–Japanese stand-off. After drawing out Japan's forces, the Nationalists pushed the fighting as far north as possible, as the Battle of Xuzhou illustrated. Chiang

Kaishek's desire to exploit Japanese–Soviet tensions is clear from an 18 August 1937 address entitled 'Our Political and Military Strategies toward the Enemy and the Main Ways for our Army to Win Victory in the War of Resistance'. He stated that 'the main forces of the Dwarf Aggressors [the Japanese] and their fronts must develop toward Chahar and Suiyuan. But the keener they become on an offensive toward Chahar and Suiyuan, the more effort they will have to put into their front with Soviet Russia'.[13] Strategically, other important elements were to seize the initiative, fight where Japanese advantages in fire power and mobility would be reduced, and rally international support behind China to isolate Japan.

The Battle of Shanghai

The first phase

The Battle of Shanghai (Map 6.1) is normally divided into four phases, of which the Nationalist assault on Japanese positions in the city itself, discussed in Chapter 5, was the first. To what extent the Nationalists thought it possible to dislodge the Japanese from Shanghai is difficult to say. von Falkenhausen had considerable faith in the strength of the National Army. In March, he had counselled Chiang Kaishek to occupy Tianjin, Beiping, and Kalgan in a Blitzkrieg manoeuvre.[14] On 21 July, the German Embassy in Nanjing passed a message from von Falkenhausen to Berlin, which stated that 'China's chances for victory are not bad because the Japanese – mindful of the threat of Russian intervention – cannot commit all their forces against the Chinese. The Chinese infantry is good. The Chinese Air Force is about equal to the Japanese … The morale of the Chinese Army is high. They will put up a bitter fight'.[15] von Falkenhausen was bitterly disappointed with the showing of the Nationalists at Shanghai. In a secret report to Chiang Kaishek of 7 September, he stated that 'if our command had been determined and unified and the main objective had been clear, we could have achieved a quick victory'.[16]

On the other hand, Henry de Fremery, the Dutch observer who reported to military authorities in the Dutch East Indies and was especially interested in Japan's military capacities, believed that ten days would not have been sufficient even for two very good divisions to clear Japanese positions in Shanghai. Writing after the event, de Fremery maintained that even had the Nationalists driven Japanese troops out of Shanghai, they still would have lacked the firepower to force the retreat of the Japanese navy. de Fremery blamed the failure of the attack on the poor state of China's coastal defences, an issue about which he had strongly disagreed with the German advisors while in the service of Chiang Kaishek, and to that extent his analysis may have been the result of sour grapes.[17] Upon German advice, the Nationalists had decided to rely on a limited number of mobile howitzers rather than permanent coastal batteries with heavy guns. According to de Fremery, the batteries that were in existence 'were lacking in even the absolutely essential equipment in the form of instruments, while the munitions were out of date and the soldiers in charge of them were not up to firing these batteries in a modern way'.[18] The crucial Jiangyin Fortress, halfway between Shanghai and Nanjing on the Yangtze River had been fitted with thirteen guns, but no defence works had been constructed on the landward side, 'the projectiles were obsolete', 'the sights dated from

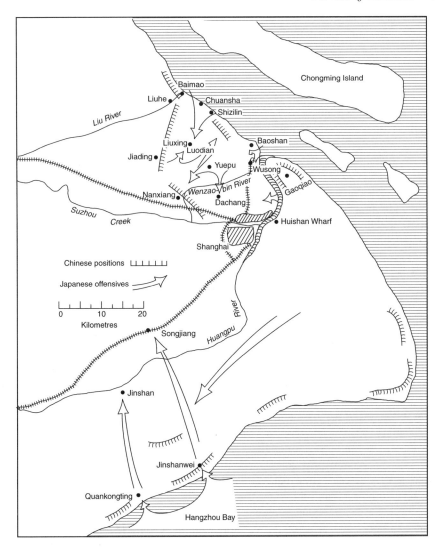

Map 6.1 The Battle of Shanghai.

1895', and 'range finders, telephones, and the like were not present'.[19] If the lack of a strong airforce was probably at least as critical, de Fremery's comments, nonetheless, are useful in highlighting the significance of Japan's naval guns in the Battle of Shanghai.

Chiang Kaishek himself did not leave unnecessary hostages to fortune. He stated that the aim at Shanghai was to 'defeat the enemy's plan of a rapid decision in a quick war by carrying out a war of attrition and wearing out the enemy'.[20] He did not hold out the prospect of victory and made clear that this was only the beginning of a longer campaign. That, of course, does not mean that no hope existed for a significant tactical victory and greater success than, in fact, were obtained. Chiang did want his army to do its very best. He issued an order to the General Staff to make clear to all officers and soldiers that 'those who retreat without an order will be charged with treason and no matter what their position, they will be executed without mercy'.[21]

The second phase

The second phase of the Battle of Shanghai began with Japanese landings to the north of Shanghai on 23 August and lasted until 12 September when Japan had assembled enough forces to begin a flanking manoeuvre aimed at encircling China's forces in Shanghai. On 15 August, the Japanese government approved the creation of the Shanghai Expeditionary Army, as the navy had wanted. The force consisted of three divisions, and its task was defined as securing together with the navy 'the destruction of the enemy at Shanghai as well as the occupation of Shanghai and the region to its north'.[22] The first two divisions reached Shanghai on 22 August and landed the next day in three different places – Chuansha Harbour, Shizilin, and Wusong – between 80 and 140 kilometre north of the city. They established a beachhead running from Baimiao on the Liuhe River to Luodian, Wusong, and North Station in Shanghai.

Both Japan's skill at amphibious operations and its ample naval guns, capable of hitting targets 13 kilometres inland, contributed to the success of these landings critical to the outcome of the Battle of Shanghai.[23] de Fremery described Japan's 'motorised landing craft' as if they were something that he had never seen before, noting that they had a 'steering mechanism' at the front that was 'surrounded by a semi-circular armoured shield'.[24] He wrote that they carried 80 men and 20 tons of cargo, including tanks, armoured cars, horses, and artillery, and possessed a 'tailboard section which can be lowered' so that the landing craft upon grounding could discharge their cargo quickly. He wrote that the craft had high armoured sides so that they 'protect against infantry and machine gun fire'.[25]

In landing craft, the Japanese were indeed far ahead of both the USA and Britain. As we have seen, landing craft remained the great limiting factor in Allied campaigning as late as the Normandy invasion. The British War Office's *Periodical Notes on the Japanese Army* of 1943 stated that the Japanese remained 'a long way in advance numerically' in terms of landing craft and the notes lauded their 'excellence of design, reliability, and adaptability'.[26] Clearly, much training and thought had gone into preparations for amphibious operations, which required rapid communications by the airforce, the navy, and the infantry and needed a highly skilled officers corps. Given that Japan had to use amphibious operations to be able to fight in the South and South-east Asia, it is no surprise that they were far ahead in this aspect of modern campaigning.

The Japanese also possessed some of the best aircraft of the time. The Mitsubishi A5M, with a top speed of 440 kilometres per hour and armed with two machine guns and two bomb racks for 30 kilogram bombs, was a fighter capable of operating from aircraft carriers. The Japanese further had Yokasuka B4Y bombers operating from carriers, while the Mitsubishi G3M operated from Taiwan, Korea, and Japan itself.[27] That von Falkenhausen was perhaps not entirely without knowledge about Japan's air power and the capacity of the Chinese airforce is suggested by the fact that the A5M was new, that the Chinese did inflict losses on its first version, and that it was its second version, with a stronger engine, that achieved air superiority and forced the Chinese airforce to withdraw.

China had the advantage in numbers. It is unsurprising that the best Nationalist Group Armies, including those of Chen Cheng, Lo Zhoying, and Hu Zongnan were present. These were reinforced by armies mostly from south China, although not by the Guangxi Clique. The Guangdong-ese General Xue Yue was Commander-in-Chief of the Left Flank under Chen Cheng. Included in his 19th Group Army were forces from Sichuan, a different Guangdong-ese faction, and a division loyal to Chiang Kaishek. The Central Front Army under Zhu Shaoliang was strengthened by divisions from Henan, Hunan, and Guangdong. Zhang Fakui was Commander-in-Chief of the Right Wing. Under him served divisions from Hunan, Henan, and Fujian, besides a core Chiang Kaishek division. Five of Liu Xiang's divisions were also at Shanghai, where they were to guard Hangzhou Bay. Tang Shengzhi was appointed Commander of the Capital Garrison Forces, made up mostly of divisions loyal to Chiang Kaishek but also two Guangdong-ese ones.[28]

It should be noted here that Japanese divisions consisted of 20,000 troops. The official troop strength of a Chinese division was 10,000, but most were seriously under-strength. Although there were wide divergences, half the figure might be more realistic. In response to the massive increase of Chinese troops at Shanghai, on 6 September, the Japanese transferred three further divisions as well as units from north China and Taiwan. They also changed their war goal to 'beginning an offensive in north China and Shanghai … and bringing about the submission of the enemy'.[29] The stage was set for a gigantic clash.

The third phase

On 13 September, the Japanese went on the offensive. From then until 18 October the two sides fought each other in positional warfare of the First World War variety. In the intense fighting, some areas switched hands almost daily. The Japanese had landed 100,000 troops, 300 tanks, and 300 pieces of land-based artillery. Their airforce numbered 200 planes.[30] The Japanese made their first breakthrough at Liuxing on 17 September. The same day, the Chinese left flank withdrew south to form a new defensive line running from North Station through Dachang, Guangfu, and Luodian to Baimiao. On 30 September, a new Japanese offensive broke through this line at two places, forcing the Chinese left flank to retreat to the south of the Wenzaobin River. The fighting then died down for a week, a period used by the Japanese to strengthen their forces to 200,000.

On 1 October, the Japanese cabinet adopted the 'Guideline for dealing with the China Incident' which declared that 'in order to cause China to lose the will to fight quickly, we must adopt appropriate measures and use the military to occupy strategic places'.[31] On 7 October, the Japanese resumed the offensive. They succeeded in crossing the Wenzaobin River and threatened to cut off the lines of retreat of the National Army at Shanghai. On the 19th, China's troops at the Wenzaobin River, reinforced by the 21st Group Army, began a counter-offensive. Although they drove the Japanese back 2 kilometres in some places, the counter-offensive failed because of bad co-ordination, with the result that Chinese ended up fighting Chinese. Panic set in as Japanese smoke screens provoked fears of poison gas attacks.[32] Bad intelligence also was a factor: a meeting of the day before involving von Falkenhausen, Bai Chongxi, and

Gu Zhutong had concluded that the Japanese were defending the front with few troops who had 'only staged limited attacks' and had been defeated easily.[33] In reality, the Japanese had amassed infantry, artillery, and air force units for their own offensive.[34] By the 22nd the Chinese offensive had run out of steam. On 24 October, the Chinese retreated all the way to Suzhou Creek.

The final phase

The final phase of the battle lasted from then until 9 November. Suzhou Creek offered considerable advantages to the defenders. The 40–50 metre wide river was not fordable and its dikes were 2–2.5 metres high. The retreat from the Wenzaobin River, conducted at night, had proceeded in good order. However, the defensive positions left much to be desired. Machine gun and artillery cannon had been fitted on top of high buildings vulnerable to Japanese artillery barrages. Usually only a single line of trenches had been dug, with no provision for machine guns and without communication trenches to the rear. Barbed wire was sporadic. In various places, due to obstacles, it was impossible to place the river under fire and so prevent crossings. Villages and hamlets, used for quartering the troops, had not been fortified.[35]

The Japanese attacked Suzhou Creek with six divisions or about 120,000 troops. The Nationalists defended it with forty-seven divisions, which nominally had close to 500,000 troops but in actuality perhaps 220,000.[36] The first Japanese attacks on 29 October failed, but two days later they succeeded in breaking through at two separate points. Despite desperate counter-attacks, the Japanese breakthroughs held and three bridges were thrown across Suzhou Creek, allowing the Japanese to pour men and equipment across. The Chinese position in Shanghai became hopeless.

The Japanese landing at Hangzhou Bay to the south of Shanghai on 5 November sealed Shanghai's fate, although it was probably not as important as previous scholars have argued. The Japanese had decided on the Hangzhou Bay operation on 20 October, when the fighting at the Wenzaobin River still was raging without an immediate conclusion in sight and the Japanese had become ever more anxious to force a speedy end to the conflict. It is likely that even without the Hangzhou Bay landing the Chinese defenders would have had to retreat once the Japanese had broken through at the Suzhou Creek.

On 8 November, the Chinese ordered a general withdrawal, after two days of hesitation. Demoralisation, the disintegration of the chain of command, Japanese bombing, and close Japanese pursuit on the ground destroyed the plans for an orderly retreat. Chinese units could often move only by night and they lost contact with their commanders. Highways and railroads were too dangerous to use. Panic spread as the Japanese threatened to trap the fleeing Chinese forces in an encirclement from which they could not have escaped. In mid-November, the Japanese landed forces which occupied the prepared Chinese defensive lines mid-way between Shanghai and Nanjing. At the same time, Japanese commanders on their own initiative began a disorderly race to Nanjing to gain glory by capturing the Chinese capital. This was an unplanned operation well beyond Japanese logistical capacities, with the result that chaos descended over the battlefield, with horrible consequences when standing orders were issued to take no prisoners and not to distinguish between combatants and non-combatants.[37]

I shall not discuss here the Battle for Nanjing, both because it was of little strategic significance, even if the casualties were high, and because a good literature in English, including about Japan's military atrocities, is now available.[38] The Nationalists themselves did not believe that Nanjing could be defended. The National Government moved to Chongqing and the MAC to Wuhan before the battle began. Chiang Kaishek bounced Tang Shengzhi into assuming command of the defence of the city,[39] mostly for symbolic and political reasons.[40] Nanjing was the capital of Republican China and Sun Yatsen's grave was on Purple Mountain, just outside the city. Abandoning the city without a fight would have jarred with Chiang Kaishek's insistence on unselfish sacrifice for the nation. If that defence could be undertaken by an erstwhile opponent of Chiang, so much the better. Displaying the attitude required of him, Tang stated that abandoning Nanjing would be 'a betrayal of the spirit of Sun Yatsen' and vowed 'I will spare no sacrifice in the defence of the city of Nanjing'.[41]

The Battle of Xuzhou

Let me first explain the strategic significance of Xuzhou. The city was located at the junction of the east–west running Long–Hai Railroad from west of Xi'an to the coastal port of Lianyungang and the north–south running Tianjin–Pukou Railroad. With Xuzhou in their hands, Japanese logistical problems would be greatly eased, as they could then make use of the harbour at Lianyungang. Japanese strategic options would also multiply. They could either continue with the occupation of the entire Tianjin–Pukou Railroad to Nanjing or move east along the Long–Hai Railroad to Kaifeng and Zhengzhou, where the Long–Hai and Beiping–Hankou Railroads intersected and from where Wuhan lay 600 kilometres to the south by rail with no significant natural obstacles. The occupation of Xuzhou too would remove the danger to the flanks of Japanese forces already advancing south down the Beiping–Hankou Railroad (Map 6.2).

The Xuzhou region offered several advantages to the Chinese defenders. It was at a distance from Japanese troop concentrations in the north. Lakes such as the Nanyanghu to the north of Xuzhou, the Loumahu to the east, and the Hongzehu to the south sheltered the city, which unlike Shanghai was beyond the reach of Japan's naval artillery. Japan's airforce too played less of role than at Shanghai, partly because of problems of range, but also because at this time the Japanese did not yet pursue strategic bombing offences, as they would later.

In a January 1938 address to officers of the 1st and 5th War Zones, Chiang stated that our strategy 'is in the east to defend the Tianjin–Pukou Railroad ... if lost, Wuhan will be without its protective shield'.[42] On 9 February, von Falkenhausen similarly argued that the safety of Wuhan depended on Xuzhou; Bangbu in northern Anhui to the north-west of Nanjing; and Anyang in northern Henan.[43] These were all railroad junctions. The Nationalists had long prepared for a battle at Xuzhou. According to de Fremery, 'years ago the Chinese military authorities had already foreseen the possibility of a Japanese attack on Nanking from the north. At the Chinese military academy, this subject was eagerly discussed and there were many staff exercise trips to the area around Xuzhou'.[44] Xuzhou was militarily important to keep the Japanese forces divided, concentrate the war in the north, protect northern railroad lines, and keep the Japanese from taking control of the Yangtze River.

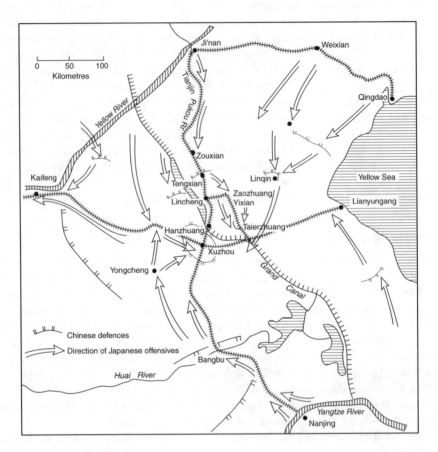

Map 6.2 The Battle of Xuzhou.

To defend Xuzhou, the Nationalists concentrated massive numbers. By January 1938, some 200,000 troops were at Xuzhou, 150,000 troops were deployed between Kaifeng and the Tongguan Pass, while 250,000 troops invested south Shanxi.[45] Among them were strong National Army divisions, but also a great number of troops from regional armies, of which the Guangxi Clique forces were the most important.

Chiang Kaishek was determined that the armies concentrated in the north would make a real fight of Xuzhou. His decision to arrest Han Fuju in front of the assembled high officers of the 1st and 5th War Zones was a clear indication that further retreats would be punished severely. At the military conference where he arrested Han, Chiang told his audience that despite recent defeats, the war was not over and that in fact China's position had real advantages, which would ultimately lead to victory. He portrayed Japanese strategy as a Schlieffen plan that had come unstuck. According to Chiang, Japan had planned to destroy China's military first in a quick war, using 15 divisions out of a total of 50, and then to turn around to take on the Soviet Union. But, he stated, Japan had already sent 26 divisions to China without achieving a decisive victory. Chiang concluded that Japan 'cannot send more troops to China … its strategy has been completely defeated by us'.[46]

Chiang also elaborated on a new operational strategy. On 13 December, the MAC had issued a new operational plan, which stated that 'in order to safeguard Wuhan as our centre, wage a war of attrition, and obtain the final victory, the National Army must begin guerrilla warfare in the peripheral areas in each war zone. At the same time, it must construct new strong battlefield positions in the hilly areas of eastern Hunan, western Jiangxi, and southern Henan and position strong forces there, in order to await the enemy entering in deep and defeat them'.[47] The plan called for the arming of the population, the defence in depth of China's major communication lines, and guerrilla warfare in the Japanese rear.[48]

Political significance

Chiang needed China's armies to fight well at Xuzhou also because of political reasons. Following a punishing series of defeats and the loss of the capital, Chiang Kaishek and the Nationalists had to make the case that the war was worth all the sacrifices that would be demanded and that they continued to have the policies and personal qualities to see it through. The KMT convened an extra-ordinary national party congress in Wuhan from 29 March until 1 April. Party congresses always were moments of potential volatility as they could lead to leadership and policy changes. In addition, many foreign reporters had now arrived in Wuhan and Chinese diplomats and public figures, including Jiang Baili and Gu Weijun, made great play of China's heroic resistance against Japanese aggression in Europe in the hope of gaining increased foreign aid as well as support at the League of Nations, scheduled to discuss the 'China Incident' on 10 May.[49]

In Wuhan, Chiang linked the War of Resistance with national redemption. On 3 April, two days after the closing of the extra-ordinary KMT party congress, Chiang addressed a large mass rally and stated:

> As the war progresses, we must gradually complete the creation of a state based on the Three Principles of the People. You must fully realise that the only goal of the War of Resistance and the Revolution is to rebuild the country. To achieve this goal, we need to implement five types of reconstruction. The first is spiritual reconstruction, the second is material reconstruction, the third is social reconstruction, the fourth is political reconstruction, and the fifth is military reconstruction. Only if we succeed in carrying out these five types of reconstruction will we be able to realise the Three People's Principles and only then can a modern nation be truly established.[50]

On 4 April 1938, the KMT made public the Organic Law for the War of Resistance and National Reconstruction that had been passed by the Party Congress.[51] This was a wartime constitution guiding domestic and international policy during the war. The preamble was careful to state that this was not a war by and for the KMT, but one that involved everybody : 'Success in the great tasks involved in the War of Resistance and rebuilding the nation will depend on the efforts of all comrades of this party, but even more requires all people of the country to join together in our common cause and shoulder these tasks together. This party therefore requests that all people make compromises and break through old barriers so that we may combine our will and act in unison.'[52]

The Organic Law stated that the War's purpose was to realise the 'Three People's Principles and the Testament of Sun Yatsen'. These formed 'the supreme guideline for all our actions during the War of Resistance and for national reconstruction'. It set out in broad strokes the political, economic, social, and military measures that the Nationalists proposed to adopt. These included the establishment of a National Political Consultative Council 'to unite all forces in the country and bring together all ideas and views to benefit the formulation of national policies'.[53] This institution, which will be discussed further in Chapter 7, was a proto-parliament of considerable influence and vitality during the first years of the War. The bureaucracy would be simplified and rationalised to improve efficiency. Officials would be held to strict codes of conduct and punished according to military law for violations. A 'planned economy' would be created to supply the military by developing militarily significant industries but also to improve people's livelihoods by encouraging agricultural production, regulating the supply and prices of food, and stabilising the currency. Profiteering, speculation, and hoarding were to be combated through 'a price stabilisation system'.

With respect to the military, the Organic Law promised that all forces would undergo political training 'so that officers and soldiers understand the significance of the War of Resistance and national reconstruction and will fight together for the country'. The population would be armed and behind enemy lines 'a broad guerrilla war will harass and tie down the armed forces of the enemy'. The state would support War casualties and families of soldiers at the front would be given various privileges. Socially, the population would be organised in associations for peasants, workers, students, and so on, so that each could contribute in an organised fashion to the War on the basis of the principle 'those with money contribute money and those with labour contribute labour'.

The Organic Law sought to define a community based on the War of Resistance. The critical dividing line was no longer between the KMT and the CCP, or between Chiang Kaishek and Li Zongren, but between those committed to fighting for the idea of China as a culture, race, and nation and 'Hanjian', national traitors, an idea discussed with great insight by Frederic Wakeman in an article of his.[54] The Organic Law stated that Hanjian 'would be punished with the utmost severity and their property confiscated'.[55] In August 1938, regulations for the punishment of traitors ordered the death penalty or hard labour for life for all those who 'conspired with or assisted the enemy in any way'.[56]

The Organic Law sought to settle the vexed issue of leadership for the duration of the War. It required that 'all War of Resistance forces unite under the leadership of this Party [the KMT] and Generalissimo Chiang Kaishek'.[57] This condition put all before the question of whether to accept this dispensation or to reject it and hence run the risk of being seen as Hanjian. This was difficult. The CCP, in December 1937, felt compelled to suggest that it had been genuine when on 22 September 1937 it issued a public statement declaring that 'the Three Principles of Mr Sun Yatsen are what is required for China today'.[58] One high-ranking member, Zhang Wentian, acknowledged that many believed that 'the CCP's co-operation with the KMT is false' because 'the CCP hopes to struggle with the KMT for the leadership position during our co-operation'. Zhang sought to eradicate such suspicions by arguing that the CCP had changed its attitudes because Chiang Kaishek and the National Government had 'begun to shoulder the responsibilities of national defence and represent our nation's interest. We will support honestly and energetically the National Government led now by Mr Chiang Kaishek'.[59]

The Battle of Xuzhou, then, was militarily important because it was the last opportunity to prevent a Japanese conquest of north China and the Yangtze River up to Wuhan. Domestically, the Nationalists needed a victory after the defeats they had suffered, give lustre to the deal they offered in Wuhan, and inspire confidence in their leadership of the war. Internationally, a military success would bolster the propaganda drive that then was being mounted in Europe.

The Taierzhuang victory

The Battle of Xuzhou would be lost, but before this the Nationalists scored a useful tactical victory at Taierzhuang, a town to the north-west of Xuzhou on a spur of the Tianjin–Pukou Railroad. This victory came on 6 April, just after the conclusion of the KMT's extra-ordinary party congress and the publication of the Organic Law; and in advance of the League of Nation's discussions of the War of Resistance. Chiang Kaishek made clear to his commanders that he wanted a success: 'If [Taierzhuang] is lost, not only will all officers and soldiers of the 20th Group Army [of Tang Enbo] be punished, but Commander-in-Chief Li Zongren, Vice Chief-of-Staff Bai Chongxi, and Assistant Chief-of-Staff Lin Wei will also be punished.'[60] Tang Enbo was the main Nationalist force at Taierzhuang. Han Fuju's recent execution made it inadvisable to regard Chiang's words as an empty threat.

In his memoirs, published in 1979 thirteen years after his death, Li Zongren claimed the credit for the victory, suggesting that through patriotic appeals he had succeeded in bringing regional military leaders such as Zhang Zizhong together and convinced them to fight for the nation, that he had lured the Japanese into a carefully laid trap, and that he then had organised the retreat of all Chinese forces before the Japanese could strike back.[61] Li's memoirs originated from interviews conducted by Tong Te-kong with Li, in the late 1950s and early 1960s, in New York as part of Columbia University's Oral History Project. According to Tong, rather than having his words recorded and archived, Li wanted 'an autobiography patterned on those in the US at the time'.[62] Tong, who had served Li as a lieutenant, agreed to help Li produce such a biography. He and Li worked on the project until Li decided to return to China in 1964, in a symbolic recognition of the PRC. Legal issues prevented publication of Li's memoirs for many years.

Li's memoirs have shaped interpretations of the Taierzhuang victory.[63] It is not surprising that Li made much of the battle in memoirs designed to establish his name in history and that he downplayed the role of others. This included Bai Chongxi, the number two figure in the Guangxi Clique who unlike Li decided to travel with Chiang Kaishek to Taiwan after 1949. In a letter to Tong, Bai stated that although Li failed to mention his contribution, he 'had been one of the principle architects of that brilliant campaign'.[64]

Li Zongren also denigrated the role of the Nationalists. He charged Tang Enbo, a Chiang Kaishek man, with disobeying orders to turn his forces south on 27 March and stated he had threatened to bring him to justice as he had Han Fuju and that he had to ask Chiang Kaishek to order Tang to move.[65] While Tang was ordered to move south by Chiang, Li played up this issue to hide his own failings. As well, the tactical situation was subject to rapid change. Bai Chongxi in his own later memoirs lauded Tang for 'flexibly and appropriately deploying his forces when the enemy attacked Taierzhuang'.[66] At Taierzhuang, Li did not, in fact, deploy Guangxi units, he seems to have been ill-informed about Japanese moves, and during the Battle of Xuzhou he consistently refused to concentrate his own forces for offensive operations, including a counter-offensive for which Chiang Kaishek pressed after the Taierzhuang victory. It was Tang's forces that did most of the fighting, as of course they should have, given that they were the best trained and equipped. At the time, Li was more generous in his appraisal of Tang. On 4 April, Li Zongren noted in a telegram to Chiang Kaishek that 'after Tang Enbo attacked the enemy at Taierzhuang from the north-east to the south-west, the main forces of the enemy retreated to the east of Taierzhuang'.[67] On 25 April, he commended him for 'creating the basis for our victory'.[68] Li too obscured the role of Liu Fei, who in his own memoirs claimed that he too had contributed to the Taierzhuang victory.[69] In reality, all these men contributed to the victory of Taierzhuang, and it seems that Chiang Kaishek had to pressure all to commit themselves fully to the battle.

The victory was made possible by Japanese over-extension, a failure to co-ordinate operations in different theatres, the limits of offensive warfare, and the under-estimation of China's will to fight. In February, the Japanese Central China Expeditionary Force in the Shanghai–Nanjing area as well as its forces in north China began an operation aimed at converging at Huangkou on the Long–Hai Railroad to the west of Xuzhou to encircle and destroy the forces of the 5th War Zone. In late January, forces under General Matsui crossed the Yangtze River to strike north along the Tianjin–Pukou Railroad towards Bangbu. In the first week of February, they crossed the Huai River, but then their advance was checked. Facing encirclement by Chinese forces rushed to the region, by 16 February the Japanese were compelled to withdraw to the south of the Huai River.[70]

In the north, two Japanese columns, each of about divisional strength, began their advances towards Xuzhou only after Japan's forces in the south had run into trouble. In January, General Itagaki had taken Shandong after Han Fuju's withdrawal. On 21 February, a column of Lin's forces marched south towards Linyi, in the hope of being able to assault Xuzhou from the east. They arrived on 10 March, but then were resisted by Pang Bingxun and Zhang Zizhong, so that by late March Linyi remained in Chinese hands.[71] Further to the west, in early March the Isogai Column began to move down the Tianjin–Pukou Railroad from Ji'nan, Tai'an, and Ji'ning. Guangxi units attacked Japanese all along this front, but the Isogai Column, nonetheless, pressed on.

On 5 March, Li Zongren informed Chiang Kaishek that instead of moving straight down the Tianjin–Pukou Railroad, as he had expected, the Japanese had amassed 150,000 troops to attack Xuzhou from south Shandong and Ji'ning.[72] In response to this call for help, Chiang ordered Tang Enbo as well as Sun Lianzhong to strengthen their armies in the 5th War Zone and assist Li.[73] Tang Enbo and Li Zongren had different ideas about how best to use Tang's 20th Group Army consisting of five divisions, an issue which may have been behind Li Zongren's charge of disobedience. On 14 March, Tang stated in a telegram to Chiang Kaishek that Li wanted to divide up his forces to plug holes at various fronts. Tang instead suggested that his forces should remain together, because 'if they are dispersed it will not be of any benefit to the campaign. They will be wasted without any purpose'. He proposed a massed offensive towards Tengxian to stop the southward thrust of the Isogai Column, which had begun to attack the city on the same day.[74] Tang asked Chiang's permission the next day for an offensive with all his forces 'to deal with the remaining enemy forces in the northern section of the Tianjin–Pukou Railroad'.[75] Tang did not shirk from battle.

While this issue was being debated, the Isogai Column took not only Tengxian but also Lincheng, Hanzhuang and Yixian. From Hanzhuang, about 50 kilometres north of Xuzhou, a branch line of the Tianjin–Pukou Railroad travelled to Taierzhuang. Xuzhou, where Li was, was now threatened, and the defenders of Linyi became vulnerable to an attack in their rear.

Confronted with this perilous situation, on 21 March, Chiang Kaishek ordered a re-organisation of the front and created a new Chief-of-Staff Unit to help Li Zongren direct the battle. With two divisions, Tang Enbo was to make a feint towards Yixian, while using his three remaining divisions to fight back westward from Yixian to the Tianjin–Pukou Railroad to attack the flank of the Isogai Column. Zhang Zizhong and Sun Lianzhong were to continue to defend Linyi. North of Xuzhou, other forces were to defend the Grand Canal, while simultaneously guerrilla attacks were to harass the Japanese rear at Zouxian.[76] Chiang himself visited Xuzhou on the 24th and appointed Bai Chongxi and Lin Wei, respectively, as Vice and Assistant Chiefs-of-Staff to the 5th War Zone, while Liu Fei, the Director of the Operations Bureau of the Ministry of War, also was sent to the front.[77]

The Isogai Column reached Taierzhuang on 23 March. Tang Enbo's forces attacked the Japanese at Yixian and Zaozhuang while Sun Lianzhong's forces, which had been sent to invest Taierzhuang, engaged the Japanese to the north of the city. Li Zongren reported, on 25 March, that Tang's offensives had thrown back the Japanese at both Yixian and Zaozhuang.[78] Li furthermore informed Chiang that Sun Lianzhong had forced the Japanese back at Taierzhuang and that only a few isolated Japanese units continued to resist there.[79] On the 27th, Li reported that the Japanese had regrouped and again tried to take Taierzhuang, but that 'in heroic street fighting, our forces dealt with almost all of them'.[80] Li feared continued Japanese attacks, and therefore ordered Tang to rush south and clean up resistance in two days.[81] On 28 March, Li reported that local militia had attacked the Japanese at Lincheng, where they had entered the city, destroyed ammunition dumps and supply stores, and even attacked the local Japanese headquarters, but then had been forced out by Japanese forces sent in relief.[82]

Li's tone changed to alarm on 29 March. He then reported that the previous day the Japanese had sent 4,000 extra troops, 40 artillery guns, and 30–40 tanks to attack Taierzhuang and that more and more Japanese forces appeared to be concentrating. He went on to state that the Japanese now had entered the city in force, and that while the railroad station remained in Chinese hands, 'casualties are high'.[83] His report of that day concluded with 'Yesterday and today, wherever we tried to make progress, the enemy attacked with ferocity using their numerous tanks so that we were defeated'. That same day, a telegram to Chiang Kaishek by Lin Wei and Liu Fei stated that the previous day the Japanese had also attacked at Lincheng.[84]

Lin and Liu also reported that on 'the evening of 27 March the whole of Tang's Group Army struck south in order to attack the enemy at Taierzhuang together with Sun [Lianzhong]'. Tang himself reported on 29 March that he had ordered two divisions to make a feint towards Yixian, reinforce the Linqin front, and protect the right flank of the Chinese position, while he had transferred two divisions and one brigade to Taierzhuang to attack the Japanese.[85]

Over the next few days, the outcome of the Battle of Taierzhuang hung in the balance. Street fighting in the city lasted for several days and the Japanese gradually pushed the Chinese defenders into a corner. However, Chiang Kaishek would not give up, insisting in a 1 April telegram to the 5th War Zone Headquarters at Xuzhou that 'the enemy at Taierzhuang must be destroyed'.[86] On 2 April, Li Zongren ordered a general counter-offensive and four days later, the Japanese had been forced out of Taierzhuang. If not the 20,000 that Li Zongren claimed,[87] some 8,000 Japanese troops had become casualties.[88] In this battle, as de Fremery reported, the Chinese 'used for the first time 15 cm batteries'. They also used tanks and anti-tank guns, while thirty aircraft bombed Japanese positions.[89] It may well be that Soviet aid made a telling difference.

The fall of Xuzhou

The successful defence of Taierzhuang led Chiang Kaishek to push for a determined counter-offensive. In a series of telegrams he urged the defenders of Taierzhuang to capitalise on Japanese problems. He admonished Tang Enbo, writing in a telegram of 5 April that 'At the Battle of Taierzhuang, we have as many as fifteen divisions to deal with only one-and-a-half enemy divisions. Even after a week we have not yet achieved victory. Your Group Army is stationed in the rear and at the flank of the enemy. How will you account for yourself if your offensive is not successful?'[90] Over the next week he continued to send similar messages to various commanders at the front, including Li Zongren.[91] Chiang increased troop deployment to about 450,000 men, including six of the best divisions of the National Army.[92] von Falkenhausen strongly supported this attempted counter-offensive and may well have helped design it.[93]

The Chinese counter-offensive soon petered out. After being thrown back at Taierzhuang, the Japanese retreated to the south Shandong hills to await the arrival of reinforcements. They used their superior artillery and the protection of city walls to defend themselves.[94] Lack of intelligence about Japanese movements and the threat of Japanese poison gas attacks blunted the counter-offensive.[95] A lack of co-ordination, sufficient air support, and the concern for an attack on the Chinese flank by Japanese forces along the Beiping–Hankou Railroad were no doubt also important in preventing the Chinese from making significant inroads into Japanese positions.

Li Zongren refused to commit his Guangxi forces. On 12 April, Chiang once more urged Li Zongren to press ahead. Li's response the next day was that 'I fear that the complete defeat of the enemy will be difficult'. He added that the agreed operational strategy for this phase of the war had been to avoid positional warfare; it was clearly on this condition that he had agreed to the deployment of his forces in north China. He proposed to 'place a few guarding units at the periphery of the battle field while concentrating the main forces in several places where they can be used flexibly. On the one hand we should destroy the communications in the enemy's rear and on the other carry out small-scale guerrilla warfare'.[96] Chiang did order Tang Enbo and Sun Lianzhong to press ahead regardless, but moving alone they ran the risk of ending up in too forward a position from which they would not have been able to retreat.[97]

It is impossible to know whether Li Zongren was right or whether, as Chiang Kaishek and von Falkenhausen believed, a real opportunity for a meaningful counter-offensive existed, with the Japanese in disarray in north China, with massive forces concentrated in the north, and with a public firmly behind the war. That Chiang tried, in these conditions, to push forward is certainly understandable. The failure of the offensive makes clear that the price of bringing regional forces such as of the Guangxi Clique into the war was to accept limitations on operational strategy.

As at Shanghai, time had been of the essence. After the Taierzhuang debacle, Japanese reinforcements were rushed to Qingdao from Manchuria and Japan.[98] On 7 April, the Japanese Supreme Staff Headquarters adopted a new war plan for the Xuzhou campaign.[99] This called for a co-ordinated operation of four divisions in the north and two in the south. A fresh group of staff officers was sent from Tokyo. A new war plan called for the Second Army of the North China Expeditionary Force, strengthened by two new divisions as well as heavy artillery and tank units, to strike south to the west of Xuzhou to cut the Long–Hai Railroad. The Central China Expeditionary Army was to restart its northward march, simultaneously this time, so as to achieve the broad encirclement of all Chinese forces now assembled in the 5th War Zone.[100]

The Japanese advanced rapidly and, on 17 May, General Terauchi's Headquarters claimed that 400,000 men had been trapped in a ring of steel so that they could only surrender or die. Japanese military leaders began to assert that the impending destruction of Chinese forces caught in their trap would be a military feat outshining even the famous battles of Tannenberg and Cannae.[101] However, by this time, the Chinese had already begun their withdrawal, which was authorised by Chiang Kaishek on 15 May.[102] Li Zongren and Bai Chongxi left Xuzhou together with the forces of Tang Enbo before going their own way.[103] Most Chinese divisions, divided into small detachments, escaped in various directions, finding gaps between the Japanese columns, which rushed towards Xuzhou. The lack of sufficient numbers of troops to make the encirclement watertight and timely dust storms that rendered Chinese movements invisible to Japanese reconnaissance made the escape possible.

The fall of Xuzhou had a profound impact on the public mood in China. When news of the Taierzhuang victory reached Wuhan, the press had been jubilant and hundreds of thousands of people marched through the streets in celebration.[104] After the Battle of Xuzhou, despondency set in again. As Mao Zedong stated in 'On Protracted Warfare', consisting of a series of lectures delivered between 26 May and 3 June just after the fall of Xuzhou, before the beginning of the War of Resistance 'there was a great deal of talk about national subjugation'.[105] The first ten months of the war had seen faith restored and the victory at Taierzhuang had made people believe that the Battle of Xuzhou 'marks the last desperate struggle of the enemy' and that 'if we win, the Japanese warlords will be demoralised and able only to await their Day of Judgment'.[106] Following the loss of Xuzhou, according to Mao, the question in people's minds again was 'will China be subjugated?'[107]

The Battle of Wuhan

In late May, after Xuzhou had been taken, the Japanese formulated concrete plans 'to bring the war to an end at the earliest possible opportunity'. A Japanese cabinet meeting in July resolved to take Wuhan to 'overthrow the current National Government' and establish 'a new government opposed to war, opposed to Chiang Kaishek, and opposed to the Communists'.[108] The Japanese were convinced that after conquering the north China plains, Wuhan, and Canton, which would be attacked simultaneously, the Nationalists would lose the will to fight and that then 'it will be possible to control China'.[109]

After the Battle of Xuzhou, the Japanese immediately struck westward along the Long–Hai Railroad, with the intention to fall upon Wuhan by descending down the Beiping–Hankou Railroad. After they had taken Kaifeng and had begun an assault on Zhengzhou, Chiang Kaishek on 9 June ordered the destruction of the Yellow River dikes at Huayuankou. The resulting floods, affecting Henan, Anhui, and Jiangsu, wrecked the Japanese plan and postponed the seizure of Wuhan by five months, but also led to the devastation of large areas.[110]

Some strategic justification existed for the decision. Combined with the heavy rainfall of the spring of 1938, the floods turned the north China plains into fields of mud, which increased Japanese logistical difficulties and prevented them from using tanks and mobile artillery. Airfields were inundated.[111] The deluge prevented the Japanese from linking up their forces in north China and the Yangtze Valley and from cutting off Chinese lines of retreat running through Wuhan. The floods, then, made it impossible for the Japanese to capitalise quickly on their victory in the Battle of Xuzhou and gained China's forces the time to withdraw and regroup in war zones that were then being built up to continue resistance in the future.

At the same time, the floods forced the Japanese military south. The Yangtze River as a result was again brought into play. During the Battle of Wuhan, the Japanese navy functioned in some way like a German Panzer force. It repeatedly broke through China's defences along the Yangtze River and advanced beyond their own infantry divisions operating along the shores as well as China's defenders. It then could land forces to attack Chinese fortresses and troops from the flanks and the rear.

By this time, the Japanese had fourteen divisions in China south of the Great Wall, of which nine, divided into two corps, would participate in the Battle of Wuhan. The 11th Corps deployed four divisions south of the Yangtze and on the river's north shore. As it advanced towards Wuhan, units fighting to the south of Yangtze separated themselves from the main force to occupy cities on the main Yangtze tributaries. The operations of the 11th Corps were greatly helped by the 120 naval vessels of the Third Fleet as well as 300 airplanes.

As at Shanghai, the ability to conduct combined naval, infantry, and air operations was important. Bombing drove Chinese troops into the hills from low-lying cultivated areas without natural protection. Naval artillery dislodged Chinese troops along the Yangtze and secured this supply line against which guerrilla operations could make little impact.

As during the Shanghai campaign, the Chinese were let down by their failure to build strong shore batteries along the Yangtze River. The loss of the Madang, Matouzhen, and Tianjiazhen fortresses were all key events. None was able to withstand Japanese combined arms operations for very long. Madang, to the east of Jiujiang, was well situated: the Yangtze was narrow here and high cliffs gave the advantage to the defenders. Thirty-nine vessels had been sunk and 1,600 mines laid to block the Japanese. Nonetheless, Madang fell as early as 26 June when the Japanese landed marines nearby and attacked the fort in the rear from its landward side. Reinforcements ordered to assist with the defence arrived too late. The Japanese navy gained access to Lake Poyang and therefore was able to support Japanese units attacking the main forces of the 9th War Zone to the south of the Yangtze River.[112]

Chen Cheng was the Commander-in-Chief of the 9th War Zone. Chen concentrated his forces between the cities of Jiujiang, Ruichang, Dechang, and Nanchang in Jiangxi south of the Yangtze River, in the belief that the Japanese would have to advance through this area on their way to Wuhan and that here the best opportunities for a counter-offensive were available. The fighting in this area began in late July and would continue until mid-September. As at Xuzhou, the Japanese attempted to encircle the Chinese forces, but failed to make serious headway and in fact were several times thrown-back by counter-offensives. When, on 14 September, the Japanese took the Matouzhen Fortress upriver from Ruichang, the defenders of the 9th War Zone were left in an isolated position. The Japanese then assaulted Tianjiazhen, the last bottleneck on the Yangtze River before Wuhan. In this case, resistance was tough and even saw the Chinese airforce inflicting some damage on the Japanese navy while Chinese field forces offered resistance to Japanese landings. But on 28 September, the defenders, having sustained punishing aerial attacks, naval bombardments, and artillery barrages, withdrew.[113] Further resistance south of the Yangtze became impossible.

North of the river, the Japanese 2nd Corps with four divisions was concentrated at Hefei and Anqing. Unable to use the Long–Hai Railroad, beginning in late August they advanced in two separate columns along the northern foothills of the Dabie Mountains. Although harassed by 5th War Zone forces, by late September the Japanese had broken through to the Beiping–Hankou Railroad.[114] The Japanese then advanced on Wuhan in a pincer movement. On 21 September, Tokyo reported that air reconnaissance suggested that Chinese troops had begun to withdraw from all fronts.[115] On 25 October, Wuhan was in the hands of the Japanese. A week earlier they had also taken Canton.

The Nationalist military performance

The first phase of the war illustrated the strengths of the Japanese military. They had the navy, the artillery, the tanks, the amphibious skills, and airforce to deploy rapidly and massively. It also highlighted Japanese weaknesses. First and foremost, the Japanese lacked a clear political strategy so that they became embroiled into a conflict which they did not want, and were drawn in deeper step by step. The battle of Taierzhuang formed a good illustration of the fact that the Japanese found it difficult to impose a common strategic view over forces operating at different fronts. Individual divisional commanders, eager for glory, had a tendency, as happened at Nanjing as well as at Taierzhuang, to rush forward beyond their supply lines, endangering the cohesion of the whole front.

The Battle of Taierzhuang showed that without the support of the navy and the airforce and at a distance from supply lines, the Japanese were vulnerable, especially to an army using a mix of positional, mobile, and guerrilla warfare. The Japanese, too, were unable to develop the international alliances that would prove the crucial determinant to victory and defeat during the Second World War.

As to the Nationalists, the fighting exposed the tactical and logistical weakness of the Chinese forces. In November 1938, at the first Nanyue Military Conference in Hunan, Chiang launched a scathing attack on the assembled high-level officers of the 3rd and 9th War Zones. He stated that large numbers of troops had deserted and that in many areas where the National Army operated the locals had fled. He criticised the use of outmoded defensive tactics. Rather than building up a position in depth, he stated, officers had created just a single defensive line, knowing nothing better than simply building up the numbers. According to Chiang, orders had frequently not been implemented, commanders had been unable to deploy units quickly and flexibly, and they had failed to gather intelligence about enemy movements. Plans had not been kept secret and no sentry posts had been set out, so that the Japanese could easily reconnoitre Chinese positions. Opportunities for counter-offensives had been lost because commanders threw in reserves too quickly. Chiang was irate about staff work: staff officers had failed to file battle reports, war diaries, and divisional accounts, so that higher level officers did not know what equipment and ammunition had been spent where, what had been allocated to what units, and how much remained. Staff officers had failed to rotate troops in a co-ordinated way, so that parts of a front had been left empty as replacements had not arrived after a particular unit had withdrawn. Communications within divisions had usually been good, according to Chiang, but it had not been uncommon, he lamented, for divisions not to lay telephone and telegraph cables to higher command centres or neighbouring units. This was one way of avoiding orders to attack.[116]

Alexander von Falkenhausen's reports on the Battle of Shanghai confirm Chiang's assessment. von Falkenhausen argued that tactical errors, staff deficiencies, and command failures had caused the defeat of China's assault on Shanghai. The divisions involved in the assault had not been assigned a specific battle area and had operated as individual units. Little contact had existed between them so that they had not co-ordinated their attacks. Artillery units and other special forces had not co-operated with the infantry in any effective way. They had fired a great deal of ammunition, but they had done so from their maximum range without guidance from forward outlook posts so that they had essentially fired at random. Chinese artillery simply had not mastered the skill of indirect fire. Japanese naval vessels on the Huangpu as well as enemy barracks at Hongkou therefore had suffered little damage.[117]

According to von Falkenhausen, command headquarters had been badly organised. Staff officers were rotated by a system of shifts rather than a rolling programme of duty and rest, so that after the end of one shift, the new duty officers had to familiarise themselves with the situation at the front. Intelligence was so bad that no accurate maps of either Chinese or Japanese positions were available. von Falkenhausen also commented on the fact that communications within divisions often had been good, but that contact with neighbouring divisions and higher command levels had been intermittent. Intelligence reports had omitted crucial details. Fearing Japanese artillery and air assault, divisional commanders had set up command posts in villages at considerable distance from the front and had relied on telephones, whose cables were easily cut, to communicate with the front and with higher levels. Rapid and flexible responses to changing situations therefore had been impossible.[118]

von Falkenhausen also criticised the adoption of tactics dating from the late nineteenth and early twentieth centuries. National Army training manuals, von Falkenhausen noted, detailed how units should spread out under attack and deploy in depth rather than in a single line. These tactics had not been adopted and Chinese forces had continued to defend a single front line, with the consequence that a Japanese breakthrough would lead to the collapse of the whole position. National Army manuals seem simply not to have been studied or made the basis of training and field exercises. In his January 1938 address to 5th War Zone officers, Chiang Kaishek dramatically stated that 'only two of all of you assembled here today have come with a copy of the *Infantry Manual* and only one with a copy of *Command Guidelines*'.[119]

von Falkenhausen also reported that the deployment of reserves had been handled incompetently. No reconnaissance had been conducted before fresh troops were sent to the front and no protecting fire had been arranged. Losses had been high because of this but also because troops were usually sent to the front in large concentrations, so that any hit had led to massive casualties. Reserves had been poured into the area where a frontal attack took place, von Falkenhausen noted, while they would have been better deployed on the flanks.[120]

Henry de Fremery's reports confirm von Falkenhausen's assessment of the tactical inadequacies of the National Army, including the disastrous habit of defending a front with a single line of trenches. Officers, according to de Fremery, could 'form their troops up in a line and have them dig in. However, they are not able to bring in reserves in a flanking position to threaten the enemy'.[121] He too noted that staff skills were simply not good enough for rapid troop movements. Following the Hangzhou Bay landings, the National Army had announced its intention to hem in the invading Japanese forces, but, according to de Fremery, 'neither the Chinese general staff, nor the divisional commanders, nor the organisation of the railways could cope with bringing these plans to fruition'.[122]

The Nationalist military had not shone. Neither the attack on Japanese positions in Shanghai nor the counter-offensive at Taierzhuang had come off. The Nationalist attempt to bring about a major battle in north China after having drawn the Japanese forces apart had ended in failure. A degree of co-operation had been established between Chiang Kaishek's forces and those of the regional militarists. They had been mixed together in orders of battle. But it had not been possible to make them fight coherently, as the refusal of individual divisions to establish communications with their superior headquarters and neighbouring divisions illustrates so well. An early victory had proved well beyond the reach of China's military.

Nonetheless, the Japanese hope of destroying Nationalist resistance in a quick victory had been dashed. The Nationalists had secured the material support of the Soviet Union and the foreign press spoke with sympathy and even admiration about Chinese resistance. The Nationalists had made shrewd use of Soviet–Japanese tensions. In contrast, the Japanese were paralysed by their fear of the Soviet Union and this had pushed them in seeking a Blitzkrieg type victory which was probably an impossible goal in a country as large as China and well beyond Japanese logistical capacities.

The First Nanyue Military Conference

The First Nanyue Military Conference took place between 25 and 28 November 1938. During the war, a series of such conferences, where high-level military officers were called together from several war zones, took place. At these conferences, Chiang Kaishek usually presented himself as a tough teacher. He lectured his audience, gave instructions, spelt out meanings, and criticised his students for their errors. The First Nanyue Conference, coming in the wake of fifteen months of defeats and the loss of the economic, cultural, and political centre of China was especially significant.

The Japanese hoped to capitalise on their victories by sidelining Chiang Kaishek and finding a Chinese interlocutor with whom to achieve a peace accord. On 21 October, a Japanese cabinet paper criticised 'the tendency of our citizens to rely only on military activities to resolve the China Incident and to hope for a quick conclusion'. It then went on to argue that 'from now on, we shall not only use military means, but shall exhaust our national political, economic, and cultural forces to advance toward a new China'.[123] On 3 November, the Japanese Prime Minister announced his intention to build a 'New Order in East Asia', declaring that 'the Empire seeks to establish a new order ... based on the basis of co-operation between Japan, Manchuria, and China and mutually supportive relations in political, economic, and cultural affairs. ... We will not reject the National Government if it abandons its past policies and changes its personnel'.[124]

In response to these announcements, on 12 November, Wang Jingwei sent Gao Zongwu, the Director of the Asian Affairs Bureau of the Ministry of Foreign Affairs, to Shanghai for negotiations with the Japanese. On 20 November, a communiqué was agreed in which the Japanese promised to withdraw their forces from all areas in China south of the Great Wall except where Communists formed a threat, abandon extraterritoriality, and return leased territories to China. Japan in return demanded that Japan and China co-operate in the defence against Communism, that China recognise Manchuria, agree to economic co-operation, and guarantee Japanese preferential rights in the exploitation of the natural resources of north China.[125] Wang Jingwei himself left Chongqing for Hanoi in December to begin his peace movement, no doubt hoping that large numbers in the military, the government, and the KMT would find Japan's conditions attractive enough to abandon Chiang Kaishek.

At this juncture, when the settlement of the spring of 1938 about Chiang Kaishek's leadership, the policies to be followed in the war, and political relations generally were again cast into doubt, Chiang had to deliver a bravura performance. Chiang continued to work the themes first elaborated in Wuhan of moral re-armament, political reform, and national reconciliation and reconstruction to argue that his way remained the only one that could deliver a decent future in which the pride of Chinese civilisation would be restored.

In his opening address, Chiang Kaishek argued that the war had proceeded so far according to plan. He stated that 'in accordance with the strategy that we had determined before the War, we have forced the enemy into a crisis situation which will lead to its defeat and from which it will not be able to extricate itself'.[126] Chiang maintained that he had opened up a second front in Shanghai rather than concentrate all forces in north China because then 'our main forces would probably have been defeated and China might well have been destroyed'. 'In order to use our main forces flexibly, wage resistance at every stage, and gradually wear out the enemy', he added, 'we had to force the enemy to fight in the Yangtze River valley'.[127] Now, he went on, Japan 'had been lured in deep' and China's armies would be able to determine when and where they would fight. He stated that with the conclusion of the Battle of Wuhan, the time had arrived 'in which we will switch from defence to offence and turn defeat into victory', because 'now the enemy has deployed its greatest number of troops…and as they dispersed while the war area expanded, their forces have become exhausted so that they could not go on and their combat strength is no longer very great'.[128]

Chiang also evoked memories of the suppression of the Taiping Rebellion, turning the event into a legend of how Chinese civilisation was saved even after huge defeats. 'Seventy years earlier', he explained, 'shamed by his defeat, Zeng Guofan contemplated suicide after the Taiping had taken Wuhan, Yuezhou [contemporary Yueyang] had fallen, and the Hunan Army had been totally destroyed'. Zeng had been dissuaded and had fled to Changsha, Chiang went on, where officials and gentry had ridiculed him. But 'after thorough self-reflection and analysis', Zeng 'had recruited and trained new armed forces, established an inland navy, and had led his troops out of Hunan, subjugating the great cities along the Yangtze'. According to Chiang, the 'bravery in unwaveringly withstanding all setbacks' that had characterised Zeng Guofan had again been displayed during the previous phase in the War of Resistance when 'the army and the people became fully united, followed the government, and had wholeheartedly and harmoniously co-operated'. This, he stated, 'is a spiritual victory which will provide the basis for our inevitable victory over the Japanese'. Chiang finished his opening address by reminding his audience that Zeng had argued that 'the Hunan Army had no equal because we looked after each other and assisted each other. Although animosities were plentiful, on the battlefield we co-operated closely'.[129] Without such co-operation, according to Chiang, Japan would not be defeated.

On the second day of the conference, Chiang turned tough. He declared that 'this is our shame: because we military men were unable to do our duty, the enemy invaders were able to commit aggression against us and we were unable to protect the country and safeguard our soil. As a result, our compatriots – women, men, the aged, and the young – were raped and murdered and suffered inhuman cruelty'.[130] He then enumerated 'twelve points of shame', including the failure to bury battlefield casualties, to care for the wounded so that casualties became beggars, and to supply enough food so that soldiers harassed the population or became deserters and beggars. It was during this speech that Chiang criticised commanding officers, urging them to transcend local interests and abandon selfish interests to become like those officials and gentry who had joined the fight against the Taiping.[131] These themes Chiang would belabour again and again during future military conferences.

In a second speech on the same day, Chiang Kaishek urged his officers to become both capable at modern warfare and to transform themselves into embodiments of the values and practices of a reborn China. He urged them to study closely the *Battle Guidelines* and the *Infantry Manual*, which provided detailed guidelines for the deployment of troops in various stages of a battle. He rebuked his commanders for corruption, logistical ineptness, and haphazard organisational practices. He called for the dismissal of superfluous commanders and staff officers; strict accounting practices; careful collection of intelligence; and a good communications and reporting system, both within but also between units. He insisted on strict implementation of rewards and punishments, the submission of honest and regular accounts so that both the troops and the people would come to trust the army, and the creation of good personnel systems to avoid instability and unnecessary jockeying for position in the army.[132] He held up the anti-Taiping leaders as unselfish heroes who had not fought for themselves, had been plain, honest, straightforward and reliable, and had not blamed others but analysed their own mistakes. Similarly, he went on, 'at this meeting, ... we must fully discuss the lessons and experiences of our past mistakes. On the basis of a spirit of self-criticism, we must completely analyse any mistake by colleagues, by friends, and also myself, in military affairs, in the party, in politics, and in foreign relations'.[133]

All this led up to the announcement of important measures that would undercut the power of individual commanders during the last day of the conference. Chiang had already made clear that command and staff organisations would be re-organised, troop levels reduced, and financial expenditures curtailed. He made clear that recruitment would be centralised and a special bureaucracy created to make sure that reports on troop establishments confirmed to reality. Chiang further made known that all forces would be re-trained under central auspices in a year-long programme. Every four months, one-third of the troops would be brought to the rear for re-training and then re-deployed, while one-third would be assigned to guerrilla warfare and one-third to front-line duty. Chiang explained the reform programme as essential to raising the prestige of the army in the country and increasing its effectiveness.[134]

Held when many had to choose between Chiang Kaishek's call for continued resistance and Japan's accommodation offer, one purpose of the First Nanyue Conference was to make the case that victory would yet be possible. Chiang did so by reviving, and re-fashioning, the history of the suppression of the Taiping and linking it to a vision of national redemption and the recovery of military vigour, as he had done in Wuhan. Wang Jingwei did depart Chongqing, but few would follow him. If a variety of reasons shaped individual decisions, Chiang's Nanyue performance no doubt was important as well. As Churchill showed, leadership during the Second World War was about mobilising words as well as about mobilising men.

The second phase of the war: from the Battle of Wuhan to Japan's Southern Advance

From the fall of Wuhan to the beginning of Japan's Southern Advance, the fighting went through three periods. The first lasted until the conclusion of the Nazi–Soviet Pact and the Nomonhan Ceasefire between the Soviet Union and Japan in August and September 1939. In this period, the Soviet Union remained an important factor in the War of Resistance and the Nationalists continued to seek to locate the fighting in north China. Japanese operations in this period were concerned with securing the Yangtze River and cutting communications between the Nationalist base at Sichuan and the north.

From September 1939 until the spring of 1941, the Nationalists could count on no meaningful foreign support. Internationally, the situation was highly fluid, with no one clear about the final shape of the international alliances that would slug it out on the battlefield. During this period, with the Japanese no longer threatened by the Soviet

Union, the fighting moved to south China. The Japanese redoubled their efforts to bottle the Nationalists up in Sichuan, including by large-scale strategic bombing campaigns, and build up Wang Jingwei as an alternative to Chiang Kaishek. The Nationalists continued their efforts to keep the war going across China, including by the Winter Offensive of late 1939 and early 1940. They were able to defeat a Japanese offensive aimed at taking Changsha.

The final period began in the spring of 1941 when both Britain and the USA became increasingly concerned about Japan and began to involve themselves more closely in the War of Resistance, the USA by means of Chennault's American Volunteer Group and the British through a covert programme to arm and train 30,000 Chinese guerrillas. In this period, the Japanese sought to end meaningful Nationalist resistance before war with the USA and Britain, but they were unsuccessful because they had to reduce their forces in China.

The period between the fall of Wuhan and the beginning of Japan's Southern Advance has often been characterised as a stalemate. It is certainly true that after the Battle of Wuhan the choreography of the war changed. Beforehand, hundreds of thousands of Chinese and Japanese troops engaged each other in the deathly dance of set-piece battles on a stage hundreds of miles long and wide. Afterwards, the war became diffuse and dispersed, with little activity in some areas for long periods of time.

Nonetheless, the idea of a stalemate is problematic. Statistics on Nationalist casualty rates, however unreliable, give some indication. In the year-and-a-half before December 1942, they were nearly 50,000 per month, only 10,000 less than between the Battle of Shanghai and the fall of Wuhan.[135] Similarly, if by Nationalist reckoning there were 5 major and 276 minor battles in the first phase of the war, the second one saw 9 major and 496 minor battles as well as more than 20,000 smaller clashes.[136]

The altered nature of the war was the result of changes in Japanese and Chinese strategy. A document of the Japanese General Staff office of 6 December 1938 stated that it no longer expected a quick end to the war.[137] It also declared that no new territory would be occupied and that no major new offensives would take place unless 'the enemy concentrates his forces for an offensive'. The task of Japan's forces in China was to conduct mopping up operations in the rear and suppress Nationalist and Communist guerrillas while reducing deployment from 750,000 to 400,000 'in preparation for changes in the international situation', which, it was estimated, would not come until a further two years had gone by.[138] Rather than seeking the military annihilation of the Nationalists, the hope was to make them irrelevant by fostering sympathetic regimes such as that of Wang Jingwei.

Neither side, then, desired to continue with the large-scale military operations that had characterised the first phase of the war. If the Japanese had come to the conclusion that they could not secure a quick military victory and also had to rely on political means, for the Nationalists it was even more true that a military victory in the short term was impossible. But, prevailing in the war and imposing their visions remained the goal for both.

The Nationalist approach during the second phase of the War of Resistance can be described as establishing a series of fortress zones across China designed to interdict Japanese lines of communication, offer a multiplicity of targets so that the Japanese were forced to dilute their forces, and keep the war going across China as a national endeavour. The major base was Sichuan, which provided, as we shall see in Chapter 7, by far the most recruits for the army as well much of its food. Other base areas were established in terrain that would always be difficult for the Japanese to take, which was important for the Nationalists to hold, such as recruitment grounds and food surplus areas, and from which military operations could be undertaken that would make it difficult for the Japanese to consolidate their positions.

The first period

After the Battle of Wuhan, the Japanese re-deployed their forces into four Group Armies. The 11th, consisting of seven divisions, was headquartered in Wuhan. Its aim was to secure the Japanese position at Wuhan, including by eliminating resistance in north Hubei, along the Yangtze River west of Wuhan, and in Hunan. The 21st Army Group with four divisions and two independent brigades invested Canton and Southern Guangdong to cut off supplies to the Nationalists carried on the Canton–Hankou Railroad. The 13th Army Group secured the Lower Yangtze region, and the North China Army with nine divisions and twelve brigades was assigned the task of securing Hebei, Shandong, north Shanxi, and Mongolia.[139]

As to the Nationalists, a Revised MAC Draft War Plan of December 1938 indicated their assessments.[140] As mentioned, the MAC first of all believed that it was unlikely that Japan would attack southern China for fear of provoking a premature conflict with European colonial empires. Sichuan, abutting the British Empire, was also protected by high mountains and lacked the rivers and railroads that had made Japan's penetration of north China possible. It therefore was thought to offer the safest basis from which to continue resistance. The MAC further believed that Japan's major concern was to 'transfer their main forces to north China to defend against Russia and make use of the weaknesses of our armies in the north to advance westward'. The MAC expected that Japan would invade western and eastern Shanxi and press west along the Beiping–Suiyuan Railroad into Gansu and Ningxia.

Further to the south, according to the MAC, the Zhongtiao Mountains in southern Shanxi as well as the Chinese Communist area in hilly northern Shaanxi would prove difficult for the Japanese to seize. But the Japanese, according to the MAC, would try to break through the Tongguan Pass to occupy the fertile plains of central Shaanxi and advance towards Xi'an. In central and south China, Japan might attempt to secure the Canton–Hankou Railroad from Canton to Wuhan, and conquer Hunan with its productive agricultural areas.

In response to these threat perceptions, in the north-west the Nationalists created the 8th War Zone under General Zhu Shaoliang. He commanded ten divisions which invested Gansu with its large airbase used by the Soviets at Lanzhou and Ningxia 'to secure international lines of communication' with the Soviet Union.[141] In addition, the 8th War Zone deployed forces in western Suiyuan and along the north bend of the Yellow River. The 10th War Zone under Jiang Dingwen secured the Tongguan Pass with ten divisions to prevent the Japanese from breaking into the south Shaanxi plains. Yan Xishan's 2nd War Zone was to secure the Zhongtiao Mountains, create strong points to interdict Shanxi railroads, and secure the eastern shore of the Yellow River. The importance attached to the north-west is clear from the fact that in February 1939, plans were drawn up for actions in all war zones to 'transfer troops and create a military base in north China'.[142]

As to China north of the Yangtze River, the 'Guide Plan for the Second Period of the War of Resistance' described the new policy as follows:

> The National Army will use part of its troops to strengthen our forces in areas occupied by the Japanese in order to develop a broad guerrilla war to pin down and exhaust the enemy. Its main forces will be allocated to the border regions of Zhejiang–Jiangxi, Hunan–Jiangxi, west Hunan, west Henan, and west Hebei as well as the Beiping–Hankou and Long–Hai Railroads to actively maintain the present situation.[143]

The 1st War Zone under Wei Lihuang controlled parts of Henan and Anhui and commanded thirteen divisions. The Guide Plan defined its tasks as impeding Japan's use of the Long–Hai Railroad and safeguarding the Nanyang basin in south-west Henan and the Loyang plains in the north. The 3rd War Zone, commanded by Gu Zhutong, included southern Jiangsu, southern Anhui, as well as Zhejiang and Fujian. Twenty-two divisions were deployed in this war zone, which concentrated its activities on interdicting Japanese traffic on the Yangtze. Li Zongren's 5th War Zone with thirty-five divisions included west Anhui, north Hubei, and south Henan. Li was to safeguard the Dabie Mountains and conduct guerrilla raids into eastern Hubei, south Henan, and north Anhui. Xue Yue was in charge of the 9th War Zone in north-west Jiangxi, Hubei south of the Yangtze, and Hunan. He had fifty-two divisions under his command. Xue's tasks were to harass Japanese traffic along the Yangtze and create difficulties for the Japanese around Wuhan, while it also was to establish a base in the Jiugongshan Mountains on the Hubei–Jiangxi border near the Yangtze River. In addition, two guerrilla zones were designated. Yu Xuezhong commanded guerrilla operations involving seven divisions in the south Shandong–north Jiangsu region. Lu Zhonglin's guerrilla zone with six divisions was located in the Hebei–Chahar border area.[144]

The south was relatively lightly defended, for the reasons explained. Zhang Fakui headed the 4th War Zone of Guangdong and Guangxi. He commanded nineteen divisions. The heaviest concentration of forces was in the East River Area, but others were deployed along the North and West Rivers. Interdicting the Canton–Hankou Railroad and harassing the Japanese near Canton were its major tasks.[145]

For the Nationalists, an important objective in this phase was to increase their forces in the north-west and to transfer troops to north China for guerrilla warfare. A February war plan outlined these objectives and made clear that the operations of the 5th War Zone, including guerrilla warfare along the Beiping–Hankou Railroad, and of the 9th War Zone along the Yangtze River must be seen in this context.[146] Similarly, in a telegram of June setting out operational plans for the summer, Chiang Kaishek stated that their aim was 'to strengthen forces in Shanxi and Suiyuan and increase the quality of our forces in Hebei, Chahar, Shandong, and Jiangsu'.[147] He explained that 'the consolidation of Shanxi is necessary to defend Xi'an. If we loose Shanxi, the area to the east of Xi'an cannot be defended, and if Xi'an is surrendered, the north-west will be in danger'.[148] That would mean the loss of lines of communication to the Soviet Union as well as the plains around Xi'an, which were economically important to the Nationalists.

The first of the two major battles of this period took place in Jiangxi. During their march to Wuhan, the Japanese had by-passed Nanchang, the capital of Jiangxi Province, as they had encountered strong resistance there. The city, on the western shore of Lake Poyang, dominated the fertile plains of north Jiangxi and was a base for the 9th War Zone under Xue Yue. Located along the south shore of the Yangtze River, the 9th War Zone was a major threat to the Japanese. The battle for Nanchang took place between April and May 1939. The Japanese quickly took the city. Although Lo Zhoying counter-attacked with ten divisions, he was driven back after briefly taking the airport and the train station.[149] This campaign in some ways still belonged to the first phase of the war and was important for the Japanese to secure the Yangtze up to Wuhan.

The second Japanese offensive aimed at countering the expansion of the 5th War Zone into north Hubei and its harassment of the Beiping–Hankou Railroad. The 5th War Zone, to the north of the Yangtze River, defended the Yangtze River from Shashi to Badong on the Sichuan border. It guarded the entrance into Sichuan and protected routes for the transfer of troops and supplies to the north. It made use of the Battle of Nanchang to transfer a substantial number of its forces to the west of the Beiping–Hankou Railroad and established strong bases in the Dahongshan and Tongbai Mountains in north Hubei. From these, it threatened the rivers, railroads, and highways to the north-west of Wuhan. It began to conduct guerrilla operations south of the Wushengguan Pass along the Beiping–Hankou Railroad. Fifth War Zone forces launched an offensive towards Suixian, while Tang Enbo's forces, still part of the 5th War Zone battle order, moved from north Hunan into north Hubei to attack Zaoyang, a key strategic city. On 1 May, the Japanese began an offensive towards Suixian and Zaoyang. They took both cities and held them against counter-offensives.[150] Chiang Kaishek again was infuriated by the failure of these counter-offensives.[151] Nonetheless, the Japanese made no further gains and they were unable to eliminate the 5th War Zone bases in north Hubei. Nationalist connections with its war zones in north China remained intact.

The two Japanese offensives, which clearly had limited objectives, took place at the same time that the Kwantung Army from April had become involved in a border war with the Soviet Union. These conflicts culminated in the Battle of Nomonhan at the Manchurian–Mongolian–Chinese border. The Japanese attacked first with an infantry division, but encountering stiff resistance, in July the Japanese assembled 475 aircraft, including Mitsubishi A5Ms and Nakajima Ki-27s. The Soviets's 1st Army Group commanded by General Georgii Zhukov had poured troops into the area and had 580 aircraft available, including 125 SB-2s, 25 TB-3s, and 150 I-16s. In August, the Japanese and Soviets were engaged in the biggest air confrontation since the First World War.[152] When the Japanese brought in tanks and infantry forces, on 23 August, General Zhukov struck back and crushed the Japanese 23rd Division in one week. The Kwantung Army then began to prepare for a major offensive against the Soviet Union. Had this taken place and the Soviets been drawn for a longer period into war with Japan, the advantages to China would have been great and the Second World War might have followed a very different course as then the Soviets might well have ended up fighting a war on two fronts.

It did not, in part, as the result of the outbreak of war in Europe and the conclusion of the Nazi–Soviet Pact. To invade Poland, Hitler sought a non-aggression pact with the Soviet Union. He feared that the invasion of Poland might lead to war with France and Britain and therefore did not want a conflict with the Soviets as well. Stalin was amenable to Hitler's overtures, in part because he was happy to share in the spoils of the destruction of Poland but also because he wanted to avoid simultaneous conflicts with the Germans at a time when he faced an escalating border war in Asia. During negotiations in Moscow, the Germans promised the Soviets to restrain the Japanese.

In early September 1939, bewildered by the German decision to conclude a non-aggression pact with the Soviet Union, deeply disappointed with the performance of the Kwantung Army, and facing the possibility that the Soviets might decide to strike into Manchuria now that they no longer had to worry about their western front, the Japanese government and Imperial General Staff agreed to negotiate a cease-fire and ordered the Kwantung Army to desist from any further operations against the Soviets. From then on, the Kwantung Army, which only weeks before had secured agreement to its requests for considerable reinforcements from China, would more or less sit out the war. The Japanese could concentrate on bringing to a close the fighting in China.[153]

The second period

The Nationalists were the great losers: what they needed was continuous and serious fighting between the Soviets and the Japanese. This ceased to be a possibility. In June 1939, the Soviets had still granted the Nationalists a new credit line of 200 million US dollars. Following Nomonhan, Soviet supplies to the Nationalists were sharply reduced. One consequence was a reduction in air power. In 1939, the Nationalists had 215 aeroplanes available to defend against about 600 Japanese aeroplanes. A year later, the Nationalists only had 65 aeroplanes.[154] In 1941, the Nationalists did receive a further 100 bombers and 148 fighters from the Soviets, but these were of inferior quality.[155] Supplies of other material, including tanks and artillery, were also reduced. Politically, the Soviet withdrawal meant that a restraint on conflict between the Nationalists and the Communists was removed. What Chinese historians refer to as the first high tide in friction between the two occurred in the fall of 1939.

The beginning of the Second World War in Europe and the Nomonhan Ceasefire Agreement affected the Nationalists in other ways as well. As a Chinese operational plan put it, 'the enemy will use the inability of the European Powers to pay attention to the East to launch a rapid offensive on Changsha to impress the world and enhance the prestige of the criminal traitor Wang Jingwei'.[156] Following the embarrassing defeat at Nomonhan, Japan needed to do something dramatic to restore morale. A 9th War Zone war plan of 1 September 1939 stated that the 'Nazi–Soviet Agreement has created great unease amongst Japanese officials and the public. In order to cover up their defeat and invigorate popular morale, the Japanese militarist will again begin an offensive against China'.[157]

An offensive against Changsha now became a logical operation for the Japanese, a Chinese operational plan explained, because the Canton–Hankou Railroad made it possible for them to transfer from Wuhan significant numbers of troops into northern Hunan.[158] The rolling hills of the area provided terrain suitable to Japan's mobile forces. Furthermore, the occupation of Changsha would make it possible for the Japanese to undertake follow-up offensives on Yichang and Shashi, the key cities to the west of Wuhan on the Yangtze River blocking Japan's entrance into Sichuan. The capture of these cities would allow Japan to secure the entire Yangtze up to the Sichuan border and sever connections between Sichuan and Nationalist War Zones in the rest of China.[159] Hunan furthermore was important to the Nationalists for its agricultural productivity as well as its use as a recruitment ground.[160] To take Hunan would be a major step forward in the Japanese strategy of rendering Chiang Kaishek an insignificance and giving impetus to Wang Jingwei's peace movement.

Before the 1939 Battle of Changsha, the Japanese placed their forces in China south of the Great Wall under the unified command of the Headquarters of the China Expeditionary Command in Nanjing. In September, the Japanese concentrated six divisions with about 100,000 troops. Four were sent by rail and boat to Yueyang in north Hunan on the Yangtze River, in preparation for an attack on Changsha from the north. From recently captured Nanchang two divisions moved west, one following the valley of the Xiushui River through two mountain ranges in north-west Jiangxi and one through the plains south of these mountains.[161] From there they could approach Changsha from the east while also attacking Chinese troop concentrations in the mountain ranges of north-west Jiangxi.

The Battle of Changsha (Map 6.3) began on 13 September, lasted for a month, and ended with a comprehensive Japanese defeat. Chinese tactics proved effective. In April 1938, Chiang had sent a telegram to Xue Yue, the Commander of the 9th War Zone, stating that if the Japanese attempted to attack Changsha, the best strategy would be to avoid a frontal confrontation but instead allow the Japanese 'to enter Changsha

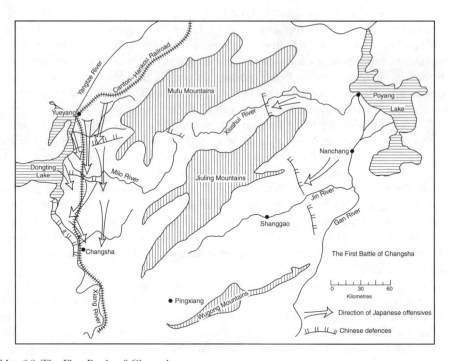

Map 6.3 The First Battle of Changsha.

and then counter-attack with a mighty assault before they have consolidated their positions'.[162] Before the Battle, Xue Yue created three lines of defences north of Changsha and deployed forces to block the approaches to Changsha from the east. He furthermore divided his forces into what he called a field army, a garrison force, an assault force, and a reserve. The garrison force was deployed in the three defensive lines. Its task was to resist while gradually falling back, drawing the Japanese into areas where ambushes had been prepared. The field force conducted guerrilla operations in the Japanese rear 'to destroy their transport and communication lines, attack their logistical facilities, and cut off their supply lines'.[163] The assault forces attacked the Japanese flanks and also slipped into the battlefield in civilian clothes to 'set ambushes, kill commanding officers at various levels, destroy communications, and create chaos'.[164] Reserve forces defended strategic areas and reinforced the assault forces during counter-offensives. The Chinese also cleared the countryside to deny supplies to the Japanese, removed populations to the hills, and mobilised locals for transport, scouting, sabotage, and messaging services.[165]

Key to the victory had been the idea 'to slow a Japanese advance down for at least a week so that they exhaust their rations and ammunition'.[166] Once they had moved beyond railheads, ports, and staging points, the Japanese found it difficult to sustain their infantry forces for very long in the field. If they failed to reach their objectives and secure their supply lines within a week, Japanese offensives quickly petered out. This would become a pattern repeated regularly through the rest of the War of Resistance. This may well have been one reason why in 1942 Chiang Kaishek did not want to mount a counter-offensive against Rangoon, easily supplied by sea, but wanted to take the Japanese on at Mandalay.

The Winter Offensive

In late November 1939, the Nationalists began a nation-wide offensive involving all war zones and as many as eighty divisions. Coming after the Battles of Nomonhan and Changsha, the completion of two cycles in the re-training programme of the National Army, and a reduction in the establishment of Japanese troops in China, according to Ch'i Hsi-sheng, the Nationalists attached considerable hope to the operation.[167]

When planning began for the Winter Offensive (Map 6.4) in October, it certainly was presented as a major operation. The 2nd, 3rd, and 5th War Zones all were to undertake major offensives, while the 1st, 4th, 8th, and 9th were to engage in subsidiary actions. In the 2nd War Zone in Shanxi, the objective was to cut railroads and re-occupy south Shanxi. In the 3rd War Zone, eleven divisions were to advance between Japanese strong points and occupy the shores of the Yangtze River at various points to interdict river traffic and so isolate Japanese forces in Wuhan. The 5th War Zone was to cut the southern section of the Beiping–Hankou Railroad and drive the Japanese from north Hubei. Troops of the 1st War Zone were to attack Kaifeng to tie down Japanese forces in Henan. The 4th War Zone was to cut the southern section of the Canton–Hankou Railroad while also moving into Guangxi to assist with the defence of Nanning. The 8th War Zone was to attack Guisui and so assist the 2nd War Zone. The 9th War Zone was to focus its offensive on the northern section of the Canton–Hankou Railroad and

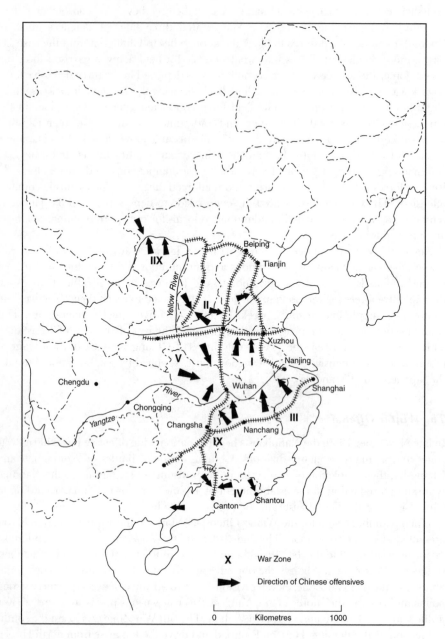

Map 6.4 The Winter Offensive.

assault Wuhan itself. While these offensives were under way, the guerrilla areas in the Shandong–Jiangsu and Hebei–Chahar border areas were to expand their areas.[168]

The Winter Offensive, nonetheless, took place when the international and domestic situations were unfavourable. In September, Chiang stated to US diplomats that following the German–Soviet Non-Aggression Treaty he feared that Britain might seek to revive the Anglo-Japanese Alliance.[169] That idea was certainly being mooted. The British Ambassador in Japan responded to a proposal by Sir A. Clark Kerr for an increase in military aid to China by arguing that this could only fuel Japanese militarism. Instead, he argued, 'in the course of the struggle in which we are now engaged in Europe we already have to deal with the USSR as a covert enemy and may soon have to fight her in the open. One of our natural allies in such circumstances would be Japan, who can ill afford to see the Soviets emerge enlightened and strengthened from the present struggle …. In certain circumstances it might suit Japan's book to make a peace with China such as Chiang Kaishek could accept in order to join a strong combination of Powers bent on settling accounts with the USSR'.[170] Chiang remarked to US diplomats that China now could only depend 'on the friendship and justice' of the USA.[171]

If the international context was not favourable for a major offensive, neither was the domestic situation. Wang Jingwei's peace movement gained new force. In December 1939, Wang Jingwei and the Japanese signed the 'Guidelines for the Re-adjustment of Relations between China and Japan' and a series of other documents. In January, Wang met others favouring an accommodation with Japan at Qingdao. This meeting resolved to establish a rival National Government in Nanjing, which would continue the Nationalists' political institutions, nomenclature, symbols, and laws. To attract support, Wang promised to abolish one-party rule. The Wang Jingwei government also had its own National Army. Japan's conditions for agreeing to Wang's proposals was that it would have the right to send military instructors and advisors to Wang Jingwei's National Army and conduct military operations against the Communists. Japan and China would also co-operate in the exploitation of Chinese economic resources and China would pay an indemnity to Japan.[172] In March 1940, Wang's National Government was formally inaugurated.

An accommodation between Yan Xishan and the Japanese undermined the Winter Offensive even before it had begun. In November 1939, Yan proposed to the Japanese that in return for their withdrawal from a number of areas in Shanxi and Japanese supply of arms and ammunition, he would cease resistance and help the Japanese in campaigns against the Chinese communists. In December, Yan began an offensive against the Communists' Eighth Route Army.[173]

Nationalist relations with the Communists also were strained in the latter half of 1939. The Communists had fanned out over north China during the first phase of the War of Resistance and had established base areas in the Shanxi–Suiyuan, Shanxi–Chahar–Hebei, and the Shanxi–Hebei–Henan Border Regions as well as in Shandong. By late 1939, the Communists feared that Nationalists favouring an accommodation with Chongqing had gained the upper hand because 'the British and French are instigating an accommodation between Japan and China' and because 'the military power and the international position of the Soviet Union have greatly advanced'.[174] The Communists redoubled their efforts to strengthen their armies, including by 'recruiting several hundred thousand troops in Shandong and central China'.[175] Co-operation between the Nationalist and Communists could not be expected.

Japan's unexpected invasion of Guangxi further weakened the prospects of the Winter Offensive. On 15 November a Japanese invasion force landed at Qinzhou Bay on the south coast of Guangxi Province. Nanning fell on 23 November and by early January the Japanese had built up a force of 100,000 troops in the province. This invasion came as a surprise to the Nationalists. At the Liuzhou Military Conference of February 1940, Chiang Kaishek apologised for having failed to anticipate it.[176] It encountered little resistance because two divisions had been moved from Guangxi to the West River area in Guangdong in advance of the Winter Offensive.[177] Many Guangxi troops had already been deployed to the 5th War Zone and hence the Qinzhou coast was left virtually defenceless. Bai Chongxi, in charge of the Guilin Headquarters of the MAC and hence responsible for the defence of Guangxi, was unable to bring the Japanese advance to a halt. Nineteen divisions were transferred to Guangxi, including the 200th Division of Du Lüming that would be lost at Toungoo. One hundred planes and a number of tanks were also deployed in Guangxi against the Japanese. The fighting in Guangxi was tough and would go on for two months, during which the 5th Army lost 16,000 troops and control of the Kunlun and Gaofeng Passes switched hands twice. While the Chinese were able to prevent any further Japanese inroads, the consequence for the Winter Offensive was that an important part of Chinese forces, including those with the best offensive capabilities, were tied down in Guangxi.

The circumstances outlined above made it unlikely that the Winter Offensive could have succeeded in driving the Japanese out of China. Chiang Kaishek convened the Second Nanyue Military Conference in late October to rally morale in advance of the Winter Offensive. His address indicates that the Offensive was less ambitious than the war plan suggested. On 29 October, Chiang first sought to make clear that the international situation was not as unfavourable as the conclusion of the Nazi–Soviet pact might suggest. He admitted that 'the accommodation between the Soviet Union and Germany goes against what we had anticipated at the beginning of the war and prevents the realisation of an alliance between the Soviet Union, France, and Britain'.[178] But, according to Chiang, 'even though since the outbreak of war we always believed that the War of Resistance had to be linked with the inevitable World War as the problem between Japan and China is one link in a chain of global problems', the recent changes in the global context should not cause defeatism. Chiang even insisted that 'the Soviet attitude remains as before. There has been no change. In this beginning phase of the war in Europe, they simply do not want to join any side and just want to remain neutral'.[179] Chiang further stated that not every development on the international front had gone against China. The US Ambassador in Japan had spoken out against Japanese aggression while Cordell Hull had stated that US–Japanese relations would break down if Japan did not change its policies. The USA had also reinforced its bases on the Philippines and Hawaii to safeguard safe navigation in the Pacific.[180]

Chiang sought to inspire his audience by arguing that Japan's forces in China had weakened. Its experienced units had been replaced with lesser quality ones and during the attack on Changsha, according to Chiang, 'officers and troops became afraid because of our heroic resistance'. They had not followed orders 'to strike straight to Changsha even though they realised that we had at most two divisions there. Their relief forces too did not obey orders to advance'.[181] Chiang argued that the 'enemy's war weariness and fear means that we must choose for offensives and advance with determination'. If China just sat still, according to Chiang, 'the enemy will advance'.[182]

However, Chiang also sought to re-assure his audience that he would not ask for any 'excessively dangerous operations: our strategy has always been one of prudence.

During the Battle of Changsha, at first we did not go on the offensive but followed a defensive strategy. We advanced only when the opportunity arose'.[183] He explicitly stated that he only wanted small offensives: 'Although our arms and equipment are still such that we cannot engage in a thorough large-scale counter-offensive', he argued, 'as in the case of Changsha, we must examine methods to avoid their strong points while attacking weak points and make use of opportunities as well as the enemy's mistakes to attack them in various places'.[184]

Given the international and domestic situation and Chiang's address, it seems probable that the Winter Offensive was mostly an exercise at keeping the war alive. If the Nationalists adopted a wholly passive stance, the Great Powers would have found it all the more easy to sell a policy of acquiescing in a Wang Jingwei Government and an East Asia dominated by Japan. To counter Wang Jingwei's peace movement, prevent others from following Yan Xishan's example, and restrict the Communists, domestically too the Nationalists had to demonstrate that they were determined to continue the fight. A failure to do so would have left it isolated as regional military forces could have thrown in their lot with the Wang Jingwei Government or accepted local accommodations with the Japanese. One reason to send Du Lüming's forces into Guangxi may well have been to prevent such developments there. A more immediate military concern was to forestall a renewed Japanese offensive at Yichang or Changsha.[185] Nation-wide offensive operations, even of a limited scale, would make it difficult for the Japanese to concentrate their forces for a new attempt to take Changsha and cut communications between Sichuan and the war zones elsewhere.

Even if the Winter Offensive was probably not undertaken in the belief that it could be successful in defeating Japan in China, it nonetheless was intended as a serious campaign and it did give the Japanese a real scare in some places. The Japanese history of the war commented that one Army Corps 'from 12 December was attacked from all sides on a scale never seen before'. It praised the Chinese offensive spirit and noted that the Chinese use of night-fighting tactics to get close to Japanese strong points and attack with hand grenades had been effective.[186] The use of that tactic, however, illustrated also the fact that the Nationalists simply did not have the air force or the artillery to seriously threaten the Japanese.

Even if the objectives of the offensive were limited, it is nonetheless true, as Ch'i argued, that Chinese forces performed very badly.[187] Most operations petered out within days and as at Shanghai, the co-ordination between divisions was virtually non-existent. Chiang Kaishek was uncommonly irate about the forces of the 3rd War Zone. Fourteen of its divisions and artillery units had been assigned to cut the Yangtze River. However, according to Chiang, 'although they were completely unaffected by the fighting in south Guangxi, after three days they stopped the offensive'.[188] Chiang lambasted commanders for retreating once the Japanese came close and preferring to offer their resignations rather than leading their troops into battle. He also stated that widespread smuggling and gambling affected combat morale in many areas.[189] Clearly, the Winter Offensive had not gone to plan.

After the Winter Offensive

After the Winter Offensive, in the remainder of 1940, the Nationalists would not again launch a major operation against the Japanese. This was the result in part of a further deterioration in the international situation. In July 1940, Britain agreed to stop the supply of arms, ammunition, petrol, trucks, and railroad building materials through Burma and Hong Kong.[190] In the same month, the French Vichy Government permitted the stationing in Hanoi of a Japanese military mission. Several bridges of the Hanoi–Yunnan Railroad were destroyed to prevent military supplies reaching China from Vietnam. No new military supplies necessary for an offensive could reach the Nationalists.[191]

Domestically, the second half of the year was dominated by further conflict between the Communists and the Nationalists. During the Winter Offensive, the Communists attacked Yan Xishan's forces in Shanxi and those of Shi Yousan in south Hebei and on the Shandong–Hebei border.[192] By the summer of 1940, the Communist Eighth Route Army operated across north China, the New Fourth Army had penetrated south of the Yangtze River, and the two armies were about to link up.[193]

In July, Chiang appointed He Yingqing and Bai Chongxi to conduct negotiations with Zhou Enlai and Ye Jianying, the Communist representatives in Chongqing, to limit the base areas that the Communists had build up in the previous years and curtail Communist troop strength. The Nationalists' proposal was to rename the Shaan-Gan-Ning Base Area, more commonly known as Yan'an, as the North Shaanxi Special Administrative Zone and to subordinate it to the Shaanxi Provincial Government. The Communist base areas in north China were to be incorporated in the order of battle of the 2nd War Zone, of which Yan Xishan would continue to be the Commander-in-Chief, while Zhu De, the highest ranking Communist military commander, would be appointed Vice Commander-in-Chief. Communist forces were to be restricted to an establishment of nine divisions and all forces that had moved south of the Yellow and Yangtze rivers were to be moved to areas north of the Yellow River in several stages.[194]

Rumours about and also actual contact between the Japanese and the Nationalists in Chongqing were perhaps useful to the Nationalists to put pressure on the Communists but also made agreement more difficult. John Leighton Stuart, the American President of Yenching University, was the conduit for what were probably the most serious negotiations between the Japanese and the Nationalists. He had earlier relayed messages between Japan and Chiang. Stuart was in close touch with the Tada Shun, the Chief-of-Staff of Japan's North China Area Army, who believed that the only way to bring an end to the war in China was through a deal with Chiang Kaishek. In March, Tada Shun instructed Stuart to inform Chiang that if Chiang would stop fighting Japan and end his collaboration with the Communists, Japan would compel Wang Jingwei to negotiate with him. During his conversations with Chiang, Stuart claimed to have the support of the most influential figures in Japan and suggested that Japan was willing to recognise Chiang's National Government.[195]

In making this claim, he was overplaying his card. If Japan's North China Area Army might be willing to go as far as ditching Wang Jingwei in favour of Chiang Kaishek, the Government in Tokyo was not. Tokyo pointedly recognised Wang's government at the same time that Stuart was holding his discussions with Chiang.[196] Neither was Chiang Kaishek willing to contemplate the Japanese offer. According to Stuart, Chiang insisted that Wang Jingwei be excluded from peace negotiations, that the USA act as mediator, which the USA was not willing to do, and that Japan withdraw from all areas south of the Great Wall.[197]

Insecurity all around contributed to the worst clash between the Communists and the Nationalists of the war. The Winter Offensive, the establishment of the Wang Jingwei Government, and Japan's campaign, discussed below, to take Shashi and Yichang to isolate the Nationalists in Sichuan made it clear that the Nationalist position was fragile, while negotiations between them and the Japanese suggested the possibility that the Nationalists would yet decide to accept defeat. As Ch'en Yung-fa has described lucidly, negotiations went on through the fall of 1940. In January 1941, after the New Fourth Army refused to accept an ultimatum to move their forces north of the Yangtze River and also did not obey orders from Yan'an to cross the Yangtze, perhaps because it was simply out of control, Nationalist units destroyed one of its divisions.[198] The Nationalists were able to prevent the spread of the Communists south of the Yangtze,[199] but Communist strength was not affected significantly and the Communists used the opportunity to suggest that the Nationalists preferred fighting them to offering resistance to the Japanese.

Besides this conflict with the Communists, the Nationalists in 1940 further faced major Japanese offensive. The Zaoyang–Yichang campaign went through two phases.[200] The first, beginning on 1 May, consisted of a Japanese drive towards Suixian, Zaoyang, and Xiangyang. One Japanese line of advance followed the valley between the Tongbaishan and Dahongshan mountains, which were important strongholds of the 5th War Zone. Another Japanese column advanced along the eastern side of the Han River. The hope was to draw the main forces of the 5th War Zone into a battle at Zaoyang in a pincer operation to encircle and destroy them. The second phase began in late May and consisted of an offensive from north Hubei, rather than along the Yangtze River where Tang Enbo's forces were stationed, towards Yichang itself. Nationalist tactics were based on the avoidance of positional warfare and, as during the first Battle of Changsha, to let the Japanese move beyond their supply bases, avoid defeat for a week, and then strike back. Chiang Kaishek stated to Tang Enbo before the battle, 'if the Japanese attack, they cannot sustain an offensive for longer than a week before they have to retreat'.[201] He ordered him to place ambushes at regular 30–50-kilometre intervals along the anticipated lines of Japanese retreat and attack their flanks and rears.[202] However, the Japanese moved around Tang's forces.

The Japanese were determined in making a success of this offensive, which took place at the same time that the Germans overran the Netherlands, Belgium, and France. They transferred a division from the Kwantung Army for the purpose. The fighting, which continued for two months, was intense and may have cost the Japanese 30,000 or 40,000 deaths.[203] When it was over, the Japanese had taken the fertile north Hubei plains and captured Yichang, while the forces of Li Zongren's 5th War Zone had to retreat. The Japanese capture of Yichang was an extremely serious blow to the Nationalist position. The Nationalists launched determined counter-attacks, expending one-fourth of their remaining ammunition,[204] but the Japanese were equally committed to take this city, through which ran the most important transport lines from the Sichuan base to fronts elsewhere in China. The Japanese also hoped to use Yichang as an airbase to conduct strategic bombing campaigns.[205]

The Japanese accompanied this offensive with a strategic bombing campaign against the Nationalist rear. They increased the number of aeroplanes in China to 800 just when the Soviet airforce was withdrawn.[206] If previously the Japanese airforce had been used tactically in support of infantry operations, it now began a strategic bombing campaign against the Chinese rear. The introduction of the famous Zero fighter with its longer range made this possible. The first fifteen were deployed in China in the summer of 1940 and the aeroplane demonstrated its value when in August 1940 it shot down all Chinese aeroplanes defending Chongqing, thus making it possible for Japanese bombers to attack unopposed. During the long summer of 1940, cities such as Chongqing, Chengdu, Xi'an, Changsha, and Lanzhou were subjected to virtually continuous Japanese air assault. Between May and September, the Japanese airforce flew nearly 5,000 sorties and dropped more than 27,000 bombs.[207]

The year 1940 was calamitous for the Nationalists. It began badly with the Winter Offensive. The Japanese invasion of Guangxi brought even the southernmost regions of China into the war. The Zaoyang–Yichang campaign and Japan's strategic bombing offensive in support of the newly inaugurated Wang Jingwei Government were disastrous for the Nationalist strategic position. During the second half of the year, conflict with the Communists led to the New Fourth Army Incident. The Nationalists were on their knees.

Towards the Southern Advance

In 1941, the Nationalist position improved. The Japanese conducted three offensives aimed at destroying the most important three war zones in China that now had been virtually cut off from Chongqing. Only one of these offensives ended in a Japanese victory. The Japanese conducted them without adequate logistical support and already with reduced numbers and support by specialised units. The Nationalists were helped by the delivery of a new batch of Soviet aeroplanes while in September 1941 the Japanese redeployed many air units to Indo-China and elsewhere as the likelihood of war with the USA and Britain increased.[208]

For the Battle of Southern Henan, lasting from 25 January until 10 February, the Japanese mobilised 150,000 troops, 300 tanks, and 100 aeroplanes. Besides securing the southern section of the Beiping–Hankou Railroad, the Japanese sought to weaken the 5th War Zone, which continued to be a threat after the Zaoyang–Yichang Campaign. On 25 January, the Japanese began the operation. Its central column advanced north along the Beiping–Hankou Railroad, while its left and right flanks advanced simultaneously on either side of the railroad.[209] As before, Nationalist strategy was to avoid a decisive confrontation in the first phase of the operation, cut off the Japanese rear, and wait until the Japanese had run out of supplies. This strategy again proved successful, and during this campaign, the Japanese suffered more casualties than the Chinese. Instead of Chinese forces becoming encircled, the Japanese suffered this fate.[210] By 10 February, the Battle ended with the Japanese, minus their casualties, back at their jumping off points.

The Battle of Shanggao in Jiangxi lasted from mid-March to early April. This Japanese offensive came in response to the programme of re-training and re-arming of the 9th War Zone. Lo Zhoying's Group Army in this war zone remained a major threat to Japanese positions in Hunan and Jiangxi as well as the Yangtze River. Shanggao was a city of considerable strategic significance. For the 9th War Zone forces in the Wugongshan and Jiulingshan mountains, it was a forward protection point. Furthermore, it was located on the old land route from Nanchang to Changsha, and was therefore important for the Japanese to take if they wanted to attack Changsha from the west. The Japanese in this case too advanced along three different routes for a converging attack on Shanggao. The Nationalists had built three lines of defences. At first they concentrated on harassing the Japanese flanks. They succeeded in preventing the Japanese columns from linking up near Shanggao, and they then cut the rear of the Japanese central column and finally encircled the Japanese division and the independent brigade that made up its main force. The Japanese were compelled to dispatch a relief force from Wuhan, but nonetheless lost nearly half the forces they had committed. The Battle of Shanggao was a Chinese victory that is much less well known than the Battle of Taierzhuang but which was at least as impressive, especially given the disasters that had befallen the Nationalists in 1940.[211]

This victory was soon overshadowed by the defeat of the 1st War Zone under Wei Lihuang in the Zhongtiao mountains of Southern Shanxi. From this area, the Nationalists threatened Japanese flanks in north China and kept pressure on Yan Xishan. The Zhongtiao Mountains protected routes into Shaanxi Province and to Xi'an itself. It was also important for the Nationalists to hamper communications between Yan'an and Communist bases elsewhere. In this campaign, the Japanese were able to achieve their objectives in one week and to firm up supply lines. This made it possible for the Japanese to cut through Nationalist positions, isolate various Chinese forces, and then destroy them. The Nationalists were forced to retreat from the Zhongtiao Mountains.

The final Japanese operation of 1941, lasting from 7 September to 2 October, was a second attempt to conquer Changsha. Japan, constrained by the need to increase its force strength in Vietnam and Manchuria, mobilised 120,000 troops, which were supported by 20 naval ships, 200 motorboats, and 100 planes.[212] As with the first battle of Changsha, these forces were concentrated near Yueyang. They descended south in separate columns, one of which used the Dongting Lake and the Xiang River, a second the Canton–Hankou Railroad, and the third three roads to the east. Rather than seeking to encircle Changsha, the Japanese attempted to take the city by a quick offensive, including by deploying airborne assault forces. Chinese tactics relied on a gradual withdrawal at the front, attacks in the rear, and in this case large-scale attacks on the eastern flank of the Japanese. Once the Japanese reached the outskirts of Changsha, the Chinese were able to cut their supply lines and counter-attacked. As at Shanggao, the Japanese lost nearly half of their forces without making substantial gains.[213]

Despite desperate attempts, the Nationalists, however, were not able to break the Japanese hold on Yichang. Seeking to make use of the Japanese attack on Changsha and the fact that Yichang was defended by only two incomplete divisions, Chen Cheng in September began a counter-offensive on Yichang. He succeeded in isolating one Japanese division outside the city and surrounded the city itself. Chinese forces launched several offensives. They did manage to enter the city, and with their rice supplies nearly exhausted, the Japanese commanders had begun to burn documents and made preparations to commit suicide. However, a Japanese column rushed back from north Hunan to Yichang and was able to break the Nationalist siege by the end of September.[214]

Once in 1941 the geo-political situation began to reach its final shape, both Britain and the USA initiated covert programmes to provide military aid to China. The British initiative to train and arm a guerrilla force in China fitted this purpose.[215] In August 1941, Chiang Kaishek approved a proposal by Ambassador Clark Kerr and Valentine Killery, the head of the Oriental Mission of the Special Operations Executive, which would see the British supply arms and ammunition through Burma as well as train and lead 30,000 Chinese guerrilla troops. Although the China Commando Group was a Special Operations Executive (SOE) initiative, to avoid creating a *casus belli*, as instructors it recruited non-British European nationals from countries occupied by Germany. Tens of tons of military aid was delivered and training camps were set up, but in April 1942 Chiang Kaishek aborted the China Commando Group. British involvement with regional commanders such as Long Yun in Yunnan, Fu Zuoyi in Suiyuan, and Chan Chak near Hong Kong; disputes about the control over British military aid delivered to China and command over operations; and perhaps a Nationalist desire to avoid provoking Japanese reprisals in China just when the Burma war was reaching its climax led to the collapse of the scheme. It would have a long-term consequence in that it set a precedent for the Sino-American Co-operative Organisation (SACO), which was similar except that it was under the firm control of Dai Li, the head of China's Military Intelligence Service, and replaced the British with American navy personnel.[216]

Claire Chennault's American Volunteer Group served a similar purpose as the China Commando Group.[217] Chennault, who was retired from the US air force as the result of a hearing problem, had in 1937 accepted an invitation from Madame Chiang Kaishek, who was a member of the board overseeing China's air force, to become an air defence advisor to the Nationalists. He advocated what at the time were revolutionary air tactics involving independent fighter operations and fighter escorts for bombers. He was impressed with the activities of Soviet fliers in the first phase of the war. After the US began to make financial aid available in 1940, Chennault through Song Ziwen proposed an airforce with 500 aeroplanes in China with the task of aiding China's resistance and carrying out long-range bombing mission to Japan.

During discussions in Washington, the plan was actively supported by Morgenthau and Lauchlin Curry, but Marshall feared that it would provoke Japan and objected to the dispatch of bombers. Roosevelt approved his suggestion that only 100 fighters would be made available and that these would be the Curtiss P-40s, which had been intended for Britain but where experience had shown that they would not be able to hold their own in air combat and where they had been used only in low-flying reconnaissance missions. Pilots and the first shipment of planes arrived in Burma in September 1941. The White House did approve the dispatch of thirty-three Lockheed Hudsons and an equal number of DB-7 bombers, but the attack on Peal Harbor prevented delivery. Neither the British nor the US initiative led to significant military aid before Japan's Southern Advance.[218]

The German invasion of the Soviet Union in June 1941 was the most decisive development internationally in 1941. It put the Japanese before the question whether to join Germany in the war against the Soviet Union. Significant voices in Japan did favour such a course of action. One situation report for the Japanese High Command stated that it was likely that Germany would succeed quickly in forcing the Soviet Union to surrender, as US war planners also expected. The Minister of the Army maintained that Germany would prevail over both the Soviet Union and Britain in a matter of months. He advocated immediate action.[219] US support for China in 1941 was in part designed to provide indirect aid to the Soviet Union by threatening the Japanese elsewhere in the Pacific.[220]

However, the leaders of the Kwantung Army in Manchuria, who would have to conduct the campaign, opposed Japanese participation in the attack on the Soviet Union. They believed that 'it will take time to prepare for military action against the Soviet Union'. The General Staff agreed, stating that at least nine months would be needed to complete the preparations and that no action should be undertaken until the German offensive had forced the Soviets to reduce the number of forces facing Japan from 700,000 to 350,000.[221] The Japanese navy too favoured the Southern Advance; its role would have been limited in an attack on the Soviet Union

The issue was debated during an Imperial Conference on 2 July. It determined that Japan 'must hold firm to the policy of establishing the Greater East Asia Co-prosperity Sphere, regardless of what changes might take place in the world situation'.[222] The meeting therefore decided to give priority to the Southern Advance. Japan repeatedly declined German requests to join the war against the Soviet Union and instead deployed 125,000 troops in Vietnam, after an armed uprising against the Vichy Government.

The second phase of the War of Resistance was perhaps the most difficult of the entire war. In the first half of 1939, the Soviet Union remained a significant factor and provided substantial military aid, but after the Battle of Nomonhan, the Nationalists became isolated, a situation that did not change until the second half of 1941. When Britain and the USA then began programmes to assist the Nationalists military, neither the China Commando Group nor the American Volunteer Group provided significant support. Behind both projects was a strategy aimed at avoiding war with Japan and providing indirect support to the Soviet Union. The Japanese, in the meantime, were increasingly desperate to reduce their troop commitments in China. Promoting the Wang Jingwei National Government and conducting infantry offensives and strategic bombing campaigns against the Nationalists served this purpose. Japanese supply problems, making it difficult for them to sustain ground offensives deep into China, made it possible for the Nationalists to survive and even inflict significant casualties. Although the Nationalists were incapable of mounting significant counter-offensives, largely because they lacked the necessary airforce as well as heavy artillery, nonetheless, had they given up, the consequences would have been serious. As Churchill feared, the Japanese could then have joined the Soviets or begun the Southern Advance earlier, and perhaps they might have been able to do both. The importance of the second phase of the War of Resistance is therefore difficult to overestimate.

Conclusion

Even if I expect, and hope, that subsequent scholarship will make this chapter quickly obsolete, I nonetheless have presented this revisionist account to restore intent and rationality to the Nationalists, move beyond descriptions of Nationalist incompetence as a foil to justify Allied geo-strategic choices, and integrate the War of Resistance into the Second World War. Only in this way, I believe, can we better grasp that this was a war fought for the future of China and East Asia, with the Japanese, the Communists, the Nationalists, and others, such as Wang Jingwei, each seeking to make manifest their own aspirations for that future. During the first phase of the War of Resistance, the Nationalists articulated their vision clearly. In Wuhan, they wrote the texts, including the Organic Law, and established the institutions, such as the National Political Council, meant to express that vision, give it institutional reality, and rally the country.

In terms of the actual fighting, I have suggested that during the first phase of the war, the Nationalists followed a coherent strategy. Threatened first by a Japanese attempt to detach north China, then Japan's naval threat on their own base in the Lower Yangtze, and finally the Japanese decision to annihilate their armies, they drew the Japanese forces apart across north China by attacking Shanghai. They then concentrated forces in the 5th War Zone to prevent the Japanese from linking up and taking China north of the Yangtze River. They failed to hold Xuzhou, however. The Battle of Wuhan became an exercise in buying time to establish a base in the rear, construct war zones across China, transfer human and material resources to the rear, and make the Japanese pay a high price for their conquests.

During the second phase, Japan's aim was to consolidate the areas in its control, localise the war, and foster a rival government to the Nationalists in Chongqing. Fighting without significant international support, the Nationalists protected their war zones, on which they depended for recruits and food, maintain communications between Sichuan and the war zones at the front, keep the war going, and prevent the rival Wang Jingwei Government from becoming a viable alternative. The years 1940 and 1941 were very difficult, with Japan doing its best to reduce the Nationalists to insignificance and with both the Wang Jingwei Government and the Communists developing into serious threats.

The battles of the first and second phases of the war involved two unequal forces. The Japanese had by far the better fighting forces. But the Japanese found it difficult to impose a common strategy on their forces, their logistical capacity was limited so that they could not operate at a distance of their supply lines, army discipline could break down disastrously, and commanders at the front were wont to take precipitous action. The Japanese were decidedly not good at alliance warfare, an ability that was critical in the Second World War. Nor were the Japanese able to develop truly powerful local supporters in mainland China, which made it hard for them to consolidate their position in China and in fact left them, as we will see in Chapter 7, with a number of collaborators who were noted for their viciousness and who therefore undermined Japan's cause in China.

The fighting revealed serious weaknesses on the Chinese side. The Nationalists nonetheless survived, in part, because of Japanese strategic choices and political failures. Nationalist defensive strategies too were important. They avoided a decisive campaign, spread the war out over large areas, offered a multiplicity of targets, and withdrew into areas in which it was difficult for the Japanese to operate. During the second phase of the war, Nationalist tactics of withdrawing in advance of a Japanese penetration and countering by hitting the Japanese flanks and rears were frequently successful.

I have stressed Nationalist geo-political strategy because it was a consistently critical element of the Nationalist prosecution of the war. Like Britain, the Nationalists were well aware that alone they would not be able to defeat Japan and that they had to link the war in China with global conflicts. Although there is no evidence for this, the decision to accept war in 1937 may well have been influenced by the belief that with a new world war virtually inevitable, China should not again be left on the sidelines of a conflict that would at a post-war conference determine the shape of a new world order. The Nationalists' first sought to profit from Japanese conflicts with the Soviet Union and then with Britain and the USA. The Nationalists were, to a degree, successful, but also, as Chapter 1 has made clear, paid a huge price.

In conclusion, I have hoped to suggest that the Nationalists, despite a military that could fight as badly as any other, performed better than has been suggested. Especially during the second phase of the war, which ought to be studied far more than it has been, the Nationalists fought with tenacity but also within their own means against an enemy that sought its destruction by military, political, and economic means. Above all, I have hoped to suggest that the Nationalists fought to realise their vision of the future. Given the means available, the international context, and local conditions, that inevitably meant assuming defensive attitudes, avoiding unnecessary confrontations, and waiting for changes in the future. That did not mean that the Nationalists were not serious. The view that the China theatre was an embarrassing backwater in the glorious story of the Pacific War simply misses the point.

7   Wartime mobilisation

The previous chapter has emphasised the international context and the domestic political situation in analysing the first two phases of the War of Resistance. This chapter turns to an issue equally fundamental to Nationalist war-making: wartime mobilisation. I shall discuss military recruitment, the collection and distribution of grains, other agricultural products, and primary sources for industry, setting out Nationalist approaches to these tasks and analysing their effects on the Nationalists' military capacity, Chinese society, and the position of the Nationalist state.

Until 1941, I suggest, the Nationalists coped with the problems of wartime mobilisation reasonably well. Initial chaos in recruitment was overcome when the Nationalists abandoned their pre-war efforts to implement a national military service system. Instead, recruitment was located in areas that traditionally had produced most army recruits and mercenary recruitment was permitted but also subjected to a degree of central control. The Nationalists further followed agricultural policies that kept productivity at reasonable levels and shielded the rural population from the cost of war. These policies enabled the Nationalists to continue resistance to the Japanese invasion.

Afterwards, however, the Nationalists were hit by a broad economic, fiscal, and financial crisis as a result of developments on the battlefield, the tightening of the Japanese economic embargo, Japan's strategic bombing offensive, financial policies of the Japanese and Wang Jingwei's rival National Government, and China's isolation from world markets. The severe disruption of markets and the destruction of transport lines worsened the crisis, as did the collapse of fiscal structures and ballooning bureaucracies. In addition, Nationalist recruitment had exhausted the pool of men who could be easily recruited without damage to local economies.

In response, the National Government reduced recruitment, off-loaded forces it could not sustain, and encouraged armies to live off the land. It located the war out of the country so that others would take some of the strain, Chinese armies could be armed by foreigners, which no longer was possible in China itself, and the Nationalists would last the course until the end of the war in Europe. This background explains Nationalist strategy better than easy assumptions about a patriotic deficit, an obsession with Communism, or a backward cultural preference for the defence. The Nationalists also switched to taxation in kind of the land tax. This shielded public finance from the imploding financial and monetary systems. The National Government at the same time sought to discipline the bureaucracy, ration scarce goods, and provide social services to key constituencies such as officials, industrial workers, and educators.

The Nationalists could not prevent a radical decline in the combat effectiveness of most of their forces. Troops living off the land do not easily move to far-away fronts for offensive duties. Nationalist guerrilla forces became indistinguishable from bandit troops and became a liability. Many war zones became independent satrapies of limited allegiance to Chongqing. The Communists accumulated substantial armies, as did the Wang Jingwei government. In addition, taxation, which now hurt the population directly, and military recruitment, which relied increasingly on force, alienated the population, creating social resentment and distrust, with especially the *baojia* becoming a hated institution. The Ichigo Offensive was disastrous for the Nationalists because it led to the loss of areas on which the National Government depended for recruitment and food supplies.

This perspective is useful to develop a new understanding of the effects of the war on the National Government. In the 1930s, the National Government aimed to establish bureaucratic control over the means of violence, demilitarise local society, bureaucratise military recruitment, and eliminate the social and economic bases of warlordism. In preparing for wartime mobilisation, they attempted to develop strong bureaucratic structures with a monopoly on military recruitment to prevent a resurgence of warlordism. During the crisis of the War of Resistance, the demands imposed by wartime recruitment overwhelmed the Nationalists. Although during the first 3–4 years, they were able to continue the war by a return to traditional recruitment practices, in the end they were not able to avoid the risks inherent in arming the population in a period of extreme crisis. Because we yet lack much understanding of how the War of Resistance was experienced individually and digested socially and culturally, an investigation of mobilisation, even if only in the generalised way pursued here, offers some insight into the debilitating and dehumanising effects that the War of Resistance had on all levels of society.

Mobilisation until 1941

Initial chaos

Throughout the war, the National Government had to find a balance between the need to sustain large armies in the field, its financial resources, and the risks inherent in the broad mobilisation of society. The introduction of national military service, the creation of Divisional Conscription Commands, and the military reforms implemented after 1935 suggest that the Nationalists had hoped to be in a position to fight Japan with a standing army kept separate from the population and recruited from the settled population through disciplined bureaucracies. Their own armies were to be reinforced by regional militarists who functioned like auxiliaries.

After the outbreak of the fighting, it became clear that the recruitment system as it existed in 1937 would never be able to supply the necessary number of troops. On 31 July 1937, the Ministry of Military Administration gave approval to 9 divisions to recruit 10 battalions of 1,000 men from Peace Preservation forces in the Lower Yangtze. It also ordered the 20 existing Divisional Conscript Commands to train 20 new battalions.[1] The total number of recruits that could be produced in this way came to 30,000.

The army's needs were far higher. The Ministry of Military Administration claimed that 900,000 men were conscripted in 1937.[2] The armies themselves reported a total recruitment figure of 305,000 men.[3] One explanation for the discrepancy between the two figures is that many recruits remained in training camps, although lousy book-keeping, false claims, and bureaucratic chaos were probably the real reasons. However, there is no doubt that the military thirsted for recruits, in part because of casualties and to bring units up to strength but also because 'the number of deserters has been enormous', as He Yingqin stated in early 1938,[4] something which, incidentally, makes casualty figures unreliable as they included deserters. With bureaucratic structures unable to meet demand, armies went on a recruitment binge after the outbreak of war. In January 1938, new regulations for recruitment by the Ministry of Military Administration acknowledged that 'army units require vast numbers of troops to replenish their numbers. Because of the great urgency, many did not follow procedures'.[5]

Recruitment was also lucrative. For each battalion, an Establishment Fee of 1,200 *yuan* was made available. In addition, a Recruitment and Transfer Fee was paid of 6 *yuan* per soldier and 7,160 *yuan* per month was allocated to each battalion of recruits during its 3 months training programme.[6] These funds were paid either to Conscription Commands where they did exist or to armies and divisions when they carried out their own recruitment.

Large-scale recruitment, sanctioned or not and even if partially fictitious, generated social upheaval, led to widespread evasion, created opportunities for malfeasance, and fuelled banditry. Writing in 1938, one commentator by the name of Yu Xuehan sought to explain why 'in many provinces peasants do not want to be conscripted' despite the fact that China was fighting for its survival.[7] He believed that few peasants were aware of the significance of the War of Resistance because the Nationalists had not explained the Japanese menace out of fear of triggering a premature conflict. Many peasants, according to Yu, evaded conscription and some fled into the hills to join bandit gangs. Yu also blamed local government and *baojia* staff. Afraid of local trouble, but also under pressure to meet government directives, they sent toughs into the countryside to round up 'those without money or influence'. Although the regulations had excused from conscription the ill, families with only one son, and the main breadwinner, these were 'forcibly seized'. Social resentment resulted from 'urban and rural gentry and landlord families, who *baojia* heads cannot control, exploiting their skills and money to prevent their own children from being drafted'.[8]

An article of January 1939 in a Sichuanese newspaper described how the introduction of conscription after the beginning of the war had brought with it impressment, trade in substitutes, malfeasance by conscription officials, and maltreatment by army recruiters who pocketed conscription fees and sent recruits to their units without training.[9] This article argued that the point of conflict tended to be at the local district office. It explained that if the *bao* head at the village level could not find a solution in a conscription matter, he would then go one step up the hierarchy, to a *lianbao* head, who oversaw several villages. This man was responsible to the district office, where staff came from outside the county, and to county offices where the Nationalists had appointed new county heads. This had angered local gentry who therefore 'stayed aloof and no longer looked after local affairs'. With the *lianbao* head responsible for decisions about military recruitment as well as tax collection, with his office or home within travelling distance, and with no protection from local gentry, he came to bear the brunt of local anger, despite the fact that tax rates under the Nationalists had come down.

The beginning of the War of Resistance, in short, led to a wave of unregulated recruitment. If for some an entrepreneurial opportunity, for local officials it was a burden that put them into a difficult situation. With Nationalist recruitment structures unable to cope and with casualty rates and desertion at high levels, many army units recruited independently. For the Nationalists, the challenge was to recover control over recruitment and limit the impact on society and the economy.

Military recruitment

In January 1938, the Ministry of Military Administration issued the 'Scheme for the Unified Management of Mercenary Recruitment and National Military Service' (Table 7.1).[10] Its aim was to adjust recruitment to the reality that conscription on the basis of universal military service was not practicable, but also to restrain mercenary recruitment by individual army units. The Programme set monthly quotas for recruits by province. Where Conscription Commands existed, these quotas, after being broken

Table 7.1 Wartime Nationalist recruitment for the standing army (in '000s)

Province	1937	1938	1939	1940	1941	1942	1943	1944	1945	Total
Sichuan	104	174	296	266	345	367	353	391	283	2,578
Xikang	31		5	5	5	3	4	5	2	31
Yunnan		96	26	0.9	35	59	58	63	36	375
Guizhou	47	35	65	79	72	70	84	64	56	580
Guangxi	107	239	38	105	65	76	76	90	25	808
Guangdong	35	80	132	126	100	122	104	189	36	925
Fujian	29	33	60	58	56	51	49	29	50	425
Zhejiang	33	30	95	108	66	49	59	62	47	550
Anhui	44	23	54	69	69	95	78	74	56	564
Jiangxi	43	154	178	120	98	108	92	92	59	947
Hunan	191	221	223	217	170	208	184	102	54	1,570
Hubei	76	95	98	64	67	88	87	73	42	691
Henan	127	324	264	384	242	215	206	110	25	1,898
Shaanxi	37	69	126	127	80	100	118	145	85	888
Gansu	24	41	55	54	50	56	43	32	29	384
Shanxi					34	23	60	60	40	217
Shandong	13	16				4				33
Jiangsu	19	20								39
Suiyuan							5			5
Ningxia		4			4	4	4	4	4	24
Qinghai		3				1	2	6	6	18
Other			264	116	106	10				497
Total	938	1,649	1,976	1,901	1,667	1,711	1,667	1,611	939	14,051

Source: He Yingqin, *Riju Qin Hua Banian Kangzhan Shi*, table 10.

Notes
The figures in Table 7.1 can only give a rough picture of recruitment. Statistics and reports by War Zone Commands and army units during the War of Resistance claimed that they in reality received 12.1 million recruits, or more than 12 per cent less than Table 7.1 suggests.[11] This figure too cannot be taken as precise, as allocations of rations, weapons, ammunition, and money depended on a unit's complement of troops. If that made overstatement likely, at the same time, army units likely continued unsanctioned recruitment.

down by county and passed on to local authorities, were first to be filled from local forces.[12] Where no Conscription Commands existed, hence in the majority of places, mercenary recruitment was permitted. Before carrying out such recruitment, however, army units were to report the number of recruits they needed to the Ministry. The Ministry then allocated quotas to Special Administrators and county governments. Army units were to send Escort Teams with the necessary provisions of food, bedding, uniforms, and travel money to their assigned counties. Impressment was strictly proscribed.[13]

The Nationalists abandoned the pre-war policy of recruiting equitably from across the country. That was bureaucratically beyond their capabilities. As Table 7.1 shows, recruitment was concentrated in provinces such as Henan, Hunan, Jiangxi, Guangxi, Shaanxi, and Sichuan. Until 1941, Henan was the most important Nationalist recruitment ground. Although then overtaken by Sichuan, the province remained important for Nationalist recruitment until 1943, when first a disastrous famine, surely connected to years of recruitment and warfare, and then Japanese occupation made further Nationalist recruitment difficult. If Henan was well known as an area that produced many bandits and soldiers, the same was true for Hunan, where Zeng Guofan had recruited the Hunan Army to fight the Taiping. After Sichuan and Henan, Hunan was the third most important recruitment area. The rapid decline of Guangxi to Nationalist recruitment was perhaps the result of reticence by the Guangxi Clique about their recruitment. It may also have been the case that recruitment became difficult in this province with a relatively small population. Guangdong and Anhui took up some, but by no means all, of the slack after 1941. Table 7.1 further makes clear that Shaanxi province, most populous in the south, was an important recruitment ground for the Nationalists. After 1943, it was one of the three or four most significant provinces for Nationalists recruitment. Nationalist forces in north and north-west China likely depended on this area to replenish their forces.

Provincial reports suggest that after the initial wave of unrest recruitment became a difficult and unpopular but nonetheless a broadly accepted reality. Besides permitting mercenary recruitment and concentrating recruitment in areas where the population had traditionally proved willing to take up the life of arms, the abandonment of an attempt to recruit by lottery, financial support for recruitment and for army families, and other local measures eased the stresses created by recruitment. Recruitment would never be a clean or fair process, and malpractices, abuses, and resistance were common. But the Nationalists were nonetheless able to staff their armies and calm social unrest.

Dai Gaoxiang was Chief-of-Staff and then the head of the Sichuan Conscription Command until 1942. He wrote in an overview Sichuan's recruitment history that after initial difficulties, recruitment took place without many problems until 1941.[14] In Sichuan, as in other provinces, the introduction of a lottery proved unpopular. If in the past, the recruiters of warlord armies came around occasionally to seize the village poor, leaving them undisturbed at other times, the lottery gave rise to a constant anxiety because suddenly every *zhuangding* became liable to military service. The lottery, moreover, was disliked precisely because it was blind to local conditions. According to Dai, once the lottery was abandoned, army recruitment ceased to be a major source of rural unrest.

Dai stated that the real criterion followed in recruitment was to leave no family without enough labour to support itself.

A report on Hunan, which began by stating that 'bribery and the purchase of substitutes do occur, although we are no worse than other provinces',[15] argued that recruitment had exceeded provincial quota in 1939 and 1940 by 50 and 25 per cent, respectively.[16] The report suggested that responsible for this success were in part central grants to support recruitment in Hunan, but also local efforts to organise aid to families with sons in the army. For recruitment, Hunan received 288,000 *yuan* per month for management expenses. In addition, it was allocated 1 *yuan* per month for each recruit. That money was divided in the following way. The county government, the district office, and the *bao* office each received 10 cents per recruit. From this, office expenditures and costs involved in accommodating new recruits when they were called up were to be paid. Each conscript received on average 30 cents per day for subsistence, with the actual amount depending on travel distance, and 10 cents to purchase straw sandals.[17] Counties had organised War Family Support Committees, in which local elites participated. These committees provided towels, toothpaste, and soap to conscripts – perhaps best seen as luxury gifts – and organised send-off meetings, and at New Year provided salt and pork to army families. According to this report, the Committees had also collected grain and money, amounting on average to 140,000 *yuan* per county and 20,000 kilos of rice, from which grants were made to poor army families.[18]

A 1941 report on Jiangxi too stated that it had been able to exceed recruitment quotas by significant amounts. In Jiangxi, army families were given, in addition to a Conscription Stipend, 10 *yuan* as a Family Support Stipend as well as 300 kilos of rice.[19] A Zhejiang report similarly argued that immediately after the outbreak of fighting, army recruitment had caused incidents, but that subsequently things had settled down. Zhejiang too had decided not to implement the lottery. It had organised Military Service Propaganda Units, made up of representatives from the government, the KMT, school teachers, and local public organisations, which had travelled through the countryside. Army Family Support Committees had also been established in Zhejiang, which provided 30–50 *yuan* to army families, who were also excused of certain surtaxes and labour duties, while the government provided them with support for burial expenditures. Children were entitled to free education, although few probably took up the offer.[20]

The Nationalists sought to keep service in the army attractive. At the beginning of the war, army pay had been cut by 20 per cent in order to limit expenditures. In 1939, a Senior Class soldier received 8.5 *yuan* per month while a Second Class Soldier received 7 *yuan*. Chen Cheng argued at an MAC Senior Staff Meeting in 1939 that inflation 'makes it difficult for a soldier to afford food expenditures, let alone anything else. Furthermore, it is now impossible for troops that have been called up to assist their families'.[21] That of course had been a major attraction for many poor families to send their sons to the army. Chen secured pay increases for the lowest ranks by more than 40 per cent and for the lowest level officers by 30 per cent.

A system, endorsed by the NPC and sanctioned as an example of 'the rich contribute money and the poor contribute labour', allowed the wealthy to purchase 'temporary relief from military service'. Upon introduction, rates were set high, from 200 to more than 1,000 *yuan* depending on wealth.[22] Revenues were to be used to support army families and improve local government. In Zhejiang, one county collected 400,000 *yuan*. This particular report lambasted famous Shaoxing with its 1.2 million residents for only having raised 50,000 *yuan*.[23]

In February 1939, the government adopted regulations that made service in the *baojia* more attractive. *Baojia* staff were exempted from labour duties and military service as long as they held office. Expenses related to their posts were paid from the county budget, their taxes were reduced, and their children, including daughters, were entitled to free primary school education.[24] In addition, they were given merit rewards, insignia, banners, and plaques – the usual device by which Chinese states sought to increase the status of its local agents.

As provincial reports indicate, abuses certainly existed in recruitment and it was never free from exploitation for personal profit or abuse by local officials. Nonetheless, what is interesting in the Nationalists' approach is the return to traditional methods. Conscription on the basis of universal military service and a draft conducted by means of a blind lottery proved unworkable. Instead, the Nationalists focused recruitment in areas well known for readily producing men with military skills, used bureaucratic means to keep control over recruitment, and used local officials to mobilise local elites to support and finance the cost of recruitment. All this makes clear that there was more to Nationalists recruitment than impressment. There was no way that the Nationalists could have recruited 2 million men annually before 1941, and more than 1.5 million afterwards, by force alone. It stands to reason that if the Taiping, Zeng Guofan, and the warlords could amass large numbers of forces, the Nationalists could do so as well at least for a number years. During the first two phases of the war, the greater difficulty was less recruitment itself than retaining control over it. Like the Taiping, Zeng Guofan, the Qing, and the warlords, the Nationalists would face the problem of how to keep these forces from degenerating in quality, from becoming abusive, from becoming tools in the hands of those opposed to their rule, and from spawning informal but abusive fiscal institutions.

It should be mentioned as well that war zones were located in or near areas with surpluses of food and men. The limited logistical capabilities of the Nationalists made it inevitable that troops were stationed where they could most easily be sustained. It is also clear that the campaigns of the second phase of the War of Resistance were shaped by this reality. Operations were limited by the ability of Nationalist forces to move away from the areas on which they depended and the hardest fighting took place to protect these areas without which Nationalist resistance would become impossible.

Agricultural policy

China was a large agricultural country in which the maintenance of rural productivity was the first concern of any government in peace and in war. To maintain the food supply was important to sustain armies in the field and to secure social stability. Once panic about the food supply set in, it was inevitable that rural producers would hoard grain and food, black markets would develop, and inflation go up. It is equally important to realise that many areas, especially the richer provinces along the coast such as Jiangsu and Guangdong in the south were grain-deficit areas, dependent on food imports from elsewhere in China and from abroad. Furthermore, because of the lack of granaries and logistical bureaucracies, the relevant time horizon was usually only the next harvest.

Before 1941, the Nationalists sustained agricultural productivity remarkable well. In the first year of the war, the Nationalists lost their principle sources of revenue. The Maritime Customs Service, the Salt Gabelle, and the Consolidated Tax had been budgeted to deliver 67 per cent of central revenue in 1937.[25] In 1938, following the loss of the Lower Yangtze and China's largest cities, only 18.7 per cent of central revenue came from these taxes and in 1939 this figure had further declined to 6.3 per cent.[26]

The Nationalists did not turn to rural taxation to finance the war. Before the beginning of the war, Chiang Kaishek had brought leading economists such as Jia Shiyi and Ma Yinchu together at Mount Lushan to discuss wartime finance. The general policy formulated there was not to raise taxes on rural society, but to develop direct taxes on salaries and property; to issue public debt, which was justified as spreading the cost of defending China over several generations; and to borrow from banks and print money.[27] In other words, the Nationalists sought to place the cost of war on urban areas and the rich while shielding its impact on rural society. Table 7.2 reflects that general policy.

This thinking was reflected in the section on financial measures of the 'Implementation Programme of the Organic Law of the War of Resistance and National Reconstruction'.[28] It announced the introduction of new taxes on consumption, excessive wartime profits, and inheritance, and also extended the income tax. Wartime financial budgets show that revenue from direct taxes rose from 5.1 per cent of total tax revenue to 27 per cent in 1943, after which it declined to 16.1 per cent in 1945.[29]

Financial policy makers understood that the risk was rising inflation. They combated this by reducing state expenditures and by measures to maintain trade and commerce. From the beginning of the war, salaries were issued at 80 per cent. The Implementation Programme called for the consolidation of all tax bureaucracies into two centralised revenue collection agencies, one for direct and one for indirect taxation to reduce personnel in central and provincial tax collection agencies. The Programme also called for the introduction of a national accounting system and a state treasury, which through its branch agencies was to handle all state financial transactions.[30]

Maintaining trade was probably the more promising way of fighting inflation. Tax rates on international trade were reduced and China's international trade routes were protected to the extent that the military was capable. The Nationalists invested in construction of highways to facilitate domestic trade, protected and built railroads,

Table 7.2 Indices of purchasing power of monetary income of several income groups, 1937–41

Year	Professors	Soldiers	Civil servants	Industrial workers	Farmers	Rural workers (Sichuan)
1937	100	100	100	100	100	100
1938	95	95	77	124	87	111
1939	64	64	49	95	85	122
1940	25	29	21	76	96	63
1941	15	22	16	78	115	82

Source: Eastman, 'Nationalist China during the Sino-Japanese War', 591.

supported riverine transport, and established agencies to finance domestic trade and assist with their transport.[31]

Access to international grain markets was critical to the China's food supply and hence for economic stability. Before the war, China had consistently depended on grain imports. In the early 1930s, imports reached as high as between 10 and 20 million piculs of 60 kilograms per year.[32] Guangdong's grain deficit, the worst in the country by a considerable margin, amounted on average to 15 million *Shidan* (of 50 kilograms) per year, equalling a supply of 40 days. The shortfall was met almost entirely by imports from South-east Asia. Without these imports, more than 2 million people in Guangdong would experience famine and starvation.[33] From the middle of the 1930s, rice imports declined, but in the first years of the war they increased.[34] From 1941, after the Japanese had strengthened the economic embargo against the National Government and international trade routes were cut, rice imports became impossible.

Table 7.3 shows that inflation of rice prices was limited until 1940.

Although Lloyd Eastman heavily criticised the Nationalists' treatment of the peasantry, he did also write that 'during the first two years of the war, virtually all farmers – and especially the poorer segments of the farm population – enjoyed relative prosperity'.[35] The Taiwanese historian Hou Kunhong, using the archives of the Ministry of Finance, has recently confirmed this general picture and showed that conditions did not begin to deteriorate until 1941.[36] Table 7.4 on per capita rural consumption, originally compiled by the Economic Research Section of the Central Agricultural Bank, bears out Hou's analysis and shows that rural consumption did not suffer until 1941.

That calorie intakes remained stable or even improved was not just the result, as Eastman suggested, of favourable weather conditions in the first two years of the War of Resistance.[37] According to Hou, important too were measures aimed at stimulating the cultivation of fallow land, resettling refugees, introducing better pesticides, and promoting the cultivation of crops such as potatoes, which could be grown on marginal land or could be planted as a winter crop.[38] A British intelligence report confirms that if favourable weather conditions had produced a bumper crop in 1938, in subsequent years this was not the case and in 1941 a disastrous year was avoided because of a 'considerable increase of the rice acreage'.[39]

Documents of the Ministry of Economic Affairs provide detail on the Nationalists' efforts to keep the rural economy going. Its Work Report for 1938 mentioned the introduction of new seed varieties for rice, assistance with the building of rice paddies, and the use of pesticides as important in improving rice cultivation. In Sichuan, peasants

Table 7.3 Price of mid-quality rice in major cities, 1937–9 (*yuan* per *Shijin* of half-a-kilo)

	Chongqing	Chengdu	Lanzhou	Loyang	Ganzhou	Guiyang	Guilin	Hengyang
1937 (first half)	1.32	1.25	2.44	1.79	0.75	1.41	1.0	0.6
1937 (second half)	1.25	1.19	2.55	1.83	0.74	1.2	0.98	0.61
1938	1.2	1.11	2.86	2.13	0.69	0.89	1.3	0.76
1939	1.3	1.24	3.4	2.99	0.76	1.72	1.89	1.41

Source: *Liangzheng Shiliao*, VI, 487.

Table 7.4 Per capita rural consumption of main food items in the fifteen provinces under National Government control, 1938–41

	1938	1939	1940	1941
Rice	288.3	299.2	294.6	289.2
Wheat	69.6	78.8	73.3	86.5
Corn	47.4	48.5	56	66.3
Sorghum	10.5	11.3	10.7	11.3
Soyabean	16.9	18.1	17.3	16.9
Fava bean	8.1	9.8	9.8	9.8
Peas	11.3	12.1	11.8	11.7
Sweet potato	65.2	62.3	61	63.4
Potato	17.9	19	18.1	20.3
Pork	18.3	18.3	18	18.1
Beef	3.2	4.3	3.3	3.5
Lamb	6.1	6.6	5.8	5.6
Chicken and ducks	5.6	5.5	4.8	5.1
Fish	7.8	6.7	6.2	5.7
Eggs	41	43	38	35

Source: *Liangzheng Shiliao*, VI, 483–4.

Note

Eggs are in single units. All others figures are in *Shijin*.

were encouraged to grow winter wheat in rice fields. In Jiangxi, Sichuan, Hunan, Fujian, Shaanxi, and Henan, populations were resettled to bring fallow land into cultivation. The report mentioned that the Ministry had engaged in a project to rear oxen in Guangxi. In 1937, many oxen, important for ploughing, had died, according to the report because of an epidemic but perhaps also because many had been commandeered by the army for haulage duties. Peasants were given loans to purchase the oxen reared in Guangxi. Inoculation was introduced to prevent animal diseases. The Ministry also promoted agricultural co-operatives. According to the report, 55,000 managed granaries, financed irrigation schemes, promoted new seed strains, and pushed the cultivation of specific crops such as wheat and potatoes.[40]

The Ministry's report for 1939 suggested that it continued these activities in that year. It stated that the Ministry had focused its activities on rice and wheat cultivation, again by introducing new seed varieties, pressing the use of pesticides, and extending sown acreage. It had supported schemes to move peasants into uncultivated areas in Jiangxi, Shaanxi, Fujian, Henan, Sichuan, and Hunan, and in 1939 had extended this effort to Guangxi and Tibet. The number of co-operatives had grown to 78,000, which had made 51 million *yuan* available in loans.[41] As in 1938, the prevention of the spread of animal diseases and the promotion of the use of pesticides were also important activities of the Ministry. No longer feeling the need to elaborate, the Ministry's report for the first half of 1940 stated that it was continuing such policies.[42]

Tables 7.5 and 7.6 illustrate the effect of these measures. The first shows that, with the exception of sweet potato and corn, agricultural yields increased significantly until 1940.

Table 7.5 Yield per *Shimou* for the winter harvest of major crops (in *Shijin*) for the fifteen provinces of Nationalist China

	1937	1938	1939	1940	1941	1942	1943	1944
Wheat	125	183	173	169	132	157	141	169
Peas	100	137	143	130	113	124	110	129
Fava beans	111	159	176	161	141	156	142	161
Rice	316	362	369	311	325	313	306	
Corn	236	214	215	197	189	163	176	
Sweet potato	1,229	1,098	971	933	957	814	939	
Sorghum	156	211	218	200	189	153	185	

Source: *Liangzheng Shiliao*, VI, 477.

Table 7.6 Index of sown area, 1936–42, for the thirteen provinces of Ningxia, Gansu, Shaanxi, Henan, Hubei, Sichuan, Yunnan, Guizhou, Hunan, Jiangxi, Zhejiang, Fujian, and Guangdong

	1936	1937	1938	1939	1940	1941	1942
Wheat	108.7	100	79.3	80.5	83.3	87.5	93.9
Rice	104.7	100	95.7	95.8	91.6	91.4	92.6
Corn	91.8	100	82.1	82.7	84.9	87.9	89.9
Glutinous Rice	106	100	87.5	84.6	77.6	68.9	64.6
Potato	90.2	100	84.7	86.5	93.3	97.5	101.4
Sorghum	90.5	100	60.2	58.8	58.6	58.7	58.7
Peas	109.6	100	88.1	90.9	90.4	89.6	91.3
Fava Beans	96	100	84.3	83.2	82.6	82.6	84.8
Soyabean	99.9	100	71.5	72	75	73.4	72.4
Cotton	104.8	100	62.5	63.7	76.1	74.9	71.4
Tobacco	95.2	100	86.1	88.1	94.3	86.6	83
Peanuts	95	100	75.2	78	83.1	83.6	84
Rape	100.7	100	89	94	111.1	115.1	113.6

Source: *Liangheng Shiliao*, VI, 471.

Note
1937 is 100.

Table 7.6 shows that following a drop in the first year of the War of Resistance, sown acreage increased substantially. The results were most pronounced for wheat, potatoes, peanuts, and rape seed.

Finally, Table 7.7 gives absolute data on harvests from 1937 to 1944. It makes clear that especially the increase in wheat production was critical to sustaining food supplies. Given that the yield per unit of sown area for potatoes declined while harvests remained stable, measures to increase sown acreage were especially important. Table 7.7 shows that rice remained the most important food crop during the war by far, but that in 1940 rice harvests plummeted and never recovered.

Table 7.7 Harvest of selected crops, 1937–44 (in '000 *Shidan*)

	1937	1938	1939	1940	1941	1942	1943	1944
Wheat (winter crop)	131,156	202,911	198,188	201,110	165,120	209,729	199,196	248,264
Peas (winter crop)	27,666	43,694	47,172	43,064	37,548	42,217	37,925	43,675
Fava beans (winter crop)	33,872	47,644	52,759	47,715	41,906	47,617	43,871	49,135
Rape seed (winter crop)	32,466	35,846	43,411	48,539	45,630	44,140	48,527	49,650
Rice (summer crop)	689,112	747,569	753,331	618,863	643,519	635,229	609,488	
Sorghum (summer crop)	34,991	33,997	34,229	31,624	29,665	24,040	28,055	
Soyabean (summer crop)	38,396	36,470	37,646	38,576	34,714	29,406	33,334	
Sweet potato (summer crop)	282,259	276,550	248,662	256,404	277,096	242,606	290,284	
Peanuts (summer)	21,406	21,901	22,420	22,799	22,848	20,147	21,834	

Source: *Liangzheng Shiliao*, VI, 475–6.

The figures in Table 7.7 hide gross regional differences and do not show areas of great misery, such as those affected by the Yellow River floods unleashed by the Nationalists after the fall of Xuzhou. But they also belie the image of a militarist regime unconcerned about the population. To prosecute the war, to carry out recruitment without destroying the social order completely, and to maintain the loyalty of its armies, the Nationalists had to pay attention to rural productivity. Even if benign weather conditions in 1937 and 1938 were favourable, the efforts of the Nationalists themselves were also important.

Feeding the army

The Nationalists estimated that the daily food requirement of a soldier was 20 *Shiliang* (one-tenth of a *Shijin*) of rice, coming to 360 *Shidan* per year.[43] Current nutritional experts agree that such an allowance was adequate.[44] The document stated that an army of 5 million men would therefore require 18 million *Shidan* per year, but in reality military grain procurement aimed at feeding 3 million troops. Coming to about 2.5 per cent of the rice harvest, this may not seem a large amount. However, the amount came on top of already existing taxes and had to be collected in a few regions with grain surpluses. In addition, reserves had to be built up and extra amounts had to be collected to offset the cost of wastage and transport costs.

A 1939 document outlining military grain procurement policies argued that Hunan, Jiangxi, and Anhui were the most important rice surplus provinces in south China outside of Sichuan. Hunan on average exported 2 million *Shidan* of rice each year and in good years 3.5 million *Shidan*. Jiangxi could usually export 2.6 million *Shidan* of rice.

Anhui was the province with the largest rice surplus, exporting in normal years 3 million *Shidan* of rice. However, the document noted, the Japanese had seized important parts of Anhui and transport lines had been destroyed, hindering rice procurement in the province. Although it did not give specific amount, the document did state that Shaanxi and Gansu were the most important wheat surplus areas, that could be used to provide the war zones in the north-west.

The document did not discuss Sichuan, Nationalist China's rice basket during the war, on the grounds that a separate policy, already endorsed by Chiang Kaishek, had already been instituted. A report of the Ministry of Economic Affairs suggests that Chiang had essentially demanded a raid on the Sichuan grain harvest. Two million *Shidan* of grain was to be collected for storage in public granaries and 5 million *Shidan* for price management and sale in other areas.[45] Sustaining rice production in Sichuan and maintaining its lines of communication to the front were critical to Nationalist military effectiveness.

Following the first phase of the war, with important parts of the railroad network and the Yangtze River in Japanese control, the Nationalists had little option but to station their armies in areas that could sustain them. The withdrawal of one-third of the army for retraining had the advantage that it reduced significantly pressure on food supplies at the front. The remaining two-third was stationed in war zones geographically situated close to grain surplus areas.[46] The danger was that these forces would become dependent on their localities. The Nationalists had to build up a supply system that would enable them to release their forces at least to a limited degree and for a certain span of time.

The policy that Nationalists adopted was to build up grain reserves for 1 year for 3 million troops. One-fourth would be kept near the front, a further one-fourth in relative safe areas behind the front, and half in the rear area provinces of Sichuan, Guizhou, Guangxi, Hunan, Jiangxi, Shaanxi, and Gansu.[47] Given that soldiers could carry a week's supply of cooked rice, this system, in which only limited supplies were kept near the front and which created a series of magazines from which troops on the move could draw, denied supplies to the Japanese, kept troops in war zones dependent on the Nationalists, and provided them with some mobility.

The Office of Military Supplies in combination with War Zone Commands was given the responsibility to oversee the procurement, storage, and transport of grains at the front, while the Bureau of Agricultural Affairs of the Ministry of Economic Affairs was responsible for the rest.[48] The Bureau of Agricultural Affairs was also responsible for the procurement, storage, and transport of grain for non-military purposes such as price stabilisation. In 1937, it had begun to collect grain for these purposes in Hunan and Jiangxi. After the outbreak of the war it significantly expanded the geographic scope of its activities, procuring wheat in Shaanxi and Sichuan, and rice in the latter province as well as in Hunan and Jiangxi. In 1938, rice from Jiangxi was used to deal with food panics that had broken out in Guangdong, the province most depended on grain imports, following Japan's seizure of Canton.[49] Centralised supply of grain and wheat was important also to prevent armies from setting up tax stations, exacting *tankuan*, and involving themselves in smuggling operations, all of which would affect civil–military relations.[50] Army units further received a certain amount of money for the local purchase of vegetables and meat, products that were difficult to store and hence could not be supplied centrally.[51]

For 1939, the military grain procurement policy allocated quotas to grain surplus provinces. Hunan was to provide 4 million *Shidan*, Jiangxi 1.3 million *Shidan*, north Anhui 1.5 million *Shidan*, south Anhui 2 million *Shidan*, with another 2.5 million coming from other areas. A wheat procurement quota of 1.5 million *Shidan* was set for parts of Anhui, Shaanxi, and other places.[52] As mentioned, Sichuan was to deliver 2 million *Shidan*. The total would have provided for one year's consumption of 3 million troops and half of the reserve of 1 year's supply that the policy demanded. The total budget for the procurement and transfer of grain as well as the building and management of granaries was set at 88.3 million *yuan*.[53]

In October 1939, the Ministry of Economic Affairs reported optimistically about the implementation of the policy.[54] In its report for the first-half of 1940, the Ministry reported that the construction of granaries had been completed in most war zones. It also reported success in accumulating reserves for three months and their storage in granaries in the rear areas of war zones. The general granaries had been filled successfully in Shaanxi and Gansu. However, procurement had been halted in Guangxi and Guizhou, as the price of rice had risen sharply in these two provinces. The quotas for Hunan and Sichuan had been reduced for the same reason.[55] In August, a report by the government agencies involved in military grain procurement reported that despite these shortfalls, the system had begun to operate with reasonable success. It proposed a budget allocation of 200 million *yuan* to continue the programme the next year.[56]

The National Political Consultative Conference

Mobilisation is not a matter of establishing bureaucratic structures alone. Success also depends on making the case that the war is justified and building a political consensus. This was especially important in a country that remained deeply divided and where control over military force could easily be lost. The promulgation of the Organic Law, the establishment of the Supreme National Defence Council, and the creation of the NPC, National Political Consultative Conference, in Wuhan served this purpose. The NPC was a proto-parliament meant to integrate the Nationalists' political opponents, including the Communists, into the new war community that the Nationalists hoped to bring about. As long as it would hold and its legitimacy was acknowledged, the dangers inherent in military mobilisation would be minimised.

The Regulations for the NPC, provided for in the Organic Law, were promulgated on 12 April. At its initial meeting in July, its first act was to accept the Organic Law in a symbolic acceptance of the Nationalists' leadership and the principles it had laid down that would guide the war effort. The NPC had to be inclusive. The first NPC was made up of Communists, including Mao Zedong, Wang Ming, Qin Bangxian, Dong Biwu, Lin Zuhan, and Deng Yingchao; minority party members such as Zhang Junmai, Zuo Shunsheng, Li Huang, Zeng Qi, Zhang Shenfu, Lo Longji, and Chen Qitian; the Confucian revivalist Liang Shuming; luminaries and activists such as Jiang Baili, Hu Shi, Fu Sinian, Wang Yunwu, and Liang Shiqiu; entrepreneurs such as Chen Jiageng and Hu Wenhu, who also were important because of their South-east Asian connections; and finally prominent regional figures such as Qin Gonglai, associated with the anti-Japanese movement in Manchuria. Ch'ien Tuan-sheng, author of a famous English language history of the KMT and an NPC member himself, wrote that the NPC was the result of 'a conscientious effort by the party to appoint well-known leaders of the country, regardless of political proclivities'.[57] Lawrence Shyue, who has written about the NPC from the perspective of the minority parties, stated similarly that it 'included the best group of people modern China has had'.[58]

According to its April 1938 regulations, 'the national Government must submit before implementation all important policies relating to international and domestic affairs to the NPC'. The NPC further listened to reports by ministries, questioned ministers, and made its own proposals. In 1940, it was given the right to establish investigative committees, and from 1944 it also reviewed the national budget.[59] The Council was to meet four times a year, a schedule later changed to two times and after 1942 to one time per year. When not in session, a Resident Committee of 15–25 members exercised the rights of the NPC.

The first membership regulations allowed for 200 NPC members. Provinces were represented by 88 'persons of proper repute who had served for three or more years in public or private institutions or in social organisations'. Each province had from 1–4 representatives. Mongolia and Tibet were represented by 4 and 2 members respectively. Overseas Chinese were allowed 6 members. The largest group of 100 members 'had served for at least three years in important cultural or economic organisations, are of proper repute, and have made important contributions to national affairs'.[60]

Until 1941, NPC meetings were public forums where serious criticisms of the National Government could and was made; one of its uses is as an indicator of public opinion during the war. Military recruitment figured as a prominent topic throughout the war. NPC members, with, in this case, Liang Shuming in the lead, criticised impressment and abuses by local officials regularly. They also made suggestions for improvement. Liang advocated the involvement of local elites and the flexible local implementation of national rules. Typical of the way the NPC operated, such proposals were subjected to a vote and passed on to the National Government which then elicited responses from the relevant bureaucracies and reported back to the NPC at a later session on implementation of those proposals that had been accepted.[61]

Other regular topics were fiscal policy, the problems caused by inflation, central government inefficiency, the *baojia* system, and the slow progress in building up local level assemblies. For instance, in October 1938 the NPC's resolution on the report by the Ministry of Finance stated that 'after listening to Minister Kong's Secret Report on Financial Affairs, we have gained a clearer understanding and are to a degree re-assured'. However, 'although we continue to have faith in our financial authorities, it is undeniable that they have not done everything possible and have not always acted as well as they might have'.[62] The criticism focused on haphazard planning, excessive reliance on bank borrowing, the inability to reform fiscal administration, and inflation. In April 1940, the NPC's resolution on financial affairs stated that 'the Government remains capable of achieving increases in revenue collection, securing international loans, reforming the fiscal administration, conducting monetary planning, and re-allocating material resources,' but also expressed concern over the steep decline in revenues, mentioning that the abandonment by tax collectors of their posts had led to the rapid spread of tax avoidance, illicit taxation, and corruption.[63]

During these years, the NPC was most critical of the Ministry of Domestic Affairs. In October 1938, the NPC resolution criticised the National Government for working too slowly, with many proposals receiving the standard bureaucratic response: 'this cannot yet be implemented. We have not yet been able to consider the proposal fully due to a lack of proper guidance'. The *baojia* came in for severe stricture: 'the implementation of all measures depend on the *baojia* as the basic level of government administration. But once we investigate real conditions, it is not implemented effectively, it exists only in name, or inappropriate people serve in it. The *baojia* has hundreds of problems'.[64]

Until 1941, the NPC members usually bracketed such criticisms with polite expressions of understanding for the problems faced by the National Government and support for the war. While no doubt aware that the Winter Offensive had been a disappointment, the NPC declared, in April 1940, that the recent 'battles have made us believe that the enemy is gradually being exhausted and that it will be difficult for them to increase their forces to undertake large offensives. This is the result of the profound understanding of the enemy by our Commander-in-Chief'.[65]

Like the PRC's Political Consultative Conference, of which the NPC was a forerunner, the NPC was not a democratic institution, although it sought to borrow from the cachet of democracy to strengthen the reputation of the Nationalists. It could not change National Government policy, nor did it play a role in the election of political leaders. Members were vetted by the KMT's Political Council. Attempts to make it more democratic failed. However, the NPC should not be dismissed as mere gesture politics.

Like the Organic Law, the NPC was symbolically important in suggesting that the Nationalists represented a new China and had broad support. It staked territorial claims by including representatives from many areas occupied by the Japanese and asserted an understanding of the Chinese nation incorporating Tibet, Mongolia, Manchuria, and overseas Chinese. The debates during NPC meetings and criticisms of National Government officials showed that many did chose to avail themselves of the NPC to press their concerns, something which made them a part of the world that the Nationalists hoped to embody. For Chiang Kaishek, it created a new source of legitimacy besides the KMT, useful to curtail a party that so often had created difficulties for him. When Wang Jingwei left Chongqing, the NPC adopted resolutions condemning his step. The NPC further was useful as a device to give those outside the KMT a stake in the Nationalists government, allow them to air their grievances and concerns, and create an orderly hierarchy of political relations.

The NPC was only one of the devices the Nationalists used in the hope of maintaining cohesion. Speech-making, propaganda, rallies, and rituals, such as commemorations for Sun Yatsen, were also important. One of the most intriguing ritual acts of the war was the sacrifice for Chenghiz Khan performed on 28 June 1942. With the Vice-President of the Committee for Mongol and Tibetan Affairs in the lead, the ceremony was attended by the Provincial Chairman of Gansu Province, senior military officers of the north-west, and Mongol leaders. Before a silver coffin in a temple on top of a mountain, banners hailed Chenghiz Khan as a 'national hero' who had 'awed Asia'.[66] The point, of course, was to undermine Japanese claims and bring Mongolian leaders into the world of the Nationalists.

Crisis

A British intelligence report written just after the outbreak of the Pacific War suggested that its consequences for the Chinese economy would be disastrous.

The scarcity of consumers' and producers' goods will be accentuated by the outbreak of the general Pacific War. British and American goods reaching Shanghai found their way to Free China by devious routes; these supplies will now be cut off. Japanese goods were also smuggled into Free China, but Japan will have to ration her exports to China very stringently. Consequently, the prices of clothing, household goods, metal ware, industrial and agricultural implements, kerosene, and matches may be expected to register further very steep price increases. The food situation in Free China will depend on the state of the next rice harvest and on whether the symptoms of peasant revolt in Szechwan develop in serious rebellion.[67]

The author of this grim message, full of foreboding about the ability of the National Government to economically last the course, focused on the Pacific War. Yet, Japan's Southern Advance only worsened an already deteriorating situation.

In 1940, the Japanese had, as mentioned, seized the agriculturally productive Hubei plains, occupied Yichang, invaded Guangxi, and cut the Yunnan–Hanoi Railroad by stationing troops in north Vietnam. As Weng Wenhao, the head of the NRC and Minister of Economic Affairs, reported to a KMT meeting in March 1941, the loss of Yichang was serious because the city was the key transhipment point between Sichuan and the war zones. From then, the transfer of grain and troops from Sichuan to the front would be difficult. The loss of Yichang was an extremely serious blow to the Nationalists. It was of course for this reason that the Nationalists put so much effort in seeking to recapture it during the Second Battle of Changsha. The war zones therefore were left increasingly to their own devices to secure the food and money they needed to sustain resistance against Japan.

Weng further reported that the Japanese had intensified the economic blockade along the coast by closing Hangzhou Bay in Zhejiang, the major ports of Fujian, and severing connections from Guangdong to Hong Kong.[68] With China cut off from international grain markets, on which Guangdong depended, and with domestic trade difficult, it was predictable that grain shortages would occur.[69] As important as real shortages was the expectation of shortages in the future. Few would not understand the consequences of isolation from international grain markets, the destruction of harvests due to warfare, or the severing of connections between Sichuan and the front. Food panics had already occurred in Guangdong in the first few years of the war;[70] in the far more serious situation that followed 1940, such panics and real shortages there and elsewhere would be of greater scope and intensity.

War affected rural production in different ways. In north China, the Japanese sought to prevent the cultivation of sorghum as it provided good hiding places for guerrillas. Recruitment withdrew good labour from farms. Industrial mobilisation drove up the cost of rural wage labour, important to larger farms, in the south-west. The great shortage of transport equipment meant that the military commandeered carts and animals, making the transport and marketing of harvests or of seeds difficult. Warfare too led to a reduction in the availability of tools and draft animals. As marketing systems broke down, peasants increasingly aimed at survival rather than seeking a profit in the market.[71]

In a sign of the times, in 1940 authorities in Guangdong, Fujian, Guangxi, Hunan, Anhui, Zhejiang, Gansu, and Shaanxi proscribed the use of rice for the brewing of alcohol, which was a lucrative enterprise but also wasteful of grain.[72] Table 7.7 on harvests makes clear that in 1940 rice harvests dropped to 618 million *Shidan* from

753 million the year before, at a time when rice imports became impossible. Subsequent years showed little improvement in rice harvests, which remained by far the most important source of calories in most of China. In 1941, the wheat harvest too fell by nearly 40 per cent, although it recovered later.

Changes in Japan's financial and monetary policies contributed to the crisis. Japanese Military Notes were issued after 1937, but initially were not able to replace the Fabi other than in large cities. To stem the flow of Fabi to Nationalist areas, the Nationalist kept the Nationalists' currency, the Fabi, convertible on international exchange markets in the International Concession of Shanghai, occupied only at the time of the Southern Advance. This helped to limit inflation and the Japanese in fact bought up Fabi to exchange it for Western currencies in Shanghai. However, the Fabi was proscribed after the formal establishment of the Wang Jingwei National Government. The Japanese and Wang Jingwei hoped to make Wang's Central Reserve Bank note the standard currency to foster acceptance of Wang's government. Between March and December 1941, the Central Reserve Bank issued 140 million *yuan* of Central Reserve Bank notes and used murder, bombs, and kidnapping to terrorise the population into accepting them.[73] The Fabi became useless in occupied areas and therefore fled to Nationalist areas, contributing to inflation there.[74] In short, just as food became scarce and worries about the future supply of grain intensified, the amount of Fabi rapidly increased.

Money is both a store of value and a social construct for the distribution of resources. To be able to function as such, trust must exist in the currency. Table 7.8 makes clear that people lost faith in the Fabi, with disastrous consequences for the distribution of goods and hence human relations. The misery implied in the figures discussed in this chapter is difficult to overestimate.

Table 7.8 shows that inflation began first in Chongqing and Chengdu, and that other cities followed. Ganzhou, in the wheat consuming north, was most isolated from its effects. Regional differentials in inflation make clear that transport systems had broken down and that markets were not functioning. They also implied enormous arbitrage opportunities for speculators and smugglers.

The growing economic crisis made it impossible for the Nationalists to continue state expenditures at a decent level. Table 7.9 makes clear that by 1941, Government expenditures already were less than half of what they had been in 1937. By 1944, they had declined to one-fifth of that figure.

One important sign of the crisis was a decline in the purchasing power of the wages of civil servants and educators. It reached to less than 15 per cent of the pre-war standard already by 1941.[75] Chiang Kaishek wrote in his diary on 11 April 1943 that 'the poverty of government employees has reached an unbelievable point. Unable to raise families, many let their wives have abortions .... What misery; I cannot bear it! Heavens! If the Japanese bandits are not defeated soon, or the war should drag on for another year or two, then China cannot make it, and I must fail in the mission that God commands me to perform'.[76] The following sections examine the consequences of the crisis for recruitment, the military, and industrial mobilisation.

The decline in recruitment

The figures presented in Table 7.1 show that in 1941 annual recruitment dropped from somewhat less than 2 million to between 1.6 and 1.7 million per year. The declines

Table 7.8 Price of mid-quality rice in major cities, 1940–2 (*yuan* per Shijin)

	Chongqing	Chengdu	Lanzhou	Loyang	Ganzhou	Guiyang	Guilin	Hengyang
1940								
February	2	2.23	5.55	4.1	1.9	4.27	2.83	1.6
March	2.2	2.83	5.75	4.5	2	4.04	2.9	1.65
April	2.8	2.86	3.8	5.2	2.6	3.88	2.95	1.75
May	3.2	3.44	3.92	5.56	2.2	3.92	2.95	1.9
June	4.8	3.54	4.2	6.2	2.2	4.36	3.1	1.95
July	6.36	4.56	4.5	6.8	3.5	5.11	3.15	1.85
August	8.3	4.13	4.5	7.6	3.4	5.58	3.4	2.4
September	8.7	5.16	4.9	8.8	5.8	5.14	3.6	2.5
October	10.6	9.6	7.5	9.2	5.8	5.69	3.7	2.7
November	15.7	11.34	7.83	8.6	5.8	5.73	3.7	3
December	18.35	10.7	8.13	7.8	5.8	5.83	3.7	3.5
1941								
January	19.17	12.74	9	7.9	6.09	6.5	3.95	3.6
February	21.53	14.24	11.17	8	6.95	7.91	4.11	3.53
March	19	15.53	14.33	9.2	9.16	9.04	4.76	4.17
April	27.07	19.87	15	11.2	11.57	10.12	5.98	8.07
May	38	29.77	15	15.17	10.9	11.49	9.67	9.83
June	41.87	38.48	15.67	15.83	12.27	23.62	10.57	15.47
July	45.33	37	22	18.17	13.17	23.83	10.76	17.33
August	40.8	26.33	26.83	25.65	11.5	16.9	12.51	17
September	34.13	24.07	28.5	29.33	12.67	14.95	17.73	13.83
October	37	28	29.17	31	12.2	16.47	17.34	13.5
November	45.33	33.67	29.83	27	10.93	28.17	16.63	14.77
December	42.67	28.67	30	26.03	10.33	26.65	18.11	16.93
1942								
January	39.83	26	31	24	11	38.57	22.1	23.83
February	41.33	29.67	32	32.33	12.23	37.27	26.57	28.5

Source: *Liangzheng Shiliao*, VI, 487–8.

Table 7.9 Government expenditures on military and civil tasks (in million *yuan*), in absolute numbers and as percentages

	Military expentitures	Civil expenditures	Debt	Price index	Index of government expentitures	Index of government expenditures adjusted for inflation
1937	1,388	161	374	103	106	100
1938	698	93	242	131	119	91
1939	1,627	258	546	220	154	70
1940	3,911	448	346	513	273	53
1941	5,159	2,500	480	1,296	548	42
1942	11,945	7,625	1,587	3,900	1,339	34
1943	30,219	19,526	3,493	12,936	3,188	25
1944	92,936	51,488	5,220	43,197	9,201	21
1945	8,28,275	1,47,230	87,268	1,63,160	79,765	49

Source: ZHMGDAZL, V: 2 (Finance and Economics), 1, 317–25.

were most marked in Henan as well as Zhejiang, where recruitment halved following the Japanese attack on that province. In Hunan and Shaanxi recruitment also fell back. The only significant increase, from 266 million to 345 million, took place in Sichuan. Recruitment in this province was clearly stepped up to make up for shortfalls elsewhere.

According to Dai Gaoxiang, after 1941 in Sichuan few households remained with surplus labour. Yet, recruitment quotas were increased in this province, and it is therefore not surprising that, as Dai stated, from 1941 impressment became a common phenomenon.[77] Xu Siping, who succeeded Dai in 1942, noted in 1944 that in the previous year the authorities had made the fight against impressment their highest priority, indicating that impressment had become common.[78] Reports on Hunan and Jiangxi attributed the decline in recruitment to reductions in central grants. In these provinces, provincial authorities were asked to raid budgets of local security offices and to press Escort Teams to supply rations to recruits. In both provinces, the training of citizen soldiers and their mobilisation in local security forces were cancelled.[79] In February 1941, this became national policy.[80]

Ray Huang, the famous historian of the Ming, has described evocatively the gruesome realities of recruitment by this time. He served in the National Army during the War of Resistance. He recollected that after he had completed his military training and was assigned to the 14th Division at the Yunnan–Vietnam border in the summer of 1941, he was ordered to accompany the Division's Escort Team to fetch 1,500 recruits in Hunan after the Ministry of Military Administration had approved this number. He wrote that 'the armed soldiers from the Escort Team accompanied the *baojia* elders to comb through villages to round up men. The conscription law had reached the bottom of the manpower barrel. The purchases of substitutes became increasingly abused and human cargo degenerated in quality'.[81] Due to disease and desertion, only 500 of the new recruits reached the 14th Division. The reason that the army went through the huge trouble of transporting recruits over such a large distance was because if troops were recruited locally at the front and fought battles in their own home areas desertion was easy.[82]

The Nationalists did try to reduce the social impact of recruitment. Regulations for 1941 stipulated that decisions of who would be liable to military service could be taken only once a year, in January, and that actual call-ups could take place only quarterly. The actual determination of who might be called up in any one year was to take place at a public meeting at the *bao* level attended by all local residents as well as by officials from the county, the party, and Conscription Commands. The latter were to explain not only the significance of the War of Resistance, but also privileges for army families, the entitlements of conscripts, local arrangements for assistance to army dependants, and the punishments for officials violating conscription laws. Selection was then to be made first on a voluntary basis and then on the basis, once again, of a lottery. In case of desertion, another member of the *bao* would be forced to take the deserter's place.[83] According to Dai Gaoxiang, this new attempt to switch to a lottery system again produced riots and was therefore halted.[84]

The National Government also sought to fund recruitment in new ways. In March 1941, the National Government with the approval of the NPC decided to replace the system that allowed the rich to purchase relief from military service. Instead, the government sold certificates for relief of military service for payments of 1, 3, and 6 *yuan*.

All families of which no member had been recruited into the army were compelled to purchase these certificates. The revenue of this tax was supposed to be allocated to conscription centres to increase their budgets.[85]

Effects on the army

One consequence of the growing financial and recruitment crisis was the deterioration of living standards in the military. Chiang Kaishek addressed this problem at two military conferences in 1942. At the Xinglongshan Military Conference for military leaders of the North-west in August, Chiang responded to concerns raised about 'the difficulty of finding replacements for troops and horses'. He remarked that 'after five years of bloody battles, the finances of the government and the national economy have become extremely difficult. If we lack something, we must make arrangements to solve it locally'.[86] He encouraged his armies to live off the land: 'there is land that can be cultivated and there are the masses who can be employed; there is no reason not to have clothes to wear or food to eat'.[87] He told his commanders to reduce rations, telling the story of how while a cadet in Japan he had to be satisfied with one bowl of rice at the mid-day meal and advising them that 'you will first feel hungry, but after a month, the habit will become natural and the feeling will go away'. He insisted that while serving at a military academy in Yunnan, shortened rations had also been introduced and that 'research showed that before restrictions on food, the cadets frequently fell ill, but three months later, no one became ill anymore. This shows that we Chinese become ill because we are undisciplined in consumption and eat too much. Foreigners speak about having enough to eat and not about eating to the full'.[88] The polite thing to do at the end of a meal in China is to say 'I am full'. Only desperation can have led to such statements by Chiang.

In early September at a Xi'an Military Conference, Chiang told his audience that 'senior commanders at the front in all war zones must fully understand the difficulties we now face. The food and clothing of officers at the front must be solved on the basis of the principle of self-reliance. At most fronts in all war zones, cotton can be grown and wheat and rice cultivated. There is no reason to be hungry or cold as long as troops have the skills for and are engaged in bringing land into cultivation, herding, forestry, irrigation, and weaving'.[89]

In an address to the Xi'an Military Conference, Chiang denied the idea that shortages were the result of corrupt officials seizing military grains. Simply everybody was short. He announced that troops in the 1st, 2nd, 5th, and 8th War Zones were to dedicate most of their energies to agricultural cultivation and taking care of their own needs as little warfare would take place in these areas before a general counter-offensive. He stated that the performance of county officials would for 35 per cent be judged on their delivery of military grains and 35 per cent on their management of military recruitment. He made known as well that Grain Investigation Offices would be established in all war zones. These had the task of investigating local production and requisitioning grains from the largest landholders. Suggestive of the state of affairs was that at the Xi'an Conference Chiang devoted the larger part of one speech to the problems of 'smuggling, opium consumption, engagement in commerce, joining secret societies, dependents of officers living close to army units, new soldiers beating Escort Officers, mutinies among recruits' and other problems.[90]

A report on an inspection tour of Yunnan and Guizhou by He Haoruo of 1942 confirms the dark picture suggested by Chiang's speeches. He reported that many army units in the two provinces subsisted on low quality rice without vegetables and that they had just one cup of boiled water per day. According to He, many units cultivated their own lands and some mined their own coal.[91] A January 1944 report of the National Mobilisation Committee analysed supplies to the military in 1943. The report argued that living standard of troops had remained low. It issued regulations for the local requisitioning of edible oils, fuels, doufu, and animals and urged the army to develop projects to cultivate their own food and cotton supplies.[92]

Ray Huang expressed his shock when he arrived at the 14th Division:

> All battalions and companies were down to half strength. Obviously the division had at one time been lavishly equipped. There were German-style helmets, gas masks, and canvas tenting sheets. But they appeared in a way that you would find in a flea market: one piece here and another there .... Two or three shared one blanket. They had no tooth brushes and used bamboo sticks for toilet paper. They washed their face by sharing a common towel, so that if one man's eye became inflamed, the whole platoon caught the infection.[93]

In the spring of 1945, a Second Class soldier received 50 *yuan* per month in pay. With inflation having eroded the value of the *yuan*, this amount of money no longer bought much. A pair of straw sandals cost 50 *yuan*, a pound of cabbage 30 *yuan*, and *doufu* 50. The monthly stipend for food supplementary to rice was 350 *yuan*.[94]

The result was that the attraction of army service declined and that therefore force was needed to obtain recruits. In January 1945, Chiang Kaishek ordered the circulation of a bitter report by Feng Yuxiang that bluntly described the cruelties to which recruits were habitually subjected. Feng wrote:

> Local recruitment organs and the staffs responsible for their transport and training treat recruits terribly. Using the pretext of preventing desertion, they cruelly treat recruits like animals and thieves. ... And local government organs, which have the task of leading the masses, have become accustomed to evil practices. They do not respect the military nor offer any help. They see the soldiers who protect the country like strangers and refuse to give them spiritual or material succour.[95]

Relations between the military and local society suffered, while morale in the army plummeted. Within armies, officers and troops must have seen each other like enemies.

The Nationalists, of course, had to keep some forces combat ready. Chiang's speeches came after a plan had been worked out for a general reduction in the number of military forces while keeping a small number of divisions ready for action. Chiang Kaishek had sent the following telegram on 29 November 1941, to the MAC:

> I hope that within ten days you call a meeting of the Senior Staff of the MAC to seriously examine the following and come forward with concrete plans: (1) a plan for reducing the National Army; (2) re-adjustments in personnel systems at the level of the division and above; (3) reform of our guerrilla forces; (4) ways to promote serious implementation of regulations regarding military training; (5) the reduction

of the military budget for next year; and (6) improving the discipline of our forces, paying special attention to the prevention of smuggling, gambling, claims of rations for non-existent soldiers, opium trade, requisitioning of grain, and the illegal sale of army rations, as well as to the custom of accommodating kinsmen.[96]

The MAC suggested to reduce the army to 240 divisions, consisting of 120 divisions of the standing army and 120 divisions of Citizen Soldiers.[97] This implied a standing army divorced from production of only something like 1.2 million troops. Four armies with twelve divisions were to be designated as Offensive Divisions.[98] In 1942, three of these division were deployed in Burma – and lost.

Industrial mobilisation

The economic crisis put paid to the hope of building up a military–industrial complex to provide China's armies. Responsible for industrial mobilisation was the NRC, whose pre-war history was discussed in Chapter 4 and whose task was to make China 'self-sufficient in materials needed for national defence'.[99] The NRC's scope of activities after the beginning of the war was expanded to include the iron and steel industries, the electronics industry, the machine industry, mining operations, the chemical industry, and the energy sector. It also was responsible for the export of mineral products such as tungsten and antimony, which were bartered for weapons and ammunition, petrol, steel, copper, cement, and cotton. The NRC's establishment expanded quickly. Before the war, it oversaw only 25 work units. In 1938, it managed directly or was involved in 37 new units. This number grew to 96 in 1942 and 131 in 1945.[100] The NRC's personnel increased from a few thousand before the war to 1,355 office staff and 9,317 workers in 1939 and to 8,169 office staff and 60,538 workers in 1943. Some recollections put the NRC's total workforce, including factories in which it had only a stake, at perhaps 200,000.[101]

William Kirby has described the sterling efforts of the NRC under the redoubtable Weng Wenhao to build up basic industries in difficult conditions. As Kirby explained, the NRC was important because it sought to create a 'national defence economy' (*guo-fang jing ji*) and developed an establishment of experts and patterns of operation that would have an impact after 1949 in the PRC as well as Taiwan.[102] The NRC was certainly an important institution, collecting some of the best and brightest in the land. Its exports made possible the import of arms and ammunition, manufacturing equipment, and other scarce resources that kept the Nationalists going during the first two phases of the War of Resistance. However, the NRC was never able to create the industrial capacity capable of sustaining the Nationalists armed forces. Its pre-war decision to locate its subordinate industries in central China proved a costly mistake. The Japanese invasion meant, as Qian Changzhao, the NRC's number two, stated, that 'the efforts of two years were wiped out in one day.'[103]

A comparison of information provided by German advisors in the 1930s on the production of chemicals and minerals needed to sustain thirty divisions with actual NRC production makes clear that wartime production of such items as nitrocellulose, sulphuric acid, nitric acid, and other chemicals fell far short of what was needed.[104] If in a few categories, production was at an appropriate level, in most it was not. To produce a bullet, one needs all the necessary ingredients.

NRC reports confirm that production was never sufficient to meet the needs of the military. A Work Report of the Economics Ministry of December 1940 noted serious shortages in iron and steel production as well as coal.[105] Another report, covering the 1937–41 period, noted shortages in the production of sulphuric acid, iron, and liquid fuels.[106] In 1940, a report compared goals as set out in a Three Year plan and actual results.[107] It noted that the production of pig iron fell short by 50 per cent. The plan had called for the production of 2 steam generators, 8 coal generators, 100 truck frames, 25 drilling machines, 20 weaving machines, and the installation of 200 gas engines in trucks at the Central Machine Plant in Kunming. These limited goals were not achieved. The sodium carbonate factory at Kunming had only achieved 10 per cent of its scheduled output. Production at the Yumen Oil Fields in Gansu fell short by 50 per cent, but that was probably on purpose since due to the lack of trucks oil could not be transported in any case. In a report of 17 December 1941, Weng Wenhao noted that the NRC had built up a productive capacity of 19,000 tons of chemicals at forty-four different sites. Shortages of primary resources restricted actual output to 2,000 tons.[108]

As Kirby argued, after 1941 industrial mobilisation faltered and by 1943, Nationalist China was in the midst of an industrial depression.[109] Financial shortages and the inability to transport raw materials forced the Nationalists to cut back investment and production. Because of the Japanese blockade and the Southern Advance, China was unable to import foreign equipment and other resources. Domestic transport was difficult as China had virtually no trucks and Japanese bombing made rail and water transport difficult. Inflation too made industrial planning and orderly management difficult and undermined private business. On 21 June, Stilwell recorded in his diary that Yu Dawei, the Director of Ordnance, had told him that following the battle of Yichang, only 30 million bullets remained available and that 'without raw materials, arsenals will close down'.[110] Yu expected that by November, stocks would have run out.

By the autumn of 1944, arsenals were operating at only 55 per cent of capacity. Eighty per cent of the iron and steel plants were forced to cease or curtail production between 1943 and early 1945.[111] An NRC report stated that in the first quarter of 1942 production declined of hand grenades, bullets, mines, generators, chemicals, flour, paper, and leather.[112] During the Ichigo Offensive of 1944, coal production decreased by 17 per cent, pig iron by 23 per cent, petrol substitutes by 81 per cent, radios by 30 per cent, and generators by 61 per cent.[113] The production of weapons and ammunition was not conducted by the NRC but by arsenals controlled by the MAC. These employed 9,000 managers and 70,000 staff. When I first read Ray Huang's statement that the Nationalists produced only 15 million bullets per month, or 5 per soldier if the army was indeed 3 million men strong, I doubted that the situation could be as bad as that.[114] However, a table produced at the end of the war of MAC arsenals, excluding ammunition production by war zone commands, suggests that the situation was as bad. The arsenals of a regime keen to maintain supremacy in arms production manufactured only 12.8 million bullets, 15,300 rifles, 232,150 mortar shells, and 510 heavy machine guns.[115]

The response

The Nationalists' responded to the crisis in a number of ways. Besides reducing the army and demanding that it supplied its own needs, the Nationalists took the radical step of returning to a reliance on the land-tax and collecting it in kind so as to develop a new source of revenue and isolate public finance from the imploding fiscal and monetary system. They took steps to reduce the bureaucracy and increase its discipline. They introduced rationing systems for state dependants. They also used diplomacy, symbolic measures such as confirming or denying appointments, and secret services to maintain a degree of influence with the army and with provincial bureaucracies.

Yet, they could not prevent much of the military from slipping out of their grasp. The Nationalists had to limit their military, scale down recruitment, off-load substantial numbers of troops, and tolerate participation in smuggling and other nefarious activities. They became involved in a complex struggle for control over military force with the Communists, the Japanese, and the Wang Jingwei Government, with none able to maintain a firm control over their forces. Nationalists armies became scourges on local society and most were of no military value. Taxation and recruitment, which now drew the state and society in direct conflict, made the *baojia* an universally abhorred institution and led to a deep resentment of the Nationalists. The bureaucracy continued to be divided with each section concerned with safeguarding its own resources.

The land tax

The most important measure that the Nationalists took in the financial area was to re-centralise the land tax and to collect it in kind. From 1942, the Nationalists collected about 60 million *Shidan* of grain annually. Table 7.10 provides a geographical breakdown of taxation in kind during 1942–5. The reported figures in the table likely overstated collection as a result of pressures to report successful implementation of the policy. In addition, it was easy to fiddle tax returns and practices such as altering weights and mixing in sand were common.

Table 7.10 makes clear that the National Government was heavily dependent on a few provinces for grain collection, as was the case for recruitment. Sichuan was especially important. Besides this province, Anhui, Jiangxi, Hunan, and Shaanxi were areas critical to the survival of the Nationalists, while other provinces in the south, such as Yunnan, Guangxi, and Guangdong, were of lesser but nonetheless substantial significance. The measure not only sought to secure a reliable supply of grain to the state and the army, but also was an effort to dampen inflation by reducing the need to issue currency. Arthur Young, a financial advisor to the Nationalist, wrote after the war that 'as a financial measure, it was an indispensable means of covering war costs, and an item to the government's credit'.[116] Table 7.11, produced by Young, illustrated that it helped bring down the amount of currency the Government needed to issue. Arthur Young's breakdown of inflation makes clear that inflation of food prices was substantially below that of other categories such as clothing, metals, fuel, and building materials.[117] By removing the role of the market in grain redistribution, the effects of inflation were limited.

As Hou Kunhong argued, the decision to re-centralise the land tax was also an effort to bring provincial taxation under control. After the beginning of the war, provincial governments faced rising expenditures on policing, recruitment, social mobilisation, and the provision of armed forces in their jurisdictions. In a pattern well known from the Taiping Rebellion, this they met by taxing local trade, with the result that goods had to

Table 7.10 Taxation in kind by province, 1942–5 (in million *Shidan*)

	Type of grain	1942 quotas	1942 total	1943 quota	1943 total	1944 quota	1944 total	1945 quota	1945 total
Sichuan	Rice/wheat	16	16.5	16	15.9	20	19.5	20	18
Guizhou	Rice	2.9	2.5	2.9	2.5	3.1	2.6	3.2	2.3
Yunnan	Rice	3.5	3.8	2.5	2.3	3.6	3.6	3	2.3
Guangdong	Rice	2.5	2.7	2.2	2.07	2.1	1.5	1.8	
Guangxi	Rice	2.9	3	2.8	3	2.3	1.5	2.3	
Hunan	Rice	10	10.6	7.5	7.6	4.5	4.6	4.5	0.02
Hubei	Rice	2	1.8	1.8	1.8	1.9	1.5	2.1	
Jiangxi	Rice	6.5	6.3	7.8	8.5	7.5	5.6	6.8	
Fujian	Rice	2.3	3	2.8	3.3	3	2.9	3.3	2.2
Zhejiang	Rice	1.5	1.6	2.6	2.6	2.5	2.1	2.4	0.004
Anhui	Wheat/rice	2.7	3	2.5	3	2.6	2.3	2.6	0.001
Shanxi	Wheat	0.6	0.6	0.6	0.3	0.4	0.4	0.4	0.03
Henan	Wheat	2.4	2.5	3	3	1.5	1.5	0.7	
Shaanxi	Wheat	4.6	3.6	4.4	4.1	4.4	3.9	2.7	2.1
Gansu	Wheat	2	1.6	1.6	1.6	2	1.7	0.7	0.7
Ningxia	Wheat	0.5	0.5	0.4	0.4	0.4	0.4	0.4	0.4
Qinghai	Wheat	0.1	0.2	0.1	0.1	0.1	0.2	0.09	0.09
Suiyuan	Wheat	0.5	0.5	0.5	0.5	0.2	0.3	0.3	0.006
Xikang	Wheat	0.7	0.6	0.5	0.5	0.6	0.5	0.6	0.4
Jiangsu	Wheat	0.3	0.3						
Shandong	Wheat	0.4	0.8				0.002		
Xinjiang	Wheat			0.5	1.2	0.5	0.4	1.4	1
Total		65	66.1	63.1	64.7		57	59	30

Sources: *Liangzheng Shiliao*, VI, 494–605; ZHMGDAZL, V: 2 (Finance and Economics), vol. 2, 240–5.

Table 7.11 The financial impact of taxation in kind

Year (ending June 30)	Cash receipts other than from bank credit	Collections in kind	Total receipts other than from bank credit	Expenditure in cash	Expenditure in kind	Total expenditure	Expenditure covered other than by bank credit (per cent)
1937	870		870	1,167		1,167	75
1938	1,314		1,314	2,091		2,091	63
1938 2nd half	341		341	1,169		1,169	29
1939 calendar	580		580	2,797		2,797	21
1940	1,589		1,589	5,288		5,288	30
1941	2,024		2,024	10,795		10,795	19
1942	6,254	6,326	12,580	25,149	6,326	31,475	40
1943	20,768	26,561	47,329	67,234	26,561	93,795	50
1944	61,046	60,000	121,046	193,619	60,000	253,619	48
1945	216,519	280,000	496,519	1,257,733	280,000	1,537,733	32

Source: Arthur Young, *China's Wartime Finance*, 29.

pass many transport tax stations as they moved from one province to the next. Provinces further issued their own debt, amounting to 23 million *yuan* in 1937, 86 million in 1938, 23 million in 1939, 95 million in 1939, and 69 million in 1940. They further borrowed from provincial banks and issued subsidiary coins, something to which they were legally entitled.[118] The lack of unified budgetary, accounting, and treasury systems meant that the central government could not effectively control provincial finances. The centralisation of the land tax was an attempt to establish discipline over provincial finances and increase the central take of total tax collection.[119]

Several further comments are in order. First, these data, like those on recruitment, illustrate again why the war zones of the central and south China were so important to the Nationalists. With the exception of Shaanxi in north China, northern provinces were not able to sustain large numbers of troops for long periods. Second, the loss of Hunan, Henan, and Jiangxi during the Ichigo Offensive led to a radical increase of collection in Sichuan. Sichuan society was put through the wringer because by the end of the war it was the only place where the Nationalists could step up grain collection and recruitment.

If the new land tax policy enabled the Nationalists to continue resistance after 1941, its price was that with the return to taxation of the land tax in kind came all the problems associated with the land tax in imperial times. The Nationalists state lacked accurate knowledge about landholdings, productivity, and population. Those with power and influence could easily find ways to avoid the tax, while *baojia* personnel, responsible for making sure that enough was collected, resorted to extortionist methods to meet quotas set at higher levels while at the same time they made false returns and hoarded grain. The cost of transport was high and formed a much criticised additional burden on taxpayers who had to haul grain over long distances to meet their tax quota. Spillage during collection and transport and decay in storage wasted an unknown but no doubt substantial part of what was collected.[120] Perhaps most importantly, the measure shifted the burden of financing the war on the shoulders of the peasantry, while tax collectors and officials abused the opportunities that the tax brought for private gain.

Wartime *tanpai* (unapproved and incidental levies) too made *baojia* personnel hated figures. It has been estimated that one-fourth of *tanpai* was instituted by central and provincial governments, another fourth by local elites and religious organisations, and half by *baojia* personnel.[121] With the central government having seized control of the land tax, local government became heavily dependent on *tanpai* after 1941. The situation was exacerbated by the fact that in many areas, government officials had fled to the rear and fiscal bureaucracies had evaporated. Government *tanpai* were levied for a host of purposes, such as disaster relief, self-government, granary maintenance, stipends for students at normal schools in the county and provincial capital, local militia, road repair, training courses, elementary schools, local self-government expenditures, and so on.[122] The army collected *tanpai* as well. Army agents, not knowing the local situation, had the *baojia* collect their *tanpai*. They demanded food, animal feed, draft animals, wood, coal, clothing, transport equipment, and cooking utensils. They also pressed men and women into service as porters, cooks, and for other duties. Especially in the later stages of the war, resentment against such behaviour spilled over into local revolts.[123]

To what extent aggregate food supplies were enough to feed the population in Nationalist areas is difficult to know. Hou Kunhong estimated that even after 1941 they remained just about sufficient. He based his calculations on a total population in Nationalist areas of 203 million, a figure based on 1941 Ministry of the Interior assessments. He then calculated how much food this population would have needed, taking into account different calorie requirements according to age and sex and then compared the result with data on harvests.[124]

Several problems exist with this analysis. Given the imperfection of the *baojia*, on which population data were based, it is unlikely that the Ministry's information was anything but a guess. Ho Ping-ti puts the population figures for the relevant provinces after the war substantially higher.[125] Using 1938 Ministry of the Interior figures, British intelligence estimated in 1942 that the population in the eight completely unoccupied provinces of China numbered 95.5 million, while another 182.6 million lived in provinces of which only small parts had been occupied, making a total of over 278 million people under National Government rule. A 1941 *China Air Mail* estimate, which used county data, put the figure at 250 million.[126] Hou's calculations do not take into account spoilage, the breakdown of the transport infrastructure, over-reporting, and Japanese raiding. Averages furthermore can hide huge regional discrepancies, as the well-known Henan Famine of 1943–4 illustrates. In short, it seems likely that food supplies became short in many areas after 1941 and were unlikely to have been sufficient, even in the aggregate, after the beginning of Operation Ichigo and likely earlier.

The General State Mobilisation Law

On 29 March 1942, the Nationalists promulgated the General State Mobilisation Law to 'concentrate and use all human and material forces in the country to strengthen national defence and implement the War of Resistance'.[127] The law gave the state far-ranging powers in all areas of life, ranging from the economic and financial to the social and cultural. It also gave the state the power to assign people to tasks and places as it saw fit. It could procure and commandeer material resources without making payments, settle labour disputes, determine prices and wages, and allocate land and stipulate its use. Violations were punishable by military law.[128] The slogan advanced to justify the new law was 'Military First; Victory First'.[129]

Behind the promulgation of the law was the desire to improve bureaucratic efficiency, deal with the economic crisis, strengthen defence industries, and dampen bureaucratic rivalries.[130] To implement it, in June a National Mobilisation Committee was established.[131] The purpose of the committee, as its Secretary explained in 1944, was to 'pressure, investigate, coordinate, and facilitate cooperation' of various state organs. The Implementation Guidelines of the National Mobilisation Law stressed that the National Mobilisation Committee would serve as an overarching organisation to co-ordinate all government departments. Each ministry had to set up a unit to liaise with the Committee. It drew up departmental implementation schemes and reported regularly to the National Mobilisation Committee.[132] In conformity with the stress on efficiency, the committee adopted detailed regulations about the flow of documents, their registration, as well as the time limits by which correspondence had to be answered.

The National Mobilisation Committee oversaw a staff divided into sections. The Military Section dealt with issues such as planning for and mobilisation of military supplies, the co-ordination of economic and military warfare, military industries, procurement and allocation of military and human resources for the army, and co-ordination of transport. The Human Resources Section concerned itself with military recruitment, training and employment of experts, the settlement of conflicts between labour and capital, as well as the organisation and training of professional and mass organisation. The Spiritual Mobilisation Section was responsible for propaganda, the promotion of science, and the development of various forms of technical expertise, culture and the arts, education, and mass training programmes. It also supervised the mass media.

One purpose of the committee was to deal with bureaucratic factionalism. It was established after a review of government operations triggered by a letter from Weng Wenhao. The War of Resistance had produced a rapid increase in the size of the central government. Weng wrote to Chiang Kaishek on 10 December 1941 that the Executive Yuan alone had 300,000 people on its pay-roll.[133] Weng believed that 45,000 would be sufficient. Chiang Kaishek's comment on Weng's letter shows that he was surprised by Weng's estimate, but the investigation proved Weng right. The Executive Yuan employed 308,207 personnel, of which the Ministry of Military Administration's, with 139,937 people on its pay-roll, employed almost half. The Ministry of Finance had 43,169 persons on its staff, the Ministry of Economic Affairs 11,000, and the Ministry of Communications 39,000.[134] If this growth was driven in part by the increase in tasks handled by the bureaucracy, it also was the result of the fact that employment in the government or in government factories was a way to escape military recruitment.

In his letter, Weng argued that bureaucratic expansion had come at the expense of efficiency. Many civil servants were incompetent, busied themselves with creating forms, demanding their completion, and convening long meetings. According to Weng, the size of the bureaucracy made it impossible to raise salaries to adequate levels so that 'the morale of administrative circles is declining daily'. Anticipating that the Southern Advance would mean the further deterioration of central finances, Weng counselled Chiang Kaishek to avoid the temptation simply to cut budgets of ministries without reducing staff.

Another issue highlighted by Weng was the emergence of '*xitong*', or systems developed by a bureaucracy to ring-fence scarce resources, provide for its own personnel, and protect its influence and power from incursion by other *xitong*. A response to shortages, the result was the creation of a myriad of agencies at provincial and local levels which each belonged to a separate *xitong*. Weng focused his criticism on Kong Xiangxi's Ministry of Finance. He argued that it controlled nearly five thousand subordinate offices at the provincial and local level.[135] Weng's own Ministry of Economic Affairs was of course also a *xitong* and he was no stranger to bureaucratic infighting: he omitted mention of the personnel figures of the NRC in his report about his own ministry's personnel figures. If the Ministry of Finance and the Ministry of Economic Affairs were competitors, so were the Executive Yuan as a whole and the Supreme Defence Council. Commenting from a provincial perspective, Fang Ce, the head of the Civil Administration Office of Henan Province, complained that each new government initiative resulted in the creation of a new office. Consequently, there was no unified control over policy and local bureaucracies proliferated, each pursuing their own initiatives.[136]

The National Mobilisation Committee was designed to bring order to this bureaucratic mess by spreading the NRC's planning methods to all government activity. The Committee was to become the central organisation where all information was brought together, detailed plans worked out, tasks assigned to various parts of the bureaucracy, and progress reports reviewed and checked. A June 1942 meeting ordered all bureaucratic organs to draw up work plans and work guidelines for the remainder of 1942 and for the 1943 calendar year.[137] The military was ordered to do the same and provide detailed statistical tables of all materials it would need. The information so collected would then be broken down into subsidiary tables of the required primary resources, so that the National Mobilisation Committee could then assign these to the relevant ministries.

The National Mobilisation Committee would not become the mechanism that would curb bureaucratic infighting. In the fall of 1942, Chiang Kaishek established a Standing Committee of three persons to speed up decision making. Chiang Kaishek's move was opposed from various quarters on the ground that decisions of the Standing Committee had to be approved by the plenary meeting of the committee. In March 1943, new regulations were adopted that included in the Standing Committee the Vice-Head of the Executive Yuan, the Secretary of the Central Party Office, as well as the Ministers of Military Administration, Finance, Economics, Communications, Agriculture and Forestry, Social Affairs, and Grain Administration. This Standing Committee would meet every two weeks.[138] The ministries had effectively blunted the attempt to centralise power and improve bureaucratic efficiency. In June 1944, Chiang again ordered the Secretary of the Committee, Zhang Lisheng, to find ways to improve efficiency. Chiang's personal secretary, Chen Bulei, commented that institutional tinkering would not work. Personal conflict between the major figures on the committee was the real cause of the lack of effective progress.[139]

State involvement in the distribution of scarce resources

Shortages, inflation, and the disintegration of markets meant that the state was drawn ever more deeply into the distribution of scarce resources. This was true not only for the distribution of energy and other inputs to industry, but also for food and other items of daily necessity. Since the National Government did not have the bureaucratic apparatus to supply rations to the whole population, it instead privileged certain state dependents as well as some factory workers.

Dependents of the central government received rations of food and other daily necessities, had access to subsidised housing and free healthcare, and their children were given privileged access to education. In February 1942, Chiang Kaishek ordered the Material Resources Bureau of the Ministry of Economic Affairs to device a rationing system for rice, salt, cotton cloth, edible oil, and coal to state dependents. They were made available at subsidised prices or for free. Some products, like coal, oil, and cotton cloth were provided at state stores at 10 per cent of official prices. Rations were also allocated through the work unit, with amounts depending not only on status but also age to reflect the family cycle. Subsidised healthcare was provided from 1943.[140]

An August 1942 report by He Haoruo, the head of the Material Resources Bureau of the Ministry of Economic Affairs, provides insight both in the type of shortages that existed as well as how the National Government dealt with them. The report reviewed supplies of coal, cotton, edible oils, paper, leather, soap, candles, toothbrushes, and toothpaste. According to He, cotton shortages were most critical. Cotton was used in China not only for clothing but also for bedding as little wool was available. After reviewing China's cotton production and industrial and household spinning and weaving capacity, He concluded that China could produce 1.8 yard of cotton cloth per capita, which according to He amounted to one-third of actual need assuming a population size of 200 million people.[141] As He mentioned, cotton demand was elastic: it was possible to forego purchase of new clothes for a while. Over the long run, however, there was no escaping the fact that cotton supplies would never be able to meet demand. To optimise supply, He suggested various schemes to transport cotton from Shaanxi and Henan, where most cotton was grown, to the cotton industries of Sichuan. He also suggested some plans to increase production. He rejected, however, a complete state monopoly on the ground that the bureaucracy would never be able to capture more then 10 per cent of finished cotton goods and because it would not be able to deliver their equitable dispersal. Instead he advocated a limited rationing system to the army and state officials.[142]

Coal was used for industry, railroads, salt production, cooking, and heating. According to He, production was about enough to meet requirements, but transport difficulties prevented efficient use of the available types of coal and led to shortages in some areas, especially in Sichuan where industry was concentrated. He suggested switching domestic users to lesser quality coal in order to make high grade coal available to industry. He also proposed that industries be required to register their needs with the Ministry, which would then organise supply from coal mines at prices determined by the state. The mines themselves were to register with the state and report their production on a monthly basis.

As to cooking oils, critically important to the Chinese diet, He reviewed production capacity and consumption in each province, concluding that the shortfall was about 10 per cent of existing production, affecting mostly the urban population because peasants could extract oil from seed. He recommended measures to increase cultivation of seeds from which cooking oils could be derived, with the state procuring about half of the amount needed to supply urban centres to stabilise prices.

With respect to paper production, He differentiated between handicraft and industrial production. He advocated that handicraft production be sustained through loans, with all production procured by the state. Industrial production was to be supervised by the state, with a representative of the ministry stationed at each factory to oversee production and allocation. All private marketing of paper was to be eliminated. Users were to register with the Ministry and made allocations from available stocks.

In including toothbrushes, toothpaste, leather shoes, and candles in his report, He was aware that 'these are not items of daily need for most people'. However, according to He, for urban elites they had become customary. He advocated their inclusion in the state rationing system 'to avoid an increase in their burdens resulting from merchants hoarding these items and driving up prices'.[143] He probably realised as well that a failure to do so would mean that elites in Chongqing would find other and far more costly and corrupting ways to import items of great value as status indicators and gifts with which to cultivate connections.

If it is clear that the Nationalists state tried to set up a rationing system, only further research can reveal the reality of its implementation. Even as conceived, it was divisive as it defined an urban elite who worked in central government offices or for units managed by it. Even amongst this circumscribed group, rationing no doubt created or re-enforced social divisions, between bureaucratic levels and between management, technical or professional workers, and regular workers. Rationing also inevitably fuelled corruption, as rationed goods could be sold for a high price on the market. Not only individuals, but also bureaucracies or *xitong* were involved in this, often on a substantial scale.[144]

The military

Out of the War of Resistance would not emerge a new unified military that recovered China's martial pride, but one more divided than before, militarily ineffective, and socially and economically parasitic. Demobilisation was difficult. The Nationalists did not have the financial means to pension off soldiers. Rural poverty meant that soldiers who returned to their homes might not be welcomed with open arms. Nationalist guerrilla forces illustrate well the problems thrown up by troops that the Nationalist could not supply or control. According to the minutes of an MAC meeting of May 1941, the Nationalists then had 467,200 guerrillas. After the first phase of the War of Resistance, guerrilla units had been attached to war zones and two large guerrilla bases had been set up in north China. Guerrilla units, however, often soaked up deserters, bandits, local militia members, and hoodlums and local toughs. They operated beyond Nationalist supply lines in occupied territories without administrative organs and were difficult to control. According to the minutes of the meeting, many became bandits gangs doing little in the way of fighting the Japanese. The minutes noted that their abusive behaviour had become so detested that local populations fled just upon the mention of the word guerrilla.

Nationalist guerrilla units, then, became a liability. The Nationalists were not the only ones who faced such problems. The same was true for the Japanese.[145] The Communists were better at balancing available resources with guerrilla warfare and keeping control over them, but they too were not always successful. Elise DeVido noted in her detailed study of Shandong that 'throughout the 1940s Shandong cadres' reports ceaselessly critiqued a wide range of abuses, broadly categorised as 'corruption and waste', committed by Communist 'regimes' and 'troops'. In 1941 and 1942, when Communist areas were subjected to Japanese and puppet mopping-up campaigns, according to DeVido, the Communists too resorted to *tanpai*. In 1944, one veteran Shandong Communist lamented that Communist troops 'acted like bandits, violated party and government policy, and did not know the difference between the army they served and the Nationalist army' and in September 1945 a top cadre of the Shandong Military District still criticised the 'tribalism,' localism, and 'guerrilla bad habits' of Shandong's military forces.[146] In south China, the Communists had considerable difficulty in imposing discipline over their forces, and some which had once belonged to the Red Army had escaped Communist disciplines altogether.[147] The possibility that behind the New Fourth Army Incident lay a Communist army that was out of control, if true, suggests the same.

The MAC decided that although guerrillas had played a useful role in several battles during the second phase of the War of Resistance, they had become such a liability that their number should be reduced by 40 per cent and that their name should be changed to Shock Troops.[148] It is unlikely that this measure achieved anything more than a symbolic distancing between the Nationalists and guerrillas they now disowned.

Not to demobilise troops was often a better way of limiting the social and economic damage that guerrillas inflicted. A British intelligence report of 1 August 1945 noted that after the fall of Burma the border area between Yunnan and the Kengtung and Manglun states of north Burma became 'a happy hunting ground for Chinese bandits' which carried out 'a scorched-earth policy', razing villages as they roamed through the area.[149] It is likely that included in such bandit gangs were former National Army soldiers. After the 93rd Division incorporated two of the main bandit groups into its army and provided them with arms and equipment, they had 'settled down' and had begun trading, including in opium and gold.

The report focused on one of the bandit leaders, Lo Zhengming. By the summer of 1945, he claimed that the Manglun state had been handed by the Burmese government to China and that he had been appointed Military and Civil Administrator. He financed his forces by imposing a house-tax payable in opium. Although a heavy burden, nonetheless, according to the report

> A very noticeable change has taken place in the daily routine of Loh Chung-ming [Lo Zhengming]'s guerrillas. A year ago they were ill-disciplined, poorly clothed, and devoted no time to any kind of training. At Pangyang the guerrillas are now summoned to their various duties by bugle call. The morning starts with P.T. and is followed by other forms of training. In the late afternoon they are given more training. After the evening meal they spend 2–3 hours singing army songs and anthems. The men are all well equipped in full army uniform and discipline appears to be strict.[150]

The report drew a contrast between Lo Zhengming's bandit group and 'a strong force of Chinese bandits' without any connection with Nationalist officials which had entered the Manglun and Wa states and 'looted the countryside'.[151]

If guerrilla units imposed huge problems of control, more disciplined Nationalist units too could end up preying on local society. Tang Enbo's forces were stationed in Henan in 1943. In *Thunder out of China*, Theodore White described Tang as a 'relatively pleasant man, gracious, good humoured, energetic', who tried 'to mitigate the curse of the famine without upsetting the army system in which he was enmeshed', but who was unable to do so and therefore became the object of popular anger.[152] Henan sustained perhaps some 300,000 Nationalist troops, whose presence was of course one of the reasons for the famine. Army officers went around pressing civil officials and *baojia* personnel to make the peasants pay their land taxes, even when they were starving. When the Japanese attacked in the spring during Operation Ichigo, Tang's troops in the area were too diseased and demoralised to offer resistance and peasants used primitive weapons such as hunting rifles, knives, and pitchforks to vent their anger on them.

Other army units involved themselves in local trade and smuggling. The National Government had declared a complete embargo on trading with the Japanese in 1937, but this embargo was modified in 1939 when it became clear that the result was a scarcity of important resources, including technical equipment but also daily necessities such as salt and cotton. From 1939, trade under government licence was allowed, with the military made responsible for enforcing it. 1941 reports from the 1st, 2nd, 4th, and

8th War Zones as well as form the 3rd and 22nd Group Army make clear that for many the sale of trade licences, the extortion of bribes, the levying of fees, confiscation, and the erection of tax barriers became an important source of income. Army units competed among themselves for business, as well as with local traders, bandit gangs, and secret societies, often in violent ways.[153]

Dai Li's secret service, the *Juntong*, became a powerful organisation because its task was to police smuggling and maintain National Government influence over localised armed forces. In 1942, responsibility for the prevention of smuggling was taken away from the military and assigned to the Bureau for the Prevention of Smuggling of the Ministry of Finance. Headed by Dai Li, the Bureau had an office staff of four thousand men and commanded 120,000 troops.[154] Dai Li's *Juntong* was a highly disciplined and hierarchical organisation in which personal bonds and absolute obedience to Dai were key features. In 1943, it dealt with 31,598 cases, imposed 3.5 million fines, and confiscated 7 million pounds of salt, 2,000 ounces of gold, and 1 million ounces of silver. The Bureau executed 359 members of its own staff for corruption.[155]

The struggle between the Communists, the Nationalists, and the Japanese for hegemony over armed force in the Lower Yangtze illustrates that establishing discipline over armed force was difficult for all, that all used secret services, and that the Communists did not have it all their own way. A British intelligence report of February 1945 indicated the tenuous position of the Nationalists when it stated that 'there are reports that General Tai Li has recently organised a campaign to contact Puppets, but had met with a reaction that has indicated a lack of confidence in the present KMT regime'.[156] But, Dai Li's *Juntong* was successful in securing the co-operation of puppet forces of the Wang Jingwei National Government. After its establishment, Wang Jingwei had to accumulate military power, something that was not easy given the doubtful loyalty of most puppet forces in the region. Wang turned to his own secret service. Its head was Li Shiqun, who had worked for both the Communist and Nationalist secret service, but joined the Wang Jingwei Government soon after its establishment. Using his knowledge of the *Juntong* presence in Shanghai as well as his Shanghai secret society connections, Li first destroyed much of the *Juntong* in one of the nastiest turf wars of the whole War of Resistance. Having thus made himself indispensable to Wang Jingwei, Li quickly rose to become Governor of Jiangsu Province, the most wealthy in China, and was put in charge of country-side pacification campaigns to bring puppet forces under control.

Li then made two mistakes. The first was to engage Zhou Fohai, one of the three most ranking leaders of the Wang Jingwei Government, in a factional struggle for control of the Wang Jingwei Government's armed forces. The second was to alienate his Japanese backers, in part by failing to deliver promised supplies for the Japanese but also by behaving in such a ruthless fashion that he became a liability to Japanese. His heinous reputation undermined their hopes of bringing order to the Lower Yangtze region and securing a degree of respectability for the Wang Jingwei Government.

Zhou Fohai became convinced in 1942 that the Japanese would lose the war and that therefore the Wang Jingwei Government was doomed. Through the *Juntong* he re-established contact with Chongqing and then provided intelligence to the Nationalists, protected *Juntong* agents, and made funds available from his Ministry of Finance for Nationalist guerrilla forces in the area. The result was that one faction in the Japanese military, the *Juntong*, and Zhou Fohai collaborated in the assassination of Li Shiqun in September 1943. Thereafter Zhou increased his control over the military forces of the Wang Jingwei Government. Following Japan's surrender, Chongqing agreed to accord him lenient treatment if he helped secure the Lower Yangtze region for the Nationalists. On 27 August 1945, after Japan's surrender, British intelligence reported that the Nanjing Garrison of Wang Jingwei, the Beiping Garrison, Manchurian troops, as well as warlords in north China had contacted Chongqing, promising to accept its leadership and resist Communist efforts to take over their areas.[157]

The great losers in these machinations were the Communists. The assassination of Li Shiqun was an important factor. The Communist spy-master Pan Hannian spent most of his time after 1940 in the Shanghai area. He established contact with Li and his operatives were active in Li Shiqun's as well as Japan's secret services. The result was a useful flow of intelligence about Japanese as well as puppet military activities and a degree of security for CCP secret service agencies. Following the beginning of the Southern Advance, Pan decided to intensify his dealings with Li, meeting him several times. Pan stayed in Li's house in Nanjing to escape the attentions of the Japanese and even accepted a blank cheque book. In 1943, Li arranged a meeting between Pan and Wang Jingwei during which the two discussed collaboration against the Nationalists and Pan offered Wang a promise of safety if future events turned against him. Li Shiqun's assassination and Zhou Fohai's victory in their factional battle seriously damaged CCP prospects in the Lower Yangtze region.

The *Zhongtong*, the Central Bureau of Investigation and Statistics under the control of the KMT party headquarters, followed similar strategies as the *Juntong*. One of its successes was the elimination in 1942 of the CCP party apparatus from provinces in south China such as Jiangxi, Guangxi, Fujian, and Zhejiang. This followed the *Zhongtong* capture of the CCP Jiangxi Provincial Committee, which allowed it to undertake a counter-intelligence operation which would net it important members of the CCP's Southern Work Committee. Some of these were turned so that the *Zhongtong* gained the necessary information to roll up CCP party organisations and destroy CCP guerrilla forces in south China.[158]

Without the *Juntong* and the *Zhongtong*, the position of the Nationalists would have been more difficult than it was. At the same time, the reliance on such organisation, which could not but damage the reputation of the National Government, also illustrates the essential weakness of the Nationalists. They needed to use extreme measures to establish what was only a limited influence over troops to have any chance of returning to their former heartland.

In the provinces of the south, the position of the Nationalists became equally fragile. In the years before the War of the Resistance, the National Government had focused on strengthening its position in north China. During the War itself, Nationalist strategy had initially been premised on the belief that the Japanese would not enter south China. If in the beginning of the War, southern generals, including Li Zongren, decided that their futures were best served by participating in the War of Resistance on the Nationalist side, by the end of the War this was no longer the case. We know of at least one instance when southern generals in 1944 made a serious bid to overthrow Chiang Kaishek. Li Jishen in August 1944 contacted the Americans to sound out their attitude towards a possible coup in the south against Chongqing under his leadership.[159]

If such would have been an extreme step, and one that would have left those who carried it out with the same difficult problems that Chiang Kaishek faced, far more common was the adoption of ambiguous attitudes. Those provided rich opportunities to gain from all sides. A British intelligence report of January 1945 described the situation, perhaps not correctly in its details but nonetheless insightfully.

> Central Government authorities continue to deny the report of the secession of Marshal Li Chai Sen [Li Jishen], but unofficial sources claim that the Marshal's entry into the Puppet camp is an established fact. These sources assert that the Japanese have formed a so-called 'People's Self Defence Commission of the Province of Kwangtung and Kwangsi, with Mr Liang Sou Min [unidentified, but perhaps Liang Shuming] as Chairman and Marshall Li Chai Sen [Li Jishen] as Military Commander. General Hsueh Yueh [Xue Yue], Commander of the Chungking Army's Ninth War Zone, is reported to have succumbed to Japanese intrigue and is believed to have retired to Lechang.... The Chungking regime reacted by appointing a successor to General Hsueh Yueh as Governor of Hunan, but it was later decided to withhold action in view of the probability that General Hsueh is merely 'sitting on the fence' and the interests of the Kuomintang regime could be best served by an attitude of indulgence. Likewise the assumption of Puppet status by General Hsia Wei [Xia Wei] is also believed to have received the tacit cognisance of Chungking leaders.... The situation in Gugong [in north Guangdong] is obscure but there is every evidence that General Yu Hanmou is ably contributing to the present hiatus by a policy of passive loyalty to all concerned.... In Western Kwangsi, General Chang Fa Kwei [Zhang Fakui], Chief of the Fourth War Zone, is reported to be establishing new Headquarters. The degree of his recognition of the status quo remains unclear.[160]

In short, during the War of Resistance the Nationalists were unable to prevent what had often happened in the past once a serious military crisis compelled the arming of large numbers of people. They lost control over many of their armies, these rapidly deteriorated in combat effectiveness, and many became scourges on local society. Describing the same process with reference to the much hailed Hunan Army of Zeng Guofan, K.C. Liu noted that by the late 1850s 'the discipline of the Hunan Army steadily deteriorated. The capture of a town was followed invariably by pillage, if not also by indiscriminate killing. Hunan troops [behaved] so badly that local militia corps often engaged them in battle. By 1856, [Zeng] found that most officers of the Hunan Army "cannot avoid fattening their private purse somewhat" '.[161]

The end to the dream

The always limited unity of the first phase of the war did not hold. Wang Jingwei made his move perhaps too early and history did not work out for him. He died in a Japanese hospital before the end of the war. He was buried on Purple Mountain near Nanjing, between the mausoleum for the founder of the Ming Dynasty who had ended Mongol rule and that of Sun Yatsen. Although heavily reinforced by concrete, Chiang Kaishek had Wang's grave destroyed upon his return to Nanjing.[162] In the mid-1990s, however,

Wang was re-incorporated into history, even if not in a flattering way. A statue of him could be found at Purple Mountain again, but it had Wang kneeling in a cage with his head bowed in shame and facing in the direction of the grand mausoleum of Sun Yatsen. The inscription condemned Wang as 'The Worst Traitor of All Time Kneels in Shame to All Generations'.[163] Today, this statue has made way for a Japanese-financed garden.

The withdrawal of the CCP from the NPC in March 1941 marked a more decisive turn in the dissipation of unity. The affair followed the New Fourth Army Incident. Just before the opening of the March 1941 session of the NPC, Mao Zedong sent a telegram to the NPC secretariat setting out a series of conditions for a reconciliation and the CCP's continued participation in the NPC. Mao demanded 'the punishment of the three principal culprits of the New Fourth Army Incident, He Yingqin, Gu Zhutong and Shangguan Yunxiang'; the release of political prisoners; 'the abolition of one party dictatorship and the introduction of democracy'; and 'the implementation of Sun Yatsen-ism'.[164] In demanding that the National Government implement Sun Yatsen-ism, Mao asserted that the Nationalists had turned against their own ideology that had been enshrined in the Organic Law, thus challenging the core claim underpinning the Nationalists' right to leadership.

The NPC spring 1941 meeting gave a full airing to the Communist withdrawal and the negotiations that had taken place between its representatives and Zhou Enlai. Most councillors expressed the wish to find a compromise while maintaining the prestige of the NPC as the organ expressing the will of the people.[165] In a speech to the NPC, Chiang Kaishek compared the CCP's behaviour to the Japanese, who, Chiang stated, also always demanded that the Nationalists accepted responsibility for an incident that it had provoked itself and then demanded special privileges as a condition for reconciliation. He charged the Communists with violating their promises made at the initiation of the United Front. He commented that 'CCP members are citizens of the Republic of China, just like us. The fact that, at this time when we are struggling for our survival in the War of Resistance, they make these demands of our country and of the NPC, which expresses the will of the whole people, means that they oppose both'.[166] The schism became expressed rhetorically in the adoption in Nationalist parlance of the adjective 'bogus' (wei) in references to Communist organisations. The Nationalists used the same adjective for the Wang Jingwei Government.[167]

This was not the final breakdown of relations. In January 1944, at a time when both the Nationalists and the Communists were experiencing severe economic difficulties, serious negotiations once more began. In May, discussions in Xi'an led to an outline agreement in which the Communists consented to accepting incorporation of their forces in the Nationalist battle order, a limit of twelve on the number of their divisions, and nominal incorporation of Yan'an in the Nationalist administrative order. The Communist negotiator Lin Boqu also agreed to Communist recognition of Chiang Kaishek. The Nationalists, on their side, agreed to make no substantial changes in Yan'an, release political prisoners, carry out democratisation, protect family members of Communist forces in Nationalist areas, end the economic boycott of Yan'an, and solve any further problems by political means.[168]

By September, this attempt at reconciliation had broken down. On 4 September, the CCP Politburo sent a telegram to its negotiator stating that 'the moment has arrived to demand the re-organisation of the Government'.[169] On 10 October, Zhou Enlai in

Yan'an elaborated in a public address that the CCP wanted the convocation of a national emergency conference attended by representatives of all parties, local governments, and armies that would 'end one party rule' and establish a 'united government' with the right to make its own military appointments.[170] As the 4 September CCP directive stated, 'it will be absolutely impossible for the KMT to accept these proposals, but minor parties, local power holders, progressive people in China and abroad, and even enlightened people of Allied governments will approve'.[171] It is unlikely that the Ichigo Offensive, the moves to unseat Chiang Kaishek in south China, and the support expressed for Yan'an by some US officials were irrelevant in convincing the Communists that their future was best served by abandoning the earlier agreement.[172]

A final twist

At the Fourth Nanyue Conference of February 1944, Chiang Kaishek declared that 'the Second Period of the War of Resistance has come to an end, and the Third Period, that of a decisive counter-attack on the enemy, has arrived'.[173] Chiang outlined two scenarios for a counter-offensive. Arguing that three months were needed to conclude preparations, the first scenario was based on the assumption that the Japanese would begin their own offensive before preparations had concluded while in the second the Japanese would sit back. In both cases, the recovery of Yichang and Wuhan along the Yangtze River and the grain and recruitment areas around them stood central.[174]

Chiang instructed each of the 9th, 5th, and 6th War Zones along the Yangtze River to prepare two armies made up of their best divisions for immediate offensive operations. If the Japanese attacked, these were to advance through the openings in the Japanese position. With respect to the second scenario, Chiang ordered all forces to select 'vanguard units' at all levels, citing Sunzi's principle that 'if an army has no vanguard, it will be defeated'. Thus, a war zone would have a vanguard army, an army a vanguard division, and so on. He ordered preparations to be complete by May 1944.[175] Chiang pointed out as well that the military would have to take responsibility for economic and social rehabilitation in recovered areas, which would be especially difficult at the time of spring shortages. He referred to Zeng Guofan and instructed his audience to familiarise themselves with Zeng Guofan's measures after recovering Nanjing to restore social order, provide material relief, organise *baojia*, and register households. He also told them to read the *Kang Jilu*, an 18th century version of a compendium of writings on relief, restoring government, and reviving agriculture as well as *New Knowledge about Self-Defence* (Ziwei Xinzhi), also full of historical examples about what to do and what not to do in restoring local order after warfare.[176]

The address makes clear that Chiang's suggestion that a counter-offensive would be possible encountered considerable scepticism. Chiang referred to a report made at the conference which argued that 'the fortifications at Yichang are very strong and Japanese fire-power is arranged tightly. When our forces reach their battle-field fortifications, we will not be able to get through'.[177] Chiang commented that this was 'true' and agreed that a strong airforce and heavy artillery would have to participate in the offensive.[178]

Chiang Kaishek's agreement that offensives were impossible without the support of the airforce and the participation of heavy artillery, his warning that Japan might go on the offensive first, the tactic of moving into gaps left in Japanese positions if they did attack, and the fact that no concrete war plans were formulated suggest that Chiang did not believe that his armies could take on the Japanese unaided. His purposes at the Fourth Nanyue Conference was probably to ensure that there would be enough forces ready to move once a Japanese collapse set in and to keep the war in the mind of his generals, who were thinking about many other things. The Ichigo and Ugo offensives put paid to any hope of a Nationalist offensive in the spring of 1944.

In the spring of 1945, once the tide had turned in Europe and in Burma and Ichigo had run its course, Chiang Kaishek again argued for an offensive in China during a meeting with Mountbatten in Chongqing in March 1945. Chiang requested Mountbatten's agreement to the withdrawal of Chinese forces from Burma for this purpose. In explaining the situation, according to the British minutes of the meeting, one 'able' Nationalist general, a reference to Chen Cheng,

> wished to emphasize how greatly China has suffered, both in personnel and in materiel and in national prestige, by the loss of Henan, Hunan, and Guangxi. He had said that they had taken the risk of moving their best troops to [Burma] and that they were then attacked by the Japanese elsewhere. By the capture of Hunan and Kwangsi, they had lost not only a most important granary, but also a valuable recruiting area, as these areas produced very good soldiers. In fact, were it not for the extremely good crops in the last year in Szechuan, which had been almost miraculous, the situation would have been most difficult. The 3rd, 7th, and 9th War Zones are cut off from the central government. Their only salvation lies in a counter-offensive against the Japanese.[179]

Mountbatten refused, arguing that China's Expeditionary Army in Burma was needed to keep pressure on the Japanese flank while General Slim fought his way to Rangoon. Although General Slim would take the city as early as 3 May, Mountbatten in Chongqing had not sounded confident. He told Chiang that Rangoon would either be captured quickly or that British forces would have to retreat to the north-west. He further explained that no amphibious landings would take place and no US forces would be deployed. Chiang Kaishek argued that China could not 'afford to let the Hunan and Kwangsi Provinces remain in Japanese hands much longer and from both the economic and political points of view they must be reconquered',[180] but the Nationalists again had to confront the reality that their best troops were deployed in Burma while their position in China disintegrated.

Albert Wedemeyer, after succeeding Stilwell, was more than a little angry with Mountbatten. He wrote on 14 May 1945 that

> last winter and this spring when I was so urgently in need of air-planes, the British were using them for clandestine operations in great numbers within French Indo China. Representations were made by Mountbatten to the British Chiefs of Staff that if one airplane were removed from India-Burma by me that his operations against Rangoon would be jeopardised.... When the Japanese were driving west-ward last winter against Kweiyang, we had definitive evidence of the fact that Kunming was their objective. They had the capability of driving on, and the Generalissimo – in fact, even Mountbatten's representative here, Lieutenant

General Carton de Wiart – urged me to withdraw all five CAI [Chinese Army in India] divisions from Burma. I took more than a calculated decision and only withdrew two, which I carefully interposed to block the Jap advance.[181]

Yet, Wedemeyer himself also prevented a Chinese counter-offensive, not because he did not want to fight in China but because he had to fit in with US strategy against Japan and in conformity with US operational doctrine believed that overwhelming force had to be concentrated on a single point before taking action. Serious planning for a counter-offensive in China began in late 1944.[182] In December, a General Command of the Chinese Army was established under He Yingqin in Kunming.[183] This followed the USA's agreement to supply thirty-six divisions with US weapons for the counter-offensive. At Guilin, various training facilities were established. US aid began to flow in significant amounts in the spring, reaching 70,000 tons per month, but then, Wedemeyer lamented, declined 'when the War Department found it necessary to reduce our hump tonnage by approximately 25,000 tons a month',[184] while in July 'the Stilwell Road [as the Ledo Road had been renamed] was closed due to slides and inundations. Also the pipelines on which we counted so heavily for POL [petrol, oil, and lubricants] have been out of order'.[185]

Throughout the spring and summer, Wedemeyer worked to build up 'approximately 20 divisions of the standard of the five CAI divisions',[186] for an offensive, named variously Iceman and Pagoda, in the fall, not along the Yangtze, but towards Canton. This operation fitted overall US strategy against Japan. It wanted the Soviet Union to take on the Kwantung Army in the north-east. If the counter-offensive in China would cut off lines of Japanese retreat from south-east Asia, a US offensive on Japan by the Pacific Fleet would be made easier and it would be impossible for the Japanese government to relocate to the Asian mainland.[187] Had that happened, US infantry operations would have had to fight on the Asian mainland after all.

To be in a position to carry out this offensive, in May Wedemeyer prohibited the Nationalists from following up their defeat of a Japanese offensive in western Hunan with 70,000 troops. On 14 May, he wrote George Lincoln, the Chief of the Strategy and Operations Section of the Operations Division of the US Army, that the 'successes we have enjoyed have greatly heartened both Americans and Chinese. The Japs suffered approximately 11,000 casualties. Spirit was so high that the Supreme Field Commander, General Ho Ying-chin [He Yingqin] ... and the Chinese commanders at the front all wanted to undertake an offensive drive eastward to sever enemy lines of communication'.[188] But to preserve forces for the later campaign, Wedemeyer wrote, 'I ... have forbidden large scale offensive action'.[189]

When in June and July the Nationalists recovered Guilin, Nanning, and Liuzhou in Guangxi Province, Wedemeyer became more optimistic. On 1 August he wrote to Marshall that 'we now look forward confidently toward a successful drive to the coast'.[190] But he also stated that 'instructions have been issued to follow up and press enemy withdrawals but to avoid large-scale commitment, air or ground' before the US had secured Manila and operations could be supported by airforces operating from there.[191] No real counter-offensive, in short, ever took place before the Japanese surrender on 15 August. When that surrender came, Wedemeyer appealed for the deployment of US forces to occupy key positions, but when this was refused, he was left pleading for the retention of fifty C-54 transport planes, which had been ordered to be removed, because 'Chinese troops are being alerted for move to secure the most critical areas; however, their arrival will be matter of weeks or months if airlift is not employed'.[192] The Nationalists were left in a disadvantageous position to re-establish their rule throughout China.

Conclusion

The idea that war could lead to the re-birth of China proved the great illusion. The Nationalists admitted as much on 3 September 1945, just after the end of the war, when they issued an order that announced 'this year's land taxes will be remitted for the whole year in all provinces that fell to the enemy. We depend on the remaining provinces in the rear for military rations and the people's food needs this year, but their land taxes will be remitted the following year. All military recruitment will be stopped throughout the country from today'.[193] In explaining the measure, the text hailed the defeat of Japan as a great historical achievement. But it also mourned the enormous loss of life and the destruction of property and concluded that 'although the War of Resistance has now ended, the task of national reconstruction has only just begun'.[194] The hopes expressed at Wuhan in 1938 had not been realised.

More than one reason existed for this outcome. The international element of Nationalist strategy never worked out as the Nationalists had hoped. The Nationalists were right in believing that they could not win without outside support. However, if the Soviet Union supported the Nationalists actively until 1939, following the Battle of Nomonhan, their involvement was scaled down and ended completely after 1941. As I hope the first chapter has made clear, the support of the USA and Britain was at best of ambiguous value to the Nationalists and their interests were consistently subordinated to those of their Allies.

Domestic factors were as important. Although the Nationalists began the war claiming that China could outlast Japan in a war of attrition, in reality that did not prove the case. This chapter has focused on the political economy of wartime mobilisation. It has argued that following the disappointments of the first year of the war, the Nationalists were able by a mix of political and economic measures to switch their approach to the war and mobilise Chinese society for a protracted conflict. After 1941, the situation became much more difficult. The Japanese occupation of Yichang, its economic embargo, the proscription of the Nationalist currency, and bad weather led to a deep economic crisis which precipitated the collapse of the fiscal and monetary order. The Nationalists' response was not that of regime holding back to let others do the fighting nor one of demoralisation. They limited their armies, scaled down recruitment, and effectively demobilised many divisions by making them live off the land in various ways. They switched to the collection of the land tax in kind, sought to discipline their sprawling bureaucracies, and introduced state supply of key resources to state dependents and industry. Thus, the Nationalists showed a considerable determination to overcome the difficult problems generated by the economic crisis. Yet, what they could not prevent was the oozing away of military power into the hands not only of major domestic competitors such as the Communists and the Wang Jingwei National Government but also in those of bandit gangs and secret societies. During the War of Resistance the Nationalists failed to escape from the pattern in which the militarisation of society to deal with a military crisis created as many dangers as it solved. What they also could not prevent was the destruction of social and political relations, as the monetary system imploded, the economy was destroyed, transport systems collapsed, Nationalist armies competed with local society for very scarce resources, Nationalist bureaucracies fought with each other and local society, and *baojia* staffs were placed in an impossible position.

The year 1944, it seems to me, was a critical year. If beforehand the situation was hugely difficult, it became virtually irretrievable afterwards. The Ichigo Offensive meant that the Nationalists lost their main granary and recruitment areas. Stilwell's haphazard search for new partners, in the south among the prominent generals there and in the north among the Communists, undermined the Nationalists' political prestige and gave their competitors new opportunities. The increasing centrality of the Soviet Union in US strategic thinking meant that the Soviets re-entered Xinjiang and occupied Manchuria. The Burma campaign led to the withdrawal of much of Chennault's 14th Airforce from China as well as many of the best Nationalists' divisions. Mountbatten's insistence that three be kept there through the spring of 1945, the sharp reduction of hump tonnage in May 1945, the breakdown of the Stilwell road during the monsoon season, the refusal to deploy more airpower in China and despatch ground forces, and the decision to rely on the Soviet Union to take on the Japanese Kwantung Army in Manchuria all had serious repercussions of the military position of the Nationalists at the end of the war.

Above all, this chapter has hoped to suggest that the War of Resistance mattered profoundly. Far too little attention has been paid to the enormous scale of suffering in China itself. Politically, the Nationalists were debilitated. They were left with countless armies of little utility or loyalty. Vital bureaucracies that would have had to shoulder the task of rebuilding the country were destroyed. Fiscal systems, without which no state can survive, ceased to function. Local society was in disarray. Institutions and routines that oriented the population to a centre of legitimate power lost their meaning. Analyses that focus on Nationalist incompetence, corruption, or militarism, or on the Nationalist–Communist rivalry, do not begin to come to terms with the War's utterly destructive effects on the Chinese economy, social relations, and culture – of humanity itself.

Conclusion

The reason that I have criticised the Stilwell–White paradigm in this book is not simply because many of Stilwell's actions were badly designed and executed and general Allied strategy often detrimental to Chinese interests. I have suggested that this paradigm obscured that the Nationalists themselves opposed Japanese aggression and that they mobilised their own society to confront it. My aim has been to bring to the fore how they mobilised Chinese society themselves in the 1920s, then to resist Western imperialism, eliminate warlordism, and build a new nation, and how in the 1930s they turned to confront Japanese aggression and finally faced it on the battlefield. The consequence of the dominance of the Stilwell–White paradigm has been that these efforts were pressed to the sidelines by a version of events that I have hoped to have shown was of debatable historical accuracy.

I have presented the story not as an unambiguous triumph of Chinese nationalism. I have shown how during the Northern Expedition cultures of violence became entrenched and have stressed the harmful effects of factionalism within the KMT, debilitating struggles for power, the resort to intrigue, and the reach for nasty and illegitimate forms of violence. I have also stressed the destabilising effects of more or less autonomous militaries in the 1930s and during the War of Resistance itself, the brutalising effects of warlordism that the Nationalists found it difficult to bring under control, and Nationalist bureaucratic shambles and logistical incompetence.

Nonetheless, I have also suggested that the problems the Nationalist confronted were not subject to easy solutions and that the strategies they adopted after the Japanese occupation of Manchuria were not without promise. I have also argued that when war came in 1937, the Nationalists followed military strategies that were appropriate to the conditions they faced and that the Nationalists then mobilised their society in a war that would determine the future shape of Asia with considerable initial success. I have suggested that the Soviet withdrawal from the war in East Asia after the Battle of Nomonhan, the loss of critical grain and recruitment areas, and Allied strategic choices had enormous consequences for the Nationalists' military position.

Once we move away from a Stilwell and US or British centred analysis of the war, it becomes possible to develop a new understanding of the Second World War in East Asia, one in which domestic mobilisations against Japanese aggression take a central place. These mobilisations were rooted in longer struggles of local populations seeking to recapture ownership over their own societies and civilisations and refashioning them according to their own insights. These struggles in India, Burma, Malaysia, Vietnam,

Korea, and China predated the war, but found new opportunities in it. In most cases, these mobilisations fuelled older and created newer divisions. Different parties envisioned quite different outcomes and sought to make these manifest. VJ-Day meant an end to the fighting against Japan and in China the withdrawal of US forces, but peace did not break out as conflicts then erupted in struggles to gain control over the new states born by the war.

An important question is why in the end the Nationalists were not able to meet the challenges of war against the Japanese. Contrary to their own belief, or perhaps better, their hope, they could not outlast Japan in a war of attrition. Essentially, it seems to me, the problem was not incompetence, a lack of will, corruption, or authoritarianism, but the reality that China was an agrarian society that could not cope with the demands imposed by modern warfare.

Such warfare during the Second World War required the ability to sustain large numbers of well-trained men at the front and supply them with adequate amounts of food and medicine as well as aeroplanes, artillery, mechanised transport, mortars, machine-guns, rifles, and ammunition. It also depended on an industrial and agricultural base able to produce these resources and a bureaucratic and logistical apparatus able to keep up a steady stream of them to the front. Necessary too was the existence of a unified bureaucracy, a vast amount of money, and a reasonably solidaire population.

Those conditions simply did not exist. The Nationalists could sustain active military operations for a short period of time. Chiang Kaishek was in fact good at this type of warfare, in which the quick and effective exploitation of a positive but temporary opportunity was key. He proved this during the Northern Expedition and the civil wars of the early 1930s. But Chiang depended on informal and unstable networks of often temporary allies among Lower Yangtze financial circles, parts of the military, secret societies, and elite Republican families. Because there was no logistical infrastructure and because troops, even if badly paid and treated, consumed vast amounts of money, important also was the possession of territorial base. Such warfare could not be sustained for long because momentary partners could and did withdraw their support, because different parts of the military each pursued their own objectives, because supplies were quickly exhausted, and because sustained recruitment and training was impossible.

The Nationalist effort to drive the Communists to north China lasted longer, but was characterised by short campaigns that had to be halted when resources dried up. The decisive military encounters lasted days or weeks, rather than months and let alone years. Their ultimate success depended on a careful effort to deny local resources, including people, to the Communists, and on restricting the Communists to a small area unable to sustain them. The Communists' defeat in the 1930s was also the result of their own internal political purges and their alienation of the local population through intense recruitment, purges, and grain collection campaigns.[1]

Warfare against the Japanese did require the Nationalists to train and equip a modern military and sustain military operations for a long period of time. They were not able to do this. Following the Battle of Wuhan, the Nationalists withdrew into war zones and limited offensive operations to campaigns of short duration usually in one particular area alone, with local forces reinforced by a few elite divisions. Even this type of warfare the Nationalists were not able to sustain indefinitely. With the areas under their control increasingly limited, it became impossible for the Nationalists to secure what they needed for continued military action without taken recourse to brutal methods that alienated the population, wrecked the combat effectiveness of their own forces, and harmed their own institutions.

The Communist of course faced the same realities. When, in 1930, they launched a serious offensive aimed at capturing large cities in central China, they too found that they could not sustain the operation for a long enough period of time. In resisting Nationalist efforts to dislodge them from their base areas along the Yangtze, Mao Zedong was determined to avoid large-scale warfare and he concentrated his forces only for the short period needed to deal a blow to Nationalists units drawn to the end of their supply lines. During the first year of the War of Resistance, when many Chinese Communists understandably wanted to dispatch large numbers to the front, Mao insisted that the Communist would not concentrate in large numbers and that they would only engage in guerrilla operations. During the One Hundred Regiment Offensive, the Communists still did not concentrate in units of larger than regiment size, as the name suggest. As Lyman Van Slyke has written, the Offensive was a series 'sprawling, decentralised engagements – large and small – over a huge area, rather than a "battle" or even a clearly defined campaign'.[2] During the Civil War, they did do so, but again the decisive encounters did not last for a long time. And the Communists feared for a long period that their victory was not secure and that the Nationalists, or another force, might as quickly re-emerge as they had been driven away.

War often makes nations. With respect to the War of Resistance, Chalmers Johnson argued that the Japanese invasion caused the rise of Chinese peasant nationalism. The Communists, according to him, captured the patronage of this nationalism because the Nationalists themselves were driven away. The Chinese Communists filled the gap and turned the story of heroic guerrilla warfare against the Japanese and Nationalist incompetence into the founding myth of their rule. Mark Selden opposed this interpretation, arguing that the pressure of war led the Communists to develop the economic, social, and political programmes that gained them the support of the peasantry. If Selden and Johnson differed in many ways, both did see the War of Resistance as historically creative.[3]

If decisive in some major ways, it seems to me that it is as right to say that the War of Resistance unmade China as that it made China. As an agricultural but commercialised society, the Chinese economy depended on the maintenance of domestic and international trade links, regional specialisation, local and regional marketing networks, flourishing urban centres, and the availability of money and credit. These did not survive the war, with at least three enduring consequences.

First, to maintain and increase food production would remain a key problem after the war, both for the Nationalists and the Communists. Food supplies remained desperately short in the years after the war, and China received little foreign assistance. Just before the spring shortages, in February 1946 H. H. Lehman of the UN informed Song Ziwen that 'a very serious situation has arisen in relation to world food supplies .... It is my responsibility to warn you that available supplies over the next few months are likely to be very greatly reduced. I trust that you and your Government will continue to take every possible measure to ensure that available supplies of food are controlled with the greatest possible care'.[4] If the food situation made recovery difficult, so did international economic difficulties, domestic financial and monetary problems, and Nationalist bureaucracies gathering up resources often in competition with each other. In the first decades of the PRC, Communist policies, aimed at self-sufficiency, were partly ideologically driven but were also attempts to recover from the economic destruction caused by war. Only after Deng Xiaoping's reform programme after 1978 did the situation begin to improve.

Second, with respect to industrial development, the wartime economy, especially as pioneered by the NRC, possessed many features of the Planned Economy. In part the result of a belief in the potential of scientific or modern management under state guidance, it also was a response to the reality that markets could not deliver the goods. If the Communists in emulation of the Soviet model continued the practices that the NRC had pioneered in China, wartime experiences and economic destruction, as well as international isolation, were also factors.

Third, the centralised procurement and allocation of scarce goods through work units became a feature of Chinese life in urban areas during the War of Resistance and remained so in the PRC until recently. While on the one hand one can see in this development a new commitment by the state to take care of the population, it extended this care only to a small section and locked it into work units and made its members dependent on the skill and whim of their superiors. Work units were usually closed entities. To have dealings with members of other work units was difficult, while the allocation of resources generated abundant internal jealousies and grievances.

Socially, the effects of the war were profound. Refugee movements have been evoked literarily by Maxine Kingston Hong to great effect, but have not yet been studied academically in detail.[5] Similarly, little is known about the dislocations caused by army recruitment or the return of soldiers from the front on individual families. With recruitment concentrated in only a number of regions, it is likely that different regions were affected in quite distinct ways. The importance of the issue of the demographic and political effects of the war is readily apparent from the sharp political division on Taiwan between Mainlanders – those who decamped with Chiang Kaishek to the island – and original Taiwanese residents.

One of the first items of business after the end of the war was the exaction of retribution on those who had passively or actively co-operated with the occupiers, who had made inordinate profits from the national crisis, or who had abused their power. Anger was easily mobilised against those who had collaborated with the Japanese, puppet forces, the *baojia* staff, the Nationalist military, and local officials. A recent paper by Julia Strauss makes clear that in the purges of the 1950s, in which officially the language of class warfare dominated, resentments generated by wartime behaviour were not far below the surface.[6] When the Nationalists returned to the coastal areas, they demanded the return of their jobs, their positions, and their property. They also demanded first dips on what the Japanese had left behind. Bureaucratic organs and companies competed with each other, as they had done during the war, to gain for themselves as much as possible.

Social order was difficult to restore, because of the ubiquity of arms, the shortages, and the collapse of authority in most areas. Perhaps the most important literary work in English to have come out of the War of Resistance, J. G. Ballard's *Empire of the Sun*, evokes the terrible realities that prevailed around Shanghai not just during but also after the Japanese surrender. Armed bands marauded in the area around the city, looting and looking for food. There was no police to keep order, safety and security were unavailable, Communist and Nationalist armed units were already at war with each other, and no one was able to offer leadership or guidance. Society itself had come unstuck. Ballard himself, interned as a boy from 1942 in a Japanese Prisoner of War camp, after having left that camp to find his parents in Shanghai returned to it as a safer place than the 'peace' he found outside it.

Following the Taiping Rebellion, China's social order re-established itself remarkably quickly and the elites who traditionally had governed local society were able not only to recover their positions but even extend their power. Several developments before the War of Resistance had begun to undermine their role, including the extension of state authority and the spread of warlordism. But the War of Resistance, especially recruitment and grain collection practices, was perhaps also important in the final elimination of traditional local elites.

Finally, the effects on Chinese culture and the patterns of daily life deserve more research than they have received so far. It seems clear that the war embedded a culture of scarcity. Spending on leisure, entertainment, ceremonies marking important transitions, clothing, religion, and luxuries all declined and became disreputable. People carried their own chop sticks and toilet paper, while work units provided extra cooking oil or pork at New Year. In addition, the war strengthened militarising tendencies in language, imaginations, and social organisation. Society was regimented, disciplined, and homogenised. The language of mobilisation and struggle, ideals of heroic action, the fear of enemies within, and the use of military forms of organisation to achieve social or political goals continued for many decades. They found their culmination during the Cultural Revolution. Red Guards were its Shock Troops; Model Operas celebrated military exploits; Lei Feng became the great hero; the Red Army was held up as a source of norms and attitudes while its uniforms became the approved attire; and struggle sessions took place against supposed internal traitors. The new culture then held up for emulation was decidedly militaristic.

The above has only sketched out some of the possible post-war effects of the War of Resistance. More work will need to be done before we can be more precise. But it does seem that it left legacies from which China has begun to move away only during the last decades. However, in one respect the War of Resistance has gained a new centrality. Memories of the war have replaced those of Communist guerrilla warfare in the 1930s, the Long March, and the Civil War as a central component of contemporary national identity. Museums are dedicated to the Japanese occupation of Manchuria, the Marco Polo Bridge Incident, and the Nanjing Massacre. In 1997, the first display in the Museum of Revolution on Tiananmen Square did not celebrate the CCP's founding, as was the case earlier, but showed a distressed child in soot sitting on a railway during a Japanese bombing attack. This image, based on a Nationalist propaganda photograph designed to whip up support for the war, is now known to be a fake, but that is irrelevant. The centrality of the War of Resistance to Chinese national identities is also clear from the continuing controversies over the treatment of the war in Japanese textbooks and Chinese demands for a fuller or more honest apology from Japan. The war too appears frequently in movies, memoirs, novels, and historical works, sometimes in commercialised forms. In some ways, the dead of the war, never properly buried and put to rest when the history of CCP revolution dominated public memory, are again about. The War of Resistance will not soon be forgotten.

Notes

Abbreviations

FRUS	*Foreign Relations of the United States.*
KRZZZ	*Kang Ri Zhanzheng Zhengmian Zhanchang.*
MP	*The Papers of George Catlett Marshall.*
PRO	*Public Record Office (London).*
USMI	*US Military Intelligence Reports: China 1911–1941.*
ZHMGSDAZL	*Zhonghua Minguo Shi Dang'an Ziliao Huibian.*
ZHMGSZYSL	*Zhonghua Minguo Zhongyao Shiliao Chubian.*

Introduction

1 Lary, 'Defending China', 408.
2 Andersson, *China Fights the World*, 261.
3 Ibid., 103–4.
4 Herzstein, *Henry Luce*, 194.
5 Ibid., 195.
6 Ibid., 193.
7 Klehr, *et al.*, *The Secret World of American Communism*, 336–41.
8 Snow, *Red Star over China*, 448.
9 Ibid., 449.
10 Epstein, *The People's War*.
11 Bertram, *North China Front*.
12 Tuchman, *Stilwell*, 320.
13 Quoted in Tuchman, *Stilwell*, 321.
14 Quoted in Tuchman, *Stilwell*, 646.
15 White, *Thunder*, cover.
16 Ibid., 315.
17 Ibid., 214.
18 Ibid., 126.
19 White, ed., *Stilwell Papers*, 340.
20 Ibid., 315.
21 Ibid., 214.
22 Ibid., 151.
23 Ibid., 305.
24 Ibid., 60.
25 White, ed., *Stilwell Papers*, 313.
26 Acheson, 'Letter of Transmittal' (30 July 1949), in Department of State, *China White Paper*, xv.
27 Van Slyke, 'Introduction', in Department of State, *China White Paper*, no page numbers.
28 'General Hurley to President Truman', in ZHMGZYSL, V: 3, 8.
29 Weinstein, *et al.*, *The Haunted Wood* and Haynes, *et al.*, *Venona*.
30 Lowenthal, 'Venona and Alger Hiss', *Intelligence and National Security*, XV: 3 (2000).
31 Young, *Wartime Finance*, 282–96; Haynes and Kehr, *Venona*, 141–5.

32 Acheson, in Department of State, *China White Paper*, iii–xviii.
33 Tuchman, *Stilwell*, xvi.
34 Ibid., xv.
35 Ibid., 678.
36 Ibid., 649.
37 Ibid., 678.
38 Ibid., 678.
39 Romanus and Sunderland, *Stilwell's Command Problems, Stilwell's Mission to China, Time Runs Out in CBI*; On Aslop, see Schaller, *The US Crusade in China*, 134–7.
40 Chennault, *Way of a Fighter*.
41 Romanus and Sunderland: *Stilwell's Mission to China*, 395.
42 Dorn, *Walkout*, vii.
43 Eastman, 'Nationalist China during the Sino-Japanese War', 901.
44 Dreyer, *China at War*, 173–311.
45 Eastman, 'Nationalist China during the Sino-Japanese War', 547–88. Stilwell also uses Liu, *A Military History of Modern China*.
46 Elleman, *Modern Chinese Warfare*, 202–14.
47 Ch'i, *Nationalist China at War*, 236.
48 Eastman, *Seeds of Destruction*, 3.
49 Ibid., 225.
50 Ibid., 156. On Eastman's assessment of the Nationalists before the War of Resistance, see also his *Abortive Revolution*. Its purpose was to criticise Sih, *The Strenuous Decade* and Domes, *Vertagte Revolution*.
51 Coble, *Shanghai Capitalists*.
52 Coble, *Facing Japan*.
53 Wei, *Counter-revolution*.
54 Rawski, *Economic Growth*, Faure, *Rural Economy*, Brandt, *Commercialisation*.
55 Kirby, *Germany and Republican China*.
56 Henriot, *Shanghai, 1927–1937*. For a different perspective, see Wakeman, *Policing Shanghai*.
57 Strauss, *Strong Institutions*.
58 A burgeoning field which has produced, among other important contributions, Wakeman, *Policing Shanghai* and *The Shanghai Badlands*; Bickers, *Britain in China*; Lee, *Shanghai Modern*; Honig, *Sisters and Strangers* and *Creating Ethnicity*; Smith, *A Road is Made* and *Like Cattle and Horses*; Goodman, *Native Place, City, and Nation*; Henriot, *Shanghai* and *Prostitution and Sexuality*; and Martin, *The Shanghai Green Gang*.
59 Fitzgerald, *Awakening China*; Dikötter, *Discourse of Race*; Widmer and Wang, eds, *From May Fourth to June Fourth* and Daruvala, *Zhou Zuoren*.
60 'Re-appraising Republican China', *China Quarterly* 150 (1997).
61 But see Waldron, *China's Turning Point*; Lary and MacKinnon, eds, *Scars of War*; Chang-tai Hung, *War and Popular Culture*; McCord, *Power of the Gun*; Levine, *Anvil of Victory*; Hsiung and Levine, eds, *Bitter Victory*; Jordan, *Trial by Fire*; Elleman, *Modern Chinese Warfare*; Graff and Higham, eds, *Military History*; van de Ven, ed., *Warfare*, 'Lifting the Veil of Secrecy', and 'War in Modern China', special issue of *Modern Asian Studies* XXX: 4 (1996). Professor Ezra Vogel is leading an international group of scholars to research the War of Resistance. The Chinese Military History Society organises regular conferences and publishes an electronic newsletter.
62 Snyder, *Ideology of the Offensive*.
63 Stoler, *Allies*, 8–13.
64 Ibid., 31.
65 Larrabee, *Commander in Chief*, 110.
66 Parker, *Cambridge Illustrated History*, 294.
67 Larrabee, *Commander in Chief*, 112.
68 Ibid., 101.
69 Stoler, *Allies*, 57.

70 Ibid., 74–76.
71 Dorn, *Sino-Japanese War*, 128.
72 Ibid., 113.
73 Ibid., 120.
74 Ibid., 185.
75 Tuchman, *Stilwell*, 155–6.
76 White, ed., *Stilwell Papers*, 77.
77 Stoler, *Allies*, 265–6.
78 Ibid., 49.
79 For an introduction and excerpts, see Wedemeyer, *Wedemyer on War and Peace*, 10–26.
80 Larrabee, *Commander in Chief*, 122.
81 van de Ven, 'Introduction, in van de Ven, ed., *Chinese Warfare*, 2–11. For a fine treatment of China in the Treaty Port imagination, see Bickers, *Britain in China*, 22–60. See also Isaacs, *Scratches on our Mind*.
82 For an interesting study of Western perceptions of war in the nineteenth century, see Pick, *War Machine*, 1–165. There were, of course, counterveiling voices.
83 If these were general trends, realities were more complex and war proved difficult to contain. But see McNeill, *Pursuit of Power*, 117–261; Tilly, *Coercion, Capital, and European States*, 67–95; Brewer, *Sinews of Power*; Fuller, *Strategy and Power*, 265–451; van Creveld, *Supplying War*, 109–41; Keegan, *A History of Warfare*, 301–15; and Kolko, *Century of War*, 44–60, 65–72.
84 Dorn, *Sino-Japanese War*, 128.
85 Ibid., 65.
86 Ibid., 6.
87 Ibid., 231.
88 Ibid., appendix.
89 Ibid., for example, 61, 77, 115–6, 128, 202–3, 220–1, 231, 332–4.
90 Hinsley, *British Intelligence*, 9, 11.
91 Dorn, *Sino-Japanese War*, 39.
92 Ibid., 83.
93 Ibid., 83.
94 Ibid., 86.
95 See, for example, the Situation Reports (6 November 1936–16 July 1937) reproduced in USMI, reel 10, frames 0470-0552.
96 See, for example, Lewis, *Sanctioned Violence*; Waldron, *China's Turning Point*; Johnston, *Cultural Realism*. See also van de Ven, 'Introduction', in van de Ven, ed., *Warfare in Chinese History*, 1–11.
97 The term should not be taken too seriously. For a brief and critical overview, see Paret, 'The History of War and the New Military History'. For some examples, see n. 88. Other noteworthy contributions have been Parker, *Military Revolution*; Fussell, *War and Modern Memory*; Beevor, *Stalingrad*; Winter, *Sites of Memory*; Keegan, *The Face of Battle* and *The Mask of Command*.
98 van de Ven, 'Military and Financial Reform', 37–8.
99 Liang Qichao, 'Zhongguo zhi Wushidao' (China's Bushido), in *Yinbingshi Congzhu*, vol. 2, part 7.
100 Liang Qichao, 'Lun Shangwu' (On Respecting Martial Qualities), in 'Xinmin Shuo' (On the New Citizen) (1904) *Yinbingshi Congzhu*, vol.1, part 1, 183; Fang Guo'an, *Junguomin Jiaoyu*; 9–16, 31–62; Tien, *Military Theory*, 119–34; Fung, *Military Dimension*, ch. 4.
101 Shi Quansheng, ed., *Zhonghua Minguo Wenhua Shi*, I, 397–8.
102 Fung, *Military Dimension*, ch. 4.
103 Chiang, *Zeng Hu Zhibing Yulu*.
104 'Instruction by Telegraph from Chiang Kaishek to Wang Boling and other Commanders' (6 August 1926), Academia Historica, Daxi Dang'an, 0012. The Daxi Dang'an, named after Chiang Kaishek's temporary resting place, consist of Chiang Kaishek's papers originally held by the KMT Historical Commission but now transferred to the Academia Historica.

105 For Jiang's reports to Chiang Kaishek, see *Jiang Baili Xiansheng Quanji*, I, 1–78. For his ideas about Chinese conditions and defensive strategies, see 'Ruhe Shi Yiwu Minbing Zhi' (What is Compulsory Military Service', ibid., I, 205–7; 'Caibing Jihua Shu' (Plan for Demobilisation), in ibid., IV, 37–9; and 'Zhongguo zhi Xin Shengming' (China's New Life), in ibid., 89–94.

1 Stillwell revisited

1 Parker, *Cambridge Illustrated History of Warfare*, 333.
2 Ibid.
3 Heinrichs, *Threshold of War*, 118–45.
4 *Miandian Gonglue Zuozhan*, 16–20.
5 'MAC Chief-of-Staff He Yingqin Reports on Military Preparations in South Yunnan' (23 August 1940), ZHMGZYSL, II: 3, 198; 'Long Yun, Chairman of the Kunming Field Headquarters, Reports on Changes on the Vietnam Border and Requests Advice' (26 August 1940), ibid., II: 3, 200; 'Telegram from Generalissimo Chiang to MAC Chief-of-Staff He Yingqin Regarding Supply of Troops Entering Yunnan and Notification of Kunming of the Central Government's Intentions' (4 August 1941), in ibid., vol. II: 3, 206.
6 Ibid., and 'Personal Order by Generalissimo Chiang to Xu Yongchang, Head of the MAC Department of War, Regarding Suggestions to Re-adjust Deployment in Yunnan' (28 October 1941), in ibid., 206–7.
7 'Order by Generalissimo Chiang to MAC Chief-of-Staff He Yingqin Regarding Supply of Troops Entering Yunnan and Notification of Kunming' (4 August 1941), in ibid., II: 3, 206.
8 Ibid.
9 Churchill, *Second World War*, III, 373–9; Aldrich, *Intelligence and the War against Japan*, 59.
10 'Report by Telegram of Shang Zhen, Head of the Military Delegation, and Lin Wei, Member, on Conversations with the British Commander-in-Chief, Far East, Brooke-Popham' (20 May 1941), ZHMGZYSL, II: 3, 202–3.
11 *Miandian Gonglue Zuozhan*, 22.
12 Parker, *Cambridge Illustrated History*, 333; Addington, *Patterns of War*, 244–5.
13 *Miandian Gonglue Zuozhan*, 105–36.
14 Ibid., 136–7.
15 Larrabee, *Commander in Chief*, 114; Stoler, *Allies*, 25.
16 Marshall, 'Memorandum for Harry Hopkins' (15 January 1942), MP, III, 66.
17 MP, III, 30–2. The quote is in Stoler, *Allies*, 270.
18 MP, III, 157.
19 Stoler, *Allies*, 75–6.
20 Stoler, *Allies*, 71–3, 265.
21 Stoler, *Allies*, 79; Marshal, 'Memorandum for Admiral King' (15 July 1942), MP, III, 276–7 and 277, n.1.
22 Stoler, *Allies*, 79–80, 265.
23 Ibid., 81.
24 Ibid., 88.
25 Ibid., 84.
26 'To General Douglas MacArthur' (8 February 1942), MP, III, 101–2.
27 'Memorandum for the President' (6 May 1942), MP, III, 184.
28 'Memorandum for the Secretary of War' (12 January 1942) MP, III, 57–9
29 Tuchman, *Stilwell*, 155–6.
30 Ibid., 164.
31 Stafford, *Roosevelt and Churchill*, 175–6.
32 Ibid., 168–91.
33 Tuchman, *Stilwell*, 315.

34 Ibid., 315.
35 Ibid., 312.
36 'Memorandum for the CCS' (25 August 1942), in MP, III, 319–20.
37 Stoler, *Allies*, 267–8.
38 Slim, *Defeat into Victory*, 5–7.
39 Aldrich, *Intelligence*, 200.
40 Lin Wei, 'Report on the Burma Campaign, the Reasons for Our Defeat, and Assessments of the Strengths and Weaknesses of our Forces' (30 September 1942), in 'Miandian Zhanyi Deshi Pipan' (Evaluation of the Burma Campaign)', Academia Historica, 055/0996-1.
41 'India Office to Lockhart' (21 January 1943)', in 'Overseas: China: Chinese Troops in China: Conditions', PRO: WO 32/10248.
42 'Record of Conversation between Generalissimo Chiang and General Stilwell, Chief-of-Staff of the Allied Forces in the China Theatre Following a Welcoming Banquet' (9 March 1942), ZHMGZYSL, II: 3, 222–3.
43 Thorne, *Allies of a Kind*, 187.
44 Quoted in Tuchman, *Stilwell*, 346.
45 'Record of Conversation between Generalissimo Chiang and General Alexander, Commander of the British Army in Burma' (25 March 1942), in ZHMGZYSL, II, 265–6.
46 'Record of Conversation between Generalissimo Chiang and General Stilwell', in ibid., II: 3, 223, and 'Record of Conversation at a Meeting between Generalissimo Chiang and Stilwell, Chief-of-Staff of the Allied Army in the China Theatre' (10 March 1942), ZHMGZYSL, III: 2, 246.
47 'Record of Conversation of Generalissimo Chiang and Mrs Chiang with Generals Stilwell, Chief-of-Staff of the Allied Forces in the China Theatre, Alexander, Commander of the British Army in Burma, and Smith, Governor of Burma' (6 April 1942), in ibid., II: 3, 282.
48 Ibid., 283.
49 Ibid., 282.
50 'Record of Conversation between Generalissimo Chiang and General Stilwell' (20 March 1942), in ZHMGZYSL, II: 3, 258–60.
51 'Record of Conversation between Generalissimo Chiang and General Stilwell' in ZHMGZYSL, II: 3, 221–4.
52 Allen, *Longest War*, 52.
53 'Record of Conversation between Generalissimo Chiang and Generals Alexander and Stilwell', ZHMGZYSL, II: 3, 280–3.
54 'Record of Conversation between Generalissimo Chiang and General Stilwell', ZHMGZYSL, II: 3, 224.
55 Ibid., ZHMGZYSL, II: 3, 225.
56 'Record of Conversation between Generalissimo Chiang and General Stilwell' (10 March 1942), ZHMGZYSL, II: 3, 242–9.
57 White, ed., *Stilwell Papers*, 53.
58 Ibid., 64.
59 'Record of Conversation between Generalissimo Chiang and General Stilwell' (19 March 1942), ZHMGZYSL, III: 2, 256–7.
60 *Miandian Gonglue Zuozhan*, 433–7.
61 Huang, 'Chiang Kaishek', Part II, 15–17; Romanus and Sunderland, *Stilwell's Mission*, 97–8; Allen, *Longest War*, 59–60; *Miandian Gonglue Zuozhan*, 431–66; White, ed., *Stilwell Papers*, 69; and Tuchman, *Stilwell*, 351.
62 Zhang Xianwen, *Kang Ri Zhanzheng de Zhengmian Zhanchang*, 269–71.
63 Allen, *The Longest War*, 59–6; *Miandian Gonglue Zuozhan*, 467–73.
64 Huang, 'Chiang Kaishek', Part II, 17–19.
65 Huang, 'Chiang Kaishek', Part II, 19.
66 White, ed., *Stilwell Papers*, 77.
67 'Record of Conversation between Generalissimo Chiang and General Stilwell' (4 June 1942), ZHMGZYSL, II: 3, 325.

68 White, ed., *Stilwell Papers*, 115–6.
69 Huang, 'Chiang Kaishek', Part 2, 17–18.
70 'Political Review 1942', British Library, India Office Records, L/PS/2300.
71 Slim, *Defeat into Victory*, 17–18.
72 Ibid., 18.
73 Tuchman, *Stilwell*, 386–7.
74 Romanus and Sunderland, *Stilwell's Mission*, 152–8; Allen, *Longest War*, 156.
75 'Report on Situation in China' (June 1942), PRO: PREM 3/143/1.
76 'To Colonel John Hutchins' (29 October 1942), 'To William Harm' (4 November 1942), 'Memorandum for the Undersecretary of War' (22 April 1943), in MP, III, 416, 425–6, 657–8.
77 Schoppa, 'Self-Inflicted Wounds', 15.
78 'Memorandum for General Arnold', and 'To William Harm' in MP, III, 197, 197 n. 2, 425–6, and 426 n.1.
79 Schoppa, 'Self-Inflicted Wounds', 18–20; *Zhongguo Kang Ri Zhanzheng Shi*, III, 186–90. Some in the USA did describe the raid at the time as 'an ineffective, politically motivated gesture', see MP, 426 n.1.
80 Tuchman, *Stilwell*, 384.
81 Ibid., 360.
82 White, ed., *Stilwell Papers*, 106, 116–17.
83 Tuchman, *Stilwell*, 366.
84 Ibid., 394.
85 Ibid.
86 'Record of Conversation between Generalissimo Chiang and General Stilwell' (15 June 1942), ZHMGZYSL, II: 3, 327.
87 Ibid., 327.
88 Addington, *Patterns of War*, 250.
89 'Memorandum for the Joint US Chiefs of Staff' (7 December 1942), MP, III, 475–6.
90 Tuchman, *Stilwell*, 257–81.
91 Bagby, *Eagle–Dragon Alliance*, 74.
92 Romanus, *Stilwell's Mission*, 252–3; Bagby, *Eagle–Dragon Alliance*, 74.
93 Bagby, *Eagle–Dragon Alliance*, 75.
94 Hsu and Chang, *Sino-Japanese War*, 509–10.
95 'To Lieutenant General Joseph Stilwell' (5 January 1943), MP, III, 503–4.
96 'Memorandum for the President' (16 March 1943), MP, III, 587.
97 Quoted in MP, III, 585–6; Romanus and Sunderland, *Stilwell's Mission*, 279–80; and Tuchman, *Stilwell*, 520.
98 'To Lieutenant General Joseph Stilwell' (9 April 1943), MP, III, 637.
99 Bagby, *Eagle–Dragon Alliance*, 68–78; Tuchman, *Stilwell*, 468–78; and MP, III, 675–8.
100 'Memorandum for General Stilwell' (3 May 1943), MP, III, 675.
101 'Memorandum for the President' (4 October 1943), MP, IV, 141.
102 Bagby, *Eagle–Dragon Alliance*, 77.
103 Romanus and Sunderland, *Stilwell's Mission*, 329–30.
104 'Memorandum for General Stilwell' MP, III, 675.
105 'Combined Chiefs of Staff: Proposals to be Made to Generalissimo Chiang Kaishek' (8 July 1933), ZHMGZYSL, II: 3, 377–8.
106 'Generalissimo Chiang's Reply to the Proposals of the Combined Chiefs-of-Staff Transmitted by General Stilwell, Chief-of-Staff of the Allied Forces in the China Theatre' (8 July 1943), ZHMGZYSL, II: 3, 379.
107 Idem, and 'Generalissimo Chiang's Telegram to Song Ziwen, Minister of Foreign Affairs' (6 August 1943); 'Major General Cai Wenzhi of the MAC Department of War to Chairman Lin Wei of the First Bureau of the Personal Staff Office' (17 August 1943), and 'Report from Gu Weijun, Ambassador to Britain, to Generalissimo Chiang' (27 September 1943), ZHMGZYSL, II: 3, 379, 382–3, 384.
108 Churchill, *Second World War*, V, 82.

109 Ibid., 75.
110 Ibid., 82.
111 Aldrich, *Intelligence*, 180.
112 'Minutes of Conference Held at the Generalissimo's Residence on 18 October', ZHMGZYSL, II: 3, 395–411.
113 Ibid., 410.
114 MP, IV, 159 n.2.
115 MP, IV, 159 n.1,2, and 3; Bagby, *Eagle–Dragon Alliance*, 80. Marshall in fact drafted a message to relieve Stilwell, see 'Proposed Message for General Stilwell' (19 October 1943), MP, IV, 158–9.
116 Ibid., and White, ed., *Stilwell Papers*, 231–5. Wu Jingping, *Song Ziwen Pingzhuan*, 368–73.
117 Wu Jingping, *Song Ziwen Pingzhuan*, 372.
118 White, ed., *Stilwell Papers*, 230–4; MP, IV, 159, n.2.
119 See 'Moutbatton to PM' (10 October 1943); 'Mountbatten to Ismay' (12 October 1943); 'Chongqing to London' (19 October 1943), and 'Mountbatten to Ismay' (26 October 1943) in 'Stilwell/Wedemeyer', PRO: PREM 3/52/12; Marshall, 'Proposed message to General Stilwell', (19 October 1943), in MP, IV, 158.
120 Wu Jingping, *Song Ziwen Pingzhuan*, 364–7.
121 'Mountbatten to PM' in 'Stilwell/Wedemeyer', PRO: Prem 3/53/12.
122 'Mountbatten to Ismay', in 'Stilwell/Wedemeyer', PRO: PREM 3/53/12.
123 Stoler, *Allies*, 166. Sainsbury, *The Turning Point*, 66–72.
124 Stoler, *Allies*, 123–9.
125 Ibid., 265.
126 Sainsbury, *Turning Point*, 131.
127 MP, IV, 191–3.
128 Ibid., 130, 181.
129 Ibid., 150.
130 Ibid., 9–10.
131 Ibid., 131.
132 Ibid., 132–5.
133 Churchill, *Second World War*, V, 289–90.
134 Churchill, *Second World War*, V, 290.
135 Thorne, *Allies*, 420–1.
136 Sainsbury, *Turning Point*, 146.
137 Alanbrooke, *War Diaries*, 477.
138 Sainsbury, *Turning Point*, 166–7.
139 Churchill, *Second World War*, V, 291.
140 Thorne, *Allies*, 60–2. The quote is on p. 62.
141 'Record of Conversation at the Meeting of Generalissimo Chiang with Nehru, Member of the Executive Committee of the Congress Party During Which He Expressed That The Two Great People of China and India Can Only Achieve Liberation if they Join Together' (20 February 1942), ZHMGZYSL, III: 3, 424–30; Venkaratamani, *Roosevelt, Gandhi, Churchill*, 46; Conolly, 'China and Britain', 21.
142 'General Mountbatten, Supreme Allied Commander South East Asia, Reports to Generalissimo Chiang on the British Offensive Plans' (23 November 1943), ZHMGZYSL, II: 3, 419–20.
143 Churchill, *Second World War*, V, 290.
144 'Minutes of Conference Held at Generalissimo's Residence', ZHMGZYSL, II: 3, 410.
145 Churchill, *Second World War*, V, 290; 'Major General Cai Wenzhi to Lin Wei, Director of the First Office of the Personal Staff Office', ZHMGZYSL, II: 3, 382; 'Letter of Director Lin Wei of the First Bureau of the Personal Staff Office with his Views about the Burma Offensive' (27 December 1943), ZHMGZYSL, II: 3, 427; Tuchman, *Stilwell*, 509–17; 'Meetings of the Combined Chiefs of Staff' (26 November 1943), FRUS, 1943, Cairo and Tehran, 364; White, ed., *Stilwell Papers*, 242–53; Thorne, *Allies*, 335.
146 Sainsbury, *Turning Point*, 185.

147 Ibid., 186.
148 Ibid., 202.
149 Ibid., 206.
150 'Proceedings of Meetings Regarding Political Matters [at Cairo]', ZHMGZYSL, III: 3, 528–35; Thorne, *Allies*, 311–12; Tuchman, *Stilwell*, 514–15.
151 Schaller, *US Crusade*, 455; 'Ambassador in China (Gauss) to the Secretary of State' (6 January 1944) and 'Ambassador in China (Gauss) to Secretary of State' (3 February 1944) in FRUS, 1944, VI, China, 302–3 and 319–26.
152 White, ed., *Stilwell Papers*, 252–3.
153 Dorn, *Walk-out*, 75–9; Schaller, *US Crusade*, 153.
154 MP, IV, 193–4; 'Combined Chiefs of Staff Minutes' (28 November 1943), FRUS, 1943 (Cairo and Tehran), 499–501, 505–7; Churchill, *Second World War*, V, 317–60.
155 Stoler, *Allies*, 168.
156 Ibid., 169.
157 Conolly, 'China and Britain', 37–8.
158 Churchil, *Second World War*, V, 364; Tuchman, *Stilwell*, 523–4; White, *Stilwell Papers*, eds., 264–5; 'Meeting of the Combined Chiefs of Staff' (6 December 1943), FRUS, 1943, Cairo and Tehran, 737; 'Memorandum for: The Prime Minister' (5 December 1943), ibid., 803, and 804, n.3.
159 'Carton de Wiart to PM' (18 December 1943), in 'Use of Yunnan Force', PRO: PREM 3/148/6.
160 'PM to Mountbatten' (21 December 1943), in ibid.
161 Slim, *Defeat into Victory*, 213–4.
162 'Memorandum to Her Excellency Madame Chiang Kaishek', ZHMGZYSL, II: 3, 425.
163 'C-of-S to PM' (23 December 1945) in 'Use of Yunnan Force', PRO: PREM 3/148/6.
164 Slim, *Defeat into Victory*, 214.
165 'Views Regarding the Burma Offensive of Lin Wei', ZHMGZYSL, II: 3, 427.
166 MP, IV, 195.
167 Churchill, *Second World War*, V, 495.
168 'Marshall to Stilwell' (1 January 1944)' in 'Use of Yunnan Force', PRO: PREM 3/148/6.
169 'Chiang Kaishek to Roosevelt' (1 January 1944), in 'Use of the Yunnan Force', PRO: PREM 3/148/6.
170 'Generalissimo Chiang's Address at the Fourth Nanyue Military Conference' (12 and 13 February 1944), ZHMGZYSL, II: 1,504.
171 'JIC (44) 14 (O) Final' (12 Jan 1944) in ' Hostilities – Far East II' in PRO: PREM 3/591/1.
172 *Zhongguo Kang Ri Zhanzheng Shi*, III, 462–3.
173 Ibid., 464.
174 Huang, 'Chiang Kaishek', II, 86–8.
175 Stoler, *Allies*, 248.
176 Drea, *In the Service of the Emperor*, 188.
177 'Telegraphic Report by General Sun Liren, Commander of the New 38th Division of the Chinese Army in India' (31 December 1943), ZHMGZYSL, II: 3, 430–1; Slim, *Defeat into Victory*, 248–58.
178 Churchill, *Second World War*, 496–503; Slim, *Defeat into Victory*, 296–346; Keegan, *Second World War*, 549; Tuchman, *Stilwell*, 560–6.
179 'SACSEA to Air Min' (21 February 1944) in 'Stilwell/Wedemeyer', PRO: PREM 3/53/12.
180 Bland, *Marshall Papers*, vol. 4, 278; Churchill, *Second World War*, VI, 145.
181 Churchill, *Second World War*, V, 504–6 and VI, 145; Thorne, *Allies*, 409–11.
182 'Memorandum of Mr Denning, Mountbatten's Political Advisor' (2 March 1944), in 'Stilwell/Wedemeyer', Prem 3/53/12.
183 Ibid.
184 'Mr Denning, Mountbatten's Political Advisor' in 'Stilwell/Wedemeyer', PRO: PREM 3/53/12.
185 Tuchman, *Stilwell*, 449–50.
186 'Wedemeyer/Stilwell', in PRO: PREM 3/5/12.

187 Churchill, *Second World War*, VI, 145–7.
188 *Time* Magazine, 14 February, 1944, quoted in Stillwell/Wedemeyer', PRO: PREM 3/53/12; see also MP, IV, 322, n.1.
189 'To Lieutenant General Joseph Stilwell', MP, IV, 321.
190 'Memorandum by Mr Dening' and 'War Cabinet Office to JSM John Dill' (29 February 1944) in 'Stilwell/Wedemeyer', PRO: PREM 3/53/12.
191 'SACSEA to JSM' (28 February 1944), in 'Stilwell/Wedemeyer', PRO: PREM 3/53/12.
192 'War Cabinet Office to JSM' (30 February 1944), in 'Stilwell/Wedemeyer', PRO: PREM: 3/53/12. Sir John Dill was head of the British Joint Staff Mission in Washington.
193 'To Lieutenant General Joseph Stilwell', MP, IV, 321–2.
194 'The Secretary of State to the Secretary of War' (26 August 1943), FRUS, 1943, China, 102–4.
195 'JSM to War Cabinet Offices' (1 March 1944), PRO: PREM 3/53/12.
196 'WSC to JSM' (2 March 1944), PRO: PREM 3/53/12.
197 Addington, *Patterns of War*, 263, Allen, *Longest War*, 320–3.
198 Huang, 'Chiang Kaishek', Part 2, 80; Tuchman, *Stilwell*, 568; 'Mountbatten to PM', in 'Myitkina', PRO: PREM 1/148/11.
199 Tuchman, *Stilwell*, 568–9.
200 'CIGS to PM' (17 February 1944), in 'Myitkina', PRO: PREM 3/148/11 and 'Mountbatten to PM' in ibid. CIGS stands for Chief of the Imperial General Staff.
201 Huang, 'Chiang Kaishek', II, 79–83.
202 Allen, *Longest War*, 364–79; Slim, *Defeat into Victory*, 271–5.
203 Slim, *Defeat into Victory*, 274.
204 Huang, 'Chiang Kaishek', II, 79–83.
205 Slim, *Defeat into Victory*, 280.
206 White, ed, *Stilwell Papers*, 305.
207 Allen, *Longest War*, 331–79.
208 'Major General Claire Chennault to President Roosevelt' (19 April 1944), FRUS, 1944, VI, China, 57–9.
209 Stoler, *Allies*, 266.
210 'The Ambassador in China (Gauss) to the Secretary of State' (20 May 1944), FRUS, 1944, VI, China, 77.
211 'Consul at Kweilin (Ringwalt) to the Ambassador in China (Gauss) (25 My 1944), FRUS, 1944, VI, China, 83.
212 'The Ambassador to China (Gauss) to the Secretary of State' (18 January 1944), FRUS, 1944, VI, China, 7. Gauss quoted a report from Everett Drumright, an Embassy Secretary at Xi'an.
213 'Ambassador to China (Gauss) to Secretary of State' in FRUS, 1944, VI, China, 77–8.
214 Huang, 'Chiang Kaishek', II, 94–5; 'To Lieutenant Joseph Stilwell' (7 June 1944) in MP, IV, 472–3.
215 'To Lieutenant Joseph Stilwell' (26 May 1944), in MP, 465.
216 Quoted in MP, IV, 475.
217 'Generalissimo Chiang Informs President Roosevelt of the Recent Situation in the China Theatre' (27 March 1944), ZHMGZYSL, II: 3, 440–1.
218 Tuchman, *Stilwell*, 567.
219 'Memorandum for the President' (13 April 1944) in MP, IV, 408; Tuchman, *Stilwell*, 567 and n.1.
220 MP, IV, 414 n.1; 'PM to General Carton de Wiart' and 'PM to Chiang Kaishek', in ZHMGZYSL, II: 3, 469–71. English texts.
221 'The Ambassador in China (Gauss) to the Secretary of State' (20 May 1944), FRUS, VI, China, 77–8; 'The Consul at Kweilin (Ringwalt) to the Ambassador in China (Gauss))' (25 May 1944), in ibid., 83–4.
222 'Memorandum by the Chief of the Division of Chinese Affairs (Vincent) to the Under Secretary' (15 May 1944), FRUS, 1944, VI, China, 72–3.
223 The memorandum is reproduced in Davies, *Dragon by the Tail*, 313.

224 Ibid., 312.
225 'Ambassador in China (Gauss) to Secretary of State' (2 April 1944), in FRUS, 1944, VI, China, 48–9.
226 'To Lieutenant General Joseph Stilwell' (7 June 1944), in MP, IV, 472–3 and n.1 and 2.
227 'Major General Claire Chennault to President Roosevelt' (14 July 1944), FRUS, 1944, VI, China, 127–8.
228 Tuchman, *Stilwell*, 603–4.
229 'Memorandum for the President' (4 July 1944) in MP, IV, 503–4.
230 Tuchman, *Stilwell*, 600–1.
231 Ibid., 302.
232 'To Lieutenant General Joseph Stilwell', MP, IV, 473; White, ed., *Stilwell Papers*, 321, 329–30; MP, IV, 586, n. 2; Romanus and Sunderland, *Stilwell's Command Problems*, 435.
233 Tuchman, *Stilwell*, 625.
234 Churchill, *Second World War*, VI, 134.
235 Ibid., 145–7.
236 Ibid., 130.
237 'Proposed Message from the President to the Generalissimo' (16 September 1944), MP, 584–5 and n.1.
238 'Major General Claire Chennault to President Roosevelt' (21 September 1944), FRUS, 1944, VI, China, 158–60.
239 'Generalissimo Chiang's Address at the Fourth Nanyue Military Conference' ZHMGZYSL, II:1, 502–9.
240 Message from Chiang Kaishek, passed on by Hurley, see 'Major General Patrick Hurley to President Roosevelt', FRUS, 1944, VI China, 167–9.
241 Schaller, *US Crusade*, 172.
242 Tuchman, *Stilwell*, 636–7.
243 'Generals Shu Shicuan, Chief of Staff of the Chinese Army in India, Sun Liren, Commander of the New 38th Division, and Others Report on Conditions in the Sino-American Army in India' (25 August 1943), ZHMGZYSL, II: 3, 516–17.
244 'Report from Kunming of General Du Lüming, Vice Commander in Chief of the First Route Army of the Expeditionary Army, to Generalissimo Chiang' (12 September 1942) and 'General Zheng Tongguo, Vice-Commander in Chief of the Chinese Army in India, Reports to Generalissimo Chiang' (14 August 1943)', ZHMGZYSL, II: 3, 515–16, 517.
245 Shao, 'Japan's Last Peace Illusion', 7–8; *Zhou Fohai Riji*, II, 1079; Bix, *Hirohito*, 492–3.
246 See Yick, 'Communist Puppet Collaboration, 70–81; Martin, 'Shield of Collaboration', 131–3.
247 Shao, 'Japan's Final Peace Fantasy'.
248 Ibid., 8.
249 Tuchman, *Stilwell*, 495–7.
250 Yu, *OSS in China*, 159–60.
251 Ibid., 187.
252 Elleman, *Modern Chinese Warfare*, 208.
253 Yick, 'Communist Puppet Collaboration', 76–8.
254 'Weekly Intelligence Summary no 19' (17 Jan 1945), in 'Airfields in Yunnan; Progress Reports; Intelligence Reports', PRO: HS1/137.
255 'Guofangbu Baomiju Han Song Kangzhan Qijian Zhonggong Gexiang Ziliao' (Various Materials Related to the CCP Transferred by the Intelligence Bureau of the National Defence Ministry [to the Academia Historica]), Second Historical Archives, 787/1914.
256 'Diary of Fu Bingchang', entry of 7 April 1945.
257 Katz, 'The polls and the 1944 election', in *Public Opinion Quarterly*, VIII (1944–5), 468, 481.
258 *Public Opinion Quarterly*, VIII (1944–5), 567–8.
259 MP, IV, 618, n.1.
260 Ibid.
261 'President Roosevelt to Generalissimo Chiang Kaishek', FRUS, 1944, VI, China, 165.
262 Passed on by Hurley, see 'Major General Patrick Hurley to President Roosevelt' (10 October 1944), FRUS, 1944, VI, China, 167.

263 'Draft of Message from the President to the Generalissimo' (16 October 1944), MP, IV, 627.
264 MP, 628, n. 3; Romanus and Sunderland, *Stilwell's Command Problems*, 468.
265 MP, 652, n.1.
266 Ibid.
267 Tuchman, *Stilwell*, 642–3.
268 Rand, *China Hands*, 246.
269 Tuchman, *Stilwell*, 646.
270 Ibid., 645.
271 Thorne, *Allies*; Aldrich, *Intelligence*; Sbrega, *Anglo American Relations*; Tonnesson, *The Vietnamese Revolution*; and Watt, *Succeeding John Bull*.
272 Allen, *Longest War*, 320–1.
273 *Penguin New Writing*, 1941, 114.

2 Raising the National Revolutionary Army

1 Waldron, *Turning Point*, 280.
2 Wilbur, 'Nationalist Revolution'; Brandt, *Stalin's Failure*; Galbiati, *P'eng P'ai*; Hofheinz, *Broken Wave*; Whiting, *Soviet Policies*; Isaacs, *Tragedy*; Schwartz, *Chinese Communism*; Saich, ed., *Origins of the First United Front*; Luk, *Origins of Chinese Bolshevism*; Smith, *A Road is Made*. Pantsov, in *The Bolsheviks*, using newly available archival sources in Russia, argued that neither Stalin nor Trotsky in the mid-1920s offered policies that could have ensured a Chinese Communist victory during the Northern Expedition, but also argued that both abandoned Lenin's original strategy of an independent Communist party and that its renewed use in the 1940s led to victory. Using Chinese, Japanese, and Russian sources, Elleman, in *Diplomacy and Deception*, argued that Soviet imperialist policies rather than a genuine commitment to world revolution drove Soviet policy including during the 1920s.
3 Lü Fangshan, *Geming zhi Zaiqi*. See also Dirlik, *Chinese Communism*, 61–73; and van de Ven, *From Friend to Comrade*, 9–54.
4 Hou Yijie, *Yuan Shikai Quanzhuan*, 308–540; Young, *Presidency*, 105–76; Ch'en, *Yuan Shih-kai*, 46–62, 166–218; and MacKinnon, *Power and Politics*, 90–136. Documents on the Confucianism movement can be found in *Zhongguo Jindaishi Zun Kong Niliu*, 33–61. For documents and contemporary writings on the monarchical movement, see *Beiyang Junfa*, II, 919–1124.
5 A broad literature exists: Chow Tse-tsung, *May Fourth Movement*; Lin Yü-sheng, *Crisis of Chinese Consciousness*; Schwarcz, *Chinese Enlightenment*; Grieder, *Hu Shih*; Fitzgerald, *Awakening China*; Daruvala; *Zhou Zuoren*; Lee, *Romantic Generation*; Tang, *Chinese Modern*; and Shih, *The Lure of the Modern*.
6 Liu Shuya, 'Junguo Zhuyi' (Militarism), in *Xin Qingnian*, II: 3 (1 November 1916), 5–8.
7 Liu Shuya, 'Ouzhou Zhanshi yu Qingnian Juewu' (The War in Europe and the Awakening of the Youth), in *Xin Qingnian*, II: 2 (1 October 1916), 1–8.
8 Wang Xinggong, 'Qubing' (Abolish the Military), *Xin Qingnian*, V: 6 (15 December 1918), 565–70.
9 Hu Shi, 'Wuli Jiejue yu Jiejue Wuli' (Armed Resolution and the Resolution of Armies), in *Xin Qingnian*, V: 6 (15 December 1918), 571–4.
10 McCord, 'Warlords against Warlordism', 795–892. For international pressure to convene the conference, and primary documents related to it, see *Beiyang Junfa*, III, 1001–32.
11 'Zhi Liang Qichao' (To Liang Qichao) (2 July 1920), in *Jiang Baili Xiansheng Quanji*, I, 35.
12 'Ruhe Shi Yiwu Minbingzhi' (What is Compulsory Military Service), *Jiang Baili Xiansheng Quanji*, I, 205–8 and 'Caibing Jihuashu' (A Plan For Demobilisation), ibid., IV, 11–144.
13 For the relevant documents, see *Shanhou Huiyi*, 210–370 and *Beiyang Junfa*, V, 13–3.
14 *Zhou Zuoren Jiwai Wen*, I, 510.
15 See Shi Quansheng, *Zhonghua Minguo Wenhua Shi*, I, 407.
16 'Yuandan Shibi' (Essay on New Year's Day), in *Yutian de Shu*, 121. I am grateful to Susan Daruvala for pointing out this article to me.

17 'Wenming yu Yeman' (Civilisation and Barbarity) (June 1925), in *Zhou Zuoren Jiwai Wen*, I, 716.
18 Wen Gongzhi, *Zuijin Sanshi Nian Zhongguo Junshi shi*, 1–7.
19 Mao Zedong, 'Tiyu zhi Yanjiu' (Physical Education and Study), in *Mao Zedong Zaoqi Wengao*, 65, 71. A partial translation can be found in Schram, *Political Thought*, 94–5, 99.
20 Jin Chongji, *Mao Zedong Zhuan*, 22.
21 Chen Jin, ed., *Mao Zedong Dushu Biji*, I, 6–7. On other readings by Mao, see Jin Chongji, *Mao Zedong Zhuan*, 18–21.
22 Chen Jin, ed., *Mao Zedong Dushu Biji*, I, 121–5.
23 Chiang Kaishek, ed., *Zeng Hu Zhibing Yulu*, 6.
24 'Guanyu Diguozhuyi zhi Taidu' (Attitudes about Imperialism), in *Zhongguo Junren*, VII, 2–4.
25 'Guomin Geming Jun Junwu Shanhou Huiyi' (NRA Military Rehabilitation Conference) (1–7 January 1927), KMT Archives 441/9.
26 Lovell, *China's Search for a Nobel Prize*, 76–8. Hay, *Asian Ideas*, 164–245.
27 'To Liao Zhongkai', in Sun Yatsen, *Sun Zhongshan Quanji*, V, 570–72.
28 'Zhonghua Minguo Guofang Jihua Gangling yu Guofang Zhengce Shishi Yijian Shu' (Paper Suggesting a National Defence Plan for the Chinese Republic and the Implementation of a National Defence Policy) (April/May 1929), in Second Historical Archives of China, 787/1955.
29 *Jiangguo Fanglue* (Basic Strategy for National Reconstruction), 39–151.
30 Ibid., 18–31, 32–8. See also 'To Act is Easy, To Know is Difficult', in Wei, *Selected Writings of Sun Yatsen*, 199–222.
31 Wei, commentary, *Selected Writings*, 314 and Bergere, *Sun Yatsen*, 280–1.
32 Quoted in Huang, Chiang Kaishek, I, 21. See also *Jiang Jieshi Nianpu*, 113–15, 154–8. Chiang poured out his dissatisfaction with current policies in long letters to Liao Zhongkai.
33 Sun Yatsen, 'The Doctrine of Sun Yatsen' (December 1918) and 'History of the Chinese Revolution' (1923) in Wei *et al.*, tr, *Prescriptions for Saving China*, 200–3, 255–7, 257–66; Bergere, *Sun Yatsen*, 246–86; and Fitzgerald, *Awakening China*, 181–213.
34 Quoted in Bergere, *Sun Yatsen*, 275.
35 'Letter to Chiang Kaishek', *Zhu Zhixin Ji*, I, 321.
36 'Lun Junguan zhi Gaiye' (On Re-employment of Officers) (30 June 1919), in ibid., I, 336–9.
37 'Gebing Gejing Zishi zhi Wenti' (December 1919), in ibid., II, 625–8.
38 'Lun Junguan zhi Gaiye', and 'Wei Dujun Huace' (Strategies for Military Governors) (n.d.), ibid., I, 336–9, II, 873–7; Lü Fangshan, *Geming zhi Zaiqi*, 462–3.
39 'Suowei Shilipai zhi Heping' (The Peace of the So-called True Powerholders) (1919), 'Zhuzhang Junguozhuyi de Liu Mei Xuesheng' (Students in America Advocating Militarism) (January 1920), and 'Junfa de Pochan Xuangao' (Declaration on the Bankruptcy of the Warlords) (March 1920), *Zhu Zhixin Ji*, I, 479–85; II, 667, 733–4.
40 'Bing di Gaige yu Qi Xinli', in ibid., II, 836–41.
41 'Cong Jingjishang Guancha Zhongguo zhi Luanyuan' (China's Chaos Examined from an Economic Perspective) (June 1919); Lü Fangshan, *Geming zhi Zaiqi*, 459.
42 Lü Fangshang, *Geming zhi Zaiqi*, 459.
43 *Jiang Jieshi Nianpu*, 86–93.
44 Lü Fangshan, *Geming zhi Zaiqi*, 471.
45 'Jiang Zhongzheng zhi Su'E Dang Fuzeren Yijianshu' (Chiang Kaishek's Paper for Soviet Leaders) (5 August 1923), Academia Historica, Daxi Dang'an, 2010/4450.01-001.
46 Chiang Kaishek, ed., *Zeng Hu Zhi Bing Yulu*, 6.
47 Bergere, *Sun Yatsen*, 378.
48 Ibid., 256–9.
49 Ibid.
50 'Jianguo Dagang Xuanyuan', in *Guofu Quanshu*, 155.
51 Waldron, 'The Warlord', 1073–100.
52 For a discussion of the literature on warlordism, see McCord, *Power of the Gun*, 24–45; McCord, 'Warlordism in Early Republican China'; and van de Ven, 'The Military in the Republic', 357–61. Waldron, *Turning Point* and McCord, *Power of the Gun* are the best recent

Western writings on the subject. Recent valuable studies in Chinese are Jiang Kefu, *Minguo Junshishi Luegao*; Lai Xinxia, *Beiyang Junfa Shigao*; Li Xin and Li Zongyi, *Beiyang Zhengfu Tongzhi Shiqi*; Jiang Shunxing, *et al.*, *Shanxi Wang Yan Xishan*; Lu Weijun *et al.*, *Feng Guozhang he Zhixi Junfa*; Shen Xiaoyun, *Li Zongren de Yisheng*. Important collections of primary sources are *Beiyang Junfa; Beiyang Lujun Shiliao; Qingmo Xinjun*.

53 Sheridan, *Feng Yü-hsiang*, 14–16.

54 See Zhu Shuli, 'Power Sharing between Central and Local Government' for the suggestion that the revival of warlordism remained a key political concern after 1949.

55 'Report: Organisation of Commissioned Officers' (January 1927), USMI, reel V, frame 518–21; 'Report: Recruitment of Enlisted Personnel' (May 1926), USMI, reel V, frame 724–8.

56 van de Ven, 'Military and Financial Reform', 21–65.

57 Luo Erh-kang, 'Qingji Bing Wei Jiang You de Qiyuan'; Franz Michael, 'Regionalism'.

58 McCord, *Power of the Gun*, 310.

59 See van de Ven, 'Introduction' in *Warfare in Chinese History*, 3–11.

60 Rich, 'Warlords, State Fragmentation, and the Dilemma of Humanitarian Intervention', 78–80; Iriye, *After Imperialism*.

61 Waldron, *Turning Point*, 161–80, 277–8; Iriye, *After Imperialism*, 25–56.

62 Slack, *Opium, State, and Society*, 4, 9–26.

63 Ibid., 16–28, 63–85. 'Guangxi Caizheng Baogao Shu' (Report on Financial Reforms in Guanxi) (1926), 32–3, 11, KMT Archives 439.2/3. On the Communists, see Ch'en Yung-fa, 'The Blooming Poppy under the Red Sun', 271–91.

64 League of Nations Report, *Statistical Information on the Trade in Arms* (1926), 89.

65 Ibid., 1929, 159.

66 See 'Returns on Arms and Ammunition Imported and Exported for the Chinese Government' (1901–25), in (Zhongguo Haiguan Dang'an) Chinese Maritime Customs Service Archives, Second Historical Archives of China, 679(7)/232 to 291.

67 See 'Memorial of the Grand Council' (29 October 1894), 'Precis of von Haneken's Memorandum'; 'Imperial Edict' (15 November 1894); 'Hu Yufen's Memorials' (22 November and 3 and 17 December 1894), 'Zhang Zhidong's Memorial' in *Qingmo Xinjun*, 6–7. On Russian influence, see 'Beiyang Lianbing An' (The Training of the Beiyang Army) in *Qingmo Dang'an Shiliao Congbian*, X (1984), 249–66.

68 See Liu Fenghan, 'Wan Qing Xinjian Lujun', 215–24; van de Ven, 'Military and Financial Reform', 38–44. For primary sources, see *Qingmo Xinjun*, 45–54.

69 Fung, *Military Dimension*, ch. 5.

70 van de Ven, 'Military and Financial Reform', 65–79.

71 Ibid., 73–95.

72 Brewer, *Sinews of Power*.

73 Kuhn, *Origins of the Modern Chinese State*, 80–90.

74 Ibid., 23, 80–90. Wang, *Land Taxation*, 5–17; Zelin, *Magistrate's Tael*, 88–123, 167–200, 220–308; Mann, *Local Merchants*, 95–144.

75 Chen Feng, *Qingdai Junfei Yanjiu*, 159–93, 288–345.

76 van de Ven, 'Military and Financial Reform', 42–65. Documents for the New Army in the provinces can be found in *Qingmo Xinjun*, 93–296.

77 Siu, *Agents and Victims*, 74–695.

78 Bliukher and Kuibishev, 'A Short History of the NRA', in Wilbur *et al.*, *Missionaries*, II, 481.

79 Siu, *Agents and Victims*, 74–6, 87, 88–97.

80 See Jiang Baili, 'Caibing Jihua Shu', 12–18.

81 Bliukher and Kuibishev, 'Short History', in Wilbur, *et al.*, *Missionaries*, II, 484.

82 Ibid., 484.

83 'Beiyang Zhengfu Gesheng Bingli Zuijin Diaocha Biao' (Most Recent Table of the Beiyang Government's Military Forces in the Provinces), Second Historical Archives, 787/1049.

84 See also Perry, *Rebels and Revolutionaries*, 152–247.

85 Guo Hengyu, *E Gong Midang*, I, 19–26.

86 Wou, *Militarism in Modern China*, 198, 211; van de Ven, *From Friend to Comrade*, 112–14.
87 Schwartz, *Documentary History*, 70.
88 See Guo Hengyu, *E Gong Midang*, I, 13–22; Maring, 'Bericht des Genossen H. Maring fur die Executive' (11 July 1922), in Saich, ed., *Origins of the First United Front*, 286–303.
89 Quoted in Wou, *Militarism in Modern China*, 215.
90 Bergere, *Sun Yatsen*, 311–12.
91 Ibid., 312–13.
92 Ibid., 310.
93 Guo Hengyu, *E Gong Midang*, I, 59.
94 Ibid., I, 63.
95 Ibid., I, 28–9.
96 Ibid., I, 64–9.
97 Ibid., I, 28–32, 60, 66–8.
98 Ibid., I, 18–33, 59–62.
99 Ibid., I, 68.
100 Bergere, *Sun Yatsen*, 316.
101 Guo Hengyu, *E Gong Midang*, I, 87.
102 Ibid., I, 87.
103 Ibid., I, 87; Wilbur, *et al.*, *Missionaries*, I, 89–99.
104 'Baogaoshu Diyihao' (First Report) (December 1923?) and 'Wu Liu Yuefen Zuzhi Gongzuo Baogao' (Work Report on Organisational Activities for May and June) (1924), KMT Archives, 439.2/1.1 and 439.2/1.
105 Wilbur *et al.*, *Missionaries*, I, 94; Shitianzhefu, 'Kangzhan Shiqi Guomindang Dangyuan Chengfen' (The Background of KMT Members during the War of Resistance), *Minguo Yanjiu*, VI (2001), 83.
106 Guo Hengyu, *E Gong Midang*, I, 85–101; Wilbur *et al.*, *Missionaries*, I, 91–99; Bergere, *Sun Yatsen*, 325–31.
107 Bergere, *Sun Yatsen*, 325–32.
108 Guo Hengyu, *E Gong Midang*, I, 105–25; Bergere, *Sun Yatsen*, 332–7.
109 Bergere, *Sun Yatsen*, 349–50.
110 Guo Hengyu, *E Gong Midang*, I, 126.
111 Ibid., I, 125–6, 137–8.
112 Wagner, 'Ritual, Publicity, and Politics', 11–14, 19–22.
113 Wilbur *et al.*, *Missionaries*, I, 96.
114 Ibid.
115 *Jiang Jieshi Nianpu*, 157–74.
116 Wang Huaizhou, 'Liao Zhongkai yü Huangpu Jianjun' (Liao Zhongkai and the Establishment of an Army at Whampoa), 85.
117 'Liao Zhongkai zhi Jiang Jieshi Yizu Handian' (Letters and Telegrams from Liao Zhongkai to Jiang Kaishek', in *Minguo Dang'an*, VII (1987), 3–8.
118 Ibid., 85–6.
119 *Jiang Jieshi Nianpu*, 168–9.
120 Ibid., 168–9. Wang Huaizhou, 'Liao Zhongkai yu Huangpu Jianjun', *Minguo Dang'an*, VII (1987), 85.
121 *Jiang Jieshi Nianpu*, 170.
122 Wilbur *et al.*, *Missionaries*, I, 96–7, and Bliukher and Kuibishev, 'Short History' in ibid., II, 484.
123 'Statistics on Graduates of the First to Fifth Classes of the Academy', *Huangpu Junxiao Shiliao*, 93
124 'Simple Recruitment Rules' (1925), *Huangpu Junxiao Shiliao*, 35–6; Patay, 'Plan and Regulations for the Central Military–Political Academy of the NRA', in Wilbur *et al.*, *Missionaries*, II, 585–93. The latter suggests that the course lasted eight months.
125 'Statistics on the Graduates from the First to Seventh Classes of our Academy', in *Huanpu Junxiao Shiliao*, 93.
126 'Simple Recruitment Rules' (1925), *Huangpu Junxiao Shiliao*, 36; 'Regulations for the Military School for Officers of the National Guard in Canton', in Wilbur *et al.*, *Missionaries*, II, 491–3.

127 'Simple Recruitment Rules', *Huangpu Junxiao Shiliao*, 36–7; 'Regulations for the Military School', in Wilbur *et al.*, *Missionaries*, II, 491–3.

128 'Introduction to the Whamoa Military Acdemy', *Huangpu Shiliao*, 5.

129 Sun Yatsen, 'Address at the Initiation of Instruction at the Military Academy', *Huangpu Junxiao Shiliao*, 44–58; 'Speech by Zhou Enlai, Head of the Political Department' (1 July 1925), ibid., 224.

130 Li Jishen, 'Opening Speech at the New Years Reception of the Academy' (1926), *Huangpu Junxiao Shiliao*, 235–6.

131 Fang Dingying, 'Overview of Instruction at the Academy' (1927), *Huangpu Junxiao Shiliao*, 80–83.

132 Yun Daiyiang, 'Methods of Political Work in the Army' (1926), *Huangpu Junxiao Shiliao*, 225–9.

133 'Regulation of the Military School', in Wilbur *et al.*, *Missionaries*, II, 491–5.

134 Wilbur *et al.*, *Missionaries*, I, 114–15.

135 'Introduction', *Huangpu Junshi Shiliao*, 3.

136 Wilbur *et al.*, *Missionaries*, I, 115–18.

137 Ibid., I, 143–4.

138 Ibid.

139 Ibid., I, 154.

140 'Hu Hanmin's Announcement Regarding the Resolution on the Implementation of Government Reform' (24 June 1925), ZHMGSDAZL, IV: 1, 35.

141 'Organisational Law of the MAC of the Chinese National Government' (5 July 1925) *Junzheng Shiliao*, I, 7–8.

142 Wilbur *et al.*, *Missionaries*, I, 155.

143 'Junshi Weiyuanhui Huiyi Jilu' (MAC Minutes), KMT Archives 0013/6.

144 'Chiang Kai-shek's Letter to Bliukher', in Wilbur *et al.*, *Missionaries*, II, 502–05.

145 Luo Ming, 'Guanyu Beifa Zhanzheng de Junfei Wenti', 77.

146 Bliukher *et al.*, 'Short History', and 'Instructions to the Commissions for the Re-organisation of the NRA' (November 1925), in Wilbur *et al.*, *Missionaries*, II, 487–8 and 562–3.

147 'Regulations Governing Political Commissaries in the NRA', in Wilbur *et al.*, *Missionaries*, II, 679–81.

148 Kuibishev (?), 'The Revolutionary Army of Canton' (February 1926?) in Wilbur *et al.*, *Missionaries*, II, 599–616. For authorship and dating, see commentary, ibid., 598.

149 'General Characteristics of the Armed Forces of the National Government', 'The Training of the NRA for War', Characteristics of the Officer Personnel of the NRA', 'Organisation of an Army Corps', 'Organisation and Function of Army Staffs', 'Report on Sanitary Conditions', 'Aviation', and 'The High Sea and River Patrol Fleet', all in Wilbur *et al.*, *Missionaries*, II, 619–53. Probably all written in February–March 1926. See commentary, ibid., 619.

150 Wilbur *et al.*, *Missionaries*, 517 state that the MAC minutes are in the hand of Tan Yankai. They did not have access, but refer to the historian Chiang Yung-ching as source for this information.

151 I am grateful to Kip Liev and Boping Yuan for assistance with deciphering and translating this poem.

152 See Radtke, *China's Relations with Japan*, 23–4.

153 Ibid., 23–36.

154 See 'Resolutions of the Financial Committee of the Supreme Headquarters' (30 December 1923–9 December 1924), ZHMGSDAZL, IV: 2, 1206–99.

155 Ibid., July 1924, ZHMGDA, IV: 2, 1057.

156 Ibid.

157 Quoted in Wang Huaizhou, 'Liao Zhongkai yu Huangpu Jianjun', 87.

158 Ibid., 86.

159 Ibid., 87.

160 Ibid.

161 Wilbur *et al.*, *Missionaries*, I, 167–8.
162 Ibid., I, 167–8; and Wang Huaizhou, 'Liao Zhongkai yu Huanpu Jianjun', *Minguo Dang'an* VII (1987), 87.
163 Wilbur *et al.*, *Missionaries*, I, 167–8.
164 Song Ziwen, 'Report on Last Year's Treasury Income and Financial Reforms' (5 November 1926), ZHMGSDAZL, IV: 2 1400–4.
165 Ibid.
166 Luo Ming, 'Beifa Zhanzheng de Junfei Wenti', 79.
167 Ibid., 79–82.
168 Song Ziwen, 'Report on Last Year's Treasury Income and Financial Reforms', ZHMGS-DAZL, IV: 2, 1401.
169 Luo Ming, 'Beifa Zhanzheng de Junfei Wenti', 82.

3 Cultures of violence during the Northern Expedition (1926–8)

1 Isaacs, *The Tragedy of the Chinese Revolution*; Brandt, *Stalin's Failure*; and Jordan, *The Northern Expedition*.
2 Wilbur *et al.*, *Missionaries*, 1.
3 Wilbur, 'Nationalist Revolution', 527.
4 For an overview of the literature, see Chapter 2, n. 2.
5 Waldron, *Turning Point*, 59.
6 'Chiang Kaishek's Northern Expedition Oath' (9 July 1926), in ZHMGSDAZL, IV: 1, 917.
7 'Circular Telegram By Chiang Kaishek Regarding his Assumption of the Post of the NRA Supreme Commander' (9 July 1926), ZHMGSDAZL, IV: 1, 916.
8 For a brief overview of the issues, see Wilbur *et al.*, *Missionaries*, 252–63.
9 'Hu Hanmin's Telegram Announcing the Establishment of a Government' (1 July 1925), ZHMGSDAZL, IV:1, p. 35.
10 Wilbur *et al.*, *Missionaries*, 167–8.
11 Wagner, 'Ritual, Politics, and Publicity', 8–15, 19–22.
12 Wilbur *et al.*, *Missionaries*, I, 188–9.
13 'Record of Wang Jingwei's Explanation at the Second KMT Congress of the History of the Acceptance of Sun Yatsen's Testament', ZHMGSDAZL, IV: 1, 267–71.
14 Bergere, *Sun Yatsen*, 405–6; Wilbur *et al.*, *Missionaries*, 124–5.
15 Bergere, *Sun Yatsen*, 406.
16 'Speech of Chairman Wang Jingwei' (4 January 1926), ZHMGSDAZL, IV: 1, 301–2.
17 Wilbur *et al.*, *Missionaries*, 31.
18 'Record of Song Qingling's Statement at the KMT Second Congress' (8 January 1926), ZHMGSDAZL, IV: 1, 330–1.
19 *Junshi Weiyuanhui Huiyi Jilu* (MAC Minutes), 7 Jan 1926, KMT Archives, 0013/6.
20 As reflected in *Junshi Weiyuanhui Huiyi Jilu*. See also Wilbur *et al.*, *Missionaries*, 248–9 and Kuibishev, 'Report on the NRA and the Kuomintang' (early 1926), in ibid., II, 599–615.
21 Kuibishev, 'Report on the NRA', in Wilbur *et al.*, *Missionaries*, II, 602.
22 Ibid., 608–9.
23 Jin Chongji, *Zhou Enlai Zhuan*, 100–14.
24 Kuibishev, 'Report on the NRA', in Wilbur *et al.*, *Missionaries*, II, 606–8 and 'Numbers of Members of the CCP in the NRA' (mid March 1926), in ibid., II, 688.
25 Li Tsung-jen, *Memoirs*, 136–40; *Jiang Jieshi Nianpu*, 529, 534, 535, 539, 540.
26 Jordan, *Northern Expedition*, 72.
27 'Yue Haiguan Dang'an' (Archives of the Canton Customs House), *Minguo Dang'an* XVIII (1996), 14.
28 *Jiang Jieshi Nianpu*, 540; Guo Hengyu, *E Gong Midang*, II, 84.
29 *Jiang Jieshi Nianpu*, 539, 545,
30 Jacobs, *Borodin*, 168–9.
31 Sheridan, *Feng Yü-hsiang*, 149–68.

32 Ibid., 183–5.
33 Ibid., 185–92.
34 Jacobs, *Borodin*, 193–8.
35 For the raid, Wilbur *et al.*, *Missionaries*, I, 1.
36 Kuibishev, 'Report on the NRA', in Wilbur *et al.*, *Missionaries*, II, 599–613.
37 Kuibishev, 'General Characteristics of the Armed Forces of the National Government', in Wilbur *et al.*, *Missionaries*, I, II, 619–21.
38 'The Training of the NRA', in Wilbur *et al.*, *Missionaries*, II, 624.
39 'Letter from Chiang Kaishek to Wang Jingwei' (9 April 1926), *Minguo Dang'an* XVIII (1996), 11.
40 'Chen Duxiu's Report to the Fifth Congress' (April 1927), Saich, *Rise to Power*, 234.
41 *Jiang Jieshi Nianpu*, 528; Guo Hengyu, *E Gong Midang*, II, 81.
42 *Jiang Jieshi Nianpu*, 528, 537; Guo Hengyu, *E Gong Midang*, II, 82.
43 *Jiang Jieshi Nianpu*, 536; Guo Hengyu, *E Gong Midang* II, 81.
44 *Jiang Jieshi Nianpu*, 536.
45 Ibid., 539.
46 Ibid., 540.
47 Ibid., 541.
48 Ibid., 546; Guo Hengyu, *E Gong Midang*, II, 82.
49 Wilbur *et al.*, *Missionaries*, 262.
50 *Jiang Jieshi Nianpu*, 80.
51 'Yue Haiguan Dang'an', *Minguo Dang'an* XVIII (1996), 15.
52 Ibid., 15.
53 'Letter from Chiang Kaishek to Wang Jingwei', in *Minguo Dang'an* XVIII (1996), 11–12.
54 'Yue Haiguan Dang'an', in ibid., 14–15.
55 Ibid., 15.
56 Ibid., 15.
57 Ibid., 15.
58 Ibid., 15.
59 *Jiang Jieshi Nianpu*, 535, 542.
60 'National Government Order Proscribing the Western Hills Faction to Convene Congresses in Beijing, Shanghai, and Elsewhere' and 'Strict Order of the KMT Central Executive Committee's Secretariat for the Arrest of Pesonnel Coming to Guangdong', ZHMGS-DAZL, IV: 1, 362–3, 364–5.
61 *Jiang Jieshi Nianpu*, 535; van de Ven, *From Friend to Comrade*, 171–3.
62 'Letter from Wang Maogong to Zhang Jingjiang' (7 March 1927), ZHMGDAZL, IV: 1, 358–60.
63 'Letter from Chen Duxiu to Chiang Kaishek' (30 August 1926), in *Chen Duxiu Shuxin Ji*, 407.
64 'Letter from Chiang Kaishek to Wang Jingwei', *Minguo Dang'an*, XVIII (1996), 10–11.
65 Ibid., 12. 'Letter from Chen Duxiu to Chiang Kaishek', in *Chen Duxiu Shuxin Ji*, 406–7.
66 *Jiang Jieshi Nianpu*, 540.
67 Yang Tianshi, 'Zhongshanjian Shijian zhi Mi' (The Riddle of the Sun Yatsen Gunboat Incident), 118–9.
68 'Letter from Wang Maogong to Jiang Jingzhang', ZHMGDAZL, IV: 1, 359.
69 *Jiang Jieshi Nianpu*, 540. Guo Hengyu, *E Gong Midang*, 83.
70 Guo Hengyu, *E Gong Midang*, II, 74–75.
71 Yang Tianshi, 'The Riddle of the Sun Yatsen Gunboat Incident', *Lishi Yanjiu*, II (April 1988), 116–30.
72 *Mingguo Dang'an*, XVIII (1996), 3–12.
73 'Letter from Ouyang Zhong to Deng Yanda' (23 March 1926), ibid., 5.
74 'Report from Li Shiyong to Deng Yanda' (24 March 1926), in ibid., 6.
75 'Report from Wang Xuechen to Deng Yanda', (26 March 1926), in ibid., 7.
76 'Li Zhilong's Testimony' (March 1926), in ibid., 8.
77 Idem, 9.
78 'Chiang Kaishek's Report to the MAC', in ibid., 4.
79 Yang Tianshi, 'The Riddle of the Sun Yatsen Gunboat Incident', 122–3.

80 Wilbur *et al.*, *Missionaries*, I, 255–64.
81 'Chiang Kaishek's Report to All Circles', *Minguo Dang'an*, XVIII (1996), 10.
82 'Letter by Chiang Kaishek to Wang Jingwei', *Minguo Dang'an*, XVIII (1996), 12.
83 Ibid., 11.
84 Ibid., 11–12.
85 Wilbur *et al.*, *Missionaries*, I, 256, 261.
86 Jiang Kefu, *Minguo Junshishi Luegao*, I, 254–8; 'General Characteristics of the Armed Forces of the National Government' in Wilbur *et al.*, *Missionaries*, 620–1.
87 Jiang Kefu, *Minguo Junshishi Luegao*, I, 256–7.
88 Wilbur *et al.*, *Missionaries*, I, 312.
89 Jiang Kefu, *Junguo Junshishi Luegao*, I, 286–7.
90 Wilbur *et al.*, *Missionaries*, I, 317; Jordan, *Northern Expedition*, 72–3.
91 Wilbur, *et al.*, *Missionaries*, I, 318.
92 Ibid., 316–9; Dreyer, *China at War*, 134; Jordan, *Northern Expedition*, 81–2.
93 'Qu Qiubai's Report Upon Returning from Guangdong' (15 September 1926), in *Guangdong Qu Dang Tuan Yanjiu Shiliao*, 417.
94 Jordan, *Northern Expedition*, 93–7.
95 Ibid., 83–92.
96 Wilbur *et al.*, *Missionaries*, I, 321–2.
97 Ibid., 325–6.
98 Jordan, *Northern Expedition*, 92.
99 Wilbur *et al.*, *Missionaries*, I, 326.
100 Ibid., 362–3.
101 Li Tsung-jen, *Memoirs*, I, 201–2.
102 'Letter from the CCP Central Bureau to the Guangdong Region' (9 November 1926), in *Guangdong Dang Tuan Yanjiu Shiliao*, 471.
103 Wilbur *et al.*, *Missionaries*, I, 359–61.
104 Ibid., 362–3.
105 Jacobs, *Borodin in china*, 273.
106 'Report on the Split between Chiang Kai-shek and Tang Sheng-chih' (5 March 1927), Wilbur *et al.*, *Missionaries*, II, 831–2.
107 Wilbur *et al.*, *Missionaries*, I, 375.
108 Ibid., 377.
109 Ibid., 377.
110 Ibid., 385.
111 Ibid., 387.
112 Ibid., 374.
113 Ibid., 374–5.
114 Ibid., 398–407; Jordan, *Northern Expedition*, 93–117.
115 Wilbur *et al.*, *Missionaries*, I, 360–3; van de Ven, *From Fried to Comrade*, 202–14.
116 'Letter from the CCP Central Bureau to the Guangdong Region' (4 October 1926), in *Guangdong Dang Tuan Yanjiu Shiliao*, 450. 'Qu Qiubai's Report Upon Returning from Guangdong', in ibid., 417.
117 'Chen Duxiu's Report to the CCP's Fifth National Congress' (29 April 1927), in Saich, ed., *Rise to Power of the CCP*, 234.
118 van de Ven, *From Friend to Comrade*, 106–8.
119 Quoted in Jacobs, *Borodin in China*, 211.
120 'Chen Duxiu's Report', Saich, ed., *Rise to Power*, 233.
121 Jacobs, *Borodin in China*, 211–12.
122 Quoted in ibid., 211.
123 'Chen Duxiu's Report', in Saich, ed., *Rise to Power*, 233.
124 Ibid., 233.
125 Chen Duxiu, 'Political Report of the Central Committee' (July 1926), in Saich, ed., 172–4.
126 Ibid., 173.
127 'Resolution on the Question of Relations Between the CCP and the GMD' (July 1926), in ibid., 174–5.

128 Ibid., 174–5.
129 Ibid., 176–7.
130 'Letter from the CCP Central Bureau to Guangdong' (22 September 1926), in *Guangdong Qu Dang Tuan Yanjiu Shiliao*, 412.
131 Ibid., 413.
132 'Lun Guomin Zhengfu zhi Beifa' (On the National Government's Northern Expedition) (7 June 1926), in *Chen Duxiu Wenzhang Xuanbian*, III, 250.
133 'Qu Qiubai's Report Upon Returning from Guangdong', *Guangdong Qu Dang Tuan Yanjiu Shiliao*, 413–4.
134 'Central Bureau Report', in *Zhonggong Zhongyang Zhengzhi Baogao Xuanji*, I, 134–5.
135 'On the Northern Expedition of the National Government', *Chen Duxiu Wenzhang Xuanbian*, III, 251.
136 'Draft of a Peasant Political Manifesto', in *Zhonggong Zhongyang Zhengzhi Baogao Xuanji*, I, 148.
137 Ibid., 149–50.
138 'Comrade Chen Duxiu's Letter to al Party Offices', in ibid., 134.
139 'Central Bureau Report', in ibid., 142.
140 Jin Chongji, *Mao Zedong Zhuan*, 99–101.
141 Ibid., 105.
142 Ibid., 119.
143 Ibid., 119.
144 'Central Bureau Report', in *Zhonggong Zhongyang Zhengzhi Baogao Xuanji*, I, 135.
145 Ibid., 137–9.
146 Ibid., 140.
147 Benton, *China's Urban Revolutionaries*, 10.
148 'Stalin on the Future of the Chinese Revolution' (30 November 1926), in *Gongchan Guoji Youguan Zhongguo Geming de Wenxian Ziliao*, I, 264.
149 Ibid., 270.
150 Ibid., 279.
151 Ibid., 267.
152 'Qu Qiubai's Report Upon Returning from Guangdong', in *Guangdong Dang Tuan Yanjiu Shiliao*, 419.
153 'Political Report' (13 December 1926), in *Zhonggong Zhongyang Zhengzhi Baogao Xuanji*, I, 175.
154 'Qu Qiubai on Borodin' (1928), in *Baoluoting Zai Zhongguo*, 237.
155 'Cai Hesen on Borodin' (1927, 1931), in ibid., 214–5.
156 Li Weihan, *Huiyi yu Yanjiu*, I, 103.
157 'How to Solve the Land Problem' (26 April 1927), in *Baoluoting Zai Zhongguo*, 206.
158 Wilbur, 'The Nationalist Revolution', 645.
159 Schwartz, *Chinese Communism*, 74.
160 Schram, ed., *Mao's Road to Power*, II, 426.
161 Ibid., 427.
162 Ibid., 427.
163 'Comments on the Report of the Comintern Representative', in Saich, ed., *Rise to Power*, 316–17.
164 Schram, ed., *Mao's Road to Power*, II, 429–30. I have translated Hankou as Wuhan.
165 Wilbur, 'The Nationalist Revolution', 644–5.
166 'Report on an Investigation of the Peasant Movement in Hunan' (28 March 1927), in Saich, ed., *Rise to Power*, 201.
167 Wilbur, 'The Nationalist Revolution', 644–7.
168 Ibid., 645.
169 Smith, *A Road is Made*, ch. 7.
170 Ibid., 141.
171 Ibid., 130–44.
172 Ibid., 149.
173 Ibid., 157.
174 Ibid., 158.
175 Ibid.

176 Ibid., 161–3.
177 Ibid., ch. 9.
178 Ibid., 163–4.
179 'Resolutions of the Joint Meeting of the Central and Regional Committees' (23 February 1927), *Dangshi Ziliao*, XI (1982), 10–11.
180 Smith, *A Road is Made*, 173.
181 'Record of Special Committee Meetings' (5 March 1927), *Dangshi Ziliao*, XI (1982), 14–5.
182 Ibid., 13.
183 Wilbur *et al.*, *Missionaries*, 399.
184 Smith, *A Road is Made*, 174–87.
185 Ibid., 187.
186 Ibid., ch. 9.
187 Ibid., 188–9.
188 Warlord forces left, but the city was not brought under control of regular NRA forces (as opposed to irregular Communist ones) until 26 March. Wilbur *et al.*, *Missionaries*, I, 399–400.
189 'Joint Declaration of Wang Jingwei and Chen Duxiu', *Zhonggong Zhongyang Wenjian Xuanji*, III, 593–4.
190 Wilbur *et al.*, *Missionaries*, 402–3.
191 Ibid., 404–5.
192 Smith, *A Road is Made*, 188.
193 *Nanjing Guomin Zhengfu Jishi*, 7.
194 Wilbur *et al.*, *Missionaries*, 402.
195 Martin, *Green Gang*, 99–108.
196 Wilbur *et al.*, *Missionaries*, 405.
197 van de Ven, *From Friend to Comrade*, 193.
198 Wilbur, 'Nationalist Revolution', 625–39.
199 Ibid., 650–7.
200 Ibid., 667.
201 Sheridan, *Feng Yü-hsiang*, 224–33.
202 Wilbur, 'Nationalist Revolution', 648–9.
203 Ibid., 657.
204 Quoted in ibid., 657.
205 Ibid., 657; Schwartz, *Chinese Communism*, 67.
206 van de Ven, 'New States of War', in van de Ven, ed., *Warfare in Chinese History*, 331.
207 Wilbur, 'Nationalist Revolution', 673–6.
208 Ibid., 673–81.
209 Ibid., 690–6.
210 Jordan, *Northern Expedition*, 126–37. A detailed description of the battle is Chang Shih-ying, 'Longtan Zhanyi de Pingjia yu Fansi', 147–80.
211 'Linshi Lianxi Huiyi Jilu' (Minutes of the Provisional Joint Council), minutes of 16, 19, and 21 August, KMT Archives 010/3.1 and 3.2.
212 Chang Shiying, 'Longtan Zhanyi', 154–60.
213 *Nanjing Guomin Zhengfu Jishi*, 35–37.
214 Li Tsung-jen, *Memoirs*, 23.
215 *Nanjing Guomin Zhengfu Jishi*, 37.
216 Jordan, *Northern Expedition*, 149.
217 'Linshi Lianxi Huiyi Jilu', KMT Archives, 010/3.1 and 3.2. Nearly all meetings discussed the shortage of funds.
218 Li Tsung-jen, *Memoirs*, 242–5.
219 Liu, *Military History*, 12–13.
220 'Chiang Kaishek to Zhang Zhizhong' (13 November 1926), Academia Historica, Daxi Dang'an, 0113.
221 Liu, *Military History*, 12–13.

222 Jordan, *Northern Expedition*, 70. Wilbur *et al.*, *Missionaries*, 334, 396.
223 Chiang copied the letter to Tan Yankai. See 'Chiang Kaishek to Tan Yankai' (10 March 1927), Academia Historica, Daxi Dang'an, 0419-1.
224 *Minguo Renwu Da Cidian*, 1059.
225 'Chiang Kaishek to Tan Yankai' (10 March 1927), Academia Historica, Daxi Dang'an, 0419-1.
226 'Chiang Kaishek to Li Jishen' (23 April 1927), in Academia Historica, Daxi Dang'an, 0496.
227 'Letter from the Guangdong Regional Committee of the CCP to the Central Bureau Regarding Relations between Chiang Kaishek and Wang Jingwei as well as the Chairmanship of the KMT' (24 October 1926), in *Guangdong Qu Dang Tuan Yanjiu Shiliao*, 460–1. Jordan, *Northern Expedition*, 98. Jiang Kefu, *Minguo Junshishi Luegao*, I, 255.
228 'Chiang Kaishek to He Yingqin' (18 February 1927), Academia Historica, Daxi Dang'an, 0381.
229 'Chiang Kaishek to Chen Qian and All Armies' (1 August 1926), Academia Historica, Daxi Dang'an, 0004.
230 'Chiang Kaishek to Borodin' (12 November 1926), Academia Historica, Daxi Dang'an, 0111.
231 'Chiang Kaishek to Deng Yanda' (23 September 1926), Academia Historica, Daxi Dang'an, 0064.
232 'Chiang Kaishek to Li Zongren' (14 November 1926), Academia Historica, Daxi Dang'an, 0116.
233 'Chiang Kaishek to Jiangnan Arsenal' (12 May 1927), Academia Historica, Daxi Dang'an, 0554.
234 'Telegram to Yuezhou' (14 September 1926), Academia Historica, Daxi Dang'an, 0052.
235 For example, telegrams of 20 and 28 September; 10 and 28 October; 8 November; 20, 28, and 31 January; 2, 19, and 22 February; 1, 2, 5, and 9 March; 14 April; and 13 May in Academia Historica, Daxi Dang'an, 0060, 0066, 0079, 0092, 0105, 0299, 0336, 0353, 0346, 0384, 0391, 0408, 0409, 0412, 0414, 0420, 0474, 0557.
236 'Chiang Kaishek to Huang Fu' (9 April 1927), Academia Historica, Daxi Dang'an, 0459.
237 Coble, *Shanghai Capitalists*, 29–41, 57–65.
238 'Chiang Kaishek to Li Jishen' (August 1926), Academia Historica, Daxi Dang'an, 0005.
239 'Chiang Kaishek to Cheng Qian' (23 August 1926), Academia Historica, Daxi Dang'an, 0035.
240 'Chiang Kaishek to Zhang Renjie' (23 August 1926), Academia Historica, Daxi Dang'an, 0034.
241 'Chiang Kaishek to Song Ziwen' (20 September 1926), Academia Historica, Daxi Dang'an, 0060.
242 'Chiang Kaishek to Xu Fu' (17 August), Academia Historica, Daxi Dang'an, 0021.
243 Wilbur *et al.*, *Missionaries*, I, 362–3.
244 'Chiang Kaishek to Zhang Yipeng' (19 January 1927), in Academia Historica, Daxi Dang'an, 0282.
245 'Chiang Kaishek to Tan Yankai' (12 February 1927), Academia Historica, Daxi Dang'an, 0368.
246 'Chiang Kaishek to Song Ziwen' (1 March 1927), Academia Historica, Daxi Dang'an, 0408.
247 'Chiang Kaishek to Song Ziwen' (18 October 1926), Academia Historica, Daxi Dang'an, 0079.
248 Zhong Xiaoguang, 'Jiang Zhe Caifa zhi Chuyi', 86–9.
249 'Chiang Kaishek to Huang Fu' (21 April 1927), in Academia Historica, Daxi Dang'an, 0490.
250 *Minguo Renwu Dacidian*, 1028.
251 'Chiang Kaishek to Chen Qicai' (29 May 1927), Academia Historica, Daxi Dang'an, 0608
252 Zhong Xiaoguang, 'Jiang Zhe Caifa zhi Chuyi', 89–90.
253 'Chiang Kaishek to Zhang Yipeng and Yu Feipeng' (20 January 1927) and 'Chiang Kaishek to Zhang Yipeng' (24 January 1927), Academia Historica, Daxi Dang'an, 0297, 0327.
254 'Chiang Kaishek to Zhu Shaoliang' (23 February 1927), Academia Historica, Daxi Dang'an, 0393.
255 'Chiang Kaishek to Song Ziwen', (30 April 1927), Academia Historica, Daxi Dang'an, 515.
256 Zhong Xiaoguang, 'Jiang Zhe Caifa', 90–1.
257 Ibid., 90–2.
258 Qiu Shulin, ed., *Xinbian Zhongguo Tongshi*, IV, 175–8.
259 'Linshi Lianxi Huiyi Huiyi Jilu' (Minutes of the Provisional Joint Council), KMT Archives 010/3.1 and 3.2.
260 Qiu Shulin, ed., *Xinbian Zhongguo Tongshi*, IV, 175–8.
261 *Nanjing Guomin Zhengfu Jishi*, 2.

4 Nationalism and military reform during the Nanjing Decade (1928–37)

1 Li Wenhai, *Zhongguo Jindai Shi Da Zaihuang*, 168–237, 339–41.
2 Harrison, *The Making of the Republican Citizen*, 176.
3 Ibid., 187.
4 'Report: The Second National Military Re-organization Conference' (15 August 1929), USMI, reel VI, frame 0058.
5 'Report: The Disbandment of Chinese Troops' (13 December 1928), USMI, reel VI, frame 0027.
6 'Chiang Kaishek's Report on the Staged Implementation of Reducing Armies to Divisions and the Organisation of the Re-organisation Committee' (15 March 1929), ZHMGSDAZ, V: 1 (Military), 1, 638–50.
7 Eastman, 'Nationalist China During the Nanking Decade', 125.
8 Jiang Kefu, *Minguo Junshishi Luegao*, II, 7.
9 Li Tsung-jen, *Memoirs*, 554–5.
10 Ibid., 556.
11 Harrison, *The Making of the Republican Citizen*, 185–6.
12 *Nanjing Guomin Zhengfu Jishi*, 66–7. Coble, *Shanghai Capitalists*, 49–51.
13 Nanjing Guomin Zhengfu Jishi, 67.
14 Ibid., 68.
15 Ibid., 68–9; 'Chiang Kaishek's Report on Demobilization Conferences with Feng Yuxiang and others at Beping and Tangshan', ZHMGSDAZL, V: 1 (Military), 603–4.
16 ZHMGZYSL, Xu (supplement) III, 167ff.
17 Zhang Xianwen and Fang Qingpiu *Jiang Jieshi Quanzhuan*, I, 259.
18 'MAC Proposal Regarding Military Reform at the Fifth Plenum of the KMT and the Relevant Resolution' (14 August 1928), ZHMGSDAZL, V: 1 (Military), 1, 606–9.
19 Quoted in Jiang Kefu, *Minguo Junshishi Luegao*, II, 7–8.
20 'Introduction', in *Guomin Zhengfu Junzheng Zuzhi Shiliao*, I, 5–6 and 'Guomin Zhengfu Ling' (7 November 1928), in ibid., I, 36; *Nanjing Guomin Zhengfu Jishi*, 70–1.
21 Jiang Kefu, *Minguo Junshishi Luegao*, II, 7.
22 'The KMT Convenes A Demobilisation and Re-organisation Conference' (1–6 January 1929), ZHMGSDAZL, V: 1 (Military), 1, 619.
23 'Declaration at the Opening of the Conference of the Demobilisation and Rehabilitation Committee' (5 January 1929), ZHMGZYSL, Xu (supplement) III, 177–9.
24 'Report: The Disbandment of Chinese Troops', in USMI, reel V, frames 0027ff.
25 'The KMT Convenes a Demobilisation and Reorganisation Conference', ZHMGSDAZL, V: 1 (Military) 1, 620; T.V. Song's Memorandum is in 'Report: The Disbandment of Chinese Troops', USMI, reel VI, frames 0027ff. See also Song Jingping, *Song Ziwen Pingzhuan*, 83.
26 'The KMT Convenes a Demobilisation and Reorganisation Conference', ZHMGSDAZL, V: 1 (Military), 1, 620–1.
27 Ibid., 625–6.
28 Li Tsung-jen, *Memoirs*, 267.
29 Furuya, *Chiang Kai-shek*, 273–4.
30 Li Tsung-jen, *Memoirs*, 266–7.
31 Eastman, 'Nationalist China during the Nanking Decade', 126.
32 'Chiang Kaishek Requests the National Government to Abolish the Fourth Demobilisation Area Because Bai Chongxi, Claiming Illness, Has Resigned his Post' (26 March 1929), ZHMGSDAZL, V: 1 (Military), 1, 650.
33 Ibid. Basic primary documents on the war can be found in ZHMGSDAZL, V: 1 (Military), 1, 685–840.
34 Basic primary documents for this conflict are in ZHMGSDAZL, V: 1 (Military), II, 1–85. For a short description, see Jiang Kefu, *Minguo Junshishi Luegao*, II, 24–9.
35 'Chiang Kaishek Reports to the National Government' (18 July 1929), ZHMGSDAZL, V: 1 (Military), 1, 661. See also subsequent documents.

36 'Table Submitted to the National Government by the National Army Demobilisation Committee For Stipends to Retired Officers and Demobilisation Fees for Officers and Soldiers' (12 August 1929), in ibid., 661–2.
37 'Resolution of the Demobilisation Committee on the Number of Divisions to be Demobilised at each Stage in the Various Demobilisation Regions' (12 August 1929), in ibid., 663–4.
38 Jiang Kefu, *Minguo Junshishi Luegao*, II, 33.
39 Ibid., 33.
40 Ibid., 33–4.
41 Ibid., 34. Li Tsung-jen, *Memoirs*, 278–9.
42 Jiang Kefu, *Minguo Junshishi Luegao*, II, 42.
43 Li, *Memoirs*, 279–80.
44 Jiang Kefu, *Minguo Junshishi Luegao*, II, 38.
45 Ibid., 40–1.
46 Ibid., 41–2.
47 Zhang Xianwen and Fang Qingqiu *Jiang Jieshi Quanzhuan*, I, 289.
48 Hans van de Ven, 'New States of War', 346–50.
49 For regulations approved on 12 December 1930, see *Guomindang Zhengfu Zhengzhi Zhidu*, I, 389–92. They legislated for Pacification Commissioner Bureaus (Suijing Duban Gongshu) for the Border Areas of Yu E Wan (Henan, Hubei, and Anhui), Yu Shan Jin (Henan, Shaanxi, and Shanxi), and for Jiangsu. See also Shen Huaiyu, 'Xingzheng Ducha Zhuanyuan Zhidu zhi Chuanshe, Yanbian, yu Gongneng', 428.
50 'Communication from the General Command of the Army, Navy, and Airforce to the National Government in the Matter of Determining the Personnel Establishment of the Beiping Headquarters of the Vice-Commander' (29 June 1931), in *Guomindang Zhengfu Zhengzhi Zhidu*, I, 392–5. See also 'Rewards and Punishments in Bandit Suppression' (May 1932), in ibid., 397–8; and 'Public Letter 6151 of the Secretariat of the Central Executive Committee of the KMT' (18 June 1932), ibid., I, 398–9.
51 'Basic Law for the Organisation of the Nanchang Field Headquarters' (20 June 1933) in ibid., I, 466.
52 Weng Jingqiu, 'Yang Yongtai Changqing Xiansheng Zhuanji Chugao' (Preliminary Biography of Yang Yongtai,' in *Yang Yongtai Xiansheng Yanlun Ji*, 1–7.
53 Yang Yongtai, 'Geming Xian Ge Xin, Bianzheng Xian Bian Su' (To Make Revolution One Must First Change Mindsets, To Change the Government one Must First Change Customs), in ibid., 1–19. Dated June 1934.
54 Yang Yongtai, 'Xian Xing Xianzhi yu Xianzheng de Chongchong Sese' (The Contemporary County Sytem and Various Aspects of County Government), in ibid., 75.
55 'Communication from the Chairman of the Military Affairs Committee of the National Government to the Executive Yuan Regarding the Date of Establishment and Initiation of the Seal' in *Guomindang Zhengfu Zhengzhi Zhidu*, 457. Dated 24 May 1933.
56 Ibid., 457.
57 'Letter to the National Government from the Political Counsel of the Central Executive Committee Regarding the Establishment of the MAC', in *Guomin Zhengfu Junzheng Zuzhi Shiliao*, II, 24.
58 'MAC Organisational Regulations', ibid., I, 38–9.
59 'Provisional Basic Law for the MAC of the National Government' (9 March 1932), in ibid., I, 42.
60 *Junshi Weiyuanhui Weiyuanzhang Xingying Zhengzhi Gongzuo Bao* (Political Work Report by the Field Headquarters of the MAC Chairman), KMT Archives, 440/21, 4–13. Officially written by Chiang Kaishek, it is likely that Yang Yongtai drafted it.
61 Shen Huaiyu, 'Xingzheng Ducha Zhuanyuan', 430–6.
62 Yang Yongtai, 'Xianxing Xianzhi yu Xianzheng de Chongchong Sese' (The Contemporary County System and Various Aspects of County Administration), in *Yang Yongtai Xiansheng Yanlun Ji*, 74.
63 *Junshi Weiyuanhui Weiyuanzhang Xingying Zhengzhi Gongzuo Bao*, 6–12 and Shen Huaiyu, 'Xingzheng Ducha Zhuanyuan', 438–41.
64 *Junshi Weiyuanhui Weiyuanzhang Xingying Zhengzhi Gongzuo Bao*, 3–4.

65 'Generalissimo Chiang's Instruction to the Governments of the Seven Yangtze Provinces and Municipalities to Regard Land Redistribution and the Baojia as Policies of the First Priority' (6 October 1932), ZHMGZYSL, Xu (supplement), III, 406.

66 *Junshi Weiyuanhui Weiyuanzhang Xingying Zhengzhi Gongzuo Bao*, 17–18.

67 Ibid., 13; Yang Yongtai, 'Xianxing Xianzhi', in *Yang Yongtai Xiansheng Yanlunji*, 74–6.

68 'Telegram of Commander in Chief Chiang to Jiang Bocheng, Acting Chairman of Zhejiang, to Perform Household Checks, Raise Militia, and Draw Up Baojia Regulations' (23 May 1928) and 'Telegram from Commander-in-Chief Chiang to Sun Qi, Acting Chairman of Anhui, to Perform Household Checks, Raise Militia, and Draw Up Baojia Regulations (23 May 1928), ZHMGZYSL, Xu (supplement), III, 399, 400–1.

69 'Personal Order of Generalissimo Chiang Instructing County Heads in Hubei Province to Vigorously Implement the Policies of Our Party's Manifesto' (14 July 1932), ZHMGZYSL, Xu (supplement), III, 402–3.

70 See for instance Jun Tian, *Zhongguo Baojia* and Huang Qiang, *Baojia Lianggui*.

71 'Personal Order of Generalissimo Chiang Instructing County Heads in Hubei Province to Vigorously Implement the Policies of Our Party's Manifesto' (14 July 1932), ZHMGZYSL, Xu (supplement), III, 404–6.

72 He Yingqin, 'Gaixing Zhengbing Zhidu zhi Ti'an' (Proposal to Change to National Military Service) (September 1928), in *Yizheng Shiliao*, I, 1–47.

73 Ibid., 4–14.

74 Ibid., 1–25.

75 'Instruction of Generalissimo Chiang to Vice Chairman Lin Wei Stating That the Training and Organisation of Militia Must Be Completed in Stages in Two Years' (15 January 1933), ZHMGZYSL, Xu, III, 407.

76 'Telegram of Generalissimo Chiang to Liu Shi, Chairman of Henan, Instructing Him to Urgently Organise Local Defence Forces' (16 March 1933), ZHMGZHSL, Xu (supplement), III, 407–8.

77 Ibid., 407.

78 'Regulations for the Investigation of Baojia Households in Bandit Suppression Regions' (August 1932), *Guomindang Zhengfu Zhengzhi Zhidu*, I, 407–14; *Junshi Weiyuanhui Weiyuanzhang Xingying Zhengzhi Gongzuo Bao*, 18.

79 *Yu E Wan Jiaofei Zong Silingbu Gongzuo Baogao Shu*, 1–2. See also Yang Yongtai, 'Xianxing Xianzheng' in *Yang Yongtai Xiansheng Yanlun Ji*, 75–7.

80 Duara, *Culture, Power, and the State*, 217–43.

81 'Scheme for Closing Off Bandit Areas', *Guomindang Zhengfu Zhengzhi Zhidu*, 458–9.

82 'Anhuisheng Zhengli Gexian Baojia Gaikuang Biao' (Tables Showing Baojia Re-organisation in the Counties of Anhui Province), Second Historical Archives, 795/173. Undated. The first check was carried out in May 1933 (*Junshi Weiyuanhui Weiyuanzhang Xingying Zhengzhi Gongzuo Bao*, 18) and the table may have been produced at that time.

83 'Henansheng Baojia Banli Qingkuang Baogao ji Jinxing Yilanbiao An' (Overview Table of Baojia Implementation in Henan), Second Historical Archives, 795/125. Dated June 1933. See also 'Henansheng Dier Xingzheng Ducha Zhuanyuan Bangongshu Chen Yu E Wan Sansheng Jiaofei Zong Silingbu' (Report by the Special Intendent of the Number Two Region of Henan to the Yu E Wan Bandit Suppression Command), Second Historical Archives, 795/152.

84 'Hubeisheng Chengbao Yi An Qi Wancheng Baojia Bianzhi An' (Reports on Baojia Completion in Hubei), Second Historical Archives, 795/68. The file contains an overall report, dated October 1932.

85 Ibid.

86 'Hubeisheng Ge Xian Biancha Baojia Hukou Qingkuang An' (The Re-organisation of Baojia Households in Hubei Counties), Second Historical Archives 796/60. Dated 1933.

87 Huang Qiang, *Baojia Lianggui*, 219–55.

88 'Provisional Service Regulations for Divisional and Regimental Recruitment Areas', in *Zhengyi Shiliao*, I, 61–8. See also 'Minister He Yingqin's Report on Military Affairs to the Third Plenum of the Fifth Central Executive Committee' (February 1937), ZHMGZYSL, Xu (supplement), III, 350–87.

89 'Implementation Regulations for the Duties of Citizen Soldiers' (27 October 1936), in *Yizheng Shiliao*, I, 79–85.

90 For a sample syllabus of 1938, see 'Comprehensive Study and Training Syllabus for Military Service Staff in All Provinces) (3 May 1938), in *Yizheng Shiliao*, I, 168–80.

91 'The Training of Zhuangding' (15 May 1937), in *Yizheng Shiliao*, II, 186.

92 'Political Work Report of the Generalissimo's Field Headquarters' (November 1935), ZHMGZYSL, Xu, III, 502–3.

93 Ibid.

94 Ibid., and 'Regulations for the Reform of Militia in Provinces in Bandit Suppression Regions' (April 1933), in *Guomindang Zhengfu Zhengzhi Zhidu*, I, 450–7; *Yu E Wan Jiaofei Zong Silingbu Gongzuo Baogao Shu*, 17–26.

95 *Nanchang Xingying Zhaoji Dierci Baoan Huiyi Jilu*.

96 Yang Yongtai, 'Gongzuo Zongping' (Overall Evaluation of Our Work), *Nanchang Xingying Zhaoji Dierci Baoan Huiyi Jilu*, 6–8.

97 Ibid., 5–7.

98 Ibid., 23.

99 *Junshi Weiyuanhui Weiyuanzhang Xingying Zhengzhi Gongzuo Bao*, 22–4.

100 *Nanchang Xingying Zhaoji Dierci Bao'an Huiyi Jilu*, Supplement.

101 Yang Yongtai, 'Gongzuo Zongping' (Evaluation of our Work), *Nanchang Xingying Zhaoji Dierci Baoan Huiyi Jilu*,15–16.

102 *Junshi Weiyuanhui Weiyuanzhang Xingying Zhengzhi Gongzuo Bao*, 39–41.

103 Ibid., 28.

104 Ibid., 36.

105 'Political Work Report of the Generalissimo's Fieldheadquarter' (November 1935), ZHMGZYSL, Xu, III, 509–515.

106 *Junshi Weiyuanhui Weiyuanzhang Xingying Zhengzhi Gongzuo Bao*, 29–33, 37.

107 Ibid., 28.

108 Ibid., 29.

109 Ibid., 34–5.

110 'Selected Historical Documents for the Peasant Bank of Henan, Hunan, Anhui, and Jiangxi', *Minguo Dang'an*, III (1986), 40–52.

111 'Political Work Report of the Generalissimo's Fieldheadquarter' (November 1935), ZHMGZYSL, Xu (supplement), III, 551–6.

112 Duara, *Culture, Power, and the State*, 253.

113 Ibid., 85.

114 Ibid., 249.

115 See also Zhang, *Social Transformation*, 229; Ch'i, *Warlord Politics*, 229; Kuhn, *Origins of the Modern Chinese State*, 101; Siu, *Agents and Victims*, 88–115.

116 Chen, *Junfei Yanjiu*, 228–76.

117 See also Zhang, *Social Transformation*, 235.

118 Coble, *Facing Japan*, van de Ven, 'Diplomacy of Chinese Nationalism'.

119 Ma Zhendu, *Cansheng*, 8.

120 Ibid., 24.

121 'Guofang Sheji Weiyuanhui Gongzuo Gaikuang' (Overview of the Work of the NDPC) (1934?), in *Minguo Dang'an*, XX (1990), 28–37; Ma Zhendu, *Cansheng*, 22.

122 Ma Zhendu, *Cansheng*, 22–23.

123 Ibid., 23.

124 'Chairman Chiang's Telegram to Chairmen Gu Zhutong and Lu Diping with Instructions for Discussions about Sea, River, and Air Defences in Jiangsu and Zhejiang' (3 April 1932), ZHMGZYSL, Xu, III, 290.

125 'Chairman Chiang's Telegram to Vice-Minister He Yaozu with Instructions to Assess Expenditures for the Reform and Expansion of Arsenals and the Aircraft Factory' (2 August 1932), ZHMGZYSL, Xu (supplement), III, 291–2.

126 'Telegram from Generalissimo Chiang Kaishek to Vice-Minister He Yaozu with the Instruction to Draw Up a Comprehensive Plan for Coastal and Yangtze Fortifications and

Gradually Implement a Plan for their Repair' (31 October 1933), in ZHMGZYSL, Xu, III, 298.

127 Ma Zhendu *et al.*, *Di Hu? You Hu?*, 100–4.

128 Ibid., 108–12.

129 'Proposals of Wetzell, the Chief German Advisor' (14 February 1933), in *Zhong De Waijiao Midang*, 136–45; Ma Zhendu *et al.*, *Di Hu? You Hu?*, 120–39.

130 Ma Zhendu *et al.*, *Di Hu? You Hu?*, 139–73.

131 Ibid., 144.

132 Ibid., *Di Hu? You Hu?*, 146–9.

133 Ibid.; Kirby, *Germany and Republican China*, 234–51.

134 Ma Zhendu *et al.*, *Di Hu? You Hu?*, 150–4.

135 'Overview of NDPC Work' in *Minguo Dang'an* XX (1990), 28–37; Wu Zhaohong, 'Wo Suo Zhidaode Ziyuan Weiyuanhui', 68–74.

136 'Ziyuan Weiyuanhui Ershisan Niandu Gongzuo Baogao' (1934 NRC Work Report) in Second Historical Archives, 28(2)/1819. The covering letter is dated 16 July 1935. See also 'Overview of NDPC Work' in *Minguo Dang'an* XX (1990), 28–37.

137 See 'Ge Sheng Shi Difang Yijiusansan Niandu Caizheng Diaocha Baogao' (Report on an Investigation of Procincial, Municipal, and Local Finances for 1934) (June 1935), Second Historical Archives, 28(2)/354.

138 Wu Fuyuan, in 'Ziyuan Weiyuanhui de Renshi Guanli Zhidu', 198–9.

139 'Guofang Sheji Weiyuanhui Guling Huiyi Junshi Caizheng Jingji Jiaotong deng Cailiao' (Materials on the Military, Finance, the Economy, and Communications for the Guling Conference of the NDPC), Second Historical Archives, 28(2)/1896; Kirby, *Germany and Republican China*, 122.

140 Wu Zhaohong, 'Wo Suo Zhidaode Ziyuan Weihuanhui', 72–3.

141 'Canmou Benbu Guofang Weiyuanhui Huiyi Jilu' (Minutes of the NDPC Meeting of the General Staff) (August 1934), Second Historical Archives, 28(2)/1892.

142 NDPC Work Report quoted in Ma Zhendu, *Cansheng*, 22.

143 'Chouhua Guofang Ding Zhongxin Quyu' (Planning for Determining a Central National Defence Region' (no date), Second Historical Archives 28(2)/1913.

144 'Guofang Gongye Chubu Jihua' (Preliminary Plan for a National Defence Industry) (1936?), Second Historical Archives, 28(2)/928; Kirby, *Germany and Republican China*, 206–7 and 'China's War Economy', 188–9.

145 Kirby, *Germany and Republican China*, 106–8.

146 'Chief Advisor von Falkenhausen's Proposals for Policies to Meet the Current Situation' (20 August 1935), *Zhong De Waijiao Milu*, 171–9.

147 'The 1937 National Defence War Plan of the KMT Government', *Minguo Dang'an*, X (1987), 40–52; and KMT 1937 National Defence War Plan (Version Two), *Minguo Dang'an* XI (1988), 34–41.

148 'Friend or Enemy' (October 1943), ZHMGZYSL, Xu (supplement), III, 617–8.

149 *Jiang Baili Xiansheng Quanji*, IV, 152–3.

150 'Chen Cheng to Chiang Kaishek' (19 December [1934?]) in 'Zhengjun Fang'an' (Proposals for Army Reform) (February to September 1935), Academia Historica, 055/0720.

151 'Generalissimo Chiang Personally Approves a National Army Reform Plan for Sixty Divisions', in ZHMGZYSL, Xu (supplement), III, 324–6. See also 'Zhengjun Fang'an', Academia Historica, 055/0720; 'Chen Cheng Cheng Guofang Jianshe Jihua Gangling' (Chen Cheng's Outline Plan for the Creation of a National Defence Army) (no date), Academia Historica, 055/0991.

152 'Minister He Yingqin's Report to the Third Plenum of the Fifth Central Executive Committee', ZHMGZYSL, Xu (supplement), III, 376.

153 'Generalissimo Chiang's Personally Approved National Army Reform Plan for Sixty Divisions', ZHMGZYSL, Xu (supplement), III, 324–6. 'Chen Cheng 's Memoirs', *Minguo Dang'an* VII (1987), 9–12.

154 'Generalissimo Chiang's Personally Approved National Army Reform Plan for Sixty Divisions', ZHMGZYSL, Xu (supplement), III, 326.

155 Ibid., 326. For the number, see Ma Zhendu, *Cansheng*, 38.

156 Kirby, *Germany and Republican China*, 91–9.

157 'Minister He Yingqin's Report to the Third Plenum of the Fifth Central Executive Committee', ZHMGZYSL, Xu (supplement), III, 365–6.

158 Ibid., 383–4.

159 Ibid., 366–72.

160 Ibid., 355.

161 Ibid., 351–64.

162 'Chen Cheng Huiyilu' (Chen Cheng's Personal Recollections), *Minguo Dang'an*, VII (1987), 12–14.

163 Zhang Xianwen, *Kang Ri Zhanzheng de Zhengmian Zhanchang*, 12–13.

164 'Commissioned Strength, Classification as to training' (28 January 1936), USMI, reel V, frame 521.

165 Hsu Long-hsuen and Chang Ming-kai, *Sino-Japanese War*, 169; F.F. Liu, *Military History*, 82–91; Chang Yü-fa, *Zhongguo Xiandaishi*, 463–4.

166 He Yingqing, *Ri jun Qin Hua Banian Kangzhan Shi*, 580–1; Chang Yü-fa, *Zhongguo Xiandaishi*, 641.

167 Chang Yü-fa, *Zhongguo Xiandaishi*, 462–3.

168 von Falkenhausen, 'Year End Report [for 1936]', in 'Fakenhausen Jianyi Kuochong Junbei' (von Falkenhausen's Proposals for Military Enhancement), Academia Historica, 055/0994.

169 *Nanjing Guomin Zhengfu Jishi*, 321; Chen Ronghua *et al.*, *Lushan Junguan Xuanlian Tuan*, 47–60.

170 *Nanjing Guomin Zhengfu Jishi*, 342–3.

171 'Xin Shenghuo Yundong Gangyao', ZHMGZYSL, Xu (supplement), III, 58.

172 ZHMGZYSL, Xu (supplement), 64–5; Zheng Yuanzhong, 'Xin Shenghuo Yundong zhi Zhengzhi Yiyi', 36.

173 Eastman, *Abortive Revolution*, 66.

174 Ibid., 69–71.

175 'Xin Shenghuo Yundong Cujinhui Zhanshi Gongzuo Jianbao' (Brief Report on Wartime Activies of the Society for the Promotion of the New Life Movement) (1942), KMT Archives, 483/33; *Xinyuan Shinian* (Ten Years of the New Life Movement), 1–2; and 'Yunnansheng Xinshenghuo Yundong Cujinhui Gongzuo Gaikuang' (Overview of the Activitities of the Yunan Promotion Committee of the New Life Movement), KMT Archives, 483/22.

176 Eastman, *Aborted Revolution*, 67. See also Dirlik, 'The Ideological Foundations of the New Life Movement,' *Journal of Asian Studies*, 34:4 (1975). Dirlik argued that the movement aimed at 'mobilising the population to improve public and private hygienic and behavourial standards' for 'national renaissance' (945–6). He argued that it was an ideology of 'counter-revolution' (947) opposed to social revolution of the Communists (974). If this was one goal, to create an ideology around which to unite the country militarily was another.

177 Maria Hsia Chang, *The Chinese Blue Shirt Society*, 9–11, 13–29.

178 Wakeman, 'Confucian Fascism', 431–2.

179 Ibid., 432.

180 Ibid., 398.

181 Ibid., 397–403.

182 Wakeman, ibid., 410.

183 'The Basic Programme of the New Life Movement', ZHMGSYSL, Xu, III, 65.

184 Ibid., 57.

185 'Shiying's Address at the Central Party Headquarters', Sun Yatsen Remembrance Ceremony Regarding the Importance of Improving Customs' (5 October 1935), ZHMGSDAZL, V: 1 (Culture), vol.1, 449.

186 'Standards for Preserving or Abolishing Deities and Temples' (30 April 1930), in ibid., 495–506.

187 'Documents relating to the Promulgation of a New and the Proscription of Old Calenders' (May–June 1930), ZHMGSDAZL, V: 1 (Culture), vol.1, 425–427.

188 'Implementation of the National Calendar' (26 June 1930), ZHMGSDAZL, V: 1 (Culture), vol.1, 435.
189 'Detailed Regulations of Nanjing Municipality Regarding Wedding and Burial Rituals' (1930), ZHMGSDAZL, V: 1 (Culture), vol.1, 438–9.
190 'Shanghai Municipal Regulations for Collective Wedding Ceremonies' (1935), ZHMGS-DAZL, V: 1 (Culture), vol.1, 456–60.
191 Orders to Chen Bulei of 29 and 30 August, 'Jiang Weiyuanzhang Shouling Ludi' (Copies of Generalissimo Chiang's Personal Orders), Academia Historica, 0555/2025. Orders of 29 and 30 August and 1 September, 1935.
192 Eastman, 'Nationalist China during the Nanking Decade', 155.
193 Ibid., 162.

5 A forward policy in the north

1 Besides the war plans discussed earlier, see also 'Chen Cheng Cheng Guofang Jianshe Jihua Gangling' (Basic Plan for Establishing National Defence Submitted by Chen Cheng) (no date), Academia Historica, 055/0991.
2 Garver, *Chinese–Soviet Relations*.
3 Getty and Naumov, *The Road to Terror*, 247–491.
4 Yan Jun, 'Jiang Tingfu Shengping Shilue' (Biographical note on Jiang Tingfu), *Minguo Dang'an*, 14) (1989), 134–6.
5 'Chiang Kaishek's Secret Telegram to Kong Xiangxi Regarding the Assignment of Jiang Tingfu to Hold Discussions with the Soviets' (1 October 1934), ZHMGSDAZL V: 1 (Foreign Relations), 2, 1425.
6 Garver, *Chinese–Soviet Relations*, 18; Chen Lifu, *Storm Clouds*, 121–4.
7 Chen Lifu, *Storm Clouds*, 121.
8 *Zhongguo Kang Ri Zhanzheng Shi*, I, 354.
9 'August 1 Declaration', *Zhonggong Zhongyang Wenjian Xuanji*, X, 486–8; Chi Yue, 'The Proposal by the CCP for a War of Resistance by all the People', ibid., 29; *Guo Gong Liangdang Guanxi Shi*, 334–5.
10 See, for example, 'Resolutions on the Current Situation and the Party's Task' (18 January 1934), in *Zhonggong Zhongyang Wenjian Xuanji*, X, 34.
11 Li Liangzhi, 'Zhongguo Gongchandang Quanmin Kangzhan de Tichu', 22.
12 Garver, *Chinese–Soviet Relations*, 64–76.
13 'Jiang Tingfu's Report on Sino-Soviet Relations', ZHMGSDAZL, V:1 (Foreign Relations), vol. 2, 1427–39.
14 Gilbert, *A History of the Twentieth Century*, II, 109.
15 'Jiang Tingfu's Report on Sino-Soviet Relations', ZHMGSDAZL, V:1 (Foreign Relations), vol. 2, 1434.
16 Ibid., 1434–6.
17 Garver, *Chinese–Soviet Relations*, 17.
18 Garver, *Chinese–Soviet Relations*, 15–26.
19 'Ambassador in the Soviet Union (Davies) to the Secretary of State' (26 March 1937), FRUS, 1937, III, Far East, 59.
20 'The Consul General at Shanghai (Gauss) to the Ambassador in China (Johnson)' (21 April 1937), FRUS, 1937, III, Far East, 70 and 'The Ambassodor in China (Johnson) to the Secretary of State' (30 April 1937), in ibid., 79–80.
21 Garver, *Chinese–Soviet Relations*, 15, 19.
22 Garver, *Chinese–Soviet Relations* 19.
23 Eastman, 'Nationalist China during the Sino-Japanese War', 551.
24 Dorn, *Sino-Japanese War*, 67, 78.
25 Ch'i, *Nationalist China at War*, 43.
26 'Chief Advisor von Falkenhausen's Proposals to Meet the Current Situation', *Zhong De Wai Jiao Midang*, 174.

27 Ch'i, *Nationalist China at War*, 47.

28 '1937 National Defence War Plan (Version 1)', *Minguo Dang'an*, X (1987), 40.

29 'Draft Revised War Plan Proposed by the MAC' (14 December 1938), KRZZZ, I, 24.

30 'Ambassador in China (Johnson) to the Secretary of State' (9 March 1937), FRUS, III, 1937, Far East, 36–7; 'Counsellor of Embassy in China (Lockhart) to the Secretary of State' (13 April 1937), ibid., 63–4; 'Ambassador in China (Johnson) to the Secretary of State' (28 April 1937), ibid., 78; 'Consul General at Shanghai (Gauss) to the Secretary of State' (25 June 1937), ibid., 121; 'Professor John Lossing Buck to the Chief of the Division of Far Eastern Affairs', FRUS, III, 1937, Far East, 157. Undated, but relaying a telegram from Shanghai of 13 July.

31 'The Counsellor of Embassy in China (Peck) to the Secretary of State' (1 July 1937), FRUS, 1937, III, Far East, 125.

32 'The Chargé in the Soviet Union (Henderson) to the Secretary of State' (21 December 1937), FRUS, III, Far East, 827.

33 Passed on via John Lussing Buck to Henry Morgenthau, Secretary of the Treasury. See 'Ambassador in China (Johnson) to the Secretary of State' (23 August 1937), FRUS, 1937, III, Far East, 460.

34 'Memorandum by the Chief of the Division of Far Eastern Affairs (Hornbeck) (16 July 1937), FRUS, 1937, III, the Far East, 189–90; Borg, *The US and the Far Eastern Crisis*, 286–7; 'The British Embassy to the Department of State' (13 July), in FRUS, 1937, III, Far East, 158–9; 'The Ambassador in Tokyo (Grew) to the Secretary of State' (13 July 1937), ibid., 157; Memorandum by the Advisor on Political Relations' (24 August), ibid., 464–5.

35 See 'The Ambassador in Japan (Grew) to the Secretry of State' (27 August 1937) (15 September 1937), FRUS, 1937, III, Far East, 485–8; 525–30.

36 Borg, *The US and the Far Eastern Crisis*, v–vi.

37 'Quanguo Lujun Shuliang Biao' (Table of Strengths of All Armies) (March 1935), Academia Historica, 055/0720.

38 'Composition and Distribution of Troops' (21 May 1937), USMI, Reel V, frames 0483-95.

39 For the circumstances, see Yang Tianshi, *Haiwai Fangshi Lu*, 337–8, and 403.

40 Wang Chaozhu, *Zhang Xueliang he Jiang Jieshi*, 300–26.

41 'Chen Cheng Cheng Guofang Jianshe Jihua An' (Chen Cheng's Scheme for National Defence' (no date), Academia Historica, 055/0991.

42 *Guo Gong Liang Dang Guanxi Shi*, 365–6.

43 Yang Kuisong, 'Jiujing Shi Shei Shuofule Shei' (Now Who Did Convince Who?), *Kang Ri Zhanzheng Yanjiu*, XIX (1996), 41.

44 Ibid., 41–2.

45 Ibid., and *Guo Gong Liangdang Guanxi Shi*, 369.

46 *Guo Gong Liangdang Guanxi Shi*, 369–71.

47 Ibid., 372.

48 Ibid., 360–3.

49 Yang Kuisong, *Shiqu de Jihui*, 4–5.

50 Ibid., 5–6.

51 Ibid., 6.

52 Ibid., 8.

53 Ibid., 7–8.

54 Yang Kuisong, *Shiqu de Jihui*, 8–10.

55 Ibid., 10.

56 Ibid., 13.

57 Ibid., 15.

58 Ibid., 23.

59 Ibid., 23.

60 Conform Wakeman, 'Hanjian', 298–304, 323–5.

61 *Zhongguo Kang Ri Zhanzheng Shi*, I, 389.

62 Ibid., 389.

63 Ibid., 390.

64 Chiang Yung-ching, 'Xi'an Shibian Qian Zhang Xueliang Suowei "Yi Er Yue Nei Ding You Biandong" Zhi He?' (What did Zhang Xueliang Mean When He Said Before the Xi'an Incident 'There Will Be a Change In One or Two Months), *Jindaishi Yanjiu* I (1997), 269; *Zhongguo Kang Ri Zhanzheng Shi*, I, 390; Hsu Long-hsuen and Chang Ming-kai, *Sino-Japanese War*, 162–3.

65 *Guo Gong Liangdang Guanxi Shi*, 375; 'Situation Report, 24 Octobter–6 November, 1936', USMI, reel X, frames 0470-2.

66 Chiang Yung-ching, 'Xi'an Shibian Qian', 269–71.

67 Yang Kuisong, *Shiqu de Jihui*, 20.

68 Ibid., 19–22; 'Central Committee Directive Regarding the Issue of Forcing Chiang to Resist Japan' (1 September 1936), *Zhonggong Zhongyang Wenjian Xuanji*, XI, 89–91; *Guo Gong Liangdong Guanxi shi*, 337, notes that the slogan 'compel Chiang to resist Japan' was used by Mao in *National Salvation* in January 1936.

69 Chiang Yung-ching, 'Xi'an Shibian Qian', 268.

70 Yang Kuisong, *Shiqu de Jihui*, 24–6; *Guo Gong Liangdang Guanxi Shi*, 351–2.

71 *Guo Gong Liangdang Guanxi Shi*, 352.

72 'Situation Report, 10 December 1936', USMI, reel X, frames 483-4.

73 *Nanjing Guomin Zhengfu Jishi*, 521–2.

74 'Situation Report, 10 December 1936', USMI, reel X, frame 484.

75 Ibid., 484.

76 'Hongjun Sanda Zhuli Shanchengbao Zhanyi Qianmie Guomindang Jun Shiliao Xuanji' (Selected Historical Sources for the Destruction of the KMT Army by the Three Main Red Army Forces at Shanchengbao', *Minguo Dang'an*, XLV (1996), 3–12. *Guo Gong Liangdang Guanxi Shi*, 352.

77 Ibid., 372–4.

78 Chiang Yung-ching, 'Xi'an Shibian Qian', 1997:1, 266.

79 *Guo Gong Liangdang Guanxi Shi*, 372.

80 Chiang Yung-ching, 'Xi'an Shibian Qian', 268.

81 Ibid., 271.

82 *Zhongguo Kang Ri Zhanzheng Shi*, I, 398.

83 Ibid., I, 399.

84 Ibid., I, 399.

85 Ibid., I, 399.

86 Ibid., I, 375.

87 Ibid., I, 397–8.

88 Li Haiwen, 'Xi'an Shibian Qian Guo Gong Liang Dang Jiechu he Tanpan', 359; Yang Kuisong, *Shiqu de Jihui*, 26.

89 *Guo Gong Liangdang Guanxi Shi*, 353.

90 Yang Tianshi, *Haiwai Fang Shi Lu*, 403–4.

91 Ibid., 471.

92 Ibid., 471. On debates within the CCP about how to deal with Chiang and what precise attitude to adopt, see also Chen Tiejian, 'Xi'an Shibian Jianlun' (Some Remarks on the Xi'an Incident), 156.

93 Ibid., 471.

94 Ibid., 472.

95 'Copy of Jiang Tingfu's Report to the Ministry of Foreign Affairs Regarding Sino-Soviet Relations', ZHMGSDAZL, V: 1 (Foreign Relations), vol. 2, 1433–4.

96 'Jiang Tingfu yu Sulian Waijiao Weiyuanhui Fu Weiyuanzhang Tanhua Jilu' (Record of Conversation Between Jiang Tingfu and the Vice-Chairman of the Soviet Foreign Relations Commission) (3 December 1936), *Minguo Dang'an*, XVIII (1989), 23.

97 Ibid., 23.

98 Ibid., 23–4.

99 Yang Tianshi, *Haiwai Fang Shi Lu*, 473.

100 'Jiang Tingfu's Report to the Ministry of Foreign Affairs Regarding Sino-Soviet Relations', ZHMGSDAZL, V: 1 (Foreign Relations), vol. 2, 1437–8.

101 Furuya, *Chiang Kai-shek*, 516.

102 Wang Chaozhu, *Zhang Xueliang he Jiang Jieshi*, 439.
103 Eastman, 'Nationalist China during the Nanking Decade', 162–3; Coble, *Facing Japan*, 356–7 for splits within Zhang Xueliang's army.
104 Coble, *Facing Japan*, 360.
105 Huang, 'Chiang Kaishek', I, 84–5.
106 Bix, *Hirohito*, 317–18.
107 Eastman, 'Nationalist China during the Sino-Japanese War', 518.
108 Bix, *Hirohito*, 321.
109 Ibid., 319–20.
110 Berger, 'Politics and Mobilisation', 112.
111 Nakamura, 'Depression, Recovery, and War, 1920–1945', 470.
112 Berger, 'Politics and Mobilisation', 123.
113 Quoted in Montgomery, *Imperialist Japan*, 385.
114 Iriye, 'Japanese Aggression', 514; Ikuhiko Ato, 'Continental Expansion', 300–1; Berger, 'Politics' 112–32; Spector, *Eagle against the Sun*, 47. Ienage, *Japan's Last War*, 69–70; *Zhongguo Kang Ri Zhanzheng Shi*, I, 311–52.
115 'Composition and Distribution of Chinese Troops' (21 May 1937), USMI Reel V, frame 488.
116 Ma Zhendu, *Cansheng*, 68.
117 Zhang Xianwen, *Kang Ri Zhanzheng de Zhengmian Zhanchang*, 18.
118 'Secret Telegram from Song Zheyuan to Chiang Kaishek' (9 July 1937), KRZZZ, I, 163.
119 Zhang Xianwen, *Kang Ri Zhanzheng de Zhengmian Zhanchang*, 18.
120 These can be found in KRZZZ, 163–75.
121 'Report by Yang Xuancheng to He Yingqin' (22 July), KRZZZ, I, 175.
122 Zhang Xianwen, *Kang Ri Zhanzheng de Zhengmian Zhanchang*, 19.
123 'General Order by Generalissimo Chiang', ZHMGZYSL, II: 2, 37.
124 Ma, *Cansheng*, 64.
125 *Nanjing Guomin Zhengfu Jishi*, 562–3.
126 'Report of the Fourteenth Joint Meeting Regarding the Marco Polo Bridge Incident', KRZZZ, I, 230.
127 'Report of the Fourth Joint Meeting Regarding the Marco Polo Bridge Incident' (14 July 1937), ibid., I, 215.
128 Idem.
129 Ma Zhendu, *Cansheng*, 92–3.
130 'Report of the Fifteenth Joint Meeting Regarding the Marco Polo Bridge Incident' (25 July 1937), KRZZZ, I, 234.
131 Ma Zhendu, *Cansheng*, 96.
132 Ibid., 155–6.
133 Dorn, *Sino-Japanese War*, 84–5.
134 *Zhongguo Kang Ri Zhanzheng Shi*, II, 5–6; Jiang Kefu, *Minguo Junshishi Luegao*, III: 1, 58–9.
135 *Zhonguo Kang Ri Zhanzheng Shi*, II, 9.
136 Jiang Kefu, *Minguo Junshishi Luegao*, III: 1, 62.
137 *Zhongguo Kang Ri Zhanzheng Shi*, II, 6–16; Jiang Kefu, *Minguo Junshishi Luegao*, III: 1, 5–21.
138 Hsu Long-hsuen and Chang Ming-kai, *Sino-Japanese War*, 181–2; Jiang Kefu, *Minguo Junshishi Luegao*, III: 1, 27–39.
139 *Zhongguo Kang Ri Zhanzheng Shi*, II, 12–16.
140 Ibid., II, 22.
141 Ibid., II, 22–3.
142 Ibid., II, 27; Zhang Xianwen, *Kang Ri Zhanzheng de Zhengmian Zhanchang*, 43–8; Jiang Kefu, *Minguo Junshishi Luegao*, III: 1, 88–94.
143 Telegram, recorded in 'Feng Yuxiang Han Chen Kanluan Jiaofei Yijian' (Feng Yuxiang's Suggestions Regarding Pacification and Bandit Suppression), p. 157, Academia Historica, 055/194.
144 'Fakenhausen Cheng Fushang Zuijin You Jin Hui Jing Guwen Jianduan Baogao' (Short Report by an Advisor Recently Returned from Shanxi to the Capital Forwarded by von Falkenhausen), Academia Historica, 055/0994.

145 Ma Zhendu, *Cansheng*, 144–54.
146 Ibid., 166.
147 Ibid., 164–9.
148 Letter of 2 November 1937, in 'Feng Yuxiang Han Cheng Kanluan Jiaofei Yijian', Academia Historica, 055/1964.
149 Jiang Kefu, *Minguo Junshishi Luegao*, III, 126–9.
150 de Fremery, 'Report No. 6', Teitler and Radtke, eds., *Dutch Spy in China*, 97–100.
151 On the Nankou–Zhangjiakou battles, see *Zhongguo Kangzhan Zhanzheng Shi*, II, 25–9. Ma Zhendu, *Cansheng*, 111, states that Japan needed twenty days. After Japan issued mobilisation orders on 15 August, the Japanese 3rd and 11th Divisions reached Shanghai on 22 August.
152 Ma Zhendu, *Cansheng*, 105.
153 'Zhang Zhizhong's Secret Telegram to Chiang Kaishek and Others', KRZZZ, I, 253.
154 'Secret Telegrams from Zhang Zhizhong to Chiang Kaishek and He Yingqin', KRZZZ, I, 266.
155 'Report of the Thirteenth Joint Meeting Regarding the Marco Polo Bridge Incident' (23 July 1937), KRZZZ, I, 228.
156 'Report of the Fourteenth Joint Meeting Regarding the Marco Polo Bridge Incident' (26 July 1937), KRZZZ, I, 236.
157 Zhang Xianwen, *Jiang Jieshi Quanzhuan*, 438.
158 'Guofang Lianxi Huiyi Jilu' (Minutes of the Joint Defence Council) (7 August 1937), in *Minguo Dang'an*, XKIII, 28–33.
159 *Nanjing Guomin Zhengfu Jishi*, 566.
160 Ma Zhendu, *Cansheng*, 112.
161 Ibid., 112.
162 'Generalissimo's Exhortation Regarding the True Military and Political Strategies of the Enemy and the Fundamental Strategy for Victory of Our Forces', ZHMGZYSL, II: 1, 47.
163 Idem.
164 Idem.
165 'Chen Cheng Siren Huiyilu' (Chen Cheng's Personal Recollections), *Minguo Dang'an*, VII (1987), 14.
166 Jiang Kefu, *Minguo Junshishi Luegao*, III: 1, 63.
167 Ma Zhendu, *Cansheng*, 109; Jiang Kefu, *Minguo Junshishi Luegao*, III: 1, 63; 'Personal Order by Generalissimo Chiang Instructing Cheng Qian, MAC Chief-of-Staff, to Re-adjust the Order of Battle' (3 August 1937), ZHMGZYSL, II: 1, 40.
168 Letter of 19 August 1937, in 'Feng Yuxiang Han Cheng Kanluan Jiaofei Yijian', Academia Historica, 055/1964.
169 'Copy of Order by the Supreme Headquarters Promulgating the National Army's Basic Guide War Plan', KRZZZ, I, 3.
170 The text spoke of only four war zones, but later documents (see next note) outlined five.
171 'Copy of Order By the Supreme Headquarters Promulgating Basic War Plan for the Third War Zone' and 'Instruction Promulgated by the Supreme Headquarters Regarding Guide Campaign Plan of the National Army' (both 20 August 1937), KRZZZ, I, 6–16.
172 Zhang Xianwen and Fang Qingqiu, *Jiang Jieshi Quanzhuan*, I, 436–7.
173 Ibid., 437.
174 Garver, *Chinese–Soviet Relations*, 38.
175 Garver, *Chinese–Soviet Relations*, 41.
176 'Situation Report, 25 January 1937', USMI, reel X, frames 0499-0505.
177 Yang Kuisong, *Shiqu de Jihui*, 27–9.
178 Ibid., 41.
179 Ibid., 57.
180 Ibid., 59; 'Central Committee Directive Regarding the Issue of Forcing Chiang to Resist Japan' (1 September 1936) and 'Central Committee Directive Regarding the Movement to Resist Japan and Save the Nation as well as the Democratic Republic' (17 September 1936), *Zhonggong Zhongyang Wenjian Xuanji*, XI, 89–91 and 92–9.
181 Shen Xiaoyun, *Li Zongren de Yisheng*, 225–9.
182 Ibid., 225.

183 Dai Ruxian and Li Liangzhi, *Kangzhan Shiqi de Wenhua Jiaoyu*, 242.

184 Ma Zhendu, *Cansheng*, 162.

185 Ibid., 162–3; 'Generalissimo's Exhortation Examining the War of Resistance and the Fundamental Strategy for Victory', ZHMGZYSL, I: 1, 61–74.

186 Ibid., 61–2.

187 Ma Zhendu, *Cansheng*, 163.

188 Ibid., 163.

189 Ibid., 167–8.

6 The War of Resistance before Japan's Southern Advance

1 Huang Meizhen *et al.*, 'Jianguo Yilai Kang Ri Zhanzheng Yanjiu Pingshu' (A Review of Research into the War of Resistance Since the Founding of the PRC), 95.

2 Ibid., 96.

3 Ibid., 96.

4 For example, Zhang Xianwen, *Kang Ri Zhanzheng de Zhengmian Zhanchang*; Guo Hong, *Kang Ri Zhanzheng Shiqi Guomindang Zhengmian Zhanchang Zhongyao Zhanyi Jieshao*; *Zhongguo Kangri Zhanzheng Shi*; *Kang Ri Zhanzheng Shiqi Guomindang Zhanchang Shiliao Xuanbian*; and Ma Zhendu, *Cansheng*.

5 Hence, Zhang Xianwen *et al.*, *Zhongguo Kang Ri Zhanzheng Shi* begins in 1931. At a July 2002 Conference at Harvard, Wei Hongyun opened his paper by stating matter of factly that 'the Sino-Japanese War broke out in 1931' ('Commerce in Jin Ji Lu Yu', 1).

6 Huang Meizhen *et al.*, 'Jianguo Yilai Kang Ri Zhanzheng Yanjiu Pingshu', 96–105.

7 Chi Jingde, *Zhongguo Dui Ri Kangzhan Sunshi Diaocha Shi Shu*, 208–16.

8 For a review of the debate, see Ma Zhendu, *Cansheng*, 2–11.

9 Yick, 'Communist Puppet Collaboration', 67–84; Elleman, *Modern Chinese Warfare*, 205, 208; 'Fu Bingchang Diary', entry of 1 April 1945; 'Guofangbu Baomiju Han Song Kangzhan Qijian Zhonggong Gexiang Ziliao' (Various Materials Related to the CCP Transferred by the Intelligence Bureau of the National Defence Ministry [to the Academia Historica]), Second Historical Archives, 787/1914.

10 Hsu Long-hsuen and Chang Ming-kai, *Sino-Japanese War*, preface and 172; *Zhongguo Kang Ri Zhanzheng Shi*, II, 5; Chen Cheng, 'Banian Kangzhan Jingguo Gaiyao' (Overview of the Eight Year War of Resistance), in *Kang Ri Zhanzheng Shiqi Guomindang Zhanchang*, 2–4; He Yingqin, 'Banian Kangzhan zhi Jingguo' (History of the Eight Year War of Resistance), ibid., 44–5.

11 *Kang Ri Zhanzheng de Zhengmian Zhanchang*.

12 ZHMGZYSL.

13 'Generalissimo Chiang's Instructions Regarding the True Situation of the Enemy's Military and Political Strategies and the Fundamental Strategy for Our Army's Victory', ZHMGZYSL, II: 1, 46.

14 Liang Hsi-huey, *The Sino-German Connection*, 127.

15 Ibid., 126–7.

16 von Falkenhausen, 'Our experiences during the Battle for Shanghai from 19–31 August 1937' in 'Fakenhaosen Jianyi Wo Kuochong Junbei' (von Falkenhausen's Proposals for Strengthening the Military Preparedness of Our Country), Academia Historica, 055/0994; 'Report by von Fallkenhausen, Chief German Advisor, to Generalissimo Chiang' (29 August 1937), ZHMGZYSL, II: 2, 181–2.

17 de Fremery, 'Report No. 6', in Teitler *et al.*, eds, *Dutch Spy*, 110–11.

18 de Fremery, 'Report No. 4', ibid., 58.

19 de Fremery, 'Report No. 7', ibid., 129.

20 'Generalissimo Chiang's Instructions Regarding the True Situation of the Enemy's Military and Political Strategies', ZHMGZYSL, II: 1, 44.

21 Ibid., 41.

22 *Zhongguo Kang Ri Zhanzheng Shi*, II, 143–4.

23 de Fremery, 'Report No.6', in Teitler *et al.*, eds, *Dutch Spy*, 111–12.
24 Ibid., 101.
25 Ibid., 101.
26 'Periodical notes on the Japanese Army (1943)', British Library, India Office Records, L/Mil/17/20/25/3.
27 Jackson, *The Guinness Book of Air Warfare*, 66 and Bix, *Hirohito*, 323–4.
28 For the order of battle at Shanghai, see Hsu Long-hsuen and Chang Ming-kai, *Sino-Japanese War*, 201; Jiang Kefu, *Minguo Junshishi Luegao*, III: 1, 82–7; For identification, see Jiang Kefu, ibid., III: 2, 28–50.
29 *Zhongguo Kang Ri Zhanzheng Shi*, II, 145.
30 'Overview of the Fighting in the Third War Zone' (no date), in KRZZZ, I, 378.
31 Quoted in Ma Zhendu, *Cansheng*, 117.
32 'Overview of the Fighting in the Third War Zone', KRZZZ, I, 379.
33 'Report by von Falkenhausen, Chief German Advisor, to Generalissimo Chiang' (19 October 1937), ZHMGZYSL, II: 2, 205–6.
34 *Zhongguo Kang Ri Zhanzheng Shi*, II, 145–7.
35 de Fremery, 'Report No. 7', 114–16.
36 Ibid., 116.
37 Ibid., 127–31.
38 See the bibliography to Fogel, ed., *The Nanjing Massacre*. An important new addition is Yamamoto, *Nanking: Anatomy of an Atrocity*.
39 *Zhongguo Kang Ri Zhanzheng Shi*, II, 153; *Bai Chongxi Xiansheng Fangwen Jilu*, I, 149–53. Chen Cheng does not even mention Nanjing in his 'Overview of the Eight Year War of Resistance' in *Kang Ri Zhanzheng Shiqi Guomindang Zhanchang*.
40 'Personal Order From Generalissimo Chiang to the Supreme Nanjing Defence Commander Tang Shengzhi' (12 December 1937), ZHMGZYSL, II: 2, 219–20.
41 *Zhongguo Kangri Zhanzheng Shi*, II, 153–4.
42 'Generalissimo Chiang's Address Reviewing the War of Resistance and Our Basic Strategy for Victory' (11 January 1938), ZHMGZYSL, II: 1, 68.
43 'Assessment of the Situation Along the Tianjin–Pukou Railroad Submitted by von Falkenhausen, Chief German Advisor, to Generalissimo Chiang' (9 February 1938), ZHMGZYSL, II: 2, 252.
44 de Fremery, 'Report No. 10', in Teitler *et al.*, eds, *Dutch Spy*, 172.
45 Ibid.
46 'Generalissimo Chiang's Address Reviewing the War of Resistance and Our Basic Strategy for Victory', ZHMGZYSL, II: 2, 64–5.
47 'Copy of Guide War Plans for the Seventh, Second, and Eighth War Zones' (November 1937), in KRZZZ, I, 18.
48 Ibid., 18–19.
49 Gao Ming, 'Taierzhuang Zhanyi de Guoji Yingxiang yu Guonei Diwei Wenti' (The International Influence of the Taierzhuang Battle and its Domestic Position), 145–7.
50 Quoted in 'Introduction', ZHMGZYSL, IV: 1, 2.
51 'Record of Fourth Meeting of the Extra-Ordinary KMT Congress) (1 April 1938), ZHMGZYSL, IV: 1, 47. The other members of the Presidium were Feng Yuxiang and Kong Xiangxi.
52 'Draft Wartime Organic Law of the KMT' (1 April 1938) ZHMGZYSL, IV: 1, 39–44. For the text passed by the Congress, see ibid. 48–51. The quote is on ibid., 48.
53 'Introduction', ZHMGZYSL, IV: 1, 2.
54 Wakeman (2000), '*Hanjian* (Traitor)!', 298–309, 323–5.
55 'Wartime Organic Law', ZHMGZYSL, IV: 1, 50.
56 'Revised Regulations for the Punishment of Traitors', ZHMGSDAZL, V: 2 (Politics), I, 153.
57 'Wartime Organic Law', ZHMGZYSL, IV: 1, 48.
58 'Propaganda Plan' (8 July 1937) and 'CCP Declaration Regargding KMT CCP Cooperation' (15 July 1937) in *Zhongguo Xiandaishi Ziliao Xuanji*, V, 10–12 and 214–15.

59 Luo Fu (Zhang Wentian), 'Strengthen CCP KMT Cooperation' (21 December 1937), in ibid., 219, 222–3.

60 Quoted in Gao Ming, 'Taierzhuang Zhanyi de Guoji Yingxiang' (The International Influence of the Taierzhuang Battle), 147.

61 Li Tsung-jen, *Memoirs*, 352.

62 Tong, foreword, in ibid., xii–xiv.

63 Lary, 'Defending China'; Gao Ming, 'Taierzhuang Zhanyi de Guoji Yingxiang' (The International Influence of the Taierzhuang Battle).

64 Tong, foreword, in Li Tsung-jen, *Memoirs*, xxv.

65 Li Tsung-ren, *Memoirs*, 353; Ma Zhendu, *Cansheng*, 175, 181–5.

66 *Bai Chongxi Xiansheng Fangwen Jilu*, I, 174–5.

67 'Secret Telegram from Li Zongren to Chiang Kaishek', KRZZZ, I, 608.

68 'Telegram from Li Zongren, Supreme Commander of the Fifth War Zone, Recommending Commanders Because of Outstanding Performance during the Battle of Taierzhuang', ZHMGZYSL, II: 2, 263.

69 Liu Fei, 'Overview of the Xuzhou Battle', in *Xuzhou Huizhan*, 24.

70 *Zhongguo Kang Ri Zhanzheng Shi*, II, 161–2.

71 Ibid., II, 163–5.

72 'Secret Telegram from Li Zongren to Chiang Kaishek', KRZZZ, I, 563.

73 'Secret Telegram from Tang Enbo to Chiang Kaishek' (14 March 1938) and 'Secret Telegram from Chiang Kaishek to Cheng Qian' (15 March 1938), KRZZZ, I, 567 and 569.

74 'Secret Telegram from Tang Enbo to Chiang Kaishek', KRZZZ, I, 568.

75 'Secret Telegram from Tang Enbo to Chiang Kaishek' (15 March 1936), KRZZZ, I, 569.

76 'Copy of Chiang Kaishek's Secret Telegram to Li Zongren', KRZZZ, I, 582.

77 *Zhongguo Kangzhan Zhanzheng Shi*, II, 165.

78 'Secret Telegrams by Li Zongren to the War Department' (25 March 1938), KRZZZ, I, 588, 589.

79 Ibid., I, 589.

80 *Taierzhuang Zhanyi Ziliao*, 154. See also 'Secret Telegrams by Li Zongren to Chiang Kaishek' (27 March 1938), KRZZZ, 592–4.

81 Ibid., KRZZZ, I, 593.

82 Ibid., KRZZZ, I, 594.

83 'Secret Telegram for Li Zongren to the Department of Military Operations' (29 March 1928), KRZZZ, I, 595–6.

84 'Secret Telegram by Lin Wei and Liu Fei to Chiang Kaishek', KRZZZ, I, 595.

85 'Secret Telegram by Tang Enbo to Chiang Kaishek', I, KRZZZ, I, 596.

86 'Secret Telegram by Chiang Kaishek to Li Zongren', KRZZZ, I, 604.

87 Li Tsung-ren, *Memoirs*, 355.

88 Gao Ming, 'Taierzhuang Zhanyi', 147.

89 de Fremery, 'Report No. 10, Teitler *et al.*, eds, *Dutch Spy*, 176.

90 'Secret Telegram from Chiang Kaishek to Tang Enbo', KRZZZ, I, 608.

91 'Secret Telegram from Chiang Kaishek to Li Zongren' (12 April 1938), KRZZZ, I, 618.

92 Zhang Xianwen, *Zhongguo Kang Ri de Zhengmian Zhanchang*, 110.

93 Ma Zhendu, *Cansheng*, 184–5.

94 de Fremery, 'Report No.10', Teitler *et al.*, *Dutch Spy*, 178.

95 'Report by Li Zongren, Supreme Commander of the Fifth War Zone, Reporting that According to Reports from Hong Kong, the Japanese Army Will Use Poison Gas during the Attack on Xuzhou' (8 May 1938), ZHMGZYSL, II: 2, 267.

96 'Secret Telegram from Li Zongren and Others to the Department of Military Operations' (13 April 1938), KRZZZ, I, 618.

97 'Secret Telegram from Chiang Kaishek to Sun Lianzhong and Others' (13 April 1938), KRZZZ, I, 619.

98 de Fremery, 'Report No. 11', in Teitler *et al.*, eds, *Dutch Spy*, 183.

99 *Zhongguo Kang Ri Zhanzheng Shi*, II, 167.

100 Jiang Kefu, *Minguo Junshishi Luegao*, III: 2, 143–4.
101 de Fremery, 'Report No. 11', in Teitler *et al.*, eds, *Dutch Spy*, 193, 200.
102 Zhang Xianwen, *Kang Ri Zhanzheng de Zhengmian Zhanchang*, 114.
103 de Fremery, 'Report No.11', in Teitler *et al.*, eds, *Dutch Spy*, 194.
104 Lary, 'Defending China', 407.
105 Mao Zedong, 'On Protracted War', 115.
106 Ibid., 116.
107 Ibid., 117.
108 *Zhongguo Kang Ri Zhanzheng Shi*, II, 181–2.
109 Ibid., 180–1.
110 Ibid., 168; Li Wenhai, *Zhongguo Jindai Shi Da Zaihuang*, 238–67.
111 Ma Zhendu, *Cansheng*, 187–91. On primary sources related to the decision making, see 'Wuhan Huizhan Changjiang Juekou Shiliao' (The Breaking of the Dikes of the Yangtze River during the Battle of Wuhan), *Minguo Dang'an*, XXXVI (1994), 20–30.
112 *Zhongguo Kang Ri Zhanzheng Shi*, II, 189–203.
113 de Fremery, 'Report No.13', in Teitler *et al.*, eds, *Dutch Spy*, 222–3.
114 *Zhongguo Kang Ri Zhanzheng Shi*, II, 199–203.
115 de Fremey, 'Report No.13', in Teitler *et al.*, eds, *Dutch Spy*, 225.
116 'Generalissimo Chiang's Address at the First Nanyue Military Conference' (26 November 1938), ZHMGZYSL, II, I, 139–49 and 150–8.
117 'Dui Minguo 26 Nian Ba Yue Shijiu Ri zhi Sanshiyi Ri Jian Shanghai Fangmain Zuozhan Jingguo' (Experiences of the Fighting on the Shanghai Front, 19–31 August 1937) (7 September), in 'Fakenhaosen Jiangyi Wo Kuochong Junbei' (von Falkenhausen's Suggestion to Strengthen Our Country's Military Preparedness), Academia Historica 055/0994. See also 'Report by von Falkenhausen, Chief German Advisor, for Chiang Kaishek' (29 August 1937), ZHMGZYSL, II: 2, 181–2.
118 Ibid., and 'Guanyu Shanghai Zhengmian Zuozhan Jingyan zhi Di Sanci Baogao' (Third report on our Battle Experiences at the Shanghai Front), in 'Fakenhaosen Jianyi Wo Kuochong Junbei', Academia Historica 055/0994.
119 'Generalissimo Chiang's Address Examining the War of Resistance and the Reasons for our Inevitable Victory', ZHMGZYSL, II: 1, 57. It was a common complaint. See, for example, 'Generalissimo Chiang's Address at the First Nanyue Military Conference', ibid., II: 1, 150.
120 'Guanyu Shanghai Zhengmian Zuozhan Jingyan zhi Di Sanci Baogao' (Third report on our Battle Experiences at the Shanghai Front), in 'Fakenhaosen Jianyi Wo Kuochong Junbei', Academia Historica 055/0994.
121 de Fremery, 'Report No.9', in Teitler *et al.*, eds, *Dutch Spy*, 155.
122 de Fremery, 'Report No. 5', ibid., 81.
123 *Zhongguo Kang Ri Zhanzheng Shi*, II, 412.
124 Ibid., II, 412.
125 *Nanjing Guomin Zhengfu Jishi*, 627.
126 'Generalissimo Chiang's Address at the First Nanyue Military Conference', *Zhongyao Shilioa Chubian*, II: I, 127.
127 Ibid., 129.
128 Ibid., 129.
129 Ibid., 129–33.
130 Ibid., 140.
131 Ibid., 139.
132 Ibid., 157.
133 Ibid., 135.
134 Ibid., 174.
135 *Kang Ri Zhanzheng Shiqi Guomindang Zhanchang Shiliao Xuanbian*, 336–7.
136 Ibid., 329–30.
137 *Zhongguo Kang Ri Zhanzheng Shi*, II, 414.
138 Ibid., 413–4; 557; Ma Zhendu, *Cansheng*, 209.
139 *Zhongguo Kang Ri Zhanzheng Shi*, II, 415.

140 'MAC Draft Revised War Plan' (14 December 1938), KRZZZ, I, 23–9.
141 'Guide Plan for the National Army for the Second Phase of the War Promulgated by Order of Chiang Kaishek', in KRZZZ, I, 33.
142 Ibid., I, 34.
143 Ibid., I, 32. See also 'Guide War Plan Drafted by the Guilin Field Headquarters' (1 January 1938), KRZZZ, I, 30.
144 *Zhongguo Kang Ri Zhanzheng Shi*, II, 425.
145 'Measures to Switch the National Army to Offensive Operations' (February 1939), in KRZZZ, I, 35.
146 Ibid., I, 34–5.
147 Ibid., I, 36.
148 Ibid., I, 36. See also 'Substitute Telegram, Chiang Kaishek's Order Promulgating Measures to Switch the National Army to Offensive Operations' (1939), in ibid., 49.
149 Ma Zhendu, *Cansheng*, 217. *Zhongguo Kang Ri Zhanzheng Shi*, II, 487–90.
150 Ibid., II, 493.
151 'Secret Telegram from Chiang Kaishek' (undated), KRZZZ, I, 37.
152 Jackson, *The Guinness Book of Air Warfare*, 67–8.
153 Coox, *Nomonhan*, 853–99.
154 Hsu Long-hsuen and Chang Ming-kai, *Sino-Japanese War*, 509–10. 'Ambassador in the Soviet Union (Steinhardt) to the Secretary of State' (22 September 1939), FRUS, III, 1939, Far East, 261.
155 Hsu Long-hsuen and Chang Ming-kai, *Sino-Japanese War*, 510.
156 'Ninth War Zone Report on the Fighting during the Battle of Changsha' (11 October 1939), in KRZZZ, II, 1028.
157 'Outline Battle Plan for Western Jiangxi of the Supreme Field Commander of the Ninth War Zone' (1 September 1939), KRZZZ, II, 1036.
158 'Ninth War Zone Report on the Fighting during the Battle of Changsha', ibid., II, 1028.
159 'Outline Battle Plan for Western Jiangxi', ibid., 1036.
160 'Overview', ZHMGZYSL, II, 2, 435.
161 'Ninth War Zone Report on the Fighting during the Battle of Changsha', KRZZZ, II, 1027.
162 'Personal Order by Generalissimo Chiang to Xue Yue about First Abandoning Changsha and then Counter-attacking the Enemy' (15 April 1939), ZHMGZYSL, II: 2, 433.
163 'Ninth War Zone Report on the Fighting during the Battle of Changsha' (11 October 1939), in KRZZZ, II, 1078.
164 Ibid., II, 1078–9.
165 Ibid., II, 1079–80.
166 Ibid., II, 1078–9; and 'Secret Telegram from Xue Yue to Chiang Kaishek', in KRZZZ, II, 1032.
167 Ch'i Hsi-sheng, *Nationalist China at War*, 56–7.
168 'Generalissimo Chiang's Address at the First Nanyue Military Conference', ZHMGZYSL, II: 1, 196–7.
169 'The Ambassador in China (Johnson) to the Secretary of State' (30 August 1939) and (6 September 1937), FRUS, 1939, III, Far East, 217–8 and 235.
170 'Telegram of Sir R. Craigie' (26 February 1940), in 'Future Military Policy', PRO: WO 106/122.
171 'The Ambassador in China (Johnson) to the Secretary of State', FRUS, 1939, III, Far East, 218.
172 *Zhongguo Kang Ri Zhanzheng Shi*, II, 538–9.
173 *Nanjing Guomin Zhengfu Jishi*, 672.
174 'Central Directive Regarding Forming an Advanced Force to Secure a Turn for the Better' (1 Decmber 1939), *Zhonggong Zhongyang Wenjian Xuanji*, XII, 203.
175 This order was issued on 8 November. See 'Concentrate all Forces to Develop Our Armed Forces and Fight for the Establishment of Base Areas' (28 January 1940), *Mao Zedong Junshi Wenji*, II, 509.
176 'Generalissimo Chiang's Address at the Liuzhou Military Conference' (24 February 1940), ZHMGZYSL, II: 1, 217–18.
177 Ibid., II: 1, 218; *Zhongguo Kang Ri Zhanzheng Shi*, II, 501.

178 'Generalissimo Chiang's Address at the Second Nanyue Military Conference', ZHMGZYSL, II: 1, 195.
179 Ibid., II:1, 191.
180 Ibid., II:1, 195–6.
181 Ibid., II:1, 193.
182 Ibid.
183 Ibid.
184 Ibid., II:1, 193–4.
185 Ray Huang, *Chiang Kaishek*, I, 109–10; Hsu Long-hsuen and Chang Ming-kai, *Sino-Japanese War*, 319–20.
186 *Zhongguo Kang Ri Zhanzheng Shi*, II, 511.
187 Ch'i Hsi-sheng, *Nationalist China at War*, 59–60.
188 'Generalissimo Chiang's Address at the Liuzhou Military Conference', ZHMGZYSL, II: 1, 248.
189 Ibid., II: 1, 231–44.
190 *Zhongguo Kang Ri Zhanzheng Shi*, II, 561.
191 Ibid.
192 Jiang Kefu, *Minguo Junshishi Luegao*, III: 1, 332–54.
193 Ch'en Yungfa, *Making Revolution*, 40–67; van de Ven, 'The Kuomintang's Secret Service in Action', 207–8.
194 *Zhongguo Kang Ri Zhanzheng Shi*, II, 580.
195 Shaw, *Stuart*, 125–6.
196 Ibid., 126.
197 Ibid., 126–7.
198 Ch'en Yung-fa, *Making Revolution*, 40–67.
199 van de Ven, 'The Kuomintang's Secret Service', 213–22.
200 'Overview of the Zao Yi Battle', ZHMGZYSL, 478–53; *Zhongguo Kang Ri Zhanzheng Shi*, III, 511–20.
201 'Personal Order of Generalissimo Chiang to Tang Enbo, Commander-in-Chief of the 31st Group Army, to Attack the Enemy from the Flanks' (12 April 1940), ZHMGZYSL, II: 2, 454.
202 Ibid., II: 2, 454.
203 Hsu Long-hsuen and Chang Ming-kai, *Sino-Japanese War*, 334–9; *Zhongguo Kang Ri Zhanzheng Shi*, II, 511–9; Zhang Xianwen, *Kang Ri Zhanzheng de Zhengmian Zhanchang*, 193–9.
204 White, ed., *Stilwell Papers*, 207–8.
205 *Zhongguo Kang Ri Zhanzheng Shi*, II, 513–9.
206 Hsu Long-hsuen and Chang Ming-kai, *Sino-Japanese War*, 509.
207 *Zhongguo Kang Ri Zhanzheng Shi*, II, 519.
208 Hsu Long-hsuen and Chang Ming-kai, *Sino-Japanese War*, 509.
209 *Zhongguo Kang Ri Zhanzheng Shi*, III, 168–9.
210 Hsu Long-hsuen and Chang Ming-kai, *Sino-Japanese War*, 347–9; *Zhongguo Kang Ri Zhanzheng Shi*, III, 168–71.
211 Hsu Long Hsuen and Chang Ming-kai, *Sino-Japanese War*, 351–3; *Zhongguo Kang Ri Zhanzheng Shi*, III, 171–4; Zhang Xianwen, *Kang Ri Zhanzheng de Zhengmian Zhanchang*, 216–29.
212 Hsu Long-hsuen and Chang Ming-kai, *Sino-Japanese War*, 359.
213 Hsu Long-hsuen and Chang Ming-kai, *Sino-Japanese War*, 361; *Zhongguo Kang Ri Zhanzheng Shi*, III, 178–82.
214 Zhang Xianwen, *Kang Ri Zhanzheng de Zhengmian Zhanchang*, 250–3.
215 Maochun Yu, 'The China Commando Group of SOE', 37–57.
216 Ibid., 55–7. On SACO, see Shen, 'SACO Re-examined'.
217 Schaller, *US Crusade*, 65–85.
218 Ibid.
219 *Zhongguo Kang Ri Zhanzheng Shi*, III, 9–10.
220 Stoler, *Allies*, 80.
221 *Zhongguo Kang Ri Zhanzheng Shi*, III, 10.
222 Ibid., III, 11.

7 Wartime mobilisation

1 'Implementation Scheme Submitted by the Ministry of Military Administration for Wartime Troop Replacement' (31 July 1937), *Yizheng Shiliao*, I, 96.
2 See Table 7.1, and He Yingqin, *Ri Jun Qinhua Banian Kangzhan Shi*, table 10.
3 Ibid., table 9.
4 'Scheme Submitted by the Ministry of Military Administration to Improve Prevention and Treatment of Desertion' (23 December 1938), *Yizheng Shiliao*, II, 389.
5 'Scheme for Wartime National Military Service Recruitment' (13 January 1938), *Yizheng Shiliao*, I, 145.
6 'Table of Regular Fees for Replacement Troop Battalions' (30 April 1938), *Yizheng Shiliao*, I, 164; 'Wartime Scheme for Troop Replacements' (31 July 1937), *Yizheng Shiliao*, 99.
7 Xu Xuehan, 'Zhengbing de Kunnan ji qi Jiejue Banfa' (The Problems of Recruitment and Ways to Resolve It), in *Yizheng Shiliao*, II, 365.
8 Ibid., 365–6.
9 'Reasons for Shortcomings in Recruitment Personnel', *Yizheng Shiliao*, II, 464–72.
10 'The Department of Military Administration Submits Secretly the Scheme for the Unified Management of Mercenary Recruitment and National Military Service as well as Replacements' (13 January 1938), *Yizheng Shiliao*, I, 141–6.
11 He Yingqin, *Ri Jun Qinhua Banian Kangzhan Shi*, table 9.
12 Ibid., I, 145.
13 Ibid., I, 146–7.
14 Dai Gaoxiang, 'Kangzhan Shiqi zhi Sichuan Yizheng' (The Sichuan Military Service Administration during the War of Resistance) (1963), *Yizheng Shiliao*, I, 477–9.
15 Liao Ming'ou, 'Liangnian Lai de Hunan Yizheng' (The Hunan Military Service System during the Last Two Years) (1941), *Yizheng Shiliao*, I, 503.
16 Ibid., I, 504–5.
17 Ibid., I, 521.
18 Ibid., I, 522–3.
19 Li Sisu 'Jiangxi zhi Yizheng' (The Jiangxi Military Service Administration) (1941), *Yizheng Shiliao*, I, 491–502.
20 'Zhejiang Bingyi' (The Zhejiang Military Service Administration) (no date), *Yizheng Shiliao*, I, 529.
21 'Zuigao Muliao Ershiba Niandu Huiyi Huibian' (Minutes and Papers of the Senior Staff Meeting during 1939), 14–15 and 30–1, Academia Historica, 510/199.1.
22 'The Implementation of Resolutions of the Third Session of the First NPC', ZHMGZYSL, IV: 1, 534.
23 Huang Shaohong, 'Zhejiang Bingyi de Yiban Jiantao' (General Review of the Zhejiang Military Service Administration) (1940), *Yizheng Shiliao*, I, 539.
24 'Renumeration of Baojia Heads in War Time', ZHMGZYSL (January 1939), I, 637 and 636.
25 On their importance, see 'Implementation Scheme for the Basic Law of the War of Resistance and National Reconstruction' (August 1938) and 'General Budget for Annual State Revenues, 1937–1944' (1945) ZHMGSDAZL, V: 2 (Finance and Economics), vol. 1, 13–14 and 314.
26 'Kong Xiangxi's Secret Report on the True Financial Situation, July 1937–June 1939' (June 1939), ZHMGSDAZL, V: 2 (Finance and Economics), 345. See also Jia Shiyi *et al.*, *Kangzhan yu Caizheng Jinrong*, 2–4.
27 Ibid., 14–16.
28 'Implementation Scheme for the Basic Law of the War of Resistance and National Reconstruction', ZHMGSDAZL, V: 2 (Finance and Economics), vol. 1, 13–19.
29 Hou Kunhong, 'Kangzhan Shiqi de Zhongyang Caizheng yu Difang Caizheng', 73.
30 'Implementation Scheme for the Basic Law of the War of Resistance and National Reconstruction', ZHMGSDAZL, V: 2 (Finance and Economics), vol. 1, 13–17.
31 Ibid., 13–69.
32 Hsiao Liang-lin, *China's Foreign Trade Statistics*, 33, 160.

33 Huang Linsheng, 'Kangzhan Sannian de Liangshi Xingzheng' (The Grain Administration during Three Years of the War of Resistance) (1940), *Liangzheng Shiliao*, I, 472.
34 Hou Kunhong, 'Kangzhan Shiqi Liangshi Gongqiu', 18; See also Hiao Liang-lin, *Foreign Trade Statistics*, 33, 160, but note that Hsiao omits data after 1941.
35 Eastman, *Seeds of Destruction*, 46.
36 Hou Kunhong, *Kangzhan Shiqi Liangshi Gongqiu*, 152–3.
37 Eastman, *Seeds of Destruction*, 45.
38 Hou Kunhong, 'Kangzhan Shiqi Liangshi Gongqiu', 48–50.
39 'The Economic Situation in Free China: The Food Situation in Szechuan' (1942), PRO: HS 1/48.
40 '1938 Work Report of the Ministry of Economic Affairs' (October 1938), ZHMGSDAZL, V: 2 (Finance and Economics), vol. 5, 88–98.
41 'The 1939 Work Report of the Ministry of Economic Affairs' (October 1939), ZHMGS-DAZL, V: 2 (Finance and Economics), vol. 5, 117–30.
42 Ibid., 129–30.
43 Fu Weiruo, 'Tianfu Zhengshi yu Junliang Buji' (Lang Taxation in Kind and Supply of Military Grain) (1942), *Liangheng Shiliao*, VI, 148, 160.
44 A man of 50 kilograms engaged in heavy work needs 3,425 calories per day, which can be derived from about 1 litre of rice per day. This is the current recommended dietary allowance for Indians. See Indian Council of Medical Research, *Nutrient Requirements and Recommended Dietary Allowance for Indians*, 31. I am grateful to Professor Kim Chung of the Michigan State University for information on this topic.
45 '1939 Work Report of the Ministry of Economic Affairs', ZHMGSDAZL V: 2 (Finance and Economics), vol. 5, 126–7.
46 He Yingqin, *Ri Jun Qin Hua Banian Kangzhan Shi*, table 9.
47 '1939 Work Report of the Ministry of Economic Affairs', ZHMGSDAZL, V: 2 (Finance and Economics), vol. 5, 127. It referred to an army of 1 million troops, but this was an error, corrected in the Ministry's report for the first half of 1940, see 'Work Report for the First Half Year of 1940 of the Ministry of Economic Affairs' (June 1940), ZHMGSDAZL, V: 2 (Finance and Economics), vol. 5, 167.
48 '1938 Work Report of the Ministry of Economic Affairs' (1938), ZHMGSDAZL, V: 2 (Finance and Economics), vol. 5, 96.
49 Ibid., 96.
50 See provincial reports, but also 'Secret Letter from the Ministry of Domestic Affairs to the Executive Yuan' (12 April 1938), *Liangzheng Shiliao*, VI, 1.
51 Zhang Zhu, 'Wo Guo Zhanshi Junliang zhi Buji ji qi Gaijin' (The Wartime Supply of Military Grains and its Improvement) (1942), *Yizheng Shiliao*, VI, 160.
52 'Scheme for the Management of Grain Procurement in War Zone Provinces' (December 1939), *Yizheng Shiliao*, VI, 28.
53 The text mentions a total budget of 62 million *yuan*, but the higher figure is mentioned in '1939 Work Report of the Ministry of Economic Affairs', ZHMGSDAZL, 5.2 (Finance and Economics), vol. 5, 127. This also has somewhat higher quotas, reaching to 14.4 million *Shidan*.
54 Ibid., 126–7.
55 'Work Report for the First Half of 1940 of the Ministry of Economic Affairs', ZHMGS-DAZL V: 1 (Finance and Economics), 5, 167–8.
56 'The Ministries of Military Administration, Finance, Economic Affairs, Agriculture and Forestry, and Rear Area Logistics Jointly Request Generalissimo Chiang to Order the Ministry of Finance to Pre-allocate 100 Million *Yuan*' (August 1940), *Liangzheng Shiliao*, VI, 46–48. For the approval, see *Liangzheng Shiliao*, VI, 51–2.
57 Ch'ien Tuan-sheng, *Government and Politics*, 283.
58 Shyu, 'China's Minority Parties', 154.
59 'NPC Regulations', in *Guomin Canzhenghui Ziliao*, 7, 14, 15.
60 Ibid., 8.
61 See ZHMGZYSL, IV: 1 and IV: 2.

62 'Resolution on the Report of the Ministry of Finance', ZHMGZYSL, IV: 1, 742–3.
63 'Resolution on the Report of the Ministry of Finance', ZHMGZYSL, IV: 1, 825–9.
64 'Resolution on Various Items in the Report of Ministry of Domestic Affairs', ZYMGZYSL, IV: 1, 358–9.
65 'Resolution on the Report on Military Affairs', ZHMGZYSL, IV: 1, 820.
66 *Nanjing Guomin Zhengfu Jishi*, 792.
67 'The Economic Situation in Free China; the Food Situation in Szechuan' (January 1942). PRO, HS1/48.
68 'Jingji Gongzuo Baogao Gaikuang' (Overview Report of Ministry of Economic Affairs), Second Historical Archives, 787/331.
69 'Financial Administration during the War of Resistance' (February 1946), ZHMGSDAZL, V: 2 (Finance and Economy), vol.1, 459.
70 'Papers for Joint Report Meetings at the Official Presidential Residence', KMT Archives, 'Tezhong Dang'an' (Special Files), 027/1.
71 Myers, 'Agrarian System', 266–9.
72 Hou Kunhong, *Kangzhan Shiqi de Zhongyang Caizheng yu Difang Caizheng*, 44–5.
73 Martin, 'Shield of Collaboration', 116–9.
74 Lin Meili, *Kangzhan Shiqi de Huobi Zhanzheng*, 36–50, ch. 3, 154–70.
75 Eastman, 'Nationalist China during the Sino-Japanese War', 591.
76 Huang, 'Chiang Kaishek', I, 127–8.
77 Dai Gaoxiang, 'The Sichuan Military Service Administration', *Yizheng Shiliao*, I, 477.
78 Xu Siping, 'The History of the Mobilisation of Students and Civil Servants by the Sichuan Conscription Command to Enrol in Military Service Voluntarily', *Yizheng Shiliao*, II, 427.
79 Liao Ming'ou, 'The Hunan Military Service Administration', *Yizheng Shiliao*, I, 520. Li Sisu, 'The Jiangxi Military Service Administration', *Yizheng Shiliao*, I, 493–502. Chen Gan, 'The Anhui Military Service Administration during the Last Eight Years' (1946), *Yizheng Shiliao*, I, 486.
80 'Zuigao Muliao Huiyi Sanshi Niandu Huibian' ([Minutes and Papers of] the Senior Staff Meetings of 1941), 161–2. KMT Archives, 501/199.3.
81 Huang, 'Chiang Kaishek', I, 119.
82 'Generalissimo Chiang's Address at the Xinglongshan Military Conference' (22 August 1942), ZHMGZYSL, II: 1, 411.
83 'Schemes for Military Recruitment and Replacement in 1942', *Yizheng Shiliao*, I, 371–2.
84 Dai Gaoxiang, 'The Sichuan Military Service Administration', *Zhengyi Shiliao*, I, 478.
85 'Table Showing Implementation of Resolutions of the First Session of the Second NPC', ZHMGZYSL, IV: 1, 996.
86 'Generalissimo Chiang's Address at the Xinglongshan Military Conference' (23 August 1942), ZHMGZYSL, II:1, 404–5.
87 Ibid.
88 Ibid., 406.
89 'Opening Address by Generalissimo Chiang at the Xi'an Military Conference' (6 September 1942), ZHMGZYSL, II: 1, 426.
90 'Lecture by Generalissimo Chiang at the Xi'an Military Conference' (9 September 1942), in ZHMGZYSL, II: 1, 455.
91 These were not grain-rich areas and logistical problems made supply of the Burma Expeditionary Force very difficult.
92 He Haoruo, 'Ri Yong Bixupin Gongying Jihua yu Wu Wu Jiaoyi' (A Plan for the Supply of Daily Necessities and Barter Trade), Academia Historica, 055/1267. 'Report to Generalissimo Chiang' (20 January 1940), in *Guojia Zongdongyuan Huiyi* (The National Mobilisation Council), Academia Historica, 055/0169.
93 Huang, 'Chiang Kaishek', I, 118–9.
94 Hou Kunhong, *Kangzhan Shiqi de Zhongyang Caizheng yu Difang Caizheng*, 156–9.
95 'The MAC Forwards the "Draft General Order of the National Government" by Feng Yuxiang', *Yizheng Shiliao*, 434–5.
96 '[Minutes and Papers] of the Senior Staff Meeting of 1941', 34, KMT Archives 510/199.3.

97 Ibid., 23–64.

98 Ibid., 88–108.

99 'Ziyuan Weiyuanhui 1941 Niandu Gongzuo Baogao' (1941 NRC Work Report), Second Historical Archives, 28(2)/45.

100 Wu Zhaohong, 'Wo Suo Zhidaode Ziyuan Weiyuanhui' (The NRC I Knew), *Huiyi Guomindang Zhengfu Ziyuan Weiyuanhui*, 73–4.

101 *Ziyuan Weiyuanhui Dang'an Shiliao Chubian* (Preliminary Collection of Archival Sources for the NRC), I, 123–4; Zheng Youkui, 'Weng Wenhao Dui Guoying Qiye de Guanli Fa' (Weng Wenhao's Management of State Enterprises), in *Huiyi Guomindang Zhengfu Ziyuan Weiyuanhui*, 145.

102 For historical overviews, see Kirby, 'Chinese War Economy', and the historical introduction provided in *Ziyuan Weiyuanhui Dang'an Shiliao Chubian*, 5–129.

103 'History of and Reflections on Two And A Half Years of Establishing Heavy Industry' (May 1939), ZHMGZYSL, IV: 3, 656.

104 On German estimates, 'Chouhua Guofang Zhongxin Quyu' (Demarcating A Central National Defence Area) (no date) and '1934 Nian Guanyu Diaocha Binggong Junxu Fangmian Xuyao Yuanliao yu Zhipin zhi Zhonglei ji Suoxu Shuliang Baogoao' (1934 Report Regarding an Investigation into the Categories and Amounts of Primary Sources and Products Required by Military Industry) (no date); Second Historical Archives of China, 28(2)/1913 and 28(2)/1929; For NRC production, see 'Ziyuan Weiyuanhui Fushu Shiye Linian Zhuyao Chanpingliang Tongji' (Main Annual Production Statistics for NRC Enterprises, 1936–1949), Second Historical Archives, 28(2)/3538.

105 'Jingjibu Gongzuo Baogao' (Work Report of the Ministry for Economic Affairs) (1938–40) (no date), Second Historical Archives, 787/329.

106 'Jingjibu Ziyuan Weiyuanhui Gongzuo Baogao' (Work Report of the NRC of the Ministry of Economic Affairs, 1936–1941), Second Historical Archives, 28(2)/44.

107 'Guofang Gongye Zhanshi Sannian Jihua ji Youguan Ziliao' (Three Year War-time Plan for National Defence Industries and Related Materials) (1940), Second Historical Archives, 28(2)/929.

108 'Work Report of the Ministry of Economic Affairs delivered by Weng Wenhao, Minister, to the Ninth Plenum of the Fifth KMT Congress' (27 December 1941), ZHMGZYSL, IV: 3, 688–9.

109 Kirby, 'China's War Economy', 192–8.

110 White, ed., *Stilwell Papers*, 208.

111 Kirby, 'China's War Economy', 196–7; 'Jingjibu Sanshisan Niandu Gongzuo Jiantao' (Critical Examination of Our Work in 1944) (June 1945), Second Historical Archives, 787/331.

112 'Jingji Gongzuo Baogao Gaiyao' (March 1941–November 1942) (Overview Work Report of the Ministry of Economic Affairs), Second Historical Archives, 787/331.

113 'Jingjibu Gongzuo Baogao, Gongzuo Gaiyao, ji Gongzuo Gaijin Jihua Yaodian' (1944– June 1945) (Work Report, Overview of Work, and Plans for Improvement of the Ministry of Economic Affairs), Second Historical Archives, 787/332.

114 Huang, 'Chiang Kaishek', I, 106.

115 ZHMGSDAZL, V: 2 (Finance and Economics), vol. 6, 515–8.

116 Young, *China's Wartime Finance*, 26.

117 See Young, *China's Wartime Finance*, 353, table 53.

118 Hou Kunhong, *Kangzhan Shiqi de Zhongyang Caizheng yu Difang Caizheng*, 101–5.

119 Ibid., 38–43, 81–5, 100–41.

120 Young, *China's Wartime Finance*, 25; Hou Kunhong, *Kangzhan Shiqi de Zhongyang Caizheng yu Difang Caizheng*, 100–5.

121 Ibid., 139–40.

122 Hou Kunhong, *Kangzhan Shiqi de Zhongyang yu Difang Caisheng*, 137–40.

123 Ibid., 116–17.

124 Hou Kunhong, *Kangzhan Shiqi Liangshi Gongqiu*, 172.

125 Hou Ping-ti, *Studies on the Population of China*, 94–5.

126 'The Economy of Free China,' in 'Former British Residents; Siamese Personalities; Agents', PRO: HS 1/48.

127 'The National State Mobilisation Law' (29 March 1942), ZHMGZYSL, IV: 3, 476–81.

128 'Fanghai Guojia Zongdongyuan Chengfa Zhanxing Tiaoli' (Provisional Regulations To Punish Violations of National Mobilisation) (1 August 1942), in 'Guojia Zongdongyuan Huiyi Zuzhi Tiaoli' (Organisational Regulations of the National Mobilisation Law), Academia Historica 055/0066.

129 'Guojia Zong Dongyuan Fa Shishi Gangyao' (Implementation Guidelines of the National Mobilisation Law) (22 June 1942), in ibid.

130 See the reports by Wu Tiecheng, Chen Yi, and He Yaozu and record of activities, May–July 1942, in 'Guojia Zong Dongyuan Huiyi' (The National Mobilisation Committee), Academia Historica, 055/0169.

131 'Implementation Guidelines of the National Mobilisation Law', Academia Historica, 055/0066.

132 Ibid.

133 'Letter of Weng Wenhao to Chiang Kaishek' (10 December 1941), in 'Tiaozheng Zhongyang yu Difang Xingzheng Jiguan' (Re-adjusting Central and Local Administrative Organs', Academia Historica, 055/0044-1.

134 See tables on central KMT and government institutions in 'Re-adjusting Central and Local Administrative Organs', Academia Historica, 055/0044-1.

135 Hou, *Kangzhan Shiqi de Zhongyang Caizheng yu Difang Caizheng*, 214–5.

136 'Report from Fang Ce to Chiang Kaishek' (December 1912), in ibid.

137 'Schedule of Activities' (May–July 1942), in 'The National Mobilisation Committee', Academia Historica, 055/0169.

138 See the relevant schedule of activities, reports by Shen Honglie (2 December 1942) and Chen Bulei (5 December 1942); and the 'Implementation Guidelines' in 'Organisational Regulations of the National Mobilisation Committee', Academia Historica, 055/0066. See Regulations of 11 March 1944, in 055/0066.

139 See Chen Bulei's Summary of Zhang Lisheng's proposals (June 1944) in ibid.

140 'Gongwuyuan ji qi Jiashu Shenghuo Bixupin Shishi Peigei' (The Implementation of Allocation of Daily Necessities to Civil Servants and Their Dependents', Academia Historica 055/0086.

141 He Haoruo, 'Plan for the Supply of Daily Necessities' (June 1942), Academia Historica, 055/1267.

142 Ibid.

143 Ibid.

144 Hou Kunhong, *Kangzhang Shiqi de Zhongyang Caizheng yu Difang Caizheng*, 117–25.

145 Yick, 'Communist Puppet Collaboration', 67–77.

146 DeVido, 'The Making of the Communist Party State', 78–81.

147 The New Fourth Army was a case in point for the first. For an example of the latter, see Warren Kuo, *Analytical History*, IV, 452.

148 (Minutes and Papers of the Senior Staff Meeting during 1941), 39–46, Academia Historica, 510/199.3.

149 'Report of Chinese Guerrilla Activities in relation to Kengtung and Manglun states, 1942–1945', in 'China General; Chungking General; Guerrillas', PRO HS1/180.

150 Ibid.

151 Ibid.

152 White and Jacoby, *Thunder out of China*, 177.

153 For the reports, see ZHMGSDAZL, V: 2 (Finance and Economics), vol. 5, 720–31.

154 'Work Report of the Bureau for the Prevention of Smuggling of the Ministry of Finance' (25 October 1943), ZHMGSDAZL, V: 2 (Finance and Economics), vol. 2, 274–6.

155 Ibid., 274.

156 'Weekly Intelligence Summary no. 28' (22 February 45), 'Airfields in Yunnan; Progress Reports; Intelligence Reports', PRO: HS 1.137.

157 'I.I.S. Intelligence' (27 August 1945), in 'Airfields in Yunnan; Progress Reports; Intelligence Reports', PRO: HS1/157.

158 van de Ven, 'The Kuomintang's Secret Service', 213–21.

159 Tuchman, *Stilwell*, 607.

160 'Weekly Intelligence Summary, No. 18' (10 January 1945), 'Airfields in Yunnan; Progress Reports; Intelligence Reports', PRO: HS1/137.

161 Liu, 'The Ch'ing Restoration', 414–5.

162 Wagner, 'Ritual, Politics, and Publicity', 33.

163 Personal observations and photograph, 1997 and 2002.

164 'Reports on the Non-attendance of Mao Zedong and Six Other NPC Members and the Opinion of Other NPC Members' (3 March 1941), ZHMGZYSL, IV: 1, 967.

165 'Reports on the Non-attendance of Mao Zedong', ZHMGZYSL, IV: 1, 969–72.

166 'Speech by Generalissimo Chiang' (6 March 1941), ZHMGZYSL, IV: 1, 674.

167 Shyu, 'China's Minority Parties', 155–9; Ch'ien Tuan-sheng, *Government and Politics*.

168 *Zhongguo Kang Ri Zhanzheng Shi III*, 507–14.

169 'Central Directive to Lin Boqu, Dong Biwu, and Wang Ruofei Regarding Raising the Demand of National Government Re-organisation and Proposals for its Implementation', *Zhonggong Zhongyang Wenjian Xuanji*, XIV, 323.

170 'How to Resolve', in ibid. 364–5.

171 'Central Directive to Lin Boqu, Dong Biwu, and Wang Ruofei', *Zhonggong Zhongyang Wenjian Xuanji*, XIV, 323.

172 For the latter, see Schaller, *US Crusade*, 177–94.

173 'Generalissimo Chiang's Address to the Fourth Nanyue Military Conference' (12 and 13 February 1944), ZHMGZYSL, II: 1, 502.

174 Ibid., II:1, 502–6.

175 Ibid., II:1, 506.

176 Ibid., II:1, 507–8.

177 Ibid., II:1, 505.

178 Ibid., II:1, 505.

179 'Record of Meeting' (9 March 1945) in 'Supreme Allied Commander's Visit to Chungking', PRO: 203/5629.

180 Ibid.

181 'To Brigadier General George A. Lincoln' (14 May 1945), *Wedemeyer on War and Peace*, 116.

182 'He Yingqin's Guide War Plan for a Co-ordinated Counter-Offensive with Allied Armies' (1944), KRZZZ, I, 133–36.

183 *Zhongguo Kang Ri Zhanzheng Shi*, III, 541; For troop re-arrangement, see 'Secret Telegrams between He Yingqin and Chiang Kaishek' (December 1944), KRZZZ, I, 131–2.

184 'To Brigadier General George A. Lincoln' (14 May 1945), *Wedemeyer on War and Peace*, 116.

185 'To General of the Army George Marshall' (1 August 1945), *Wedemeyer on War and Peace*, 127.

186 'Brigadier General George A. Lincoln', *Wedemeyer on War and Peace*, 116.

187 'Guide War Plan of the Supreme Chinese Headquarters for an Offensive on Guilin, Leizhou, Hengyang, Canton, and Hong Kong' (14 July 1945), KRZZZ, I, 148–157.

188 'To Brigadier General George A. Lincoln' (14 May 1945), *Wedemeyer on War and Peace*, 117.

189 Ibid., 117.

190 'To General of the Army George Marshall' (1 August 1945), *Wedemeyer on War and Peace*, 129.

191 Ibid., 129.

192 'Memorandum to WARCOS' (15 August 1945), *Wedemeyer on War and Peace*, 142.

193 'Order of the National Government to Remit the Land Tax and Postpone Military Recruitment' (3 September 1945), *Yizheng Shiliao*, I, 435–6.

194 Ibid., 436.

Conclusion

1 Van de Ven, 'New States of War', 372–94.
2 Van Slyke, 'The Battle of the Hundred Regiments: Problems of Coordination and Control during the Sino-Japanese War', 979–80.
3 Johnson, *Peasant Nationalism* and Selden, *The Yen'an Way*.
4 'H.H. Lehman to T.V.Soong' (9 February 1946), in *Liangzheng Shiliao*, VI, 241–2.
5 But see MacKinnon, 'Refugee Flight', 118–35.
6 Strauss, Julia 'Bureaucracy, Political Theatre, and the Accousation of Counter-revolutionaries', paper presented at the conference on Political Practice in Modern China, July 2002, Cambridge University, 5–6.

Bibliography

Abend, Hallett, *Chaos in China* (London: The Bodley Head, 1940).

Addington, Lary, *The Patterns of War since the Eighteenth Century* (Bloomington: Indiana University Press, 1994).

Alanbrooke, Field Marshall, in Alex Danchev and Dan Todman, eds., *War Diaries, 1939–1945: The Diaries of Field Marshall Lord Alanbrooke* (London: Weidenfield & Nicholson, 2001).

Aldrich, Richard, *Intelligence and the War against Japan: Britain, America, and the Politics of Secret Service* (Cambridge: Cambridge University Press, 2000).

Allen, Louis, *Burma: The Longest War* (London: Dent, 1984).

Andersson, Johan Gunnar, *China Fights the World*, tr. Arthur G. Chater (London: Kegan Paul & Co., 1938).

Bagby, Wesley, *The Eagle–Dragon Alliance: America's Relation with China in World War II* (Newark: University of Delaware Press, 1991).

Bai Chongxi Xiansheng Fangwen Jilu (Record of Interviews with Mr Bai Chongxi), Zhongyang Yanjiuyuan Jindaishi Yanjiusuo Koushu Lishi Congshu 4) (Oral History Collection of the Institute of Modern History of the Academia Sinica, No 4) (Taibei: Zhongyang Yanjiuyuan Jindaishi Yanjiusuo, 1989).

Baoluoting zai Zhongguo de Youguan Ziliao (Sources for Borodin in China), ed., Zhongguo Shehui Kexueyuan Jindaishi Yanjiusuo (Modern History Institute of the Chinese Academy of Social Sciences) (Beijing: Zhonguo Shehui Kexueyuan Chubanshe, 1982).

Barlow, Tani, ed., *Gender Politics in Modern China* (Durham: Duke University Press, 1993).

Bayly, Christopher, *The Birth of the Modern World: Global Connections and Comparison* (Oxford: Blackwell, forthcoming).

Beevor, Antony, *Stalingrad* (London: Penguin, 1998).

Beiyang Junfa (The Northern Warlords), eds, Zhang Bofeng and Li Zongyi (Wuhan: Wuhan Chubanshe, foreword 1989).

Beiyang Lujun Shiliao (Historical Materials for the Beiyang Army), eds, Zhang Bofeng *et al.* (Tianjin: Tianjin Renmin Chubanshe, 1987).

Belden, Jack, *China Shakes the World* (New York: Monthly Review Press, 1970).

Benton, Gregor, *China's Urban Revolutionaries: Explorations in the History of Chinese Trotskyism* (New Jersey: Humanities Press, 1996).

Berger, Gordon, 'Politics and Mobilisation in Japan', in Peter Duus, ed., *The Cambridge History of Japan*, VI, (Cambridge: Cambridge University Press) 97–153.

Bergere, Marie-Claire, *Sun Yatsen*, tr. Janet Lloyd (Stanford: Stanford University Press, 1998).

Bertram, James, *North China Front* (London: Macmillan, 1939).

Bickers, Robert, *Britain in China* (Manchester: Manchester University Press, 1999).

Bix, Herbert, *Hirohito and the Making of Modern Japan* (New York: HarperCollins, 2000).

Bond, Brian, *The Victorian Army and the Staff College, 1854–1914* (London: Eyre Methuen, 1972).

Borg, Dorothy, *The US and the Far Eastern Crisis* (Cambridge, MA: Harvard University Press, 1964).

Brandt, Conrad, *Stalin's Failure in China: 1924–1927* (Cambridge, MA: Harvard University Press, 1958).

Brewer, John, *Sinews of Power: War, Money, and the English State, 1688–1783* (London: Unwin Hyman, 1989).

Caizheng yu Jindai Lishi (Finance and Modern History), eds, Jindaishi Yanjiusuo Shehui Jingji Shi Zu (Section for Social and Economic History, Institute of Modern History) (Taibei: Zhongyang Yanjiuyuan Yanjiusuo, 1999).

Chang Jui-te, *Kangzhan Shiqi de Guojun Renshi* (The Personnel System of the National Army during the War of Resistance) (Taibei: Zhongyang Yanjiuyuan Jindaishi Yanjiusuo, 1993).

Chang Shih-ying, 'Longtan Zhanyi de Pingjia yu Fansi' (Evaluation of and Reflections on the Longtan Battle), *Zhongguo Junshi Xuehui Jikan*, II (1997), 147–80.

Chang Yü-fa, *Zhongguo Xiandai Shi* (A History of Modern China) (Taibei: Donghua Shuju, 1996).

Chiang Yung-ching, 'Xi'an Shibian Qian Zhang Xueliang Suowei "Yi Er Yue Nei Ding You Biandong" He Zhi' (What Did Zhang Xueliang Mean When He Said 'There Will Be Change in One or Two Months'), in *Jindaishi Yanjiu*, I (1997), 266–72.

Chen Duxiu Shuxin Ji (Chen Duxiu's Letters), ed., Shui Ru (Beijing: Xinhua Chubanshe, 1987).

Chen Feng, *Qingdai Junfei Yanjiu* (Qing Military Finance) (Wuhan: Wuhan Daxue Chubanshe, 1992).

Chen Jieru, edited and introduced by Lloyd Eastman, *Chiang Kaishek's Secret Past: the Memoir of his Life and Times*, (Boulder: Westview, 1993).

Chen, Jerome, *Yuan Shih-kai, 1859–1916: Brutus Assumes the Purple* (Stanford: Stanford University Press, 1961).

Chen Lifu, *Storm Clouds Over China: The Memoir of Ch'en Li-fu, 1900–1993*, eds, Sidney Chang and Ramon Myers (Stanford: Hoover Institute Press, 1994).

Chen Ronghua and He Youliang, *Lushan Junguan Xuanliantuan* (The Lushan Officers Training Regiment) (Nanchang: Nanchang Renmin Chubanshe, 1987).

Chen Tiejian, 'Xi'an Shibian Jianlun' (Some Comments on the Xi'an Incident), *Lishi Yanjiu*, I (February 1997), 140–63.

Ch'en Yung-fa, 'The Blooming Poppy under the Red Sun', in Hans van de Ven and Tony Saich, eds, *New Perspectives on the Chinese Communist Revolution* (Armonk: M. E. Sharpe, 1995), 263–98.

——, *Making Revolution* (Stanford: Stanford University Press, 1986).

Chennault, Claire, *Way of a Fighter* (New York: Putnam, 1949).

Ch'i Hsi-sheng, *Nationalist China at War: Military Defeats and Politics Collapse, 1937–45* (Ann Arbor: University of Michigan Press, 1982).

——, *Warlord Politics in China, 1916–28* (Stanford: Stanford University Press, 1976).

Chi Jingde, *Zhongguo Dui Ri Kangzhan Sunshi Diaocha Shi Shu* (An Account of Investigations into China's Losses during the War of Resistance) (Taibei, Guoshiguan, 1987).

Chiang Kaishek, *Zeng Hu Zhi Bing Yulu* (Saying of Zeng Guofan and Hu Linyi about the Military) (Chengdu: Bashu Shushe, 1995). Chiang expanded an earlier version by the Yunnanse warlord Cai E.

Ch'ien Tuan-sheng, *The Government and Politics of China* (Cambridge, MA: Harvard University Press, 1950).

The China White Paper, ed., Department of State (US), introduction by Lyman Vanslyke (Stanford: Stanford University Press, 1970).

Chow, Rey, *Women and Chinese Modernity: The Politics of Reading between East and West* (Minneapolis: University of Minnesota Press, 1991).

Chow Tse-tsung, *The May Fourth Movement: Intellectual Revolution in Modern China* (Cambridge, MA: Harvard University Press, 1960).

Coble, Parks, *Facing Japan: Chinese Politics and Japanese Imperialism, 1931–1937* (Cambridge, MA: Harvard University Press, 1991).

Coble, Parks, *The Shanghai Capitalists and the National Government, 1927–1937* (Cambridge, MA: Harvard University Press, 1980).

Cohen, Paul, *History in Three Keys: The Boxers as Event, Experience, and Myth* (New York: Columbia University Press, 1997).

Churchill, Winston, *The Second World War* (London: Cassell, 1950).

Conolly, Chris, 'China and Britain between Cairo and Tehran', BA dissertation, Cambridge University, 2000.

Coox, Alvin, *Nomonhan: Japan against Russia* (Stanford: Stanford University Press, 1985).

——, *Unfought War* (San Diego: San Diego State University Press, 1992).

Dai Ruxian and Li Liangzhi, *Kangzhan Shigi de Wenhua Jiaogu* (Beijing: Beijing Chubanshe, 1995).

Daruvala, Susan, *Zhou Zuoren and an Alternative Response to Modernity* (Cambridge, MA: Harvard University Press, 2000).

Davies, John Paton, *Dragon by the Tail: British, Japanese, and Russian Encounters with China and One Another* (London: Robson Books, 1974).

DeVido, Elise, *The Making of the Communist Party State in Shandong Province, 1972–1952* (Cambridge, MA: Harvard University Press, 1995).

Dikötter, Frank, *The Discourse of Race in Modern China* (London: Hurst, 1992).

Dirlik, Arif, 'The Ideological Foundations of the New Life Movement', *Journal of Asian Studies* 34: 4 (1975), 945–80.

——, *The Origins of Chinese Communism* (Oxford: Oxford University Press, 1989).

Domes, Jurchen, *Vertagte Revolution: Die Politik der Kuomintang China, 1923–1937* (Berlin: Walter de Gruyter, 1969).

Dorn, Frank, *The History of the Sino-Japanese War: From Marco Polo Bridge to Pearl Harbor* (New York: Macmillan, 1974).

——, *Walkout: With Stilwell in Burma* (New York: Crowell, 1971).

Drea, Edward, *In the Service of the Emperor: Essays on the Imperial Japanese Army* (Lincoln, Nebraska: University of Nebraska Press, 1998).

Dreyer, Edward, *China at War, 1901–1949* (London: Longman, 1995).

Duara, Prasenjit, *Culture, Power, and the State: Rural North China, 1900–1942* (Stanford: Stanford University Press, 1988).

Dutta, Krishna, *Rabindranath Tagore: The Myriad Minded Man* (London: Bloomsbury, 1995).

Duus, Peter, ed., *The Cambridge History of Japan, Vol VI: The Twentieth Century* (Cambridge: Cambridge University Press, 1985).

Eastman, Lloyd, *The Abortive Revolution: China under Nationalist Rule* (Cambridge, MA: Harvard University Press, 1974).

——, 'Nationalist China during the Nanking Decade, 1927–1937', in John Fairbank and Denis Twitchett, eds, *The Cambridge History of China*, XIII (Cambridge: Cambridge University Press, 1986) 116–67.

——, 'Nationalist China during the Sino-Japanese War', in John Fairbank and Denis Twitchett, eds, *The Cambridge History of China*, XIII (Cambridge: Cambridge University Press, 1986) 547–608.

——, *Seeds of Destruction: Nationalist China in War and Revolution* (Stanford: Stanford University Press, 1984).

Eksteins, Modris, *Rites of Spring: The Great War and the Birth of the Modern Age* (London: Black Swan, 1990).

Elleman, Bruce, *Diplomacy and Deception: The Secret History of Sino-Soviet Diplomatic Relations, 1917–1927* (Armonk: M. E. Sharpe, 1997).

——, *Modern Chinese Warfare, 1795–1989* (London: Routledge, 2001).

Epstein, Israel, *The People's War* (London: Victor Gallancz, 1939).

Fairbank, John and Denis Twitchett, eds, *The Cambridge History of China*, X, XII, XIII, (Cambridge: Cambridge University Press, 1978, 1983, 1986).

Fang Guo'an, 'Qingmo Minchu Zhongguo Junguomin Jiaoyu zhi Yanjiu' (Educating Military Citizens in the Late Qing and Early Republic), MPhil Dissertation, Chinese Culture University, Taibei, no date.

Farmer, Rhodes, *Shanghai Harvest: A Diary of Three Years in the China War* (London: Museum Press, 1945).

Faure, David, *The Rural Economy of Pre-Liberation China: Trade Expansion and Peasant Livelihood in Jiangsu and Guangdong, 1870–1937* (Hong Kong: Oxford University Press, 1989).

Fewsmith, Joseph, *Party, State, and Local Elites in Republican China: Merchant Organisation and Politics in Shanghai, 1890–1930* (Honolulu: Hawaii University Press, 1985).

Figes, Orlando, *The Pity of War* (London: Allen Lane The Penguin Press, 1998).

Fitzgerald, John, *Awakening China: Politics, Culture, and Class in the Chinese Revolution* (Stanford: Stanford University Press, 1996).

Fogel, Joshua, ed., *The Nanjing Massacre in History and Historiography* (Berkeley: University of California Press, 2000).

Foreign Relations of the United States, ed., Department of State, Historical Office (Washington: US Government Printing Office, 1956–1967).

'Fu Bingchang Diary', private possession of Mrs Yee Wah Gates. Excerpts used gratefully with permission of Mrs Gates.

Fuller, Willam C., *Strategy and Power in Russia, 1600–1914* (New York: Macmillan, 1992).

Fung, Edmund, *The Military Dimension of the Chinese Revolution: The New Army and its Role in the 1911 Revolution* (Canberra: Australia National University Press, 1981).

Furet, Francois, *The Passing of an Illusion: The Idea of Communism in the Twentieth Century*, tr. Deborah Furet (Chicago: Chicago University Press, 1999).

Furth, Charlotte, *The Limits of Change: Essays on Conservative Alternatives in Republican China* (Cambridge, MA: Harvard University Press, 1976).

Furuya, Keiji, *Chiang Kai-shek: His Life and Times* (New York: St John's, 1981).

Fussell, Paul, *The Great War and Modern Memory* (London: Oxford University Press, 1975).

Galbiati, Fernando, *P'eng P'ai and the Hai-lu-feng Soviet* (Stanford: Stanford University Press, 1985).

Gao Ming, 'Taierzhuang Zhanyi de Guoji Yingxiang yu Guonei Diwei Wenti' (The International Influence of the Battle of Taierzhuang and its Domestic Position), *Minguo Yanjiu*, IV (2001), 144–9.

Garver, John, *Chinese–Soviet Relations, 1937–1945: The Diplomacy of Nationalism* (Oxford: Oxford University Press, 1988).

Getty, J. Arch and Oleg Naumov, *The Road to Terror: Stalin and the Self-Destruction of the Bolsheviks, 1932–1939* (New Haven: Yale University Press, 1999).

Gilbert, Martin, *A History of the Twentieth Century: Volume II, 1933–1951* (London: HarperCollins, 1998).

Green, O. M., *China's Struggle with the Dictators* (London: Hutchinson & Co., 1941).

Goodman, Bryna, *Native Place, City, and Nation: Regional Networks and Identities, 1853–1937* (Berkeley: University of California Press, 1995).

Graff, David and Robin Higham, eds, *A Military History of China* (Boulder: Westview, 2002).

Grieder, Jerome, *Hu Shih and the Chinese Renaissance: Liberalism in the Chinese Revolution* (Cambridge, MA: Harvard University Press, 1970).

Gongchan Guoji Youguan Zhongguo Geming de Wenxian Ziliao (Documents of the Communist International Concerning the Chinese Revolution), ed., Zhongguo Shehui Kexueyuan Jindaishi Yanjiusuo (The Modern History Institute of the Chinese Academy of Social Sciences) (Beijing: Zhongguo Shehui Kexueyuan Chubanshe, 1981).

Guangdong Qu Dang Tuan Yanjiu Shiliao (Historical Sources for the Party and Youth League in the Guangdong Region), eds, Guangdongsheng Dang'anguan, Zhonggong Guangdongsheng Dangshi Yanjiu Weiyuanhui (The Guangdong Provincial Archives and the CCP Guangdong Party History Committee) (Guangzhou: Guangdong Renmin Chubanshe, 1983).

Guo Gong Liang Dang Guanxi Shi (A History of KMT CPP Relations), eds, Wang Gong'an and Mao Lei (Wuhan: Wuhan Chubanshe, 1988).

Guofu Quanshu (Collected Writings of the Father of the Nation), ed., Zhang Qiyun (Taibei: Guofang Yanjiuyuan, 1960).

Guomin Canzhenghui Ziliao (Sources for the National People's Consultative Congress), ed., Sichuan Daxue Ma Lie Jiaoyanshi (Marxism Leninism Education and Research Department of Sichuan University) (Chongqing: Sichuan Renmin Chubanshe, 1984).

Guomin Zhengfu Junzheng Zuzhi Shiliao (Historical Sources for the Organisation of Military Administration of the National Government), ed., Zhou Meihua (Taibei: Guoshiguan, 1996).

Guomindang Zhengfu Zhengzhi Zhidu Dang'an Shiliao Xuanbian (Compilation of Archival Sources for the KMT Government's Political System), ed., Zhonguuo Di'er Lishi Dang'anguan (Hefei: Anhui Jiaoyu Chubanshe, 1994).

ter Haar, Barend, *The White Lotus Teachings in Chinese Religious History* (Leiden: Brill, 1992).

Harrison, Henrietta, *The Making of the Republican Citizen: Political Ceremonies and Symbols in China: 1911–1929* (Oxford: Oxford University Press, 2000).

Haslam, Jonathan, *The Soviet Union and the Threat from the East, 1933–1941: Moscow, Tokyo, and the Prelude to the Pacific War* (Pittsburgh: University of Pittsburgh Press, 1992).

Hatao, Ikuhiko, 'Continental Expansion, 1905–1946', in Peter Duus, ed., *The Cambridge History of Japan*, VI, (Cambridge: Cambridge University Press) 271–314.

Hay, Stephen, *Asian Ideas of East and West: Tagore and his Critics in Japan, China, and India* (Cambridge, MA: Harvard University Press, 1970).

Haynes, John Earl and Harvey Kehr: *Venona: Decoding Soviet Espionage in America* (Hew Haven: Yale University Press, 1999).

He Yingqin, *Ri Jun Qin Hua Banian Kangzhan Shi* (History of the Eight Year War of Resistance Against Japanese Aggression) (Taibei: Liming Wenhua Shiye Gongsi, 1982).

Heinrichs, Waldo, *Threshold of War: Franklin D. Roosevelt and the American Entry into World War II* (Oxford: Oxford University Press, 1988).

Henriot, Christian, *Prostituion and Sexuality in Shanghai* (Cambridge: Cambridge University Press, 2001).

——, *Shanghai, 1927–1937: Municipal Power, Locality, and Modernisation* (Berkeley: University of California Press, 1991).

Heinrichs, Waldo, *Threshold of War: Franklin D. Roosevelt and the American Entry into World War II* (Oxford: Oxford University Press, 1988).

Herzstein, Robert E, *Henry Luce: A Political Portrait of the Man who Created the American Way* (New York: Macmillan, 1994).

Hinsley, Hillory, *British Intelligence in the Second World War: Abridged Edition* (London: Her Majesty's Stationary Office, 1993).

Hobsbawm, Eric, *Age of Extremes: The Short Twentieth Century* (London: Michael Joseph, 1994).

Hofheinz, Roy, *The Broken Wave: The Chinese Communist Peasant Movement* (Cambridge, MA: Harvard University Press, 1977).

Holsti, K. J, *The State, War, and the State of War* (Cambridge: Cambridge University Press, 1996).

Honig, Emily, *Creating Ethnicity: Subei People in Shanghai, 1850–1950* (New Haven: Yale University Press, 1992).

Ho Ping-ti, *Studies on the Population of China*, (Cambridge, MA: Harvard University Press, 1959).

Hou Kunhong, 'Kangzhan Shiqi de Zhongyang Caizheng yu Difang Caizheng' (Central and Local Finance during the War of Resistance), PhD dissertation National Chengchi University, Taiwan, 1996.

——, 'Kangzhan Shiqi de Liangshi Gongqiu Wenti Yanjiu' (The Supply and Demand of Cereals during the War of Resistance), MA dissertation, National Chengchi University, Taiwan, 1988.

Hou Yijie, *Yuan Shikai Quanzhuan* (A Complete Biography of Yuan Shikai) (Beijing: Dangdai Zhongguo Chubanshe, 1994).

Hsia Chang, Maria, *The Chinese Blue Shirt Society: Fascism, and Developmental Nationalism* (Berkeley: University of California Press, 1985).

——, ' "Fascism" and Modern China', *The China Quarterly* 79 (1979), 553–567.

Hsiao Kung-chuan, *Rural China: Imperial Control in the Nineteenth Century* (Seattle: University of Washington Press, 1960).

Hsiao Liang-lin, *China's Foreign Trade Statistics: 1864–1949* (Cambridge, MA: Harvard University Press, 1949.

Hsiung, James and Steven Levine, eds, *China's Bitter Victory: The War with Japan* (Armonk: M.E. Sharpe, 1992).

Hsu, Immanuel, 'The Great Policy Debate in China, 1874: Maritime Defence versus Frontier Defence', *Harvard Journal of Asian Studies* XXV (1965), 212–28.

Hsu Long-hsuen and Chang Ming-kai, *History of the Sino-Japanese War*, tr., Wen Ha Hsing (Taibei: Chung Wu Publishing Co, 1972).

Huang Meizhen, Zhang Jishun, and Jin Guangyou, 'Jianguo Yilai Kang Ri Zhanzheng Yanjiu Pingshu' (The Historiography of the War of Resistance Since the Founding of the PRC), *Minguo Dang'an* X (1987), 95–110.

Huang Qiang, *Baojia Lianggui* (Great Baojia Programme) (no place, 1935).

Huang, Ray, 'Chiang Kaishek and his Diary', I and II, in *Chinese Studies in History*, XXIX: 1 and 2 (Fall–Winter 1995/6) and XXX: 1 and 2 (Fall–Winter 1996–7).

Huangpu Junxiao Shiliao (Historical Sources for the Whampoa Academy), ed., Guangdong Geming Lishi Bowuguan (Guangdong Revolutionary History Museum) (Guangzhou: Guangdong Renmin Chubanshe, 1982).

Huiyi Guomindang Zhengfu Ziyuan Weiyuanhui (Recollections of the KMT Government's NRC), ed., Quanguo Zhengxie Wenshi Ziliao Weiyuanhui (Committee for Materials for Culture and History, National People's Consultative Congress) (Beijing: Zhongguo Wenshi Chubanshe, 1988).

Hung, Chang-tai, *War and Popular Culture: Resistance in Modern China, 1937–1945* (Berkeley: University of California Press, 1994).

Hyde, Robin, *Dragon Rampant* (London: Hurst and Blackett, 1938).

Ienaga, Saburo, *Japan's Last War: World War II and the Japanese, 1931–1945* (Oxford: Oxford University Press, 1979).

Indian Council of Medical Researach, *Nutrient Requirements and Recommended Dietary Allowance for Indians* (India, Hyderabad, 1994).

Iriye, Akira, *After Imperialism: The Search for a New Order in the Far East, 1921–1931* (New York: Atheneum, 1969).

——, 'Japanese Aggression and China's International Position', in John Fairbank and Denis Twitchett, eds, *The Cambridge History of China* XIII, (Cambridge: Cambridge University Press) 492–546.

Isaacs, Harold, *Scratches on Our Mind: American Images of China and India* (New York: John Day, 1958).

——, *The Tragedy of the Chinese Revolution* (Stanford: Stanford University Press, 1951).

Jackson, Robert, *The Guinness Book of Air Warfare* (Enfield: Guinness Publishing, 1993).

Jacobs, Dan, *Borodin: Stalin's Man in China* (Cambridge, MA: Harvard University Press, 1981).

Jeans, Roger B., *Roads Not Taken: The Struggle of Opposition Parties in Twentieth Century China* (Boulder: Westview Press, 1992).

Jia Shiyi, Ma Yinchu *et al.*, *Kangzhan yu Caizheng Jingrong* (The War of Resistance and Finance) (Chongqing: Duli Chubanshe, 1938). KMT Archives 504/132.

Jiang Baili Xiansheng Quanji (The Collected Works of Mr Jiang Baili), ed., Jaing Fucong and Xue Guangqian (Taibei: Zhuanji Wenxue, 1971).

Jiang Jieshi Nianpu (Chronological Biography of Chiang Kaishek), ed., Wan Renyuan, Fang Qingqiu (Beijing: Dang'an Chubanshe, 1994).

Jiang Kefu, *Minguo Junshishi Luegao* (Draft Military History of the Republic) (Beijing: Zhonghua Shuju, 1992).

Jin Chongji, *Mao Zedong Zhuan, 1893–1949* (Biography of Mao Zedong, 1893–1949) (Beijing: Zhongyang Wenxian Chubanshe, 1996).

——, *Zhou Enlai Zhuan* (Biography of Zhou Enlai) (Beijing: Zhongyang Wenxian Chubanshe, 1996).

Johnson, Chalmers, *Peasant Nationalism and Communist Power: The Emergence of Revolutionary Power* (Stanford: Stanford University Press, 1963).

Johnston, Alistair Iain, *Cultural Realism: Strategic Culture and Grand Strategy in Chinese History* (Princeton: Princeton University Press, 1995).

Jordan, Donald, *The Northern Expedition: China's Revolution of 1926–1928* (Honolulu: University Press of Hawaii, 1976).

Jordan, Donald, *China's Trial by Fire: The Shanghai War of 1932* (Michigan: University of Michigan Press, 2001).

Jun Tian, *Zhongguo Baojia Zhidu* (The Chinese Baojia System) (Shanghai: Shangwu Yinshuguan 1934).

Kang Ri Zhanzheng Shiqi Guomindang Zhanchang Shiliao Xuanbian (Compilation of Historical Sources for the KMT Fronts during the War of Resistance), ed., Zhejiangsheng Zhongguo Guomindang Lishi Yanjiuzu (Department for KMT History of Zhejiang Province) (no details).

Kang Ri Zhanzheng Zhengmian Zhanchang (The Battlefields at the Front during the War of Resistance), ed., Zhongguo Di'er Lishi Dang'anguan (Jiangsu Guji Chubanshe, 1987).

Kaiser, David, *Politics and War: European Conflict from Philip II to Hitler* (London: I. B. Taurus, 1990).

Kang Youwei Zhenglun Ji (The Political Writings of Kang Youwei), ed., Tang Zhijun (Beijing: Zhonghua Shuju, 1981).

Katz, Daniel, 'The Polls and the 1944 Election', *Public Opinion Quarterly* VIII (1944–5).

Keegan, John, *The Face of Battle* (London: Pimlico, 1991).

——, *A History of Warfare* (London: Hutchinson, 1993).

——, *The Mask of Command* (London: Cape 1987).

——, *The Second World War* (London: Hutchinson, 1989).

Kimball, Warren, ed., *Churchill and Roosevelt: The Complete Correspondence* (Princeton: Princeton University Press, 1984).

Kirby, William, *Germany and Republican China* (Stanford: Stanford University Press, 1984).

——, 'The Chinese War Economy', in James Hsiung and Steven Levine, eds, *China's Bitter Victory: The war with Japan* (Armork: M. E. Sharpe, 1992), 185–212.

Klehr, Harvey, John Earl Haynes, and Kyrill Anderson, *The Secret World of American Communism* (New Haven: Yale University Press, 1995).

Kolko, Gabriel, *Century of War: Politics, Conflicts, and Society since 1914* (New York: New Press, 1994).

Kuo, Warren, *Analytical History of the Chinese Communist Party* (Taipei: Institute of International Relations, 1971).

Kuhn, Philip, 'Local Self-Government under the Republic', in Frederic Wakeman and Carolyn Grant, eds, *Conflict and Control in Late Imperial China* (Berkely: University of California Press), 257–98.

——, *The Origins of the Modern Chinese State* (Stanford: Stanford University Press, 2001).

Lai Xinxia, *Beiyang Junfa Shigao* (Draft History of the Northern Warlords) (Beijing, 1983).

Larrabee, Eric, *Commander-in-Chief: Franklin Delano Roosevelt, His Lieutenant, and their War* (London: Deutsch, 1987).

Lary, Diana, 'Defending China: The Battles of the Xuzhou Campaign', in van de Ven, ed., *Warfare in Chinese History,* (Leiden: Brill, 2000) 398–427.

——, *Region and Nation: The Kwangsi Clique in Chinese Politics, 1925–1937* (Cambridge: Cambridge University Press, 1985).

——and Stephen MacKinnon, eds, *Scars of War: The Impact of Warfare on Modern China* (Vancouver: University of British Columbia Press, 2001).

League of Nations, *Statistical Information on the Trade in Arms, Ammunition, and Materials of War* (Geneva, 1926–9).

Lee, Leo, *The Romantic Generation of Modern Chinese Writers* (Cambridge, MA: Harvard University Press, 1973).

——, *Shanghai Modern* (Cambridge, MA: Harvard University Press, 1999).

Lei Haizong, *Zhongguo de Wenhua yu Zhongguo de Bing* (Chinese Culture and the Chinese Military) (Changsha, Yuelu Chubanshe, 1989).

Levine, Steven, *Anvil of Victory: The Communist Revolution in Manchuria, 1945–1948* (New York: Columbia University Press, 1987).

Lewis, Mark, 'The Han Abolition of Universal Military Service', in Hans van de Ven, ed., *History of Chinese Warfare*, (Leiden: Brill) 33–76.

——, *Sanctioned Violence in Ancient China* (Albany: State University of New York Press, 1990).

Li Haiwen, 'Xi'an Shibian Qian Guo Gong Liang Dang Jiechu he Tanpan de Lishi Guocheng' (The Historical Process of Meetings and Negotiations between the KMT and the CCP before the Xi'an Incident), in *Wenxian he Yanjiu*, 1989 collected edition, 350–61.

Li Liangzhi, 'Zhongguo Gongchandang Quanmin Kangzhang Zhuzhang de Tichu ji qi Yanbian' (The CCP Proposal for National Resistance by All the People and its Evolution), *Dang de Wenxian*, IV (1995), 27–33.

Li Weihan, *Huiyi yu Yanjiu* (Memoirs and Studies) (Beijing: Zhonggong Dangshi Ziliao Chubanshe, 1986).

Li Wenhai, *Zhongguo Jindai Shi Da Zaihuang* (The Ten Great Natural Disasters of Modern China) (Shanghai: Shanghai Renmin Chubanshe, 1994).

Li Tsung-jen, *The Memoirs of Li Tsung-jen*, Te-kong Tong and Li Tsung-jen, eds (Boulder: Westview Press, 1979).

Li Xin, 'Beiyang Junfa de Xingwang' (The Rise and Fall of the Northern Warlords), in Li Xin and Li Zongyi, eds, *Zhonghua Minguo Shi Di'er Bian: Beiyang Zhengfu Tongzhi Shiqi* (Volume Two of the History of the Chinese Republic: The Period of Beiyang Government Rule) (Beijing: Zhonghua Shuju, 1987).

Li Zongren, see Li Tsung-jen.

Liang Hsi-huey, *The Sino-German Connection: Alexander von Falkenhausen between China and Germany, 1900–1941* (Assen: Van Gorcum, 1978).

Liang Qichao, *Yinbingshi Congzhu* (Collected Writings from the Ice-Cream Parlour) (Shanghai, Shangwu Yinshuguan, 1916).

Liangzheng Shiliao (Historical Sources for the Grain Administration), ed. Hou Kunhong (Taibei: Guoshiguan, 1988).

Lin Maosheng, *Chen Duxiu Wenzhang Xuanbian* (Collected Articles by Chen Duxiu) (Beijing: Sanlian, 1984).

Lin Meili, 'Kangzhan Shiqi de Huobi Zhanzheng' (The Currency War of the War of Resistance), PhD Dissertation, Guoli Shifan Daixue, Taiwan, 1995).

Lin Yü-sheng, *The Crisis of Chinese Consciousness: Radical Anti-Traditionalism in the May Fourth Movement* (Madison: University of Wisconsin Press, 1979).

Link, Perry, *Mandarin Ducks and Butterflies* (Berkeley: University of California Press, 1981).

Liu Fenghan, *Qingji Ziqiang Yundong yu Junshi Chubu Gaige* (The Late Qing's Self-Strengthening Movement and Initial Military Reform), in Zhongyang Yanjiuyuan Jindaishi Yanjiusuo (Institute of Modern theory of the Academia Sinica), eds, *Qingji Ziqiang Yundong Yantaohui Lunwen Ji* (Proceedings of a Conference on the Late Qing's Self-Strengthening Movement) (Taibei: Institute of Modern History, 1988), 343–95.

——, 'Wan Qing Xinjun Lianbian ji Zhihui Jigou de Zuzhi yu Bianqian' (The Training of the New Army in the late Qing, the Organisation of its Command Institutions, and their Evolution), *Jindaishi Yanjiusuo Jikan*, IX (1980), 201–53.

Liu, Frederick Fu, *A Military History of Modern China, 1926–1956* (Princeton: Princeton University Press, 1956).

Liu, Kwang-ching, 'The Ch'ing Restoration', John Fairbank and Denis Twitchett, eds, *The Cambridge History of China*, X, 409–490.

Lovell, Julia, 'China's Search for a Nobel Prize in Literature: Literature and National and Cultural Identity in Twentieth Century China', PhD dissertation, Cambridge University, 2002.

Lowenthal, John, 'Venona and Alger Hiss', *Intelligence and National Security* XV: 3 (2000), 98–130.

Lü Fangshan, *Geming zhi Zaiqi* (The Second Rise of Revolution) (Taibei: Zhongyang Yanjiuyuan Jindaishi Yanjiuyuan, 1989).

Luk, Michael, *The Origins of Chinese Bolshevism: An Ideology in the Making* (Hong Kong: Oxford University Press, 1990).

Luo Erh-kang, 'Qingji Bing Wei Jiang You de Qiyuan' (The Origins of Private Armies in the Qing), *Zhongguo Shehui Jingji Shi Jikan* V: 2 (1937), 235–50.

Luo Ming, 'Guanyu Beifa Zhanzheng de Junfei Wenti' (The Warlord Issue during the Northern Expedition), *Minguo Dang'an* XXX (1992), 76–83.

Ma Zhendu, *Cansheng: Kangzhan Zhengmian Zhanchang Daxieyi* (Bitter Victory: Impressionistic Account of the Battlefields at the Front during the War of Resistance) (Guilin: Guangxi Shifan Daxue Chubanshe, 1993).

——and Qi Rugao, *Di Hu? You Hu?: Deguo yu Zhongguo Kangzhan* (Friend or Enemy: Germany and the Chinese War of Resistance) (Guilin: Guangxi Shifan Daxue Chubanshe, 1997).

McCord, Edward, *The Power of the Gun: The Emergence of Modern Chinese Warlordism* (Berkeley: University of California Press, 1993).

——, 'Warlordism in Early Republican China', in David Graff and Robin Higham, eds., *A Military History of Modern China*, 175–92.

——, 'Warlords against Warlordism', *Modern Asian Studies* XXX: 4 (1996), 795–892.

McNeill, William, *The Pursuit of Power: Technology, Armed Force, and Society since AD1000* (Oxford: Blackwell, 1983).

Machiavelli, Nicolo, *The Prince* (Oxford: Oxford University Press, 1998).

MacKinnon, Stephen, *Power and Politics in Late Imperial China: Yuan Shikai in Beijing and Tianjin, (1901–1908)* (Berkeley: University of California Press, 1980).

——, 'Refugee Flight at the Outset of the Anti-Japanese War', in Diana Lary and Stephen MacKinnon, eds, *Scars of War: The Impact of Warfare on Modern China* (Vancouver: University of British Columbia Press, 2001), 118–35.

——, 'The Tragedy of Wuhan', in *Modern Asian Studies* XXX: 4 (1996), 931–43.

Mallory, Walter Hampton, *China: Land of Famine* (New York: American Geographical Society Special Publications 6, 1926).

Mann, Susan, *Local Merchants and the Chinese Bureaucracy* (Stanford: Stanford University Press, 1987).

Mao Zedong, 'On Protracted War', in *Selected Works of Mao Zedong* (Beijing: Foreign Languages Press, 1967), 113–94.

Mao Zedong Dushu Biji (Mao Zedong's Reading Notes), ed. Chen Jin, (Guangzhou: Guangdong Renmin Chubanshe, 1996).

Mao Zedong Junshi Wenji (Collected Military Writings of Mao Zedong) (Beijing: Junshi Kexueyuan Chubanshe, 1993).

Mao Zedong Zaoqi Wengao (Early Writings of Mao Zedong) (Changsha: Hunan Chubanshe, 1990).

Martin, Brian, *The Shanghai Green Gang: Politics and Organised Crime, 1919–1937* (Berkeley: University of California Press, 1996).

——, 'Shield of Collaboration', *Intelligence and National Security* XVI: 4 (2000), 89–148.

Miandian Gonglue Zuozhan (The Burma Offensive) , tr. Zeng Qinggui (Taibei: Guofangbu Shizheng Bianyi Ju, 1997).

Michael, Franz, 'Regionalism in Nineteenth Century China', in Stanley Spector (ed.), *Li Hung-chang and the Huai Army: A Study in Nineteenth Century Chinese Regionalism* (Seattle: University of Washington Press, 1964).

Minguo Renwu Da Cidian (Biographical Dictionary of the Republic) (Shijiazhuang: Hebei Renmin Chubanshe, 1991).

Montgomery, M., *Imperialist Japan: The Yen to Dominate* (London: Methuen, 1987).

Myers, Ramon, 'The Agrarian System', in John Fairbank and Denis Twitchett, eds, *The Cambridge History of China* XIII, 230–69.

Nakamura, Takafusa, 'Depresssion, Recovery, and War, 1925–1945', in Peter Duus, ed., *Cambridge History of Japan*, VI, 451–93.

Nanchang Xingying Zhaoji Di'er Ci Bao'an Huiyi Jilu (Records of the Second Security Conference Convened by the Nanchang Field Headquarters), in Shen Yun-lung, ed., *Jindai Zhongguo Shiliao Congkan* (Collectanea of Modern Chinese History), vol. 520 (Taibei: Wenhai Chubanshe, 1966–73). Original date 1935.

Nanjing Guomin Zhengfu Jishi (Chronology of the Nanjing National Government), ed., Zhu Hanguo (no place, Anhui Renmin Chubanshe, 1993).

Ownby, David, *Brotherhoods and Secret Societies in Early and Mid Qing China: the Formation of a Tradition* (Stanford: Stanford University Press, 1996).

Pai Ch'ung-hsi, see Bai Chongxi.

Pantsov, Aleksandr Vadimovich, *The Bolsheviks and the Chinese Revolution* (Richmond: Curzon, 2000).

The Papers of George Catlett Marshall, ed. Larry Bland (Baltimore: Johns Hopkins University Press, 1991).

Paret, Peter, *Understanding War: Essays on Clausewitz and the History of Military Power* (Princeton: Princeton University Press, 1992).

——, 'The History of War and the New Military History', in Peter Paret, ed., *Understanding War: Essays on Clausewitz and the History of Military Power*, 209–26.

Parker, Geoffrey, *Cambridge Illustrated History of Warfare* (Cambridge: Cambridge University Press, 1995).

——, *The Military Revolution: Military Innovation and the Rise of the West, 1500–1800* (Cambridge: Cambridge University Press, 1996).

Pepper, Suzanne, *Civil War in China: The Political Struggle, 1945–1949* (Berkeley: University of California Press, 1978).

Perry, Elizabeth, *Rebels and Revolutionaries in North China, 1845–1945* (Stanford: Stanford University Press, 1980).

Pick, Daniel, *War Machine: The Rationalisation of Slaughter in the Modern Age* (New Haven: Yale University Press, 1993).

Pogue, Forrest, in Larry Bland, ed., *George C. Marshall: Interviews and Reminiscences for Forrest C. Pogue*, (Lexintong, Virginia: The George C. Marshall Foundation, 1991).

Pong, David, *Shen Pao-chen and China's Modernisation in the Nineteenth Century* (Cambridge: Cambridge University Press, 1994).

Qingmo Xinjun Bianlian Yange (The History of the Training of the New Army in the Late Qing), ed., Zhongguo Shehui Kexueyuan Jindaishi Yanjiusuo Zhonghua Minguo Shi Zu (Department of the History of the Republic, Insitute of Modern History, Chinese Academy of Social Sciences) (Beijing: Zhonghua Shuju, 1978).

Qiu Shulin, *Xinbian Zhongguo Tongshi* (A New General History of China) (Fuzhou: Fujian Renmin Chubanshe, 1996).

Radtke, Kurt, *China's Relations with Japan, 1945–1983: The Role of Liao Chengzhi* (Manchester: Manchester University Press, 1990).

Rawlinson, John, *China's Struggle for Naval Development* (Cambridge, MA: Harvard University Press, 1967).

Rawski, Thomas, *Economic Growth in Pre-War China* (Berkeley: University of California Press, 1989).

Rand, Peter, *China Hands* (New York: Simon and Schuster, 1995).

Reynolds, Douglas, *China, 1898–1912: The Xinzheng Revolution and Japan* (Cambridge, MA: Harvard University Press, 1993).

Rich, Paul, 'Warlords, State Fragmentation, and the Dilemma of Humanitarian Intervention', *Small Wars and Insurgencies* X: 12 (1999).

Romanus, C. F. and R. Sunderland, *Stilwell's Command Problems, Stilwell's Mission to China* and *Time Runs out in CBI* (Washington, DC: Office of the Chief of Military History, 1956, 1953, 1958).

Saich, Tony, ed., *Origins of the First United Front in China: The Role of Sneevliet (Alias Maring)* (Leiden: Brill, 1991).

——, ed., *The Rise to Power of the CCP* (Armonk: M. E. Sharpe, 1996).

Sainsbury, Keith, *The Turning Point: Roosevelt, Stalin, Churchill, and Chiang Kaishek, 1943: The Moscow, Cairo, and Tehran Conferences* (Oxford: Oxford University Press).

Sbrega, J. *Anglo American Relations and Colonialism in East Asia, 1941–1945* (New York: Garland, 1983).

Schaller, Michael, *The US Crusade in China* (New York: Columbia University Press, 1979).

Schoppa, Keith, 'Self-Inflicted Wounds', paper presented at a Scars of War conference, Univeristy of British Columbia, 1998.

Schram, Stuart, 'Mao Tse-tung's Thought to 1949', in John Fairbank and Denis Twitchett, eds, *The Cambridge History of China*, XIII, (Cambridge: Cambridge University Press), 789–870.

——, *The Political Thought of Mao Tse-tung* (New York: Praeger, 1966).

——, ed., *Mao's Road to Power*, II (Armonk: M. E. Sharpe, 1994).

Schwarcz, Vera, *The Chinese Enlightenment: Intellectuals and the Legacy of the May Fourth Movement of 1919* (Berkeley: University of California Press, 1986).

Schwartz, Benjamin, *Chinese Communism and the Rise of Mao* (Cambridge, MA: Harvard University Press, 1951).

Selden, Mark, *The Yen'an Way in Revolutionary China* (Cambridge, MA: Harvard University Press, 1971).

Service, John, *The Amerasia Papers: Some Problems in the History of US China Relations* (Berkeley, University of California Press, 1971).

Shai, Aron, *Britain and China, 1941–1947: Imperial Momentum* (London: Macmillan, 1984).

Shanhou Huiyi (The Rehabilitation Conference), ed., Zhongguo Di'er Lishi Dang'anguan (Beijing: Dang'an Chubanshe, 1985).

Shao Minghuang, 'Riben Zuihou Qiuhe de Huanmeng: Miao Bin de Gongzuo' (Japan's Last Peace Illusion), paper presented at the Fourth International Conference on Republican History, Nanjing, September 2000.

Shaw Yu-ming, *An American Missionary in China: John Leighton Stuart and Chinese–American Relations* (Cambridge, MA: Harvard University Press, 1992).

Shen Huaiyu, 'Xingzheng Ducha Zhuanyuan Zhidu zhi Chuanshe, Yanbian, yu Gongneng) (The Establishment, Evolution, and Functions of the System of Special Administrative Supervisors), *Jindaishi Yanjiusuo Jikan* XXII (1993).

Shen Songqiao, 'Wo Yi Wo Xue Jian Xuanyuan' (I Offer My Life to the Yellow Emperor), paper presented at the conference Inventing the Past and Imagining the Future, Institute of Modern History, Academia Sinica, 1997.

Shen Xiaoyun, *Li Zongren de Yisheng* (The Life of Li Zongren) (Zhengzhou: Henan Renmin Chubanshe, 1992).

Shen, Yu, 'SACO Re-Examined: Sino-American Intelligence Co-operation during World War II', *Intelligence and National Security* XVI: 4 (2002), 149–74.

Shepherd, Charles, *The Case Against Japan* (London: Jarolds, 1939).

Sheridan, James, *Chinese Warlord: The Career of Feng Yü-hsiang* (Stanford: Stanford University Press, 1966).

Shi Quansheng, ed., *Zhonghua Minguo Wenhua Shi* (A Cultural History of the Republic of China) (Changchun: Jilin Wenshi Chubanshe), 1990.

Shih Shumei, *The Lure of the Modern: Writing Modernism in Semi-Colonial China, 1917–1937* (Berkeley: University of California Press, 2001).

Shitian Zhefu, Kangzhan Shiqi Zhongguo Guomindang Dangyuan Chengfen de Tezheng he Yanbian (The Characteristics and Changes in the Background of the KMT Members during the War of Resistance), *Minguo Yanjiu* VI (2001), 82–102.

Showalter, Dennis, *Railroads and Rifles: Soldiers, Technology, and the Unification of Germany* (Hamden: Archon Books, 1975).

Shyu, Lawrence, 'China's Minority Parties in the People's Political Council', in Roger B. Jeans, ed., *Roads Not Taken: The Struggle of Opposition Parties in Twentieth Century China* (Boulder: Westview Press, 1992), 151–70.

Sih, Paul, *The Strenuous Decade: China's Nation-Building Efforts, 1927–1937* (Jamaica, NY: St John's University Press, 1970).

Siu, Helen, *Agents and Victims in South China: Accomplices of Rural Revolution* (New Haven: Yale University Press, 1989).

Slack, Edward, *Opium, State, and Society: China's Narco-Economy and the Guomindang, 1924–1937* (Honolulu: University of Hawaii Press, 2001).

Slim, William, *Defeat into Victory* (London: Pan Books, 1999).

Smith, Robert, 'History of the Attempt of the US Army Medical Corps to Improve the Effectiveness of the Chinese Army Medical Service, 1941–1945', PhD dissertation, Columbia University, 1950.

Smith, Stephen, *A Road is Made: Communism in Shanghai, 1920–1927* (Honolulu: University of Hawaii Press, 2000).

——, *Like Cattle and Horses: Nationalism and Labor in Shanghai* (Durham: Duke University Press, 2002).

Snow, Edgar, *Red Star Over China* (New York: Random House, 1938).

Snyder, Jack, *The Ideology of the Offensive: Military Decision Making and the Disasters of 1914* (Ithaca: Cornell University Press, 1984).

Spector, Ronald, *Eagle Against the Sun: The American War with Japan* (Harmondsworth: Viking, 1985).

Stafford, David, *Roosevelt and Churchill: Men of Secrets* (London: Abacus, 2000).

Stoler, Mark, *Allies and Adversaries: The Joint Chiefs of Staff, the Grand Alliance, and US Strategy in World War II* (Chapel Hill: University of North Carolina Press, 2000).

Stranahan, Patricia, *Underground: The Shanghai Communist Party and the Politics of Survival* (New York: Rowman and Littlefield, 1998).

Strauss, Julia, *Strong Institutions in Weak Politics: State Building in Republican China* (Oxford: Clarendon, 1998).

Strauss, Julia, 'Bureaucracy, Political Theatre, and the Accusation of Counterrevolutionaries', paper presented at the conference on Political Practice in Modern China, July 2002, Cambridge University.

Sun Yatsen (Sun Zhongshan), *Sun Zhongshan Quanji* (Collected Works of Sun Yatsen) (Beijing: Zhonghua Shuju, 1981–6).

Sutton, Donald, *Provincial Militarism and the Chinese Republic: The Yunnan Army, 1902–1925* (Ann Arbor: University of Michigan Press, 1980).

Tang Xiaobing, *Chinese Modern: The Heroic and the Quotidian* (Durham: Duke University Press, 2000).

Taylor, Jay, *The Generalissimo's Son: Chiang Ching-kuo and the Revolutions in China and Taiwan* (Cambridge, MA: Harvard University Press, 2000).

Teitler, Ger and Kurt Radtke, *A Dutch Spy in China: Reports on the First Phase of the Sino-Japanese War (1937–1939)* (Leiden: Brill, 1999).

Thompson, Roger, *China's Local Councils in the Age of Constitutional Reform, 1898–1911* (Cambridge, MA: Harvard University Press, 1995).

Thorne, Christopher, *Allies of a Kind: The US, Britain, and the War against Japan* (London: Hamilton, 1978).

Tien Chen-ya, *Chinese Military Theory* (Stevenage: SPA Books, 1992).

Tilly, Charles, *Coercion, Capital, and European States* (Oxford: Blackwell, 1975).

——, *The Formation of National States in Western Europe* (Princeton: Princeton University Press, 1975).

Timperley, Harold, *What War Means: The Japanese Terror in China: A Documentary Record* (London: Victor Gallancz, 1938).

Tonesson, S., *The Vietnamese Revolution of 1945: Roosevelt and Ho Chi Minh in a World at War* (Berkeley: Sage, 1991).

Tuchman, Barbara, *Stilwell and the American Experience in China* (New York: Bantam Books, 1972).

US Military Intelligence Reports: China 1911–1941 (Frederick, MD: University Publications of America, 1983).

van Creveld, *Supplying War: Logistics from Wallerstein to Patton* (Cambridge: Cambridge University Press, 1977).

van de Ven, Hans, *From Friend to Comrade: The Founding of the Chinese Communist Party* (Berkeley: University of California Press, 1991).

——, 'The Kuomintang's Secret Service in Action: Operational and Political Aspects of the Arrest of Liao Chengzhi', *Intelligence and National Security* XVI: 4 (2001), 205–37.

——, 'Military and Financial Reform in the late Qing and Early Republic', in Zhongyang Yanjiuyuan Jindaishi Yanjiusuo Shehui Jingji Shi Zu (Section of Social and Economic History, Modern History Institute, Academia Sinica), ed., *Caizheng yu Jindai Lishi* (Finance and Modern History), 17–103.

——, 'The Military in the Republic', *The China Quarterly*, 150 (1997), 352–74.

——, 'New States of War: Communist and Nationalist Warfare and State Building (1928–34)', 321–97.

——and Tony Saich, eds, *New Perspectives on the Chinese Communist Revolution* (Armonk: M. E. Sharpe, 1995).

——, 'Public Finance and the Rise of Warlordism', *Modern Asian Studies* XXX: 4 (1996), 829–68.

——, 'Some Historical Aspects on the Diplomacy of Chinese Nationalism', *Issues and Studies* XXXVI: 6 (2000), 52–79.

——, ed., *Warfare in Modern Chinese History* (Leiden: Brill, 2000).

Vanslyke, Lyman, 'The Battle of the Hundred Regiments: Problems of Coordination and Control during the Sino-Japanese War', in *Modern Asian Studies* XXX: 4 (1996), 979–1005.

Venkatarami, M. S., *Roosevelt, Gandhi, Churchill: America and the Last Phase of India's Freedom* (London: Sangram, 1997).

Wagner, Rudolph, 'Ritual, Politics, and Publicity during the Republic: The Enshrining of Sun Yatsen', paper presented at the Conference on Political Practice in Modern China, Cambridge, June 2002.

Wakeman, Frederic 'Hanjian (Traitor)!: Collaboration and Retribution in Wartime Shanghai', in Yeh Wen-hsin, ed., *Becoming Chinese*, 298–341.

——and Carolyn Grant, eds, *Conflict and Control in Imperial China* (Berkeley: University of California Press, 1975).

——, *The Great Enterprise* (Berkeley: University of California Press, 1985).

——, *Policing Shanghai: 1927–1937* (Berkeley: University of California Press, 1995).

——, 'A Revisitionist View of the Nanjing Decade: Confucian Fascism', *The China Quarterly* 150 (1997), 395–432.

Wakeman, Frederic, *The Shanghai Badlands: Wartime Terrorism and Urban Crime, 1937–1941* (Cambridge: Cambridge University Press, 1996).

Waldron, Arthur, *From War to Nationalism: China's Turning Point, 1924–1925* (Cambridge: University of Cambrige Press, 1995).

——, 'The Warlord: The Twentieth Century Chinese Understanding of Violence, Militarism, and Imperialism', *American Historical Review*, 96 (October 1991), 1073–100.

——, 'China's New Remembering of World War II', *Modern Asian Studies* XXX: 4 (1996), 946–78.

Wang Chaozhu, *Zhang Xueliang he Jiang Jieshi* (Beijing: Zhongguo Qingnian Chubanshe, 1992).

Wang, David Der Wei, *Fin-de-Siecle Splendour* (Stanford: Stanford University Press, 1997).

Wang Huaizhou, 'Liao Zhongkai yu Huangpu Jianjun' (Liao Zhongkai and the Founding of an Army at Whampoa), *Minguo Dang'an* VII (1987), 85–90.

Wang Yeh-chien, *Land Taxation in Imperial China* (Cambridge, MA: Harvard University Press, 1973).

Wasserstrom, Jeffrey, *Student Protest in Twentieth Century China: The View from Shanghai* (Stanford: Stanford University Press, 1991).

Watt, D. C., *Succeeding John Bull: America in Britain's Place, 1900–1975* (Cambridge: Cambridge University Press, 1984).

Wedemeyer, Albert, *Wedemeyer on War and Peace* (Stanford: Hoover Institution Press, 1987).

Wei, William, *Counter-Revolution in China* (Ann Arbor: University of Michigan Press, 1985).

Wei Yongyun, 'Commerce in the Jin Ji Lu Yu Anti-Japanese Base Area', Conference on Wartime China: Regional Regimes and Conditions, July 2002, Harvard University.

Wei, Julie Lee, Ramon Myers, and Donald Gillin, eds, *Presciptions for Saving China: Selected Writings of Sun Yat-sen* trs. Julie Lee Wei, E-zu Sen and Linda Chao (Stanford: Hoover University Press, 1994).

Weinstein, Allen and Alexander Vassiliev, *The Haunted Wood: Soviet Espionage in America – the Stalin Era* (New York: Random House, 1999).

Wen Gongzhi, *Zuijin Sanshi Nian Zhongguo Junshi Shi* (The Military History of China during the Last Thirty Years), in Wu Xiangxiang, *Zhongguo Xiandaishi Congshu* (Collectenea for Modern Chinese History), IV (Taibei: Wenxing Shudian).

Westad, Odd Arne, *Decisive Encounters: The Chinese Civil War, 1945–1950* (Stanford: Stanford University Press, 2002).

White, Theodore, ed., *The Stilwell Papers* (New York: William Sloane, 1948).

—— and Annalee Jacoby, *Thunder out of China* (New York: William Sloane, 1946).

Whiting, A., *Soviet Policies in China, 1927–1924* (New York: Columbia University Press, 1954).

Widmer, Ellen and David Der-wei Wang, eds, *From May Fourth to June Fourth* (Cambridge: Harvard University Press, 1993).

Wilbur, C. Martin, 'The Nationalist Revolution: From Canton to Nanking', in John Fairbank and Denis Twitchett, eds, *The Cambridge History of China*, XII, 527–720.

Wilbur, C. Martin and Julie Lien-Ying How, eds, *Missionaries of Revolution: Soviet Advisors and Nationalist China, 1920–1927* (Cambridge, MA: Harvard University Press, 1989).

Winter, Jay, *Sites of Memory, Sites of Morning: The Great War in European Cultural History* (Cambridge: Cambridge University Press, 1995).

Wong, R. Bin, *China Transformed: Historical Change and the Limits of the European Experience* (Ithaca: Cornell University Press, 1997).

Wou, Oderic, *Militarism in Modern China: The Career of Wu Pei-fu, 1916–1939* (Folkestone: Dawson, 1978).

Wu Fuyuan, 'Ziyuan Weiyuanhui de Renshi Guanli Zhidu' (The NRC's Personnel System), *Huiyi Guomindang Zhengfu Ziyuan Weiyuanhui*, 197–205.

Wu Jingping, *Song Ziwen Pingzhuan* (Critical Briography of Song Ziwen) (Fuzhou: Fujian Renmin Chubanshe, 1992).

Wu Zhaohong, 'Wo Suo Zhidaode Ziyuan Weiyuanhui' (The NRC I Knew), *Huiyi Guomindang Zhengfu Ziyuan Weiyuanhui*, 63–141.

Xin Qingnian (The New Youth) (Annual Compilation Reprint) (Shanghai: Qunyi Shushe, various).

Xu Xiaoqun, *Chinese Professional and the Republican State* (Cambridge: Cambridge University Press, 2001).

Xuzhou Huizhan: Yuan Guomindang Jiangling Kang Ri Zhanzheng Qinliji (The Battle of Xuzhou: Recollections of the KMT Commanders Themselves), ed., Zhongguo Renmin Zhengzhi Xieshang Huiyi Wenshi Ziliao Weiyuanhui (Committee for Sources for Culture and History, Chinese People's Consultative Conference) (Beijing: Zhongguo Wenshi Chubanshe, 1985).

Yamamoto, Masahiro, *Nanking: Anatomy of an Atrocity* (London: Praeger, 2000).

Yang, Benjamin, *From Revolution to Politics: Chinese Communists on the Long March* (Boulder: Westview, 1990).

Yang Kuisong, *Shiqu de Jihui: Zhanshi Guo Gong Tanpan Shilu* (Lost Chance: True Record of Wartime KMT CCP Negotiations) (Guilin: Guangxi Shifan Daxue Chubanshe, 1992).

——, 'Jiujing shi Shei Shufule Shei' (Now Who Did Convince Who?), *Kang Ri Zhanzheng Yanjiu*, I (1996), 35–51.

Yang Tianshi, *Haiwai Fangshi Lu* (Visiting History Abroad) (Beijing: Shehui Kexue Wenxian Chubanshe, 1998).

——, 'Zhongshanjian Shijian zhi Mi' (The Riddle of the Zhongshan Gunboat Incident), *Lishi Yanjiu*, II (April 1988), 116–30.

Yang Yongtai Xiansheng Yanlun Ji (Speeches and Writings of Mr Yang Yongtai), ed., Yang Runxi, (Taibei: Wenhai Chubanshe, no date).

Yeh, Wen-hsin, ed., *Becoming Chinese: Passages to Modernity and Beyond* (Berkeley: University of California Press, 2000).

Yick, Joseph, 'Communist Puppet Collaboration in Japanese Occupied China: Pan Hannian and Li Shiqun, 1939–1949', *Intelligence and National Security* XVI: 4 (2001), 61–88.

Yizheng Shiliao (Historical Sources for the Military Service Administration), ed., Zhu Huisen, (Taibei: Guoshiguan, 1990).

Young, Arthur, *China's Wartime Finance and Inflation, 1937–1945* (Cambridge, MA: Harvard University Press, 1965).

Young, Ernest, *The Presidency of Yuan Shih-k'ai: Liberalism and Dictatorship in Early Republican China* (Ann Arbor: University of Michigan Press, 1977).

Yu E Wan Jiaofei Zong Silingbu Gongzuo Baogao Shu (Work Report of the E Yu Wan Bandity Suppression Command) (no details, availabe in National Central Library, Taiwan).

Yu, Maochun, 'The China Commando Group of SOE' *Intelligence and National Security* XVI:4 (2001), 37–60.

——, *OSS in China: Prelude to the Cold War* (New Haven: Yale University Press, 1996).

'Yue Haiguan Dang'an Youguan Zhongshanjian Shijian Qingbao' (Intelligence Reports of the Canton Customs House Relevant to the Sun Yatsem Gunboat Incident), *Minguo Dang'an* XVIII (1996), 13–23.

Zelin, Madelein, *The Magistrate's Tael: Nationalizing Fiscal Reform in Eighteenth Century Ch'ing China* (Berkely: University of California Press, 1984).

Zhang Xianwen, *Kang Ri Zhanzheng de Zhengmian Zhanchang* (Battles at the Front during the War of Resistance against Japan) (Zhengzhou: Henan Renmin Chubanshe, 1987).

Zhang Xianwen and Fang Qingqiu, *Jiang Jieshi Quanzhuan* (A Complete Biography of Chiang Kaishek) (Zhengzhou: Henan Renmin Chubanshe, 1996).

—— et al., *Zhongguo Kang Ri Zhanzheng Shi* (History of China's War of Resistance against Japan) (Nanjing: Nanjing Daxue Chubanshe, 2001).

Zhang, Xin, *Social Transformation in Modern China: The State and Local Elites in Henan* (Cambridge: Cambridge University Press, 2000).

Zheng Yuanzhong, 'Xin Shenghuo Yundong de Zhengzhi Yiyi' (The Political Meaning of the New Life Movement), in *Kangzhan Qian Shinian Guojia Jianshe Shi Yantaohui Lunwenji* (Proceedings of the Conference on Nation Building in the Ten Years Before the War of Resistance) (Taibei: Zhongyang Yanjiuyuan Jindaishi Yanjiusuo, 1984).

Zhong De Wai Jiao Midang, 1927 Nian–1947 Nian (Secret Archival Documents for Sino-German Foreign Relations, 1927–1947), ed., Zhongguo Di'er Lish Dang'anguan (Second Historical Archives of China) (Guilin: Guangxi Shifan Daxue Chubanshe, 1994).

Zhong Xiaoguang, 'Jiang Zhe Caifa zhi Chuyi' (Comments on the Zhejiang and Jiangsu Lords of Finance), *Minguo Dang'an* XXVII (1992), 86–93.

Zhonggong Zhongyang Wenjian Xuanji (Selected CCP Central Committee Documents), ed., Zhongyang Dang'anguan (CCP Central Committee Archives) (Beijing: Zhonggong Zhongyang Dangxiao Chubanshe, 1989–1992).

Zhonggong Zhongyang Zhengzhi Baogao Xuanji (Selected CCP Central Committee Political Reports), ed., Zhonggong Zhongyang Dang'anguan (CCP Central Committee Archives) (Beijing: Zhonggong Zhongyang Dangxiao Chubanshe, 1981).

Zhongguo Jindaishi Zun Kong Niliu (The Counter Current of Venerating Confucius in Modern China) ed., Zhonguo Kexueyuan Jindaishi Yanjiusuo (Modern History Institute of the Chinese Academy of Sciences) (Beijing: Zhonghua Shuju, 1974).

Zhongguo Junren (China's Soldier) (Reprint, Beijing: Rennion Chubanshe, 1983).

Zhongguo Kang Ri Zhanzheng Shi (History of China's War of Resistance against Japan), ed., Junshi Kexueyuan Junshi Lishi Yanjiubu (Military History Department of the Chinese Military Academy) (Beijing: Jiefangjun Chubanshe, 1994).

Zhongguo Xiandaishi Ziliao Xuanji (Selected Sources for Modern Chinese History), ed., Peng Ming (Beijing: Zhongguo Renmin Daxue Chubanshe, 1989).

Zhonghua Minguo Shi Dang'an Ziliao Huibian (Compendium of Archival Sources for the History of the Republic of China), ed. Zhongguo Di'er Lishi Dang'anguan (Second Historical Archives of China) (Jiangsu Guji Chubanshe, 1991–).

Zhonghua Minguo Zhongyao Shiliao Chubian (A Preliminary Collection of Historical Sources for the Republic of China), ed. Ch'in Hsiao-i (Taibei: Guomindang Zhongyang Zhixing Weiyuan Dangshi Yanjiu Weiyuanhui, 1981–1988).

Zhou Fohai Riji (Diary of Zhou Fohai), ed., Cai Dejin (Beijing: Zhongguo Shehui Kexueyuan Chubanshe, 1986).

Zhou Yumin, *Zhongguo Huibang Shi* (History of Chinese Secret Societies and Lodges) (Shanghai: Shanghai Renmin Chubanshe, 1993).

Zhou Zuoren Jiwai Wen (Further Writings of Zhou Zuoren), eds, Chen Zishan and Zhang Tierong (Hainan: Guoji Xinwen Chubanshe, 1993).

Zhou Zuoren, *Yutian de Shu* (Rainy Day Writings) (Hong Kong, 1967).

Zhu Shoupeng, ed., *Guanxu Chao Donghualu* (The Vermillion Gate Record for the Guangxu Reign) (Beijing: Zhonghua Shuju, 1958).

Zhu Shuli, 'Power Sharing between Central and Local Government in China', paper presented at the conference on Political Practice in Modern China, Cambridge, July 2002.

Zhu Zhixin Ji (Collected Writings of Zhu Zhixin), ed., Guangdongsheng Zhexue Shehui Kexue Yanjiusuo (Guangdong Institute for Philosophy and Social Sciences) (Beijing: Zhonghua Shuju, 1979).

Index